Professional SQL Server® Reporting Services

Professional SQL Server® Reporting Services

Paul Turley
Todd Bryant
James Counihan
George McKee
Dave DuVarney

WILEY

Wiley Publishing, Inc.

Professional SQL Server® Reporting Services

Published by
Wiley Publishing, Inc.
10475 Crosspoint Boulevard
Indianapolis, IN 46256
www.wiley.com

ISBN: 0-7645-6878-7

Manufactured in the United States of America

10 9 8 7 6 5 4 3 2 1

For general information on our other products and services or for technical support, contact our Customer Care Department within the U.S. at (800) 762-2974, outside the U.S. at (317) 572-3993 or fax (317) 572-4002.

Wiley also publishes its books in a variety of electronic formats. Some content that appears in print may not be available in electronic books.

About the Authors

Paul Turley

Paul is an instructor for Netdesk Corporation in Seattle. As a consultant, he has worked with Microsoft Consulting Services on enterprise-scale development projects and has created reporting solutions using Crystal Reports, Active Reports, and Access. Since 1988, he has managed IT projects, designed and programmed applications using Visual Basic 3, 4, 5, 6, ASP.NET, ADO.NET, and SQL Server. He obtained his MCSD certification in 1996. Other certifications include MCDBA, IT Project+ and Microsoft Solutions Framework (MSF) Practitioner.

He designed and maintains www.Scout-Master.com, a web-based service that enables Boy Scout units to manage their membership and advancement records online using ASP.NET, SQL Server 2000, and Reporting Services. Paul has been a contributing author on books and articles including *Professional Access 2000 Programming*, *Beginning Access 2002 VBA*, and *SQL Server Data Warehousing with Analysis Services* from WROX Press.

> *My deepest appreciation goes to my wife, Sherri, and our children: Josh, Rachael, Sara, and Krista for their support and understanding while barricading myself in my office for four months. Thanks to Todd Shelton, Lance Baldwin, and the rest of the Netdesk team for supporting our efforts and putting up with this madness.*

> *For their contributions, special thanks to:* **Tommy Joseph**, *Disney Internet Group;* **Andrew Bryan**, *Dundas Software;* **Dennis Higgins**, *Strafford Technology;* **Mario Raia**, *Combined IQ.*

Paul Turley contributed Chapters 1, 3, 4, 5, 10, 14, and Appendices D and E to this book.

Todd Bryant

Todd has been creating custom data-focused applications and reporting solutions since the early eighties. He began using Microsoft technologies in 1998 and the love affair began. Todd has been contract programming, teaching, and developing custom courseware every since. He is currently working as a trainer at Netdesk Corporation, where he concentrates on Enterprise Solutions, Com+ Services, and Object Oriented Programming using both VB.NET and C#. His certifications include the MCSD, MCSE, MCDBA, and MCT certifications from Microsoft, the CNA certification from Novell, and both CompTIA's A+ and CTT+.

> *I would like to thank my parents Janice, Gary, and Abby for believing in me. I was not always who I am today. Secondly, I would like to thank my daughter Ali for putting joy in my life, Christine for showing me love, and Tommy and Stephanie for teaching me the true meaning of the word compromise. Lastly, I would like to thank the Lord above who placed so many good people in my life and made all this possible.*

Todd Bryant contributed Chapters 11 and 12 and Appendix C to this book.

James Counihan

James started working with databases and reporting applications when doing research for the government back in 1979. Since then his program management and development experience has been primarily in the retail and energy industries. He's been teaching development courses at Netdesk Corporation in Seattle for the past three years, focusing on integrating LOB applications using Microsoft application servers and web services.

Thanks to my wife and family. It was only with their understanding and support that I was able to participate in this project. With my deepest love and appreciation, thank you!

James Counihan contributed Chapters 6 and 8 and Appendix B to this book.

George McKee

George McKee is a Solution Developer for Avanade Inc., a Seattle-based integrator for Microsoft technology that's a joint venture between Accenture Ltd. and Microsoft. George specializes in the in-house financial systems of Avanade. He has a degree in Chemical Engineering from Brigham Young University and has been using computers and databases to resolve technical and business problems for 25 years. George has MCAD and MCSD certifications. When not sitting in front of a computer, George likes to be found in backcountry skiing in the Washington Cascade Mountains. He can be reached via email at georgem@avanade.com.

I would like to thank my wife Becky for tolerating various forms of computing at meal times and my physical and mental absence from many family activities while writing this book. My children (George Jr., Ben, Rosie, and Emily) deserve an honorable mention for patience with my generally distracted interest in their activities during the production of this book.

George McKee contributed Chapter 13 and Appendix A to this book.

Dave DuVarney

Dave DuVarney is a Senior Consultant at Aspirity, LLC where he provides consulting and training services in the fields of business intelligence and software development. He brings over 5 years of finance, programming, and development methodologies experience to high technology business intelligence solutions. Prior to joining Aspirity, Dave was a development instructor teaching a wide range of Microsoft technologies. Dave also spent his early career working for a Seattle-based CPA firm.

When Dave is not working, he enjoys running. At the time of publishing, he is training for his first full marathon.

I would like to thank my wife, Stephanie, for all the love and support she has provided in this process. I would also like to thank my parents, Marcus and Trudy, for giving me the opportunities that have helped me succeed in life.

Dave DuVarney contributed Chapters 2 and 9 to this book.

Credits

Authors
Paul Turley
Todd Bryant
James Counihan
George McKee
Dave DuVarney

Acquisitions Editors
Sharon Cox
Katie Mohr

Vice President and Executive Group Publisher
Richard Swadley

Vice President and Executive Publisher
Robert Ipsen

Vice President and Publisher
Joseph B. Wikert

Executive Editorial Director
Mary Bednarek

Editorial Manager
Kathryn A. Malm

Production Editor
Pamela Hanley

Book Producer
Peer Technical Services Pvt. Ltd.

Foreword

Jason Carlson

Many people have asked me, "How can you be so passionate about reporting when it is so mundane?" To me the most exciting thing about reporting is that it is so very common. Like basic transportation, everybody uses it in some way or another. A report is a piece of art, meant to covey a message; but unlike traditional art, that message changes based on the data driving it. The potential to help, and be used by, millions of people and companies is one of the reasons I started writing software and eventually joined Microsoft. No other company can reach out to so many people by making great products accessible.

Reporting is a very broad topic covering areas ranging from packing lists and telephone bills to ad hoc analysis and Excel spreadsheets. When designing Microsoft SQL Server Reporting Services, I started with a simple definition for it: an information delivery platform. While this definition is also very broad, it did allow us to focus on our design while leaving us significant room to expand in later versions. This book will help you understand the power of Reporting Services and fully to utilize its capabilities.

Information is not just data; it is data that has been transformed into something meaningful. This transformation is important. Any tool can read and display data; what people really need for doing their jobs is well thought out, correct, and pertinent information. There are many tools that allow anyone with access to data to build "views" or "reports". However, many times these users are unfamiliar with all of the nuances of the data storage and can produce inaccurate results or inadvertently affect the performance of the data engine. Reporting Services acts as the official source so that there is only one version of the truth that everyone uses.

In future, Microsoft plans to take this even further by integrating with Information Rights Management so that not only does the information come from a single source, but is also certified, can expire, and is access-controlled even after it is delivered to the end user. The data does not always exist in one database or even come from a database. For those of us who have spent careers working with corporate data, this is a painful truth. Very few reports (or sets of reports that give you sufficient insight) come from a single source. Building some type of data mart or data warehouse is the best solution, but not always possible due to timing, policy, or budgetary constraints. Reports must be able to retrieve data from any source and combine them in a single report.

What good is information if you do not have it when you need it? Delivering information is more than just processing it and making it available; it is providing information when you need it, in any format, and on any device that you have. The common case today is the ubiquitous online access via HTML in a browser. This is perfect when you have a computer and connectivity to the server. However, as we all know, nothing is perfect. We need the reports when we are on a plane, in a car, with the customer, at the game, on the production floor, etc. This may include your pager, telephone, fax machine, laptop, paper, and other devices. We also need different capabilities: interactivity, pixel perfect printing, integration into applications like MS Excel for "What if" scenarios and additional analysis, universal access via PDF, etc. A single format and a single delivery channel is not enough, but how do you know which ones you will need? Reporting Services insulates you from these choices. All reports may be distributed in any channel or rendered in any format. Report design is independent of how it will be consumed. It is the responsibility of the system to provide the report as accurately as possible, given the constraints of the specific format or channel requested.

Building a platform is very different from building a solution. In fact the goals are in many cases completely opposed. A platform is successful if the developers and administrators have complete access to all aspects of the product. They need to be able to optimize, extend, restrict, embed, and replace parts of the product to meet their needs. This means that all of the APIs are available and documented, all formats are open and described, and every component is configurable or replaceable. While there are always restrictions due to the many tradeoffs in software design, this was the goal when building Reporting Services. Very much like Windows, SQL Server, or Visual Studio, Reporting Services is designed to enable developers to build on a solid foundation and mold it to meet the business needs in significantly less time and with more functionality, but without losing the flexibility and power of building it themselves.

Looking to the future, there's an endless list of features and scenarios that Microsoft will add to make the platform more powerful with little or no additional in-house development required. I have mentioned some, and there are many that haven't even been considered yet.

We look forward to hearing from all of our customers about what is important to them and how we can make designing, building, and operating their information delivery systems easier, faster, and (I hope) more fun.

Jason Carlson
SQL Server Reporting Services Product, Unit Manager, Microsoft

Jason Carlson is the Product Unit Manager for SQL Server Reporting Services. He joined Microsoft in 1996 as a Program Manger for Visual Source Safe and Repository. In 1997, the Repository team joined SQL Server and Jason became the development manager for SQL Server Meta Data Services. In 2001, he built a team and started work on V1 of Reporting Services. Before joining Microsoft, Jason owned and operated an independent software development company. This company provided consulting and vertical software solutions for healthcare and telecommunications.

Foreword

David Cunningham

Agility. In business today, key decisions must be made daily or weekly rather than monthly or quarterly. Leading companies realize that to increase the speed of competitive response, their corporate agility, they need to delegate as much decision-making authority as possible to employees on the front lines. Real-time bidding systems, reverse auctions, accurate costing on spot production, build-to-order manufacturing, a world-wide labor force, and globalization. These are just a handful of the trends in today's business climate that demand better decisions faster.

To be successful in this new model, employees need the best quality information they can possibly get. Information must be accurate, timely, and reliable; and it must be the information they need. Whether your employees are trying to maximize revenues by intelligently attacking new markets, or minimizing expenses through astute purchasing, they absolutely must have the right information at their fingertips.

Microsoft's release of SQL Server 2000 Reporting Services marks an important milestone in the world of business intelligence: information truly accessible to the masses. By building reporting functionality directly into Microsoft's Enterprise Data Platform, SQL Server 2000, software developers and information architects can now count on the availability of a high quality, scalable, and robust architecture on which to build their reporting systems.

For the past 20 years Business Intelligence (BI) has been working its way deeper and deeper into the Enterprise. Previously, the domain of a handful of highly skilled analysts high in the corporate ivory tower, BI is now in the hands of line managers, department heads, and knowledge workers at the very edge of today's organizations.

In the past, dependable reporting systems could be horrendously expensive, with organizations forced to deploy robust reporting services only where the greatest gains could be realized. Microsoft's long-standing objective of reducing information technology cost to spur adoption is again evident in the SQL Server 2000 Reporting Services licensing model. This technology is licensed to anyone currently licensed for SQL Server 2000 and so essentially represents no additional cost. This is a fantastic development for software developers and users alike; it will dramatically increase the adoption and distribution of detailed, accurate, and timely reporting and will push quality BI even further down into the Enterprise.

In this excellent book, the authors walk us through SQL Server 2000 Reporting Services from the basics of practical reporting through deployment and management of reporting solutions written for BI Solution architects, designers and developers; it is certainly a most valuable resource.

David Cunningham
President & CEO, Dundas Software

Dundas Software has provided charting and graphing technology under license to Microsoft for inclusion in SQL Server 2000 Reporting Services and is readying additional data visualization extensions for the next version of SQL Server, code-named 'Yukon'.

Contents

Contents

Contents

Contents

Contents

Contents

Contents

Contents

Contents

Contents

Introduction

SQL Server Reporting Services is a serious reporting platform that delivers real business intelligence to knowledge workers and business decision makers. It has the ability to render reports in many different formats and also to execute those reports on demand, cache, archive, or automatically deliver them to users. Whether you need reports to extend a custom desktop application, web site or a simple out-of-the-box reporting solution, Reporting Services can make it happen. The fact that Microsoft makes this capability available as an extension to their flagship database product with no additional investment is exciting news.

Whether you're a novice or an advanced-level programmer, you'll learn to create reports with the right tools for the job. We start with the architecture of Reporting Services and learn about its foundation of .NET and XML web services. You will learn how easy it is to design reports practically for any data source. We cover the basics thoroughly and show you everything you need to get started, working through the processes of report authoring, management, and delivery. You'll create dynamic, interactive reports with drill-down and drill-through features. With the use of tables, groupings, subreports, matrices, images, and charts, reports can be attractive and to-the point. You'll use the Report Manager to configure and execute reports. Next, we'll extend the capabilities of advanced reports using .NET programming code and custom expressions.

After several comprehensive exercises in report design, we will build custom viewing and management tools for advanced reporting solutions. You'll learn to use objects in code and script to render reports, create custom data processing extensions, and manage security and subscriptions. You'll learn how to design and extend reports with the Report Definition Language (RDL).

Finally, we'll put all the pieces together and discuss designing complete solutions and deploying reports and Reporting Services in your business environment. Five experienced authors have worked very hard over several months to make this book a comprehensive tutorial and source of useful information. We sincerely hope it will be a valuable addition to your reference library.

Who Is This Book for?

William Shatner once said that the needs of the many outweigh the needs of the few. We've done our best to dispel this myth and wanted this book to meet the needs of as many people as possible. As some of us have traveled around the United States teaching and presenting Reporting Services, we've come to realize that there isn't a "typical" Reporting Services user. This book was written to address the needs of developers, serious reporting professionals who may be less experienced programmers or non-programmers, system administrators, and solution designers. To meet this objective, we begin with the basics of report design and then progress, chapter-by-chapter, through more advanced design and programming techniques. We sincerely hope it will be a valuable addition to your reference library.

What Does This Book Cover?

Introduction to Reporting Services

In *Chapters 1* and *2*, you will learn what Reporting Services really is and what makes it a unique and powerful reporting solution. We will introduce the stages of the reporting lifecycle and frame the steps and tasks necessary to create a functional reporting solution.

Authoring Reports

This section spans *Chapters 3, 4,* and *5*. These three chapters will teach you how to design reports using the report project template in Visual Studio .NET and the report designer tools. Using all of the available report items and data range items, you will create powerful reports with data groupings, conditional formatting, drill-down and drill-through features.

In *Chapter 3,* you will learn the basics and shows you how to use the Report Wizard and Report Designer environment in Visual Studio.NET.

In *Chapter 4,* you will learn how to plan and create data sources, design queries, and work with parameters and filtering techniques.

Chapter 5 will introduce you to advanced programming techniques using in-line expressions, custom code, and reusable code assemblies.

Managing Reports

In *Chapter 6,* you will use the Report Manager to configure, secure and manage the execution of reports organized by business units or categories. You will also learn the basics of caching, creating snapshots and history, and creating subscriptions.

In *Chapter 7,* you will learn how to manage reports using the Reporting Services Web Service through custom program code.

In *Chapter 8* you will learn how to manage and administer all reports and your Report Server using command line and batch scripting.

Report Delivery

In *Chapter 9,* you will learn you how to render reports using program code with the Reporting Services Web Service. This powerful feature can be used to integrate reporting into custom business applications, creating a seamless user experience.

In *Chapter 10,* you will learn the details of subscriptions—giving users the ability to have reports delivered to them on a regular schedule. Using custom program code, subscriptions and snapshots may be used to deliver important business information to users when data changes and as conditions arise.

Advanced Topics

Chapter 11 explores the details of RDL and shows you how to define reports in file-based XML. Using custom tools and programming, reports may be designed and created outside of the Visual Studio.NET environment. You will walkthrough an end-to-end solution using a third-party tool.

Chapter 12 will take you into the core of Reporting Services and show you how to replace and enhance its fundamental capabilities. You will create a custom data processing extension and see how the architecture supports the ability to build your own data access, security, and rendering extensions.

Chapter 13 discusses the nuts and bolts of deployment and report server administration. You will learn to plan and design a scalable and secure Reporting Services solution.

Finally, Chapter 14 offers a birds-eye view of Business Intelligence (BI) and discusses the concepts and issues involving database design, indexing, and delivering enterprise-wide decision-support systems.

What You Need To Use This Book

In order to use SQL Server Reporting Services and to run the samples in this book, you will need:

- ❑ SQL Server 2000, any edition. An evaluation version of SQL Server and Reporting Services may be downloaded from Microsoft at http://www.microsoft.com/sql.

- ❑ Windows 2000, Windows Server 2003, or Windows XP.

- ❑ Visual Studio .NET 2003, any edition.

- ❑ Pentium II class PC with a 500 MHz processor and 256 megabytes of RAM.

The complete source code for the samples is available for download from our web site at http://www.wrox.com/. There are versions available in both Visual Basic .NET and C#. (See the *Source Code* section later in this introduction.)

Conventions

To help you get the most from the text and keep track of what's happening, we've used a number of conventions throughout the book.

> **Boxes like this one hold important, not-to-be forgotten information that is directly relevant to the surrounding text.**

Tips, hints, tricks, and asides to the current discussion are offset and placed in italics like this.

As for styles in the text:

- ❑ We *highlight* important words when we introduce them

- ❑ We show keyboard strokes like this: Ctrl+A

- ❑ We show file names and code within the text like so: `persistence.properties`
- ❑ We present code in two different ways:

```
The Code Foreground style shows new, important, pertinent code. We indent
            the 2nd line to show that you should enter both lines on one
            line.
The Code Background style shows code that's less important in the present
            context or has been shown before.
```

Occasionally, code that needs to be placed all on one line is split over two because of the layout of the book, as shown in the preceding highlighted code. However, make sure you type it all on one line.

Source Code

As you work through the examples in this book, you may choose either to type in all the code manually or to use the source code files that accompany the book. All of the source code used in this book is available for download at http://www.wrox.com. Once at the site, simply locate the book's title (either by using the Search box or by using one of the title lists) and click the **Download Code** link on the book's detail page to obtain all the source code for the book.

Because many books have similar titles, you may find it easiest to search by ISBN; for this book the ISBN is 0-7645-6878-7.

Once you download the code, just decompress it with your favorite compression tool. Alternately, you can go to the main Wrox code download page at http://www.wrox.com/dynamic/books/download.aspx to see the code available for this book and all other Wrox books.

Errata

We make every effort to ensure that there are no errors in the text or in the code. However, no one is perfect, and mistakes do occur. If you find an error in one of our books, like a spelling mistake or faulty piece of code, we would be very grateful for your feedback. By sending in errata you may save another reader hours of frustration and at the same time you will be helping us provide even higher quality information.

To find the errata page for this book, go to http://www.wrox.com and locate the title using the search box or one of the title lists. Then, on the book details page, click the **Book Errata** link. On this page you can view all errata that has been submitted for this book and posted by Wrox editors. A complete book list including links to each book's errata is also available at www.wrox.com/misc-pages/booklist.shtml.

If you don't spot your error on the Book Errata page, go to www.wrox.com/contact/techsupport.shtml and complete the form there to send us the error you have found. We'll check the information and, if appropriate, post a message to the book's errata page and fix the problem in subsequent editions of the book.

p2p.wrox.com

For author and peer discussion, join the P2P forums at p2p.wrox.com. The forums are a web-based system for you to post messages relating to Wrox books and related technologies and interact with other readers and technology users. The forums offer a subscription feature to email you topics of interest of your choosing when new posts are made to the forums. Wrox authors, editors, other industry experts, and your fellow readers are present on these forums.

At http://p2p.wrox.com, you will find a number of different forums that will help you not only as you read this book, but also as you develop your own applications. To join the forums, just follow these steps:

1. Go to p2p.wrox.com and click the Register link.
2. Read the terms of use and click Agree.
3. Complete the required information to join as well as any optional information you wish to provide and click Submit.
4. You will receive an email with information describing how to verify your account and complete the joining process.

You can read messages in the forums without joining P2P, but in order to post your own messages, you must join.

Once you join, you can post new messages and respond to messages other users post. You can read messages at any time on the Web. If you would like to have new messages from a particular forum e-mailed to you, click the Subscribe to this Forum icon by the forum name in the forum listing.

For more information about how to use the Wrox P2P, be sure to read the P2P FAQs for answers to questions about how the forum software works as well as many common questions specific to P2P and Wrox books. To read the FAQs, click the FAQ link on any P2P page.

Acknowledgments

Our thanks to the members of the product team for making themselves accessible and responsive. We appreciate you allowing us to participate—in a small way—in the process of making this a great product. You've done a fantastic job! To Jason Carlson and the rest of his team, thanks taking the time to field questions and support our efforts with this book.

Kudos to Andrew Bryan and David Cunningham at Dundas Software for your help with the charting features. The integration in the product is awesome and your assistance has been invaluable. Thanks to Dennis Higgins from Strafford Technology and Mario Raia from Combined IQ for your business perspectives. To Tommy Joseph from Disney Internet Group: thanks for starting all of this madness. We owe you cheesecake with bacon. A big thank you goes to Eric Smith for contributing his code generation tool, CodeSmith, to the development community and the RDL templates to generate custom reports.

Special thanks goes to the Todd Shelton, Lance Baldwin, and the rest of the Netdesk team for your patience and support as we've tested the limits of time, energy, and human sanity.

Getting Started with Reporting Services

SQL Server Reporting Services is an amazing offering from Microsoft that will change the way you create and deploy reporting solutions. It's difficult to fully appreciate the revolutionary nature of this product until you understand its architecture. The look and feel of the Report Designer environment and the functionality of a particular report view window have little to do with its full capabilities. Like your favorite media player program, you can always bolt-on another skin or façade, but it's what's inside that really matters. The product group has done a stellar job by providing a design environment and a nice web-based report management and viewing application. The impressive part is the underlying architecture that makes SQL Reporting Services a fully scalable and extensible solution that is also surprisingly easy to work with.

If you are impressed by the capabilities of the .NET Framework, web services, SQL Server, and ASP.NET, you should know that by using these technologies Reporting Services takes data accessibility to the next level. Microsoft is making good on their promise of making information available "*any time, any place, and on any device*." Reports may be designed using specific rendering formats and page sizes to support mobile devices. There are many other reporting tools with impressive capabilities but none of them are quite like this one.

This chapter will introduce several topics that will be covered in greater detail later in the book. This will be a high-level view of the need for, purpose, capabilities, and mechanics of SQL Server Reporting Services.

In short, this chapter includes a discussion on the following main topics:

- ❑ The history of reporting
- ❑ *Business Intelligence (BI)* and decision support in current and past reporting solutions
- ❑ Reporting solutions and application types used to deliver reports

❑   Installing Reporting Services, setup options, resources, and tools

❑   *Report Definition Language (RDL)*

Who Is This Book for?

Since you've picked up this book, you may be in need of a reporting solution. You may be an application developer, solution architect, project manager, database administrator, or business owner. Maybe you're not a technical professional and you just need reports for your business. Perhaps you are the executive sponsor of a project and you need to know what kinds of capabilities are available for IT professionals to build a solution for you. We assume that you have made (or are considering making) an investment in Microsoft products to manage a business process of some kind. You may need SQL Server or Visual Studio .NET.

We have made it a point to address several aspects of reporting from the perspectives of executives and business managers who need to have solutions developed for them; project managers, business analysts, and software developers who will design and create solutions; and for database and system administrators who will configure, deploy, and maintain databases and business reporting infrastructure.

After spending a couple of months with the early beta release versions of Reporting Services and building solutions with them, I had the opportunity to conduct some early adopter classes for BI and report solution professionals before the product was released. For most, this was their first look at SQL Reporting Services. Everyone was impressed and excited about putting it into practice. I was taken back by a handful of non-developers who complained that they wanted to use Visual Studio to create reports. *"Why should we have to buy this product and learn to use it?"* they asked.

In Chapter 11 you will see how designing reports isn't restricted to the Visual Studio .NET design environment. There will likely be other design tools for building reports in the market soon. The fact is that designing reports is easy. If you have used other report design tools, I'm sure you will agree. One nice thing about using the Visual Studio report designer is that it feels like the other Microsoft products you already know how to use. If you are a Microsoft developer, you'll love it. If you're not a developer, you'll love it when you realize how easy it is to design, deploy, and manage very powerful reporting solutions with it.

Agility

Imagine that you are sitting in a presentation meeting at the corporate office of a key customer. You are a senior sales representative for a company that sells high volume data backup systems, and the solution they decide on will be implemented in several regional data centers around the world. Your team has been preparing for this meeting for months. Your success depends on your ability to demonstrate your competence to the customer and a clear understanding of their needs. Your team has done their homework, and you know the customer has a history of scanning printed medical records and storing them as image files. Based on this information, you are certain that a particular product will adequately provide the file backup facilities for their moderate volume of image files. You have made it a point to familiarize yourself with the capabilities of the system that appears to be the best fit.

During your customer's opening presentation, they tell you that they have recently made a huge investment into full motion video imaging equipment. Now they need a backup system that can handle large file capacities. They are prepared to make an investment that is substantially larger than what you had anticipated for a capable backup solution. Your company began to offer a large-scale solution just a couple of weeks ago but you aren't very familiar with its capabilities. You've spent so much time preparing to sell the smaller system that you haven't had time to learn more about this new product. Your associate is doing introductions, and it will be your turn in about 15 minutes.

Discretely, you open your Pocket PC Phone and access the World Wide Web. You login to your company's secure report server, select the product catalog report; choose the product category and then *drill-down* to the new product. The report has a *drill-through* option that lets you quickly view a detailed specification report for the new, high-volume backup system. After noting the pertinent specifications, you save this report to a PDF file and then choose the customer sales inquiry history report. Looking up this customer, you learn that someone named Julie made an inquiry about two months ago regarding video media backups from this very company.

Looking around the room, you find a name card with her name on it. You explore the details of this call, and you find that she had asked if you offer a solution comparable to a very expensive product from a competitor. Checking the competition's web site, you discover that the competing product Julie had mentioned uses older technology, has a smaller capacity than the new system, and it costs considerably more. You save a report with all of the pertinent specifications to your memory card, hand the card to the administrative assistant sitting next to you, and ask that he make printed copies of the PDF file it contains.

Your colleague finishes her presentation and then introduces you. Taking another quick glance at the new product specs, you begin your introduction. You explain that one of your team's greatest strengths is your real experience and understanding of how business can change day-to-day. In order to be responsive and competitive, it's necessary to adapt to these changes. You show the brochure for the mid-scale product and explain that this product would be an excellent solution for a company that just scans documents. But for digital video, a more capable solution is required. You share the product specification and qualify the product to your customer's needs. During your presentation, the administrative assistant returns with the printed specification report. Not missing a beat, you distribute these to everyone and conclude. Making brief eye contact with your colleague, he raises an eyebrow just before your customer's chief decision maker, Julie, aggressively shakes your hand, and thanks you profusely for your time and effort.

The Way We Were

In many business applications, reports were an afterthought. This lack of planning often forced developers to build ad-hoc reports with little opportunity for significant planning and design. Queries became complicated and difficult to support. Reports ran slowly and were prone to errors. To avoid these difficulties, you really need a plan. In a perfect world, you would architect the database and application around your reporting needs, and would completely understand your users' requirements before designing the system. In the real world, you may understand some of the users' needs ahead of time but chances are that new reports will be requested long after the other features are in place.

According to Frederick P. Brooks' *The Mythical Man-Month*, it's usually a good idea to learn from and throw away your first few attempts at almost any design. I typically try to develop reports in stages realizing that the first attempt will be a prototype. My experience has been that when you gather the initial requirements, users will ask for a handful of different reports based on some specific criteria. After the solution is deployed and people begin to use it, others will almost inevitably realize that they too would like reports to help make their jobs as easy as their associates. As users realize what kinds of information they can get, they will find new and exciting ways to sort, filter, group, pivot, and slice and dice their data – in ways they never thought possible. That is, until you show them the possibilities.

That Was Then, This Is Now

Static, printed reports may be an acceptable format for a list of products and prices or for a company, but not for the majority of the information people use to make important decisions today. Business decision makers need pertinent information, and they need to view it in a manner that applies to that person's role or responsibility. Since most users deal with information in a slightly different manner, you can create hundreds of reports, each designed for a specific need. Alternatively, you can create flexible reports that serve a broader range of user needs. For example, a sales summary report could be grouped or filtered by the sales person's region, by customer type, and include information for the week, month, quarter or year, or for a specific product category. To produce individual reports for each of these needs would be time-consuming and cost prohibitive. Besides, computer users are savvier than they were a few years ago and need to have tools that help them take informed decisions, not just look at the numbers.

I recall working at Hewlett-Packard several years ago in a manufacturing site IS group. Every Thursday a report cart would come around. There were several regularly scheduled reports that the mainframe system produced on a weekly and monthly basis. Users, typically department managers, would subscribe to these reports that were then printed in another building and delivered by hand to each subscriber. Many of these reports were little more than a huge list of numbers and text printed on continuous, fan-fed paper – some as large as 500 pages. I watched inquisitively as managers would meticulously scan through the pages, highlighting and circling figures of interest. Some would bind them into large books and give them to their administrative assistants to go through with a ten-key calculator and add up all of the figures they had highlighted.

At the end of the month dumpsters full of these reports were hauled off to landfills and recycling centers as their usefulness quickly came to an end. I spent nearly two years developing a reporting application for this group using Microsoft Access. We originally planned for eight to ten reports in this application. But as time went on, and users began to rely on the reports to perform their jobs, they would ask for the same reports with different sorting, grouping, and selection criteria. In the end, we deployed some 25-30 reports, most of which were variations on the few original reports.

Business Intelligence and Decision Support

Dennis Higgins is a BI Consultant with Strafford Technology, Inc. in Windham, NH. He says, *"I think one of the greatest challenges to providing BI Solutions is to educate the customer as to the extent of the long-range problems (and the associated business costs) caused by disjointed attempts to derive information from corporate data. Closely related to that is to correct the normal tendency to apply band aids. Foresight and planning with a BI Strategy is the most effective means of halting the creation of stove-pipe data analysis systems. Once management perceives the benefits and buys into the process, a 'master plan' strategy can be formulated, that will guide the process of developing the solution. Integration of existing systems, new tools, or BI Platform migration can then be tackled based on priority and available resources."*

Business executives understand that it's important to have good data. They reason that good data should lead to good decisions, and good decisions mean good business. This makes sense, right? A very common scenario today is that businesses trying to get that edge will invest in expensive ERP systems that effectively gather and store mountains of customer, product, and sales information. Mission accomplished? Wrong! These days, the time between data entry and consumption is very short, almost instant. More effective data-gathering mechanisms result in data silos and data warehouses populated to the gills with all kinds of facts.

The new generation of business workers are informed and empowered to make decisions. They need tools to get useful information and respond to changes. Having data available is useless unless it has business value and can be used to effectively take informed decisions.

A fundamental fact in business is that the people who gather and collect data are often not the people who use that data or need access to the information that the data represents. Business executives, managers, and analysts make strategic decisions everyday that may affect many people, the direction of their organizations, and ultimately, the way people and organizations will go about conducting business in the industry. These decisions are largely driven by the relative height of a bar displayed in a chart or a few numbers printed on a piece of paper. Having capable reporting tools doesn't necessarily solve this problem. Most businesses don't know how to effectively use the products they own. A reporting tool is of little value if it's complicated and difficult to use.

This presents some fundamental challenges such as collecting comprehensive, accurate and meaningful information, storing it in a form so it continues to represent the facts, and presenting the information in a concise and unbiased form. On the surface, it seems like a simple task.

Automation to the Rescue – A Scenario

I'll share an example of this kind of challenge. Several years ago, I spent a few months developing a reporting system for the operations group at a paper mill in the Pacific Northwest. The old mill is located in a small, remote town and many of the people operating the mill have been working there all of their lives. As is common in the pulp and paper industry, the mill has changed ownership a few times and is currently operated by a very large paper and office supply company.

As time went by and technology changed, several different computer systems were incorporated into the operation of this mill; an IBM 360 and an AS400 system were used to manage customer orders and production history records. The original inventory management system is still in place. It's a very old, special-purpose computer that stores most of its data in a single, flat text file. All of its components are redundant and it hardly ever needs significant maintenance. Shortly before I arrived, a Windows server box was installed with a SQL Server database and an application that would replicate production and inventory data from the existing database systems. Management within the parent company believed that they didn't have a handle on the rates of material consumption and product quality. They wanted a reporting system that would give them the figures they needed to make adjustments to their ordering and pulp production processes.

Over a period of time, orders would be placed for certain grades of pulp. The system would calculate quantities of ingredients to produce a batch – typically to fulfill an order for a customer. The order would be sent to the production floor where workers had newly installed controls used to assure the accurate delivery of pulp ingredients. Different batches of product continued to be produced with varying degrees of quality and their ability to track the consumption of these materials didn't significantly improve. Management continued to invest in reporting solutions. They bought and developed software to look for trends and perform statistical analysis but to no avail.

After several months and hundreds of thousands of dollars invested, the product quality didn't really improve much. Finally, one of the IT managers put on a hard hat and walked down to the production floor to observe the process. What he learned was a simple lesson: when the orders arrived on their computer workstations, workers were printing the orders and then putting them aside. They had overridden the automated controls and were using the same manual techniques to make paper that earlier generations had been using for decades. It was a matter of tradition and pride, and they weren't about to let some computer do their job for them.

The initial reporting solution was elegant and technically capable. The calculations were accurate and the report presentation was appropriate. However, the solution didn't fully support the process. This cultural hurdle was eventually overcome (workers were instructed to use the automated systems if they wanted to keep their jobs) and the product and process improved. A report is only as good as the data it presents, and the data is only as good as the information used for collection. The information is only as good as the process that it represents.

Challenges of Existing Reporting Solutions

For over ten years, Microsoft has offered only one product with substantial reporting capabilities. Designed to run as a single-user or a small workgroup, desktop application, Microsoft Access is a capable database and reporting solution. In Access 2000, Access Data Projects were added. This extension of the product works well against a SQL Server back-end, in a LAN environment. In Visual Studio 6, an integrated reporting tool was offered for Visual Basic 6 but its capabilities were meager at best. Developers at that time thought this was a glimpse of things to come in subsequent versions of Visual Studio.

Due to the lack of a unified, consistent approach for reporting, many developers have had to revert to creating their own custom solutions. One case in point is the reports starter kit project available on the ASP.NET development support site (www.asp.com). The developers did a bang-up job creating a web-based reporting solution using ASP.NET datagrids and datalist controls. They even made their own pie charts using line drawing objects. This effectively proves that .NET is a powerful arsenal of programming tools. However, it also makes the point that we have lacked a strong reporting solution to round out Microsoft's front-line development and database suite.

When Visual Studio .NET was released in 2002, I was a little disappointed because the only integrated reporting component was a limited-use version of *Crystal Reports*. Now, before I get myself into too much trouble with folks who may be loyal to this product, I'll say that Crystal Reports is a capable reporting tool. However, it's neither a part of Microsoft's strategic direction nor does it behave like, or integrate tightly with other Microsoft products. The version of Crystal Reports that installs with Visual

Studio is limited to five concurrent users (and the term *concurrent* is subject to some serious interpretation). Now that Crystal Reports has changed hands once again (recently acquired by Business Objects), it will be interesting to see how this affects the direction of this well-known product.

Notably, the most remarkable change in the industry over the past few years has been the opportunity and need to exchange information over the Internet. Previous technologies simply don't provide the means to access application components across the Internet. Component architectures such as COM, DCOM, and CORBA were designed to communicate across secure LAN and WAN systems, which required a substantial infrastructure investment. Connecting business trading partners and even regional sites was often cost prohibitive and logistically infeasible. Few options existed for reporting over the web. At best, a list or table filled with data could be viewed in custom-built, server-side web page solutions using ASP or CGI. Each page had to be carefully designed and scripted at the cost of dozens, or sometimes hundreds of programming hours.

With the recent maturity of the web, a new generation of mobile devices is evolving that can connect users to company resources, email, documents, and databases. These laptop, hand-held, palm-top, and wrist-worn devices open new doors of opportunity and present new challenges for data presentation. Perhaps, it will soon be common for people to stagger around the streets, talking to themselves and staring blindly into space in a zombie-like trance as they are connected to the world through web-enabled cerebral implants! We can only hope!

To gain access to useful and readable information, data must be accessible over available communication channels (such as corporate networks and the Internet), easy to access, secure, and available in a variety or formats so that it may be viewed using available document readers or browsers – all compatible with different devices. Did I mention the need to support different *Operating Systems (OS)*, applications, and perhaps, without the installation of any custom software on the client device? This is the challenge.

How Does SQL Server Reporting Services Meet This Challenge?

SQL Server Reporting Services is a server-side reporting solution that meets all of these requirements and more. It can obtain its data from a variety of data sources that you can access using modern programming tools. That data may be grouped, sorted, aggregated, and presented in dynamic and meaningful ways. The structure of the data and the presentation elements may be transmitted across practically any communication medium, using an industry standard format, to just about any type of client or server computer or device. The resulting content may then be displayed in many standard formats using browsers and document readers. Further, the data itself may be consumed by standard and custom applications to be further parsed, imported, manipulated, and consumed. It's a truly remarkable innovation with incredible possibilities.

Since Reporting Services is based on .NET, it offers the advantage of integrating tightly with the Windows platform and benefits from the performance, scalability, and security inherent to the .NET Framework. When used in concert with BackOffice products like Share Point Portal, it can provide a comprehensive enterprise solution with little programming effort. Reporting Services can be used with ASP.NET and other .NET programming tools to produce highly customized, special-purpose solutions.

In Chapter 2, we will discuss the specific Reporting Services architecture that is used to perform all of this magic. In brief, functionality is exposed through an XML web service that may be accessed across a LAN or across the web. Reports may be rendered in program code or they may be accessed through a simple web address – like any other web page. Reports may be rendered in several formats. These include different flavors of HTML to provide compatibility with different browsers and devices, the Adobe Acrobat *Portable Document Format* (*PDF*) for uniform presentation and printing, as a graphic file, and in Microsoft Excel so users can slice, dice, pivot, and re-analyze the data. Content may also be rendered in XML and CSV formats to import and exchange data with a variety of applications.

Business Intelligence Solutions

Traditionally, BI solutions have been very costly and only accessible to large businesses that could afford them. *Customer Relations Management (CRM)* systems, *Online Analytical Processing (OLAP)* systems (or data warehouses), and analysis solutions have been available for many years from specialized vendors. However, they require costly deployment, training, and maintenance. By contrast, (this is the part I like the best) Reporting Services is available at no additional cost if you install it on a computer with a licensed instance of SQL Server. Reporting Services is an add-on to SQL Server rather than a stand-alone product. In a single server installation, you don't need an additional license and you can use it royalty free – so long as your database, and server products are appropriately licensed. For additional information regarding licensing and deployment options, please refer to Chapter 13.

Comparatively speaking, collecting data is the easy part. Most companies have been doing this for decades, but how they utilize all of this data is often another story. There is no doubt that effectively collecting data may not be so easy but it's something businesses have been doing for quite some time. Most companies have untold mega-, giga-, or even peta-bytes of "important" archived data residing in documents, spreadsheets, and various databases on backup tapes, disks and folders throughout their enterprise – with no hope of fully utilizing and gaining significant value from it all.

According to Tommy Joseph of Disney Interactive Group, "*BI is about more than just tracking product sales. It's about measuring performance, discovering patterns and trends; and measurable forecasting through statistical analysis.*"

An effective BI solution provides visibility to important facts at all levels of an organization, and gives people access to uniform data from different sources using familiar and easy to use applications. It ties together applications, documents, and data sources in a manner that lets people collaborate and communicate effectively.

BI systems are no longer a luxury but a necessity in many business environments. Today, having access to timely information can make the difference between having a competitive edge and being left in the dust behind competitors.

Who Uses Reports and Why?

In almost any organization, there is a universal condition that people in different roles and at different levels have different perspectives on information. This is typically most apparent in large corporations, where executive leaders who make financial and market-direction decisions have less exposure to the daily processes of the company than the line-level workers. Ask any executive and they will tell you that the line-level worker doesn't have a broad perspective regarding the challenges and direction of the organization at a high level. Conversely, ask most of the line-level workers in the organization and they will tell you that the upper management and executives don't share their perspective of "real problems" and the daily pulse of the company. To a point, this is the natural condition of a healthy organization.

Bill Gates has spoken extensively about the *information worker* of the twentieth century. At all levels within an organization, people who have convenient access to accurate and appropriate information are empowered to take informed decisions that benefit the organization and the individual. This is rapidly becoming the case throughout many industries today and continues to change the way people work and are managed. Although this paradigm shift may be occurring for many people, organizations often struggle to provide the resources necessary to support workers who are eager to use information to make a difference in their environments.

Executive Leadership

Leaders simply must make informed decisions. They must fully understand their business environment and the competitive climate in which they operate. Access to market conditions, customer needs, and financial information can often make the difference between decisions that produce success or jeopardize the organization.

Decision support systems provide interfaces for executive leadership through dashboards called *Executive Information Services (EIS)*. Reporting Services installs them with a simple web interface and enhances integration with executive consoles through SharePoint Portal services and third party solution integration.

Managers

Inefficient business processes can no longer remain the status quo. Customers demand results and simply will not tolerate services or products that don't meet their expectations. Customers have choices and will quickly switch to a competitor if their needs are not met. Managers need the information necessary to drive customer satisfaction and make corrections, directing business processes and the effective use of people and other important resources.

Information Workers

In businesses today, workers are educated and given more freedom to solve problems and effect change. This category could be applied to workers at various levels within an organization, including the managers and higher level workers. Often, the customer service representative or service provider will be the only human interface a customer has with an organization. That person must be empowered to collect and retrieve information quickly and accurately. They must also be empowered to make corrections to - and to work with, not against - unyielding business processes. In the past, workers simply had to accept the way information was presented to them, as well as the inefficiencies of most automated systems. With greater demands on businesses, workers simply must have the means to acquire accurate and concise information that meets their needs – in order to work efficiently.

Customers

Many businesses can't afford to put people in front of their customers on a routine basis. Customers who can get the information, services and assistance they need may not demand that someone help them when it's not warranted. By making regular services available through customer-friendly automation and information portals, you can afford to offer assistance to customers who really need special attention. Customers often need to look up account and transaction histories, order status, and shipping information. Making these services available through a web browser, email, or a mobile device can provide a greater degree of customer satisfaction.

Vendors and Partners

Like customers, business vendors may need to interface with an organization to place orders, schedule service calls, and obtain status information. Making this information available in the most appropriate form will improve efficiency and ultimately business-vendor partnerships. Business vendors are often more accepting of special procedures and automated systems. Vendors can be trained to use more sophisticated systems to obtain product information, service orders, invoices, and other business-related information. Systems may be designed to interface and automate the download or exchange of information that enable a partnering business to work cooperatively.

Reporting with Relational Data

Transactional databases are designed to capture and manage real data as it is generated; for example, as products are purchased and as services are rendered. Relational databases are designed according to the rules of normal form and typically have many tables, each containing fragments of data rather than comprehensive information or business facts. This helps preserve the integrity and accuracy of data at the detail level, but it presents challenges for deriving useful information from a large volume of transactional data. In order to obtain information with meaningful context, tables must be joined and values must be aggregated. Although relational database systems may support complex queries, reporting against these queries routinely could prove to be slow and inefficient.

Reporting for Decision Support

Optimized data storage systems are for analysis and don't use normalized tables, and don't contain details at the transactional level. Tables typically have more columns and fewer rows and often contain descriptive values that would otherwise exist only in lookup tables. The purpose of a decision-support data store is to drive meaningful reports and analysis tools with a sampling of read-only, historical, data and not for keeping up-to-the minute details.

Data Warehouses

The usual approach for maintaining a decision-support system is to copy only necessary data from relational, transaction-support databases to a separate data store at regular intervals. Depending on an organization's reporting needs, this data dump (or import) is performed daily, weekly, or even monthly.

The transactional tables are joined and pre-aggregated to eliminate unnecessary detail. Surrogate key values and codes have little use since the transformed data is readable in a more concise form.

Data warehouses (and smaller subsets of data analysis called *data silos*), can simply be implemented as relational data stores that have been designed for analysis. There can also be special purpose data structures that store data in hierarchal or multi-dimensional structures. These specialized data storage structures are optimized for performing pivots and extensive calculations and aggregations against a large volume of decision-support data.

A data warehouse is typically a large, central store of decision-support data whereas smaller, more specialized *data marts*, effectively divide analysis data into business unit and divisional data warehouses. *SQL Server Analysis Services* (see http://www.microsoft.com/sql/evaluation/bi/bianalysis.asp) is capable of storing and analyzing data in both relational and multi-dimensional structures. Data warehouse systems often use special query expressions that have capabilities beyond that of SQL. The *Multidimensional Expressions (MDX)* language supports pivoting and slicing data cubes to derive informational facts for comparative analysis.

Eventually most businesses that generate reports from live data will experience a common anomaly. As the data in a transactional database is ever growing and changing, reports will reflect these subtle changes and show up on the bottom line. Different users may produce similar reports in a short period of relative time and will notice that totals and summary values slightly vary. With no other explanation, users question the accuracy of report data and assume that there is a problem with their data. Believe it or not, the technical term for this condition is known as "twinkling data". As this phrase suggests, the totals and data points aren't typically way out of line. They just seem to fluctuate slightly. Reporting Services helps this situation by "freezing" report data through *caching* and report *snapshots*.

You might not perceive this to be a problem but consider what might happen if a user had made data entry mistakes and in an effort to correct the errors, entered duplicate, corrected data and then deleted the old records. Or, they deleted the erroneous records and then re-entered corrected information. If a report were produced at the wrong time, summary values could be skewed significantly. Statistically speaking, the chances of this condition causing a crisis may not be significant, but over time, they may increase. Data analysis should therefore be performed on unchanging values that are updated at regular, predictable intervals. This problem is often addressed by building separate OLAP data stores used only for analysis and reporting against snapshot data imported from transactional databases at regular intervals.

The Reporting Lifecycle

Chapter 2 will discuss the reporting lifecycle in greater detail with the architecture that supports this process. Briefly, creating a functional reporting solution requires an understanding of user and business requirements. Existing data sources must be considered and new data stores must be designed to meet reporting needs. From this perspective, the process of creating useful reports consists of three activities:

❑   **Authoring**: With the available tools, reports are authored using the *Report Designer* in Visual Studio .NET. This interface is used to create data sources, queries and datasets, and the report definition.

❑   **Management**: Report management is performed using the *Report Manager*, a web browser interface used to manage and deploy report definition files, shared data sources, and configuration settings; it can also be used to view and export report data.

❑   **Delivery**: Reports may be delivered to a user *on-demand* through the Report Manager or a custom application; it can also be scheduled for delivery through *subscriptions*. Reports can be delivered in the form of a web page, document, file, or even via email.

Report Delivery Application Types

In the past, reporting solutions were typically delivered through a desktop application of some kind. Data was queried in real time, and of course the application had to be connected to the data source. Users also had limited opportunity to save reports for later viewing and usually printed them on paper.

Now we have many opportunities to view and interact with reports in environments where it may not be possible (or feasible) to connect to data stores. Reports may also be presented in different forms that offer multiple capabilities and compatibility with various devices and software.

Web Browser

Web browser-based solutions have become popular for a number of reasons. User accessibility takes on a whole new definition when special software isn't required on the client computer. Of course, a web browser makes information available for viewing over the World Wide Web, but browser-based solutions are also a compelling means to deliver information in a controlled business enterprise environment. Whether users access resources within their corporate intranet environment or over the web, the browser paradigm has significantly changed the approach to application delivery.

Some of the traditional challenges with browser-solutions are the lack of consistent support for client-side script and components. These issues have largely been resolved with server-side rendering mechanisms that output product-independent HTML content. For viewing offline content, HTML documents require links to external files, such as images, sounds, and video. These issues have also been resolved by using a MIME-encoded format call *MHTML* or *Web Archive* to encapsulate binary content within the page definition. Although not supported in all browsers, this format is a viable means to deliver extensible report content for live and off-line viewing. HTML 4.0 works on different types of computers across the Internet, within a LAN on newer web browsers and HTML 3.2 works with older browsers and on a portable or hand-held device.

Office Applications

Microsoft Office brings together a tremendous assortment of capabilities to assist report users at all levels. Microsoft Excel has been the mainstay tool for data collection and analysis. By rendering a report into Excel, the data may easily be reformatted, modified, or analyzed using formulas and calculations. This capability has been around for several years but it required writing custom code to use the Excel object model from Access or Visual Basic to produce report data in Excel; in addition, this process was tedious at best. Now, pushing complex report data into a useful and well-formatted Excel document is simple.

Microsoft Access continues to be the office worker's database of choice. Data tracking and management solutions can be created with minimal cost and effort. Report Services may be used to exchange and import data into an Access database using XML or CSV formats. Access and Excel both provide the Office Web Components that may be used to view pivot tables and charts. These components duplicate the functionality of the Matrix and Report Services *chart* items but might give users a more convenient option for analyzing data.

Programmability

The possibilities for incorporating report features in your own applications are impressive. All of the features of the Report Manager can be duplicated in many cases and can be extended through program code. Reports may be viewed in place within an application by using an external web browser window, integrated browser control, or a custom report viewer component. Report content may be rendered to a file for persistent storage to directly into a viewer or browser.

Subscriptions

Subscriptions allow users to receive or gain access to reports on a regular schedule. Reports are delivered by email or saved to files where they may be viewed offline at the users' convenience. Report subscriptions may be setup for an individual user or large groups of users using data-driven subscriptions. To put this into perspective, effectively reports may be delivered to any individual or size group of users in practically any readable format at any place and any time.

Report Formats

In addition to the three HTML rendering formats, you can use document types to control formatting elements, printing layout and adding other capabilities. The PDF document format remains the most popular means for assuring that documents are formatted exactly as they were intended. Rendering a report to a Microsoft Excel workbook gives users the ability to continue to message data and perform calculations.

Importing Data/Exchanging Data

Not all "reports" may be intended to be read or printed. Reporting Services provides two report rendering formats that can be used for export/import and data exchange. Using either the *Comma Separated Values (CSV)* or XML formats, Reporting Services provides a very convenient mechanism for inter system data exchange or pushing data out to a trading partner. Imagine your system automatically sending invoices and shipping manifests to your order fulfillment vendor at end of the day via XML file attachments to email.

System Requirements

The hardware system requirements for Reporting Services are very similar to those for SQL Server. The default installation will place the Report Manager, Reporting Services, and the Report Server database on the same physical server but this configuration is not a requirement. These components may be installed on three separate servers.

The Report Server and the Report Manager servers must be running *Internet Information Services (IIS)* 5.0 or higher with ASP.NET, and the .Net Framework 1.1 or higher. The Report Server Database requires any edition of SQL Server 2000 with Service Pack 3. The SQL *Agent* and the *Distributed Transaction Coordination (DTC)* services must be running.

Editions of Reporting Services correspond to editions of SQL Server and include Evaluation, Standard, Development, and Enterprise editions. Like SQL Server, Standard Edition is a good solution for a single-server environment with a moderate number of users.

The Enterprise Edition has additional capabilities to support many users in a scalable environment using web farms and clustering technology. Subscriptions may be managed for users and recipients whose names and email addresses are stored in any accessible database.

The following table shows the requirements and features for each edition of Reporting Services:

SRS Edition	Operating System	Requirements
Enterprise	Windows 2003 Server	Must be configured as an Application Server SQL Server 2000 Standard or Enterprise with SP3
	Windows 2000 Server	Windows 2000 SP4 SQL Server 2000 Standard or Enterprise with SP3
Standard	Windows 2003 Server	SQL Server 2000 Standard or Enterprise with SP3
	Windows 2000 Server	Windows 2000 SP4 SQL Server 2000 Standard or Enterprise with SP3
Developer	Windows XP Professional	Windows XP SP1 SQL Server 2000 Developer, Standard or Enterprise with SP3 limited to 10 database connections
	Windows 2000 Professional	Windows 2000 SP4 SQL Server 2000 Developer, Standard or Enterprise limited to 10 database connections
Evaluation	Windows XP Professional	Windows XP SP1 SQL Server 2000 Evaluation, Developer, Standard or Enterprise with SP3 limited to 10 database connections
	Windows 2000 Professional	Windows 2000 SP4 SQL Server 2000 Evaluation, Developer, Standard or Enterprise with SP3 limited to 10 database connections

Installing Reporting Services

This section describes the steps for installing Reporting Services for SQL Server 2000. Reporting Services may be installed using one of two methods. A standard, Windows setup package provides a wizard dialog to guide the user through the entire process. It will prompt for file paths, server and other resource names and allow for optional component selection. The other installation method is a command-line utility and may be used, typically by system administrators, to script or automate the installation process. This method is not quite as user-friendly and requires more planning and a better understanding of the product and its components.

Setup Options

The following options are offered during setup as shown in Figure 1-1:

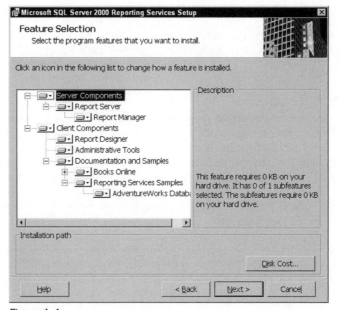

Figure 1-1

You can select the feature options that you want to install. Some features are related to others and appear as expandable branches of the feature tree. A plus sign next to a feature indicates that the branch includes related features. You can also specify that all related features under a branch should be installed by choosing the option labeled Entire feature will be installed on local hard drive. Likewise, selecting Entire feature will be unavailable will set this mode for all features under this branch. See Figure 1-2:

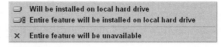

Figure 1-2

A few options can be installed so the content is located on a central network fileshare. Choosing this option for Books Online, for example, will not copy these files to the local disk but will refer to files at a central location. In order to use this option, it is necessary for the setup disk image to be copied to a folder that will be accessible whenever this feature is used. Some features include the option to install and run from the network displaying the drop-down list shown in Figure 1-3:

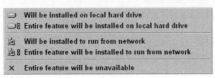

Figure 1-3

Adding and Removing Options

After the initial product installation, features may be added or removed by running setup again from the Control Panel | Add or Remove Programs applet. The currently installed start is displayed for each feature. Any changes made in the setup dialog will cause features to installed or removed.

Server Components

Server components include the Report Server and the Report Manager. It consists of a Windows service that runs continually on the server computer, a .NET web service hosted in IIS and a SQL Server database. The Report Server database can be installed on only one instance of SQL Server per physical database sever computer. The database need not reside on the local Report Server computer but the server must be a member of the Windows domain or a server trusted by the domain.

Report Manager is an ASP.NET application that exposes reports, configuration, and administrative features through a web browser interface.

The Report Manager requires IIS 5.0 or greater to be running on the Report Server computer. The .NET Framework version 1.1 also must be installed on the server. This is an included feature of Windows Server 2003. On a Windows XP Professional system, SP1 is required. Windows 2000 Professional, Server, and Advanced Server require SP4. Windows XP Home Edition is not supported.

Client Components

This includes the Report Designer. This option installs the *Report Project* and *Report Wizard Project* templates and *BI Projects* project group into Visual Studio .NET 2003 or greater. The Report Designer enables developers to create report projects in Visual Studio to create reports and related data sources. A report project generates definition files in Report RDL, an XML grammar that defines report content, layouts, and data sources. These reports may be deployed directly from Visual Studio into the Report Server. Reports may also be deployed manually using the Report Manager.

The Report Designer and Report Server can reside on different computers to support a separate development environment. The installation requirements for the Report Designer are the same as those for Visual Studio .NET 2003.

Let's look at the documentation and samples for Reporting Services.

Books Online

The documentation for Reporting Services is the Reporting Services Books Online. Its format and behavior are similar to that of SQL Server Books Online. All Reporting Services - related documentation is contained in only one source. If you plan to install the server and client tools on different computers, you should consider including the Books Online with both installations.

Reporting Services Samples

The samples include example projects for Visual Studio .NET, SQL Server databases, import data files, report definitions, and scripts. The projects include Visual Basic and C# code samples to manage and render reports using program code. The samples also include several reports exemplifying various design techniques.

AdventureWorks Database

The AdventureWorks2000 sample database was created for demonstration and instructional purposes in future versions of SQL Server and related products. Like the Northwind and Pubs databases, it will include design elements and sample objects for SQL Server developers and administrators. Unlike Northwind and Pubs, the AdventureWorks database is not a simplified design. It has been created to model the design of a highly normalized, large-scale business database containing over 60 tables. We will use this database for many of our sample reports later in the book.

Administrative Tools

Command-line utilities provide scripting and command level access to server management, deployment, and configuration features. These capabilities are thoroughly discussed in Chapter 8.

The following command-line utilities are installed with the Administrative Tools option:

Utilities	Description
rs	Used to process script files for deploying reports, managing the Report Server database, making and restoring backups, and other administrative tasks.
rsactivate	Used to manage the Report Server Windows service on a local or remote Report Server computer.
rsconfig	Used to set or modify configuration settings for a Report Server. This includes security authentication setting and database connections.
rskeymgmt	Used to allow administrators to backup and restore private keys to enable access to this secure information.

Command Line and Unattended Installation

The setup may be run using command line switch to automate the installation process. This capability is provided by the standard Windows Installer 2.0. Although there is no command-line interface, the setup process may be scripted and settings can be specified.

Log Files

Reporting Services records event information in the standard Windows Application Log and in specific log files. Report execution logging is enabled by default and may be configured in the Report Manager. Specific settings for the Report Server are stored in the `RSReportServer.config` file. More granular tracing information may be captured in log files for a variety of application and server events and system errors. These logs may be helpful in analyzing usage and debugging specific problems. The log files are auto-generated using time-stamped names. The file names, categories, and locations correspond to the configuration files mentioned in the *Configuration Files* section of this chapter.

Email Delivery

In order for Report Services subscriptions to utilize email delivery, an available server must be configured for the *Simple Mail Transport Protocol (SMTP)*. Internally, Report Services uses *Collaborative Data Objects (CDO)* to send mail. These required components are part of the standard configuration of Windows 2000 servers and Windows Server 2003 operating systems but you should verify that they are installed and working. The best way to do this is to create a test subscription in the Report Manager and verify that it has executed and the message is received in the recipient's inbox. Subscriptions are covered in detail in Chapter 10.

The SMTP service is not required on the actual report server but an accessible SMTP server must be available to the server in order for this feature to work. If you don't have an SMTP server configured, or if you don't intend to use the email delivery option, simply leave these fields blank in the setup wizard.

Designing Reports

Chapter 3 will deal with the essentials of report design and followed by Chapter 4 will take more specific design elements to the next level. Reports fall into a few design categories which will be covered next.

Form Reports

A report can display a single record on a page with data from a table, calculations and just static text. Form reports can be used to print or display a letter, invoice, contract or informational sheet.

Tabular Reports

This is a fundamental style for reports that have repeated rows of data called data regions. Tabular data is repeated in free-forum bands or table rows with rows and columns. Either the list or table items may be used to produce a tabular report in various layouts. Column headers can be displayed for each column in a table and subtotals and summary information may be displayed in table or group section footers.

Groupings and Drill-Down

Records in a report may be sorted and grouped. Each group can be collapsed and expanded to drill-down into more detail. This capability gives users the ability to explore large sets of data without the need to scroll though long, multi-page reports. The report may also be printed in its expanded form.

Drill-Through Reports

A drill-through report can be any standard form, tabular or pivot table report that contains links to a separate report. Any textbox item may used as a link to provide drill-through capability. Key values are hidden with the link and passed as a parameter to the target report for filtering.

Multi-Column Reports

A report may contain multiple columns. List or tabular rows are repeated vertically within a column and then *snake* from one column to the next, filling the page. This type of format is ideal for optimizing page space for labels and contact information.

Matrix

A matrix is like a cross-tab or a pivot table in which the rows and columns roll-up summary values and may be expanded or collapsed to expose more detail. It is a simple and easy-to-use control, much like the datagrid control in ASP.NET.

Charts

Charts are used to display a graphical representation of data, typically aggregated along at least two axes. Common types of charts are bar and column, pie and donut, line, area and scatter charts. More specific types of charts like stock and bubble charts are more specialized.

Data Sources

Reports can obtain data from standard data providers supported by the .NET Framework. In addition to SQL Server versions 7.0 and 2000, this list includes Oracle, Access, Excel, Informix, DB2, and any other databases and data sources accessible via an OLE DB provider or ODBC driver. Non-relational sources such as Active Directory Services, Exchange Server, and OLAP sources like Analysis Services can be queried. Developers can create custom data provider extensions— when an OLEDB provider or ODBC driver does not exist—to make practically any type of data accessible to a report.

Queries

Each report contains a query expression within its definition. A standard Transact-SQL query builder tool is incorporated into the report designer, capable of producing complex query expressions to be stored in the report. Although this is the defacto behavior of the designer, keeping queries in the report may not always be the best practice. Using a view or stored procedure from a SQL Server database can be a far more efficient method to query enterprise data. Parameters passed to a stored procedure cause the precompiled query to be processed on the database server before data is transferred across network connections.

OLAP Reporting

Decision-support databases come in many sizes and shapes. In its simplest form, a reporting data source can be a relational database with a few tables that can be queried more easily with some joins to other tables. Unlike transactional databases (often called online transaction processing or OLTP systems), OLAP databases are designed for efficient read-only access and reporting.

Large-scale OLAP databases require special storage and retrieval engines. Data may be managed in a cube structure, which enables values to be summarized and aggregated into slices and pivots. To query these structures effectively, MDX is used—much like SQL is used for relational structures. Reporting services supports the use of MDX queries although the reporting engine was not specifically built around this capability. When an OLAP data provider is used as a data source, the Report Designer displays the Generic Query Designer, which supports MDX expressions. The dataset resulting from this type of query is flattened into rows and columns like any other dataset. For this reason, all report items are supported for MDX queries.

Using Visual Studio .NET

Visual Studio .NET is Microsoft's integrated development environment tools for developing all types of applications. It replaces several different development tools in previous versions. Visual Studio now supports many different programming languages and file types. Whether you are an application developer or not, Visual Studio is the only tool currently available to design and build reports for SQL Server Reporting Services. Because of the extensibility of Reporting Services and the RDL XML grammar, other design tools will likely become available soon.

Report Wizard

The Report Wizard is a simple way to get started creating reports. It leads a designer though all of the steps necessary to build a simple report interface. New designers will find it an easy, uncomplicated tool for creating or choosing a data source, creating a query, selecting fields for header, grouping and display values, and choosing report styles and format options. Experienced designers will likely not find the wizard helpful as they become more familiar with the design process and prefer to have more control of these options. After completing the wizard, the report design may be extended and tuned to provide more functionality.

The .NET Framework

The Microsoft .NET Framework is a completely new direction for Microsoft, and replaces the *Application Programming Interfaces (API)* and object technology of the past. It's far more than a marketing strategy or a product. It gives application developers the objects and building blocks to create powerful applications of all kinds. Design and debugging features are also available in it to help developers through the tedious application development process. Utilities and compilers enable applications to be configured, compiled, and deployed. A runtime environment manages execution, resource allocation, security, and interoperability with other services, servers, and operating systems.

The main thing to understand about .NET is that it is a core component of Windows and it supports applications at many levels. The runtime and the development support tools are free. Visual Studio .NET is a development tool that gives developers convenient access to these design and development capabilities.

Reporting Services is built on the .NET platform. The Report Server runs as a Windows service and is a .NET-managed assembly. Rendering and management features are exposed as an ASP.NET web service. The Report Manager is an ASP.NET web forms application. Finally, the report metadata, subscriptions and configuration information is managed in a SQL Server 2000 database access through the SQL Server ADO.NET data provider. As you can see, Reporting Services is purely a .NET solution.

Custom Reporting Extensions

On the advanced end of the opportunity scale, reports can be extended and enhanced in a variety of ways. At the core of the Reporting Services architecture is a set of extendable programming interfaces that enable the use of custom components written with .NET programming tools.

Data Processing Extensions

The .NET Framework includes native support for connecting to standard data sources using the SQL Server, OLE DB, ODBC, and Oracle .NET data providers.. However, to report on non-traditional types of data, developers can create custom data processing extensions to expose practically any type of data as a data provider, for instance. If a cache of data could be held in memory rather than written to disk. Another example would be data stored in files using a proprietary format.

Delivery Extensions

Reporting Services supports subscription delivery via email or file output with no additional programming work. Additional delivery options can be added by creating a custom delivery extension. Using a custom solution, reports could be sent to a message queue, FTP site or practically any other destination.

Configuration Files

Options and settings are stored in XML-based text files that are easy to edit and maintain. The purpose, location and content of these files are detailed in Appendix E. Configuration files include the following:

File Name	Purpose
RSReportServer.config	All settings that apply to the Report Server including connections and security, caching, and subscription delivery options.
RSWebApplication.config	Settings that apply to the Report Manager web application. Most settings correspond to options in the Report Manager application configuration pages.

Table Continued on the following page

File Name	Purpose
`ReportingServicesService.exe.config`	Enables tracing and logging of certain server events that include restarts, exceptions, warnings and status messages. Some settings are used to manage the trace and log files and tracing output options.
`RSReportDesigner.config`	Used to manage and configure custom data processing and rendering extensions. Also sets designer preview and rendering options.

Scripting

Most report management and delivery features may be automated through a simple scripting interface. A single utility executable, `rs.exe`, is used to obtain access to the vast capabilities of the Report Services web service. You can create scripts to manage batch processing of reports or programmatically manipulate any exposed functionality of reporting service. Capabilities are similar to that of the web service proxy used in .NET programming code but a scripting solution is a simpler approach that doesn't require complex programming or a compiled project. Scripting is an ideal approach for system administrators to create simple maintenance, deployment and ad-hoc delivery solutions. Chapter 8 will detail report scripting options.

Subscriptions

Subscriptions allow users to request reports to be delivered to them automatically. Based on a schedule (single-instance or recurring) reports may be delivered using any available deliver extension (email, file or custom) in any available rendering format. Subscriptions can be either standard, where a user requests the scheduled delivery of a specific report, or data-driven, where a group of users can request the scheduled delivery of one or more reports. This is an extremely powerful tool that can be used to provide report content in an efficient manner to users in practically any location or work schedule. Chapter 10 will lead you through this compelling feature.

Securing Reports

Reporting Services uses a role-based security model that is installed and configured by default. This model is highly extensible and may be changed after installation to use a custom authentication component.

In order for sensitive data to be protected from intrusion, it should be encrypted both at the Report Server and in the web browser or client application. The preferred method to do this is to use Reporting Services' built-in support for certification-based encryption over the *Secure Sockets Layer (SSL)*. Implementing SSL will automatically redirect web requests to an address at the same location using the http:// prefix. This enables bidirectional encrypted streaming of all data over port 443 (by default) rather than the standard HTTP port 80. Reporting Services supports levels of automatic encryption which are detailed in the section that follows. There is currently no maintenance interface for this setting through the Report Manager or any other provided utility.

You will need to obtain a digital certificate from a certificate authority such as Verisign, AuthentiCode or Thawte. These companies will sell or lease the certificate for a specified period of time for a few hundred dollars per year. The authority will do a background check on your business to verify you are legitimate. Configuring the certificate is actually quite easy. This is performed using the IIS management console and setting the properties for the ReportServer web folder.

To enable encryption in Report Services, edit the RSReportServer.Config file using Visual Studio or a text editor and set the SecureConnectionLevel element to a value from 0 to 3.

In the RSReportServer.Config file, you will find this setting near the top of the file after the encrypted login and connection settings:

```
<Add Key="SecureConnectionLevel" Value="0"/>
```

Modify only the number value between the double quotes and save and close the file:

The values are as follows:

Value	Description
0 (default)	Disables encryption support
1	Enables minimal support but may expose credentials if a certificate isn't installed or configured properly
2	Provides an appropriate level of encryption for rendering and authentication calls
3	Encrypts all data

The Report Manager

The Report Manager (shown in Figure 1-4) is a web-based interface that provides both user-level access to reports and administrative features to configure security, subscriptions, report caching, and data access.

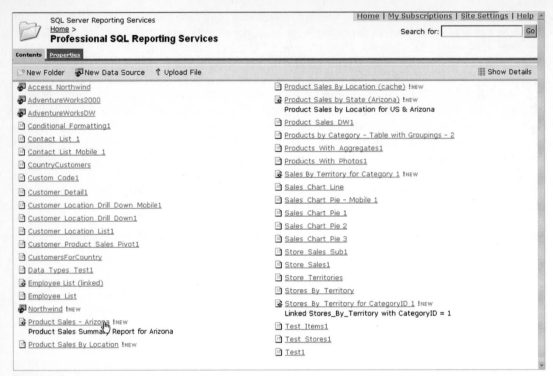

Figure 1-4

This web application is used to perform report and server administration as well as report delivery. Users may use it simply navigate to reports, provide parameter values and view them. The Report Manager will be discussed in detail in Chapter 6.

Designing Reports

In this first release of Reporting Services, reports are designed and created in Visual Studio .NET using a special type of project especially for report design. Simple reports can be built with little effort using the report wizard. The wizard (shown in Figure 1-5) leads the user through all of the steps necessary to produce a variety of useful but simple report designs.

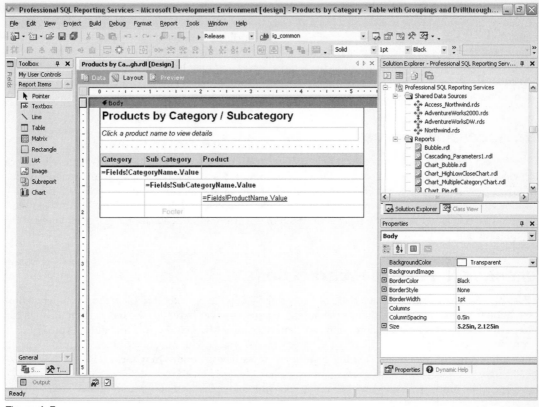

Figure 1-5

Chapter 3 will lead you through a series of exercises to get you started with simple report design and lay the foundation of the report design elements.

In Chapter 4, we will explore data sources and datasets that provide data for reports. We will discuss different query types like SQL expressions, MDX expressions, views and stored procedure. Query parameters and report parameters enable data to be filtered at the right level and to make the best use of data, server and network resources.

In Chapter 5, we cover the spectrum of report design items, data ranges and formatting tools. By using groupings, we can design multi-level, hierarchal reports. Drill-down reports let users interactively expand groupings and discover more detail without having to navigate through many pages of content. Drill-though reports let users navigate from one report to another, passing filtering parameters to obtain detail information about items in the report. Navigational links may also be used to drill-through to external resources like web pages, documents and email links.

Charts are useful for aggregating values and presenting a series of data for comparison. A number of standard charts are available including bar, column, line, area, pie and doughnut charts. Specialized charts types like scatter, bubble, and stock charts are used with multi-dimensional data and values in distinct ranges.

Report formatting and content may be enhanced by using program code in a few different ways. Custom functions may be written in a block of code that is embedded into the report. These functions may then be called in various property expressions providing conditional formatting and business rules. More complex code routines may be built into a class library and exposed to reports as custom assemblies. An assembly is deployed to the Report Server and may be shared by many reports. Finally, custom extensions may be written to replace or extend inherent data source and rendering capabilities, providing custom capabilities beyond those built-into the product.

URL Access to Reports

The Report Manager environment is the default entry point and a convenient, comprehensive interface to view reports. However, one easy method to view a report is to simply navigate to the report's web address provided by the Report Server. URL query string parameters are used to specify a variety of options including rendering formats, filtering parameter values, and display options. This is a simple method for managing and using reports right out of the box—without additional programming or configuration.

Rendering Reports in Program Code

Possibly the most unique characteristic of Reporting Services is the way it renders report content. Unlike traditional report solutions that use a proprietary, custom viewer to render the report content; at its core, Reporting Services is built on a programmatic interface (an XML web service) that outputs the entire contents of reports in several different file or rendering formats. This capability gives programmers an incredible range of options for creating custom solutions. These options may include:

- ❑ On a simple web page, users could click a link to display a custom report in their web browser using simple URL rendering.

- ❑ In a custom ASP.NET web application, users provide filtering criteria on a web page; click a button and view the resulting report in a secondary browser window without navigating off the application's web site.

- ❑ In a desktop application, users provide filtering criteria and view the report within the desktop application form.

- ❑ Custom reports are saved to an Adobe Acrobat (PDF) file that may be viewed offline on a laptop, Pocket PC or other mobile device.

An in-depth discussion of programmatic rendering may be found in Chapter 9. Even for the novice programmer, creating these kinds of solutions is relatively simple and may be accomplished with just a few lines of program code.

Report Definition Language

Rather than defining a proprietary specification for individual report definitions, our friends at Microsoft took a very different approach. They chose to publish an extensible and well documented standard. The entire set of instructions that define a report are stored in a single XML document using an RDL XML grammar. If necessary, property values for elements of a report's design could be modified with a text editor. If someone wanted to build their own report design tool, they would simply need to output the appropriate XML tags to an RDL file. This also makes it easy and convenient to send the report definition to someone or to deploy a report to another server.

In chapter eleven, we will use a third-party tool to build reports from an RDL template. This will enable us to create new reports without using Visual Studio .NET. This exercise should open your eyes to the possibilities to design and build reports from your own custom software, extending vertical business systems and making Reporting Services part of a complete business solution.

Deploying Reports

Reports are defined in an RDL file but the report's definition is stored in the Report Server database once it has been deployed to the server. Report deployment may be performed in at least three different ways. In Visual Studio .NET, the project defines a corresponding web folder on the target Report Server. Building a report project will deploy reports to a designated target Report Server. The Report Manager web interface may be used to deploy individual reports manually by simply browsing for and selecting the RDL file. The Reporting Services web service may be used to deploy reports programmatically using methods of this multi-purpose object. Chapter 13 will explore each of these options and detail deployment techniques and related considerations.

Designing and Architecting Report Solutions

Reporting Services does offer an out-of-the-box solution. Reports can be designed in Visual Studio .NET, deployed to a server and viewed using the Report Manager Web interface quite easily. However, for custom applications or to meet specific business needs, this may not be the ideal solution. Reporting Services is an extensible service with several options for designing, managing, deploying, rendering and delivering reports to users.

In Chapter 13, we will discuss these options and consider how understanding your business requirements should lead to the most ideal solution. We will look at different business cases and how a reporting solution fits into the overall picture to meet business and users' needs now and in the future.

Summary

At this point, you should understand that Reporting Services uses a new approach for report delivery. Each report has a data source that may be shared with other reports. A data source can obtain from practically any database product or data provider.

Report definitions are stored in an XML document format called RDL. Out-of-the-box, reports may be designed in Visual Studio .NET but third-party and custom solutions may be used to create and design reports as well.

Reporting Services can be completely secured and highly customized. The Report Manager is provided to simplify server, user and report management. Solutions may be simple and easy to implement or they may be completely customized and integrated into your custom-built software.

Reports may be delivered using snapshots and subscriptions that are either pulled by the user in real-time, or pushed by the server on a schedule. Using these capabilities, valuable system resources are conserved since reports are rendered less often and can be cached in the Report Server database

Setup is performed using a standard Windows Installer package. We've explored the setup options and selections. Configuration settings are stored in XML configuration files that may be modified by an administrator using a text editor.

The next chapter will help you understand the architecture that makes Reporting Services work. You will learn about the nuts and bolts that give this impressive product the ability to provide scalable and extensible reporting solutions. Throughout the book, we will build on this foundation as you learn to design, manage and deploy your own reporting solutions.

2

Reporting Services Architecture

Before writing any reports, we need to take a good look at what Reporting Services does. This chapter will introduce you to Reporting Services features and architecture.In the first part of the chapter, you will look at all the features of Reporting Services. These include the Report Designer, Report Server, and Programming Interface. The chapter will provide a surface-level overview of what you will see later in the book.

Next, we'll look at how Reporting Services is put together. We will walk you through the various processing components, data source extensions, and rendering extensions and take a closer look at how the Reporting Services Web Service works. This chapter also includes a series of illustrations to help you visualize each component.Once you have completed this chapter you will have a good understanding of the Reporting Services "big picture". This knowledge will carry you through the following chapters and help you draw it all together.

This chapter covers:

- ❏   The reporting lifecycle
- ❏   Reporting Services features
- ❏   Report Server components
- ❏   Data Processing Extensions
- ❏   Delivery extensions
- ❏   Report Server databases
- ❏   The Reporting Services Web Service
- ❏   Report Designer
- ❏   Reporting Services tools

The Reporting Lifecycle

Before digging into the architecture of Reporting Services, you need to understand the fundamentals of a reporting lifecycle. Reporting platforms can be evaluated by their support for the following areas—authoring, management, and delivery. We will take a look at what is included in each of these phases and later see how Reporting Services implements them. Take a look at the reporting lifecycle block diagram shown in Figure 2-1:

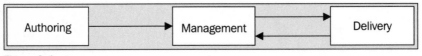

Figure 2-1

Authoring

The authoring phase is concerned with the actual development of reports. Authoring generally includes the following features:

- ❑ Connecting to a data source
- ❑ Writing database queries
- ❑ Creating report layout
- ❑ Creating report parameters
- ❑ Setting report properties such as height and width

These capabilities are important for the initial development of the report. They must be flexible enough to handle diverse reporting needs and structured enough to be easy to use.

Management

After developing the report, you move into the management phase, which is concerned with setting properties of reports specific to the production environment. These properties include:

- ❑ Data source connection information
- ❑ Default parameter values
- ❑ Security permissions
- ❑ Report caching
- ❑ Report execution schedules
- ❑ Report delivery schedules

Management phase is generally performed by the administrators. Most of the user access to reports is defined in this phase.

Delivery

The delivery phase looks at how reports get to the end users. Delivery includes:

- ❏ Providing an end user interface for browsing reports
- ❏ Publishing reports on a specific schedule
- ❏ Delivering reports to end users

A common concept in reporting platforms is *push/pull delivery*. Push delivery constitutes the reports that are sent to the user. Pull delivery constitutes reports that can be accessed on-demand by the user . Users are required to take the effort to get the report information. The report could be emailed to the requestor of the report, or published to a specified fileshare.

Reporting Services Features

Having seen the main phases in a reporting platform, let's look at the specific features in Reporting Services that make the three phases of reporting services possible. In this section, we will look at the Report Designer, Reporting Services, and the programming interface, and then move on to the specific components that make these features possible.

Visual Studio .NET 2003 Integration

Any respectable reporting platform must provide report writers with a rich set of design tools. Microsoft has created a designer to do just that. Because of the integration with Visual Studio .NET, users can take full advantage of the established development features. The designer also gives several design options to fulfill the users reporting requirements.

The Report Designer is fully integrated with Visual Studio .NET 2003. Through this integration, the Report Designer can take advantage of a number of established tools. Let's take a closer look at what the designer has to offer.

Query Designer

The query designer allows users to visually create data source queries. It works with multiple data sources and should be familiar to people already working with Microsoft products. Users can graphically drag and drop database objects to create SQL queries. They can also switch to a generic query designer to create freeform queries.

Server Explorer

The Visual Studio .NET Server Explorer allows users to view and work with multiple servers. This is extremely helpful when working with Microsoft SQL Server. Users do not have to switch from the Report Designer to other tools to view database objects. They can simply open the Server Explorer and browse for the specific object.

Visual Source Safe

Visual Studio .NET also integrates with Microsoft Visual Source Safe. Report writers can easily store and maintain the *version history* of their report files. This can be an invaluable tool when working on both large and small scale reporting projects.

Report Designer

Microsoft has created a couple of new Visual Studio .NET templates that allow you to create Reporting Services Report Projects. These Report Projects give you a graphical interface for creating their report definition. This interface displays the data sources used by the report, the layout of the report and also allows you to preview a report before it is published.

The Report Designer also provides a number of controls to facilitate report writing. You can create table reports, matrices, and freeform lists. The ability to combine these controls gives you even more possibilities.

If you want more control over the actual report definition, you can simply switch to Code view and see the XML generated by the designer. Working with the XML might seem a bit complicated, but when you need to do a search and replace a given word, this can be invaluable. It also lets you see a little more of what is created under the covers. Unlike other proprietary formats, XML allows you to easily read and debug report definitions.

Report Server Features

The Report Server is the main component of Reporting Services. It takes care of all report processing, data access, security, and rendering. For a while now, I have looked for what I truly felt was a service-based application—you hear a lot about it in development circles. I believe Microsoft has hit it on the head with this one. Reporting Services is truly a serviced application. Microsoft has elegantly encapsulated all the reporting functionality into one neat package. In this section we'll take a quick look at what's available.

Central Report Storage

Reporting Services creates one central store for your reports. This eliminates the need to deal with a bunch of messy fileshares. On a recent client engagement, I used it to help consolidate all of their different report areas into a hierarchical structure. This is easily accomplished with features available in Reporting Services. Central storage also makes it much easier for your users to access their reports—no more searching a bunch of directories for the item you want!

Security

In any reporting environment, you will have the need to secure certain items. Reporting Services integrates with Windows security to create a flexible role-based security model. This model allows you to create *roles* with a number of different permissions. You can then assign *Users* and *Groups* to these roles.

Reporting Services security is really the combination of three different items:

❑ **Role definitions**: A set number of tasks that can be performed. These include item-level roles, which apply to reports, folders, resources, and data sources, and system roles, those that apply to the Report Server site.

❑ **Securable object**: Securable objects include reports, folders, resources, data sources, and the Report Server itself.

❑ **Windows users and groups**: The combination of a role definition, securable object, and a Windows user/group creates a role assignment. This security model encapsulates the common features needed in a reporting system and gives you the flexibility to adopt it in your organization.

Report Delivery

Once you have created your reports, you will need an easy mechanism to deliver them. Reporting Services follows the standard push/pull model for reports. Push/pull refers to the ways in which a user can access information.

When you go to a web site and view stock quotes, you are pulling information, hence the push/pull part of the model. Users must be able to access information freely. Reporting Services allows users to navigate through the web to see listings of available reports.

Let's say you order a book online from http://www.amazon.com/ (hopefully this book). After you enter your credit card information, email address, and so on, and press Buy, Amazon sends a receipt to your inbox. This is an example of a push report. Email is just one delivery method for push reports. Reporting Services supports both email and fileshare push deployment along with the ability to create your own delivery extensions.

To take maximum advantage of a truly effective reporting system, users should have the ability to grab information when convenient and get information delivered on a regular basis.

Scheduling

Along with being able to deliver reports via email or a fileshare, a reporting system must have some mechanism to send these items on a regular basis. Reporting Services relies on *SQL Server Agent* to schedule and execute given tasks. Scheduling features in Reporting Services allows individual users and administrators to subscribe to reports on a schedule they define.

But, delivering information is not the only area where a scheduling tool comes in handy. If we think about what part of generating a report takes the longest, it is generally the actual retrieval of data. Reporting Services helps you eliminate some of this wait time by scheduling reports to execute (retrieve their data) on a regular schedule. So, if you update your sales information every Sunday, you could easily schedule a report to run early Monday morning. So when users come in on Monday, they'll have quick access to their information.

Programming Interface Features

When selecting a reporting platform, it is crucial to be able to extend that platform and incorporate it in existing systems. Microsoft has provided a web service interface for accomplishing these goals. Through the web service, you have complete access to the Reporting Services platform. Anything from rendering reports to creating subscriptions can be performed programmatically.

Open Architecture

Why did Microsoft use a web service interface? Web services are built on an open architecture. This means you do not need to have Microsoft development technologies to take advantage of them. The key to web services is that they are built on industry standard technologies. Through the use of XML, SOAP, and HTTP just about any platform can call and use web services.

Complete Access

Not only did Microsoft create a platform-neutral programming interface, they also let you do anything you need to through the interface. It is common to work with an API where the developer has limited control over what happens. With Reporting Services, the world is really open to you. If you just don't like the administrative tools that come with Reporting Services, you could write your own.

Most people do not go to this extreme, but it is important to have the flexibility. This means that as an application developer you can add any part of Reporting Services you need into your application. A common example would be creating your own custom interface for rendering reports. You could make it much easier for your users to get the report in exactly the format they want. Another example would be creating your own subscription interface. You might already know the users email information, so they click a few buttons and the subscriptions are done.

> *The possibilities for using the Reporting Services Web Service are only limited by what the product can do. This should be incredibly good news to all the code junkies out there.*

Report Server Components

Now that we have taken a look at what Reporting Services can do, let's get down to the nuts and bolts of how it works. In this section we will focus on the various components of Reporting Services. We'll move through processing of the report and data to rendering and delivering reports.

Report Processor

Report processing is the main driver in the Report Server. The Report Processor is responsible for handling user requests and returning the appropriate report and data. Along with this task it also performs caching of reports to improve performance. Let's take a look at the individual components that constitute report processing.

> *The main job of the Report Processor is to combine the report definition and report data to create and return this data.*

Report Request Handling

When a report request is received, the report processor takes the following steps:

1. It determines which report is being asked for and retrieves the report definition from the Report Server database.

2. The report processor asks for the report data. This is a call made into the data processing extensions (more on this in a moment).

3. The Report Server combines the two into an intermediate format. The intermediate format is then sent to the rendering extensions for delivery.

Report Definition

The report definition is an output format and a neutral representation of the report. Reporting Services was designed to support numerous output formats, so the report definition is not aware of how the report will actually be rendered. The report definition defines the query and layout of a report. These are things like the tables contained in the report, their position in the report, and number of columns. The query information is then used to retrieve data and to combine it with the layout. Once the report definition and data are combined, they form an intermediate format.

Intermediate Format

The *intermediate format* is an internal format of the report used by Reporting Services for rendering and caching. It is this format that is sent to the rendering extensions. It is a combination of both the data and report definition. The size of the intermediate format will depend mostly on the data that is returned.

Caching

The report processor also handles the caching of reports. When working with a reporting solution, the main bottleneck in report performance inevitably is the execution of queries. To solve this problem, Microsoft has developed a number of caching strategies. These strategies offer various performance gains and flexibility. The basic premise of a cached report is that we stored the report definition and data together. Thus when a user requests a report, the only thing that needs to be performed is the actual rendering. Rendering by comparison with other activities, is a relatively inexpensive part of the report processing in terms of server resources. Let's take a look at each of the caching strategies.

Session Cache

Since Reporting Services works over HTTP (we will talk more about this later), it must maintain some information about each user request. This is referred to as *session* information. If the same user asks for the same report in a relatively short period of time, it does not make sense to query that information again. So, when a user makes an initial request, the report definition and data are stored in the session cache. Session cache is used with on-demand reports (reports not cached).

Cached Instances

Cached instances also store the report definition and data, but they must expire at some given time. This time frame could be an hour, week, or month. The actual start time, however, is not defined. With a cached instance, the first user that requests the report has to wait for the query to process. After this initial request, the timeout is started. Once the report expires, the next user requesting the same information will have to execute the associated query.

This caching strategy is perfect if you have slower changing data, or even data that changes frequently but is not critical to update as soon as it changes. A good example of this would be stock quotes. They update constantly. It would be incredibly taxing on software systems if they had to keep up with this rapid rate of change. So, instead of updating every millisecond, stock quotes are generally updated every five to ten minutes.

Snapshots

The final type of caching strategy is the *snapshot*. Like the name implies, it is a snapshot of the data at a given point in time. Unlike cached instances, snapshots have a defined start time and not definite end time. Let's say you have a group of users that needs summary reports every Monday at 7:00 am for a weekly meeting. You are in the data warehousing group and have jobs that process data late Sunday night in preparation for the meeting. Once the data is processed, it does not change. This data is also very large and takes a long time to query. In that case, it makes perfect sense to store the reports right after the information is available. This way when people come in Monday morning to run the reports, they are kept ready and the users will not have to wait for any query processing. Therefore, by using snapshots, data is made available at a specific time within minimum amount of processing time.

Working again from our example above, a week goes by and you are again ready to run your reports. Would you want to get rid of the previous week's information? Certainly not—as soon as you do, someone is bound to ask for it! So, you need a mechanism to store that information away. Reporting Services gives you the ability to store a *history* of report snapshots. That way, even though the new snapshot has been created, the old one is still available.

Report Processing Illustrated

Figure 2-2 shows the process of requesting a report and moving through the Report Processor:

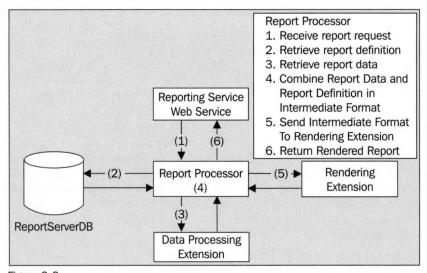

Figure 2-2

Data Processing Extensions

Now that we have seen the Report Processor, let's take a look at how the actual data is retrieved. Data is returned to the Report Processor through the *Data Processing Extensions*. The Data Processing Extension that is used will depend on the data source defined in your report. We describe the common functions of all these extensions and then those that are supported by Reporting Services.

Data Processing Defined

Data Processing Extensions are used to return data from a given data source. The architecture in Reporting Services supports the .NET managed providers and allows you to create extensions for your own particular data source.

The common functions that all Data Processing Extensions perform are as follows:

❑ Connect to the data source

❑ Pass parameters to the query

❑ Run the query on the data source

❑ Return a list of field names from the query

❑ Move through the rowset to retrieve data

Supported Providers

Reporting Services supports the .NET managed providers for returning data. These include SQL Server, OLEDB, ODBC, and Oracle. Since they are managed providers, they take full advantage of the .NET Framework. Using these four data providers, users should be able to connect to just about any data source. Let's take a look at some common providers.

SQL Server Provider

Using the SQL Server provider, users can retrieve data from SQL Server tables, stored procedures, views, and *User Defined Functions (SQL 2000)*. The SQL Server managed provider is optimized to connect to SQL Server. Extra layers such as OLEDB and ODBC have been removed for optimal performance.

Oracle Provider

Although Reporting Services uses SQL Server to store its metadata, you can use Oracle as a source for your reports. Like the SQL Server managed provider, the Oracle managed provider is optimized for Oracle and removes extra layers such as OLEDB and ODBC.

OLEDB Provider

The OLEDB provider gives report writers a great deal of flexibility. Using this provider, you can query a number of different data sources. The following is a list of just a few:

❑ Microsoft Analysis Services

❑ Microsoft Access

❑ Microsoft Excel

❑ Microsoft Directory Services

ODBC Processing Extension

ODBC works through the .NET OLEDB managed provider. The ODBC Processing Extension allows users to access any system with a compatible ODBC driver. This opens the door to reporting on a number of legacy systems, such as dBase and FoxPro. ODBC drivers have been written for most of today's database systems.

Be careful when using an ODBC driver. It is possible to connect to SQL Server, Oracle, and a number of data sources listed earlier. If you use an ODBC driver to connect to these data source instead of the native .NET managed provider or OLEDB provider, you could seriously hamper query performance. With your data sources, look for a .NET managed provider first, then an OLEDB provider, and if neither of these options is available, use an ODBC driver.

Data Processing Extensions and Data Providers

Along with the four .NET managed providers, users can also create their own custom Data Processing Extensions or data providers through the Reporting Services API. This allows users to expose the functionality of their data source to the end user and achieve some performance gains. The .NET Framework also allows the creation of .NET data providers. Since Reporting Services supports .NET data providers, this would be another viable option for connection to your custom data source. The role of Data Processing Extensions in relation to the report processor and the data source is shown in Figure 2-3:

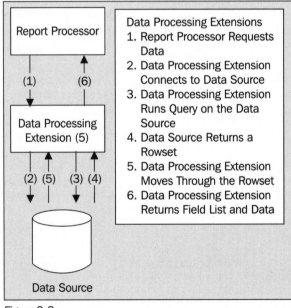

Figure 2-3

Supported Rendering Extensions

Reporting Services also supports a number of different rendering extensions. When creating a report in Reporting Services you are creating them in a neutral output format. In the report, you define the query, the fields, and how they should be laid out. It is the job of the rendering extensions to take this information combined with the data and create a useful output. Often, this is not an easy task. Let's take a look at some of the supported extensions. Microsoft has provided seven different rendering extensions. Each of these can be used to return report information.

Excel

The Excel rendering extension takes report data and outputs it to Excel. This is a common format for many users, especially for those users who will perform further analysis on the information.

The Excel rendering is more sophisticated than competing reporting platforms. Many reporting platforms lay out reports in a banded format. If you are familiar with Microsoft Access, you will understand the different bands for data detail, grouping headers and footers, page headers and footers, and report headers and footers. While this type of banded report does offer an extremely flexible report design, it does not always translate well into an Excel document.

By incorporating table and matrix controls in reports, users can create report layouts almost like they would in Excel. This type of layout lends itself nicely to rendering in Excel.

> *At the time of writing, Excel rendering is limited to Office XP and Office 11.*

PDF

Microsoft also provides a rendering extension for PDF Format, which is probably the most popular document format on the web. It is clean and easy to read and has printing capabilities. You would most likely choose this format for reports that are widely distributed but not analyzed by the end users. The reports that are in PDF format cannot be altered. Some common examples would be invoices, inventory pick tickets, weekly sales summaries, and a company's public financial documents.

PDFs also support document map functionality. This feature in Reporting Services allows you to define bookmarks within your report. Once the report is rendered, users can click on links to easily navigate to different areas of the report.

End users can download Adobe Acrobat Reader for free and you do not need a license to distribute PDF documents generated by Reporting Services.

HTML

Probably the most common output format for reports in Reporting Services is HTML. Since both the Designer Preview and Report Manager work in this view, reports can be rendered in HTML 4.0 or HTML 3.2. The .NET Framework looks at the user request to determine which browser is being used and then renders the report in the appropriate HTML format.

HTML rendering is good for interactive reports. By navigating to a web site, a user can easily manipulate report parameters to find specific information. HTML rendering also supports dynamic visibility, which gives users the ability to drill down to detailed information and supports document maps for easier navigation. Users can also render reports to HTML with *Office Web Components*. This allows for even greater manipulation of report information.

HTML rendering, however, is not good for printing. HTML pages are truly meant for displaying information. Most web applications will allow users to click a link and print printer friendly information. In Reporting Services, users can simply export a report to PDF or Excel and print it from there.

Web Archive (MHTML)

Web Archive or MHTML is commonly found in email messages. MHTML stands for *MIME Encapsulation of Aggregate HTML Documents* and these files have a .MHT extension. Generally an HTML document references a number of external resources such as images and style sheets. Although HTML allows for rich formatting of documents, it is hard to transport them when they reference other independent objects. MHTML takes care of this by encapsulating the externally referenced information such as images into one document.

MHTML documents are useful when sending out subscriptions. If users would like to view reports through email without opening an attachment, then MHTML is the appropriate format. One thing to note though is that not all email clients support this standard, so check your User Communities setup first.

CSV

The *Comma Separated Value (CSV)* format takes the report definition and data and transforms it into a *flat* file. This type of output is not appropriate for reading. It is suitable as a data exchange format. You might have customers with legacy systems that are very good at parsing and consuming flat files. In this case, you could electronically send reports in CSV format to these users. They could in turn consume the data and report on it or manipulate it how they see fit.

TIFF

The *Tag Image File Format (TIFF)* is a widely used format for storing document images. Many facsimile programs use this format to transfer data. Many organizations store documents in document management systems such as *SharePoint Portal Server*. Reports rendered in TIFF format would be excellent candidates for this type of document system. You could place historical snapshots of reports into your document management system and then remove them from the Report Server. This would allow you to take advantage of common document management features such as indexing.

XML

The *Extensible Markup Language (XML)* is very different from CSV rendering, but can serve many of the same purposes. XML is a structured markup language that lets you define data. Reporting Services uses this markup in a number of areas. When reports are rendered as XML, they include both the report definition and data, much like CSV rendered reports. Similar to CSV files, XML files are designed explicitly for the exchange of information. You could send XML rendered reports to customers or other applications for additional processing, or you could run the XML rendered report through an *XML Transform* document to control the standard formatting of the document.

Customized Extensions

Along with the seven supported rendering extensions, the Reporting Services API also allows users to create their own rendering extensions. So, if you want to output a report to a Word or a GIF file, you could create your own extension. Report rendering is illustrated in Figure 2-4:

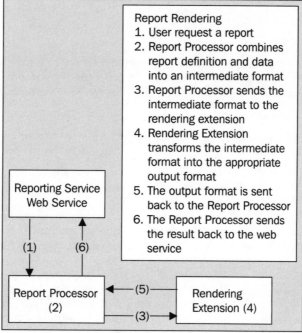

Figure 2-4

Scheduling and Delivery Processor

The Scheduling and Delivery Processor has two major functions, creating report snapshots and delivering subscriptions. These tasks hinge on the use of Microsoft's *SQL Server Agent*. The SQL Server Agent is responsible for queuing scheduled events. Reporting Services monitors these events and takes appropriate action as and when required. Scheduling and delivery have been encapsulated together because they use similar functionality. In both cases, Reporting Services is watching for a given event, processing the report, and then either storing that processed report or delivering it. Let's take a closer look at both the scheduling and delivery areas.

Scheduling

Scheduling refers to the actual setting up of the report execution and delivery schedule. When we store report schedules, this information is relayed to the SQL Server Agent to queue the request at the appropriate time. Both users and administrators can define schedules for report execution and delivery.

Delivery

Delivery deals with the mode of delivery of reports in Reporting Services. Users can have reports delivered via email, a fileshare, or a customized delivery extension, you will see more on delivery extensions in the forthcoming sections.

There are two types of subscriptions available in Reporting Services, standard and data-driven subscriptions.

Standard Subscriptions

Users can create their own subscriptions through Report Manager or a custom interface. Additionally, administrators can also create subscriptions for users. When setting up a standard subscription, information such as parameter values and rendering format can be set along with a schedule for report delivery.

With standard subscriptions, users can define their own schedule for receiving a report. This is important for small scale reports and gives users a great deal of freedom in how they receive certain information.

Data-Driven Subscriptions

Data-driven subscriptions offer a great deal of flexibility when delivering reports. You can create reports for any number of users, use different rendering formats for each user, and even change report parameters for each. This allows you to create a very custom report experience for users with a minimal amount of work.

Think of a large retail organization where each store in the organization has a store manager. Each week the store manager receives the sales numbers from the previous week. The report is identical for each manager except for the reference to the actual store. So, using data-driven subscriptions, you could dynamically set the store report parameter for each report and then email these individual reports to each manager. In the end you have created only one report, but quickly tailored it for a number of different users.

In both standard and data-driven subscriptions, the delivery of these reports is event-driven.

Schedule-Based Events

One of the common methods of determining when reports are to be delivered is doing so through some sort of schedule. The report could be delivered every month, week, day, or at any such pre-decided interval of time. Reporting Services gives users a number of different options when setting schedules. These schedules can be either specific to a given subscription or shared through Reporting Services.

Let's imagine that your organization has a set of reports that have their underlying data updated every Sunday evening. Executives for a Monday morning meeting can use this information. You could define a shared scheduled that contains information such as "Weekly, Monday, 6 am". This shared schedule could then be used for any number of reports. If later you decide that sending the report at 6 am does not meet new requirements, you could simply edit the shared schedule and thereby change the schedule for each report using it.

Snapshot Update Events

Delivery of reports can also be triggered by the update of snapshot reports. Many reports in an organization have set intervals after which they are updated. For example, data for a monthly sales report is always updated on the last day of the month. Once this has happened, the data is frozen and does not change for an entire month. If you want to create a report from this information, does it make sense to query the database each time the report runs? No, the information at this point is static. So, we create a snapshot of the data at the end of each month and store the entire report. At this point when users display the report you no longer have the overhead of a database call.

If we were going to update our reports according to a given schedule, it would only make sense to deliver them to the appropriate users when they are ready. Reporting Services allows users to set their subscriptions based on updates to snapshots. Through this method, we do not have to worry about setting a defined time when we think the report will be done processing; instead it will send off the delivery when report processing is finished.

Scheduling and Delivery Processor Illustrated

The following set of illustrations (Figure 2-5) will walk you through the various tasks performed by the Scheduling and Delivery Processor. Let's begin by handling the initial subscription and then move on to running snapshots and delivering subscriptions.

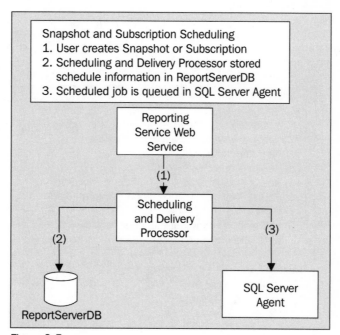

Figure 2-5

Now that we have seen how report schedules are created, we can look at both snapshot processing and subscriptions processing (Figure 2-6):

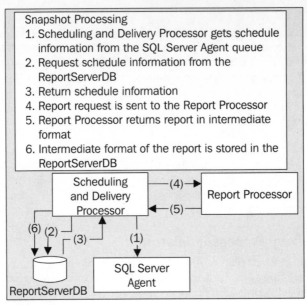

Snapshot Processing
1. Scheduling and Delivery Processor gets schedule information from the SQL Server Agent queue
2. Request schedule information from the ReportServerDB
3. Return schedule information
4. Report request is sent to the Report Processor
5. Report Processor returns report in intermediate format
6. Intermediate format of the report is stored in the ReportServerDB

Figure 2-6

The final piece of scheduling and delivering is subscription processing. In Figure 2-7, you can see the individual steps in the processing of report subscriptions:

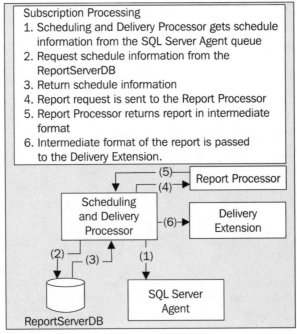

Subscription Processing
1. Scheduling and Delivery Processor gets schedule information from the SQL Server Agent queue
2. Request schedule information from the ReportServerDB
3. Return schedule information
4. Report request is sent to the Report Processor
5. Report Processor returns report in intermediate format
6. Intermediate format of the report is passed to the Delivery Extension.

Figure 2-7

Delivery Extensions

Delivery extensions are tied heavily to the Scheduling and Delivery Processor. They are used when sending subscriptions to users. Microsoft has provided two delivery extensions and given users the ability to develop their own. Reporting Services comes with two delivery extensions—email and fileshare. Let's take a look at each.

Email

The email delivery extension allows users to receive reports directly in their inbox. You can specify the rendering format that you would like the report to be delivered in and whether or not to include a web link to the report. Depending on the rendering extension used in the report, users will either see the report directly in their mailbox or receive it as an attachment. As mentioned earlier, you could use the Web Archive (MHTML format) to embed reports and their images in an email message.

To send email deliveries, Reporting Services must be able to communicate with a valid SMTP server. This setting is initially set when installing Reporting Services.

File Share

Reports can also be delivered directly to a fileshare. For this, Reporting Services must have Write permissions to the share. You can also specify credentials to use when sending reports to a fileshare.

Custom Extensions

Along with the supported extensions, Reporting Services also allows for the creation of custom delivery extensions. Say you like monthly reports to be delivered directly to a printer after they have been processed. You can create your own delivery extension and then schedule a subscription to use this delivery extension. In the Reporting Services sample folder, you can find an example for creating a delivery extension for a printer. Delivery extensions are illustrated in Figure 2-8:

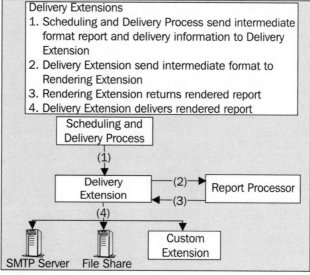

Figure 2-8

Report Server Databases

Reporting Services relies on SQL Server for storing its metadata. This allows for greater scalability in large reporting applications. This also allows you to take advantage of features inherent to SQL Server, such as backup and transaction logging.

Reporting Services uses two SQL Server databases to store data, `ReportServer` and `ReportServerTempDB`. In the next section, we will take a look at the major components of each database and describe how they are used. We will also take a quick look at a *Data Transformation Service* (*DTS*) package provided for monitoring information.

ReportServer Database

The `ReportServer` database is the main store for data in Reporting Services. It houses all report definitions, data sources, schedules and delivery information, security information, and snapshots and snapshot history. There are a series of tables for each functional area. The database schema is open and generally easy to follow.

> *Updating or querying these database tables is not recommended, but an understanding of how they are arranged should give you a better understanding of how Reporting Services works.*

The following table lists some of the tables in the `ReportServer` database and their related functions:

Table Name	Function
Resources	
Catalog	Information such as report definitions, folder locations, and data sources.
DataSources	Information about individual data sources. When reports are published, the data source information is removed to avoid inadvertent overwrites.
Security	
Users	User name and security ID (SID) information for authorized users.
Policies	User/Group role assignment information.
PolicyUserRole	User/Group role assignment information.
Roles	Role descriptions and permissions.
Snapshots and Snapshot History	
SnapshotData	Snapshot schedule information.
ChunkData	Actual report snapshots containing report definition and data.
History	Snapshot history information.

Table Name	Function
Scheduling and Report History	
Schedule	Schedule execution information.
ReportSchedule	Relates a given report to its execution schedule and subscription information.
Subscriptions	Subscription information such as owner, parameters and delivery extension.
Notifications	Subscription notification information such as date processed and last runtime and delivery extension.
ActiveSubscriptions	Information on subscription success and failure.
RunningJobs	Currently executing schedule processes.
Administrative	
Configuration	Reporting Services configuration settings.
ExecutionLog	Log of report executions including report, time started, time ended, format, and parameters.

> When working with Reporting Services, it is important to pay close attention to the ReportServer database. It contains all critical information related to Reporting Services and should be backed up on a regular schedule.

ReportServerTempDB Database

As the name implies, the ReportServerTempDB database stores temporary Reporting Services information. User session information is stored in the ReportServerTempDB. Because Reporting Services communicates using HTTP, no state is maintained between the client application and the server. Session state about the reports that the user is running must be stored between each server call. The ReportServerTempDB stores this information in a SessionData table.

ReportServerTempDB also stores report cache information. When a report is set as a cached instance, there is no definite time when that report is executed. It depends on which process requests the report first. Once the report is executed, the intermediate format and data are stored in the ReportServerTempDB database. If this database were to fail, the cached information would be lost. But, since it is executed when a user views the report, there is no real loss of information. Snapshots, on the other hand, are not stored here. Their execution time is usually at a set moment to ensure that the data on the report is correct. Therefore, this information is stored in the more permanent ReportServer database. Reporting Services will not be able to function without the ReportServerTempDB database.

It is not necessary to backup the data in the `ReportServerTempDB`.

Viewing Execution Information

As mentioned earlier, it is not recommended to view or modify the underlying SQL Server tables. It is also very difficult to analyze execution information in the ReportServer database. So, Microsoft has provided a DTS package for moving this data out of the ReportServer database.

To use the DTS package, you must first create a database to hold execution log information. Microsoft provides a number of scripts in Reporting Services to help with this task. Once the database has been created, you can use the DTS package to move information into it. Once the information has been moved to the new database, you can run queries against it or maybe even create a Reporting Service report.

The Reporting Services Web Service

One of the most outstanding aspects of Reporting Services is its open programming interface. Everything that we have seen so far can be performed through the *Reporting Services Web Service*. The Reporting Services Web Service is a set of functions you can use to render, subscribe to, and publish reports.

Reporting Services takes advantage of technologies already implemented in *Internet Information Server* (*IIS*) and the .NET Framework. Both these components provide the backbone infrastructure for web services. IIS performs web request handling and routing along with some security. The .NET Framework provides classes for consuming and publishing web service interfaces.

To understand the Reporting Services Web Service, you must first understand the underlying technology.

Web Services

Web services have really been a hot topic over the last few years. With them comes the promise of various applications exchanging information freely with one another. No more complicated interfaces for calling code on disparate systems—just one set of standards that everyone can follow.

The standards are what make web services so inviting. In the past, different companies have come up with their own standards for interfacing different sections of code. COM for example is a specification that allows code written in Visual Basic to talk to code written in C++. This is fine if you are working on Microsoft platforms, but what if you want your Visual Basic application to use functionality in a COBOL application. You would have to write some cumbersome code to make this happen. Let's take a look at the standards that make web services possible.

Open Standards

There are a number of open standards that make web services possible. When you think of code communicating with other code and all the tasks that entails, you quickly find some similarities. First of all, you need some transport mechanism for sending information.

One of the most widely adopted standards for sending information is *Hypertext Transfer Protocol* (*HTTP*) which is the default standard for web communication. It has the ability to send information back and forth between remote machines and has a huge implementation base. All major platforms today support sending information via this protocol. Now that we have a transport mechanism, we need to package (or address) the information.

Simple Object Access Protocol (*SOAP*) is a messaging protocol designed specifically for the distribution of information via HTTP. SOAP messages define a standard to package data and send it across the Internet. Some of this information includes header information for the message, security information, and the actual message body of itself. SOAP also uses XML as part of its protocol. So, you've got a package and a way to send it—now all you need is the message.

> **Web service messages are sent encoded in XML. This allows services to have richly defined interfaces and yet be able to use the structure of XML. It also allows other systems to easily read and manipulate data.**

Visual Studio .NET Integration

Visual Studio .NET has complete support for using web services. Consuming web services is almost as easy as working with objects in the .NET base classes. Using the Visual Studio .NET IDE, you can easily add web references to your projects and get full access to a web services. Using the Reporting Services Web Service through Visual Studio .NET allows you to take advantage of the IDE built-in functionality.

Although Visual Studio .NET makes it easy to work with web services, it is not the only development option. Because web services are built on open standards, any development tool supporting these standards can be used to work with them. For example, if you want to integrate Reporting Service functionality into your Microsoft Office applications, you can. Through Visual Basic for applications, you can write code that calls web services and therefore can call Reporting Services. You might want to build a list of reports into an existing Microsoft Access application. This could be easily accomplished in a few lines of code using the Reporting Services web service.

Available Features

Any feature that you use in the Report Manager interface can be used or accessed through the Reporting Services Web Service. There are no special calls from the Report Manager to Reporting Services.

Here is a list of just a few things available through the Reporting Service Web Service. The rest of the book will go into detail on these topic areas:

- ❑ Rendering reports through various rendering extensions
- ❑ Publishing reports programmatically
- ❑ Creating snapshot reports
- ❑ Adding snapshot reports to history
- ❑ Creating subscriptions
- ❑ Modifying data sources

The list could continue on with a number of different features. Just remember that anything you do in Report Manager can be done through the Reporting Service Web Service.

Report Designer

Creating reports in Reporting Services is very straightforward. Microsoft has provided a set of tools that allow you to easily build and publish your reports. In this section, we will take a look at how the Report Designer is incorporated in Visual Studio .NET and also explain the RDL file created by the designer.

Visual Studio .NET

Microsoft has chosen Visual Studio .NET as the standard development tool for their products. Along these lines, they have incorporated the Reporting Services Report Designer into Visual Studio .NET. Visual Studio .NET provides a number of other features other than the Report Designer.

Once you have installed the Reporting Services, there are a couple of project templates added to Visual Studio .NET. Inside Visual Studio .NET you will see a folder called **Business Intelligence Projects**. This folder contains both the **Report Project Wizard** template and **Report Project** template. Choosing either of these project templates will load the Report Designer.

Report Definition Language (RDL)

Now let's take a look at what exactly the Report Designer does. The Report Designer allows you to visually layout reports and build their underlying queries. This information is used to create an, RDL file. An RDL file is a XML document that defines the elements of a report. It is this file that is eventually published to the Report Server. Once the file is published, the report definition is stored in the `ReportServer` database. Any subsequent publishing of the report replaces most of the definition stored in the `ReportServer` database. You will learn more about RDL in Chapter 11.

Reporting Services Tools

There are a couple of tools included with Reporting Services. These tools allow you to publish reports, modify data sources, set security information, and a number of other tasks. Each of these tools relies on the Reporting Services Web Service. Anything that you can perform with these tools can be written in your own custom code. Let's take a look at a couple of the major tools, Report Manager and `RS.EXE`.

Report Manager

Report Manager is the main management tool for Reporting Services. It provides the following functionality:

- **Report management**
  - Uploading RDL files
  - Managing folder hierarchies

- ❑   Setting data source credentials
- ❑   Managing default parameter values
- ❑   Creating linked reports
- ❑   Creating execution snapshots
- ❑   Setting caching options

❑ **Security**

- ❑   Setting server-level and item-level security
- ❑   Defining Reporting Services Roles
- ❑   Assigning Windows Users and Groups to roles

❑ **Report delivery**

- ❑   Viewing reports
- ❑   Exporting reports to different rendering formats
- ❑   Defining report subscriptions

We will take a closer look at the Report Manager in Chapter 5.

Report Server Command-Line Utility (RS.EXE)

Reporting Services also comes with a command-line utility to simplify management of reports. After installing Reporting Services, you will find a file named RS.EXE. This utility contains a reference to the Reporting Services Web Service and allows users to call any of the service methods. To use the Reporting Services command line utility, you must first create a Visual Basic .NET input file. This file contains one main procedure and then instructions for working with the Report Server. The commands in the Visual Basic .NET file rely on the Reporting Services Web Service to perform their tasks. This file can then be passed into the command-line utility for execution.

A common example of this would be deploying development reports on a set basis. You can create a command line utility that checks for files updated in the Report Definition files. Once file changes are found, you could then use the Reporting Services command line utility to publish these files to the report server.

> *Reporting Services comes with a few samples that demonstrate how to perform various tasks using* RS.EXE.

Reporting Services Illustrated

Now that we have seen all the components that make up Reporting Services, let's take a look at an overall illustration. Figure 2-9 shows the different components of Reporting Services and how they are grouped. Notice that the actual functionality of Reporting Services is all encapsulated in one area. The databases storing data for the Reporting Service are separate. This means that we can physically separate the different components of Reporting Services to take advantage of *web farm* configurations (multiple servers combined to distribute processing), allowing us to create highly scalable applications.

Also notice that all calls to the Reporting Service go through the Reporting Services Web Service. This means that you can create your own custom front ends and have complete access to the Reporting Service.

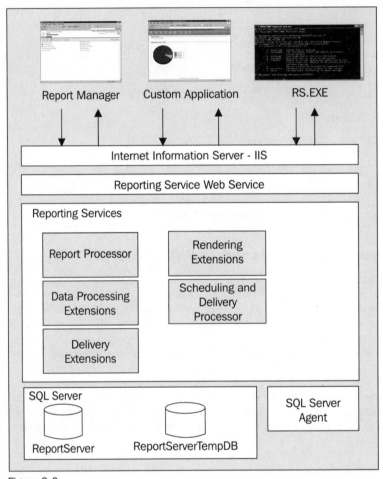

Figure 2-9

Summary

In this chapter, we covered the basics of Reporting Services. We started with a look at the three different reporting phases, authoring, management, and delivery. In the authoring phase, you dealt-with developing the report. In the management phase, you set attributes around the reports to use in the report generation phase. In the delivery phase, you specified the format in which users can view reports.

After discussing the phases, we saw the features of Reporting Services that support these phases. The Report Designer allows users to create rich reports. Once reports are created, they can be published to the Reports Server. Using Report Manager, we can update and maintain report information such as data sources and security information. If users need to view reports, they can go through the Report Manager interface or a custom interface created using the Reporting Services Web Service. Users and administrators also have the ability to create subscription information for a report.

In the final section of the chapter, we saw the specific components of Reporting Services. We started by looking at how reports definitions and data are combined by the Report Processor. The Report Processor also relies on data extensions to do the physical retrieval of information. After the data is received, the Report Processor calls the Rendering Extensions to get the formatted output of the report. Along with the Report Processor, you saw the Scheduling and Delivery Processor. This component allows execution snapshots to be created and report subscriptions to be sent out. When report subscriptions are sent out, they are sent using delivery extensions such as email and fileshare.

Now that you have seen the foundation of Reporting Services, you can move on to creating your first reports.

Designing Reports

Let's take a look at the big picture of designing reports in SQL Server Reporting Services. We will examine most of the important features of Reporting Services just to get an idea of what you can do with the product. We'll also point you to later chapters to get more information and to learn about the details. We will be using Visual Studio .NET to design and create reports. You may use any edition of Visual Studio .NET 2003 or later.

Before you read on you need to get your bearings and discuss this chapter's direction. In any technical book, it's necessary to get every reader at a basic level of understanding before moving on to advanced material. Different readers may have varying levels of expertise or experience with Visual Studio, so let's start with the basics. Don't worry whether you've never seen Visual Studio before, or if you are a tenured Visual Studio .NET developer, we're going to cover the right material at the right depth at the right time. If you have used Visual Studio for application development, please be patient as you read through the next section. If you have never written a line of code in your life or if you are new to Visual Studio .NET, you're in luck.

This chapter covers the following topics:

- ❑ Using the Report Wizard
- ❑ Importing reports
- ❑ Planning for extensibility
- ❑ Report items and data regions
- ❑ Formatting considerations
- ❑ Pagination and printing considerations

We're covering all the essentials in this section. This chapter contains a series of walkthrough exercises that are intended to lead you step-by-step through some basic report design.

Using the Report Wizard

To get acquainted with the basic mechanics of reports, let's start with a quick tour of the Report Wizard used to create a simple, tabular report. The Report Wizard will take you through all of the steps necessary to design a basic report. From that point, you can make adjustments and add more features to your report. To get started, open Visual Studio .NET as in Figure 3-1 and close any projects or solutions that you may have opened. Click the left-most button on the standard toolbar to create a new project:

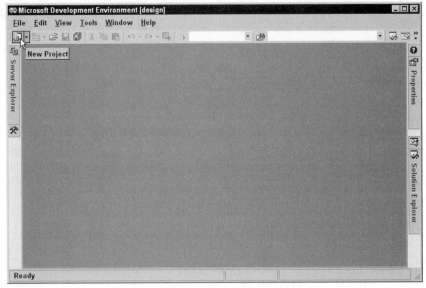

Figure 3-1

The Reporting Services installation adds a project type category called Business Intelligence Projects. Choose this group, select the Report Project Wizard template and enter a name for the project. This creates a new report project and launches the wizard as in Figure 3-2:

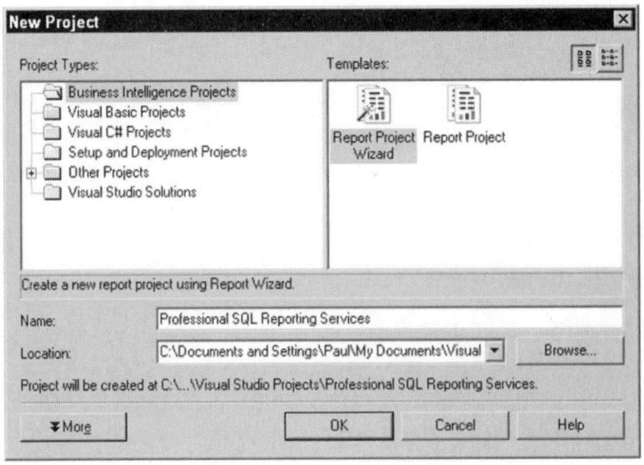

Figure 3-2

Establishing a Data Source

Since you have no data sources created yet, let's add one. It usually makes sense to use a name that means indicates the name and location of the database. In this example, you will use the AdventureWorks2000 sample database that installs with Reporting Services.

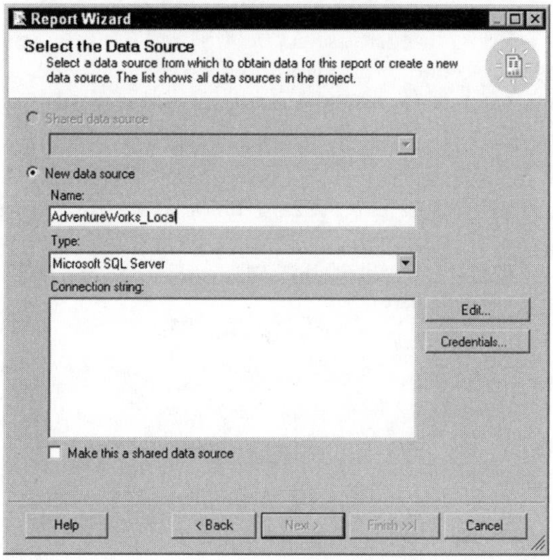

Figure 3-3

Make sure the New data source radio button is selected and enter AdventureWorks_Local for the name as shown in Figure 3-3. Leave the Type set to Microsoft SQL Server and then click the Edit button. This opens the Data Link Properties dialog to set up a connection string shown in Figure 3-4. If you have used other Microsoft products that use SQL Server, this interface should be familiar to you:

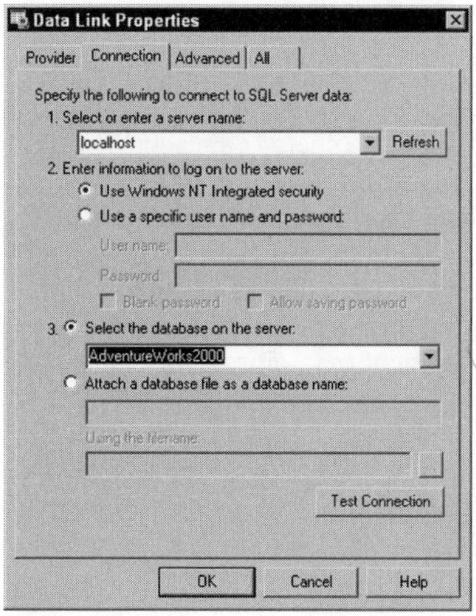

Figure 3-4

There are three steps to complete this dialog:

1. Select the database server from the drop-down list. Since you're using the database server installed on the local computer, enter localhost. If this were a production application, you could select the name of any server on your network from the list, and then type the server name or enter an IP address to connect to a server over the Internet.

2. To use integrated Windows security, select the first radio button reading Use Windows NT Integrated Security. The second option would be used if you were using the SQL Server security model. If that were the case, your database administrator would provide this information.

3. Finally, select the AdventureWorks2000 database from the drop down list. You may use the Test Connection button to validate the settings. When you click the OK button, a connection string is generated and returned to the Report Wizard dialog as shown in Figure 3-5:

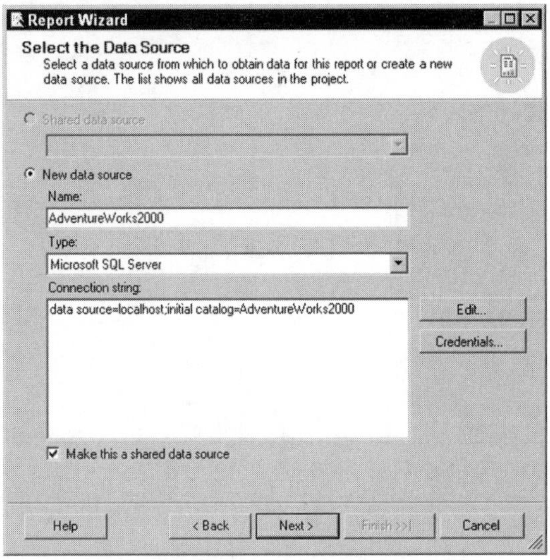

Figure 3-5

Selecting the check box labeled Make this a shared data source will cause this data source to be available to other reports. This simple but important feature is quite powerful and will save you a tremendous amount of time and effort. By creating a central data source for all reports on the server, connection and database information may be changed in only one place to affect all your reports. This is preferable to the traditional approach where each report must be updated separately. This can be very inconvenient when the system administrator moves your database to another server or when you migrate your reporting solution from the development environment to your production server.

So far, the Report Wizard has created a report project and has led you through creating a shared data source. There isn't much to see yet. You need to continue to work through the pages of the wizard before you see any results. In an established report project, you would create a new report using the shared data source you created earlier.

Building a Query

The next wizard page prompts for a query string as shown in Figure 3-6. If you are using a SQL Server database as the data source, this is a Transact SQL SELECT statement used to retrieve the data for the report.

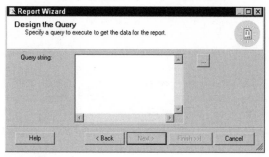

Figure 3-6

More complex reports may be based on more than one query. In fact, data can even be obtained from multiple data sources in a single report. Let's create a very simple query that will select records from only the Employee table.

Click the ellipsis (...) button to open the Transact SQL Query Builder dialog:

Figure 3-7

This is dialog box is common to several Microsoft products. There are no toolbar controls available in this dialog screen. All functionality is available from a pop up menu. If you've never created a query before, this might seem a little complicated, but it's not. The following steps will take you through the process and with a little practice you'll see that it's pretty easy. Right click the mouse while pointing to the top area of the screen shown in Figure 3-7:

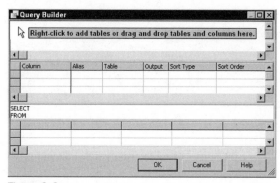

Figure 3-8

From the pop up menu, select Add Table to display the Add Table dialog as shown in Figure 3-9:

Figure 3-9

Select the Employee table from the list and then click the Add button. This adds the table to the top pane of the Query Builder as in Figure 3-10. Click the Close button on the Add Table dialog. You need to include four columns in the report so let's add them to the query.

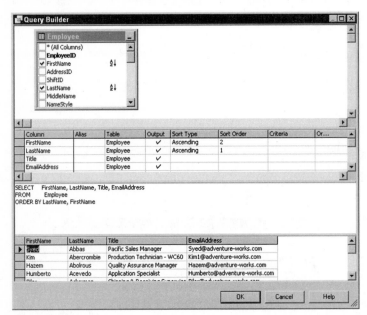

Figure 3-10

In the Employee table window, check the FirstName, LastName, Title, and EmailAddress columns. You should see them added to the column list and to the SQL statement, which is in the third pane of the Query Builder window. You will also need to sort the report by the LastName and FirstName columns. This may be done by setting the Sort Type of these columns to Ascending. Note that the Sort Order values are set in the order you selected the Sort Type. You could also set up sorting within the report definition; however, having the data presorted from the database as you have done here is far more efficient.

To test the query results, right click in the top pane again and select Run from the pop up menu. The query results are displayed in the lower pane in this window. You should see that the employees' records are ordered by the LastName and then FirstName columns.

> **When you view data in this window, system memory is allocated that uses significant resources. This tool has a built-in feature that will prompt you if the query results are viewed for several minutes and the Query Builder is not closed. Often this occurs after you switch to another application and forget about what you were doing in the Query Builder. If you receive a warning message regarding the query results, your response (to leave the results open or not) will not affect the work you have done.**

The query string is returned to the Report Wizard dialog when you click the OK as in Figure 3-11 button in the Query Builder window. Click the Next button to continue.

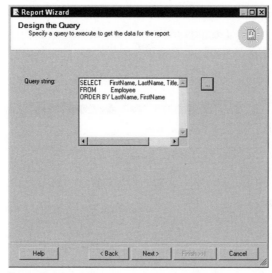

Figure 3-11

The Query Builder does one very simple thing. It creates the Transact SQL expression that you see in the Query string box in this page of the Report Wizard. If you know your way around Transact SQL, you can simply type the expression into this box or into the SQL pane of the Query Builder Window. You can also go back and make changes if necessary either directly to the query string or using the Query Builder dialog. In a later example, a stored procedure will be used in place of the query string.

Define the Report Structure

The following pages will guide you through specifying report design elements such as the style, layout, data sorting, and grouping. In an effort to keep things simple, specify a Tabular style with all data fields in a single detail section as in Figure 3-12:

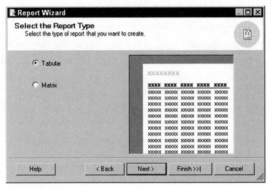

Figure 3-12

This report will simply be a list of records and is known as a Tabular report. Click the Next button to go to the next page, which is used to design a Table control that will display rows and columns of data. In this simple report, you will not be using any groupings so all four fields will be added to the Details section.

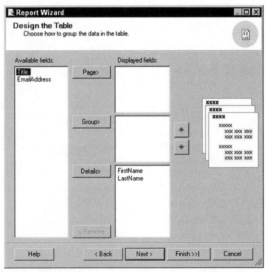

Figure 3-13

Select the four fields from the Available fields list and click the Details button in the order FirstName, LastName, Title, and EmailAddress; then click the Next button as you can see in Figure 3-13.

The Report Wizard will create controls with coordinated fonts and colors using one of five different themes. These properties may be modified in the designer later. Retain the default Bold setting and click Next as in Figure 3-14:

Figure 3-14

As you create other reports, you will have the opportunity to define your own look and feel by using fonts, colors, borders, and graphics. The Report Wizard sets many of these properties for you using the style templates you see on this page. If you like, all of these properties can be changed in the Report Designer.

Specify the Deployment Location

The first time the Report Wizard is used in a report, the dialogue box shown in figure 3-15 is displayed, prompting for the Report server path and Deployment folder name:

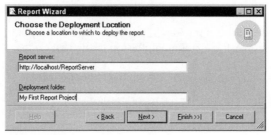

Figure 3-15

The default URL is used for the Report server. Unless you intend to use a different server, leave this value as it is. Enter a folder name for the Deployment folder. This folder will be created and displayed in the Report Manager will contain all of the reports defined within this project. It's important to note that these folders do not correspond with folders in the file system. The hierarchy of folders is actually stored in the Report Server catalog database and can be based upon functional or operational classification. This method simplifies making related reports available to various user roles. Folders may be useful for grouping reports categorically, and searching and securing reports as a group.

When Reporting Services is installed, a web folder is created on the server and is managed by *Internet Information Services (IIS)*, which exposes this path as a URL or web folder. The URL you see in Figure 3-14 is the default location, if you are developing on the Report Server. If you are developing on another computer you should enter a URL that points to that Report Server's installation path, most likely `http://yourservername/ReportServer`. If you're not sure, talk to your server administrator. The Deployment folder isn't really a physical folder. It's a virtual path that is managed and exposed by Reporting Services. You'll see this folder when you use the Report Manager later on.

Finally, enter a Report name, call this report Employee_List as in Figure 3-16. Click the Finish button.

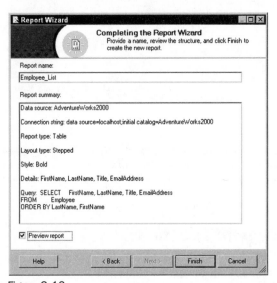

Figure 3-16

This causes the report to be built and the Report Designer to be displayed in either Layout or Preview mode. The Report Designer has three tabs along the top labeled as:

❏ Data: It displays the query designer used in the Report Wizard.

❏ Layout: It is used to create or alter the report design.

❏ Preview: This is used to view the report with data.

Visual Studio .NET contains several useful designer windows that are automatically hidden by default. These windows are accessible when you hover the mouse pointer over icons positioned along the left and right edge of the designer window. As you can see some of these icons are labeled and some are not.

Let's take a closer look at the Tool Box, Fields, Solution Explorer, and the Properties designer windows after this tour.

The Report Designer

The next thing you should see is the actual report in Layout view. The Report Designer is now a component of the Visual Studio .NET *Integrated Development Environment* (*IDE*) and uses many of the windows and tools that are built into Visual Studio. You'll be taking a look at a number of these tools as you continue. The Report Wizard can also decipher intelligent column labels from the column names. For example, the First Name column header has a space between the words First and Name as in Figure 3-17:

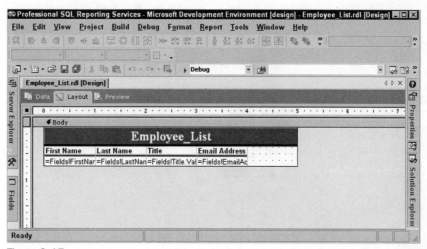

Figure 3-17

Scale Units

Let's take a short break from the wizard and discuss some important information you need to understand before you move on. Notice that these examples were created on a computer configured with US/English regional settings. As a result, all of the scaling units are set to inches. If your computer is configured for another culture or regional setting, your environment may use metric units.

It's also important to understand how a report fits onto a page. The report content fits onto a design element called the *Body*. The report defines the page for printing and displaying purposes with associated margins. The relationship between these two design elements will be shortly discussed.

American SAE, pixels, and metric scale units may be used for the report, body, margins, and control size measurements. The designer will automatically use either inches (in) or centimeters (cm) depending on the current locale setting in Windows. This example uses inches with the default US letter 8.5in x 11in page size. If you are using metric units or a different page size, please make the appropriate adjustments. For example, if you are designing reports for A4 paper, the report width and height would be set to 21cm and 29.7cm respectively.

Note that the Report Designer is currently only five inches wide and that the grid containing the fields partially fills this space. You need to make some adjustments to use the available space.

You should be able to use all of the available space to fill your target page size. Apply the following formula to calculate the report page width:

```
Report Width = Body Width + Left Margin + Right Margin
```

You can set the report size by either resizing the report body in the designer with the mouse or by setting the Height and Width values in the Properties window.

Click on the report background and view the Properties window (either right click and choose Properties or just click the Properties tab on the right side of the designer). Verify that Body is displayed in the drop down list at the top of the properties window. Now, click the small plus sign next to Size to expand this item and set the properties as shown in Figure 3-18:

Figure 3-18

To set the report margins, select Report from the drop-down list and expand the Margins item. Change the Left, Right, Top, and Bottom margins as shown in Figure 3-19:

Figure 3-19

Here's a quick review. The report body contains the actual report content. This area must fit within the area defined for a page of the report. Using the properties window set the report dimensions to be 8.5 inches wide by 11 inches tall with the left and right margins set to 0.25 inches each. This leaves 8.0 inches of available width for the report body. To use all of this horizontal space for report data, set the body to be 8.0 inches wide.

With the report and margins set correctly, you can reformat the report. For the list of repeated data, the wizard added a grid control with columns bound to the four fields you exposed in the query. Sizing these columns for optimum space is a simple matter of trial and error. The first order of business is to select the grid and resize it to fill the report body.

To select the grid, click anywhere in the grid and then click on the gray box at the intersection between the column and row headers. This is shown in Figure 3-20:

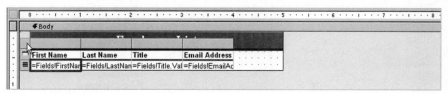

Figure 3-20

This will display a selection box around the grid with resizing handles as in Figure 3-21:

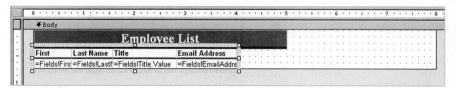

Figure 3-21

Grab the grid on the right side and drag it to fill the report body as in Figure 3-22:

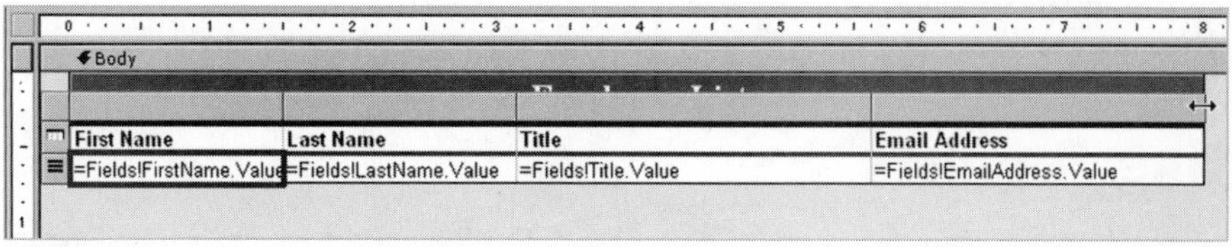

Figure 3-22

Using the column headers at the top of the grid, resize each column. You can switch between Layout and Preview to see how the data looks in the report. With a little adjustment to column sizes and text alignment, the table may easily be formatted so text in each cell doesn't wrap and the report appears balanced. Let's fix the report heading. You can edit the heading text right in the text box. Remove the underscore character and type a space between the words Employee and List.

Select the Preview tab to view the completed report as in Figure 3-23:

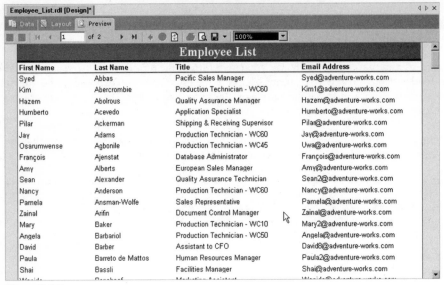

Figure 3-23

That's it! You've created your first report using the Report Wizard. You can go back and make changes to the report design by opening it from the Visual Studio Solution Explorer. In the future, you may find it more effective to create reports without the wizard where you have more control and don't have the tool making so many decisions for you. To get more practice, you may want to design additional reports using different data sources, queries, or other options. At the very least, you'll end up with a few attempts that didn't go so well and some reports that worked. On one of my kids' favorite Saturday TV programs, the teacher character would always say, "Get dirty, make messes, and don't be afraid to try things". That concept applies here.

The remainder of this chapter will focus on individual design elements and concepts rather than the overall process. You will apply this information in another walkthrough exercise in the chapter as designing more advanced reports are discussed.

Importing Reports

One very compelling aspect of this product is that the definition of each report is managed in a standard file format called *Report Definition Language* (*RDL*), which is just an XML document with a standard definition of markup tags that define all of the properties for a report. All objects placed into the Report Designer and the related property settings result in entries made to the RDL content for that report. This simple approach will make it easy for independent software vendors and custom solution developers to generate a report definition from a variety of sources and tools.

Using RDL

There is little doubt that a host of applications and products will have the ability to create report definitions for Reporting Services. Chapter 11 discusses advanced techniques for generating report definitions outside of the integrated Report Designer.

However, a small snippet of an RDL file content describing a textbox is as follows:

```
<Textbox Name="textbox1">
  <Style>
    <PaddingLeft>2pt</PaddingLeft>
    <PaddingBottom>2pt</PaddingBottom>
    <PaddingTop>2pt</PaddingTop>
    <PaddingRight>2pt</PaddingRight>
  </Style>
  <Top>0.25in</Top>
  <rd:DefaultName>textbox1</rd:DefaultName>
  <Height>0.25in</Height>
  <Width>1in</Width>
  <CanGrow>true</CanGrow>
  <Value />
  <Left>0.375in</Left>
</Textbox>
```

In the current version of Reporting Services, you have the ability to import reports from Microsoft Access. Access has an excellent report writer and has long been the only real substantial reporting tool in the Microsoft armada of products. Since the early 1990s, Access was the product of choice for creating reporting solutions and still is for many desktop solutions. Its greatest limitation, however, is that Access must be licensed and installed on the user's desktop and can effectively be used only in a single user or small network environment.

Importing Access Reports

If you are already familiar with creating reports in Access, this may be a good starting point to learn report design in Reporting Services. Most Access reports will import very nicely. There are some functions and expressions used in Access that are not supported and Access reports that run code behind them will likely not work when imported. These details are explained in Appendix B but the short version is that most basic report functionality will work. Grouping and sorting features are preserved as are most expressions and formatting. The use of domain functions and any custom code is not supported.

Plan for Extensibility

If your goal is to create a reporting solution that will work for users with different needs, there are a number of things to be considered. The users may need to:

- ❑ Access reports from a web-enabled hand-held device or cell phone
- ❑ Download reports for off-line viewing
- ❑ View reports in different web browsers

Reporting Services can meet all of these needs if you understand the requirements and plan ahead. Let's briefly discuss some of these design considerations.

Browser Compatibility

A solution should be designed to meet the needs of the least capable user or platform. The optimal design for the web has always been a moving target. If, when designing reports, you view them only in the latest version of Internet Explorer, you may not be aware of incompatibilities or design issues for other browsers. Creating solutions independent of the client platform for a diverse audience will always be challenging, with a certain degree of unpredictability.

Reports with interactive design elements like *drill-down* and *auto-hide* sections, for example, generate client-side JavaScript. This script runs in the user's browser to produce effects and interactive functionality. Theoretically, pages containing many JavaScript functions should run in newer versions of Internet Explorer, Netscape Navigator, and other browsers. In a report, scripted features include documentation maps, bookmarks, and show/hide features (used for drill-down reports). On the standard report toolbar, scripted features provide the ability to zoom, search, refresh, export, and request help.

Another variable to consider when using HTML is the font typeface and size. If you make a point to use common fonts, this is not typically an issue. However, the user's configuration isn't always predictable. Font files on the user's computer can be uninstalled or deleted and default font sizes can be changed in the browser. A popular solution for unpredictable HTML results is to use a proprietary document format typically read in a downloadable viewer. Rendering reports to an *Adobe Portable Document Format (PDF)* document will ensure that reports are displayed and printed consistently.

Offline Viewing

Reporting Services can render reports in three different forms of HTML including MHTML (or web archive). As mentioned in earlier chapters, MHTML is a fairly recent standard that encapsulates content that would normally be linked to separate files, typically graphics, into a single document. Using this format simplifies web content rendering for portability, but it isn't supported in all browsers (including Pocket Internet Explorer). Even when using standard HTML format, most report files will be self-contained with the exception of any graphics. If all of the content is contained in one file, it will be easier to download and view offline. If your users are consistently using Internet Explorer or a browser you have tested thoroughly, consider rendering reports in MHTML to preserve embedded graphics content. If you don't have that kind of control over the user's environment, PDF document rendering may be the best choice.

Another possibility is to allow the user to download report content into a storage file and then render the content using your own client-side solution. Reports rendered as *Comma Separated Values (CSV)* can be opened in Microsoft Excel where the user can format or further manipulate the data. Data saved to an XML file may be imported or read using Excel, Word, or a custom application. The Excel rendering format currently supports Microsoft Excel versions 2002 and 2003 only.

Mobile Device Support

Portable electronic devices are available in different sizes and shapes. This medium could prove to be a very convenient reporting solution for users who need to get information on the go. Web-enabled cellular phones generally fit into three categories:

❑ The Pocket PC and Palm OS devices with integrated cellular phones have the advantage of a relatively larger display (240 x 320 pixels) and a more traditional-style web browser.

❑ The new generation of *Smart Phones* runs a slightly scaled down version of the Windows CE operating system with a smaller display (176 x 220 pixels) and fewer features, but in a more convenient size.

❑ The standard web-enabled cell phone. It's hard to find a new cell phone that doesn't offer the capability to surf the web. Most of these phones have very small displays and many will only display text.

The simple fact is that you can develop reporting solutions using Reporting Services for all of these devices, making it possible and convenient for users to access information wherever they are.

Of course, screen size is one of the most significant limitations so reports may simply be scaled down to a smaller page size to fit a smaller screen size. The Pocket PC and Smart Phone browsers will run client-side JavaScript to support drill-down and other such effects. To support less capable devices, you can design simple text reports rendered in HTML.

Report Items and Data Regions

Reports consist of items and regions that define the placement and format of data from a data source. In the Report Designer, you can place items or draw them onto the report body. If you have worked with Visual Basic or Access forms, you would be familiar with the practice of placing controls on forms. This is pretty much the same environment. When you add a new report to a report project in Visual Studio .NET, the designer is displayed in the Layout view. Much of the Visual Studio functionality is exposed using various utility windows. On the left side of the designer, you will find the Toolbox that contains all of the available report items as shown in Figure 3-24. The toolbox may be set to auto hide using the pushpin icon in its toolbar.

Figure 3-24

Textbox Report Item

The Textbox item can be used to display data from a data source, calculations or expressions or static data, much like a label control in a Windows forms project. When you drag fields from the Fields list onto the Report Designer, *bound* textbox items are created. Common expressions can refer to a field in the report'

The following example in Figure 3-25 shows a textbox used as a label and another text box bound to the LastName field of the report data source:

| Last Name | =First(Fields!LastName.Value) |

Figure 3-25

Right click the Textbox and select Properties from the pop up menu to display the Textbox Properties dialog as in Figure 3-26:

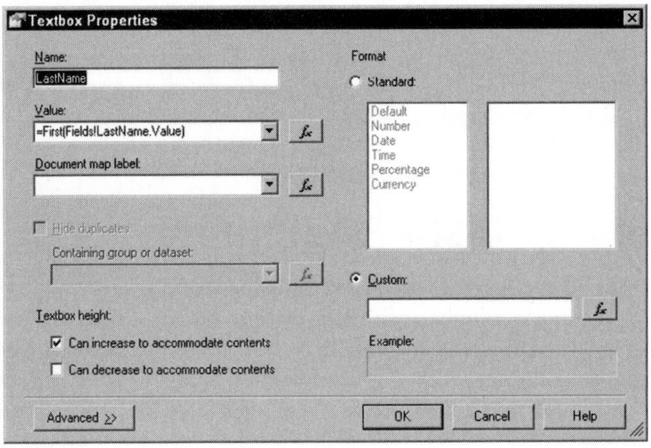

Figure 3-26

Properties may also be viewed and set using the standard properties sheet located to the right of the designer. This window may be pinned out or will auto hide by default. As in Figure 3-27, this window contains quite a bit more detail than the custom properties window. However, the property information is not as conveniently organized. Right click to get to the most common properties and use the property sheet when you need to set other properties.

Figure 3-27

Line Report Item

Lines may be drawn in any direction and may be set to a variety of styles and colors as displayed in Figure 3-27. The properties for a line are simple and mostly set using the properties window or designer toolbar.

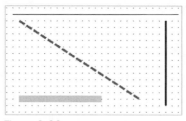

Figure 3-28

Some clever techniques are used to render lines. Reporting Services will typically try to render content using the most effective way possible. In Figure 3-28, when outputting standard HTML, the two black lines are rendered as table borders, the wide gray line is rendered as a DIV tag filled using a JavaScript function and the diagonal broken line is rendered using *Virtual Reality Modeling Language (VRML)* commands.

VRML is an industry standard extension to HTML for displaying vector-based graphics in the web browser.

Rectangle Report Item

A rectangle item can have many different uses. A rectangle is simply used to visually separate a region of the report. It may be used to visually contain other items. If items such as text boxes, grids and so on are placed into a rectangle, all these items can be moved together by simply moving the rectangle. A rectangle may also be used as a data container for data items and can be related to and repeated with a parent container.

Image Report Item

Images can be embedded into the report, linked to an external file, or obtained from a data source. Images can be of the BMP, GIF, JPG, JPE, PNG, or X-PNG type. Adding an image in the designer is pretty straightforward. A critical factor is that images are sized and cropped prior to being added to a report. You can resize the image in the Report Designer but this will not result in a smaller file size. Use a graphics editing tool like the Office Picture Library, Microsoft PhotoDraw, Adobe PhotoShop, or Macromedia Fireworks to resize or crop the image and them save it to a new file.

Drag and drop an image item from the Toolbox onto the report. This will launch the Image Wizard dialog (see Figure 3-29). Select the method you want to use; the image can be from a table or a file and may be linked or embedded into the report:

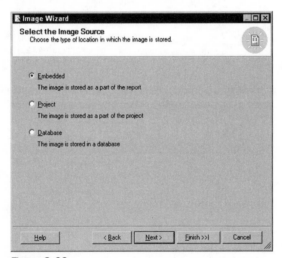

Figure 3-29

Keep the default selection Embedded and click Next to show the image selection page shown in Figure 3-30. Click New Image and find your image file.

Selecting the Project option will result in a linked image using a file found in the project. Selecting the Database option will allow you to extract an image stored in an Image or Binary type column within a database, exposed through your dataset.

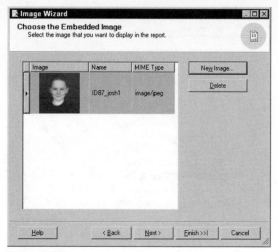

Figure 3-30

When you click **Next**, a summary is displayed with information about the image; see Figure 3-31:

Figure 3-31

If your picture data is stored in the database and the **Database** option is selected, the database field page is displayed in the wizard. This gives you the option to derive an image file type from the image as in Figure 3-32.

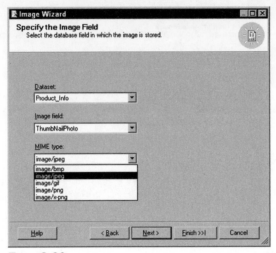

Figure 3-32

Generally, the JPEG format is most flexible. If the image uses transparency, use either the GIF or X-PNG formats. The GIF and JPEG formats are most widely used on the Internet and are supported by all web browsers.

Subreport Item

A *subreport* is a container for another report. The subreport can contain practically any other report with its own, independent data source. It can optionally have its data linked to a record in the main report often referred to as a master/detail report. Subreports are an important element in complex report designs. Figure 3-33 shows a simple report containing a master record and related detail records in the subreport:

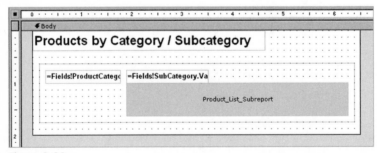

Figure 3-33

The design details of the subreport are not visible in the designer. This report is designed separately and then inserted into the main report as a subreport item.

Chart Report Item

The chart functionality in Reporting Services is really a simplified version of *Dundas Chart* that Microsoft has licensed from Dundas Software. It's very capable and easy-to-use charting solution with a variety of available chart types.

Probably the most common and most recognizable chart type is the column graph. This example as in Figure 3-34 shows store sales data grouped by year, with the total product sales grouped by product category:

Figure 3-34

If any of the sample sales data in the AdventureWorks2000 database is accurate, I'm glad that I don't own a bike shop. Let's use the same data to take a peek at some other report types.

Bar charts and column charts are pretty much the same. You can tilt your head to the side to get the same view as the other. In addition to the standard, single bar view, the stacked view provides a consolidated look at a series of values by using fewer bars or columns. Each bar is like a mini pie chart where each value in the bar's range is in proportion to the others.

Figure 3-35 shows a standard stacked column chart. A series of related values are stacked in the column to show the aggregate sum of values and their proportional values:

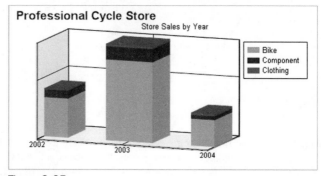

Figure 3-35

A variation, the 100% stacked bar or chart (not shown), displays each bar with the same height or length as others, regardless of the total values. This type of chart is useful for comparing values within the bar's range but not for comparing the aggregates represented by each bar.

Area and line charts are useful for analyzing trends and helping the viewer to follow data points through a series. Figure 3-36 shows a simple area chart with three points of data for each series:

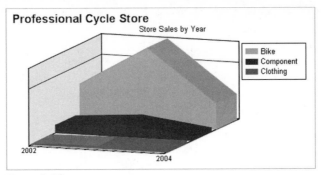

Figure 3-36

To view the proportional components of an aggregate sum, this type of chart comes in two pastry types: Pie and Doughnut. Values are presented visually as a percentage of the total for all values in a series. Pie and Doughnut chart views may be either *Simple* or *Exploded*. Figure 3-37 is an example of an exploded Doughnut (sounds messy). This presentation may help to visually separate values, especially the smaller slices. This chart looks more like PacMan undergoing a root canal than retail sales figures, but these types of charts can be useful for placing values into comparative perspective.

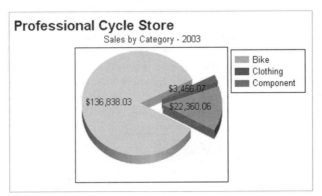

Figure 3-37

The data source for a chart can either be pre-aggregated in the underlying query using GROUPBY and SUM functions, or the chart will perform the aggregation for you. If you have a large volume of data, aggregating the values in the database, using a View or stored procedure, will be much more efficient. The chart item will be discussed in detail in Chapter 5.

Drill-Down and Drill-Through Reports

Although related, these are two different features. A drill-down report as in Figure 3-38 contains related groups or sections of information. Each section can be expanded or collapsed to show or hide pertinent information. In the following report, product categories only are displayed when the report opens. Using the expand icon next to a category, the category group (in this case, Clothing) is expanded revealing a group of related subcategories. Expanding a subcategory (such as Bib-Short) reveals individual products within the subcategory.

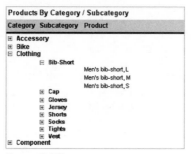

Figure 3-38

A drill-through report may or may not include some drill-down functionality. Items shown in the report may represent sections or more detailed information that may be viewed in a separate report. These key items are displayed as a hyperlink and when a user clicks the link, a separate detailed report is displayed for the item selected as in Figure 3-39:

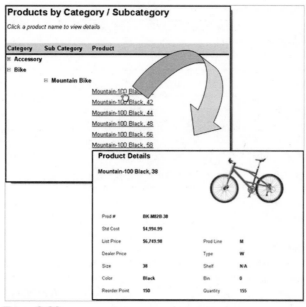

Figure 3-39

Tabular Reports

One of the most fundamental reports is a simple list of record values arranged in rows and columns. Typical tabular reports display column headers above repeated row values. Rows may also be grouped categorically and may be followed by totals, subtotals, or other aggregate values pertaining to a grouping or the entire report.

The two common techniques used to obtain this design are by using the grid or the list control. The grid control makes it easy to format rows and columns with column headers and supports groupings, headers, footers, and multiple row sections.

Grouping Data

Tabular or matrix data may be sorted and grouped on one or multiple levels. The table, list, and matrix controls support this functionality. Groupings may be based on field values or expressions that may include conditional qualifiers, functions, and combined values from multiple fields.

When values are grouped, they may need to be aggregated. This means that a row in the report layout represents a *rollup* of multiple rows from the data source (like the sum or average of a range of values). After introducing the data region items used to perform grouped operations, let's take a closer look at the aggregate functions that are used as rollup values within the group.

Table Report Data Region

The following example in Figure 3-40, using a table, contains three groupings for product records on the Category, Sub Category and Product fields:

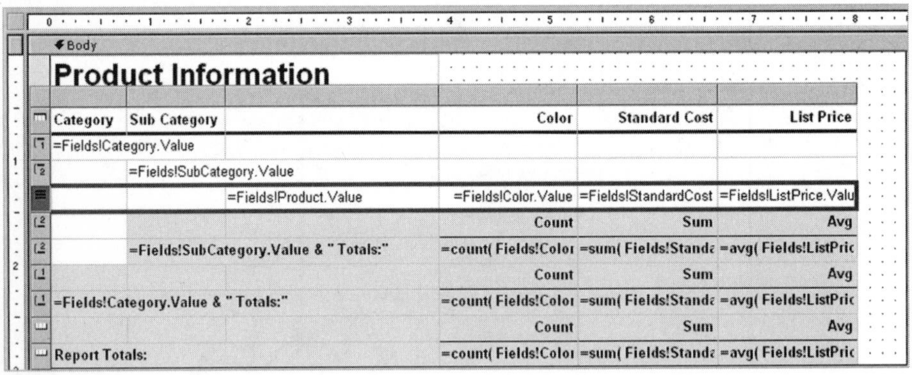

Figure 3-40

List Report Data Region

Using embedded list items allows greater flexibility over the formatting and placement of individual report items. The list control may also be used as the basis for a more complex report with embedded sub reports, lists, matrices, or grids. Figure 3-41 shows a preview of a report with groupings created using nested list items. The list item is useful for creating groups of repeated data that isn't constrained to a tabular format.

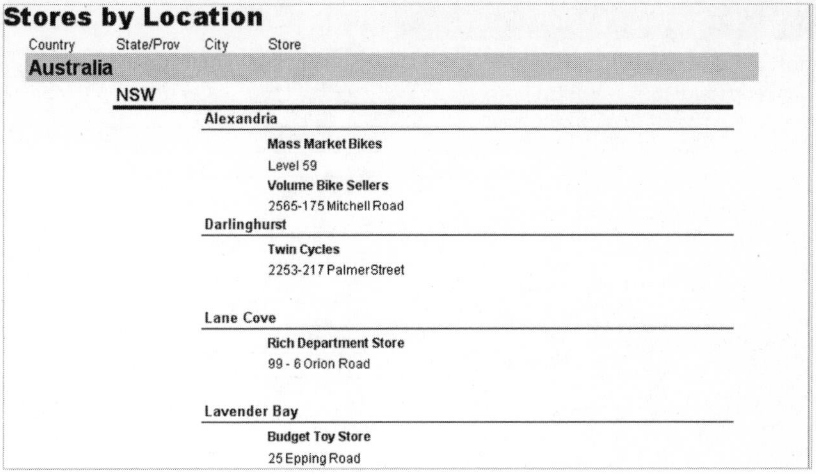

Figure 3-41

In the design for this report, there are four list controls placed inside one another. Groupings have been created for each of the lists to organize them into a hierarchy. For the sake of clarity in this demonstration, each list control is drawn well inside its parent list and the borders are made easier to see as in Figure 3-42. It is common for the list borders to share the same line space if you don't need to create additional white space around data elements typically on the right side and bottom borders.

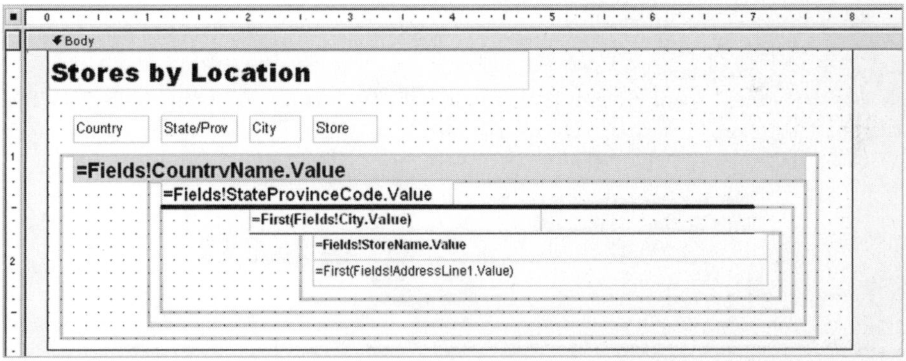

Figure 3-42

Matrix Report Data Region

The matrix item produces a pivot table with automated drill-down functionality on both axes. This matrix report contains the same groupings for row data as the previous report and also contains column groupings for Product Category and Sub Category fields. The aggregate value in the center cells is the sum of product sales for the intersection of each of the groupings. By default, values are aggregated and rolled up within groupings. To view detail values, use the plus sign (+) icon to drill-down in one axis (rows or columns) and then do the same for the other axis. Figure 3-43 shows a matrix report that has been expanded to show details on both the axes:

Customer Location / Product Sales		Accessory	Bike			Clothing	
			Mountain Bike	Road Bike	Touring Bike		
Australia		$57,196.91	$127,491.84	$71,671.20	$855,668.05	$58,002.01	
Canada	AB	$9,921.40	$769,103.75	$35,712.08	$8,469.60	$39,998.10	
	BC Burnaby	$8,997.34	$548,042.69	$292,964.97	$102,596.76	$34,362.05	
	Cliffside	$4,859.40	$539.99	$20,816.79	$11,339.96	$5,196.45	
	Haney	$2,240.98		$3,239.97		$5,938.80	
	Langford		$2,643.96	$8,934.94	$10,259.96	$13,770.49	
	Langley	$2,384.07	$3,239.94	$9,719.91		$18,767.18	
	Metchosin	$6,379.75	$4,238.93	$21,638.37	$6,749.98	$4,656.75	
	N. Vancouver	$2,384.07	$1,849.47	$6,774.96	$3,374.99	$2,699.55	
	Newton	$17,805.88	$2,103.97	$9,393.93	$6,749.98	$14,040.34	
	Oak Bay	$27,296.53	$7,889.36	$11,823.93	$23,624.93	$17,891.35	
	Port Hammond	$17,903.34	$539.99	$8,423.95	$5,669.98	$5,196.45	
	Richmond	$7,799.08	$211,825.66	$617,701.00	$131,971.03	$25,648.89	
	Royal Oak		$4,468.43	$14,309.89	$10,259.96	$9,989.57	
	Shawnee	$10,416.22	$4,009.43	$6,304.45	$6,749.98		
	Sooke	$16,825.38	$3,388.45	$21,233.34	$6,884.97	$15,927.45	
	Surrey		$55,335.03			$938.37	
	Vancouver	$7,799.45	$3,847.45	$339,775.32	$266,789.17	$12,302.74	
	Victoria	$11,296.67	$1,619.97	$9,738.98	$6,749.98	$5,227.69	
	Westminster	$7,980.83	$6,342.90			$6,613.95	
	MB		$36,642.08			$1,415.43	
	NB	$5,746.32		$227,566.85		$16,924.33	
	ON	$40,314.27	$1,650,581.93	$2,667,004.85	$126,531.70	$161,833.13	
	QC	$10,011.58	$889,257.60	$1,125,116.22	$306,553.72	$41,888.60	
Germany		$58,468.11	$152,654.49	$180,962.43	$924,034.33	$129,967.37	
United States		$839,332.57	$16,277,365.64	$20,134,766.54	$4,106,553.79	$1,549,646.75	

Figure 3-43

The matrix control takes care of the grouping functionality in this report. As in Figure 3-44, the design is fairly simple:

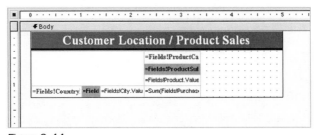

Figure 3-44

Subtotals

Although Reporting Services generically refers to these type of expressions as subtotals, they may be used to perform any aggregation of grouped data. Subtotals may be added to a table's footer row, list control, or in the detail or grouping cells of a matrix. The following table is a list of aggregate functions supported by Reporting Services:

Function	Description
Avg	Average for all values in a range
Count	Count of all non-null values in a range
CountDistinct	Count of unique values in a range
CountRows	Count of all rows in a range, regardless of null values or uniqueness
First	First value in a range based on the current sort order
Last	Last value in a range based on the current sort order
Max	Highest value in a range
Min	Lowest value in range
StDev	Standard deviation of non-null values
StDevP	Population standard deviation of non-null values
Sum	Sum of all values in a range
Var	Variance of non-null values
VarP	Population variance of non-null values

Using the table from Figure 3-40, let's take a closer look at the summary rows and their aggregated values. In this example, a table that has groupings on the **Category** and **Sub Category** fields is created. Note that the grouping numbers in the row markers next to each row indicate the grouping level. The detail row is selected and sandwiched between grouping levels 1 and 2. In the grouping footers and the report footer, the aggregate functions `Count`, `Sum`, and `Avg` are used for the **Color**, **StandardCost**, and **ListPrice** columns. In this report, an additional row is added for each of the grouping footers for the columns as shown in Figure 3-45:

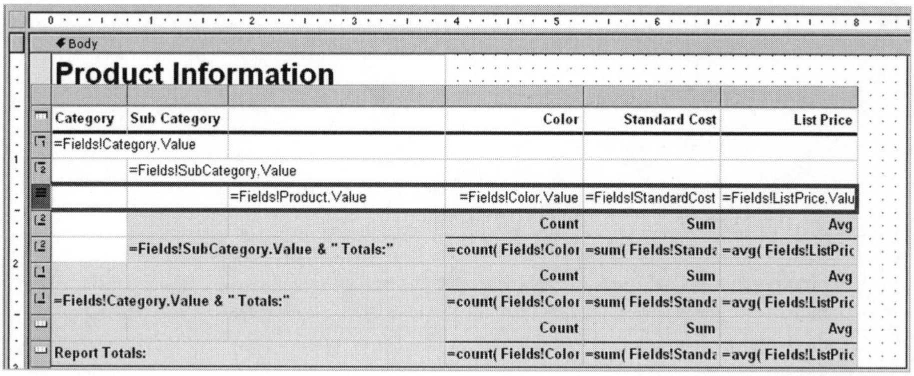

Figure 3-45

Aggregate expressions may be entered in different ways. The expression may be typed directly into the textbox, or into the value property using the property sheet window or customer property page window. Next to each applicable property, a button can be used to open the expression builder dialog, which can be used to assemble the expression. This will be discussed in detail in Chapter 5.

Here is a condensed view of the same report shown in the print preview. Since you are using the Count function on the Color field value, rows that don't have a value in this column (the value is Null) have a count of 0. First you see four sections with subtotals for the Sub Category field, and then further down the page, you see rollups for the Category and then for the entire report as shown in Figure 3-46:

Product Information

Category Sub Category		Color	Standard Cost	List Price
Accessory				
	Bike Racks			
	Hitch rack - 4 bike		$66.00	$120.00
		Count	Sum	Avg
Bike Racks Totals:		0	$66.00	$120.00
	Bike Stand			
	All-purpose bike stand		$87.45	$159.00
		Count	Sum	Avg
Bike Stand Totals:		0	$87.45	$159.00
	Bottles & Cages			
	Mountain bottle cage		$5.49	$9.99
	Road bottle cage		$4.94	$8.99
	water bottle 30 oz		$2.74	$4.99
		Count	Sum	Avg
Bottles & Cages Totals:		0	$13.18	$7.99
	Tires & Tubes			
	HL Mountain Tire		$19.25	$35.00
	HL Road Tire		$17.93	$32.60
	LL Mountain Tire		$13.74	$24.99
	LL Road Tire		$11.82	$21.49
	ML Mountain Tire		$16.49	$29.99
	ML Road Tire		$13.74	$24.99
	Mountain Tire Tube		$2.74	$4.99
	Patch kit with 8 patches		$1.26	$2.29
	Road Tire Tube		$2.19	$3.99
	Touring Tire		$15.94	$28.99
	Touring Tire Tube		$2.74	$4.99
		Count	Sum	Avg
Tires & Tubes Totals:		0	$117.87	$19.48
		Count	Sum	Avg
Accessory Totals:		5	$547.87	$34.35
	LL Mtn Rear Wheel	Black	$64.93	$87.75
	LL Road Front Wheel	Black	$63.32	$85.57
	LL Road Rear Wheel	Black	$83.30	$112.57
	ML Mtn Front Wheel	Black	$154.68	$209.03
	ML Mtn Rear Wheel	Black	$174.66	$236.03
	ML Road Front Wheel	Black	$183.80	$248.39
	ML Road Rear Wheel	Black	$203.78	$275.39
	Touring Front Wheel	Black	$161.33	$218.01
	Touring Rear Wheel	Black	$181.31	$245.01
		Count	Sum	Avg
Wheel Totals:		14	$2,288.83	$220.93
		Count	Sum	Avg
Component Totals:		292	$127,300.45	$540.62
		Count	Sum	Avg
Report Totals:		740	$621,520.41	$1,063.27

Figure 3-46

Formatting

Many data values need to be formatted appropriately as the default formats are usually not acceptable. The following table shows common SQL Server data types and their unformatted defaults:

Data Type	Default Display	Example
Float	Large number of decimal positions with no rounding or truncation. Large numbers with no thousand separators or scientific notation.	123456789.123456 1.23456789012346E+19
Decimal	Large numbers with no thousand separators. The number of decimal positions is defined by the column's scale attribute.	123456789.1234
Int, SmallInt, BigInt	Large numbers with no thousand separators.	123456789
Money	Up to four decimal positions. Large numbers with no thousand separators.	123456789.1234
Date	Always displays date and time. Seconds included.	11/1/2003 3:34:26 PM
Bit	Displays the words True or False.	True False

If these values are not what you want to see in your reports, you will need to use the Format property of each control to change them. The formatting capabilities of Reporting Services controls are based on the formatting mechanics in the .NET Framework and use a form of *regular expressions*. Regular expressions are very powerful and can be used to format values in just about any way imaginable. Expression strings can range from simple to extremely complex. If you need to learn more about the advanced use of regular expressions, search the Visual Studio .NET online help or the MSDN library for *Regular Expression Language Elements*. For most of your needs, however, we'll show you how to use the basics.

Standard Formatting

Standard, one character, strings may be used to specify formatting options for numbers and dates. One advantage of using standard format strings is that culture specific formats are automatically applied.

There is plenty of information on this subject in Reporting Services Books Online. Unfortunately, there is also a lot of extra information that just doesn't apply to most reporting needs. The objective is to keep this simple and show only what you really need to know for majority of reports. The following table lists the common format strings that apply to numeric data types:

Format	Description	Example
C	Currency	$123,456,78.9.12
D	Decimal followed by optional precision specifier	123456789 000123456789 using D12
E	Scientific notation followed by optional precision specifier	1.234568e+008 1.234567891234+008 using E12
F	Fixed-point followed by optional precision specifier	123456789.12 123456789.123400000000 using F12
P	Percent followed by optional precision specifier	12.35%

The following table lists the common format strings that apply to date and time data types:

Format	Description	Example
d	Short date	11/1/03
D	Long date	Saturday, November 01, 2003
t	Short time	3:34 PM
T	Long time	3:23:26 PM
f	Full date and time	Saturday, November 01, 2003 3:34 PM
F	Full date and time	Saturday, November 01, 2003 3:34:26 PM
g	General date and time	11/1/03 3:34 PM
G	General date and time	11/1/03 3:34:26 PM
M or m	Month	November 01
Y or y	Year	November, 2003

Explicit Formatting

In addition to the standard formatting techniques, you may also use an explicit format string to get more control and deal with specific format needs. Keep in mind that the formatted output will be the same for dates and currency even if the locale setting is changed for the server.

Again, the Reporting Services Books On-line contains detailed information about specific formats for string elements so we won't rehash that information here. What we will do, however, is show a few common examples of explicit formatting. You can find the details about this topic under the topics *Custom Numeric Format Strings and Custom DateTime Format Strings* in Books Online. The following table is a summary of some common format expression elements:

Format Element	Type	Description	Example
yyyy	DateTime	Four character year	2004
yy	DateTime	Two character year	03
MMMM	DateTime	Month, full name	August
MMM	DateTime	Month, three characters	Aug
MM	DateTime	Month, two numerals	09 or 11
M	DateTime	Month, one or two numerals	9 or 11
dddd	DateTime	Week day, full name	Saturday
ddd	DateTime	Week day, three characters	Sat
dd	DateTime	Day, two numerals	04 or 15
d	DateTime	Day, one or two numerals	4 or 15
hh	DateTime	Hour in 12-hour time, two numerals	08 or 10
h	DateTime	Hour in 12-hour time, one or two numerals	8 or 10
HH	DateTime	Hour in 24-hour time, one or two numerals	08 or 23
H	DateTime	Hour in 24-hour time, one or two numerals	8 or 23
mm	DateTime	Minute, two numerals	35
ss	DateTime	Seconds, two numerals	45
tt	DateTime	12-hour time using AM or PM	AM or PM
t	DateTime	12-hour time using A or P	A or P
0	Number	Required numeral placeholder	09
#	Number	Optional numeral placeholder	
%	Number	Percentage	95 = 95%
- , : /.	Any	Literals	123.45, 1-234, 12:34 PM

Let's use a common scenario as an example; say your company has offices around the world and follows a corporate standard to use European style dates, regardless of where users are located. Instead of letting the system decide how to format dates, you want them to be explicitly formatted using your corporate standard.

By setting the `Format` property of the date type controls to the string MMMM d, yyyy; the resulting date would be displayed in the format, November 1, 2003.

Conditional Formatting

Under certain conditions, you may need to alter the format of a value based on an expression related to other fields or conditions in the report. The use of different functions and expression will be discussed in Chapter 4. For now, let's take a look at a couple of examples to explore the concept and some techniques.

Let's say that your company has locations in England, Germany, and the US, and, for whatever reason (remember, we're making this up), you want different rows to display information formatted for the corresponding locales. Each row in the underlying table includes a column named `MyLocale` that holds your own two-character code for the locale. The industry has a five character standard known as the RFC1766. Your codes are loosely translatable to this standard. Based on the anticipated values in this column (UK, DE, or US), you will display currency and date information in the corresponding format. The objective will be to format the following date and currency values as follows:

Value	Locale	Formatted Value
November 1, 2003	US	11/1/03
November 1, 2003	UK	1/11/03
November 1, 2003	DE	1.11.03
12345.1234	US	$1,234.12
12345.1234	UK	£1,234.12
12345.1234	DE	1.234,12

A control's property may be set to an expression that will actually parse and set the property value for the row as it is rendered. There are a few techniques to do this; one is to use the *Immediate If* or *IIF* function. This works if you have one condition to test and two possible outcomes. A more powerful technique is the `Switch` function. It works like the `Switch` statement in C# and like the `Select Case` statement in VB rolled into one. This technique will be used to set the `Format` property of the date. For the textbox that will display this value, use the following expression:

```
=Switch(Fields!MyLocale.Value="DE", "d.MM.yy", Fields!MyLocale.Value="UK",
  "d/MM/yy", Fields!MyLocale.Value="US", "M/d/yy")
```

The currency value could be set the same way, except that the German form would be difficult to contend with since commas are used to designate the thousand separator and a period is used for decimals. In the German language, these characters have the opposite meaning. Fortunately each control has a `Language` property that is equipped to handle this and many other language and culture-specific idiosyncrasies. By dynamically manipulating this property in the same manner, you can reach your objective. Using the `Switch` function, you can translate your two-character codes to the industry standard that uses five-character codes. The following expression can be used to change the `Language` property of the currency text box:

```
=Switch(Fields!MyLocale.Value="DE", "de-DE", Fields!MyLocale.Value="UK", "en-GB",
    Fields!MyLocale.Value="US", "en-US")
```

Again, this is an example of one possible business problem and one possible solution. If this were a real situation, it might make more sense to store the actual culture information string in the table and simply set the `Language` property of the control to that value pulled directly from the table. By the way, all of the supported culture information strings can be found in the MSDN library under the search key CultureInfo. The sample report in Figure 3-47 shows the final result using the formatting examples just discussed:

Conditional Formatting Example

Locale	Date	Money
UK	11/1/2003	£123,456,789.12
DE	01.11.2003	123.000.000.000,01 €
US	11/1/2003	$98,765.43
DE	01.11.2003	1.234.567,12 €
US	11/1/2003	$1,234,567.12
UK	11/1/2003	£1,234,567.12

Figure 3-47

Multiple Columns

A report can display list values in multiple columns. Values in a column *snake* from top to bottom and then left to right. It's important to note that Reporting Services can only do so much in HTML and that some multi-column reports can't be rendered in some (or possibly any) versions of HTML, so your only option may be to render these reports in PDF format.

Columns are defined for the **Body** of a report. When the `Columns` property for the Body is set to a value greater than 1, the report page width should be set according to the following equation:

```
Report Page Width >= (Body Width x number of columns) + (ColumnSpacing x (number of
    columns - 1)
```

For example, a report, which has a body width of 2.5 inches with three columns and the column spacing set to 0.25 inches, this will yield a report width of 8 inches. If the report's left and right margins were set to 0.25 inches each, this should fit neatly into an 8.5 inch page width.

The following screenshot is that of a report designed with these dimensions and property settings (Figure 3-48):

Figure 3-48

This report is very simple and contains no headers or footers. You can add them to this report but the options are limited. You are limited to the width of the report body and the header will only show above the first column. In order to use a report header wider then 2.5 inches in this example, you have to create another report and use the multi-column report as an embedded sub report. Creating sub reports will be looked at in the Chapter 4.

Pagination Control

Unlike traditional reporting tools like Microsoft Access, Reporting Services doesn't have its own specific report viewer. Since reports may be rendered in different formats and viewed in different browsers or document viewers, page handling may be different for various rendering formats. The following chart shows the behavior of pagination in the supported rendering formats:

Rendering Format	Pagination Behavior
HTML	Pages are separated on specific page breaks but are not based on page length. Page handing depends on the browser and is unpredictable.
PDF	Pages are separated based on the page length and for specific page breaks. This format is good for large, page-oriented reports.
Excel	Specific page breaks cause the workbook to be split into separate worksheets. Worksheets are not split base on page length.
TIFF	Pages are separated based on the page length and for specific page breaks. This format is good for small, page-oriented reports.
MHTML	Page breaks are not supported.
XML	Page breaks are not supported.
CSV	Page breaks are not supported.

For PDF and TIFF formats, reports will naturally paginate as the content exceeds the usable page height. In cases where you need content to paginate uniformly, you can force page breaks using a number of different data containers or data ranges. For each of the following report items, right click on the item and select Properties from the pop up menu to view the related properties dialog.

Remember that forcing page breaks may have different results depending upon the rendering format used. For example, a report with forced page breaks rendered to an Excel workbook will produce separate worksheets for each page.

Page Breaks for a Rectangle

You can set a page break to occur before or after a rectangle. Using the properties dialog or properties sheet for a rectangle, set one or both of the page break properties as seen in Figure 3-49. If all you want to do is set a page break at a specific location in a static report, you can use a rectangle with no border to do this:

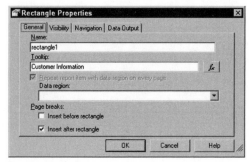

Figure 3-49

Page Breaks for a List

Since the list item is designed to repeat a group of bound report items, it is a natural place to force a page break. Set these properties using the List Properties dialog as shown in Figure 3-50. In addition to breaking before or after the entire range of listed items, you can cause a list to fit onto one page if the rendered content permits this to happen. If this property is checked, the rendering engine will test the length of the listed data and move the entire list to the next page so that it fits.

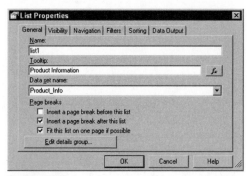

Figure 3-50

Page Breaks for a Table

The table can have page breaks defined in much the same way that they are for a list item. A page break may be set to occur immediately before or after the table. You can also try to fit all of the table data on one page, in which case a page break will occur before the table. The Table Properties page is shown in Figure 3-51:

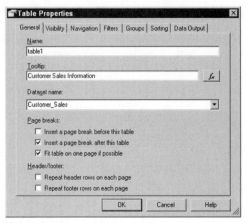

Figure 3-51

Breaks may be specified within the table at data groupings. Grouping and sorting will be covered in greater detail in the next chapter. Once a grouping has been defined for a table, the grouping and sorting properties dialog is accessible by selecting the grouping row in the table. Either right click on the row selector and select Edit | Group from the pop up menu or choose Grouping/Sorting from the standard Properties window.

Page Breaks for a Group

In the Grouping and Sorting Properties dialog, shown here in Figure 3-52, page breaks may also be forced before or after the grouping:

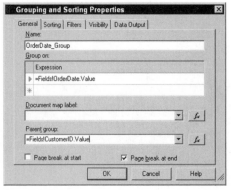

Figure 3-52

Page Breaks for a Matrix

The matrix page break options are the same as for the table report item. As the matrix rows are expanded, data will automatically span pages. If the content fits on one page and the Fit this matrix on one page if possible option is checked (Figure 3-53), a page break will be placed before the content. You can also force a page break immediately before or after the matrix content.

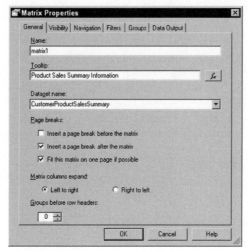

Figure 3-53

Page Breaks for a Chart

Page break properties for charts are available only in the standard Visual Studio properties window and not in the custom properties dialog for the chart. You may set a page break immediately before or after a chart by setting the Page Break At Start and Page Break At End properties respectively.

Printing Considerations

An important issue to keep in mind is that Reporting Services doesn't display reports. It generates and renders report content to be viewed in a web browser or an application. Report printing will be managed by the application that you use to view your report. This means that most reports will be printed using either Internet Explorer or the Adobe Acrobat Reader.

The Report Manager, which is an HTML interface designed to run in Internet Explorer contains printing features.

In cases where international users might need to acess and print your reports, you may need to specify a page size that will accommodate different paper sizes. For example, if you anticipate that a report will be read and printed in the United States and Great Britan, the report content should fit on both letter and A4 paper sizes.

Summary

The purpose of this chapter was to introduce the Report Designer and get you started on designing a report. Several features and design considerations were mentioned but not discussed in depth. The chapter starts by using the Report Wizard to create a simple, tabular report. This should have given you a birds view of a Report project in Visual Studio .NET and the basic features of the Report Designer. Furthermore, importing reports from Access will allow you to leverage existing report solutions. You can also use the features of Access you already understand as a learning tool. Designing reports for extensibility with different user environments, including different browsers, computers, and mobile devices, was also covered.

Different reporting formats can assure formatting control and compatibility. Report items can be used to display static values as well as data from a data source. Simple items like textboxes may be repeated and grouped in data ranges and list-type containers. More sophisticated report items like the list, table, and matrix may be used to create tabular and pivot reports that perform functions like aggregate, subtotal, and group, and provide drill-down and drill-through functionality.

Data formatting can be achieved using simple, standard format strings, explicit format expressions, and conditional logic using programming functions and expressions. Several report items can be used to paginate a report statically or based on the size andcontent of data regions.

By now, you should be comfortable using Visual Studio .NET to create and extend a simple report project. Chapter 4 will expand on what you have learned so far and take you to the next level.

Designing Data Access

This chapter will discuss the essential steps of report design—how to consume data. Although this is typically simple and straightforward, there are a number of options to be considered when designing data sources and queries. We'll discuss the following topics:

❑ Creating standalone and shared data sources

❑ Designing queries and datasets

❑ Using parameters to filter data at the database

❑ Using parameters to filter data at the Report Server

Every report will have at least one data source (with the rare exception of a static form that doesn't use any data). The simplest of reports will have a single data source to provide data for a single dataset. The data source defines a connection using a simple text string. This connection information may include security credentials information. The dataset defines a query expression or data source object reference. A data source may be shared among multiple reports or may be contained within the report definition. The dataset is also contained within the report definition. Figure 4-1 depicts how data flows to the report. The data source provides the ability to connect to the database and the dataset contains a query expression that populates the report with data:

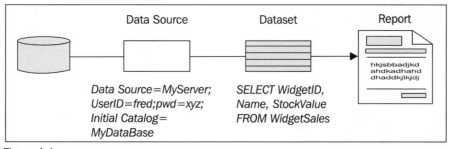

Figure 4-1

More complex reports may require multiple datasets to provide data for different data ranges or items in the report, or to feed values to parameter value selection. Datasets can be based on query expressions from the same data source as shown in Figure 4-2:

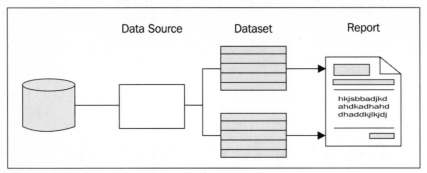

Figure 4-2

Multiple datasets can get their data from multiple data sources. This model would enable a report to have parameter selection values to be obtained from a local database and report data to be obtained from a central data store. In some cases, data regions, subreports, and various report items might obtain data from multiple sources through associated datasets as shown in Figure 4-3:

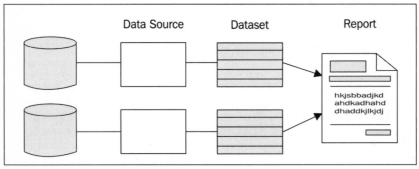

Figure 4-3

As you can see, almost anything is possible in terms of combining data sources and datasets.

A report can be a central point of data collection and aggregation.

Data sources can be practically anything you can query in program code and products that consume data. Reporting Services consumes data using the .NET data providers, which include support for SQL Server, Oracle, and all OLE DB providers. These include almost any database product that supports ODBC access or a capable ISAM driver. Datasets in Reporting Services are always read-only so there is no need to specify cursor types or locking options.

Reporting for Relational Data

In the previous chapter you briefly looked at using the Query Builder. Now you'll take a closer look at how queries are created and how data is provided for a report. At this point it's important to understand the basic building blocks for reports. We will begin by discussing some of these fundamentals. You will go through several short walkthrough exercises so you can see and experience how it works. It is assumed that you have used Visual Studio .NET and you have created a report using the Report Wizard. If this is not the case, please read Chapter 2 to get acquainted with these tools.

A Dataset Is Not a Dataset

If you are a .NET programmer as I am, you probably saw this term and thought, "I know what a dataset is and I use them all the time in .NET data access program code so I should have a leg up on doing data access in Reporting Services". If you are not a .NET programmer you're already a step ahead of those programmers who have to relearn the application of this term.

We ran out of new words in the English language a long time ago. Everyone knows that to be environmentally responsible we need to recycle so this is what we're doing—recycling words and phrases. The fact is that we just simply don't have the means to assign a unique name to every object or concept that we need to represent in written or spoken language—especially in this industry where we reinvent the technology every few years. So, we have a plethora of homonyms (two or more words that have the same sound and often the same spelling but differ in meaning) in our glossary of technical terms. The challenge is to understand the context of a term and to differentiate between their meanings.

This one is a classic example. In Reporting Services, you have the concept of a query in the report definition that provides data values for the report output; our good friends at Microsoft decided to call this a *Dataset*. If you have worked at all with programmatic data access in the .NET Framework, you should know that a Dataset is also an object that stores a cache of data (perhaps from a query) as an XML structure in memory. Although these two items may both handle data and deal with queries, result sets, and binding values displayed in a report, they are two very different concepts. Now, since we have that straightened out, try this: If you were to create a custom data source extension in program code, you might use an ADO.NET Dataset that would serve as the Dataset for a report!

Query Basics

Reporting Services has the ability to obtain data from a variety of data sources. Most database products are queried using a form of *SQL,*which means that a query created for one database product (say, Microsoft Access) may be portable to a different data source (perhaps Oracle or SQL Server). Most database products implement a form of SQL conforming to the ANSI SQL standard. SQL Server, for example, conforms to the ANSI 92 SQL standard and other products may conform to other revisions (like ANSI 89 SQL or ANSI 99 SQL). Beyond the most fundamental SQL statements, most dialects of SQL are not completely interchangeable and will require some understanding of their individual idiosyncrasies.

The main point here is that you can use whatever query language your database product understands. Reporting Services provides a query editor designed especially for Transact SQL and a generic editor that will accommodate other query languages and SQL dialects.

Data Sources

A data source contains the connection information for a dataset. Data sources can either be created only for a specific report dataset or may be shared among different reports. Since most reports will get data from a common data source, it often makes sense to create a shared data source. There are a number of advantages in using shared data sources. Even if you don't have several reports that need to share a central data source, it takes no additional effort to create a shared data source. This may still be advantageous in this case as the data source is managed separately from each report and can be easily updated if necessary. Then, as you add new reports, the shared data source will already be established and deployed to the Report Server.

In a Visual Studio report project there are three different ways to create a data source:

❑ Creating a data source in the Report Wizard

❑ Creating a data source from the Project Add Item template

❑ Creating a data source when defining a dataset

Let's look at each of these in detail.

Creating a Data Source in the Report Wizard

If you choose Add New Report from the Solution Explorer right-click menu the Report Wizard is launched. The first page in the wizard will give you the opportunity to select an existing shared data source or create a new data source as shown in Figure 4-4:

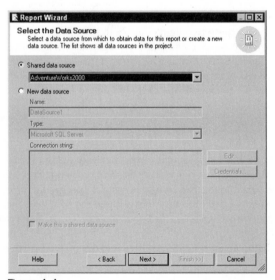

Figure 4-4

Creating a Data Source from the Project Add Item Template

Choose Add New Item from the Solution Explorer's right-click menu, new item options, and include Report Wizard, Report, and Data Source. Selecting the Data Source option creates a shared data source.

The following is an example of the standard Data Link Properties dialog used to define a data source. If your database server was named DWServer, this name would be selected or entered in the first box, under step 1 in this dialog as shown in Figure 4-5:

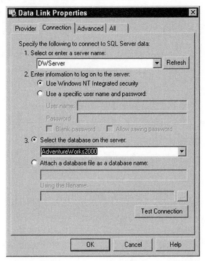

Figure 4-5

If you are working with a local development database server, installed on the same computer, you can enter local or localhost. Otherwise, enter the name of the database server.

> **You may also enter an IP address to access a SQL Server across the Internet. Connecting across the Internet requires some ports to be opened through the firewall. By default, ports 1433 and 1434 are used.**

In step 2, you choose the security authentication method to be used by the database server to check security credentials. SQL Server may be configured to use Integrated Windows Security, SQL Server security or both. In a development environment, integrated security is a simple choice.

Finally, you would select or type the database name.

Creating a Data Source When Defining a Dataset

If you create a new report without using the Report Wizard, data sources are selected or created from the Report Designer Data tab when creating a dataset. From the Dataset drop-down list, select New Dataset to get the dialog shown in Figure 4-6:

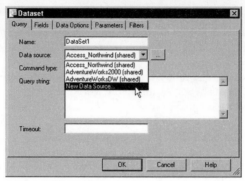

Figure 4-6

Select a shared data source from the drop-down list or click the ellipsis (...) button to create a new one. This will open the Data Link Properties dialog with the same options as selecting the Data Source new item template.

Regardless of the method used, a data source is simply a connection string saved into the report definition or shared data source file.

Data Sources and Query Languages

The examples in this chapter will all use SQL Server 2000 databases. When creating a data source, if you choose any data provider other than SQL Server, queries must be written in the query language appropriate for that product. For most relational database products, this will be a dialect of SQL. For example, Oracle uses a version of SQL called PL/SQL and Microsoft Access understands Access SQL. Some providers require unique types of query expressions or scripting code specifically designed for that data source environment.

When defining a dataset's query expression, the Designer will display one of the two similar query windows. If you are using the SQL Server data provider, the Transact SQL Query Builder will be displayed. In the case of another data provider that uses another query language or dialect of SQL, a generic query window is displayed.

To query cube structures in Analysis Services, a specialized expression language called Multidimensional Expressions (MDX) is used. The current implementation of Reporting Services supports MDX with some limitations. Unlike the Cube Browser in Analysis Services and other specialized multi-dimensional data query tools, reports are based on data that is flattened to two-dimensional structures and represented as rows and columns like a SQL query.

In this sample MDX query expression for the FoodMart2000 OLAP database (included in SQL Server 2000 Analysis Services), column data is generated from the Store Type dimension and rows are created from the Store dimension:

```
"SELECT {[Store Type].[Store Type].MEMBERS}
ON COLUMNS, {[Store].[Store State].MEMBERS}
ON ROWS FROM
```

```
[Product_Sales]
WHERE
(Measures.[Average Sales], [Time].[Year].[2003])"
```

We will discuss the use of data warehouses and specialized decision-support databases in our discussion about in Chapter 14.

Filtering Techniques

When retrieving report data from a data source, it's important to consider the most efficient means for filtering report data based on the user's selection criteria. Many databases contain large amounts of data. Therefore, it is always important to retrieve just the right amount of data required for reporting. At times, a report will only be used to view data for a narrow range of values and at other times the user may specify different criterion causing the report to render a varied range of related values. In the case of a narrow range of possible values, it makes more sense to retrieve only the associated data. However, if users will specify different criteria during a session—causing the data source to be re-queried multiple times—it could prove to be slow and also an inefficient use of resources.

In Figure 4-7, parameters presented to the data source cause data to be filtered and return only the data for a single rendering of the report. The dataset represents the database server's result set on the client side (the Report Server). As you see in the diagram, this is small volume of data since it has already been filtered at the database.

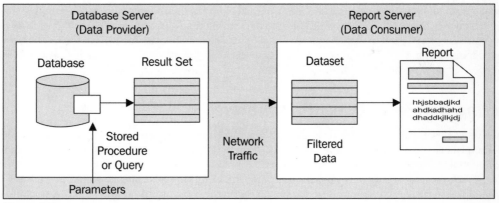

Figure 4-7

By passing selection criteria parameters at the database object level, network traffic can be greatly reduced and the report is rendered more efficiently. However, if the user will be providing different parameter values to render several views of the same report within a session, the database will be queried repeatedly, perhaps resulting in longer overall wait times and much of the same data will be moving across the network multiple times. In Figure 4-8, a larger volume of data is returned from the database server since it is unfiltered. Filtering then occurs by using report parameters on the Report Server.

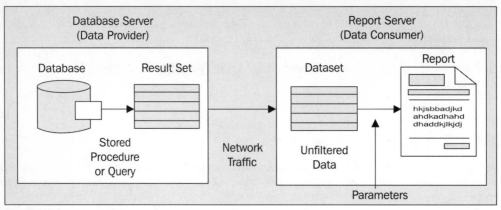

Figure 4-8

If all of the data necessary for each query to be executed in a user's session is obtained in one result set, it will result in a greater volume of network traffic for a single execution. However, it may reduce subsequent report rendering times.

Selection parameters may be applied to data at the report level rather than at the data source. Since all of the data is cached (held in memory) reports will render much faster. This technique can reduce the overall network traffic and rendering time.

You certainly don't want to retrieve unnecessary data from the data source, so a combination of these two techniques may be the appropriate solution depending upon specific reporting needs. For example, if you are a regional sales manager and you wish to get sales summaries for each of the territories within your region, you may begin your session by retrieving all of the regional sales data for a range of dates. For each territory report, this data is simply filtered down to the territory level.

Filtering Data with Query Parameters

Let's begin this discussion by talking about using parameters to filter data at the data source. Whether the data is to be filtered within the report or not, filtering at least some of the data within the database is an essential technique for most report solutions. If you have created parameterized stored procedures in SQL Server, you are already familiar with this pattern. The technique applies to stored procedures and query expressions using very similar syntax. Let's start with a simple ad hoc query expression and then we'll move on to creating a stored procedure.

Query parameters begin with the @ symbol and must conform to the naming convention standards for Transact SQL identifiers. The name should not contain spaces or certain punctuation characters and can't begin with a numeral; for simplicity, just use letters. In stored procedures, parameters must be declared before they are used. In an ad hoc query, simply make up parameter names when you need them. In the WHERE part of a SQL statement, use a parameter to represent a variable valuable as follows:

```
SELECT * FROM Products WHERE ProductID = @ProductID
```

In this case, the parameter has the same name as the corresponding field name but this isn't necessary. If you want to use the Query Builder to create a more complex query, parameters may be specified in the Criteria column of the builder grid. This is shown in Figure 4-9:

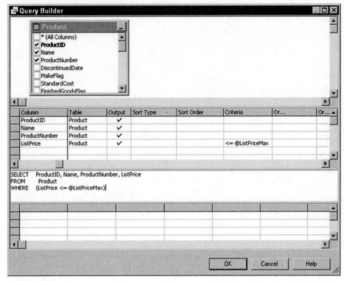

Figure 4-9

In this example, rows will be returned for records where the ListPrice column value is less than or equal to the value specified using the @ListPriceMax parameter.

Report Parameters

All query parameters specified for a dataset will automatically generate corresponding report parameters. Additionally, report parameters (that do not have corresponding query parameters) can be added to support addition report functionality.

The following example demonstrates some simple report parameters used to dynamically set values on the report. Later we'll apply this technique to some practical report features. This example is intended to demonstrate two very simple report parameters for academic purposes.

Create a new report without using the wizard. You can do this by selecting Add and then Add New Item from the Solution Explorer's right-click menu; select Report from the report item templates in the Add New Item dialog. Do not specify a dataset for the new report and then switch to the Layout view in the Report Designer.

Report parameters are added using the Report Parameters dialog. Select the Report item in the properties window and click the ellipsis (...) button next to the ReportParameters item.

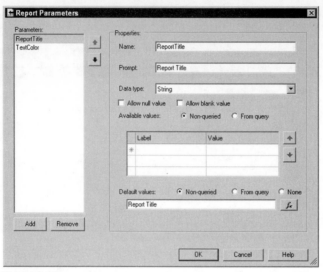

Figure 4-10

As you see in Figure 4-10, the ReportTitle parameter is a string value with the default set to Report Title. The TextColor parameter is similar and has a default value set to Blue.

Drag two text box items from the toolbox window onto the body of the report in the Report Designer. Normally it's a good idea to give items an appropriate name (especially if they are to be referenced in an expression) but this isn't necessary in this simple example.

Set two properties for these text boxes: the Value property for each text box and the Color property of the second text box. The Designer displays the value property in the text boxes but it's a good idea to change these property values in the standard properties window or the custom text box properties dialog (right click the text box and choose Properties).

The first text box will get its value from the ReportTitle parameter. Set its Value property to =Parameters!ReportTitle.Value and set the Value property of the second text box to ="This Text is " & Parameters!TextColor.Value. With the second text box selected, set its Color property to =Parameters!TextColor.Value. See Figure 4-11:

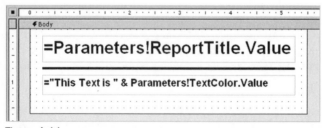

Figure 4-11

You can also change the FontSize and FontWeight properties if you prefer to dress things up a bit more. I've also added a line to the report.

Now click the Preview tab and notice what happens. The ReportTitle and TextColor parameters are displayed in the header of the preview window with the default values and these values are displayed in the report.

Try changing the ReportTitle and Color using the parameter fields in the header and click the View Report button to refresh the report preview. The first text box should display the text entered into the ReportTitle parameter and the second text box should not only display the specific color name but the text should also be displayed in that color as in Figure 4-12:

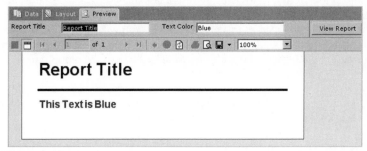

Figure 4-12

As you can see, this is an effective way to feed values to the report to be used in expressions. We will expand this technique to provide filtering and dynamic formatting.

Basing a Parameter on a Query

Whether report parameters are derived from query parameters or created within the report explicitly, they may be used for a variety of things in the report. Often, it will make sense to let your user select from a list of items to supply a parameter value. Parameter items may be populated from a static list or from a data-driven query.

Parameter values can be selected from a data source through a dataset that is set up within the Report Designer like any dataset you would use for the report itself. A report may contain any number of datasets, some to supply parameter values and others to supply data for items within the report.

Using the sample Northwind database for a simple example, your report may be driven by a dataset that selects records from the Products table where the CategoryID matches a user-specified parameter value. The CategoryID parameter values would be based on another dataset that selects the CategoryID and CategoryName columns from the Categories table. In Report Manager, the user simply selects a category name from a drop-down list and then the report is viewed showing only products that match the selected category.

In the upcoming walkthrough exercise, you will create different parameters that will not only drive the report but will filter the values for multiple, related parameters.

Cascading Parameters

The behavior I just described is what we call *cascading parameters*. This is a feature in the Report Manager that allows one parameter value selection to cause another parameter list to be populated with related values. There will be times when you may want to filter a list of parameter values based on another parameter selection. In the earlier example for product categories and products let's say that the selection from the Products table is to provide another parameter value that will be used to generate a report of sales records for the selected product. In this case, you may want to select the category first. This would give you a filtered list of products that would be used to select a specific product. The product selection would then be used to render the sales report.

We'll use another example from the AdventureWorks2000 database. We'll raise the bar just a little more and create three different parameters to drive a fairly simple walkthrough example. The outcome of this exercise will be a report showing stores in a given location. You will be prompted to select a country. When the country is selected, related states or provinces will be listed. Making a selection from this list will make cities available. Selecting an item from this list will drive the report data—a list of stores in the selected city.

This walkthrough requires that you either complete the steps in the preceding chapter or that you already know how to create a report project and a shared data source.

To begin with, add a new report to a Visual Studio report project. From the Solution Explorer, right click on Reports and choose Add and then Add New Item. Select Report from the templates list and give it any name you like. I'm calling mine Cascading_Parameters. I know it's not very imaginative but it makes the point.

In the Report Designer, you should be looking at the Data tab at this point. Drop down the list labeled Dataset and select New Dataset. The dialog as in Figure 4-13 will appear:

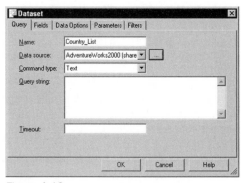

Figure 4-13

Enter the name Country_List for the new dataset. Select or create a shared data source for the AdventureWorks2000 database (created one in the previous chapter) and then click the OK button to move to the Query Builder window.

Rather than going through the whole Query Builder procedure, here is the SQL statement to type into the SQL pane. Place the cursor in the third pane down in this window (between the two grids) and type the following code:

```
SELECT      CountryRegionCode, Name
FROM        CountryRegion
ORDER BY    Name
```

Note that the carriage returns and most of the spacing are optional. The only critical spaces are between the words ORDER and BY. Everything else should have one or more spaces. This query doesn't use any parameters since it won't be filtered.

Drop down the dataset list, choose **New Dataset** and repeat the preceding steps to create a new dataset called **StateProvince_List**. The SQL expression for this dataset can also be typed into the Query Builder window:

```
SELECT      StateProvinceID, StateProvinceCode, CountryRegionCode
FROM        StateProvince
WHERE       CountryRegionCode = @CountryCode
ORDER BY    StateProvinceCode
```

If you used the Query Builder to create this expression, there may be some additional parentheses. These are unnecessary and, again, the spacing and returns are not particularly important.

This expression does include a parameter, @CountryCode, which will get its value from a row selected from the previous dataset. A corresponding parameter will be created for the report called CountryCode.

Drop down the dataset list and create a third dataset called **City_list**. Like the last dataset, this one also includes a parameter that will get its value from the selected state or province. Type the following SQL statement for this dataset:

```
SELECT      StateProvinceID, City
FROM        Address
GROUP BY    StateProvinceID, City
HAVING      StateProvinceID = @StateProvinceID
ORDER BY    City
```

There is no table exclusively for cities so you can use the Address table and grouping on the City column to eliminate duplicates. This query will return a list of cities for the selected state or province using the StateProvinceID parameter.

Finally you will need to create the dataset for the report itself. The SQL for this is going to be a little more complicated. Due to the normalized design of the AdventureWorks2000 database, it takes several tables to take you from a city to a store with the necessary report values. Let's use the Query Builder for this one.

If you prefer, you may skip the following Query Builder steps and type the SQL statement directly into the SQL pane.

Add one more dataset and call it **Stores_By_City**. Click the **Add Table** toolbar button (or right click the top pane and choose **Add Table**) and add the tables illustrated in Figure 4-14:

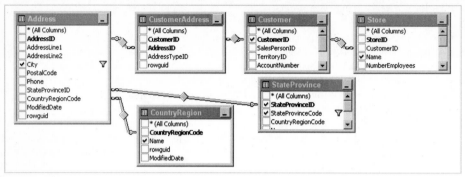

Figure 4-14

The joins will be added automatically by the Query Builder. An additional join will be added between the **StateProvince** and **CountryRegion** tables. To remove the join, click once on the line and then press the delete key.

In the second pane, select the table columns in the order you see here. You can either use the drop-down lists in the grid for the column and table or check them in the table diagram in the first pane. Since the **Store** and **CountryRegion** tables both contain columns called **Name**, you can use aliases to make these column names more descriptive. Enter the alias names as you see in the grid in Figure 4-15:

Column	Alias	Table	Output	Sort Type	Sort Order	Criteria	Or...	Or...
CustomerID		Customer	✓					
Name	StoreName	Store	✓					
Name	CountryName	CountryRegion	✓					
StateProvinceCode		StateProvince	✓			= @StateProvinceID		
City		Address	✓			= @City		
StateProvinceID		StateProvince	✓					

Figure 4-15

Finally, enter the query parameters `@StateProvinceID` and `@City` as you see here. This dataset should be complete. To check it, compare this SQL statement with the one in the Query Builder:

```
SELECT    Customer.CustomerID, Store.Name AS StoreName,
          CountryRegion.Name AS CountryName, StateProvince.StateProvinceCode,
          Address.City, StateProvince.StateProvinceID
FROM      Customer
          INNER JOIN
          CustomerAddress ON Customer.CustomerID = CustomerAddress.CustomerID
          INNER JOIN Store ON Customer.CustomerID = Store.CustomerID
          INNER JOIN Address ON CustomerAddress.AddressID = Address.AddressID
          INNER JOIN CountryRegion
              ON Address.CountryRegionCode = CountryRegion.CountryRegionCode
          INNER JOIN StateProvince
              ON Address.StateProvinceID = StateProvince.StateProvinceID
```

```
WHERE        Address.City = @City
             AND StateProvince.StateProvinceCode = @StateProvinceID
```

Let's now look into configuring parameters.

Switch to the Layout tab and select the Report item from the properties window drop-down list. Click the ellipsis button next to the ReportParameters property. This opens the Report Parameters dialog as seen in Figure 4-16:

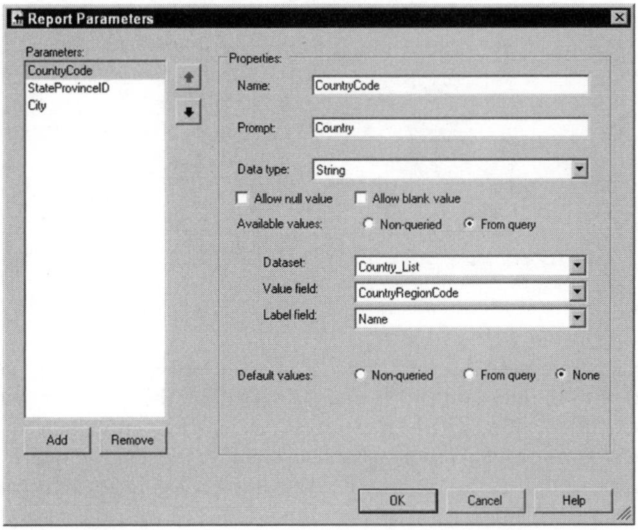

Figure 4-16

The CountryCode parameter will get its values from the Country_List dataset. Like most typical lookup tables, the key value is not intended to be a user-readable value but is used to indicate the selected country for related tables through a foreign key relationship.

Select this parameter in the Parameters list box and then enter Country for the prompt. This is the caption the user will see next to the parameter drop-down list when they view the report. Uncheck both of the check boxes to indicate that the user must select a value from the drop-down list.

The parameter drop-down list will display values in the Name column and return the corresponding value in the CountryRegionCode column. Set the Label field and Value field properties accordingly. Finally, indicate that there is no default value by selecting the last radio button and click OK when you're done.

> We will repeat this process for the other two parameters. Use the following Report Parameters screen diagram to set these properties.

The StateProvinceID parameter is configured as shown in Figure 4-17:

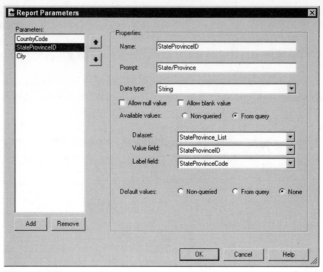

Figure 4-17

The properties for this parameter are set much like they were before. This time use the StateProvince_List dataset as the drop-down list data source. You should remember that this dataset contains a query parameter called CountryRegionCode. The reporting engine is smart enough to make the connection between the Value field of the previous parameter's dataset and this dataset's corresponding parameter. One parameter selection will filter the list for the next parameter as long as the parameters are listed in their order of dependency.

The final parameter, City, is configured as shown in Figure 4-18:

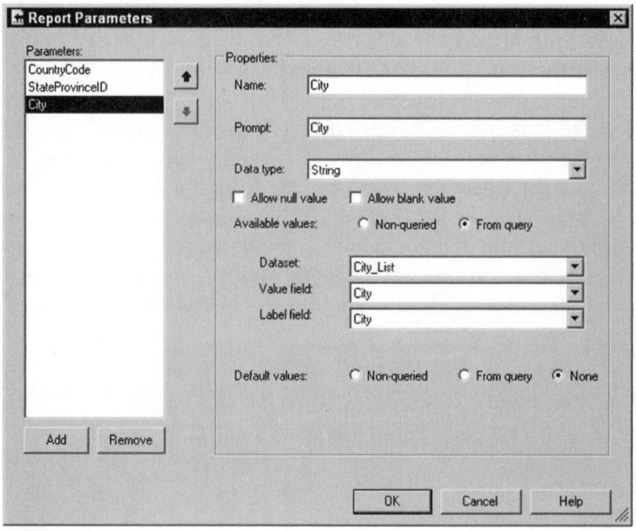

Figure 4-18

Much like the previous parameter, the City parameter gets its value list from the City_List dataset, which contains a query parameter related to the value field selection for the StateProvinceID parameter.

Designing the report is easy. I've made it a point to size the text box items so you can read their value properties in this view of the Report Designer:

Figure 4-19

The wide rectangle at the bottom of the report body is a list item. Drag this from the toolbox to the report body first and set its DataSetName property to Stores_By_City. The toolbox is located on the left side of theDesigner window and has a little wrench and hammer icon.

The easiest way to create data-bound text boxes is to drag fields from the fields list (located on the left side near the toolbox). With the fields list open, drop down the list at the top and select the Stores_By_City dataset. Now drag the CustomerID and Name fields onto the list item you created earlier.

From the Toolbox, drag two text boxes above the list and change the Value properties to Customer ID and Store like you see in the Figure 4-19. The Stores By Location, Country, State/Province, and City text boxes are also unbound and serve only as static labels.

Drag and drop the CountryName, StateProvinceCode, and City fields to the right of the corresponding label text boxes near the top of the report body.

Note the value of these three items contains some additional information. An aggregate function (like the First function used here) is necessary when an item isn't contained in a list, grid or other container item that repeats rows of data. Since this report defines more than one dataset, the dataset name is required in the second argument of the First function.

With these settings in place, you should be able to preview the report and see the results. Switch to the Preview tab and select a Country from the drop-down list.

As shown in Figure 4-20, select United States from the list and the State/Province parameter list is enabled:

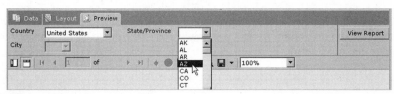

Figure 4-20

Drop this list down and you will see that it contains only states in the US. Select **AZ** for Arizona and the City parameter list becomes available.

Drop down the City list, select **Phoenix** and then click the **View Report** button as shown in Figure 4-21:

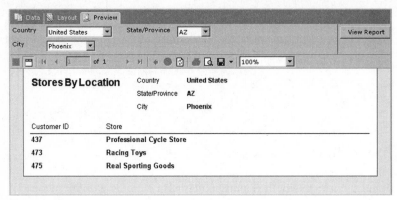

Figure 4-21

As you can see, the report manager offers a great deal of built-in functionality for using parameters without very little effort. Even in Microsoft Access, getting this kind of behavior would have required writing some code.

Using Stored Procedures

The best way to go about querying a data source will depend highly on your requirements. Refer back to our earlier discussion about filtering techniques where processing parameters (on the database server, the client or both) affects performance, efficiency, and the flexibility of your reporting solution. Handling parameters on the database server will almost always be more efficient, while processing parameters on the client will give you the flexibility of handling a wider range of records and query options without needing to go back to the database every time you need to render the report.

Using a parameterized stored procedure is typically going to provide the most efficient means for filtering data since it returns only the data matching your criteria. Stored procedures are compiled to native processor instructions on the database server. When any kind of query is processed, SQL Server creates an execution plan, which defines the specific instructions the server uses to retrieve data. In the case of a stored procedure, the execution plan is prepared the first time it is executed and then it is cached on the database server. In subsequent executions, results will be returned faster since some of the work has already been done. Stored procedures for SQL Server can be created in three different places: the SQL Enterprise Manager, the SQL Query Analyzer, or in Visual Studio's integrated Query Builder.

In the next exercise we will create a stored procedure that will be used to create columnar report. This is performed using the Server Explorer to obtain a connection to the database server and then manage objects on the server.

With Visual Studio open, you can see the Server Explorer located on the left side of the Designer by default. Click the plus sign handle to the left of these items to expand each branch of the tree. Open

Servers | (your computer name) | SQL Servers | (your computer name) | AdventureWorks2000 and then right click on Stored Procedures. From the pop-up menu, select New Stored Procedure as shown in Figure 4-22:

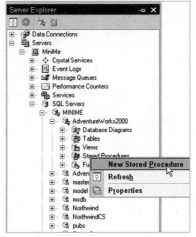

Figure 4-22

This action will open a new Designer window to create a new stored procedure. The text in Figure 4-23 demonstrates the basic structure of a simple stored procedure:

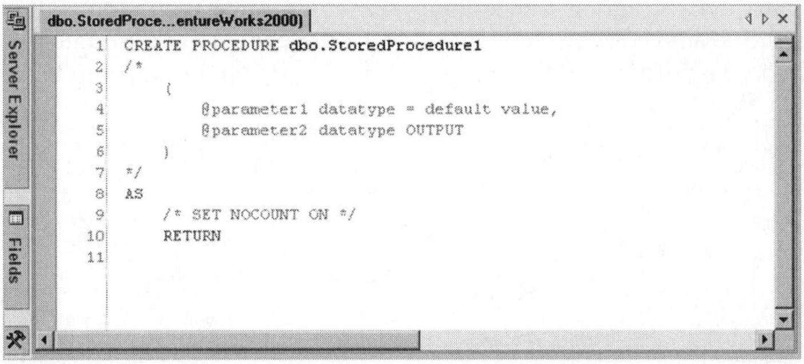

```
 1   CREATE PROCEDURE dbo.StoredProcedure1
 2   /*
 3       (
 4           @parameter1 datatype = default value,
 5           @parameter2 datatype OUTPUT
 6       )
 7   */
 8   AS
 9       /* SET NOCOUNT ON */
10       RETURN
11
```

Figure 4-23

We will replace the procedure name and parameters, and add a Transact-SQL statement to complete the procedure.

Note that the line numbers shown in the left side of the code window are an optional feature of the Visual Studio editor and are not part of the stored procedure text. If you don't see them, don't worry about it.

> **Enable line numbers in the editor, so you can easily keep track of things in your code.**

Highlight the procedure name (dbo.StoredProcedure1) and replace it with **spGetStoresByLocation**. Highlight all of the green-colored text in the block including the /* and */ and delete it and replace it with:

```
@StateProvinceCode Char(2),
@City              nVarChar(30)
```

The spacing and indentation isn't important. Highlight and delete the text /* **SET NOCOUNT ON** */ and then right click in this location. From the pop-up menu, select **Insert SQL**. In the Query Builder, type the following into the third pane down (between the grids in the second and fourth panes):

```
SELECT   Store.Name AS StoreName, StateProvince.StateProvinceCode,
         StateProvince.Name AS StateProvinceName, Address.City
FROM     Customer INNER JOIN Store
         ON Customer.CustomerID = Store.CustomerID
         INNER JOIN CustomerAddress
         ON Customer.CustomerID = CustomerAddress.CustomerID
         INNER JOIN Address
         ON CustomerAddress.AddressID = Address.AddressID
         INNER JOIN StateProvince
         ON Address.StateProvinceID = StateProvince.StateProvinceID
WHERE    StateProvinceCode = @StateProvinceCode AND City = @City
ORDER BY City, StoreName
```

Again, using spaces and indentation (as well as carriage returns) is not mandatory, but is a good practice for increasing the clarity of code and reducing errors. If you are familiar with the Query Builder, you can build this query in the table diagram and column grid panes rather than typing all of this into the SQL pane. Close this window and confirm that you want to save changes and update the stored procedure with this expression. The finished stored procedure should appear as shown in Figure 4-24:

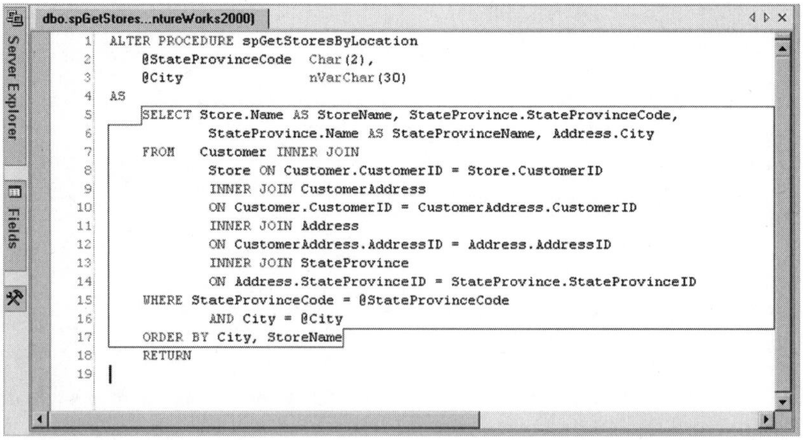

Figure 4-24

Go ahead and close this window and save any changes if prompted. The stored procedure should show up in the Server Explorer tree under the stored procedures branch.

Next create a new report and use this stored procedure as the dataset. In the Solution Explorer, right click on **Reports** and select **Add | Add New Item**. In the **Add New Item** dialog, select **Report** and enter the report name **Stores By Location**. Click **Open** to create the new report. On the **Data** tab of the Report Designer, drop down the **Dataset** list and select **New Dataset**. In this dialog, enter **StoresByLocation** for the dataset name and then select or create a data source for the AdventureWorks2000 database.

We created a shared data source for this database in the section *Establishing a Data Source*. You can refer to that exercise to create it if the shared data source isn't available in this project.

Change the **Command type** from **Text** to **Stored Procedure** and then type the stored procedure name, **spGetStoresByLocation**, into the **Query string** box. Click **OK** when you're done. See Figure 4-25:

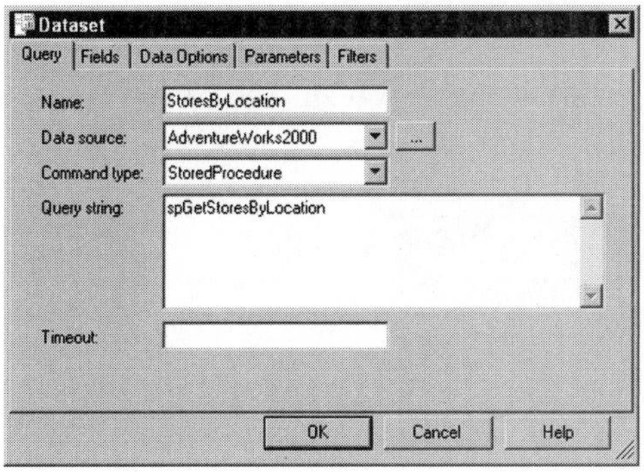

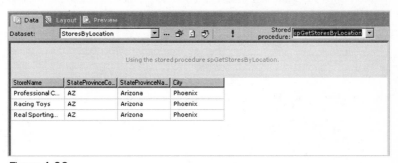

Figure 4-25

The Designer's appearance will change to a grid with the stored procedure name in a drop-down list at top-right.

Click the **Execute** button (dark red exclamation mark icon) to test the dataset and execute the stored procedure. You will be prompted for the two parameter values, **@StateProvinceCode** and **@City**. Enter two valid values and click **OK** to view the results. Figure 4-26 shows an example:

Figure 4-26

The dataset is used exactly as before. The stored procedure parameters become report parameters.

Filtering Data with Report Parameters

So far you've only filtered data at the database level. In cases where users may be using the same report in one sitting to view data for different criteria, it may be more effective to retrieve a larger result set from the data source and then filter the report data on the Report Server.

As you've already seen, parameters defined in a query or stored procedure that serves as report dataset are pulled into the report as report parameters. You can also define your own parameters and use expressions to filter data at the report level.

We're going to use both product categories and sub-categories for report parameters. The category will be filtered in the dataset (at the SQL Server) and the sub-category will be filtered in the report (on the Report Server).

Add a new report to a project. Use the AdventureWorks2000 shared data source and apply the following SQL expression in the dataset:

```
SELECT      Product.ProductID, Product.Name AS ProductName,
            ProductSubCategory.Name AS SubCategoryName,
            ProductCategory.Name AS CategoryName,
            ProductSubCategory.ProductCategoryID,
            Product.ProductSubCategoryID
FROM        Product INNER JOIN ProductSubCategory
            ON Product.ProductSubCategoryID = ProductSubCategory.
            ProductSubCategoryID
            INNER JOIN ProductCategory
            ON ProductSubCategory.ProductCategoryID = ProductCategory.
            ProductCategoryID
WHERE       ProductSubCategory.ProductCategoryID = @CategoryID
ORDER BY    Product.Name
```

You're going to create two more datasets to populate parameter drop-down lists and set up a cascading relationship between the two parameters.

Using the same data source, add another dataset and name it CategoryList. Type this text into the third pane of the Query Builder:

```
SELECT      ProductCategoryID, Name
FROM        ProductCategory
ORDER BY    Name
```

And add one more dataset named SubCategoryList using this text:

```
SELECT      ProductSubCategoryID, Name, ProductCategoryID
FROM        ProductSubCategory
WHERE       ProductCategoryID = @CategoryID
ORDER BY    Name
```

With the Report Designer Layout tab selected, select the Report item from the properties window drop-down list and find the ReportParameters property. Click the ellipsis button next to this property. This will open the Report Parameters dialog. Note that the CategoryID parameter has been added to the report parameters as expected. Click the Add button to add a new parameter and name it SubCategoryID. Leave all of the other settings at default values to keep things simple. Click OK to close the Report Parameters dialog.

Now switch back to the Data tab and click the ellipsis next to the dataset name. On the Dataset dialog change to the Filter tab. There are three required elements for a filter expression—the Expression (what you want to filter), Operator (how you're going to compare a value), and Value (the source of the filter value). For the expression, drop down the list and select =Fields!SubCategoryName.Value.

Leave the equality operator set to = then drop down the Value list and select Expression. This opens the expression builder. Use the controls to select the SubCategoryID parameter and use the Insert button to move it into the expression box on the right side of this dialog. The resulting expression should be =Parameters!SubCategoryName.Value.

Modify the first expression using the CInt function and place parentheses around the field expression. Some value comparisons don't resolve data types correctly. If such a comparison results in a data type conversion or casting error, it can be corrected by explicitly converting the expression to the correct data type as you've done here with the field expression. To be on the safe side, you can use Visual Basic type conversion functions with any expression or value. See Figure 4-27:

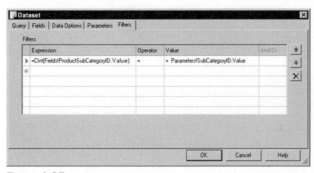

Figure 4-27

The Filters expression builder has an interesting feature. The And / Or column doesn't allow an explicit selection to be made. If you want to use a more complex expression (for example, if you wanted to bring back all products for a category if no sub-category was selected), you can enhance the expression manually as a single expression. However, you can't do it line-by-line using this tool. We'll likely see enhancements to this dialog in future version of Reporting Services.

Now that you have the datasets and parameters set up, you can actually create a report. We'll keep it simple. In the Layout tab, drag a text box to the report body, click on it to set focus and type the report title Products by Category / Subcategory. Add a table to the report just below the text box and stretch it to fill the width of the report.

Click once in the table and then select the table by clicking the top-left corner selector to select the table. Select the DatasetName property in the properties window for the table and select the dataset ProductsByCategory. From the fields list on the left of the Designer, drag the ProductName, CategoryName, and SubCategoryName fields into the detail row's first, second, and third columns respectively.

Dress up the grid by selecting the header row (click once on the grid and use the row selector on the left to select the header row) and use the report formatting toolbar to make the text bold. Use the property window to set the Border Style | Bottom property to Solid and the Border Width | Bottom to 2pt.

Switch to the Preview tab. You should be prompted to select a category using a drop-down list. The category selection will populate the CategoryID query parameter and retrieve records from the database into memory. Select any category value and you should be prompted to select a subcategory. This is the report parameter SubCategoryID. Selecting a value will cause the filter to be applied and the resulting data will be fed to the report. Click the View Report button to render the report as shown in Figure 4-28:

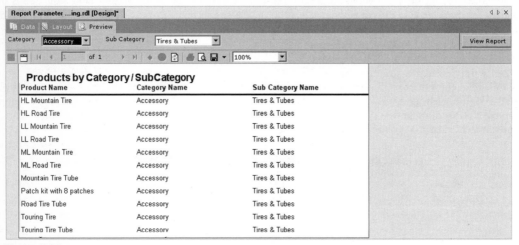

Figure 4-28

The category parameter filters data at the database. This is shown in Figure 4-29:

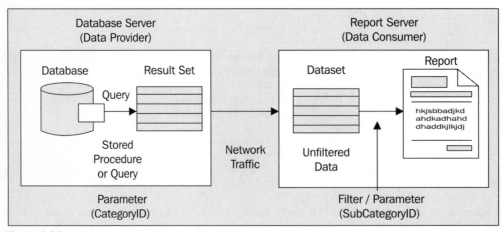

Figure 4-29

The resulting data is cached in memory on the Report Server where the subcategory filter further limits results.

You could easily extend the design of this report using more complex items, sorting, and grouping. The dataset query could also be replaced with a stored procedure. With these building blocks, you now have the capability to create efficient reports that move the appropriate volume of data across network connections and allow users to using filtering criteria without needing to re-query the entire dataset.

Summary

Defining data sources and datasets to manage data source queries is the starting point for almost any data-driven report. It's essential to understand basic data storage and query architecture to achieve the best design. Data can be filtered within the database server or in the report. Making the correct choice and finding the best combination of these options will improve performance and provide flexibility with the least degree of overhead.

Defining shared data sources in your projects makes it much easier to maintain data connections for all of your reports as a group. Changing the database location or security credentials becomes a much simpler proposition. The datasets for your reports define queries for retrieving data and may be used as the source for the report and repeatable data regions or to provide data value for report parameters.

An ad hoc query expression is stored in the report within the report definition and a stored procedure is stored in the database. Using stored procedures is an effective means for processing parameters and filtering data before sending it to the report while using a report filter lets you reuse the data you've already retrieved. A combination of these parameterized filtering techniques may be an optimal solution for more complex reporting needs.

Advanced Report Design

Picking up where we left off in Chapter 2, we will expand on the elements of report design and learn how to use a number of interesting and useful features. This chapter should serve as both a tutorial to get you started with these advanced techniques, and a reference for creating your own reports from your own data sources. The topics covered in this chapter are:

- ❑ Creating a tabular report using tables
- ❑ Links and drill-through reports
- ❑ Using charts in reports
- ❑ Using custom code to extend formatting and apply business logic
- ❑ Designing reports for mobile devices

At this point, you should be comfortable using Visual Studio .NET to create and add reports to a project and you should be familiar with the basic mechanics of the Designer. If you are new to this environment, please work through the exercises in Chapter 4 before you read on.

You will no longer be using the Report Wizard. You should be able to add a new report to a project, create or select a shared data source, create a dataset, and add items to the Report Designer by now. This chapter will provide directions for using nearly all of the design elements mentioned here.

In Chapter 4, we talked about using items and data regions in a report. In particular, you used the wizard to generate a tabular report with a *table data region*. In this chapter, you will start by repeating this exercise, only with a greater level of detail to create a report to your own specifications.

Creating a Tabular Report Using a Table

The Table data region is a very useful controland can be used to create report interfaces with multiple levels of groupings and drill-down functionality. As you briefly saw in Chapter 2, groupings give you the ability to organize repeated data within hierarchies and related groups.

Using the Products by Subcategory/Category query you created in the previous chapter, you can create a simple report that demonstrates the use of groupings within a table. After demonstrating groupings in a multi-level grouped table, drill-down and drill-through capabilities will be added.

Groupings are added directly to the table item using the right click menu and a custom properties dialog window. Table groupings can have an associated header and footer row. Cells in these rows contain textboxes (by default) that can be used to display column values for the grouping level. Different columns can be used to indent grouped values, or you can use the padding property of a textbox to achieve more precise control.

You'll use a modified version of the previous query without the parameter. Add a new report without using the wizard. For the dataset, use the shared data source for the local AdventureWorks2000 database or create a data source that points to this database.

From the Products by Subcategory/Category exercise, you can copy and paste the SQL expression from the `ProductsByCategory` dataset into the new report's dataset, and then remove the `@CategoryID` parameter reference and the two key columns, `ProductCategoryID` and `ProductSubCategoryID`. If you didn't do this exercise, type the following SQL expression into the third pane of the Query Builder:

```
SELECT     Product.ProductID, ProductCategory.Name AS CategoryName,
           ProductSubCategory.Name AS SubCategoryName, Product.Name AS ProductName
FROM       Product INNER JOIN ProductSubCategory
           ON Product.ProductSubCategoryID = ProductSubCategory.
           ProductSubCategoryID
           INNER JOIN ProductCategory
           ON ProductSubCategory.ProductCategoryID = ProductCategory.
           ProductCategoryID
ORDER BY   ProductCategory.Name, ProductSubCategory.Name, Product.Name
```

As you can see, we've simplified the expression since you're not going to use any parameters in this example.

Switch to the Layout tab and drag a Table data region item from the toolbox to the Report Designer. Click on the table and then click the gray handle on the top-left to select it. This should display a border with selection handles around the table. In the properties window, select the `DatasetName` property and in the drop-down list, select the dataset name.

The table currently contains a detail, header, and footer row. You will add two groups for the Category and Subcategory. Groups are added in top-down order so we will add the Category group first. Right click the detail row handle and select Insert Group from the pop-up menu as shown in Figure 5-1:

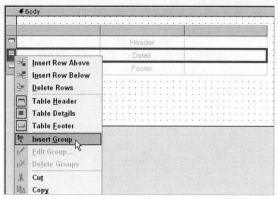

Figure 5-1

The Grouping and Sorting Properties dialog is displayed with a default name for the new grouping. For a complex report, you may want to devise a more intuitive naming convention than the one offered by the Designer. Note the features in this dialog include:

❑ Name is used for identifying and referring to this group in expressions

❑ Group on may contain one or more expressions to group on

❑ Document map label is a field value or text that will be used in the document map for the report

❑ Parent group may be used to create a hierarchy of nested groupings

❑ Page break options may be used to force a page break

❑ Header and footer options enable group header and footer rows

For simplicity, just add the group field name to the end as you see in the Figure 5-2. In the Expression box, drop down the first list and select =Fields!CategoryName.Value:

Figure 5-2

Switch to the Sorting tab and choose the same field to ensure that records are sorted correctly prior to grouping on this field value as shown in Figure 5-3:

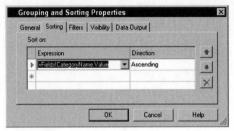

Figure 5-3

Click OK to close the Grouping and Sorting Properties dialog. Right click on the detail row handle again and repeat the same process for the ProductSubCategory field. This is shown in Figure 5-4 and Figure 5-5:

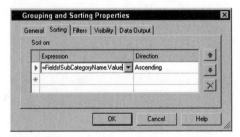

Figure 5-4

Figure 5-5

Adding the fields to the table is a snap. Just drag and drop them from the Fields window on the left. Place the CategoryName in the first cell in the group 1 row. Drag the SubCatgoryName field to the second column on the group 2 row and drag the ProductName field to the third column on the detail row as shown in Figure 5-6:

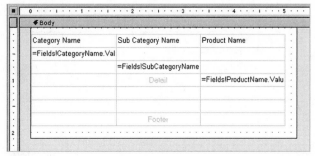

Figure 5-6

The report should be functional at this point although it needs a little cosmetic work. Select the header row by clicking in the table and then on the header row selector handle. This selects all of the textboxes in this row. Using the properties window set the BorderStyle | Bottom property to Solid and the BorderWidth | Bottom property to 2pt.

Column Placement and Indentation

One of the typical limitations of a grid is that if you want values to be indented or staggered, the values are restricted to specific column placement and widths. If you want the indentation between each level to be less pronounced, it wouldn't allow much room for values in their respective columns.

There are two common techniques for dealing with these limitations. The first technique, you'll use in this example, is to merge columns together which will give values more space, even with the column spacing reduced. To apply this technique, click and drag the mouse pointer across a group of adjacent columns to group select them. Right click and select Merge Cells. Note that this effectively extends the first cell in the range and hides other cell values. You may find it necessary to abbreviate column headings so you can resize the columns and get the desired effect. In Figure 5-7, you can see that I've changed the column headings, resized the columns, and set the Category and Sub Category textboxes to use bold text:

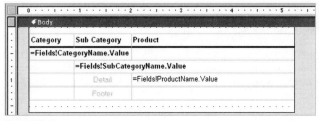

Figure 5-7

The other technique for indenting column values in a multi-level grouping is to place different group row values in the same column and change the left padding property. In Figure 5-8, the table contains only one column. The CategoryName textbox left padding is set to the default value of 2px. The SubCategoryName textbox is set to 22px and the ProductName textbox left padding is set to 42px:

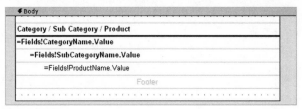

Figure 5-8

One restriction on using this technique is that the column header text can be slightly more difficult to align. The finished report (using the multi-column technique) is shown in Figure 5-9:

Category	Sub Category	Product
Accessory		
	Bike Racks	
		Hitch rack - 4 bike
	Bike Stand	
		All-purpose bike stand
	Bottles & Cages	
		Mountain bottle cage
		Road bottle cage
		water bottle 30 oz
	Cleaners	
		Bike wash - dissolver
	Fenders	
		Fender set - mountain
	Helmet	

Figure 5-9

Headers and Footers

Page headers and footers can be configured so that they are displayed and printed on all pages, or omitted from the first and/or last pages. Using the report you created for the last section on filtering, let's move the report header text into a header and show page count information in the footer on each page.

Add a page header and footer by selecting **Page Header** and **Page Footer** from the **Report** menu while the report is open in **Layout** view. Select **Report Properties** from the **Report** menu. This is where you can optionally leave a page header or footer off the first or last page of the report (see Figure 5-10):

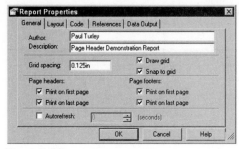

Figure 5-10

Now that the page header and footer are visible in the Designer, drag the report title textbox into the header area. You'll also replace the header row of the table with textboxes in the page header. Add three textboxes and label them with the same text as the three columns in the table header row. Let's also add a line and place it immediately below the row of textboxes. Resize the page header area as needed.

In the report body, click on the table and then right click the row selector to the left of the table header. Choose **Delete Rows** to get rid of the header row. Resize the report body as needed. Finally, in the report footer section, place a horizontal line and a textbox item below it.

You're going to set the value of the textbox so that it reads **Page X of Y**. To do this, you'll use an expression to create a dynamic value. Expressions may be used to set most property values based on a variety of global variables, fields and calculations. To display the page number and page count, select the **Value** property for the textbox in the properties window and drop down the list. Select **Expression** and use the **Edit Expression** window to create the expression. Begin by typing '="Page " & ' in the **Expression** box and then use the **Globals** item on the **Fields** list to select the PageNumber field. Next, insert the field reference into the expression using the **Insert** button. Concatenate the text ' & " of " & ', and then select and insert the **TotalPages** field. The finished expression should read as follows:

```
=''Page '' & Globals!PageNumber & '' of '' & Globals!TotalPages
```

The **Edit Expression** window, or the Expression Builder, in turn should appear as shown in Figure 5-11:

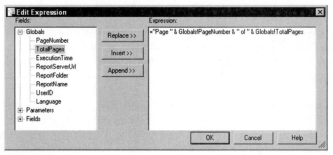

Figure 5-11

The Expression Builder is a simple tool that builds string values. You can always type the expression into the property window. The finished report in the Designer window can be seen in Figure 5-12:

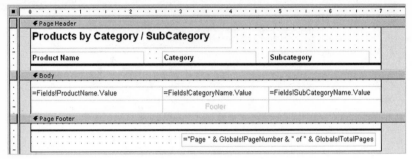

Figure 5-12

The report should be ready to preview and is shown in Figure 5-13:

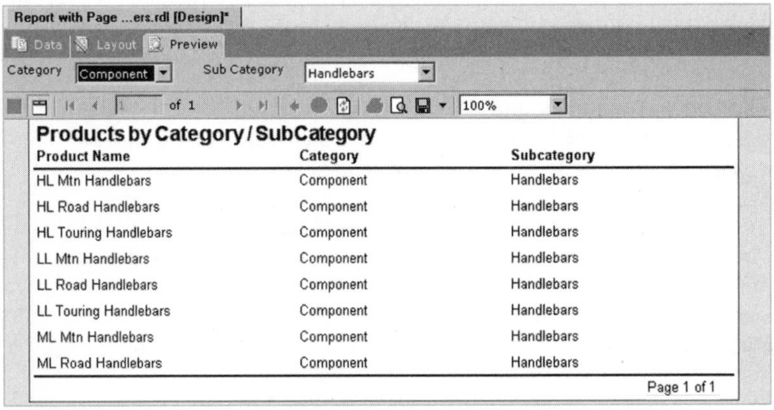

Figure 5-13

Drill-Down Reports

A drill-down report is an interactive report design that allows the user to expand and collapse sections of the report to discover more detail as needed. In recent years, users have become accustomed to this type of tree-view navigation in software, so it has become a common user interface metaphor. Interactive reports give the user more options and reduce unnecessary screen space used by data that the user need not view. They can drill down further as per their need to view more specific details.

The magic of drill-down reports is that rows and sections are simply hidden and displayed based on a toggle item. This means that a value item (like a textbox) is used to toggle the hidden property of rows and other report items. A plus sign or icon (+) is displayed to the left of the toggle item. Each time the user clicks the icon, the hidden property for the associated row items is toggled between true and false, and the toggle icon toggles between a plus (+) and minus (-) sign. The rows must also be set up to collapse when they are hidden.

Continuing from the previous example, the first thing you need to do is to remove the unused row footers in the table. Click in the table to show the row selector handles, and then right click the handle for each of the two empty footer rows and delete them. As drill-down visibility is managed at the grouping level, you need to define a grouping for the detail row. Select the detail row using the row selector and find the Grouping/Sorting property in the properties window. Click the ellipsis button (...) next to this property to show the Grouping and Sorting Properties dialog. You need to specify a name. To keep the naming consistent with the other two groupings, enter Table1_Group3_ProductName in the Name box. Select =Fields!ProductName.Value from the drop down in the first row of the Expression list box as shown in Figure 5-14:

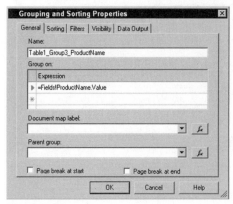

Figure 5-14

On the Visibility tab, change the initial visibility to Hidden and then check the box labeled Visibility can be toggled by another report item. This enables the report item drop-down list. Select the SubCategoryName item in the Report item drop-down list. The SubCategoryName textbox is in the second column of the subcategory group row. It will be used to toggle the visibility of the row that is being dealt with. See Figure 5-15:

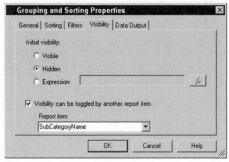

Figure 5-15

The same process should be repeated for the subcategory row grouping. Select the row using the row selector and click the ellipsis button next to the **Grouping/Sorting** property. On the dialog, choose the Visibility tab and set the initial visibility to **Hidden** and use the **CategoryName** report item to toggle the visibility of this grouping. Click **OK** to save the settings. Figure 5-16 shows the preview for this report:

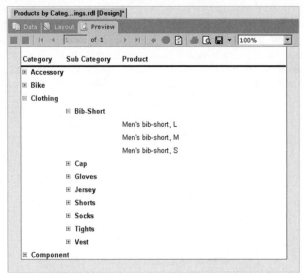

Figure 5-16

Use the (+) icons to drill-down into a category or subcategory row. As you see, the report now becomes interactive and users can customize the display of the report by viewing only the information that they need.

Creating a Document Map

This is a simple navigation feature that allows the user to find a group label or item value in the report by using a tree displayed along the left side of the report. It's sort of like a table of contents for report items, which can be used to quickly navigate to a specific area of a large report.

The document map is limited to the HTML, Excel, and PDF rendering formats. In Excel and HTML formats, the document map may not survive when saving report files to an older document format – such as Pocket Excel on a Pocket PC device.

You will add the **CategoryName** and **SubCategoryName** groupings to the document map. In the **Grouping and Sorting Properties** dialog for the Category row (group 1), drop down the **Document map label** list and choose the =Fields!CategoryName.Value item. See Figure 5-17:

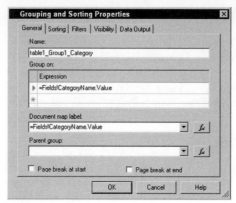

Figure 5-17

Click OK to close the dialog and then do the same for the second row group.

Be careful and specify the document map label property only for items that you want to include in the document map. For example, if you specify this property for a grouping (like you've done here), don't do the same for a textbox containing the same value. Otherwise, you will see the same value appear twice in the document map. A report with a document map is illustrated in Figure 5-18:

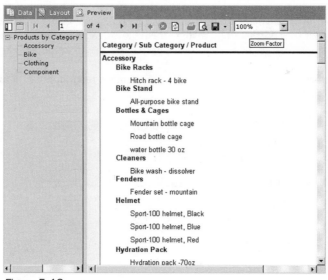

Figure 5-18

The document map may be shown or hidden using the left-most icon in the Report Designer's Preview or the Report Manager report view toolbar.

Links and Drill-Through Reports

Any textbox or image item can be used for intra-report or inter-report navigation, for navigation to external resources like web pages and documents, and also to send email. All of these features are enabled by using navigation properties that can be specified in the Textbox Properties or Image Properties dialog. In the Image Properties dialog, select the Navigation tab. In the Textbox Properties dialog, click the Advanced button to show the Advanced Textbox Properties dialog, and then switch to the Navigation tab.

Bookmarks and Links

A bookmark is a textbox or image in a report that can be used as a navigation link. If you want to allow the user to click an item and navigate to another item, assign a bookmark value to each of the target items. To enable navigation to a bookmark, set the Jump to Bookmark property to the target bookmark.

The Jump to URL property can be used to navigate to a static location (a bookmarked item, report, or URL). It can also be set to an expression that uses links stored in a database, custom code, or any other values. Any standard URL can be specified for linking to a web page, file, or even an email address.

Drill-Through

This powerful feature enables a textbox or image to be used as a link to another report by passing parameter values to the target report. The target report can consist of a specific record or multiple records depending on the parameters passed to the target report. The following example uses the Products by Category report created earlier to demonstrate the use of grouped tables. The Product Name textbox is used to link to a report that will display the details of a single product record. This report accepts a ProductID parameter to filter the records and narrow down to the record requested.

In the Advanced Textbox Properties dialog box, select the Jump to report radio button and select the target report from the drop-down list. See Figure 5-19:

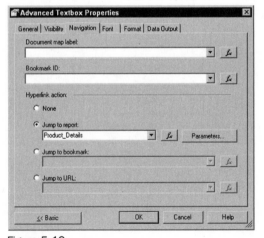

Figure 5-19

Any parameters you need to pass to the target report can be configured using the Parameters button. In the Parameters dialog, parameters for the target report are selected in the Parameter Name column. Values supplied from the current report are provided in the Parameter Value column as you can see in Figure 5-20:

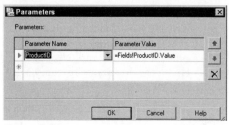

Figure 5-20

If you set an item as a link to a target, its appearance does not change.

If you need to give a cue to the user that the item is a link, you may want to display text with an underline. The resulting reports provide drill-through functionality. When a product name is clicked on the main report, the viewer redirects to the detailed report for the specific product by passing the ProductID parameter value. This is shown in Figure 5-21:

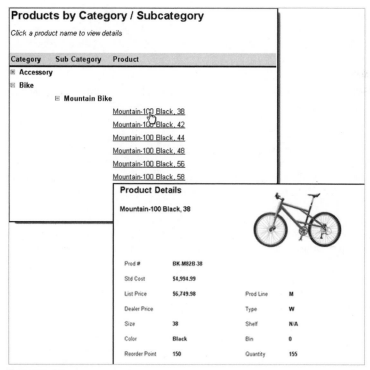

Figure 5-21

Recursive Data

Representing recursive hierarchies has always been a pain for reporting and often a challenge to effectively model in relational database systems. Examples of this type of relationship (facilitated through a self-join) may be found in the `Employees` table of the **Northwind** and **AdventureWorks2000** sample databases. Report tools were designed to work with data organized in traditional multi-table relationships. Fortunately, our friends at Microsoft built recursive support into the reporting engine to deal with this common challenge. A classic example of a recursive relationship (where child records are related to a parent contained in the same table) is the employee/boss relationship. For example, if I were to diagram the organizational hierarchy of the developer instructors group at Netdesk, it would look something like Figure 5-22:

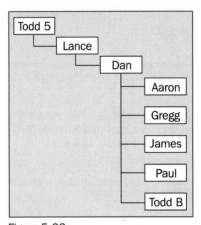

Figure 5-22

In our employee database, each of these records exists in the same table. My record (**Paul**) would indicate that my boss is **Dan**. Dan reports to **Lance**, who in turn reports to **Todd S**.

In the **AdventureWorks2000** database, you have a similar set of data. The `Employee` table contains a primary key, `EmployeeID`, that uniquely identifies each employee record. The `ManagerID` is a foreign key that depends on the `EmployeeID` attribute of the same table, and it contains the `EmployeeID` value for the employee's *manager*. The only record that won't have a `ManagerID` would be the president of the company or any such employee who doesn't have a boss.

Representing the hierarchy through a query would be quite difficult. However, defining the dataset for such a report is very simple. You simply expose the primary key, foreign key, employee name, and any other values that you want to include on the report. You'll just include these three values for our simple example.

Create a new report and define a dataset using the **AdventureWorks2000** shared data source. The name of the new dataset will be **EmployeesAndManagers**. Enter this SQL expression into the third pane of the Query Builder:

```
SELECT      EmployeeID, FirstName + ' ' + LastName AS EmployeeName, ManagerID
FROM        Employee
ORDER BY    FirstName + ' ' + LastName
```

Add a table to the report in the Layout tab. The single grouping will provide all of the recursive functionality for the table. Click on the table to show the selection handles and then click the selector to the left of the detail row. You're not adding a new grouping, but simply using the grouping that exists on this row. In the properties window, click the ellipsis next to the Grouping/Sorting property. In the Grouping and Sorting Properties dialog, enter the grouping name as OrgChart_Recursive. In the first row of the Group on list box, select the expression =Fields!EmployeeID.Value. Drop down the Parent group list and select the expression =Fields!ManagerID.Value. The reporting engine recognizes this as a recursive grouping because these fields are in the same table. Select the Sorting tab and select the expression =Fields!EmployeeName.Value in the first row of the Sort on list box. Click OK to close the dialog. See Figure 5-23:

Figure 5-23

Now the fun begins; Reporting Services recognizes that recursive groupings have special characteristics. We use the Level function that returns a group level number within the recursive hierarchy. Each row is assigned a level value that represents its relative position to parent and children rows in the hierarchy. You will also use a Count function indicating that you want the count of the recursive group's children.

Drag the EmployeeName field from the Fields list window to the first column of the detail row. Enter column headers for the second and third columns as Level and Count respectively. In the second detail cell, set the Value property to =Level("OrgChart_Recursive") + 1. You're adding 1 to this value because the Level function returns 0 for the first level, 1 for the second, and so on. The expression for the third column will use the Recursive keyword in the Count function's third argument. This indicates that the aggregate function should be applied to child rows of this grouping. Set the value to the expression =Count(Fields!EmployeeID.Value, "OrgChart_Recursive", Recursive).

Finally, you want each row's padding to be progressively greater based on the grouping level. Using the Level function you can apply some simple math to the padding property value to get the desired result. Since padding values are expressed as a string value, you will concatenate the value px to the end of a calculated numeric value.

Click on the first cell in the detail row to select the EmployeeName textbox and in the properties window, set the Padding > Left property to =Level("OrgChart_Recursive") * 15 & "pt". This will set the padding for the first level (level 0) to 0 pixels, the second to 15 pixels, and the third to 30 pixels, and so on. I've dressed up the header row using bold text, a border, text alignment, and added a title textbox as in previous examples. See Figure 5-24:

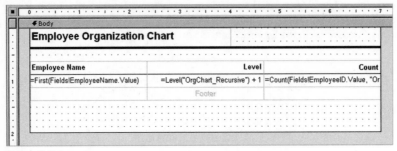

Figure 5-24

Save the report and then select the Preview tab to view the results. The generated report should appear as shown in Figure 5-25:

Employee Organization Chart		
Employee Name	Level	Employees
Ken Sanchez	1	288
Brian Welcker	2	18
Amy Alberts	3	4
Jae Pak	4	1
Rachel Valdez	4	1
Ranjit Varkey Chudukatil	4	1
Stephen Jiang	3	11
David Campbell	4	1
Fernando Caro	4	1
Garrett Vargar	4	1
José Saraiva	4	1
Linda Mitchell	4	1
Michael Blythe	4	1
Pamela Ansman-Wolfe	4	1
Shu Ito	4	1
Tete Mensa-Annan	4	1
Tsvi Reiter	4	1
Syed Abbas	3	2
Lynn Tsoflias	4	1
David Bradley	2	9
Jill Williams	3	1
John Wood	3	1
Kevin Brown	3	1
Mary Dempsey	3	1

Figure 5-25

Subreports

This feature is largely borrowed from Microsoft Access. Essentially, a subreport is a standalone report that is embedded into another report. Using parameters, you can link the contents of a subreport to the main report.

There are some limitations to the content and formatting that can be rendered for a subreport. For example, a multi-column report may not be possible within a subreport (depending upon the rendering format used). If you plan to use multiple columns in a subreport, test your report with the rendering formats you plan to use

A subreport can be linked to the main report so that it can be used like a data region, but this is not essential. A subreport could be used to show aggregated values unrelated to groupings or content in the rest of the report.

Creating a subreport is like creating any other report. The fact is that you just create a report and then add it to another report as a subreport. If you intend to use the main report and subreport as a *Master/Detail* view of related data, the subreport should expose a parameter that can be *linked* to a field in the main report. You'll build a simple report that lists products and exposes a subcategory parameter. The main report will list categories and subcategories and the products list report will then be used as a data region, like a table or list like in previous examples.

The first report, which will be used as a subreport, will include a list of products. The second report will consist of the product categories and subcategories and will contain the subreport, which renders a list of products for each subcategory.

1. Add a new report to your project called Product_List_Subreport.

2. On the Data tab, create a new dataset called Product_List using the AdventureWorks2000 data source. Add the Products table to the dataset and select the Name, StandardPrice, and ProductSubCategoryID columns to be output by the query. Sort the records by the Name column in ascending order.

3. Create a parameter for the ProductSubCategoryID column called @SubCategoryID. The easiest way to do this is to move the cursor to the grid column labeled Criteria on the row for the ProductSubCategoryID table column and type = @SubCategoryID. The SQL for the dataset should look like this:

```
SELECT     Name, StandardCost, ProductSubCategoryID
FROM       Product
WHERE      ProductSubCategoryID = @SubCategoryID
ORDER BY   Name
```

4. On the Layout tab, add a List item and set its DataSetName property to the Product_List dataset.

5. From the Fields window, drag the Name and StandardPrice fields into the List item and arrange them horizontally to form a row with sufficient room for these values. Resize the list so that it is the height of one textbox and about four inches wide. Place two textboxes to be column headings above the list and set their values to read Product and Price, as shown in Figure 5-26. Arrange the textboxes and the items in the list to line up, right justify the Price heading textbox, and then resize the report body background to fit closely around the list.

Figure 5-26

6. Add a new report called Product_List_Categories and create a new dataset with the same name using the ProductCategory and ProductSubCategory tables. Leave the join in place, alias the name columns from both the tables, and sort by first the category name and then the subcategory name. The resulting SQL expression should look like the following:

```
SELECT      ProductCategory.Name AS ProductCategory,
            ProductSubCategory.Name AS SubCategory,
            ProductSubCategory.ProductSubCategoryID
FROM        ProductCategory INNER JOIN ProductSubCategory
            ON ProductCategory.ProductCategoryID =
            ProductSubCategory.ProductCategoryID
ORDER BY    ProductCategory.Name, ProductSubCategory.Name
```

7. On the Layout tab, add a textbox for the report heading and a list item with the `DataSetName` property set to the new dataset. Drag and drop the `ProductCategory` and `SubCategory` fields from the fields window into the list data region, with the Product_List_Categories dataset selected. Size the list item to be about 6.5 inches wide by 1.5 inches tall (about 13 cm x 4 cm). Arrange the two new textboxes in a row in the top area of the list.

8. From the Solution Explorer, drag and drop the Product_List report into the list data region below the textboxes. Resize the new subreport to be about 4.5 inches wide and 0.75 inches tall (7 cm x 2 cm) and place it under the second textbox. Resize the list around the contained items. The report should be as shown in Figure 5-27:

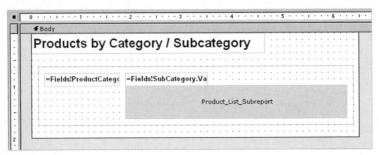

Figure 5-27

9. You need to use the subcategory parameter to associate the product list subreport with the outer list data region. Right click the subreport and select Properties. In the Subreport Properties dialog, switch to the Parameters tab and select the SubCategoryID parameter in the first row of the parameters box. In the Parameter Value column, select =Fields!ProductSubCategoryID.Value in the drop down list. See Figure 5-28:

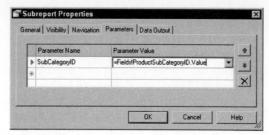

Figure 5-28

This completes the report design. You should be able to preview the report and see subcategory names followed by a list of related products as shown in Figure 5-29:

Products by Category / Subcategory

Accessory	Bike Racks	
	Product	Price
	Hitch rack - 4 bike	$66.00
	Bike Stand	
	Product	Price
	All-purpose bike stand	$87.45
	Bottles & Cages	
	Product	Price
	Mountain bottle cage	$5.49
	Road bottle cage	$4.94
	water bottle 30 oz	$2.74
	Cleaners	
	Product	Price

Figure 5-29

Charting

The charting capabilities in Reporting Services are quite impressive and as easy to use as those in Excel or Access, and in many ways, more powerful. The charting components are based on Dundas Charts developed by Dundas Software. Dundas provides a suite of ASP.NET charting components that have been available for .NET developers since .NET was in early beta stages nearly four years ago. A chart item is based on a dataset just like any data range and can use query parameters and filters in much the same way as with a table or matrix.

Some of the more common chart types (like Column, Bar, Line, and Area) can be used for different views of the same data. Pie and Doughnut charts are also quite simple but work well with fewer dimensions. The other charts are more specialized.

When a report is rendered, the chart output is rendered to a bitmap and streamed to a PNG type image. This image is then linked or embedded in the report. There are nine general chart types available and are described in the following table:

Chart Type	Description
Column	This is a classic vertical bar chart with columns representing values along the Y axis. Like-valued items along the X axis are grouped together and bars representing values for each group along the X axis have the same colors or patterns. Series values can also be grouped and sub-grouped. Columns can have point labels and the colored bars may be labeled using a legend. Columns may be arranged side-by-side (along the X axis) or in front of one another (along the Z axis). Columns may appear to be extruded from their base using a rectangular or circular shape.
Bar	This has the same functionality as a Column chart turned 90 degrees with the advantage of accurately depicting value comparisons, especially for layouts where you have more available horizontal space.
Area	This is like a Column chart with a trend line drawn from one point to the next in the series. It is appropriate for a series of values that tend to progress over a relatively even plane that describes a "level", "up", or "down" trend. It is not at all appropriate for series values that tend to jump around or fluctuate a lot. The solid shading of the charted area depicts a volume of data values.
Line	Similar to the Area chart but the area of the charted region isn't filled. It is useful for comparing multiple series (along the Z axis) without obscuring trend lines behind a series.
Pie	This is an excellent tool for comparing relative values. Unlike the above mentioned charts, the aggregate value isn't quantified. The value of each data point in a bar chart is expressed by the length of each bar, whereas only the relative values of each point are expressed by the size of each pie slice. Pie charts put comparative values into a proportional context and can help formulate quick decisions at a glance. Pie chart views can be exploded to visually separate each section.
Doughnut	This is a Pie chart with a hole in the middle. A 3-dimensional Doughnut rendering may expose smaller slices more clearly than a Pie chart since each slice has four sides rather than three.
Scatter	This chart plots several points in a range (both X and Y) to show trends and variations in value. The result is more like a cloudy band of points rather than a specific aggregated point or line.
Bubble	The Bubble chart is used to chart points on three dimensions. Values are plotted using different sized points, or bubbles, on a two-dimensional grid. The size of the bubble indicates the related value along the Z axis.
Stock	The Stock chart plots values vertically like a Column chart. For each item along the Y axis series, a vertical line indicates a start and end value for the range. A tick mark in the line can indicate a significant value in that range or an aggregation of the range. It is useful for showing trading stocks with opening, closing, and purchase values or represent wholesale, retail, and discount prices, and so on.

Column Charts

The following chart in Figure 5-30 is an example of a simple Column chart. The X axis series values are product categories and the Y axis values represent annual sales revenue. In this view, the legend at the bottom indicates the X axis series values.

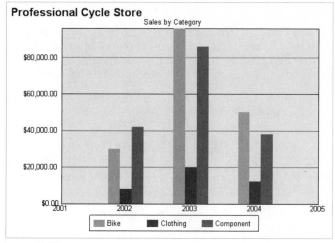

Figure 5-30

3-D Column Charts

Figure 5-31 is a three-dimensional view with cylindrical columns arranged in a clustered formation. If used correctly and in appropriate moderation, a 3-D chart adds a sense of realism (and looks cool). This type of view can be effective for making an impact, but a flatter view may be more appropriate to maintain accuracy.

Figure 5-31

I'm not suggesting that this is the most appropriate view for all column charts. I've made a point to set this chart up with a fairly extreme 3-D and perspective view, just to show you what can be done. This type of view tends to distort the values, and the clustering (stacking the columns along the Z axis) can hide some columns from view (in the preceding chart, I had to choose whether to hide the left-most column in the back row or the right-most column in the second row).

Stacked Column Chart

Column and Bar charts may have their bars stacked. This appends the different colored bars (for a like series value) into one bar with multiple colored bands. This may be an appropriate method for showing the accumulation of all values within the series point. The individual values are displayed in a different color as a percentage of the bar. In essence, each bar becomes like a linear Pie chart (see Figure 5-32):

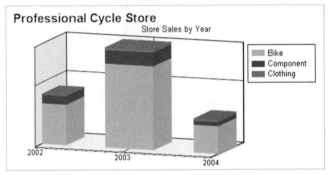

Figure 5-32

To emphasize the proportion of like values rather than the comparative accumulation, the 100% stacked view (not pictured) will make all of the bars in the chart the same length rather than depicting the sum of all the values in the bar.

Area and Line Charts

An Area chart plots the values of each point and then draws a line from point to point to show the progression of values along the series. This is an effective method for analyzing trends and works well when values tend to climb, decline, or remain level in the series. It typically doesn't work well to express a series of values that are not in a relatively uniform plane. Figure 5-33 is an example of an Area chart:

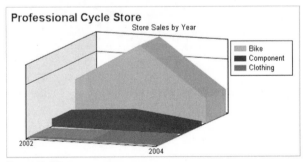

Figure 5-33

The Line chart is a variation of an Area chart using a line or ribbon rather than a solid area. The Line chart works better than the area chart for comparing multiple categories for a series of values as one layer may obscure another in the area view. In the preceding example, the Area chart works because values are sorted in a way that larger values are in the background and other points in the foreground are smaller, the trend increases back to front.

Pie Charts

A Pie chart is an excellent tool for comparing proportional values. Display options for a Pie chart include exploded and 3-D views. The following 3-D Pie chart in Figure 5-34 clearly shows that Touring Bike sales are a small percentage, around 10% of total Bike Sales, and that Road Bike sales account for about half of the total sales:

Figure 5-34

Bubble Charts

Bubble charts are essentially a point plotted in a three dimensional grid. The value of the Z axis is expressed by the size of the bubble. Image that the bubble exists in a 3-D plane and will appear large if it is closer to you. Actually the 'bubble' can be a circle, square, triangle, diamond, or cross shape. This also means that a combination of shapes may be used to represent different data elements in the same chart space.

In Figure 5-35, employees' vacation and sick hours are plotted above their names. The number of vacation hours is represented by the bubble's vertical distance from the 0 baseline and the number of sick hours is represented by the size of the bubble.

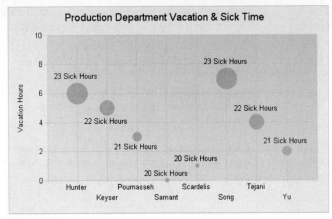

Figure 5-35

The chart shown in figure 5-36 is a Stock chart. As you see, for each product, a line is plotted to span a range of values and has a large tick mark to indicate the position of a value within the high/low range. In this example, the beginning (lowest point of the line) of the range is the standard cost of the product. The tick mark represents the last receipt cost and the high range of the line is the list price.

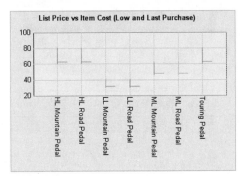

Figure 5-36

A Charting Example

To get you started on creating charts, you will create a column chart using sales information from AdventureWorks2000. This chart will include an added feature with a category grouping that shows sales associates grouped by their respective regions.

The dataset SQL expression and the steps to set up the chart have been provided for you. You need to take care of the standard report design details that were covered in the earlier sections of this chapter.

To demonstrate a Column or Bar chart, you only need a simple query with values to plot on two axes. You will also add a third value to categorize or group another set of values. To get started, add this SQL expression in a new dataset using the AdventureWorks2000 database:

```
SELECT      Employee.LastName AS EmployeeName, SalesPerson.SalesYTD,
            SalesTerritory.Name AS TerritoryName, SalesPerson.SalesLastYear
FROM        Employee INNER JOIN SalesPerson
            ON SalesPerson.SalesPersonID = Employee.EmployeeID
            INNER JOIN SalesTerritory
            ON SalesPerson.TerritoryID = SalesTerritory.TerritoryID
WHERE       SalesPerson.SalesYTD > 0 AND SalesPerson.SalesLastYear > 0
            AND SalesPerson.TerritoryID < 5
ORDER BY    SalesPerson.TerritoryID
```

Add a new Chart item to the report and resize it to fill an area about 7 inches wide and 5 inches tall (18 cm x 12 cm). Right click the chart item in the Report Designer and select Column | Simple Column for the Chart Type.

When you drag fields onto the report item, drop zones are displayed in the areas above to the right, and below the report. These areas will change depending on the report type. Switch to the Fields window and drag these fields to the drop locations indicated in the following table:

Field	Drop Zone Label
Sales YTD Sales Last Year	Drop data fields here (above the chart)
TerritoryName EmployeeName	Drop category fields here (below the chart)

This is also illustrated in Figure 5-37:

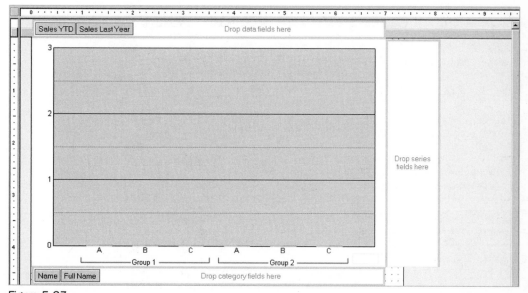

Figure 5-37

145

Verify your results using this example. It's important that the fields are dropped in this order. However, you can switch them later in the properties dialog.

Right click the chart again and select Properties to display the Chart Properties dialog. On the General tab, give the chart the name SalesPerformanceChart and for the title, enter North American Sales Associate Performance. This is shown in Figure 5-38:

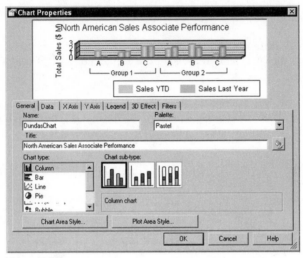

Figure 5-38

Note that the preview chart image in this dialog is the result of all the specified property settings. You can use this as a reference when you've completed all of the settings for this report.

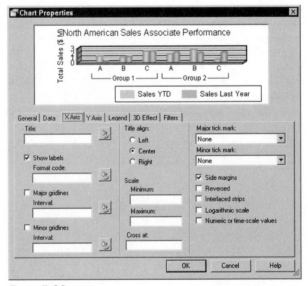

Figure 5-39

You're going to make several changes on the Y Axis tab. The title will be displayed along the left side of the chart as you see in the preview image. Set the title to Total Sales ($ M). For the Scale, set Minimum to 0 and Maximum to 3000000 and set the Format code to 0,, to indicate that this is to be a numerical value using comma separators per thousand. By providing a range of values, the tallest column will be shorter than the top of the chart (unless it exceeds the maximum value).

Gridlines can be used to make charts easier to read but can also make them more cluttered. The appropriate use of major and minor gridlines can emphasize comparable points. In this chart, you will show major and minor gridlines by using the values shown in Figure 5-40:

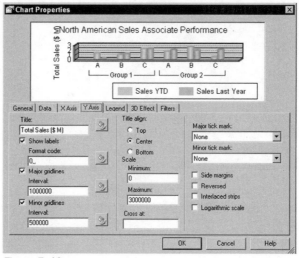

Figure 5-40

On the Legend tab, place the legend at the bottom, in the lower-right corner of the chart with labels arranged in a row (short and wide). This is shown in Figure 5-41. You can select Display legend inside plot area to maximize the size of the chart; this works well on Pie and Doughnut charts that have free corner space. However, this could cause the legend to overlap the chart area for some types of charts.

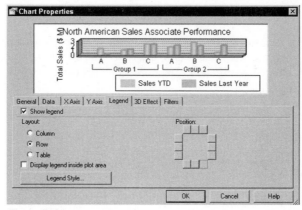

Figure 5-41

Use the 3-D Effect settings at your discretion. You often have to play with these settings to achieve the right balance between an effective 3-D rendering and an accurate display of data (see Figure 5-42):

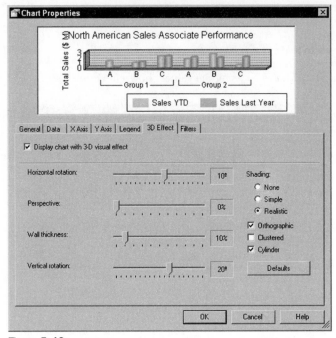

Figure 5-42

Realistic shading makes the 3-D chart appear to have a light source that casts shadows on the borders. The Orthographic property causes the 3-D effect to be slightly exaggerated. The Clustered property causes rows or columns at the same series point to be arranged in front of one another rather than side-by-side. Cylinder bars or columns are less traditional than block style bars.

Click OK on the Chart Properties dialog, save the report, and select the Preview tab to see the completed chart.

As you can see in Figure 5-43, having two related groups on the X axis causes set lines to show the regional groupings (in this case, the values Northwest, Northeast, Central, and Southwest) that you can see along the bottom of the chart. Two different values are plotted at each X axis point using differently colored, cylindrical columns.

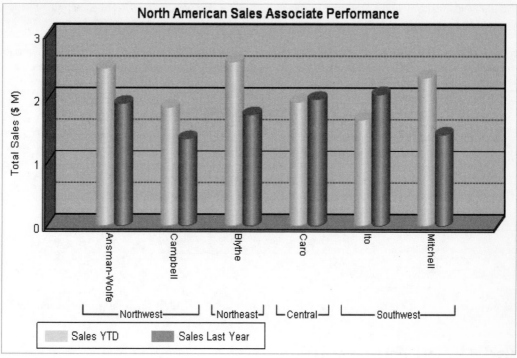

Figure 5-43

Custom Fields

Custom fields can be added to any report and can include expressions, calculations, and text manipulation. This might be similar in functionality to alias columns in a query or *view* but the calculation or expression is performed on the report server after data has been retrieved from the database. Expressions can also use globals and functions that may not be available in a SQL expression. The term *globals* applies to a set of variables built in to Reporting Services that provide useful information like page numbers. A list of available globals, fields, and parameters may be found in the Expression Builder. The global variables currently offered in Reporting Services are:

- ❑ Page Number
- ❑ Total Pages
- ❑ Execution Time
- ❑ Report Server URL
- ❑ Report Folder
- ❑ Report Name
- ❑ User ID
- ❑ Language

Use the Fields window in the Designer to select the dataset you want to use. Right click in the Fields window and select Add.

In the Add New Field dialog, enter the name you would like to use for the custom field. If you want to use an expression, select the Calculated field property as shown in Figure 5-44, and then use the builder button to create the expression:

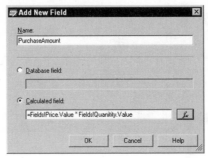

Figure 5-44

Here you can see that the price and quantity fields are used to calculate the total purchase amount.

Conditional Expressions

You've seen some simple examples of using expressions to set item values in unique ways. You can use expressions with most properties as well. In Chapter 3, you used an expression to set the Language property of a text box based on the value of a field.

Let's take a look at one more example of a conditional expression, and then we'll discuss using program code to handle more complex situations. This will be a simple list of products with current inventory values. The `Product` table in the AdventureWorks2000 database contains a `ReorderPoint` value that informs stock managers when they need to reorder products. If the inventory count falls below this value, you can set the inventory quantity to appear in red next to the name. Using a conditional expression in this manner is similar to using conditional formatting in Excel.

The following example will use a dataset with the SQL expression:

```
SELECT     Product.Name, Product.ReorderPoint, ProductInventory.Quantity
FROM       ProductInventory INNER JOIN Product
           ON ProductInventory.ProductID = Product.ProductID
ORDER BY   Product.Name
```

A table bound to this dataset has three columns, Name, ReorderLevel, and Quantity. On the Quantity textbox in the detail row of the table, the Color property is set to an expression containing conditional logic instead of to a set value. You can use the Expression Builder or just type this expression into the properties window under the Color property:

```
=IF( Fields!Quantity.Value < Fields!ReorderPoint.Value, "Red", "Black" )
```

You can do the same thing with the Font > FontWeight property, so that if the inventory quantity for a product is below the reorder point value, the quantity is displayed in both red and bold text.

Switch to the Preview tab to check the results; these should be as shown in Figure 5-45:

Product Inventory / Reorder

Name	Reorder Point	Quantity
Adjustable Race	750	324
Adjustable Race	750	408
Adjustable Race	750	353
All-purpose bike stand		144
AWC logo cap		288
BB Ball Bearing	600	443
BB Ball Bearing	600	585
BB Ball Bearing	600	324
Bearing Ball	750	318
Bearing Ball	750	427
Bearing Ball	750	364
Bike wash - dissolver		36
Blade	600	532
Blade	600	388
Blade	600	441
Cable lock		252
Chain	375	192

Figure 5-45

Using Custom Code

When you need to process more complex expressions, it may be difficult to build all of the logic into one expression. In such cases, you can write your own function to handle different conditions and call it from a property expression.

There are two different approaches for managing custom code. One is to write a block of code to define functions that are embedded into the report definition. This technique is simple but the code will be available only to that report. The second technique is to write a custom class library compiled to an external .NET assembly and reference this from any report on your Report Server. This approach has the advantage of sharing a central repository of code, which makes updates to the code easier to manage. The down side of this approach is that the configuration and initial deployment is a bit tedious.

Using Custom Code in a Report

A report may contain embedded Visual Basic .NET code that defines a function that you can call from property expressions. The code editor window is very simple and doesn't include any editing and formatting capabilities. For this reason, you may want to write the code in a separate Visual Studio project to test and debug before you place it into the report. After your code is ready, open the report in the Designer. With the Layout tab selected, drop down the Report menu and select Report Properties.

On the Report Properties window, switch to the Code tab and write or paste your code in the Custom Code box. As you can see, you can't even use the tab key to indent your code, which is why you will want to write the code elsewhere.

Here is the code along with the expressions you will need to create a simple example report on your own. The following Visual Basic function accepts a phone number or social security number in a variety of formats and outputs a standard US phone number and properly formatted SSN. The Value argument accepts the value and the Format argument accepts the values Phone or SSN. You're only going to use it with phone numbers so you can leave the SSN branch out if you wish:

```
'****************************************************************
'     Returns properly formatted Phone Number or SSN
'     based on Format arg & length of Value arg
'     PT - 12/12/03
'****************************************************************
Public Function CustomFormat(Value as String, Format as String) as String
        Select Case Format
        Case "Phone"
                Select Case Value.Length
                Case 7
                    Return Value.SubString(0, 3) & "-" & Value.SubString(3, 4)
                Case 10
                    Return "(" & Value.SubString(0, 3) & ") " _
                            & Value.SubString(3, 3) _
                            & "-" & Value.SubString(6, 4)
                Case 12
                    Return "(" & Value.SubString(0, 3) & ") " _
                            & Value.SubString(4, 3) & "-" & Value.SubString(8, 4)
                Case Else
                    Return Value
                End Select
        Case "SSN"
                If Value.Length = 9 Then
                    Return Value.SubString(0, 3) & "-" _
                            & Value.SubString(3, 2) & "-" & Value.SubString(5, 4)
                Else
                    Return Value
                End If
        Case Else
                Return Value
        End Select
End Function
```

The dataset in this report gets its data from the `Vendor` and related tables in AdventureWorks2000 and returns three columns: `FirstName`, `LastName`, and `Phone`. The SQL expression used to retrieve this information is as follows:

```
SELECT      Vendor.Name, Contact.FirstName, Contact.LastName, Contact.Phone
FROM        Vendor
            INNER JOIN VendorContact ON Vendor.VendorID = VendorContact.VendorID
            INNER JOIN Contact ON VendorContact.ContactID = Contact.ContactID
```

These three columns are used in a table bound to the dataset. The `Value` property of the `Phone` column uses an expression that calls the custom function preceded by a reference to the `Code` object:

```
=Code.CustomFormat(Fields!Phone.Value, "Phone")
```

The report preview should be as shown in Figure 5-46:

Custom Formatting with Embedded Code		
First Name	**Last Name**	**Phone**
Lorraine	Nay	(669) 519-3272
Fred	Ortiz	(275) 676-1732
Marie	Moya	(114) 998-7242
Fred	Northup	(330) 597-0115
David	Ortiz	(937) 733-0322
Deborah	Poe	(331) 771-2003
Zheng	Mu	(945) 965-9287
Randy	Reeves	(668) 833-8477
Kim	Ralls	(193) 794-1571
Tim	O'Brien	(360) 691-2653
Jack	Richins	(705) 193-8964
Jonathan	Mollerup	(859) 020-8503
Mary Lou	Quintana	(430) 860-5712
Patricia	Ping	(939) 964-9506
Paula	Moberly	(273) 461-5654
Jan	Nelsen	(905) 539-3497
Jonathan	Perera	(404) 753-1880
Gloria	Orona	(810) 973-2915

Figure 5-46

Using a Custom Assembly

Rather than embedding code directly into each report, using a custom assembly facilitates the use of a reusable central repository of code to extend the functionality of multiple reports. As I mentioned, this is a powerful technique but setting it up is a little cumbersome in the product's current form. The custom assembly feature is disabled by default and requires that you make simple but manual modifications in two configuration files. In a default installation of Reporting Services, you will find these files in the following locations:

File Name	Default Installation Path
RSReportDesigner.config	C:\Program Files\Microsoft SQL Server\80\Tools\Report Designer
RSReportServer.config	C:\Program Files\Microsoft SQL Server\MSSQL\Reporting Services\ReportServer

If you double click the file icon in Windows Explorer, it should open in Visual Studio, thus allowing you to edit and save the file. In each of the files, you will find XML elements with the following content. Comments are provided with instructions to remove a commented block of tags to enable custom assemblies.

```
<!-- Remove this comment to enable custom assemblies
<CustomAssemblies>
   <Default>
           <PermissionSet class="System.Security.PermissionSet">
              <IPermission class="System.Security.Permissions .Security
              Permission"
              version="1" Flags="Execution"/>
              </PermissionSet>
   </Default>
</CustomAssemblies>  -->
```

Remove the line beginning with <!-- and the --> at the end of the closing tag. Close and save each of these configuration files.

Create a class module project. You can write this code in any .NET language since it's going to be compiled to an assembly. The methods you create can be either static or instantiated. It's a little easier to use static methods so you don't have to manage the instancing and life of each object. This simply means is that you will declare public functions in your class using the Static keyword in C# or the Shared keyword in Visual Basic. Using the same code logic as in the previous example, the Visual Basic class code would look like:

```
Public Class Report_Formats
    '************************************************************
    '     Returns properly formatted Phone Number or SSN
    '     based on Format arg & length of Value arg
    '     PT - 12/12/03
    '************************************************************
    Public Shared Function CustomFormat(Value as String, Format as String) as String
        Select Case Format
        Case "Phone"
            Select Case Value.Length
            Case 7
                Return Value.SubString(0, 3) & "-" & Value.SubString(3, 4)
            Case 10
                Return "(" & Value.SubString(0, 3) & ") " _
                     & Value.SubString(3, 3) _
                     & "-" & Value.SubString(6, 4)
            Case 12
```

```
                    Return "(" & Value.SubString(0, 3) & ") " _
                        & Value.SubString(4, 3) & "-" & Value.SubString(8, 4)
                Case Else
                    Return Value
                End Select
            Case "SSN"
                If Value.Length = 9 Then
                    Return Value.SubString(0, 3) & "-" _
                        & Value.SubString(3, 2) & "-" & Value.SubString(5, 4)
                Else
                    Return Value
                End If
            Case Else
                Return Value
            End Select
        End Function
    End Class
```

Save and build the class library project in **Release** configuration and then copy the assembly (DLL) file to the `ReportServer\bin folder`. The default path to this folder is `C:\Program Files\Microsoft SQL Server\MSSQL\Reporting Services\ReportServer\bin`.

> **To deploy a report using custom assembly files to a production server, you will need to copy the assembly file to the same location on the server.**

In the Report Properties dialog (this is where you entered the code in the previous topic example), select the References tab and add the reference by browsing to the assembly file. The reference line shows metadata from the assembly, including the version number, as you can see in Figure 5-47:

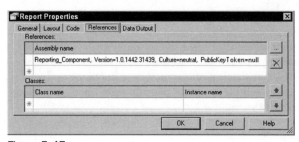

Figure 5-47

To use a custom method in an expression, reference the namespace, class, and method using standard code syntax. The expression for the **CustomFormat** method should look like:

```
=Reporting_Component.Report_Formats.CustomFormat(Fields!Phone.Value, "Phone")
```

The report should look exactly as it did in the previous example.

Designing for Mobility

The idea of making reports available in custom applications that run over the Internet or letting users access reports from desktop computers outside of the office opens many doors of opportunity that were earlier not possible. These capabilities are now very easy to achieve but the promise of this technology doesn't stop there. This brings to mind the unforgettable words of Ron Popeil, "...but wait. There's more..." Another very quotable figure, Bill Gates, announced in 2000 that the next generation of services from Microsoft would enable people to access information "any time, any place, and on any device." This product fulfills that promise making reports available to the next generation of mobile computing devices.

There are many different devices on the market that could be categorized as *mobile internet devices* or *mobile network devices* capable of viewing reports. These may include *Personal Digital Assistants (PDAs)*, palm-sized or hand-held computers, and enhanced pagers or cellular phones. The lines separating these devices are becoming quite blurred as the newest generation of cell phones can be used to surf the web and some PDAs now include integrated cell phones. There are also camcorders with built-in networking and web browsers! For our discussion, the scope of these devices will be limited to the Windows-based units. However, some Palm OS devices may be used to view online content via a wireless corporate network or the World Wide Web and can be used to view offline documents in standard formats (such as PDFs). We acknowledge that many of the capabilities may also be supported on the Palm platform.

The challenges and opportunities for delivering mobile device-enabled reports are varied but fall into the following areas:

❑ Screen size

❑ Device, browser, and viewer capabilities

❑ File portability

❑ File size restrictions

Current Windows-powered devices run a version of Windows CE called *Pocket PC* or *Windows Mobile SmartPhone*. The Pocket PC form factor has a screen resolution of 240 by 320 pixels and features a number of scaled-down desktop applications (like Pocket Word, Excel, Outlook, and Internet Explorer). The SmartPhone screen is considerably smaller at 176 by 220 pixels and is designed to function primarily as a phone with some additional PDA features. An edition of the Pocket PC called the Pocket PC Phone Edition has integrated features to support units with a built-in cell phone. All Pocket PC devices have a touch screen interface and many of the SmartPhone units are controlled only by the phone's keypad. These devices, and many non-Windows cell phone devices, may be used to view online web content.

Screen Size

The most significant restriction for most mobile devices is the limited screen size. The Pocket PC and SmartPhone can view web content with some client-side scripting support and can also cache recently viewed content for offline viewing. Most web pages designed for desktop users can be viewed on the tiny screen but it requires the user to scroll extensively just to navigate a single page. Web-based reports created with Reporting Services are no exception. Most stock reports will likely work on a Pocket PC running Pocket Internet Explorer if they can be viewed in Internet Explorer on a desktop PC. The user experience, however, is often like watching a large-screen movie through a keyhole.

To design reports optimized for the mobile user, reports must be simplified and designed for smaller page size. Some dynamic reporting features (like drill-down and drill-through) may not be supported in all rendering formats. The page size of the Pocket PC screen is about 3.25 inches (8.25 cm) wide. Simply scaling your mobile reports down to this width will resolve most screen resolution issues for mobile web users. Keep the font sizes small and avoid clutter, large graphics, and unnecessary extra space.

Figure 5-48 illustrates a simple employee email directory that was created using a Table data region on a narrow page:

Figure 5-48

The sample report shown earlier has only two columns but it could easily have several. There is no need to restrict the functionality of your reports simply because users can't see all of the information at one time. Just keep in mind that when the user navigates to the report, they will only see the information beginning in the top-left hand corner of the content. Design your reports with this in mind, placing the most important content near this entry point. Users can always scroll to find other information if the report is intuitive and easy to navigate. This is yet another reason to use interactive reporting features like drill-down.

Keep the report content size to a minimum as well. Regardless of the device or computer used to view reports, a dial-up user will always suffer a significant performance penalty from large reports. Avoid unnecessary use of graphics and filter the data whenever possible. The Pocket PC phone device pictured in Figure 5-49 can connect to the Internet using either cell phone dial-up or a wireless network connection, but broadband wireless is typically only available in close proximity to a secure wireless access point. At best, cellular dial-up connection speeds are 14400 to 19200 bps.

Figure 5-49

Offline Solutions

One of the challenges that mobile users face on a number of levels is that they typically don't have the opportunity to remain continuously connected to a network or the Internet. Mobile devices are intended to give us the ability to cut ties with the corporate network and work without wires or wireless connections. At times, report users might need to render reports on their desktops or have them pushed out to files or email via subscriptions. They can then view these reports offline on the mobile device.

Typically the best solution for off-line reporting is to save the report to a document. Pocket IE will store a cached copy of an HTML report if it has been viewed online. In the case of a drill-down report, the entire report content may not be stored in cache. When a cached drill-down report is viewed, exploring sections that have not been previously viewed may cause the device to try to connect and retrieve the newly requested content. Overall, caching HTML is not a comprehensive solution.

The PDF format is by far the most reliable method for transporting a report document and keeping content consistently formatted. After the report has been exported to a PDF document it is a simple matter to drop the file into the synchronization folder on the partnering desktop and let *ActiveSync* automatically copy it to the device the next time it is placed into its cradle. Unfortunately, Adobe Acrobat doesn't support the drill-down functionality in Reporting Services, so the report will need to be designed without dynamic drill-down and drill-through. The TIF image format also guarantees that the report will look and print consistently as the file is sent from place to place, but one drawback of this format is that files will typically be much larger than in PDF format.

The Excel rendering format is also an excellent medium for small offline reports but Pocket Excel doesn't support drill-down either. The Excel rendering format is supported only in Excel 2002 and later. One advantage to using this format is that users can make modifications to their local copy of the report content, and then sort and format the data. A user can also add calculations and other content to extend the report for their own needs. See Figure 5-50:

Figure 5-50

Summary

You have covered a lot of ground in this chapter. By using what is covered in the previous two chapters, you saw how many types of reports using data sources and filtering techniques that exposed different design strategies are created.

Data regions let you repeat and group data in a section of the report. The table organizes repeated data into specific rows and columns and provides inherent grouping capabilities with headers and footers. Using a list, you can achieve similar results with a little more formatting flexibility. With a subreport, you can essentially use a separately defined report as a data region and filter the data it contains with parameters and filters.

Drill-down and drill-through techniques optimize screen space and allow the user to interact with a report by expanding groupings of a table or list, or by using links to jump to an item, or bookmark another report. The document map provides a mini drill-down report in a separate frame that may be used to easily find headings and category labels and navigate to them in the report. Recursive relationships are easy to manage and will produce multi-level groups using a single source of data.

Charts are a powerful tool used to express aggregated values in a series and in multiple dimensions. Several chart types are available for different types of data and presentation formats.

Advanced formatting and calculations can be performed by adding customized programming code to your reports. This can be done by simply adding code in the Report Designer or by creating a compiled .NET assembly and adding a reference to the assembly in the report. Report properties can be set using expressions and program code to achieve conditional formatting.

Developing reports for mobile users is a relatively simple task, keeping in mind the limits and capabilities of devices. Reports are designed to fit smaller screen sizes and may be optimized for online or disconnected scenarios. Mobile reporting opens vast opportunities for traveling information workers using convenient wireless and synchronized devices.

Managing Reports Using the Report Manager

Now that the report authoring process is complete and reports have been deployed to the Report Server, you need some way of managing how the reports are organized and controlling who has access to them. For example, once the monthly sales report for your company has been added to the Report Server database, you may want to schedule the report to run on the first of every month and ensure that only managers have access to it. Microsoft has included an application with Reporting Services that provides access to all the functionality typically needed by a manager of the content in the Report Server database. This application is called *Report Manager*.

In this chapter, you'll learn to use the Report Manager for common Reporting Service tasks:

❑   Managing the organization of your reports and other resources

❑   Configuring report properties and adding needed resources

❑   Administrating users and implementing security policies

❑   Managing the scheduling and execution of a report

Introduction to the Report Manager

The Report Manager application is a tool that enables you to perform tasks related to managing the content in the Report Server database. This particular function is commonly referred to as *content management*. In Reporting Services, a Content Manager is a predefined role specifically for managing reports and content. While the Content Manager role is important in administering a Reporting Service platform, it might not be the same person who is responsible for administering the web server or SQL Server instances directly. The Report Manager application was built to primarily support managing the content within the Report Server database rather than performing administration of the server infrastructure.

What Is Report Management?

An effective Reporting Service platform needs to support key content management tasks. Typically, a Report Server manager handles generating reports, organizing reports, and controlling access to them. The key Report Server management responsibilities include:

- ❑ Administrating the organization and identification of content
- ❑ Managing other resources needed by reports
- ❑ Configuring users and defining access permissions
- ❑ Managing the generation and deployment of reports

Let's see how the Report Manager addresses these content management responsibilities.

Understanding the Report Manager

The Report Manager application resides on a web server and is accessed using a web browser. It provides an interface that's used to manage the contents of the Report Server database. The Report Manager is an ASP.NET Web application that acts as a graphical user interface for the Reporting Services Web Service, which also happens to be an ASP.NET Web application. Figure 6-1 shows the relationship between the Report Server exposed via the Reporting Services Web Service, the Report Manager application, and the browser running on your client machine:

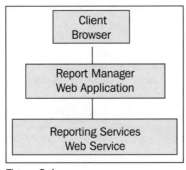

Figure 6-1

You could even build your own version of the Report Manager by creating an application that works against the same Reporting Services Web Service API. Choosing to do that might be a good opportunity to further understand the design and implementation of a service-based application architecture. For example, common tasks that were often performed in pieces using separate applications are now achievable using a single, consolidated interface, without compromising the freedom required for diverse and heterogeneous reporting. In the opinion of a noted professional, this capability is "really a piece of art in application architecture". However, the Report Manager is included with the Reporting Services package and is robust enough and suitable for most business needs.

Using the Report Manager, you have the ability to:

- ❑ Create folders and folder structures to act as *containers* for report collections
- ❑ Create and modify data sources, and add additional resources to the Report Server database

❑   Implement an identity based security model, controlling access to Reporting Services resources

❑   Configure automated report generation and delivery

Most importantly, access to all reports and resources can be flexibly managed. For example, a user can be provided access to reports that run on demand based on values supplied by that user, or they may be restricted to viewing static reports delivered by subscription. The task of managing content can also be broken up among multiple roles, each responsible for managing the functions of different reports or other resources. Using the Report Manager, you can perform create, read, update, and delete operations on almost anything in the Report Server database.

The Report Manager Interface

Although you've probably spent time surfing the web using your browser, you may not have used it as a sophisticated application for managing content and resources in a Reporting Service database. Let's see the interface in action.

For opening the Report Manager, you'll need to have Microsoft SQL Server Reporting Services installed, an updated Microsoft Internet Explorer browser running on your client machine, and permissions to access the Report Manager interface.

There are two ways of accessing the Report Manager. The first is by using the Start button on your system taskbar. If Reporting Services has been installed on your local machine, click Start | Programs | Microsoft SQL Server | Reporting Services | Report Manger as in Figure 6-2:

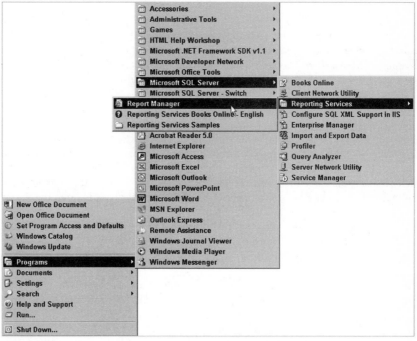

Figure 6-2

The menu item will open Internet Explorer and display the initial **Report Manager** screen, as seen in Figure 6-3:

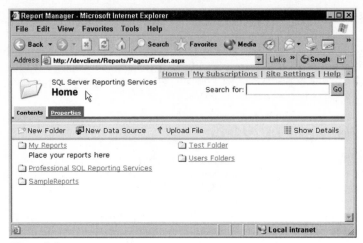

Figure 6-3

Figure 6-3 also shows that the current user location is in the Home folder. This Home folder contains several folders, called sub folders or children. The SampleReports parent folder, for example, is contained in the Home folder and could be considered a child of it. You'll take a closer look at the user interface shortly.

The second way of getting to the Report Manager is by manually typing the Report Manager URL into the address bar of your browser. If Reporting Services is not installed on your local machine, you may find this technique the easiest way to access the Report Manager. Open Internet Explorer, and type the URL of your Report Server in the address bar. By default, the address is:

http://<ServerName>/reports

Be sure to replace <ServerName> with the server hosting the Report Manager application. During installation, the name of the virtual directory containing the Report Manager can be changed from the default /reports to something that works better for you. If that's the case for your installation, you'll need to specify that virtual directory name rather than /reports. You should see the same page displayed in Internet Explorer as you saw when using the first technique to open the Report Manager.

Note that in the first technique used to access the interface, the Report Manager menu item has an Internet Explorer icon. It is, in fact, a shortcut to the same address you typed into the address bar using the second method. Some users add shortcuts to the desktop or Quick Launch toolbar for convenience.

One of the reasons the Report Manager application is so effective is because it leverages capabilities of the client browser used to access it. Specifically, working with the Report Manager requires Microsoft Internet Explorer 6.0 with Service Pack 1 (SP1) or Internet Explorer 5.5 with SP2 as the browser client. As an ASP.NET application, the Report Manager also makes use of client-side scripting to support functionality, so you'll also need to have scripting enabled.

To check the script security settings for your browser, select Tools | Internet Options | Security tab. In the Web Content Zone window, be sure that the Local intranet zone is selected. Below that window, there's an area called Security level for this zone. Click the Custom Level button to open the Security Settings dialog box, where you can view your current script settings. Scroll down to the section called Scripting to see whether Active scripting is enabled as shown in Figure 6-4:

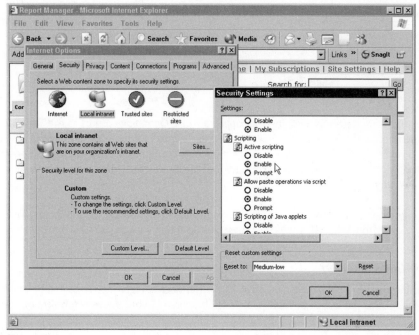

Figure 6-4

Although most browsers are already configured to support scripting, some organizations have scripting disabled as part of company policy. If so, that part of the security policy may need to be revisited for users who are responsible for using and working with the Report Manager.

Navigating the Report Manager Interface

The Report Manager uses the concept and hierarchical structure of folders extensively. In fact, when you open the Report Manager, your initial view is of the Home folder. As you move between folders, forms, and items, it's important to be aware of where you are in that hierarchical structure. To help you to move around in the Report Manager, let's take a look at the various navigational controls available.

Navigation Tools

Several navigational methods have been incorporated into the Report Manager interface. Which ones you see and which options are available vary depending on where in the folder structure you are and what permissions you've been granted. For example, if a user doesn't have permission to view certain reports or upload resources to folders, they won't be given access to the controls needed to perform those actions. Let's take a tour of the Report Manager interface by taking a look at the navigational elements and talk about a couple of global settings.

Breadcrumb Trail

Frequently referred to as *breadcrumb trail*, this control displays links to each level back up the file or in folder structure. It's in the top left corner of the browser window. Figure 6-5 shows an example:

Figure 6-5

In this figure, you are currently viewing the Employee_List_Operations report in the Staff_Listings folder, which is contained in the Professional_SQL_Reporting_Services folder, which in turn is one level below the top level Home folder. In XML terms, the Home folder could be considered the root node of the structure and everything is descendant from it. Note the hand icon indicating a hyperlink back up to the Staff_Listings folder.

This navigation tool is not always available, for example, when viewing certain forms. The breadcrumb trail is a quick way to navigate back to the parent folder when viewing an item's properties pages.

Tabs and Options Toolbar

Tabs are defined by blue and orange lines across the Report Manager interface, just below the breadcrumb trail. Available, but not active, tabs are displayed in blue. Active tabs are orange in color and flows into the orange line above the current view. The orange line borders the top of a toolbar that displays option buttons for the current view. Figure 6-6 shows an options toolbar for the Subscriptions tab and a sample option button:

Figure 6-6

In Figure 6-6, two option buttons for creating new subscriptions are displayed on the Subscriptions tab. Like tabs, the option buttons available to a user will vary depending on the permissions granted to that user on that item.

Local Menu

Under the Properties tab, local links may be available along the left side of the page. These links are used to access the different property pages for an item. The links are shown in Figure 6-7:

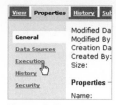

Figure 6-7

You'll be taking a closer look at each of these property pages and how they're used throughout this chapter.

Global Toolbar and Details Button

The global toolbar is available on every page in the Report Manager. It's located in the top right corner of the page, displayed as a series of links with a blue background to separate them from other items on the page. There are links to the Home folder, user-specific report subscriptions called My Subscriptions, global Site Settings, and Report Manager Help.

The Show Details button is one of those items that get more useful as you get more comfortable working with the Report Manager. The button text toggles between Show Details and Hide Details, depending on your current view as in Figure 6-8:

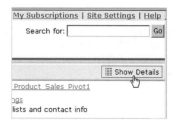

Figure 6-8

When viewing folder contents in Detail view, for example, you have direct access to Move and Delete option buttons to work with folder items as seen in Figure 6-9:

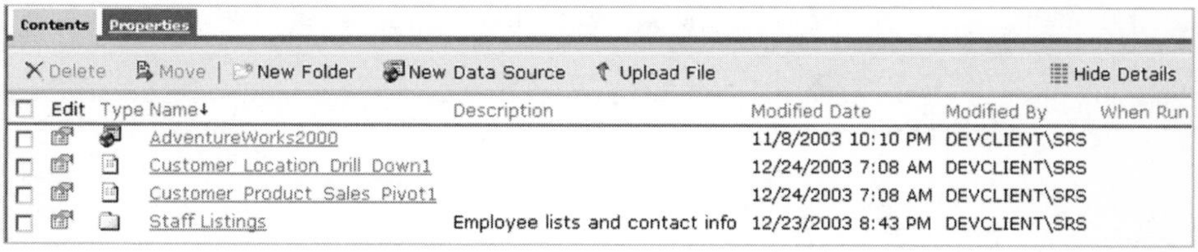

	Edit	Type	Name↓	Description	Modified Date	Modified By	When Run
☐	🔧	🗐	AdventureWorks2000		11/8/2003 10:10 PM	DEVCLIENT\SRS	
☐	🔧	🗋	Customer Location Drill Down1		12/24/2003 7:08 AM	DEVCLIENT\SRS	
☐	🔧	🗋	Customer Product Sales Pivot1		12/24/2003 7:08 AM	DEVCLIENT\SRS	
☐	🔧	🗋	Staff Listings	Employee lists and contact info	12/23/2003 8:43 PM	DEVCLIENT\SRS	

Figure 6-9

Clicking on the Properties link, seen to the left in Figure 6-9, brings you directly to the Properties tab for that item. When the details are hidden, you must first select the item and then go to the Properties tab—so you save a step with details displayed (great for frequent users).

Icons beneath the Type column head indicate the type of item listed. There are icons for:

❑ Folder

❑ Report

❑ Linked report

❑ Resource

❑ Subscription

❑ Data-driven subscription

Hold the cursor over the icon to see a descriptive tool tip. Clicking the icon will perform a default action on that item. For example, clicking the folder icon will open the folder, clicking the properties icon will access the properties pages, and clicking the report icon will open the report.

Searching for Folders and Reports

Use the search function available in the upper-right corner of the Report Manager interface to search for items. Because items (folders, reports, resources, and data sources) are stored in the Report Server database, doing a search on the file system using Windows Explorer won't return the desired results. The Report Manager search function searches the database for items matching your search keywords, whether searching by the item name or description.

Search results are only returned for items that you have permission to access, making the tool very useful even for end users. For example, Report Server allows storage of incremental snapshot reports for archival purposes. A single report design can be a source of many report items. In the Report Manager, there literally may be hundreds of available reports in a typical organization. The search function returns a filtered report set based on user permissions.

To search within a report, you can use the report toolbar displayed above the generated report in the HTML Viewer. To read more about viewing reports, see the section on *Viewing, Executing, and Scheduling Reports* later in this chapter.

The Report Manager Help

The Help link is always available to you from within the Report Manager. The link is in the far upper-right corner of the browser window. The Report Manager Help is a separate help application that provides information about every form in the Report Manager and is a valuable resource.

You'll be using those navigation tools quite a bit as you explore Report Manager. Let's start the rest of our tour by taking a look at what's behind the Site Settings link.

About System Site Settings

The Site Settings form is accessed using the Site Settings link in the global links area, in the top-right corner of the Report Manager interface. This form is used to configure default settings for the site and enable different features of the Report Manager. Usually, you won't have access to this form unless you're a member of the *System Administrator* role. Figure 6-10 shows the Site Settings form:

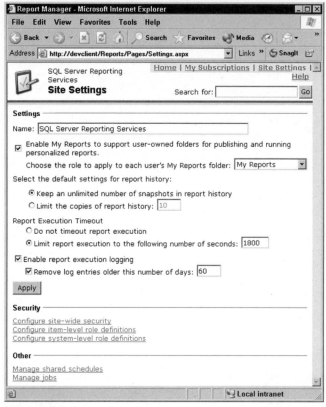

Figure 6-10

Using this form, you can change the name that's displayed in the top left corner of every page in the Report Manager. My Reports can be enabled here as you'll read about shortly. Let's briefly cover the other main properties on this page.

Report History Default Settings

This property defines the number of previously run reports to keep archived. Although this sets the default report history value for all reports, this value can be overridden by individual reports. You'll read more about configuring report histories in the *Creating a Report History* section later in this chapter.

Report Execution Timeout

Execution timeout is the length of time the Report Server will continue attempting to execute a report. When the timeout value elapses, execution will stop and rendering or delivery of the report will not occur. This value can be overridden in individual reports.

Report Logging

By default, Report Server logs information about report execution. The report log contains values such as delivery format, the parameters used, and server processing time. The report log is not viewable in the Report Manager; a SQL Server DTS package is used to obtain values from the log. For more information on viewing report logs, search for *Report Execution Log* in Reporting Services Books Online.

About My Reports

My Reports is a folder that provides a central location for the management of user-specific content and subscriptions. Rather than having to navigate through the public folders for regularly generated and referenced reports, My Reports provides a self-managed area for users to place and maintain their content, similar to My Documents. The similarity of My Reports to My Documents in both name and function is not an accident. My Documents is a concept and tool almost universally accepted by users, and My Reports is a variation of that successful theme. Building on the experience and familiarity a user has with an existing environment or feature is a good tip for feature designers and architects.

To enable My Reports, you need permission for the Manage the security settings of the Report Server task. The steps to enable this are as follows:

1. From the Home directory, click the Site Settings link in the global navigation bar in the top right corner of the browser window. You'll see the area displayed in Figure 6-11:

Figure 6-11

2. Check the Enable My Reports checkbox. Optionally, you can choose a role definition used to group users who have access to their My Reports. Microsoft created the My Reports role for this purpose, and it is the default selection. Leave that setting as My Reports, and click Apply. Then return to the Home folder view. You'll see the new My Reports folder added to the Home folder contents.

My Reports is a folder that allows users to manage their own content. Enabling My Reports lets users create and delete their own folders and reports and create personalized linked reports. Users don't have access to the My Reports folders of other users; only Report Server administrators can do that. Using My Reports, you can upload reports and other resources as well as publish reports you've created using the Report Designer.

It's important to keep in mind that there's a My Reports *folder*, and a MyReports *role*. The My Reports role defines permissions the user has in their My Reports folder. System administrators can change the permission set for all roles including My Reports. Because of that, your capabilities may be different than those just described. It's a good practice to reserve a specific role for accessing My Reports to help ensure a consistent user experience when using it. It's easy to create a shortcut to your My Reports folder, creating a portal to the reports you frequently need to work with. Functionally, the My Reports folder provides a secure area for users who need to manage and view reports as part of their regular work responsibilities.

Once a user has added items to their My Reports folder, it's important to understand the different choices available if tyou need to revoke access. That topic is covered in the *Revoking Access to My Reports* section later in this chapter.

Working with Folders and Reports

Folders represent the structure and relationship of content in the Report Server database. Folders are containers for items and other folders. Each folder is considered the *parent* of the content it contains, and items in that folder *inherit* properties of that parent. Individual folder and item properties can be set by overriding the properties inherited from the parent folder.

Working with folders requires permission to tasks that are used to support folder management. If your Report Manager application hasn't been modified since installation, the local system administrator automatically has rights to perform actions such as create and delete folders. If new roles have been created, the role you belong to will need the same task permissions in order to manage folders.

Creating New Folders

In Report Manager, folders are created *in place*, meaning it's necessary to navigate to a folder before creating a new folder inside it. For example, to create a new folder within My Reports, you have to be in your My Reports folder. Once the folder is created, you can set the properties of that new folder. Home is also a folder, so you can create folders there as well. As an example, to create a new folder within My Reports, follow these steps:

1. With Report Manager open the Home folder and click the My Reports folder to open it.

2. Be sure you're viewing the Contents tab.

3. Click the New Folder button on the option button bar. You'll be brought to the New Folder form. Verify that Create a new folder in My Reports is the action displayed at the top of the form as shown in Figure 6-12:

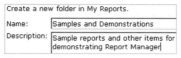

Figure 6-12

4. Type a name for your folder. A folder name can contain spaces, but because the name appears as part of the URL used to access the folder, you can't use characters that are reserved for URL encoding (such as @ & $? , ; : + * / % = < >). For testing and exploring purposes, Samples and Demonstrations works well.

5. Type a description for your new folder. This field is optional but the item description is searchable. It's good to use a description containing keywords that helps to search for items. The description used for this chapter is Sample reports and other items for demonstrating Report Manager.

6. Hide in list view refers to making the folder hidden when viewing the parent folder contents in the default view of its Contents tab. Note that when content details are listed by clicking the Show Details button, the folder will still be visible. Leave that checkbox cleared for now.

7. Click OK. The folder will be created, and you'll see it in the Contents tab of your My Reports folder. Figure 6-13 shows an example:

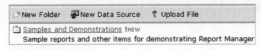

Figure 6-13

Notice the icon indicating a new item and how the folder description displays underneath the new folder link. Let's see how this works.

Your new folder inherits the security of the parent **My Reports** folder. By changing folder permissions, you can override the parent folder settings and define your own values. The changed values will in turn be applied to the contents of that folder. This application of parent settings continues to the deepest level of the folder structure. The use of configuration settings that are inherited by child nodes is used extensively in .NET.

Creating folders and modifying their security settings can degrade into an unplanned, ad hoc combination of configuration settings for different folders and users, which can be difficult to manage and maintain. Making the **My Reports** folder available to users allows them to manage settings in the context of their own **My Reports** folder, rather than modifying individual folder properties to grant the required permissions.

Moving Items into a Folder

Items can be added to folders and moved between folders. When you add an item, you've seen how it inherits the security properties of the new parent. When you move an item, its properties and contents go with it to the new location. You will need permission to manage the item type you're working with, to add or move items to a folder. Specifically, those tasks include **Manage folders**, **Manage reports**, and **Manage data sources**. For an example of how to add a report to a folder, follow these steps:

1. Open Report Manager to the Home folder.

2. Click the link to your **My Reports** folder to view its contents.

3. The Samples and Demonstrations folder you created earlier is there. Click the link to view its contents.

4. Click the Upload File button on the options toolbar. This will open the Upload File form as shown in Figure 6-14:

Figure 6-14

5. Click the Browse button to open the Choose File dialog box. Navigate to the directory on your file system containing the SQL Server Reporting Services sample reports. By default, the sample reports are located on the installed machine at:

```
C:\Program Files\Microsoft SQL Server\MSSQL\Reporting Services\Samples\Reports
```

6. Select the Company Sales.rdl file as shown in Figure 6-15:

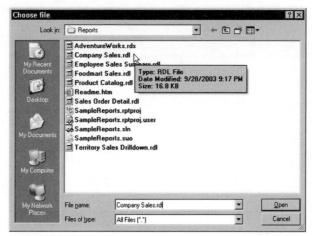

Figure 6-15

7. Enure that the Company Sales.rdl file is listed in the File name field of the form, and click Open.

8. Change the name to Company Sales Report. This changes the name displayed in Report Manager but does not change the underlying report. Note that you can choose to overwrite the item if it's already in the folder. For this example, leave that checkbox cleared.

9. Click the OK button on the Report Manager Upload File form to add the report to your folder. You'll see the Company Sales Report item added to the Samples and Demonstrations folder, with the Report and New icons alongside.

10. When you click the link to view your new report, unfortunately, you'll see the kind of message displayed in Figure 6-16:

Figure 6-16

Adding a report to a folder this way is functionally the same as a report author publishing the report using Report Designer. When a report author designs a report, a data source is configured to retrieve the desired dataset for the report-rendering engine to work with. Without the data source, the report is

173

unable to retrieve, process, or display any data. In that case, you'll need to go in and configure some properties for the report to function correctly.

You can set properties for reports in several categories. Some settings are specific to reports; others are inherited from the parent folder and overridden where necessary. For example in the General Properties of a report, you can create a new linked report based on the current report definition. Figure 6-17 shows an example of the General Properties page for a report:

Figure 6-17

In the General Properties window, you can view *metadata* about the report such as the Creation Date of the report and the user who last modified it. Using the text boxes, you can change the name or description of the report. Buttons along the bottom of the form let you apply changes, create a linked report, move or delete this report. Linked reports are extensions of an existing report definition; you'll read more about linked reports in the *Viewing, Executing, and Scheduling Reports* section later in this chapter.

In the rest of the chapter, you'll read about property settings and actions that can be performed on both the system and items contained in the Report Server. Let's start addressing that report problem by taking a look at data sources.

Working with Data Sources

A data source represents what the report definition uses to connect with the Report Server database to retrieve data from it. Data sources are generally created by the report author and added to the database content along with the report definition. At times, it may be necessary to adjust data source properties. When a database gets moved to a new machine, you may need to update data sources referencing that database to point them at the new machine. Data sources are used by reports and by data-driven subscriptions. There are two types of data sources:

❑ **Report-specific (or private) data source**: This is created for use by a single report definition and is embedded within the report definition. Since private data sources are part of the report definition file (.rdl), modifications to the data source properties must be made using the Report Designer. When making changes in the Report Designer, the author can choose to overwrite the existing data source property values in the Report Server database. In some circumstances, a report may display values returned as multiple datasets. When that happens, the property settings for each data source are contained in the report definition.

❑ **Shared data sources**: These items are separate from report definitions and can also be managed using Report Manager. Shared data sources are intended for use by reports and subscriptions that access similar datasets, giving you the ability to configure and manage a single data source for use by multiple reports. Note that the changes you make to a shared data source using Report Manager overwrite the data source properties previously held in the Report Server database.

Configuring Shared Data Sources

Shared data sources are items that can be managed from within Report Manager. You can create, delete, move, and update shared data sources. In general, it's better to rely on shared data sources rather than private ones that are hardcoded in the report design. Deployment is easier with shared data sources, and multiple reports benefit from the centralized maintenance of their data sources. For example, if a data source changes, only the required properties need to be changed. There's no need to worry about whether individual, dependent reports need to be updated and re-tested. The updating and management is all performed at a single data source location rather than within multiple reports.

The next sample exercise assumes you've completed the previous examples in this chapter, and that you have permission to manage data sources. The custom data source properties specified here are for a machine running Microsoft SQL Server in the context of the system using mixed mode security. Following are the steps to configure a shared data source:

1. From your My Reports folder, click the Samples and Demonstrations folder to open it. The report you uploaded earlier should be there.

2. Click the Company Sales Report. You'll be brought to the View tab for the report, where you'll see the error displayed earlier.

3. Click the Properties tab.

4. Click the Data Source link in the left navigation area. You'll see the Data Sources properties page, and the error indicating that shared data source reference is no longer valid. The Company Sales report is configured to use a data source called AdventureWorks, and the selected radio button shows that this data source is A shared data source.

5. Click the radio button to select A custom data source. The shared data source information greys out while the custom data source fields become enabled.

6. For the Connection Type drop-down combo box, select Microsoft SQL Server. SQL Server, SQL Server Analysis Services, Oracle, OLE DB, and ODBC data providers are all available by default.

7. Type an OLE DB connection string to the AdventureWorks2000 database location in the Connection String field. It's not a good practice to include credential information in the connection string, doing so overrides the values provided in the credentials section below. A sample connection string is as follows:

```
data source=(local);persist security info=False;initial catalog=AdventureWorks2000
```

8. In the Connect Using section, select Credentials stored securely in the Report Server. Enter the user ID and password you use to log into your system.

9. Click the Use as Windows credentials when connecting to the data source checkbox to select it. Figure 6-18 shows a completed data source Properties page:

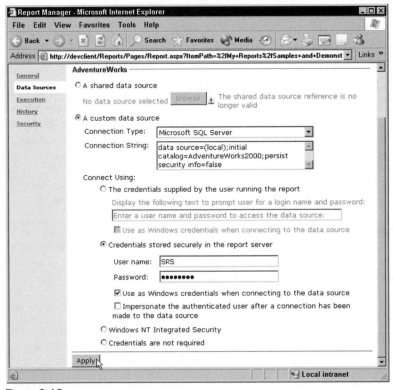

Figure 6-18

10. Click the Apply button to apply your changes.

11. Click the View tab. The report will execute, and in a few moments it's displayed as HTML in your browser. Figure 6-19 shows the rendered report:

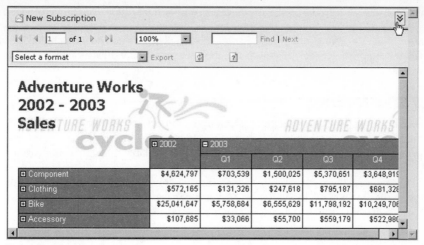

Figure 6-19

A custom data source can be configured for a report, overriding the previously published values. In the previous example, you pointed the report away from a shared data source to one that was custom configured. Creating a shared data source uses exactly the same process, except you begin by clicking the New Data Source button on the options toolbar when viewing the contents of a folder. Configuring the credentials section of the form can be confusing, so let's take a closer look at that.

Data Source Credentials

SQL Server has very effective security mechanisms in place to control access to data. When a report or subscription attempts to retrieve data from the SQL data store through a configured data source, authentication is performed to ensure that whoever is attempting to access the data has permission to do so. If your SQL Server instance is configured to use both SQL Server and Integrated Windows authentication, there are four ways that Reporting Services can handle authentication to SQL Server:

❑   NTLM

❑   Basic

❑   Kerberos

❑   Passport

In a way, how Reporting Services handles passing authentication credentials depends on which device is requesting the report. When the Report Server ultimately connects to SQL Server to retrieve data, authorization is performed on the credentials it provides. Those credentials can be obtained from the user when the report is run or can be values previously stored in the Report Server database.

Credentials Supplied by the User

By selecting this choice, the user will be prompted for a user name and password each time they run the report. The credentials can be used to identify the user as a Windows account holder, or passed directly to SQL Server for it to perform its own authentication and authorization. You'll need to instruct your users whether to provide Windows or SQL credentials, depending on whether your SQL Server is configured for Integrated Windows or SQL Server security. The Use as Windows credentials checkbox indicates whether Reporting Services should use the user-provided values as Windows account credentials or not.

Credentials Stored Securely

You can choose to have the user credentials stored in the Report Server database for use when required later. The values are stored in encrypted form in the database. Storing credentials in the Report Server is required for reports that are run on a schedule or are made available through a subscription.

It's possible to configure the security policy for an item so only certain role members can perform certain actions. This applies to all items in the Report Server database, including data sources. Let's see how you can control access to the report and data source contained in your folder.

Configuring Users and Permissions

Report Manager is an effective tool for managing access to Report Server content. Although configuring Reporting Services security is straightforward, it's not to be taken lightly. It's important to understand the effects of your decisions.

There are a number of topics to cover in this section, so here's a map of where we are going:

❑ After looking at an overview of the Report Manager security policy, you'll read about role-based security that is the foundation of how roles and tasks are implemented in Report Manager.

❑ You'll look at the Report Manager predefined roles. Each role is made up of a particular permission set, which defines the role definition. You'll read about how to create your own role definition.

❑ You'll look at assigning users to roles and how to create your own role assignments.

About Report Manager Security

Security is based on two essential elements:

❑ Identifying who or what is attempting to perform an action

❑ Determining if that user has permission to perform that action on the resource

For example, to view the Report Manager you must first log in to the system where Report Manager is running, and then you must have the correct permissions to view the Report Manager application. By default, anyone belonging to the Everyone group can view Report Manager, so the application is available to a wide group of users. Regardless of this, you still have to log in and be authenticated as belonging to that group.

Reporting Services uses a role-based security model, which can be implemented and managed through the Report Manager interface.

In Report Manager, security is addressed at two levels:

- ❑ **System-level**: This type of security addresses the tasks required to administrate the Report Server globally

- ❑ **Item-level**: This type of security addresses the tasks that can be performed on an individual item in the Report Server database

If you've worked with configuring users and groups in SQL Server, you're already familiar with adding users and groups to role definitions. Let's take a closer look at how to use it in Report Manager.

Understanding Role-Based Security

Role-based security is a security model that's based on the identity of the user who's attempting to access a resource. In a Windows environment, the user is identified by their Windows account. Users can be identified using other techniques, however. For example, user-provided values can be used to perform a database lookup from a web or Windows application.

Authentication is determining who is attempting to access a resource; authorization is determining whether they have permission to perform the requested action on that resource.

Once the users have been identified (*authenticated*), it needs to be determined if they are *authorized* to access the resource. This is done by identifying which roles the users have been placed in (*role membership*). For example, administrators have more permissions than users. Ultimately, the security settings of the resource are checked to see if the user has permission to perform that particular action.

Identifying the user is the foundation of a role-based security model. In Reporting Services, users are identified by their Windows account. The Reporting Services application itself does not authenticate the user. To use role-based security in Report Manager, you create task-based roles and then add Windows users to your defined roles. This is considered to be the best model to use when defining the security architecture for a complex application. For example, don't add overhead to your application by having it handle user authentication. Let the user be identified outside your application, using any one of the many mechanisms available. Once authentication is handled, then authorization becomes your application's responsibility. Your application is the best judge of what permissions to grant to the user, and is typically also the best place to manage those permissions.

In Report Manager, the role definition defines the permission set for each user that belongs to it. A user can belong to multiple roles, and those role permissions can be different for different items. For example, a user who has update permissions for one resource may have read-only permissions for another resource.

Role-based security works well in the case of Reporting Services, because it's both flexible and scalable while still being relatively simple to manage.

Using Report Manager Default Security

Reporting Services installs with a default set of permissions in place. These permissions provide the initial settings, so you can go in and start defining the implementation of your own security policy. Called *Default* security, it's configured so that users who belong to the local Administrator group are given System Administrator role permissions and Windows users belonging to the Everyone group are given browser role permissions.

You'll need to edit the default security settings to support other Windows users and groups depending on the permissions needed for users to accomplish their tasks. To better understand how security is configured in Reporting Services, let's take a closer look at what roles are.

Understanding Roles

Once Reporting Services is installed, you'll want to go in and change the default security configuration to support your specific access requirements. For example, you may want to create new roles, add users to those roles, or change security settings to modify access to a particular item.

At the beginning of this chapter, you read about the role of a content manager in the context of a reporting application. The content manager role is responsible for organizing the report folder structure and overseeing the generation of reports. To perform that role, a content manager has the permissions to create, update, and delete specific content items. The Content Manager role in Report Manager has been given the permissions to perform those tasks. A role might be considered a functional job description, with each role being granted the rights it needs to carry out its particular tasks. In addition to Content Manager, the Report Manager application contains a number of other predefined roles.

Understanding Tasks

In Report Server, roles are defined by the permissions they have been granted. To make managing permission sets easier, they've been grouped into subsets called *tasks*. Combinations of task permissions define the overall permission set for a role.

A task is an action that can be performed by a user or administrator. In terms of security, tasks are comprised of the permissions needed to perform that task. The tasks defined in Report Manager cannot be modified and you cannot create your own.

Tasks are essentially combinations of three elements:

- ❑ A domain user account or group that defines the user context
- ❑ The role the user belongs to that defines the allowed tasks
- ❑ Specific item properties that define whether or not permission is granted

Permissions are defined as rights to perform specific create, read, update, or delete actions on either the global Report Server system or on an individual item in the Report Server database.

A Report Server item can be one of four things:

- ❑ Folder
- ❑ Report
- ❑ Resource
- ❑ Data source

Tasks are a combination of permissions granted to perform actions on each of those items. Folders act as containers for other items. Because of this, everything contained within a folder inherits the permissions of that folder. Remember that an individual item can have its own security properties set differently, which would then override the settings of the parent folder.

System Tasks and Item Tasks

In Report Manager, a distinction is made between two groups of actions that can be performed: actions performed on the system and actions performed on items. They are referred to as system-level and item-level tasks. System-level tasks are actions that apply to the Reporting Services system as a whole, while item-level tasks are actions that can be performed on items such as folders and reports that are contained in the Report Server database. The two groups essentially form separate security zones, each containing different permission sets. Typically, system tasks are performed by administrators and item tasks are performed by users. Figure 6-20 shows a sample Edit System Role page with the system-level tasks and their descriptions:

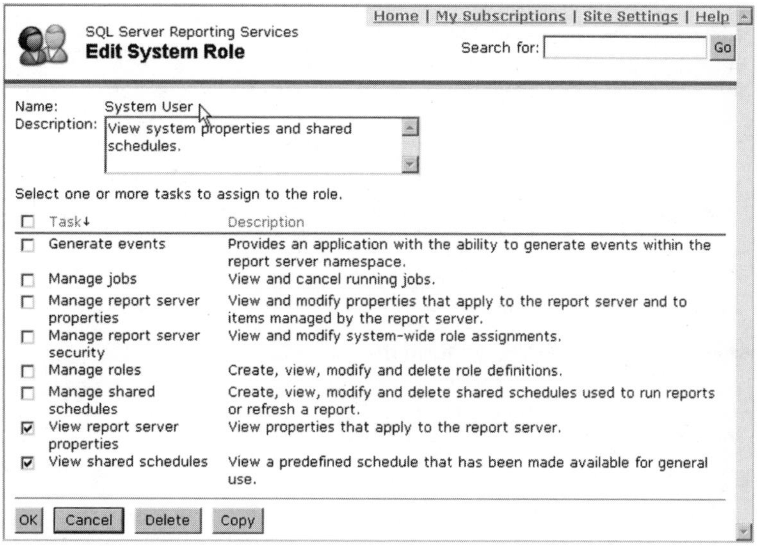

Figure 6-20

Understanding the Predefined Roles

By default, Report Manager contains definitions for six roles that act as the basis for implementing security policies in Reporting Services. You are free to modify the default role definitions, and you'll see later how to create your own roles. Continuing with the concept of grouping tasks into system-level and item-level tasks, Reporting Services has system-level and item-level roles. Different forms are used to configure each type, which are each accessed from the Site Settings page. Figure 6-21 shows the links as they appear at the bottom of the Site Settings page:

Figure 6-21

181

In each of the following sections, the displayed task permissions were taken from the **Edit Role** form of each role. Figure 6-22 shows a complete **Edit Role** form, displaying the default definition of the Content Manager item-level role:

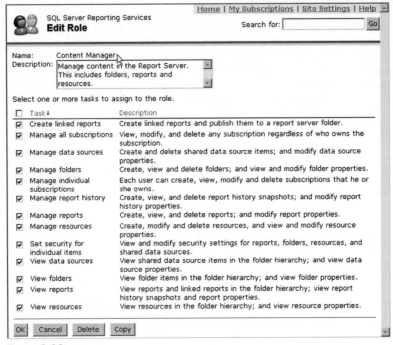

Figure 6-22

First let's look at the predefined system-level roles and then the item-level roles.

System Administrator

The system-level System Administrator role is for Report Server users who are responsible for administrating the application but might not be involved in the process of managing the actual content in the Report Server database. It's a role used by Report Manager default security, and role members include Windows accounts that are members of the Administrator group. Figure 6-23 shows the permissions granted to this role:

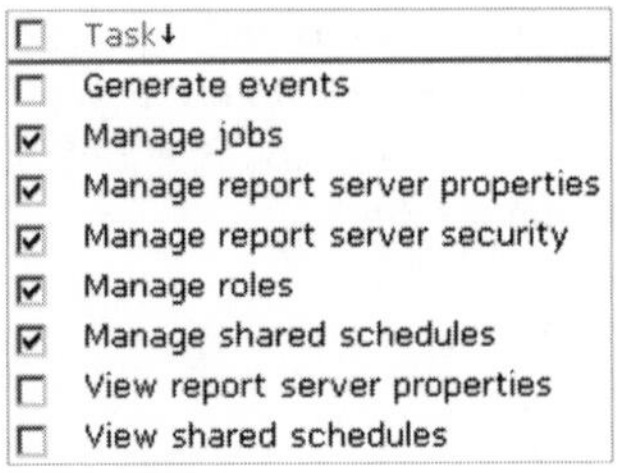

Figure 6-23

Notice how the System Administrator is not granted the View report server properties or View shared schedules task permissions. Permission to view Report Server properties is granted in the Manage Report Server properties task, and permission to view shared schedules is granted in the Manage shared schedules task. This is an example of how task permissions can overlap and how important it is to carefully consider modifying existing role permissions.

System User

System User is a system-level role, used for providing minimum access to Report Server functionality. It is one of the roles used in the Report Server default security configuration, where user accounts belonging to the Windows Everyone role are added to this role. Figure 6-24 shows the permissions granted to the System User role:

Figure 6-24

Note that although the System User role has access to Report Server properties and shared schedules, this role has read-only permissions on both.

Report Manager installs with four predefined item-level roles. Let's look at them in detail.

Content Manager

Just as it sounds, Content Manager is the primary role meant for managers of content held in the Report Server database; it is an item-level role. Figure 6-25 shows the permissions granted to this role:

Figure 6-25

Publisher

Publisher consists of a subset of the Content Manager permissions, allowing report authors to publish their reports to the Reporting Services database and manage the resources required by those reports. This is a good example of segmenting tasks and responsibilities to allow delegation. In this case, tasks related to publishing reports and uploading resources have been delegated without compromising access to security settings or user subscriptions. Figure 6-26 shows the permissions granted to this role:

Figure 6-26

My Reports

My Reports is the role for granting permissions to the My Reports folder, and defines the actions the user is allowed to perform on items within it. Figure 6-27 shows the permissions granted to this role:

Figure 6-27

The Browser Role

The Browser role is the most restrictive of the predefined roles. It's applied when you want to restrict a user to a minimum level of Report Server functionality such as viewing reports. It's a good idea to initially add new users to this role and add to their permissions as required, rather than dumping users into an "anything goes" role. A good security practice is called the *principle of least privilege*. It states that users should be granted the least privilege required to accomplish their tasks. Applying this principle is not only helpful in mitigating security threats, but it's also helpful in preventing users from wreaking unintentional havoc on the system. Figure 6-28 shows the permissions granted to the Browser role:

Figure 6-28

Creating a New Role Definition

Generally, you don't need to create many new roles. Having too many roles defined can quickly become a management headache, particularly if you start modifying role definitions that are already in use. With a complex folder and report structure, it can be difficult to tell what effects your changes will have.

To create a new role definition, you'll need to have permission to manage system security policy. An example of the steps required to create a new role definition are as follows:

1. In Report Manager, click the Site Settings link. It's a global link in the upper-right corner of the page.

2. Click the Configure item-level role definitions link. Note that you also have the ability to configure system-level roles.

3. Click the New Role button on the options toolbar. You'll be brought to the New Role form.

4. Give your new role the name, Demo User. It's a good practice to use a name that matches the job function or title for the group you're creating. The name can include spaces and special characters, though it can't be more than 256 characters long.

5. Type Role to demonstrate item-level security for the description. The description should make it easy for administrators who create role assignments to understand what purpose the role is intended for. Ideally, the description should describe the role responsibilities. Providing a complete description keeps an administrator from having to open a role definition just to figure out what task permissions it has.

6. Check the View folders, View reports, and View resources checkboxes. Figure 6-29 shows the completed New Role form:

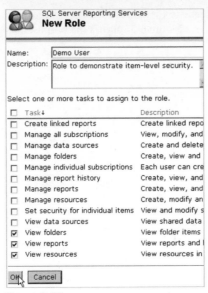

Figure 6-29

7. Click OK to save the new role into the Report Server database. You'll see the new role and its description listed on the Item-Level Roles page.

The Demo User role is now ready for user or group accounts to be added. You can go back in and modify the task permissions, if needed, but have your changes ironed out before adding users. Remember that many management headaches have started with modifying a role after users have already begun using it. If desired, you can also delete the role by clicking the Delete button on the Edit Role form. The Copy button will open a new Edit Role form with the same task permissions already selected. This way, you can easily extend an existing role to create a new one.

Creating a new role definition is straightforward, but it's important to be careful and not go overboard. Note how changing task permissions affects users. When you remove tasks or delete a role entirely, the change applies to every item in every folder in the Report Server database. Things can get tricky, because a role can be associated with a single item as well as an upper-level folder and all its children. There isn't any way to easily view how the web of user roles and permissions affect their access to different reports and folders, so use care when modifying existing role definitions. Start with an existing definition, and extend task permissions only as required.

Users are added to roles through *role assignments*.

Understanding Role Assignments

Ultimately, access to the Report Server content is controlled by role assignments. Role assignments are created when you add a Windows domain account to a role definition. Remember that Report Server doesn't perform its own authentication; it relies on Windows to perform that function. Report Manager is used to map Windows users and groups to Report Manager role definitions. As you've seen, each role is a unique collection of permissions. When a user attempts to perform an action, Report Server checks the roles that the user is a member of to determine whether to allow the action. Figure 6-30 illustrates how the Report Server permission stack maps specific domain users or groups to finally determine access permission on an item:

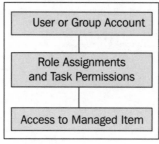

Figure 6-30

Reporting Services creates its own role assignments when it implements the default security policy upon installation. Default security allows members of the local Administrators group to perform administrative actions on the Report Server database, while restricting users in the Everyone group to viewing items only.

Creating Role Assignments

Creating role assignments is how you bring life to your role definitions. Role assignments are created in place, meaning that you must be looking at the properties for a specific item before you can make a role assignment for it. An example of how to create a new role assignment is as follows:

1. Open Report Manager and navigate to your Samples and Demonstrations folder in My Reports.

2. Be sure you're viewing the Contents tab of the Samples and Demonstrations folder. On the Options toolbar, click the Show Details button. You'll see the contents listed as in Figure 6-31:

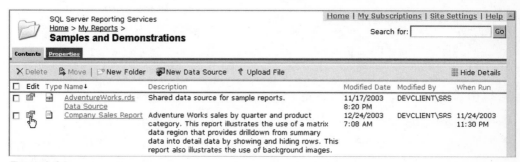

Figure 6-31

3. Click the Properties icon for the Company Sales Report. The icon is in the Edit column on the left side of the page. Click on it to go to the Properties page of the report.

4. In the left navigation area, click the Security link to view the security properties page for the report as in Figure 6-32:

Figure 6-32

5. On the Options toolbar, click the Edit Item Security button. You'll see a message box display a security message as seen in Figure 6-33:

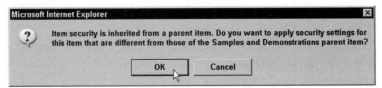

Figure 6-33

6. Click OK on the message box. The page view changes and has new buttons on the options toolbar as shown in Figure 6-34:

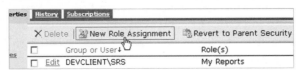

Figure 6-34

7. Click the New Role Assignment button to view the New Role Assignment form.

8. In the Group or user name field, type the username you log in with.

9. Locate the Demo User role, and click the checkbox next to it. This will add you as a user to the Demo User role, and you now have the permissions of that role on the Company Sales Report item. This role permission set is in addition to the one you are currently using as you perform this exercise. Note that you can click a role to view its task permissions. Figure 6-35 shows a completed form:

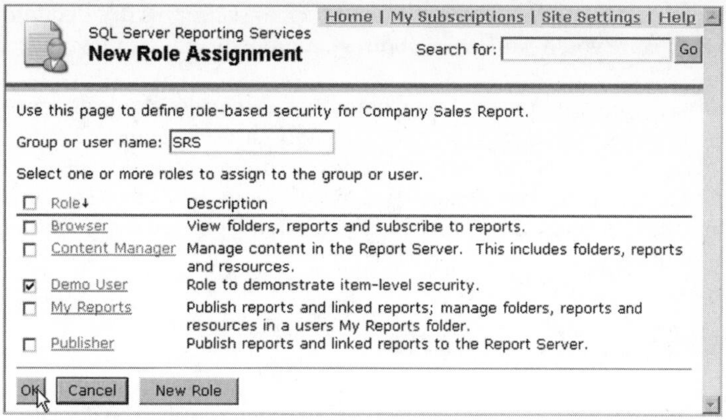

Figure 6-35

10. Click OK to apply the new assignment.

Note that you can easily revert back to the security settings of the parent folder by clicking the Revert to Parent Security button. That will cause the security settings for the Company Sales Report to be set back to *mirror* those of the parent folder. Subfolders inherit the security characteristics of their parent, so the security settings of the Home folder effectively establish the default settings for the rest of the tree unless over-ridden by a child in the structure. For example, the My Reports folder has different permission settings than the Home folder. It's a good practice to grant limited permissions on the Home folder because of the inheritance of security settings down the folder hierarchy. It's also a good idea to bear in mind that when modifying the role assignments for a folder, your new settings can affect items much further down in the folder hierarchy.

You can add multiple users and groups to a role assignment, though you can add a specific named group or user to a role only once. When accessing an item, the task permissions in allowed roles are combined for a user. For example, let's say that Mary belongs to the domain Department Managers and that both Mary and Department Managers' rights have been assigned to a folder, then she'll have the combined permissions of both Mary and Department Managers for that folder (and its contents).

Role definitions are applied across the system. Modifying them can have unforeseen consequences unless careful consideration is given to the effects of that change. If a user needs certain permissions on an item in the Report Server database, it may be better to address the issue at the item level rather than the role level. Modifying the role definition affects all assignments to that role and in every location that the role has access.

Creating roles and role assignments aren't an everyday task, but it's important to know what happens when you do make or modify one. Let's look at a couple of other important security considerations.

System Security and Network Considerations

The best-practices approach to implementing a Reporting Services security policy is to use a small number of role definitions, assign users to the roles, and make changes to the security policy on an as-needed special case basis. Remember that Reporting Services security is divided into two zones, system-level and item-level. Ensure you're addressing both system-level and item-level security zones.

Like item-level role assignments, you can create your own system-level role assignments. Reporting Services security is set at the system level by configuring user permissions for actions such as creating shared schedules and setting report security properties. To define system-level role assignments, click Configure site-wide security on the Site Settings form by accessing the Site Settings link. For more information on the specific system tasks and permissions available, see the *Understanding the Predefined Role* section in this chapter.

Revoking Access to My Reports

Consider the possible ways to prevent users from accessing their My Reports folder. First, you can clear the Enable My Reports checkbox under Site Settings. That removes the My Reports folder from the Home folder contents.

Its important to note that although clearing the checkbox removes the My Reports folder from display, it doesn't actually prevent access to the My Reports folder content. If you know the structure and path to a folder, you can still navigate to the location directly.

Another way to prevent access to the contents of My Reports is to modify the role definition used for accessing My Reports. Clearing all the task permissions will effectively lock it down and prevent a user from accessing its contents. Unfortunately, it also denies access to anyone else in that role (who doesn't already have permissions granted through other role memberships).

Finally, My Reports can be secured by removing the user's Windows account from My Reports role membership. This is the most effective way of locking out individual users, without creating potentially far-reaching side effects.

Intranet and Extranet Considerations

Reporting Services relies on *Internet Information Services* (*IIS*) and Windows to perform user authentication. Remember, users are granted access to Report Manager because their Windows account or group was added to a role assignment. To provide Report Manager access, users must have a valid Windows user account or be a member of a Windows group.

Report Manager itself is not meant for use in an extranet or Internet environment, although you can create a custom application to provide extranet access to reports and/or resources through another interface. If you build an ASP.NET Web application, for example, you have many options for configuring security and improving performance. Combinations of IIS and .NET authentication and authorization mechanisms with response output and user session caching capabilities enable you to make a custom application that's both secure and reliable. For example, you can create a subscription to deploy a rendered report out to a location on the file system and use an ASP.NET configuration file for the IIS virtual directory to require authentication to access it.

You'll want authenticate users against Active Directory and encrypt the communication to ensure privacy. Because of this, the Report Server machine should be configured as a certificate server, responding to requests over a Secure Sockets Layer (SSL) connection. Users can be authenticated against Active Directory using ASP.NET Forms authentication, or by using IIS Basic or Integrated Windows authentication mechanisms. If using Basic authentication, be sure to use an SSL connection. Certificate configuration may be the source of unexpected issues.

One note from the field refers to a Report Manager instance returning errors indicating problems accessing the `machine.config` *file, which infact turned out to be a certificate service configuration issue.*

Viewing, Executing, and Scheduling Reports

As you've seen, the first things defining the ability of a user to view a report are the permissions of the user and the security settings applied to that report. After that, there are a variety of ways that reports can be run, deployed, and viewed. Let's talk about the different options available and when to use them.

Viewing Reports

As Report Manager is a web-based management tool, the default rendering of reports is in HTML format so they render in your browser as part of the Report Manager interface. When you view a report in one of the other available formats, the rendered output is displayed in a new browser window.

The .NET Common Language Runtime (CLR) handles the job of determining whether to send HTML 3.2 or 4.0 to the client depending on the browser making the request. HTML 3.2 displays static HTML reports without client-side script. Reports with advanced functionality such as search and generation of multiple report formats are output as HTML 4.0.

Refreshing the current report view is not done by refreshing the browser window. To view the report using updated data, be sure to click the refresh button on the HTML Viewer toolbar.

Linked Reports

Linked reports are based on already existing reports. Because the base report has already been configured, a linked report uses those property values for much of the processing. Where linked reports differ is in the security properties and report parameters used to render the data. Linked reports are a way to provide filtered views of existing reports. By creating a linked report that uses predefined parameters, for example, you can control what data renderings can be viewed by your users.

You should know that deleting a report that's being used as the base for other linked reports will break the link and cause those reports to fail. Unfortunately, there's no way to globally view the connections related to linked reports. You've got to view the properties of each linked report, to see what report it's based on.

On-Demand Reports and Subscriptions

Reporting Services has two types of report execution:

- ❑ On-demand, which execute upon user request
- ❑ Subscription, which execute unattended

To begin our discussion of these report types, it's important to understand the report execution process.

The Report Execution Process

Running a report means generating a rendered version of the report definition based on values contained in the Report Server and SQL Server databases. The authored, published report is executed using retrieved data and staged in an intermediate format for further processing. Figure 6-36 shows the major steps to rendering a report:

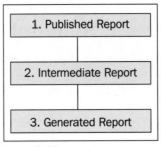

Figure 6-36

How an intermediate report is processed into a generated report depends on the type of rendering requested. Report execution properties are accessed by navigating to the report, then selecting the Properties tab for the report selected, and finally clicking the Execution link in the left of the navigation area. Figure 6-37 shows a sample report Execution property page:

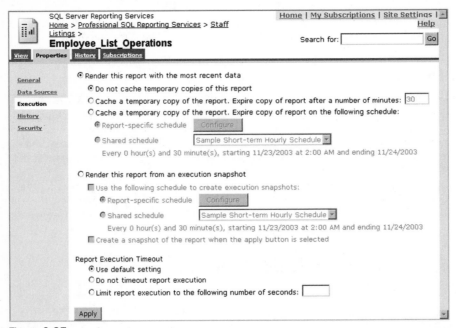

Figure 6-37

Providing Report Parameters and Credentials

As a report viewer, you may be allowed or required to provide values for the report to use when it's generated. Dates and date ranges, categories and credentials are examples of commonly used parameter values. The report author has designed the report to run using the values you provide. This is used to display a filtered view of the underlying data. After you've provided the required parameters, clicking the View Report button will run and display the resulting view.

Earlier, many reporting tools required additional coding and manual passing of values in order to accept parameters from users at runtime. Reporting Services, however, handles all the underlying tasks associated with parameter management. For example, consider some of the different parameter possibilities default values, derived parameters, cascading parameters, linked report parameters, data source parameters, and so on. Reporting Services provides an elegant solution to what was once a cumbersome process.

Credentials are special parameters the values of which determine whether the user has the correct permissions to view the report. Depending on how the report was designed, two users may see entirely different results when the reports run. Figure 6-38 shows a sample parameter bar for a report:

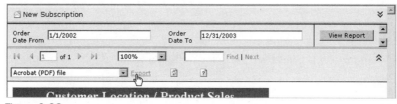

Figure 6-38

A report can contain default parameters or may run only after the user has provided values. The number and types of parameters a report takes is part of the report definition. However, you can change what values are used and whether the report viewer has the option of changing them. Figure 6-39 shows an example report Parameters property page:

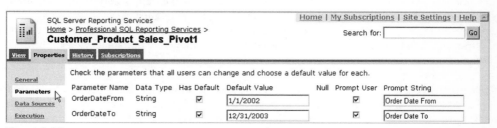

Figure 6-39

A change has been made to the report viewed in Figure 6-39. The OrderDateFrom parameter value has been set to 1/1/2002, and the users ability to change that value has been revoked. The user will still be able to specify the OrderDateTo parameter value, but the user prompt will only say Order Date To for usability. Figure 6-40 shows the resulting change rendered with the report:

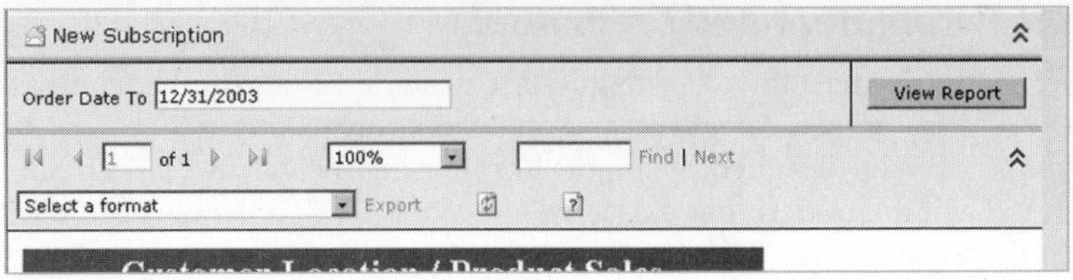

Figure 6-40

Entering a new Order Date To value and clicking the View Report button will render the report based on the new parameter value. Any parameter that has a default value can be hidden from the user. Without a default value, the user must supply a value and click the View Report button to render the report. If the Prompt User checkbox is cleared and the parameter has a default value, the user will never see the parameter. If you do allow the user to enter parameter values, the Prompt String property can be used to provide information to the user about the type of values required.

On-demand and subscription reports have different requirements when providing parameter and credential values. Let's take a look at how these two report generation techniques differ.

On-Demand Reports

When an on-demand report is generated, the following steps occur:

1. Data is retrieved from the SQL data store.
2. The data is processed according to the report definition.
3. A temporary copy of the report in intermediate form is generated and added to memory.
4. The intermediate report is rendered based on the requested format and delivered.

The temporary, intermediate copy of the report is session-specific. The individual user is tracked during the Report Manager session, and if the generated report is requested again, the user will see the cached version. This behavior is similar to using session state in an ASP.NET application, with one important point. If the underlying values of the report have changed, the user must click the refresh report icon on the parameter toolbar. Clicking the Refresh button on the browser will not cause the report to refresh and retrieve updated values; rather it will cause the browser to merely update its view of the cached report.

There currently isn't any way to define or restrict the specific report rendering format when a user views an on-demand report, except in the behavior of your own application interface. You can control the rendering of reports that are not created on demand, however, as described in the section on *Report Subscriptions* later in this chapter.

Caching the Report for Other Users

On-demand reports are executed each time the report is requested. For example, if ten users request the same report, ten connections will be made, ten sets of data will be retrieved, and the report will be generated and cached ten times. That's because the report is executed and cached for each unique user. Rather than separate copies of the intermediate report being generated for each user, you can specify that one cached version of the report be made available to all users. This is a great way to increase Report Server performance.

Generating a cached version of the intermediate report is set at the item level. For example, you must be looking at the properties of the Company Sales Report to enable and configure caching. Figure 6-41 shows the section of the Execution properties page where cache settings are made:

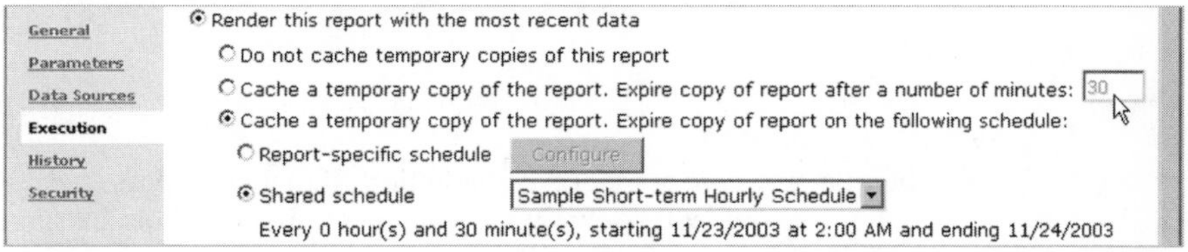

Figure 6-41

The first time this report is executed, the intermediate version of the report will be cached and be made available for another user to view. That user will not cause a data connection to be made, but rather will cause a rendering of the cached intermediate report to be made. This process saves server resources. The Report Server Web Service and Report Manager web application are then able to handle more incoming HTTP requests, while making fewer SQL connections for them.

This ability enables a Report Server instance to scale enough to support even high client loads. For example, consider an online sports site that tracks player and team statistics. These statistics are updated periodically, not continually. Because of that, cached versions of the various reports can be stored. When the processing of a web page requires a report, it's simply served up from the cache. The overhead of connecting to the data source and processing the data is avoided entirely. Few thought it was the responsibility of the reporting engine to handle caching intelligently, but here Microsoft has done a great job of blending technologies and capabilities for the best possible results.

There are two ways you can specify when the cached report expires:

❑ You can set the time after which the report must expire. When the cached copy expires, the report is executed on the next user request. The new intermediate report is then cached, expiring when the minutes specified are passed. The default value for this is 30 minutes.

❑ You can set cache expiration by scheduling a new-cached copy to be generated after a specific time. For example, you can set the Company Sales Report to run every Sunday at midnight. The generated intermediate report will be placed in the cache, available to users until the next time the report executes. This process creates what is called a *snapshot* report. Snapshot reports are discussed in the next section.

When a report takes query parameters, the cached version of the report will reflect the parameter values supplied when the report executed. If another user provides different parameter values, the new report will cause a new cache to be created. This behavior is known as *vary by parameter*. There can be as many different cached versions of the report as there are possible parameter combinations.

Reports that use filters have a slightly different behavior. For filtered reports, only one copy of the intermediate report is cached. Filtering is applied during the rendering of the report based on the intermediate version in memory.

It's important to know that cached reports require the credentials used to run a report to be stored in the Report Server database. Reports that prompt users for authentication credentials cannot be cached.

Creating and Editing Schedules

You can automate the generation of cached reports; to do this, you create a schedule item. Like data sources, there are two types of schedules:

❑   Report-specific

❑   Shared

Unlike data sources, both schedule types are managed using Report Manager. Report-specific and shared schedules are both configured almost the same way. You need to have permissions to manage schedules in Report Manager to create a shared schedule. The steps are as follows:

1.   Open Report Manager and click the Site Settings link on the global toolbar. In the bottom-left corner of the Site Settings page, click the Manage shared schedules link. This will open the Shared Schedules page, which lists the currently defined shared schedules.

2.   Click the New Schedule button on the options toolbar as shown in Figure 6-42. This will bring you to the Reporting Services Scheduling form.

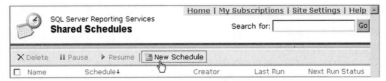

Figure 6-42

3.   In the Schedule Name field, enter a name for the schedule. Unlike other new item forms, schedules don't have a description field. Because of this, it's helpful to write a descriptive name for the schedule. For this example, type Sample Short-term Hourly Schedule.

4.   In the Schedule details section, you can set the schedule to run on an hourly, daily, weekly, monthly or one time basis. Click the various options, to see how the schedule pane changes and allows you to supply different values depending on the schedule type. Select the Hour option.

5.   The Hourly Schedule pane lets you specify how frequently the schedule runs and when the schedule begins. Set the schedule to run every 30 minutes and leave the default start time of 2:00 AM. Figure 6-43 shows a completed Schedule details section:

Schedule details

Define a schedule that runs on an hourly, daily, weekly, monthly, or one time basis.

All times are expressed in (GMT -08:00) Pacific Standard Time.

◉ Hour   **Hourly Schedule**
○ Day   Run the schedule every:
○ Week   ☐0☐ hours ☐30☐ minutes
○ Month
○ Once   Start time: ☐02☐ : ☐00☐   ◉ AM ○ PM

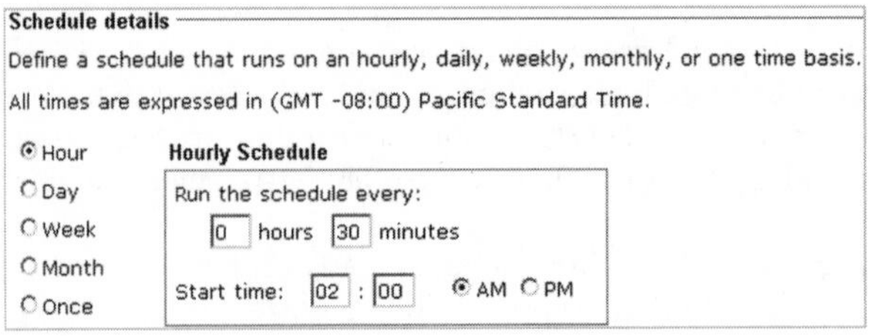

Figure 6-43

6. At the bottom of the form, set the start date of the schedule to today. This is an optional schedule setting. Click the calendar icon to the right of the textbox to display a calendar of the current month and select the date as in Figure 6-44:

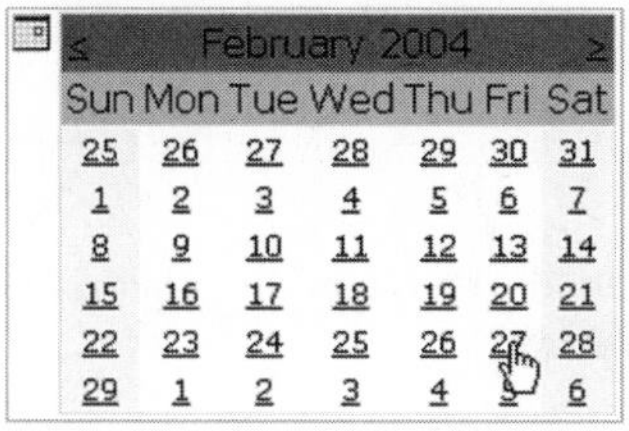

Figure 6-44

7. Check the checkbox to stop the schedule on a specific date and choose tomorrow for the stop date. Like the start date, the stop date is an optional property setting for schedules.

8. Click OK to apply the new schedule. You'll be taken back to the Shared Schedules page where the new schedule is listed. Note that it's easy to Pause, Resume, or Delete a schedule by selecting the checkbox for a schedule and then choosing the action on the options toolbar.

The Sample Short-term Hourly Schedule is now available for users to choose for scheduling a report or subscription.

Schedules are items that are stored in the Report Server database. Shared schedules differ from report-specific schedules as they are available for use by any report or subscription that needs to run on that same schedule. They are implemented as SQL Server Agent jobs, which has a very practical implication. For example, consider a company where different reports are generated on weekly or monthly schedules as required.

Using a shared schedule configured for a particular time/day/date frequency, all reports cycling on a similar schedule can be pointed to the same schedule. Then, if the schedule changes for some reason such as scheduled closings or delayed shipments, all the reports can be rescheduled at one location. Even better, both generated and subscription reports can share a schedule.

Working with shared schedules requires system-level permissions, and is done from the Site Settings page in the Report Manager. Report-specific schedules are items that can be created in-place by users who have the permissions. Creation and editing is done from the property pages for an individual report or subscription.

Shared schedules are created once and then referred to when setting the execution properties for a report or subscription. Because shared schedules are managed from a central location and enable reuse, they are usually preferred over report-specific schedules. For example, a report-specific schedule would be used when the existing shared schedules don't have the right interval settings to suit the report execution requirements.

Snapshot Reports

Snapshot reports are cached reports that are executed based on a schedule rather than on a user request. To schedule a report snapshot, the steps are as follows:

1. Open Report Manager, and navigate to the **Samples and Demonstrations** folder. If you're not already viewing the folder contents in the details view, click the **Show Details** button.

2. Click the properties icon in the **Edit** column for the **Company Sales Report** item. You'll be taken to the **General** properties page.

3. Click the **Execution** link in the local navigation area on the left. and choose the **Render this report from an execution snapshot** option.

4. Click the **Use the following schedule** checkbox. In this area, you can configure a report-specific schedule or choose an existing shared schedule.

5. Choose the **Shared schedule** option, and select the **Sample Short-term Hourly Schedule** shared schedule item in the drop-down combo box. Notice how the schedule execution properties for the schedule are displayed.

6. Leave the checkbox to allow creation of a snapshot when the user clicks the **Apply** button, manually forcing a snapshot to be generated.

7. Leave the default report execution timeout to **Use default setting**. The default value is set in the Site Settings form, and applies to all reports unless over-ridden by an individual report. Figure 6-45 shows the completed property settings:

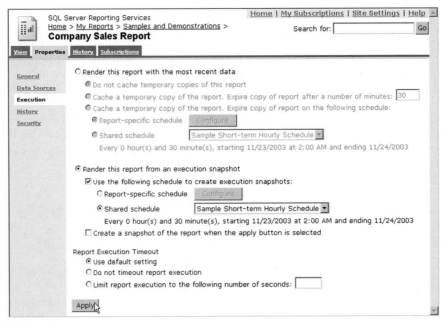

Figure 6-45

8. Click the **Apply** button to apply your updated execution settings.

Snapshot reports are cached intermediate reports. Cached reports execute when the user makes a request, but snapshot reports execute automatically based on a schedule. Like cached reports, snapshot reports are rendered from the intermediate report. Unlike cached reports, snapshots aren't required to expire after a period of time. Instead, snapshots expire and are removed when a new one is generated. Although there can only be one current snapshot, you can archive them in the report history for later viewing. Snapshots are accessed using the View tab of the report; a report history is accessed using the History tab.

The Company Sales Report will now be executed hourly, creating a new intermediate report snapshot each time. The snapshot will be served up from cache and rendered for each user request, until the new snapshot is created. To verify that the report ran, go to the Contents tab of the Samples and Demonstrations folder. The Last Run value will be displayed there.

You can specify that snapshots be archived, rather than replaced. To do that, you create report history.

Creating a Report History

Configuring report caching and snapshots is done using the Execution properties page, accessed from the Properties tab. Creating a report history is done in place, using the History tab of a report as shown in the following steps:

1. Open Report Manager and navigate to the Samples and Demonstrations folder. Display the contents in details view.

2. Click the properties icon for the Company Sales Report item to view the report Properties tab.

3. Go to the History property page.

4. By default, the Allow history to be created manually checkbox is selected. Leave the default setting.

5. Click the Use the following schedule to add snapshots to report history checkbox to select it. That will enable the option buttons below it as shown in Figure 6-46:

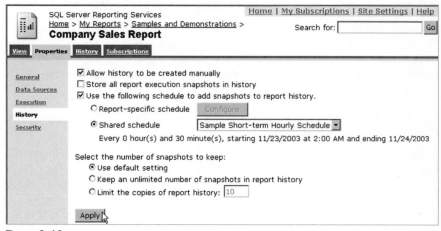

Figure 6-46

6. Click the option to use a Shared schedule and select the Sample Short-term Hourly Schedule in the drop-down combo box.

7. Note that you can define your own setting for the number of copies to be kept in History. For now, go ahead and use the default setting.

8. Click Apply to save your changes.

9. Go to the History tab and click the New Snapshot button on the options toolbar. That will force the first snapshot to be generated and added to the report history.

If you don't see the snapshot available, try refreshing your browser. To view a snapshot, click the link that indicates the date and time of the report run. To verify that a snapshot ran, check the When Run value. Report executions that raise an error will not create a snapshot and so will not be archived.

Snapshots created for a report history are subject to the same credential limitations as other snapshots. The report execution runs automatically, so the credentials used to create the intermediate report must be stored in the Report Server database. Because snapshots are historical perspectives, users can't be prompted for credentials or have their Windows account used for authorization.

Snapshots in history are items separate from the report definition. For example, changes made to the report definition or its data sources don't affect the previous snapshots kept in the report history.

However, changes made to the property value specifying the number of snapshots to be kept in report history do affect the existing snapshots. For example, if you reduce the property value setting the number of copies to be kept in a report history, any report copies older than the new property value will be deleted from the database. If current users need access to those earlier snapshots, there's a problem. Be careful when changing History property values.

Report Subscriptions

The report rendering mechanisms you've read about so far all share one requirement for the user, to initiate the action of viewing the rendered report. Subscriptions are a way to allow the automated delivery of rendered reports. The following steps demonstrate creating a report subscription. Create a folder on your C drive called RSTemp (this example builds on the previous examples in this chapter):

1. Open Report Manager and navigate to the Samples and Demonstrations folder.

2. Click the Company Sales Report item and view the report Subscriptions tab.

3. Click the New Subscription button on the options toolbar. This should bring you to the Subscription: Company Sales Report page.

4. For the Delivered by: field, select Report Server File Share. Report Manager will display the page with the appropriate properties for your selection.

5. Leave the File Name field as the default value Company Sales Report.

6. Enter a valid UNC path to the RSTemp folder you created. For this example, type the path as follows (replacing serverName with your server name):

```
\\serverName\C$\RSTemp
```

7. Select XML file with report data as the Render Format.

8. Leave the User Credentials checkbox checked, and enter your login user ID and password.

9. Leave the default Overwrite an existing file with a newer version option selected.

10. In the Subscription Processing Options section, choose to run the subscription On a shared schedule.

11. Choose the Sample Short-term Hourly Schedule in the shared schedule combo box.

The execution properties for the schedule will be displayed below the combo box. Figure 6-47 shows a completed subscription form:

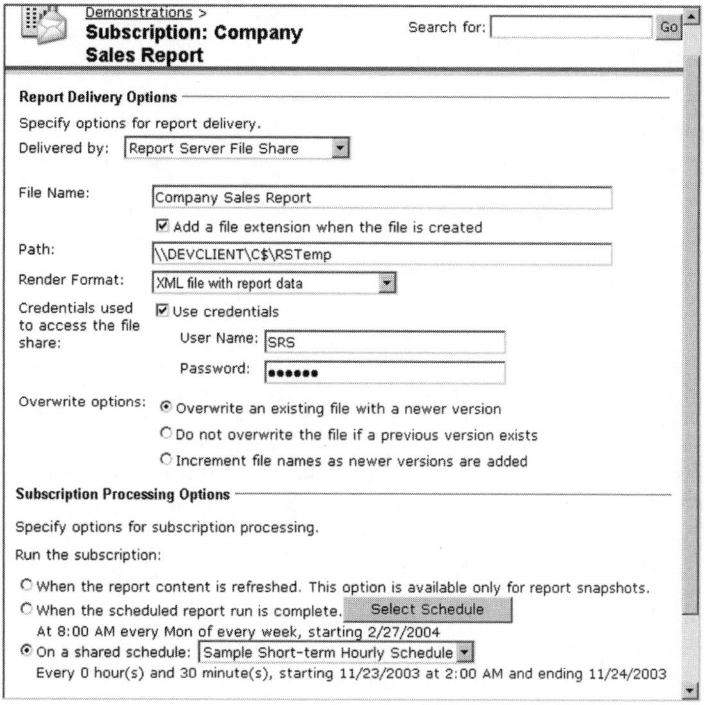

Figure 6-47

12. Click OK to create the new subscription. You'll be taken to the Subscriptions tab for the Company Sales Report where the subscription will be listed.

When the scheduled event is raised, Reporting Services will process the schedule and deliver the report using the specified channel. Out of the box, SQL Server Reporting Services provides support for file share and email delivery. You just saw the use of file share delivery in this example. When the half hour schedule event is raised, the report in the XML version will be written to the file system. This delivery of a single report to a single location, for example, a file path or email address, is considered a *standard subscription*.

Standard Subscriptions

Typically, subscriptions are user defined. To create a subscription, you need permission to Manage individual subscriptions as well as permission to view the report itself. You can choose to have the delivered report rendered in any of the available options. Email delivery provides you the option of receiving a link to the report rather than having the entire rendered report sent as an email.

Subscriptions are not considered as items, so you cannot use the Report Manager search function to find an existing subscription. There are two other ways to access a subscription. The first is by viewing the Subscriptions tab for a report. The second is by using the link to My Subscriptions, which is located on the global toolbar. My Subscriptions provides a central location to manage all your subscriptions without having to navigate to each report item with access to the subscription and the report parent folder. There, you can also verify the Status and Last Run values for the subscription. To delete an existing subscription, select it using the checkbox and click the Delete button on the options toolbar. Figure 6-48 shows the subscription you created listed on the My Subscriptions page:

SQL Server Reporting Services
My Subscriptions

Search for:

✕ Delete

☐	⚠️📄		Report↓	Description	Folder	Trigger	Last Run	Status
☐	📄	Edit	Company Sales Report	Save in \\DEVCLIENT\C$\RSTemp as Company Sales Report	/My Reports/Samples and Demonstrations	TimedSubscription	11/24/2003 11:30 PM	File Company Sal written to \\DEV(
☐	📄	Edit	Customer Product Sales Pivot1	Save in \\DEVCLIENT\C$\RSTemp as Customer_Product_Sales_Pivot1	/Professional SQL Reporting Services	TimedSubscription	11/24/2003 11:30 PM	File Customer_Produc was written to \\DEVCLIENT\C$\

Figure 6-48

Like snapshot reports, the user credentials for the subscription report must be stored in the Report Server database (or take no credentials at all). There is no way for the user to be prompted for credentials; the report must be able to run unattended. This also applies to whatever parameters might be needed by the report. These parameters must be contained in the report definition or should be supplied by the user when creating the subscription.

It's possible to change the parameters used to execute the report. When that happens, the report is considered changed, and the subscription will not run until it is saved. Re-open your subscription and save it, enabling the report to run again.

System Administrator role members have the ability to edit and delete individual subscriptions. They also can create subscriptions that are delivered to multiple users at once. These are called *data-driven* subscriptions.

Data-Driven Subscriptions

Data-driven subscriptions give you the ability to *broadcast* a report to many users in a variety of rendering formats. The delivery values and report parameters are dynamic and are read during the report execution process. Consider, for example, a utility company that as part of its business process its invoices are generated indicating utility consumption and charges. Using Reporting Services, the invoice could also include representations of comparative usage, and so on. Data-driven subscriptions then enable the distribution through direct email to the customer in an example of one to one custom mass mailing. The same process could be used to make the information available through email or secured web page. Creating data-driven subscriptions is a seven-step process and requires the Enterprise Edition of SQL Reporting Services.

Summary

Report Manager is a robust tool, and this chapter has covered a lot of ground to address it. From navigating the interface to managing content and configuring security, there's a lot to consider. Using Report Manager as a report viewing application is intuitive and flexible. However, administering security, permissions, and report execution can be more of a challenge.

It's important to understand the implications that your choices can have. For example, remember to exercise care when extending the default security model. Reporting Services, including the Report Manager interface, demonstrate a number of sophisticated and elegant design practices.

Even if you choose to develop your own Report Server interface, much can be learned from Microsoft's Report Manager. The next chapter, in fact, shows how to build your own Reporting Services interface.

Managing Reports Using Program Code

A friend of mine, who happens to be a very funny person, coined the following: "*There is very little that cannot be accomplished if you have a positive mental attitude, tons of money, and supernatural powers*". Steve's philosophy is so appropriate for much of what happens in software development. Fortunately, with Reporting Services bringing enterprise reporting to any application, it only takes the first of Steve's ingredients but the other two are always nice to have.

We discussed the use of the Report Manager web application for managing reports in Chapter 6. In this chapter you will learn how the exposed interfaces of Reporting Services can be used to develop custom applications to manage reports. All the tools that can be used in the Report Manager application are available for use through the Reporting Services Web Service. In fact the web application is just a pretty wrapper around the web service. In this chapter we will not be demonstrate all the features of the web service but will give you an understanding of what can be done and the methods necessary to create your own user interface to the service. So get ready to get your hands dirty with some code.

Professional SQL Reporting Services Manager

In order to program the web service, you'll be creating a Windows Forms application called Professional SQL Reporting Services Manager, PSRSM for short. The application will have the familiar look and feel of Windows Explorer, but instead of looking at the file system or resources on the computer, you will be looking at the objects stored in the Reporting Services database. We will develop the application with the assumption that you have installed Reporting Services on your local machine. The application will work properly when pointed to any machine on your network that has Reporting Services installed, but the example will be easier to create if the service is installed on your development machine.

Start Visual Studio .NET and create a New Project. You are going to create a Windows application in both C# and VB.NET. Name the new project PSRS_Manager and give it an appropriate location.

The location is not important, but as you can see in Figure 7-1, the application is created in C:\Professional SQL Reporting Services:

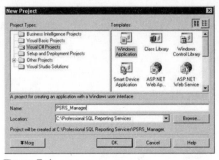

Figure 7-1

By default Visual Studio will create a form called `Form1` that will be the startup object of the application. Right click anywhere in the form **Design Window** and select **Properties**. Change the **Name** property to MainForm. It will also be necessary to right click on the **Form1.cs** file in the Solution Explorer window and rename it to **MainForm.cs**.

When creating a new Windows application, Visual Studio inserts a method named `Main` into the code behind `Form1` that will be the starting point for the application. Since you have renamed the form, the method will try and start the wrong object. Right click anywhere on the design window and select **View Code**. Scroll to the bottom of the code window until you find the `Main` method. Change the following line of code in the method so that it looks like:

C#

```
/// <summary>
/// the main entry point for the application.
/// </summary>
[STAThread]
static void Main()
{
      Application.Run (new MainForm());
}
```

If you are creating a VB.NET application as you follow along, the above step and the namespace step are both taken care of when you set the properties of the application.

While you are looking at the code window you should change the namespace for your application. Declaring your own namespace is a useful way of collecting all of your code into a single area. When you created your project, Visual Studio placed your new form into **PSRS_Manager** and change the namespace code line to the following:

```
namespace Wrox.Professional.ReportingServices
```

The final bit of housekeeping that you need to take care of in order to have the application build properly is to set the default namespace and the startup object. Click the **Project menu** and choose **PSRS_Manager Properties** menu item. This will bring up the dialog box shown in Figure 7-2. In the

General section of the Common Properties folder, change the Default Namespace property to Wrox.Professional.ReportingServices. Below the default namespace open the combo box for the startup object and choose Wrox.Professional.ReportingServices.MainFrom:

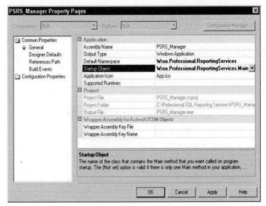

Figure 7-2

Click OK to save the settings and close the Property Pages dialog box.

Building the Visual Interface

A blank form is only a canvas on which to paint or build your application. To make your application do something worthwhile you need to place controls from the toolbox on the form. Using the following table as a reference, add the necessary controls to `MainForm`:

Control Type	Control Name	Text	Anchor
TreeView	treeViewFolders		Top, Bottom, Left
ListView	listViewReports		Top, Botton, Left, Right
MainMenu	mainMenu1		
Label	labelServerAddress	Server Address:	Top, Left
TextBox	textBoxServerPath	http://localhost/ReportServer	Top, Left, Right
Button	buttonGo	Go	Top, Right
Button	buttonClose	Close	Bottom, Right

We are working under the assumption that Reporting Services is installed on the local development machine. If you are running Reporting Services on a remote machine you may want to replace **localhost** *in the text of the TextBox with the name of your server or a placeholder such as* `<ServerName>` *to remind you that you need to specify the server.*

With all the controls you need on the form you now need to do some fine-tuning of the ListView and the MainMenu controls. Right click on the ListView control and select Properties. For the View property select Details from the drop-down list of choices. You need four columns in the ListView to display information about items in a folder. Click the Columns property in the property window and click the button with three dots to the right of (Collection), as shown in Figure 7-3:

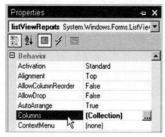

Figure 7-3

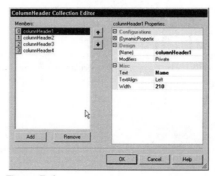

Figure 7-4

Using the ColumnHeader Collection Editor (shown in Figure 7-4), add four columns and set their properties as shown in the following table:

Name	Text	TextAlign	Width
columnHeader1	Name	Left	210
columnHeader2	Type	Left	66
columnHeader3	Size	Left	66
columnHeader4	Date Modified	Left	135

The final task required to make your form work is to add menu items to the MainMenu control you assigned to the form. The menu editor in Visual Studio .NET is intuitive and easy to use; just type where you are prompted to add menu items as shown in Figure 7-5:

Figure 7-5

The name of a menu item can be changed from the properties window. Using the Menu Editor and the properties window build the menu structure as outlined in the following table:

Menu Item Name	Text	Parent
menuItemFile	File	
menuItemEdit	Edit	
menuItemHelp	Help	
menuItemFileNew	New	menuItemFile
menuItemFileNewFolder	Folder	menuItemFileNew
menuItemFileNewDataSource	Data Source	menuItemFileNew
menuItemFileImport	Import Report	menuItemFile
menuItemFileExit	Exit	menuItemFile
menuItemEditDelete	Delete	menuItemEdit
menuItemSecurity	Security	
menuItemSecurityRoles	Roles	menuItemSecurity
menuItemSecuritySystemRoles	System Roles	menuItemSecurity
menuItemSecurityAssignments	Role Assignments	menuItemSecurity
menuItemSecuritySystemAssignments	System Role Assignments	menuItemSecurity
menuItemHelpAbout	About	menuItemHelp

This completes the look and basic construction of the main form of your application. Your `MainForm` should look similar to Figure 7-6:

Figure 7-6

Adding a Reference to the Web Service

Although the form looks correct, it is only a lifeless shell of what it needs to be. So like Gene Wilder in *Young Doctor Frankenstein* it is time to "..*give my creation LIFE!*"

In the Solution Explorer, right click on the Web Reference folder and select Add Web Reference from the menu and click the hyperlink Web services on the local machine as in Figure 7-7:

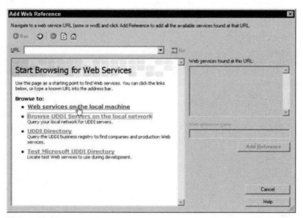

Figure 7-7

To use Reporting Services from a remote machine, you will need to enter the URL of the service in the URL textbox. The URL should be of the form http://machineName/ReportServer/ReportService.asmx.

From the list of web services on the machine, select **ReportService** as shown in Figure 7-8:

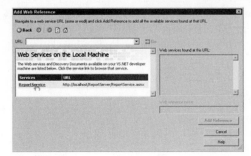

Figure 7-8

Change the web reference name to `ReportingWebService` and click the **Add Reference** button. The **Web References** folder should now look like Figure 7-9:

Figure 7-9

The process of adding the web reference to the project has created a *proxy* class in the project that is named `Reference.cs`. You can view the contents of this file by opening the **Solution Explorer**, clicking the **Show All Files** button as shown in Figure 7-10, and fully expanding the **ReportingWebService**. The proxy class does not contain the actual methods of the web service; it only has a template of the methods and the URL where the real methods can be found. When you use the web reference in design and during compilation you will be using the proxy class to assist with proper method syntax and parameters. The proxy class will then pass the information to the service at runtime.

Figure 7-10

Consuming the Web Service

Actually using the web service is where you begin to write some code for your application. First, add some namespaces and change the namespace for the form. Namespaces are the first lines of code in any class file. Namespace declarations appear above the line that declares the class.

C#

```
using System;
using System.Drawing;
using System.Collections;
using System.ComponentModel;
using System.Windows.Forms;
using System.Data;
using System.Web.Services.Protocols;
using Wrox.Professional.ReportingServices.ReportingWebService;
```

VB.NET

```
Imports System.Web.Services.Protocols
Imports Wrox.Professional.ReportingServices.ReportingWebService
```

Go back to the form **Design View** of `MainForm` and double click on the **Go** button. This will add an event handler for the click event of the button and take you to the code window with the new event handler in the window.

C#

```
private void buttonGo_Click(object sender, System.EventArgs e)
    {
        ConnectToServer();
    }
```

VB.NET

```
Private Sub buttonGo_Click(ByVal sender As System.Object,
                           ByVal e As System.EventArgs) Handles buttonGo.Click
        ConnectToServer()
End Sub
```

The `ConnectToServer` method will be where you perform the connection to the web service. A call to this method could have been placed immediately after the call to `InitializeComponent` in the constructor of `MainForm` but there are a couple of reasons for not doing that:

❑ Reporting Services is a .NET assembly. If the web service has not been called for a while, it takes time to load the assembly and run it through the JIT compiler. This will make your application slow to load. If you delay the connection until the form has loaded, your application will appear to be more responsive and you can show an hourglass to let the user know that something is happening while he waits for the service to respond.

❑ By waiting to connect until you explicitly call the connection method, you can put the name of any computer running the web service into your server address textbox and connect to the service on that computer upon clicking GO.

Create a private variable to hold a reference to the web service. You will use this private variable to call the methods of the service and to pass the connected web service to dialog forms for creating or editing items in the database.

C#

```csharp
/// <summary>
/// Required designer variable.
/// </summary>
private System.ComponentModel.Container components = null;
// User defined private variables
private ReportingService rs;
```

VB.NET

```vbnet
Public Class MainForm
    Inherits System.Windows.Forms.Form
    ' User defined private variables
    Private rs As ReportingService
```

Next add the `ConnectToServer` method to perform the actual connection. The meat of the work is done by setting your private variable to a new `ReportingService` object and setting the URL of the service to the URL you have entered in the server address text box.

C#

```csharp
private void ConnectToServer()
{
    string serverPath = textBoxServerPath.Text + "/ReportService.asmx";
    try
    {
        Cursor.Current = Cursors.WaitCursor;
        // Connect to Report Server
        rs = new ReportingService();
        // A production application would perform a complete check of
        //the url path
        rs.Url = serverPath;
    }
    catch (Exception ex)
    {
        RSUtilities.ErrorHandler(ex);
    }
    finally
    {
        Cursor.Current = Cursors.Default;
    }
}
```

VB.NET

```vbnet
Private Sub ConnectToServer()
    Dim serverPath As String = textBoxServerPath.Text + "/ReportService.asmx"
    Try
        Cursor.Current = Cursors.WaitCursor
        ' Connect to Report Server
```

```
            rs = New ReportingService()
            ' A production application would perform a complete check of
            ' the url path
            rs.Url = serverPath
      Catch ex As Exception
            RSUtilities.ErrorHandler(ex)
      Finally
            Cursor.Current = Cursors.Default
      End Try
   End Sub
```

Error handling is always a vital function of an application. As you are building a demonstration application and learning some new technology, a simple error handler for your application can help you debug problems as they occur. The web service you are consuming will throw SOAP exceptions if you try and call its methods improperly, so you should look specifically for a SoapException in your error handler.

Add a new class to the project and name it RSUtilities. You need to create a class with some static methods that you can call throughout the application to perform some common tasks associated with creating and modifying objects in the Reporting Services database.

Add the System.IO and Wrox.Professional.ReportingServices.ReportingWebService namespaces to the class file. As the class will be comprised of static methods, you won't actually need an instance of the class to use the methods; you will only need to reference its name. If you are writing your code in C#, you should delete the default constructor for the class. The default constructor is the section with the grey background in the following code:

```
public class RSUtilities
{
    public RSUtilities()
    {
      //
      // TODO: Add constructor logic here
      //
    }
}
```

Enter the following procedure to the RSUtilities class:

C#

```
private static void ErrorHandler(Exception ex)
{
  string exceptionText;
  // Find out if the exception is a SOAP exception and make
  //  use of the SOAP exception Detail property.
  if (ex is SoapException)
  {
      exceptionText = ((SoapException)ex).Detail["Message"].InnerXml;
  }
  else
  {
      exceptionText = ex.Message;
```

```
        }
    MessageBox.Show("An exception has occurred: " + exceptionText,
                "Application Error");
    }
```

VB.NET

```
Private  Shared Sub ErrorHandler(ByVal ex As Exception)
    Dim exceptionText As String
    ' Find out if the exception is a SOAP exception and make
    '  use of the SOAP exception Detail property.
    If TypeOf ex Is SoapException Then
        exceptionText = (CType(ex, SoapException)).Message
    Else
        exceptionText = ex.Message
    End If
    MessageBox.Show("An exception has occurred: " + exceptionText,
                "Application Error")
End Sub
```

Filling the Treeview

You can show the virtual folders in the Reporting Services database using **TreeView** similar to the way file system folders are shown in **Windows Explorer**. To accomplish this, open the code for `MainForm` and enter the following procedure.

C#

```
    private void GetServerFolders()
    {
        this.treeViewFolders.Nodes.Clear();

        CatalogItem[] items = null;
        try
        {
            items = rs.ListChildren("/", true);
        }
        catch (SoapException ex)
        {
            RSUtilities.ErrorHandler(ex);
        }
        TreeNode rootNode = new TreeNode("Report Server Folders");
        rootNode.Tag = "/";
        this.treeViewFolders.Nodes.Add(rootNode);
        foreach (CatalogItem item in items)
        {
            if (item.Type == ReportingWebService.ItemTypeEnum.Folder)
            {
                TreeNode newNode = new TreeNode(item.Name);
                newNode.Tag = item.Path.ToString() + "/";
                string parentPath =
                        item.Path.ToString().Replace(item.Name.ToString(), "");
```

```
                        AddNodeToTree(parentPath, newNode, rootNode);
                }
          }
    }
```

VB.NET

```vbnet
Private Sub GetServerFolders()
     Me.treeViewFolders.Nodes.Clear()

     Dim items() As CatalogItem = Nothing
     Try
          items = rs.ListChildren("/", True)
     Catch ex As SoapException
          RSUtilities.ErrorHandler(ex)
     End Try
     Dim rootNode As TreeNode = New TreeNode("Report Server Folders")
     rootNode.Tag = "/"
     Me.treeViewFolders.Nodes.Add(rootNode)
     Dim item As CatalogItem
     For Each item In items
          If item.Type = ReportingWebService.ItemTypeEnum.Folder Then
               Dim NewNode As TreeNode = New TreeNode(item.Name)
               NewNode.Tag = item.Path.ToString() + "/"
               Dim parentPath As String =
                              item.Path.ToString().Replace(item.Name.ToString(), "")
               AddNodeToTree(parentPath, NewNode, rootNode)
          End If
     Next
End Sub
```

Objects that can be contained in folders in a Reporting Services database are defined as objects of type CatalogItem. A CatalogItem can be a folder, report, resource (such as a graphic image), linked report, or a data source. Every CatalogItem has a number of standard properties:

- ❑ CreatedBy
- ❑ CreationDate
- ❑ ModifiedBy
- ❑ ModifiedData
- ❑ Name
- ❑ Path
- ❑ Size

These properties can be returned directly from the item. For a complete list of the properties of a CatalogItem and their purposes, refer to the Reporting Services Books Online.

The GetServerFolders procedure will clear all the nodes from the TreeView and call the web method ListChildren that gets an array of all the CatalogItems that are in the Reporting Services database. Then call the ListChildren method with rs.ListChildren (/, true). The first argument is a string indicating the path of the folder you want as the source for your list. You can use the root folder, which always has a value of /. The `boolean` argument indicates if you want the list to be *recursive*, meaning you want to see not only the children of an item, but also any grand children, great grand children and so on. To show all the folders in the database pass `true` for this argument.

The array of `CatalogItems` is, in essence, a read-only list of the items that the current user has permission to see in the database. New objects of type `CatalogItem` cannot be added directly to Reporting Services. To add items to the database it is necessary to create an object of the type you wish to add and then call the `add` method specific to that object type. Adding objects will be covered when we discuss adding folders and data sources.

With an array of every item that is in the database you then need to loop through the array one item at a time to find which items are folders and then add them to the tree.

The actual addition of a node to the TreeView is done with the `AddNodeToTree` procedure shown below. The TreeView control in the .NET Framework has a very rigid hierarchy. The TreeView itself only holds the nodes that are at the root level. All the other nodes are contained by their parent node. The result of this structure is that you need to use a recursive routine to traverse all the nodes and find where any given new node should be added. You are storing the path of where a node belongs in the tree into the `Tag` property for each node. The routine can then examine the contents of the `Tag` property of any node to see if it matches the destination path of the node to be added. When a match is found, the new node is added to the collection of child nodes of the tree node, which is being examined.

C#

```csharp
private void AddNodeToTree(string parentPath, TreeNode childNode, TreeNode
searchNode)
{
      if (parentPath == searchNode.Tag.ToString())
      {
          searchNode.Nodes.Add(childNode);
      }
      else
      {
          TreeNodeCollection  treeNodes = searchNode.Nodes;
          foreach(TreeNode node in treeNodes)
          {
              if (node.Tag.ToString() == parentPath.ToString())
              {
                  node.Nodes.Add(childNode);
              }
              else
              {
                  if ( node.Nodes.Count > 0)
                  {
                      AddNodeToTree(parentPath, childNode, node);
                  }
              }
          }
      }
      return;
}
```

VB.NET

```
Private Sub AddNodeToTree(ByVal parentPath As String, ByVal childNode As TreeNode,
                          ByVal searchNode As TreeNode)
    If parentPath = searchNode.Tag.ToString() Then
        searchNode.Nodes.Add(childNode)
    Else
        Dim treeNodes As TreeNodeCollection = searchNode.Nodes
        Dim node As TreeNode
        For Each node In treeNodes
            If node.Tag.ToString() = parentPath.ToString() Then
                node.Nodes.Add(childNode)
            Else
                If node.Nodes.Count > 0 Then
                    AddNodeToTree(parentPath, childNode, node)
                End If
            End If
        Next
    End If
    Return
End Sub
```

Make a change to the `ConnectToServer` procedure you created earlier so that after you connect to the server the TreeView will automatically be filled.

C#

```
private void ConnectToServer()
{
    string serverPath = textBoxServerPath.Text + "/ReportService.asmx";
    try
    {
        Cursor.Current = Cursors.WaitCursor;
        // Connect to Report Server
        rs = new ReportingService();
        // A production application would perform a complete check of
        //the url path
        rs.Url = serverPath;
        GetServerFolders();
    }
    catch (Exception ex)
    {
        RSUtilities.ErrorHandler(ex);
    }
    finally
    {
        Cursor.Current = Cursors.Default;
    }
}
```

VB.NET

```
Private Sub ConnectToServer()
    Dim serverPath As String = textBoxServerPath.Text + /ReportService.asmx"
    Try
```

```
             Cursor.Current = Cursors.WaitCursor
             ' Connect to Report Server
             rs = New ReportingService
             ' A production application would perform a complete check of
             'the url path
             rs.Url = serverPath
             GetServerFolders()
        Catch ex As Exception
             RSUtilities.ErrorHandler(ex)
        Finally
             Cursor.Current = Cursors.Default
        End Try
    End Sub
```

After saving the project, start the project to see what happens. After the project starts, click the Go button to fill the **TreeView**. Figure 7-11 shows the result of trying to call the web service without the proper credentials:

Figure 7-11

Credentials

This actually was not a mistake. When you created the `ConnectToServer` procedure you ignored an important item and this error gives us an opportunity to discuss it. By default when Reporting Services is installed the virtual web folder is created with *Anonymous* access disabled and authentication is set to **Integrated Windows authentication**. Why would this be? Remember from the previous chapter that you can set security on any object in the server. If Anonymous access was enabled you would have everyone trying to access the service identified as IUSER_<computerName> and granting or denying an individual user access would be problematic. Using integrated security permits the service to capture the identity of a user from the browser header information.

So to use the web service properly you need to tell the service who you are. The .NET Framework provides a whole set of classes to handle identity and credential issues.

Add the following namespace to the header of the `MainForm` code file:

C#

```
using System;
using System.Drawing;
using System.Collections;
using System.ComponentModel;
using System.Windows.Forms;
using System.Data;
```

```
using System.Net;
using System.Web.Services.Protocols;
using Wrox.Professional.ReportingServices.ReportingWebService;
```

VB.NET

```
Imports System.Net
Imports System.Web.Services.Protocols
Imports Wrox.Professional.ReportingServices.ReportingWebService
```

Then change the ConnectToServer procedure as shown in the following code:

C#

```
private void ConnectToServer()
{
        string serverPath = textBoxServerPath.Text + "/ReportService.asmx";
        try
        {
            Cursor.Current = Cursors.WaitCursor;
            // Connect to Report Server
            rs = new ReportingService();
            rs.Credentials = System.Net.CredentialCache.DefaultCredentials;
            // A production application would perform a complete check of
            //the url path
            rs.Url = serverPath;
            GetServerFolders();
        }
        catch (Exception ex)
        {
            RSUtilities.ErrorHandler(ex);
        }
        finally
        {
            Cursor.Current = Cursors.Default;
        }
}
```

VB.NET

```
Private Sub ConnectToServer()
    Dim serverPath As String = textBoxServerPath.Text +"/ReportService.asmx"
    Try
        Cursor.Current = Cursors.WaitCursor
        ' Connect to Report Server
        rs = New ReportingService
        rs.Credentials = System.Net.CredentialCache.DefaultCredentials
        ' A production application would perform a complete check of
        'the url path
        rs.Url = serverPath
        GetServerFolders()
    Catch ex As Exception
        RSUtilities.ErrorHandler(ex)
    Finally
        Cursor.Current = Cursors.Default
    End Try
End Sub
```

The effect of this new line of code is to take the credentials of the current user and pass them to the web service. You could also do some error trapping around this new line of code to see if the default credentials have access to the service. If the default credential fails, you could create a form to prompt the user for valid credentials. Of course it is also possible to not supply any credentials as done before, but you should provide a method to demand credentials from the user before the service can be used. For more information on .NET authentication and authorization refer to the .NET Framework and Visual Studio documentation on the `System.Net` namespace.

After adding your credentials to the to the `ConnectToServer` procedure you should be able to run the application and see any folders that have been added to the service.

Displaying the Folder Contents

This would also be a good time to add some code to display the child items of a folder in the ListView control.

Add the following procedure to the code file of `MainForm`:

C#

```
private void DisplayFolderContents( string path )
{
    if (path != "/")
    {
        path = path.Substring(0, path.Length -1);
    }
    CatalogItem[] catalogItems = null;
    Cursor.Current = Cursors.WaitCursor;
    listViewReports.Items.Clear();
    catalogItems = rs.ListChildren(path, false);
    try
    {
        // Main part of method
        if (catalogItems != null)
        {
            foreach ( CatalogItem item in catalogItems )
            {
                // Create a ListView item containing a CatalogItem
                ListViewItem newItem = new ListViewItem(item.Name);
                newItem.Tag = item.Path.ToString();
                newItem.SubItems.Add(item.Type.ToString());
                newItem.SubItems.Add(item.Size.ToString());
                newItem.SubItems.Add(item.ModifiedDate.ToShortDateString()
                            + " " + item.ModifiedDate.ToShortTimeString());
                listViewReports.Items.Add(newItem);
            }
        }
    }
    catch (Exception ex)
    {
        RSUtilities.ErrorHandler(ex);
```

```
        }
        finally
        {
            Cursor.Current = Cursors.Default;
        }
    }
```

VB.NET

```
    Private Sub DisplayFolderContents(ByVal path As String)
        If path <> "/" Then
            path = path.Substring(0, path.Length - 1)
        End If
        Dim catalogItems() As CatalogItem = Nothing
        Cursor.Current = Cursors.WaitCursor
        listViewReports.Items.Clear()
        catalogItems = rs.ListChildren(path, False)
        Try
            ' Main part of method
            If Not catalogItems Is Nothing Then
                Dim item As CatalogItem
                For Each item In catalogItems
                    ' Create a ListView item containing a CatalogItem
                    Dim NewItem As ListViewItem = New ListViewItem(item.Name)
                    NewItem.Tag = item.Path.ToString()
                    NewItem.SubItems.Add(item.Type.ToString())
                    NewItem.SubItems.Add(item.Size.ToString())
                    NewItem.SubItems.Add(item.ModifiedDate.ToShortDateString() + " " +
                                    item.ModifiedDate.ToShortTimeString())
                    listViewReports.Items.Add(NewItem)
                Next
            End If
        Catch ex As Exception
            RSUtilities.ErrorHandler(ex)
        Finally
            Cursor.Current = Cursors.Default
        End Try
    End Sub
```

The key to display the contents of a folder is the call to the web method `ListChildren`. Make this call with the code `rs.ListChildren(path, false)`. The `path` argument is the path of the folder that you want to work with. For the boolean argument pass the value of `false`. When you filled the TreeView you wanted the method to give you a list of all child generations in the database. For the ListView you only need to see the direct children of the folder you have selected. The code also examines some of the properties of each `CatalogItem` (`Name`, `Type`, `Size`, and `ModifiedDate`) and uses the property values to fill the ListView information.

To call this procedure you need to create an event handler for the TreeView control. Open the Design View of `MainForm` and double click on the TreeView control. This will open the code for the form and give you an empty event handler for the `treeViewFolders_AferSelect` event.

Insert the following code into the event handler:

C#

```
private void treeViewFolders_AfterSelect(object sender,
                                    System.Windows.Forms.TreeViewEventArgs e)
{
    TreeNode node = treeViewFolders.SelectedNode;
    string path = node.Tag.ToString();
    DisplayFolderContents(path);
}
```

VB.NET

```
Private Sub treeViewFolders_AfterSelect(ByVal sender As System.Object,
                        ByVal e As System.Windows.Forms.TreeViewEventArgs)
                    Handles treeViewFolders.AfterSelect
    Dim node As TreeNode = treeViewFolders.SelectedNode
    Dim path As String = node.Tag.ToString()
    DisplayFolderContents(path)
End Sub
```

The first line you added grabs a reference to the currently selected node in the tree. From this node you get the Reporting Services path from where it has been stored in the `tag` property. Finally call the `DispalyFolderContents` procedure you created above to show the contents of the selected folder. Run the application and click on the **Go** button to fill the **TreeView**. When the **TreeView** shows the folder structure select any folder and the **ListView** will display the contents of the folder as in Figure 7-12:

Figure 7-12

Adding/Updating Folders

While this looks good, it will currently only show you what already exists in the Reporting Services database. To really make this application useful for managing Reporting Services, you need to be able to add, edit, or delete objects in the database. With this in mind let's make changes to the application to make it more powerful.

Add the following code to the RSUtilities class:

C#

```csharp
public enum EditModeEnum
{
    add,
    edit
}

public static Property CreateProperty(string Name, string Value)
{
    Property property = new Property();
    property.Name = Name;
    property.Value = Value;
    return property;
}

public static Property[] CreatePropertyArray(int MemberCount)
{
    Property[] properties = new Property[MemberCount];
    return properties;
}
public static void SetProperty(string Name, string Value, Property[] properties)
{
    foreach (Property property in Properties)
    {
        if (property.Name == Name)
        {
            property.Value = Value;
            return;
        }
    }
    return;
}
```

VB.NET

```vbnet
Public Enum EditModeEnum
    add
    edit
End Enum

Public Shared Function CreateProperty(ByVal Name As String, _
                      ByVal Value As String) As ReportingWebService.Property
    Dim prop As ReportingWebService.Property = New ReportingWebService.Property
    prop.Name = Name
    prop.Value = Value
    Return prop
 End Function

Public Shared Function CreatePropertyArray(ByVal MemberCount As Integer) _
                As ReportingWebService.Property()
    Dim properties(MemberCount - 1) As ReportingWebService.Property
    Return properties
End Function

Public Shared Sub SetProperty(ByVal Name As String, ByVal Value As String, _
```

```
                              ByVal properties() As ReportingWebService.Property)
        Dim prop As ReportingWebService.Property
        For Each prop In properties
            If prop.Name = Name Then
                prop.Value = Value
           Return
              End If
        Next
        Return
    End Sub
```

You can use the `EditModeEnum` enumeration to set the mode for forms. This way you should be able to use the same form to add a new folder or update the information in an existing folder.

Reporting Services uses a properties collection to hold and manage information about objects in the database. While a `CatalogItem` has a description property, it cannot be set directly. To set the description property of an object, you must do the following:

1. Create a properties array.

2. Set the description property in the array.

3. Assign the properties array back to the item you want to work with.

You will need to do a lot of work with the properties array of an item. The three methods you will be using to manage item properties are as follows:

❑ `SetProperty`

❑ `CreateProperty`

❑ `CreatePropertyArray`

Folder Form

Add a new form to the application and name it `FolderForm`. Add two label controls, two textbox controls, and two button controls to the form and arrange the controls as in Figure 7-13:

Figure 7-13

Name the textboxes `textBoxName` and `textBoxDesctiption`. Name the buttons `buttonOK` and `buttonCancel`. Be sure to set the multiline property of `textBoxDescription` to `true`.

To pass information to the `FolderForm`, you are going to create some public properties of the form. To hold the property information you need to declare some private variables.

Open the code file for the form and add the following code above the default constructor of the form:

C#

```
// Private form variables
private string folderPath = "";
private string folderName = "";
private ReportingService rsWebService = null;
private RSUtilities.EditModeEnum mode;
```

VB.NET

```
Imports Wrox.Professional.ReportingServices.ReportingWebService

Public Class FolderForm
    Inherits System.Windows.Forms.Form
    ' Private form variables
    Private mFolderPath As String = ""
    Private mFolderName As String = ""
    Private mRsWebService As ReportingService
    Private mMode As RSUtilities.EditModeEnum
```

These private variables will be used by the property routines to hold the state of each property. Now add the following property procedures to the class below the constructor and the `Dispose` procedure.

C#

```
public ReportingService RsWebService
{
    set
    {
        rsWebService = value;
    }
}

public string FolderPath
{
    get
    {
        return folderPath;
    }
    set
    {
        string path = value.Substring(0, value.Length - 1);
        if (path == String.Empty)
        {
            path = "/";
        }
        folderPath = path;
    }
}
```

```csharp
public string FolderName
{
      get
      {
          return this.textBoxName.Text;
      }
      set
      {
          folderName = value;
          this.textBoxName.Text = folderName;
          this.textBoxName.Tag = folderName;
      }
}
public RSUtilities.EditModeEnum Mode
{
      get
      {
          return mode;
      }
      set
      {
          mode = value;
          string label = "";
          switch (value)
          {
                case RSUtilities.EditModeEnum.add:
                    label = "Add";
                    break;
                case RSUtilities.EditModeEnum.edit:
                    label = "Update";
                    break;
          }
          this.buttonOK.Text = label;
      }
  }
```

VB.NET

```vbnet
Public WriteOnly Property RsWebService() As ReportingService
        Set(ByVal Value As ReportingService)
         mRsWebService = Value
        End Set
End Property

Public Property FolderPath() As String
     Get
          Return mFolderPath
     End Get
     Set(ByVal Value As String)
         Dim path As String = Value.Substring(0, Value.Length - 1)
         If path = String.Empty Then
             path = "/"
         End If
```

```
            mFolderPath = path
        End Set
End Property

Public Property FolderName() As String
    Get
        Return Me.textBoxName.Text
    End Get
    Set(ByVal Value As String)
        mFolderName = Value
        Me.textBoxName.Text = mFolderName
        Me.textBoxName.Tag = mFolderName
    End Set
End Property
Public Property Mode() As RSUtilities.EditModeEnum
    Get
        Return mMode
    End Get
    Set(ByVal Value As RSUtilities.EditModeEnum)
        mMode = value
        Dim label As String = ""
        Select Case value
            Case RSUtilities.EditModeEnum.add
                label = "Add"
                Exit Property
            Case RSUtilities.EditModeEnum.edit
                label = "Update"
                Exit Property
        End Select
        Me.buttonOK.Text = label
    End Set
End Property
```

The OK button will look at the mode of the form to determine if the information the form contains relates to a new folder or to a folder that already exists in the Reporting Services database.

C#

```csharp
private void buttonOK_Click(object sender, System.EventArgs e)
{
        if (this.textBoxName.Text == String.Empty ||
                this.FolderPath == String.Empty)
        {
            throw new ArgumentException("Invalid input parameter");
        }
        else if (this.rsWebService == null)
        {
            throw new Exception("Web Service reference not set");
        }
        else
        {
            if (this.mode == RSUtilities.EditModeEnum.add)
            {
                AddFolder();
```

```
            }
            else
            {
                UpdateFolder();
            }
            this.Close();
        }
    }
```

VB.NET

```vbnet
Private Sub buttonOK_Click(ByVal sender As Object, ByVal e As System.EventArgs)
                          Handles buttonOK.Click
    If (Me.textBoxName.Text = String.Empty Or Me.FolderPath = String.Empty) Then
        Throw New ArgumentException("Invalid input parameter")
    ElseIf mRsWebService Is Nothing Then
        Throw New Exception("Web Service reference not set")
    Else
        If Me.Mode = RSUtilities.EditModeEnum.add Then
            AddFolder()
        Else
            UpdateFolder()
        End If
        Me.Close()
    End If
End Sub
```

C#

```csharp
private void AddFolder()
{
    try
    {
        //Create Property array for description
        Property[] rsProperties = RSUtilities.CreatePropertyArray(1);
        rsProperties[0] = RSUtilities.CreateProperty("Description",
                        this.textBoxDescription.Text);

        //Call RS CreateFolder() base method
        rsWebService.CreateFolder(this.textBoxName.Text,
                                this.FolderPath, rsProperties);
    }
    catch (Exception)
    {
        throw new ApplicationException("Add operation failed");
    }
    return;
}
```

VB.NET

```vbnet
Private Sub AddFolder()
    Try
        'Create Property array for description
        Dim rsProperties() As ReportingWebService.Property =
```

```
                    RSUtilities.CreatePropertyArray(1)
        rsProperties(0) = RSUtilities.CreateProperty("Description",
                Me.textBoxDescription.Text)

        'Call RS CreateFolder() base method
        mRsWebService.CreateFolder(Me.textBoxName.Text, Me.FolderPath,
                rsProperties)
    Catch
        Throw New ApplicationException("Add operation failed")
    End Try
    Return
End Sub
```

The AddFolder method calls the web service CreateFolder method. CreateFolder takes the name of
the folder, its path and properties as arguments. Since you need to set the description property of the
folder you have to use the property methods of RSUtilities first to create an array of properties and
then to add a Description property to the array.

C#

```csharp
private void UpdateFolder()
{
        Property[] properties = RSUtilities.CreatePropertyArray(1);
        properties[0] = RSUtilities.CreateProperty("Description",
    this.textBoxDescription.Text);
        try
        {
            string oldPath = folderPath + "/" +
                            this.textBoxName.Tag.ToString();
            string newPath = folderPath + "/" +
                            this.FolderName;
            // Rename Item and Create new Properties based on old properties
            // Create batch header
            BatchHeader batchHeader = new BatchHeader();
            // Set EditItem batch id and top BatchHeaderValue
            batchHeader.BatchID = rsWebService.CreateBatch();
            rsWebService.BatchHeaderValue = batchHeader;
            // update the folder info inside a transaction
            rsWebService.MoveItem(oldPath, newPath);
            rsWebService.SetProperties(newPath, properties);

            // Rollback transaction if either method fails
            rsWebService.ExecuteBatch();
            rsWebService.BatchHeaderValue = null;
        }
        catch (Exception)
        {
            throw new ApplicationException("Update operation failed");
        }
    }
}
```

VB.NET

```vbnet
Private Sub UpdateFolder()
    Dim properties() As ReportingWebService.Property =
```

```
                    RSUtilities.CreatePropertyArray(1)
        properties(0) = RSUtilities.CreateProperty("Description",
                    Me.textBoxDescription.Text)
    Try
        Dim oldPath As String = Me.FolderPath + "/" +
                            Me.textBoxName.Tag.ToString()
        Dim newPath As String = Me.FolderPath + "/" + Me.FolderName
        ' Rename Item and Create new Properties based on old properties
        ' Create batch header
        Dim batchHeader As batchHeader = New batchHeader
        ' Set EditItem batch id and top BatchHeaderValue
        batchHeader.BatchID = mRsWebService.CreateBatch()
        mRsWebService.BatchHeaderValue = batchHeader
        ' update the folder info inside a transaction
        mRsWebService.MoveItem(oldPath, newPath)
        mRsWebService.SetProperties(newPath, properties)
        ' Rollback transaction if either method fails
        mRsWebService.ExecuteBatch()
        mRsWebService.BatchHeaderValue = Nothing
    Catch
        Throw New ApplicationException("Update operation failed")
    End Try
End Sub
```

The `UpdateFolder` method introduces the Reporting Services concept of a batch and transaction. Let's take a step back for a moment to discuss transactions.

Imagine that you are going to lunch at your favorite restaurant and you need cash. There is an ATM on the way to the restaurant at which you stop to get some money from your checking account. You enter your PIN and indicate that you want to withdraw $100 from your checking account. Hitting the enter button begins a series of individual tasks (verifying that you have money in your account, debiting your account for the amount being withdrawn, crediting the ATM machine that amount and dispensing your cash) which are treated as a single transaction. Immediately after you hit the enter button a truck coming down the street loses control and crashes into the ATM machine. You saw the truck coming out of the corner of your eye and were able to jump out of the way, but the ATM was not so lucky. The ATM has been ripped from its base and now appears to be dead. What happened to your money? This is the time you are really grateful that your bank uses the concept of a transaction when handling electronic funds. If any part of the transaction fails to complete (in this case the ATM dispensing money to you) each element of the transaction cancelled or rolled back.

Reporting Services information is stored in a database. Good practice dictates that all updates or deletions to data in a database should be wrapped in a transaction to make sure that no data is lost in the event that something interrupts the process. Reporting Services uses a `Batch` object to contain all of the changes to be made to the database. Remember that you are not directly manipulating the information in the database, but asking some remote object to make these changes for you. Transmitting the transaction information to the web service in the batch object gives the service all the information it needs so that the change can all be wrapped in a SQL Server transaction.

The folder form is almost complete. You'll be using this form to add new folders to Reporting Services as well as update existing folders. You already created a property of the form that you named `Mode` to indicate if the form is new or an existing item that you are editing. To complete the form you need to get all the information you know about the folder and load it into the controls of the form. You are going to load the form as a modal dialog box, which will not relinquish focus until the form is closed. This allows you to use the activated event, which fires when the form is first visible on the screen, to see if the form is in the edit mode. If the form is in the edit mode you can get information about the folder from Reporting Services and load it into the form.

Open the Windows Form Designer generated code region of FolderForm and find the section labeled // FolderForm and add the following line of code after the last line in the section.

C#

```
this.Activated += new EventHandler(FolderForm_Activated);
```

Adding an event handler in VB.NET is much easier and more intuitive than in C#. From the code window for FolderForm just below the title bar select **FolderForm Events** in the left hand combo box. In the right hand combo box select the event you want to trap. Figure 7-14 is an example of how the event handler is created for the FolderForm.Activated event:

Figure 7-14

This will declare the event handler for the form **Activated** event. You also need to add the event handler using the following code:

C#

```csharp
private void FolderForm_Activated(object sender, EventArgs e)
{
    // look to see in the form has been placed in the edit mode
    if (this.Mode == RSUtilities.EditModeEnum.edit)
    {
        string path = this.folderPath + "/" + this.folderName;
        Property[] properties = rsWebService.GetProperties(path, null);
        foreach (Property property in properties)
        {
            if (property.Name == "Description")
            {
                if (property.Value != null)
                    this.textBoxDescription.Text = property.Value.ToString();
            }
        }
    }
}
```

VB.NET

```vbnet
Private Sub FolderForm_Activated(ByVal sender As Object,
                      ByVal e As System.EventArgs)
                      Handles MyBase.Activated
```

```
          ' look to see in the form has been placed in the edit mode
      If mMode = RSUtilities.EditModeEnum.edit Then
          Dim path As String = Me.FolderPath + "/" + Me.FolderName
          Dim properties() As ReportingWebService.Property =
                          mRsWebService.GetProperties(path, Nothing)
          Dim prop As ReportingWebService.Property
          For Each prop In properties
              If prop.Name = "Description" Then
                  If Not prop.Value Is Nothing Then
                      Me.textBoxDescription.Text = prop.Value.ToString()
                  End If
              End If
          Next
      End If
  End Sub
```

The event handler is pretty straightforward. First it looks to see if the form has been placed in the edit mode; if not, the entire routine is skipped. If the edit mode has been set, you then get the path of the parent folder, append the separator and the name of the folder to it, and call the `GetProperties` method of the web service to retrieve the properties of the folder. This form is pretty simple and you are only setting the `Description` property of the folder, so you loop through all the properties until you find this property and then place its value of the `Description` property into the description text box.

Now you have a fully functional folder form but no way to call it. Open the **Design View** of `MainForm` and click on the **File** menu to expand its members. Click on the **New** menu item and double click on the **Folder** menu item. This declares a `menuItemFileNewFolder` event and creates a procedure named `menuItemFileNewFolder_Click` to handle this event. Add the following code to the new event handler:

C#

```
private void menuItemFileNewFolder_Click(object sender, System.EventArgs e)
{
      FolderForm dialogForm = new FolderForm();
      string path = this.treeViewFolders.SelectedNode.Tag.ToString();
      dialogForm.FolderPath = path;
      dialogForm.RsWebService = rs;
      dialogForm.ShowDialog(this);
      // folder has been added show it in the tree
      string folderName = dialogForm.FolderName;
      TreeNode newFolder = new TreeNode(folderName);
      newFolder.Tag = path + folderName + "/";
      TreeNode parentFolder = this.treeViewFolders.SelectedNode;
      parentFolder.Nodes.Add(newFolder);

      // refresh the tree to show the new folder
      this.treeViewFolders.Refresh();
      // refresh the listview
      DisplayFolderContents(path);

      // dispose of the local form variable
      dialogForm.Dispose();
}
```

VB.NET

```
Private Sub menuItemFileNewFolder_Click(ByVal sender As System.Object,
                ByVal e As System.EventArgs) Handles menuItemFileNewFolder.Click
    Dim dialogForm As FolderForm = New FolderForm
    Dim path As String = Me.treeViewFolders.SelectedNode.Tag.ToString()
    dialogForm.FolderPath = path
    dialogForm.RsWebService = rs
    dialogForm.ShowDialog(Me)
    ' folder has been added show it in the tree
    Dim folderName As String = dialogForm.FolderName
    Dim NewFolder As TreeNode = New TreeNode(folderName)
    NewFolder.Tag = path + folderName + "/"
    Dim parentFolder As TreeNode = Me.treeViewFolders.SelectedNode
    parentFolder.Nodes.Add(NewFolder)

    ' refresh the tree to show the new folder
    Me.treeViewFolders.Refresh()
    ' refresh the listview
    DisplayFolderContents(path)

    ' dispose of the local form variable
    dialogForm.Dispose()
End Sub
```

The `menuItemFileNewFolder_Click` event handler perfoms the following actions:

1. Declare `dialogForm` as a new instance of the `FolderForm` class

2. Get the path of the selected TreeView node from its `Tag` property

3. Assign the path to the `FolderPath` property of the `dialogForm`

4. Assign the local instance of the web service to the `RsWebService` property of `dialogForm`

5. Open `dialogForm` as a modal dialog box

After the dialog box has closed, the data from the form will be used to create a new TreeView node, which represents this new folder. Finally the TreeView and ListView will both be refreshed.

You also need a way to initiate an edit session of existing item in a folder. In Windows Explorer you expect to double click on an item to open it, so let's implement similar functionality into our application. In order to do this you need to open the code region labeled Windows Form Designer generated code. After expanding this code region, go to the area labeled listViewReports and add an event handler for the double click event as shown:

C#

```
//
// listViewReports
//
this.listViewReports.Anchor =
((System.Windows.Forms.AnchorStyles)((((System.Windows.Forms.AnchorStyles.Top
    System.Windows.Forms.AnchorStyles.Bottom)
    System.Windows.Forms.AnchorStyles.Left)
```

```
                System.Windows.Forms.AnchorStyles.Right)));
    this.listViewReports.Columns.AddRange(new System.Windows.Forms.ColumnHeader[] {
                    this.columnHeader1,
                    this.columnHeader2,
                    this.columnHeader3,
                    this.columnHeader4});
    this.listViewReports.Location = new System.Drawing.Point(288, 40);
    this.listViewReports.Name = "listViewReports";
    this.listViewReports.Size = new System.Drawing.Size(480, 288);
    this.listViewReports.TabIndex = 1;
    this.listViewReports.View = System.Windows.Forms.View.Details;
    this.listViewReports.DoubleClick += new EventHandler(listViewReports_DoubleClick
) ;
    //
    // columnHeader1
```

Again adding this event handler in VB.NET is much easier and more intuitive than in C#. In the `MainForm` code window select listViewReports in the left combo box and double click in the right combo box.

You now need to create the event handler for the double click event. As this event handler will handle the double click event for any items in the ListView, you need to examine what type of item you have selected and then deal with each possible item type. Add the following code to the `MainForm`:

C#

```
private void listViewReports_DoubleClick(object sender, EventArgs e)
{
    string path = this.treeViewFolders.SelectedNode.Tag.ToString();
    ListViewItem item = this.listViewReports.SelectedItems[0];
    string itemType = item.SubItems[1].Text.ToString();
    switch (itemType)
    {
        case "Folder":
            OpenFolder(path, item.Text);
            break;
        case "DataSource":
            OpenDataSource(path, item.Text);
            break;
        case "Report":
            OpenReport(path, item.Text);
            break;
    }
    return;
}
```

VB.NET

```
Private Sub listViewReports_DoubleClick(ByVal sender As Object, _
                            ByVal e As System.EventArgs) Handles _
                            listViewReports.DoubleClick
    Dim path As String = Me.treeViewFolders.SelectedNode.Tag.ToString()
    Dim item As ListViewItem = Me.listViewReports.SelectedItems(0)
    Dim itemType As String = item.SubItems(1).Text.ToString()
```

```
            Select Case itemType
                Case "Folder"
                    OpenFolder(path, item.Text)
                    Exit Sub
                Case "DataSource"
                    OpenDataSource(path, item.Text)
                    Exit Sub
                Case "Report"
                    OpenReport(path, item.Text)
                    Exit Sub
            End Select
            Return
    End Sub
```

Now you will create the methods to handle each of the item types. The `OpenFolder` method will be the only one with code for the moment. Creating the stubs to handle reports and data sources will now allow the application to run and you can fill in the details of these methods, as required.

C#

```csharp
private void OpenFolder(string Path, string FolderName)
{
        FolderForm frm = new FolderForm();
        // set the form properties to set the folder that we
        // will be working with.
        frm.FolderPath = Path;
        frm.FolderName = FolderName;
        frm.RsWebService = this.rs;
        // set the edit mode of the form
        frm.Mode = RSUtilities.EditModeEnum.edit;
        // show the form that now has now had all properties set.
        frm.ShowDialog(this);
        // refresh the contents of the list view after the dialog closes.
        DisplayFolderContents(
        this.treeViewFolders.SelectedNode.Tag.ToString());
}

private void OpenDataSource(string Path, string DataSourceName)
{
        return;
}

private void OpenReport(string Path, string ReportName)
{
        return;
}
```

VB.NET

```vbnet
Private Sub OpenFolder(ByVal Path As String, ByVal FolderName As String)
        Dim frm As FolderForm = New FolderForm
        ' set the form properties to set the folder that we
        ' will be working with.
        frm.FolderPath = Path
```

```
        frm.FolderName = FolderName
        frm.RsWebService = Me.rs
        ' set the edit mode of the form
        frm.Mode = RSUtilities.EditModeEnum.edit
        ' show the form that now has now had all properties set.
        frm.ShowDialog(Me)
        ' refresh the contents of the list view after the dialog closes.
        DisplayFolderContents(Me.treeViewFolders.SelectedNode.Tag.ToString())
    End Sub

    Private Sub OpenDataSource(ByVal Path As String, ByVal DataSourceName As String)
        Return
    End Sub

    Private Sub OpenReport(ByVal Path As String, ByVal ReportName As String)
        Return
    End Sub
```

You are finally ready to try out your code to add a new folder. Run the application and click the Go button to fill the TreeView with the folders in Reporting Services. Expand the tree and click on the Professional SQL Reporting Services folder. From the File menu select New Folder. Enter your information for the folder you are creating and click the Add button as shown in Figure 7-15:

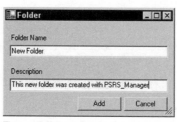

Figure 7-15

The main form should now show your new folder in the ListView and the TreeView will have a + sign in front of Professional SQL Reporting Services indicating that there is a child folder below it. You could also launch the Report Manager web application and see the new folder from that tool. Be sure to double click on the newly created folder to open it in the edit mode and modify either its name or description to verify that the edit procedures work, as in Figure 7-16:

Figure 7-16

Deleting an Item from a Folder

Before moving on to items other than folders you should investigate how folders as well as other items can be deleted from Reporting Services. Open `MainForm` in the **Design View**, expand the **Edit** menu, and double click on **Delete** menu item. This will create an event handler for the click event of this menu item. Into the newly created `menuItemEditDelete_Click` method, add the following code:

C#

```
private void menuItemEditDelete_Click(object sender, System.EventArgs e)
{
        DeleteServerItems();
}
```

VB.NET

```
Private Sub menuItemEditDelete_Click(ByVal sender As Object, ByVal e As
System.EventArgs) Handles menuItemEditDelete.Click
        DeleteServerItems()
End Sub
```

Now add the method to perform the actual deletion of the item:

C#

```
private void DeleteServerItems()
{
        if (this.listViewReports.SelectedItems.Count > 0)
        {
            bool wasFolder = false;
            string message =
                "Are you certain you want to delete the selected item(s)?";
            DialogResult result = MessageBox.Show(
                        this, message, "PSRS_Manager",
                        MessageBoxButtons.YesNo, MessageBoxIcon.Question);
            if (result == DialogResult.Yes)
            {
                Cursor.Current = Cursors.WaitCursor;
                string path = this.treeViewFolders.SelectedNode.Tag.ToString();
                try
                {
                    // Set up a reporting services batch to handle the
                    //deletes as a transaction
                    BatchHeader batchHeader = new BatchHeader();
                    batchHeader.BatchID = this.rs.CreateBatch();
                    this.rs.BatchHeaderValue = batchHeader;
                    // Call the delete items
                    foreach (ListViewItem item in
                            this.listViewReports.SelectedItems)
                    {
                        if (item.SubItems[1].Text == "Folder")
                        {
                            wasFolder = true;
                        }
```

```
                        string itemName = path + item.Text;
                        this.rs.DeleteItem(itemName);
                }
                // all the items have been marked for deletion.
                // Execute the batch.
                this.rs.ExecuteBatch();
                this.rs.BatchHeaderValue = null;
            }
            catch (Exception exp)
            {
                RSUtilities.ErrorHandler(exp);
            }
            finally
            {
                Cursor.Current = Cursors.Default;
            }
            if (wasFolder)
            {
                this.GetServerFolders();
                this.listViewReports.Items.Clear();
            }
            else
            {
                // refill the list view with the current list of
                // items
                DisplayFolderContents(
                        this.treeViewFolders.SelectedNode.Tag.ToString());
            }
        }
    }
    else
    {
        MessageBox.Show("Select an item in the list view to delete.");
        return;
    }
}
```

VB.NET

```
Private Sub DeleteServerItems()
    If Me.listViewReports.SelectedItems.Count > 0 Then
        Dim wasFolder As Boolean = False
        Dim message As String
        Dim result As DialogResult
        message = "Are you certain you want to delete the selected item(s)?"
        result = MessageBox.Show(Me, message, "PSRS_Manager", _
                            MessageBoxButtons.YesNo, MessageBoxIcon.Question)
        If result = DialogResult.Yes Then
            Cursor.Current = Cursors.WaitCursor
            Dim path As String = Me.treeViewFolders.SelectedNode.Tag.ToString()
            Try
                ' Set up a reporting services batch to handle the
                ' deletes as a transaction
                Dim batchHeader As BatchHeader = New BatchHeader
```

```
                batchHeader.BatchID = Me.rs.CreateBatch()
                Me.rs.BatchHeaderValue = batchHeader
                ' Call the delete items
                Dim item As ListViewItem
                For Each item In Me.listViewReports.SelectedItems
                    If item.SubItems(1).Text = "Folder" Then
                        wasFolder = True
                    End If
                    Dim itemName As String = path + item.Text
                    Me.rs.DeleteItem(itemName)
                Next
                ' all the items have been marked for deletion.
                ' Execute the batch.
                Me.rs.ExecuteBatch()
                Me.rs.BatchHeaderValue = Nothing
            Catch exp As Exception
                RSUtilities.ErrorHandler(exp)
            Finally
                Cursor.Current = Cursors.Default
            End Try
            If wasFolder Then
                Me.GetServerFolders()
                Me.listViewReports.Items.Clear()
            Else
                ' refill the list view with the current list of
                ' items
                DisplayFolderContents( _
                        Me.treeViewFolders.SelectedNode.Tag.ToString())
            End If
        End If
    Else
        MessageBox.Show("Select an item in the list view to delete.")
        Return
    End If
End Sub
```

You will remember the discussion of transactions from when you were working on adding folders to
Reporting Services. Here we again use a `Batch` to make sure that all the items you have marked for
deletion are indeed removed from the database. After removing the item from the database, check to see
if the item you removed was a folder; if so refresh the TreeView as well as the ListView.

Importing Report Definition Files

From the chapters about designing reports you will remember that a report file is a specially formatted
XML document, which contains the complete definition for a report. The report definition is stored in
the database in binary format. In order to save the data, a binary definition is read from a file stream into
an array of Bytes. You will begin this section by adding a new namespace reference to the `MainForm`
code file.

C#

```
using System.IO;
```

VB.NET

```
Imports System.IO
```

Open `MainForm` Design View and add an OpenFileDialog control from the toolbox. Change the name of the dialog control to open ReportDialog. While still in the design mode, open the File menu and double click on the Import Report menu item. Add the following code to the new event handler that you have just created for the click event of the menu item.

C#

```csharp
private void menuItemFileImport_Click(object sender, System.EventArgs e)
{
    Stream fileStream;
    System.Byte[] reportDefinition;
    string[] filePath = null;
    // gather the path to put the report in from the selected node
    // in the treeview
    string path = this.treeViewFolders.SelectedNode.Tag.ToString();
    // be sure to remove the trailing seperator
    if (path.Length > 1)
    {
        path = path.Substring(0, path.Length -1);
    }
    openReportDialog = new OpenFileDialog();
    if (openReportDialog.ShowDialog() == DialogResult.OK)
    {
        // get the name of the file and its extension from the dialog box
        string delimiterString = @"\";
        char [] delimiter = delimiterString.ToCharArray();
        filePath = openReportDialog.FileName.Split(delimiter);
        // get the name of the report from the path
        string reportName = filePath[filePath.Length - 1];
        string reportExt = reportName.Substring(reportName.Length - 3, 3);
        reportName = reportName.Substring(0, reportName.Length - 4);
        // make sure that the stream is not null.
        // also make sure that the file extension is rdl indicating that
        // the file is a report definition.
        if ((fileStream = openReportDialog.OpenFile())!= null &&
            reportExt == "rdl")
        {
            //Now read the file stream to get the report definition
            try
            {
                Cursor.Current = Cursors.WaitCursor;
                reportDefinition = new Byte[fileStream.Length];
                // read the report definition from the file stream.
                fileStream.Read(reportDefinition, 0,
                        (int) fileStream.Length);
    fileStream.Close();
    // the necessary information has been gathered.
    // Create the report
    this.rs.CreateReport(reportName, path, false,
                    reportDefinition, null);
    }
```

```
    catch (Exception)
    {
        MessageBox.Show(
            "This report is associated with a shared data source. " + "/" +
            "Please import the shared data source, " + "/" +
            "before importing this report.",
            "Exception");
        Cursor.Current = Cursors.Default;
    }
    finally
    {
        DisplayFolderContents(
        this.treeViewFolders.SelectedNode.Tag.ToString());
        Cursor.Current = Cursors.Default;
        string message = "Report " + reportName +
                    " imported sucessfully";
        MessageBox.Show(message);
    }
        }
        else
        {
            MessageBox.Show("Not a report format or report file is empty");
        }
    }
```

VB.NET

```
Private Sub menuItemFileImport_Click(ByVal sender As Object, _
                ByVal e As System.EventArgs) Handles menuItemFileImport.Click
    Dim fileStream As Stream
    Dim reportDefinition() As System.Byte
    Dim filePath() As String = Nothing
    ' gather the path to put the report in from the selected node
    ' in the treeview
    Dim path As String = Me.treeViewFolders.SelectedNode.Tag.ToString()
    ' be sure to remove the trailing seperator
    If path.Length > 1 Then
        path = path.Substring(0, path.Length - 1)
    End If
    If openReportDialog.ShowDialog() = DialogResult.OK Then
        ' get the name of the file and its extension from the dialog box
        Dim delimiterString As String = "\"
        Dim delimiter() As Char = delimiterString.ToCharArray()
        filePath = openReportDialog.FileName.Split(delimiter)
        ' get the name of the report from the path
        Dim reportName As String = filePath(filePath.Length - 1)
        Dim reportExt As String = reportName.Substring(reportName.Length - 3, 3)
        reportName = reportName.Substring(0, reportName.Length - 4)
        ' make sure that the stream is not null.
        ' also make sure that the file extension is rdl indicating that
        ' the file is a report definition.
        fileStream = openReportDialog.OpenFile()
        If (Not (fileStream Is Nothing) And reportExt = "rdl") Then
            'Now read the file stream to get the report definition
```

```
    Try
        Cursor.Current = Cursors.WaitCursor
        ReDim reportDefinition(fileStream.Length)
        ' read the report definition from the file stream.
        fileStream.Read(reportDefinition, 0, fileStream.Length)
        fileStream.Close()
         ' the necessary information has been gathered.
        ' Create the report
        Me.rs.CreateReport(reportName, path, False, _
                reportDefinition, Nothing)
    Catch
        MessageBox.Show( _
           "This report is associated with a shared data source. " + "/" +
           "Please import the shared data source, " + "/" + _
           "before importing this report.", _
           "Exception")
        Cursor.Current = Cursors.Default
    Finally
        DisplayFolderContents( _
              Me.treeViewFolders.SelectedNode.Tag.ToString())
        Cursor.Current = Cursors.Default
        Dim message As String = "Report " + reportName + _
              " imported sucessfully"
        MessageBox.Show(message)
    End Try
Else
    MessageBox.Show("Not a report format or report file is empty")
    End If
  End If
End Sub
```

The purpose of reading the definition into the database is to locate the file to be imported with the OpenFileDialog. Before trying to read the file make sure that a file was actually selected and that its extension is .rdl. Once you are certain that the file does exist and is the correct type, declare the Byte array to the length of the stream and read the stream into the array. Finally, call the web method CreateReport and pass the following:

❑ Name of the report

❑ Path of the parent folder

❑ Boolean value that indicates if an existing report should be overwritten

❑ Definition in a Byte array

❑ Properties array for the report (since you have not set the Properties array this is set to null or nothing)

The most common error that you might encounter in saving the report is the condition where a report is using a shared data source that is not already in the database. If saving the report creates an exception, it is assumed that the shared data source is missing and the user must be prompted to import it.

Managing Security

The next topic that you will learn about for the PSRS_Manager application is security. Reporting Services has a rich security model where permissions can be assigned to folders and individual objects contained in folders. The object model used for the securing Reporting Services items is different from those used by other Windows security models, so a bit of explanation is in order.

Tasks

At the lowest level of the model is the *task*. A task represents a particular job or action that can be done with Reporting Services, such as viewing a folder or creating a report. The list of tasks is fixed and cannot be modified. There are two distinct types of tasks:

❑ **System tasks**: This task applies to the Reporting Services as a whole.

❑ **User tasks**: This set applies to folders and their contents on a server.

Roles

A level up from the task is the *role*. Each role has an array of tasks, with at least one element, assigned to them. Roles can be created and deleted. There are pre-defined system roles that have been assigned system tasks. Users are strongly discouraged from deleting any of the system roles and those created during the installation process. User roles are assigned user tasks and can be created and deleted as needed. A role cannot be assigned both system and user tasks. The roles included in a Reporting Services installation include:

❑ Browser

❑ Content Manager

❑ Publisher

Policies

The highest level in the security model is the *policy*. In other security models this would usually be referred to as a user and indeed a security policy is given to a user or a group. A policy has an array of roles, with at least one element, assigned to it. A single policy cannot have both system and user security roles. The user/group account to which a security policy is applied can be either a local computer account or a domain account.

Building the Security Forms

To illustrate how the security model in Reporting Services works you will be adding four forms to your application. Although the model has been presented to you in a bottom up fashion, you will be building the application starting at the top level so you can test it as you go along. Let's get started by looking at how to program Reporting Service policies.

Policy Form

Add a new form to your application and name it PoliciesForm and add the following controls:

Control Type	Control Name	Text
ListView	listViewPolicies	
Button	buttonAdd	Add
Button	buttonEdit	Edit
Button	buttonDelete	Delete
Button	buttonOk	OK

Set the View property of the list view control to Details. Using the ColumnHeader Collection Editor add two columns and set their properties as shown in the following table:

Name	Text	TextAlign	Width
columnHeader1	User/Group Name	Left	130
columnHeader2	Roles	Left	200

Arrange the controls on the form so that it looks similar to Figure 7-17:

Figure 7-17

The forms you create to manage security use public properties. These are similar to those used by the FolderForm to pass the path of the folder and a reference to the connected web service.

The code bundle for Chapter 7 will contain the complete code for these properties.

It is always a good practice to reuse code rather than duplicate code. You will use the same form to manage policies for system and user security. To do this it will be necessary to create a property to indicate if you are intending to work on system or user security.

When you create the forms for managing roles and tasks you will be using similar properties to indicate whether you want to work on user or system security objects.

Open the code window for `PoliciesForm` (as shown in the Figure 7-17) and add the following private variable to the class.

C#

```
//Private form variables
private string itemPath = "";
private string itemName = "";
private ReportingService rsWebService = null;
private RSUtilities.EditModeEnum mode;
private bool systemPolicies = false;
```

VB.NET

```
'Private form variables
Private mItemPath As String = ""
Private mItemName As String = ""
Private mRSWebService As ReportingService = Nothing
Private mMode As RSUtilities.EditModeEnum
Private mSystemPolicies As Boolean = False
```

Add a public property to indicate if the form is to work on system security or object security.

C#

```
public bool SystemPolicies
{
    get
    {
      return systemPolicies;
    }
    set
    {
      systemPolicies = value;
    }
}
```

VB.NET

```
Public Property SystemPolicies() As Boolean
    Get
        Return mSystemPolicies
    End Get
    Set(ByVal Value As Boolean)
        mSystemPolicies = Value
    End Set
End Property
```

Now add the following method to get an array of policy objects for either an item or the system. The item can be a folder or an object contained in a folder.

C#

```
private Policy[] GetItemPolicies()
{
    ReportingWebService.Policy[] policies;
```

```
        bool inheritParent;
        if (! systemPolicies)
        {
          policies = this.rsWebService.GetPolicies(itemPath, out inheritParent);
        }
        else
        {
          policies = rsWebService.GetSystemPolicies();
        }
        return policies;
      }
```

VB.NET

```
      Private Function GetItemPolicies() As Policy()
          Dim policies() As ReportingWebService.Policy
          Dim inheritParent As Boolean
          If Not mSystemPolicies Then
              policies = mRSWebService.GetPolicies(mItemPath, inheritParent)
          Else
              policies = mRSWebService.GetSystemPolicies()
          End If
          Return policies
      End Function
```

The web service methods that return the array of policy objects are:

❑ GetPolicies: This method takes the path of the item you want to work on and a Boolean output parameter as arguments. The inheritParent output parameter indicates if the item inherits its permission set from its parent.

❑ GetSystemPolicies: This method takes no arguments.

Now that you have a way to get the policies from the web service, you need to show the policies in the list view control. Enter the following procedure in the code for PoliciesForm.

C#

```
    private void FillPolicyListView()
    {
        this.listViewPolicies.Items.Clear();
        ReportingWebService.Policy[] policies = GetItemPolicies();
        foreach(ReportingWebService.Policy policy in policies)
        {
          ListViewItem item = new ListViewItem(policy.GroupUserName.ToString());
          string rolesCollection = "";
          foreach(ReportingWebService.Role role in policy.Roles)
          {
             rolesCollection += "," + role.Name.ToString();
          }
          rolesCollection = rolesCollection.Substring(1, rolesCollection.Length - 1);
          item.SubItems.Add(rolesCollection);
          this.listViewPolicies.Items.Add(item);
        }
    }
```

VB.NET

```vb.net
Private Sub FillPolicyListView()
    Me.listViewPolicies.Items.Clear()
    Dim policies() As ReportingWebService.Policy = GetItemPolicies()
    Dim policy As ReportingWebService.Policy
    For Each policy In policies
      Dim item As ListViewItem = New ListViewItem(policy.GroupUserName.ToString())
      Dim rolesCollection As String = ""
      Dim role As ReportingWebService.Role
      For Each role In policy.Roles
          rolesCollection += "," + role.Name.ToString()
      Next
      rolesCollection = rolesCollection.Substring(1, rolesCollection.Length - 1)
      item.SubItems.Add(rolesCollection)
      Me.listViewPolicies.Items.Add(item)
    Next
    Return
End Sub
```

In this code, you are looping through the array of policy objects and adding the information from each policy to the list view. Each policy object contains an array of roles that the policy object has assigned to it. The code above concatenates the names of the roles assigned to a policy into the variable rolesCollection so they can be displayed in the list view. This should be somewhat familiar from the code you wrote to show the contents of folders, earlier in this chapter.

In order to show the security policies for an item you need to call the FillPolicyListView method. Add an event handler for the form Load event of PoliciesForm, as shown in the following code:

C#

```csharp
private void PolicyForm_Load(object sender, System.EventArgs e)
{
    FillPolicyListView();
}
```

VB.NET

```vb.net
Private Sub PolicyForm_Load(ByVal sender As System.Object, ByVal e As
System.EventArgs) Handles MyBase.Load
        FillPolicyListView()
End Sub
```

Now you only need a way to call the form in order to see some security policies. Open **MainForm** in the **Design View** and create an event handler by double clicking on the **System | Role Assignments** menu item. Into this new event handler enter the following code:

C#

```csharp
private void menuItemSecurityAssignments_Click(object sender, System.EventArgse)
{
    if (this.treeViewFolders.SelectedNode != null)
    {
      PolicyForm dialogForm = new PolicyForm();
```

```
        dialogForm.ItemPath = this.treeViewFolders.SelectedNode.Tag.ToString();
        dialogForm.ItemName = this.treeViewFolders.SelectedNode.Text.ToString();
        dialogForm.RsWebService = rs;
        dialogForm.ShowDialog(this);
    }
    else
    {
        MessageBox.Show("Select a folder you want to view policies for");
    }
}
```

VB.NET

```
Private Sub menuItemSecurityAssignments_Click(ByVal sender As System.Object, ByVal
e As System.EventArgs) Handles menuItemSecurityAssignments.Click
        If Not (Me.treeViewFolders.SelectedNode Is Nothing) Then
            Dim dialogForm As PolicyForm = New PolicyForm
            dialogForm.ItemPath = Me.treeViewFolders.SelectedNode.Tag.ToString()
            dialogForm.ItemName = Me.treeViewFolders.SelectedNode.Text.ToString()
            dialogForm.RsWebService = rs
            dialogForm.ShowDialog(Me)
        Else
            MessageBox.Show("Select a folder you want to view policies for")
        End If
End Sub
```

This code is very similar to the code you entered when working with folders. You declare a variable as a new `PoliciesForm`, set the form properties for the path and name of the folder, pass the reference to the web service and show the form as a modal dialog. Now is a good time to add the code for viewing the system policies. Add an event handler for the Security | System Role Assignments menu selection and add the following code to the event handler:

C#

```
private void menuItemSecuritySystemAssignments_Click(object sender,
                                            System.EventArgs e)
{
        PolicyForm dialogForm = new PolicyForm();
        dialogForm.ItemPath = "/";
        dialogForm.ItemName = "Site Settings";
        dialogForm.RsWebService = rs;
        dialogForm.SystemPolicies = true;
        dialogForm.ShowDialog(this);
}
```

VB.NET

```
Private Sub menuItemSecuritySystemAssignments_Click(ByVal sender As System.Object,
ByVal e As System.EventArgs) Handles menuItemSecuritySystemAssignments.Click
        Dim dialogForm As PolicyForm = New PolicyForm
        dialogForm.ItemPath = "/"
        dialogForm.ItemName = "Site Settings"
        dialogForm.RsWebService = rs
        dialogForm.SystemPolicies = True
        dialogForm.ShowDialog(Me)
End Sub
```

The only interesting difference between these event handlers and the event handlers for user objects is that here you set the path to the root path \, and the `SystemPolicies` property is set to `true`.

Save your changes and run the application. Click the Go button to load the folder tree and select the Professional SQL Reporting Services folder from the tree. Then select the Security | Role Assignments menu item. You should see the policy form as shown in Figure 7-18:

Figure 7-18

Adding, Editing, and Deleting Security Policies

Being able to view a list of policies is useful, but to manage Reporting Services you need to be able to make changes to the policies. Add a new form to your application and name it `UserPolicyForm`. Add the following controls to the form:

Control Type	Control Name	Text
Label	labelItemName	Item name
Label	label1	User/Group Name
TextBox	textBoxUserGroupName	
CheckedListBox	checkedListBoxRoles	
Button	buttonCancel	Cancel
Button	buttonOk	OK

Set the `DialogResult` property of `buttonCancel` to `Cancel` and the `DialogResult` property of `buttonOk` to `OK`. Arrange the controls on the form as shown in Figure 7-19:

Figure 7-19

Again we will be using properties and private member variables to hold information about the object name, object path, and a reference to the web service. Add the following private variables and properties to the form.

C#

```csharp
// Private form variables
private string itemPath = "";
private string itemName = "";
private RSUtilities.EditModeEnum mode;
private ReportingService rsWebService = null;
private bool systemRoles = false;
private ReportingWebService.Policy userPolicy = null;
private Role[] itemRoles = null;
public bool SystemRoles
{
    get
    {
      return systemRoles;
    }
    set
    {
      systemRoles = value;
    }
}

public Policy UserPolicy
{
    get
    {
      return userPolicy;
    }
    set
    {
      userPolicy = value;
      this.textBoxUserGroupName.Text = userPolicy.GroupUserName.ToString();
    }
}
```

VB.NET

```
'Private form variables
Private mItemPath As String = ""
Private mItemName As String = ""
Private mRSWebService As ReportingService = Nothing
Private mMode As RSUtilities.EditModeEnum
Private mSystemRoles As Boolean = False
Private mUserPolicy As ReportingWebService.Policy = Nothing
Private itemRoles() As Role = Nothing

Public Property SystemRoles() As Boolean
    Get
        Return mSystemRoles
    End Get
    Set(ByVal Value As Boolean)
        mSystemRoles = Value
    End Set
End Property

Public Property UserPolicy() As Policy
    Get
        Return mUserPolicy
    End Get
    Set(ByVal Value As Policy)
        mUserPolicy = Value
        Me.textBoxUserGroupName.Text = userPolicy.GroupUserName.ToString()
    End Set
End Property
```

The UserPolicy property is used to pass a policy object to the form so it can be edited and return the new or modified policy to the calling form.

The work of this form will take place in the event handlers for the two buttons and the form load event. Create these event handlers and add the following code.

C#

```
private void UserForm_Load(object sender, System.EventArgs e)
{
    if (systemRoles)
    {
        itemRoles = this.rsWebService.ListSystemRoles();
    }
    else
    {
        itemRoles = this.rsWebService.ListRoles();
    }
    foreach (ReportingWebService.Role role in itemRoles)
    {
        bool checkRole = false;
        if (this.userPolicy != null)
        {
            foreach(ReportingWebService.Role userRole in userPolicy.Roles)
```

```
                {
            if (userRole.Name == role.Name)
            {
              checkRole = true;
              break;
            }
          }
        }
        this.checkedListBoxRoles.Items.Add(role.Name.ToString(),checkRole);
    }
}
```

VB.NET

```
Private Sub UserPolicyForm_Load(ByVal sender As System.Object, ByVal e As
System.EventArgs) Handles MyBase.Load
```

```
        If (mSystemRoles) Then
            itemRoles = Me.mRSWebService.ListSystemRoles()
        Else
            itemRoles = Me.mRSWebService.ListRoles()
        End If
        Dim objRole As ReportingWebService.Role
        For Each objRole In itemRoles
            Dim checkRole As Boolean = False
            If Not (mUserPolicy Is Nothing) Then
                Dim userRole As ReportingWebService.Role
                For Each userRole In UserPolicy.Roles
                    If (userRole.Name = objRole.Name) Then
                        checkRole = True
                        Exit For
                    End If
                Next
            End If
            Me.checkedListBoxRoles.Items.Add(objRole.Name.ToString(), checkRole)
        Next
    End Sub
```

The `UserPolicyForm_Load` method shown here first determines whether or not you want to work with system or user policies by evaluating the `systemRoles` variable. The existing system and user roles are loaded into the `itemRoles` variable with either the `ListSystemRoles` or `ListRoles` methods of the web service. The `itemRoles` variable has form level scope so it can be initialized as part of the form load event but still is available when the roles are needed again when you process any changes at the time when the form is closed. The list of roles is created by looping through the array or roles found in the `itemRoles` variable. If the `UserPolicy` property has been set, you loop through the array of roles associated with the policy and compare the `name` property to the `name` property of the role from `itemRoles` to determine if the check box of an item should be checked.

The event handler for the click event of `buttonOK` either assigns an array of roles to a new policy or assignes a new array of roles to the existing policy. Add the following code into the `buttonOK_Click` and `buttonCancel_Click` event handlers:

C#

```csharp
private void buttonOK_Click(object sender, System.EventArgs e)
{
    int roleCount = this.checkedListBoxRoles.CheckedItems.Count;
    if (this.mode == RSUtilities.EditModeEnum.add)
    {
      this.userPolicy = new Policy();
      userPolicy.GroupUserName = this.textBoxUserGroupName.Text.ToString();
    }
    Role[] userRoles = new Role[roleCount];
    for (int i = 0; i < this.checkedListBoxRoles.CheckedItems.Count; i++)
    {
      foreach(Role role in itemRoles)
      {
        if (role.Name == this.checkedListBoxRoles.CheckedItems[i].ToString())
        {
          userRoles[i] = role;
          break;
        }
      }
    }
    userPolicy.Roles = userRoles;
    this.Close();
}
private void buttonCancel_Click(object sender, System.EventArgs e)
{
    this.Close();
}
```

VB.NET

```vbnet
Private Sub buttonOK_Click(ByVal sender As Object, ByVal e As System.EventArgs)
                    Handles buttonOK.Click
        Dim roleCount As Integer = Me.checkedListBoxRoles.CheckedItems.Count
        If mMode = RSUtilities.EditModeEnum.add Then
            mUserPolicy = New Policy
            mUserPolicy.GroupUserName = Me.textBoxUserGroupName.Text.ToString()
        End If
        Dim userRoles(roleCount - 1) As ReportingWebService.Role
        Dim i As Integer
        For i = 0 To Me.checkedListBoxRoles.CheckedItems.Count - 1 Step 1
            Dim objRole As ReportingWebService.Role
            For Each objRole In itemRoles
        If objRole.Name = Me.checkedListBoxRoles.CheckedItems(i).ToString() Then
                    userRoles(i) = objRole
                    Exit For
                End If
            Next
        Next
        mUserPolicy.Roles = userRoles
        Me.Close()
End Sub
```

```
Private Sub buttonCancel_Click(ByVal sender As Object, ByVal e As
                                System.EventArgs) Handles buttonCancel.Click
        Me.Close()
End Sub
```

The code behind the buttonOK click event checks the UserPolicy property. If a policy has not been assigned to the property, a new policy is created. A new variable, userRoles, is then declared as a array of roles. The number of elements in userRoles will be the number of checked items in the checked list box. The elements of userRoles are added from the itemRoles array by comparing the text property of the checked items in the checked list box to the Name property of the elements of the itemRoles array. The last step before closing the form is to assign the userRoles array to the Roles property of the policy held by the UserPolicy property of the form.

Although the code presented here has created a new policy or modified an existing one, this policy has not been applied to either the system or an item in a Reporting Services folder. The assignment of the policy takes place after form closes and control is returned to the calling form. To complete the policy assignment you need to create a couple of methods in the code of PolicyForm. Open the code window of PolicyForm and enter the following code:

C#

```csharp
private void SetItemPolicies(Policy[] NewPolicy)
{
    try
    {
        // Create the batch to handle the transaction
        BatchHeader batchHeader = new BatchHeader();
        batchHeader.BatchID = rsWebService.CreateBatch();
        rsWebService.BatchHeaderValue = batchHeader;
        // set the policies for the item to the new policy
        // array passed to the procedure
        rsWebService.SetPolicies(this.itemPath, NewPolicy);
        // execute the batch
        this.rsWebService.ExecuteBatch();
        this.rsWebService.BatchHeaderValue = null;
    }
    catch(Exception exp)
    {
        RSUtilities.ErrorHandler(exp);
    }
}
```

VB.NET

```vbnet
Private Sub SetItemPolicies(ByVal NewPolicy() As Policy)
    Try
        ' Create the batch to handle the transaction
        Dim batchHeader As batchHeader = New batchHeader
        batchHeader.BatchID = mRSWebService.CreateBatch()
        mRSWebService.BatchHeaderValue = batchHeader
        ' set the policies for the item to the new policy
        ' array passed to the procedure
        mRSWebService.SetPolicies(mItemPath, NewPolicy)
        ' execute the batch
        mRSWebService.ExecuteBatch()
```

```
        mRSWebService.BatchHeaderValue = Nothing
    Catch exp As Exception
        RSUtilities.ErrorHandler(exp)
    End Try
    Return
End Sub
```

The `SetPolicies` method of the web service is used to associate a policy that you have created with an item in the Report Server. `SetPolicies` method takes a path to an item and an array of policy objects as arguments in the Reporting Services database. Any time changes are made to database objects and setting the policies for an item makes changes to the existing policies, so it is vital that these changes be wrapped in a transaction. You will remember from the code used to create new folders, that the Reporting Services object for supporting transactions is a batch. The `SetItemPolicies` method uses the batch header and batch objects to make sure that all the database updates are completed successfully or rolled back entirely.

Adding a New Policy

Now that you have a form to create a new policy and a method to assign a policy array to an object in the database, you need methods to call the form, set its properties, and do something with the returned user policy. Create an event handler for the click event of `buttonAdd` of `PolicyForm` and add the following code:

C#

```csharp
private void buttonAdd_Click(object sender, System.EventArgs e)
{
    UserPolicyForm dialogForm = new UserPolicyForm();
    dialogForm.RsWebService = rsWebService;
    dialogForm.ItemName = this.itemName;
    dialogForm.ItemPath = this.ItemPath;
    dialogForm.SystemRoles = this.systemPolicies;
    dialogForm.Mode = RSUtilities.EditModeEnum.add;
    dialogForm.ShowDialog(this);
    if (dialogForm.DialogResult == DialogResult.OK)
    {
        Policy newPolicy = dialogForm.UserPolicy;
        if (newPolicy != null)
        {
            Policy[] currentPolicies = GetItemPolicies();
            Policy[] newPolicies = new Policy[currentPolicies.Length + 1];
            for (int i = 0; i < currentPolicies.Length; i++)
            {
                newPolicies[i] = currentPolicies[i];
            }
            newPolicies[currentPolicies.Length] = newPolicy;
            SetItemPolicies(newPolicies);
            FillPolicyListView();
        }
    }
}
```

VB.NET

```
Private Sub buttonAdd_Click(ByVal sender As System.Object, ByVal e As
                              System.EventArgs) Handles buttonAdd.Click
    Dim dialogForm As UserPolicyForm = New UserPolicyForm
    dialogForm.RsWebService = mRSWebService
    dialogForm.ItemName = mItemName
    dialogForm.ItemPath = mItemPath
    dialogForm.SystemRoles = mSystemPolicies
    dialogForm.Mode = RSUtilities.EditModeEnum.add
    dialogForm.ShowDialog(Me)
    If dialogForm.DialogResult = DialogResult.OK Then
        Dim newPolicy As Policy = dialogForm.UserPolicy
        If Not newPolicy Is Nothing Then
            Dim currentPolicies() As Policy = GetItemPolicies()
            Dim NewPolicies(currentPolicies.Length) As Policy
            Dim i As Integer
            For i = 0 To currentPolicies.Length - 1 Step 1
                NewPolicies(i) = currentPolicies(i)
            Next
            NewPolicies(currentPolicies.Length) = newPolicy
            SetItemPolicies(NewPolicies)
            FillPolicyListView()
        End If
    End If
    Return
End Sub
```

Instantiating a new form variable, setting properties, and displaying it as a modal dialog should look very familiar. When you created the buttons on UserPolicyForm you had set the DialogResult property for each button. The event handler checks to make sure that the OK button was used to close the form and that the dialog's UserPolicy property returns a valid policy. If these two conditions are met then the UserPolicy from the dialog form is added to the existing policies of the database object in a new array of policies. The last step is to set the policies of the database object to the new array of policies with the SetItemPolicies method.

Editing an Existing Policy

Another important task that PSRS_Manager should be able to do is to modify the roles of an existing user. Create an event handler for the click event of buttonEdit on PolicyForm and insert the following code:

C#

```
private void buttonEdit_Click(object sender, System.EventArgs e)
{
    if (this.listViewPolicies.SelectedItems.Count == 0)
    {
        MessageBox.Show("Select a user for which to edit roles.");
        return;
    }
    Policy[] currentPolicies = GetItemPolicies();
    Policy userPolicy = null;
    foreach (Policy policy in currentPolicies)
```

```
    {
      if (policy.GroupUserName == this.listViewPolicies.SelectedItems[0].Text.
                          ToString())
      {
        userPolicy = policy;
        break;
      }
    }
    UserPolicyForm dialogForm = new UserPolicyForm();
    dialogForm.RsWebService = rsWebService;
    dialogForm.ItemName = this.itemName;
    dialogForm.ItemPath = this.itemPath;
    dialogForm.UserPolicy = userPolicy;
    dialogForm.SystemRoles = this.systemPolicies;
    dialogForm.Mode = RSUtilities.EditModeEnum.edit;
    dialogForm.ShowDialog(this);
    if (dialogForm.DialogResult == DialogResult.Ok)
    {
      userPolicy = dialogForm.UserPolicy;
      Policy[] newPolicies = new Policy[currentPolicies.Length];
      for (int i = 0; i < currentPolicies.Length; i++)
      {
        if (userPolicy.GroupUserName == currentPolicies[i].GroupUserName)
        {
          newPolicies[i] = userPolicy;
        }
        else
        {
          newPolicies[i] = currentPolicies[i];
        }
      }
      SetItemPolicies(newPolicies);
      FillPolicyListView();
    }
    return;
}
```

VB.NET

```
Private Sub buttonEdit_Click(ByVal sender As System.Object, ByVal e As
                        System.EventArgs) Handles buttonEdit.Click
    If Me.listViewPolicies.SelectedItems.Count = 0 Then
        MessageBox.Show("Select a user for which to edit roles.")
        Return
    End If
    Dim currentPolicies() As ReportingWebService.Policy = GetItemPolicies()
    Dim userPolicy As ReportingWebService.Policy = Nothing
    Dim objPolicy As ReportingWebService.Policy
    For Each objPolicy In currentPolicies
        If objPolicy.GroupUserName = Me.listViewPolicies.SelectedItems(0).Text.
                            ToString() Then
            userPolicy = objPolicy
            Exit For
        End If
```

```
        Next
        Dim dialogForm As UserPolicyForm = New UserPolicyForm
        dialogForm.RsWebService = mRSWebService
        dialogForm.ItemName = mItemName
        dialogForm.ItemPath = mItemPath
        dialogForm.UserPolicy = userPolicy
        dialogForm.SystemRoles = mSystemPolicies
        dialogForm.Mode = RSUtilities.EditModeEnum.edit
        dialogForm.ShowDialog(Me)
        If dialogForm.DialogResult = DialogResult.OK Then
            userPolicy = dialogForm.UserPolicy
            Dim newPolicies(currentPolicies.Length - 1) As Policy
            Dim i As Integer
            For i = 0 To currentPolicies.Length - 1 Step 1
                If userPolicy.GroupUserName = currentPolicies(i).GroupUserName Then
                    newPolicies(i) = userPolicy
                Else
                    newPolicies(i) = currentPolicies(i)
                End If
            Next
            SetItemPolicies(newPolicies)
            FillPolicyListView()
        End If
        Return
    End Sub
```

The code here is very similar to the code to add a new policy. The `UserPolicy` of the dialog form is set to the policy selected with the list view. Rather than creating a new policy and adding it to the existing policy array, the modified policy replaces the original in the array before the `SetItemPolicies` method is called.

Deleting a Policy

Change is a constant in any organization. It is likely that it will be necessary to revoke user privileges as the structure of your organization changes over time. `PolicyForm` has a delete button and now would be a good time to make it functional. Create an event handler for the click event of `buttonDelete` and enter the following code:

C#

```csharp
private void buttonDelete_Click(object sender, System.EventArgs e)
{
    if (this.listViewPolicies.SelectedItems.Count == 0)
    {
        MessageBox.Show("Select a user/group to delete.");
        return;
    }
    DialogResult result = MessageBox.Show("Are you sure you want to delete this
                                policy?",
                                "Delete Policy",MessageBoxButtons.YesNo,
                                MessageBoxIcon.Question);
    if (result == DialogResult.Yes)
    {
        string userName = this.listViewPolicies.SelectedItems[0].Text;
```

```
        Policy[] currentPolicies = GetItemPolicies();
        Policy[] newPolicies = new Policy[currentPolicies.Length -1];
        int i = 0;
        foreach (Policy policy in currentPolicies)
        {
          if (policy.GroupUserName != userName)
          {
            newPolicies[i] = policy;
            i++;
          }
        }
        SetItemPolicies(newPolicies);
        FillPolicyListView();
    }
    return;
}
```

VB.NET

```
Private Sub buttonDelete_Click(ByVal sender As System.Object, ByVal e As
System.EventArgs) Handles buttonDelete.Click
    If Me.listViewPolicies.SelectedItems.Count = 0 Then
        MessageBox.Show("Select a user/group to delete.")
        Return
    End If
    Dim result As DialogResult
    result = MessageBox.Show("Are you sure you want to delete this policy?", _
            "Delete Policy", MessageBoxButtons.YesNo, _
            MessageBoxIcon.Question)
    If result = DialogResult.Yes Then
        Dim userName As String = Me.listViewPolicies.SelectedItems(0).Text
        Dim currentPolicies() As ReportingWebService.Policy = GetItemPolicies()
        Dim NewPolicies(currentPolicies.Length - 2) As ReportingWebService.Policy
        Dim i As Integer = 0
        Dim objPolicy As ReportingWebService.Policy
        For Each objPolicy In currentPolicies
            If objPolicy.GroupUserName <> userName Then
                NewPolicies(i) = objPolicy
                i = i + 1
            End If
        Next
        SetItemPolicies(NewPolicies)
        FillPolicyListView()
    End If
    Return
End Sub
```

This is very similar to the way you edited the array of policies for the edit routine; instead of performing a replacement, the policy selected for deletion is eliminated from the new array of policies sent to the SetItemPolicies method.

It's about time to check if all this code actually works. Save all your changes and run the application. After clicking Go, select the Security | Role Assignments menu item and click the Add button on the policy form to display the form for adding a new user policy. Enter a valid user or group name and assign the user some roles, similar to Figure 7-20:

Figure 7-20

After clicking the Add button the policy form should show the new policy in the list view similar to Figure 7-21:

Figure 7-21

Adding, Editing, and Deleting Security Roles

With the ability to create and modify policies, it is now time to look at how roles are created and modified. As mentioned at the beginning of this section you learned that the installation of Reporting Services creates a number of user and system roles. For most users the roles created during the installation provide all the options necessary to manage an installation. You may encounter a need to create a special purpose role so lets dive into how that is done.

RoleForm

Add a new form to your application and name it RoleForm. From the toolbox add the following controls to RoleForm:

Control Type	Control Name	Text
Label	labelRoleName	Role name
ListView	listViewRoles	
Button	buttonAdd	Add
Button	buttonEdit	Edit
Button	buttonDelete	Delete
Button	buttonOk	OK

Set the `View` property of the list view control to `Details`. Using the ColumnHeader Collection Editor add two columns and set their properties as shown in the following table:

Name	Text	TextAlign	Width
columnHeader1	Role Name	Left	130
columnHeader2	Description	Left	500

Arrange the controls on the form so it looks similar to Figure 7-22:

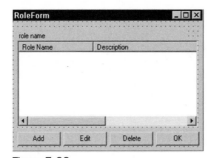

Figure 7-22

Open the code for `RoleForm` and add the following private form variables to hold form property values.

C#

```csharp
// Private form variables
private Role[] roles = null;
private bool systemRoles = false;
private ReportingService rsWebService = null;
```

VB.NET

```vb
'Private form variables
Private mRoles() As Role = Nothing
Private mSystemRoles As Boolean = False
Private mRSWebService As ReportingService = Nothing
```

Now add the following property methods shown to the form.

C#

```csharp
public bool SystemRoles
{
    get
    {
      return systemRoles;
    }
    set
    {
      systemRoles = value;
    }
}
public ReportingService RsWebService
   {
    set
    {
      rsWebService = value;
    }
}
```

VB.NET

```vb
Public Property SystemRoles() As Boolean
    Get
        Return mSystemRoles
    End Get
    Set(ByVal Value As Boolean)
        mSystemRoles = Value
    End Set
End Property
Public WriteOnly Property RsWebService() As ReportingService
    Set(ByVal Value As ReportingService)
        mRSWebService = Value
    End Set
End Property
```

Very similar to the way you displayed the policies for a folder, you will also need a method to fill the list view with role information. Enter the following method into the code window for RoleForm:

C#

```csharp
private void FillRoleListView()
{
    this.listViewRoles.Items.Clear();
    if (systemRoles)
```

```
    {
      roles = rsWebService.ListSystemRoles();
      this.labelRoleName.Text = "System Roles";
    }
    else
    {
      roles = rsWebService.ListRoles();
      this.labelRoleName.Text = "User Item Roles";
    }
    foreach (Role role in roles)
    {
      ListViewItem item = new ListViewItem();
      item.Text = role.Name.ToString();
      item.SubItems.Add(role.Description.ToString());
      this.listViewRoles.Items.Add(item);
    }
}
```

VB.NET

```
Private Sub FillRoleListView()
    Me.listViewRoles.Items.Clear()
    If (systemRoles) Then
        mRoles = mRSWebService.ListSystemRoles()
        Me.labelRoleName.Text = "System Roles"
    Else
        mRoles = mRSWebService.ListRoles()
        Me.labelRoleName.Text = "User Item Roles"
    End If
    Dim role As ReportingWebService.Role
    For Each role In mRoles
        Dim item As ListViewItem = New ListViewItem
        item.Text = role.Name.ToString()
        item.SubItems.Add(role.Description.ToString())
        Me.listViewRoles.Items.Add(item)
    Next
    Return
End Sub
```

The web service methods `ListRoles` and `ListSystemRoles` each return an array of role objects. The array or role objects returned from the calls to the web methods is used to fill the list view with information. To call the `FillRoleListView` method, create an event handler for the form load event and enter this code.

C#

```
private void RoleForm_Load(object sender, System.EventArgs e)
{
    FillRoleListView();
}
```

VB.NET

```
Private Sub RoleForm_Load(ByVal sender As System.Object, ByVal e As
System.EventArgs) Handles MyBase.Load
    FillRoleListView()
End Sub
```

Go back to `MainForm` and enter event handlers for the menu items `menuItemSecurityRoles` and `menuItemSecuritySystemRoles`. Insert the following code into the new event handlers.

C#

```csharp
private void menuItemSecurityRoles_Click(object sender, System.EventArgs e)
{
    RoleForm dialogForm = new RoleForm();
    dialogForm.RsWebService = rs;
    dialogForm.ShowDialog(this);
}

private void menuItemSecuritySystemRoles_Click(object sender,
                                        System.EventArgs e)
{
    RoleForm dialogForm = new RoleForm();
    dialogForm.RsWebService = rs;
    dialogForm.SystemRoles = true;
    dialogForm.ShowDialog(this);
}
```

VB.NET

```vbnet
Private Sub menuItemSecurityRoles_Click(ByVal sender As System.Object, ByVal e As
System.EventArgs) Handles menuItemSecurityRoles.Click
    Dim dialogForm As RoleForm = New RoleForm
    dialogForm.RsWebService = rs
    dialogForm.ShowDialog(Me)
End Sub

Private Sub menuItemSecuritySystemRoles_Click(ByVal sender As System.Object, ByVal
        e As System.EventArgs) Handles menuItemSecuritySystemRoles.Click
    Dim dialogForm As RoleForm = New RoleForm
    dialogForm.RsWebService = rs
    dialogForm.SystemRoles = True
    dialogForm.ShowDialog(Me)
End Sub
```

Save the changes you have made and run the application. When `MainForm` is displayed click **Go** and then select then **Security | Roles** menu item. You should see the `RoleForm` displayed looking similar to Figure 7- 23. These are roles that exist on the Reporting Services server.

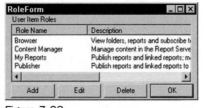

Figure 7-23

Adding, Editing, and Deleting Roles

Now that you can show the list of roles, let's add, edit, and delete roles.

Role Task Form

Add a new form to your application and name it RoleTaskForm. From the toolbox add the following controls to RoleTaskForm:

Control Type	Control Name	Text
Label	label1	Role name
Label	label2	Description
TextBox	textBoxRoleName	
TextBox	textBoxDescription	
CheckedListBox	checkedListBoxTasks	
Button	buttonCancel	Cancel
Button	buttonOk	OK

Arrange the controls on the form as shown in Figure 7-24:

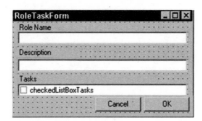

Figure 7-24

Add the following private variables to the code window of RoleTaskForm.

C#

```
// Private form variables
private ReportingService rsWebService = null;
private RSUtilities.EditModeEnum mode;
private bool isSystemRole = false;
private ReportingWebService.Role userRole = null;
private Task[] itemTasks = null;
```

VB.NET

```vbnet
' Private form variables
Private mRsWebService As ReportingService = Nothing
Private mMode As RSUtilities.EditModeEnum
Private mIsSystemRole As Boolean = False
Private mUserRole As ReportingWebService.Role = Nothing
Private mItemTasks() As Task = Nothing
```

In addition to the standard `Mode` and `RsWebService` properties that you have used with previous forms, add the following properties to your `RoleTaskForm`:

C#

```csharp
public bool IsSystemRole
{
    get
    {
      return isSystemRole;
    }
    set
    {
      isSystemRole = value;
    }
}

public Role UserRole
{
    get
    {
      return userRole;
    }
    set
    {
      userRole = value;
      this.textBoxRoleName.Text = userRole.Name.ToString();
      this.textBoxDescription.Text = userRole.Description.ToString();
    }
}
```

VB.NET

```vbnet
Public Property IsSystemRole() As Boolean
    Get
        Return mIsSystemRole
    End Get
    Set(ByVal Value As Boolean)
        mIsSystemRole = Value
    End Set
End Property
Public Property UserRole() As ReportingWebService.Role
    Get
        Return mUserRole
    End Get
    Set(ByVal Value As ReportingWebService.Role)
```

```
            mUserRole = Value
            Me.textBoxRoleName.Text = mUserRole.Name.ToString()
            Me.textBoxDescription.Text = mUserRole.Description.ToString()
        End Set
    End Property
```

Add an event handler for the form load event and enter the following code.

C#

```
private void RoleTaskForm_Load(object sender, System.EventArgs e)
{
    string description = "";
    Task[] userRoleTasks = null;
    if (isSystemRole)
    {
      itemTasks = this.rsWebService.ListSystemTasks();
    }
    else
    {
      itemTasks = this.rsWebService.ListTasks();
    }
    if (userRole != null)
    {
      userRoleTasks = rsWebService.GetRoleProperties(userRole.Name.ToString(), out
                                                     description);
    }
    foreach (ReportingWebService.Task task in itemTasks)
    {
      bool checkTask = false;
      if (this.userRole != null)
      {
        foreach(ReportingWebService.Task userTask in userRoleTasks)
        {
          if (userTask.TaskID == task.TaskID)
          {
            checkTask = true;
            break;
          }
        }
      }
      this.checkedListBoxTasks.Items.Add(task.Name, checkTask);
    }
}
```

VB.NET

```
Private Sub RoleTaskForm_Load(ByVal sender As System.Object, ByVal e As
                              System.EventArgs) Handles MyBase.Load
    Dim description As String = ""
    Dim userRoleTasks() As ReportingWebService.Task = Nothing
    If (mIsSystemRole) Then
        mItemTasks = mRsWebService.ListSystemTasks()
    Else
        mItemTasks = mRsWebService.ListTasks()
```

```
      End If
      If Not (mUserRole Is Nothing) Then
          userRoleTasks = mRsWebService.GetRoleProperties(UserRole.Name.ToString(),
                                              description)
      End If
      Dim sysTask As ReportingWebService.Task
      For Each sysTask In mItemTasks
          Dim checkTask As Boolean = False
          If Not (mUserRole Is Nothing) Then
              Dim userTask As ReportingWebService.Task
              For Each userTask In userRoleTasks
                  If (userTask.TaskID = sysTask.TaskID) Then
                      checkTask = True
                      Exit For
                  End If
              Next
          End If
          Me.checkedListBoxTasks.Items.Add(sysTask.Name, checkTask)
      Next
      Return
  End Sub
```

The `RoleTaskForm_Load` method uses the `ListSystemTasks` or the `ListTasks` web service method to fill a local array variable with a list of tasks. This variable has a wide scope so it can be used to evaluate selections when the OK button is clicked without going back to the web service to reload the values. If you are editing an existing role, the tasks for the role are returned from the `GetRoleProperites` web service method, which takes the role name and description (output parameter). Another interesting feature of tasks has to do with the name property. If you have an array of tasks from an existing role, the name property exists but will always return an empty string and is not useful for comparing to one of the built in tasks. Instead you will need to compare `TaskID` property of the role tasks to the `TaskID` property of the built in tasks. The `RoleTaskForm_Load` method uses this technique to determine if a task is already part of a role and thus its check box should be checked.

Add an event handler to the click event of `buttonOK` and `buttonCancel` and enter the following code:

C#

```csharp
private void buttonOK_Click(object sender, System.EventArgs e)
{
    int taskCount = this.checkedListBoxTasks.CheckedItems.Count;
    Task[] roleTasks = new Task[taskCount];
    for (int i = 0; i < taskCount; i++)
    {
      string taskName = this.checkedListBoxTasks.CheckedItems[i].ToString();
      foreach(Task task in itemTasks)
      {
        if(taskName == task.Name)
        {
          roleTasks[i] = task;
          break;
        }
      }
    }
}
```

```
        try
        {
          BatchHeader batchHeader = new BatchHeader();
          batchHeader.BatchID = rsWebService.CreateBatch();
          rsWebService.BatchHeaderValue = batchHeader;
          if (mode == RSUtilities.EditModeEnum.edit)
          {
              rsWebService.SetRoleProperties(this.textBoxRoleName.Text.ToString(),
                                       this.textBoxDescription.Text.ToString(),
                                       roleTasks);
          }
          else
          {
              rsWebService.CreateRole(this.textBoxRoleName.Text.ToString(),
                                  this.textBoxDescription.Text.ToString(),
                                  roleTasks);
          }
          this.rsWebService.ExecuteBatch();
          this.rsWebService.BatchHeaderValue = null;
        }
        catch (Exception exp)
        {
          RSUtilities.ErrorHandler(exp);
        }
        this.Close();
    }
    private void buttonCancel_Click(object sender, System.EventArgs e)
    {
        this.Close();
    }
```

VB.NET

```
    Private Sub buttonOK_Click(ByVal sender As System.Object, ByVal e As
                         System.EventArgs) Handles buttonOK.Click
        Dim taskCount As Integer = Me.checkedListBoxTasks.CheckedItems.Count
        Dim roleTasks(taskCount - 1) As ReportingWebService.Task
        Dim i As Integer
        For i = 0 To taskCount - 1 Step 1
            Dim taskName As String = Me.checkedListBoxTasks.CheckedItems(i).ToString()
            Dim sysTask As ReportingWebService.Task
            For Each sysTask In mItemTasks
                If taskName = sysTask.Name Then
                    roleTasks(i) = sysTask
                    Exit For
                End If
            Next
        Next
        Try
            Dim objBatchHeader As BatchHeader = New BatchHeader
            objBatchHeader.BatchID = mRsWebService.CreateBatch()
            mRsWebService.BatchHeaderValue = objBatchHeader
            If Mode = RSUtilities.EditModeEnum.edit Then
                    mRsWebService.SetRoleProperties( _
                    Me.textBoxRoleName.Text.ToString, _
```

```
                            Me.textBoxDescription.Text.ToString,
                        roleTasks)
            Else
                mRsWebService.CreateRole(Me.textBoxRoleName.Text.ToString, _
                                    Me.textBoxDescription.Text.ToString,_
                                    roleTasks)
            End If
            mRsWebService.ExecuteBatch()
            mRsWebService.BatchHeaderValue = Nothing
        Catch exp As Exception
            RSUtilities.ErrorHandler(exp)
        End Try
        Me.Close()
    End Sub
    Private Sub buttonCancel_Click(ByVal sender As System.Object, ByVal e As System.
    EventArgs) Handles buttonCancel.Click
        Me.Close()
    End Sub
```

The web methods needed for working with role objects are:

❑ `CreateRole`: This method is used to create a new role. It takes a name, a description, and an array of tasks as arguments.

❑ `SetRoleProperties`: This method is used for modifications of an existing role. It takes the same arguments as the `CreateRole` method.

In keeping with the other times that you have made modifications to the `buttonOk_Click` method, also makes use of the batch objects to make sure the changes are wrapped in a transaction.To call the `RoleTaskForm` add event handlers for click events of `buttonAdd` and `buttonEdit` buttons in the `RoleForm` and enter the following code into the event handlers:

C#

```csharp
private void buttonAdd_Click(object sender, System.EventArgs e)
{
    RoleTaskForm dialogForm = new RoleTaskForm();
    dialogForm.IsSystemRole = systemRoles;
    dialogForm.RsWebService = rsWebService;
    dialogForm.Mode = RSUtilities.EditModeEnum.add;
    dialogForm.ShowDialog(this);
    FillRoleListView();
    return;
}
private void buttonEdit_Click(object sender, System.EventArgs e)
{
    if (this.listViewRoles.SelectedItems.Count == 0)
    {
        MessageBox.Show("Select a role to edit.");
        return;
    }
    Role workingRole = null;
    string roleName = this.listViewRoles.SelectedItems[0].Text;
    foreach(Role role in roles)
```

```
      {
        if(role.Name == roleName)
        {
          workingRole = role;
          break;
        }
      }
      RoleTaskForm dialogForm = new RoleTaskForm();
      dialogForm.IsSystemRole = systemRoles;
      dialogForm.UserRole = workingRole;
      dialogForm.RsWebService = rsWebService;
      dialogForm.Mode = RSUtilities.EditModeEnum.edit;
      dialogForm.ShowDialog(this);
      return;
}
```

VB.NET

```
Private Sub buttonAdd_Click(ByVal sender As System.Object, ByVal e As
                         System.EventArgs) Handles buttonAdd.Click
    Dim dialogForm As RoleTaskForm = New RoleTaskForm
    dialogForm.IsSystemRole = mSystemRoles
    dialogForm.RsWebService = mRSWebService
    dialogForm.Mode = RSUtilities.EditModeEnum.add
    dialogForm.ShowDialog(Me)
    FillRoleListView()
    Return
End Sub
Private Sub buttonEdit_Click(ByVal sender As System.Object, ByVal e As
                         System.EventArgs) Handles buttonEdit.Click
    If Me.listViewRoles.SelectedItems.Count = 0 Then
        MessageBox.Show("Select a role to edit.")
        Return
    End If
    Dim workingRole As ReportingWebService.Role = Nothing
    Dim roleName As String = Me.listViewRoles.SelectedItems(0).Text
    Dim role As ReportingWebService.Role
    For Each role In mRoles
        If role.Name = roleName Then
            workingRole = role
            Exit For
        End If
    Next
    Dim dialogForm As RoleTaskForm = New RoleTaskForm
    dialogForm.IsSystemRole = mSystemRoles
    dialogForm.UserRole = workingRole
    dialogForm.RsWebService = mRSWebService
    dialogForm.Mode = RSUtilities.EditModeEnum.edit
    dialogForm.ShowDialog(Me)
    Return
End Sub
```

Now add an event handler for the click event of buttonDelete on RoleForm and enter the following code.

C#

```csharp
private void buttonDelete_Click(object sender, System.EventArgs e)
{
    if (this.listViewRoles.SelectedItems.Count == 0)
    {
      MessageBox.Show("Select a role to delete.");
      return;
    }
    DialogResult result = MessageBox.Show("Are you sure you want to delete this
                                          role?",  "Delete
                                          Role",MessageBoxButtons.YesNo,
                                          MessageBoxIcon.Question);
    if (result == DialogResult.Yes)
    {
      string roleName = this.listViewRoles.SelectedItems[0].Text;
      try
      {
        // Create the batch to handle the transaction
        BatchHeader batchHeader = new BatchHeader();
        batchHeader.BatchID = rsWebService.CreateBatch();
        rsWebService.BatchHeaderValue = batchHeader;
        // delete the role
        rsWebService.DeleteRole(roleName);
        // execute the batch
        this.rsWebService.ExecuteBatch();
        this.rsWebService.BatchHeaderValue = null;
      }
      catch(Exception exp)
      {
        RSUtilities.ErrorHandler(exp);
      }
      FillRoleListView();
    }
    return;
}
```

VB.NET

```vbnet
Private Sub buttonDelete_Click(ByVal sender As System.Object, ByVal e As
                              System.EventArgs) Handles buttonDelete.Click
    If Me.listViewRoles.SelectedItems.Count = 0 Then
        MessageBox.Show("Select a role to delete.")
        Return
    End If
    Dim result As DialogResult
    result = MessageBox.Show("Are you sure you want to delete this role?", _
                        "Delete Role", MessageBoxButtons.YesNo, _
                        MessageBoxIcon.Question)
    If result = DialogResult.Yes Then
        Dim roleName As String = Me.listViewRoles.SelectedItems(0).Text
        Try
            ' Create the batch to handle the transaction
            Dim objBatchHeader As ReportingWebService.BatchHeader =
                              New Reporting WebService.BatchHeader
```

```
            objBatchHeader.BatchID = mRSWebService.CreateBatch()
            mRSWebService.BatchHeaderValue = objBatchHeader
            ' delete the role
            mRSWebService.DeleteRole(roleName)
            ' execute the batch
            mRSWebService.ExecuteBatch()
            mRSWebService.BatchHeaderValue = Nothing
        Catch exp As Exception
            RSUtilities.ErrorHandler(exp)
        End Try
        FillRoleListView()
    End If
    Return
End Sub
```

The final web method that you will be using is `DeleteRole`. It will delete a role from the database; it takes the name of the role as its only argument. Again the batch is used to wrap the changes in a transaction. Save your code changes and run the application. Click the Go button to get a reference to the web service then choose the Security I Roles menu item to display the RoleForm. Click the Add button on the RoleForm to add a new role. Your RoleTaskForm should look similar to Figure 7-25. Add a name and description for your new role, assign some tasks and click the OK button.

Figure 7-25

The RoleTaskForm shown in Figure 7-25 presents a list of tasks a role may have permissions to perform. Enter a Role Name, Description for the role, and then check the appropriate Tasks as in Figure 7-26:

Figure 7-26

Clicking the OK button adds the new role to the list of user item roles in the RoleForm shown in Figure 7-27:

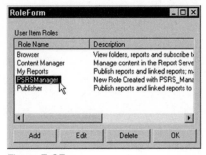

Figure 7-27

Click the OK button to close the RoleForm dialog.

Summary

In this chapter you learned how to consume the Reporting Services Web Service with a Windows application. The code throughout the application with the exception of the interface code would work just in the same way for a web application. You should now have a better understanding of the web service, its objects, and methods. The content of this chapter could be expanded to fill an entire volume by itself. In later chapters we will cover rendering reports, creating and maintaining subscriptions using program code. It is hoped that the material presented here will give you confidence to explore the web service and expand this application for your own needs.

Report Scripting

Many repetitive tasks on Report Server administration and management can be automated using script files. You can copy reports from one server to another and schedule the script to run when network traffic is low. By using scripts, the security configuration can be updated on a remote machine or the settings of a single report can be copied to multiple reports on a server. Other practical uses of scripting include:

❑   Creating a new report subscription for a role

❑   Listing the contents of a particular folder

❑   Adding a new member to a role

❑   Updating a shared data source

❑   Listing all the reports that are visible to a role

In this chapter, you'll step through a script that replicates reports and their properties from a source machine to a target machine. The script loops through a Report Server for report items and copies them to a target location just before logging the action in an XML log file. The file toggles easily between the development environment and the production environment by changing a single Boolean value.

Scripting is a powerful tool that will be increasingly used to execute common Windows and Report Server management tasks. Before getting started on the code, let's take a look at the various command line utilities available in Reporting Services.

Command Line Utilities

Reporting Services provides several utility applications that can ease the process of server management. The four main command line utilities are outlined in the following table:

Utility	Function
rsconfig	Manages the encrypted connection settings on a server
rskeymgmt	Retrieves the server encryption key-set and writes it to a file
rsactivate	Creates the encryption key to activate a server
rs	Automates common server management tasks

Let's briefly look at each of these useful tools.

rsconfig

Report Server keeps credentials and connection information encrypted in the ReportServer database. The rsconfig utility is used to manage the encrypted connection settings for a Report Server installation. For example, you can use this utility to change the username and password that Report Server uses to connect to a SQL Server database. The utility uses *Windows Management Instrumentation (WMI)* to write changes to the target machine and you must have administrator privileges to perform the actions. For reports that use data from a remote server, you can use this utility to configure the credentials used when the report runs.

Arguments passed to the rsconfig utility include username, password, server name, and authentication method.

For more information on this utility and its capabilities, refer to the rsconfig *utility topic in Reporting Services Books Online.*

rskeymgmt

Although encrypting data is a terrific way to secure it, the process has a weakness—the storing of encryption key values for later use. In reality, encrypted data is only as secure as the keys that are used to encrypt and decrypt it. Once the keys are compromised, data is no longer secure. Reporting Services securely stores encryption keys in its database.

Reporting Services documentation indicates that it uses both a public key and a symmetric key to encrypt data. Symmetric encryption is used because the data to be secured is usually private and the process is relatively quick. Symmetric encryption involves the use of a single key value for both encryption and decryption. For example, if you need to repair account information in a Report Server instance, you can use the encryption key to recover the encrypted data and restore the account. If the key is not available, the encrypted data cannot be recovered and you'll need to manually enter the account information to make the account operational again.

Reporting Services creates encryption keys during the setup process. It's important that you make a copy of the key value and store it in a secure location. The rskeymgmt utility is the tool used to retrieve the encryption key-set and write it to a file. By default the rskeymgmt executable is located in the

`C:\Program Files\Microsoft SQL Server\80\Tools\Binn` directory. The key values written to the file are encrypted using another key built from the password used when creating the file. The same password must then be used to later retrieve the decrypted keys from the storage file.

Creating a backup copy of the encryption key is straightforward. The `rskeymgmt` application must be run on the same machine as the Report Server installation. Use the `-e` (extract) argument to pull the key value from Reporting Services and the `-f` (file) argument to specify the fully qualified file name. You'll also need to supply a password using the `-p` argument. The completed command line syntax reads as follows:

```
rskeymgmt -e -f a:\ReportServerDBKey.txt -p P@ssw0rd
```

This line extracts the key value, creates a text file on a floppy disk called `ReportServerDBKey.txt`, and encrypts the key value using the password indicated.

The `rskeymgmt` utility can be used to perform other encryption key management functions as well. For example, it can be used to delete encrypted content that is no longer in use.

rsactivate

While the `rsconfig` utility can be used to add a Report Server instance to a web farm, the server instance is not considered activated until it can encrypt and decrypt data in the Report Server database. The process of activation creates the symmetric key used in the encryption process and is performed using either the `rsactivate` utility or the Reporting Services WMI provider.

rs

In this chapter we refer to this utility as the RS utility. This utility provides developers and administrators the ability to automate common, repetitive server management tasks. These scripted operations allow a wide range of tasks to be performed, such as finding all the reports being delivered to a particular user or updating the security settings on a server instance. The bulk of this chapter covers a script that performs the commonly requested task of deploying reports from one server to another.

Automating Server and Report Management

Reporting Services provides a WMI interface to the configuration files for the Report Server instance and the Report Manager application. Much like the command line utilities, these classes provide a way to programmatically perform application management. For example, you can change the credential values and authentication mechanisms that the Report Server uses to connect to the database. The same classes can be used to perform actions on remote machines. These application configuration files are XML files.

The next time the application runs, the CLR will apply the new values. The Report Server configuration file is accessed through the `MSReportServer_ConfigurationSetting` class and the Report Manager Interface web application configuration file is available through the

`MSReportServerReportManager_ConfigurationSetting` class. Both classes are accessed through the WMI interface.

Repetitive tasks can be automated using scripts and the RS utility. Common tasks that can be scripted include duplicating environment settings from one server to another or deploying resources, reports, and other database content from one environment to another. For example, migrating content from the development environment to the testing and production environments.

The file that contains the automation code is a Unicode or UTF-8 text file with an `.rss` file extension. The code itself is written in Visual Basic .NET.

Reporting Services RS Utility

The RS utility is an application that hosts scripts for execution by a scripting engine. The RS utility compiles the user-supplied script and creates instances of the objects required to run it. If the script does not compile, errors are returned to help debug the file. If the compilation is successful, execution of the script begins. The RS utility can run scripts against a local or remote sever installation.

As a script developer, you are provided access to several namespaces in the .NET Framework class library. You also have full access to the Reporting Services Web Service interface. One of the most important functions of the RS utility is the creation of a proxy class for use by the hosted script. When the RS utility is run, an argument is provided, which is the URL of the Reporting Service instance to work with. The RS utility then invokes the `wsdl.exe` utility internally, creating a proxy class that acts as the local script interface to the Reporting Services Web Service. The variable name for the web service reference is called `rs`, and is available globally to your script. All of the Reporting Service Web Service methods are available through the `rs` proxy. For this chapter, the `rs` proxy is referred to as the `rs` object.

RS Utility Command Line Syntax

Let's take a look at the RS utility command line syntax. At the command prompt, type `rs /?`. This will invoke the RS utility Help displaying the utility syntax and command line arguments as in Figure 8-1:

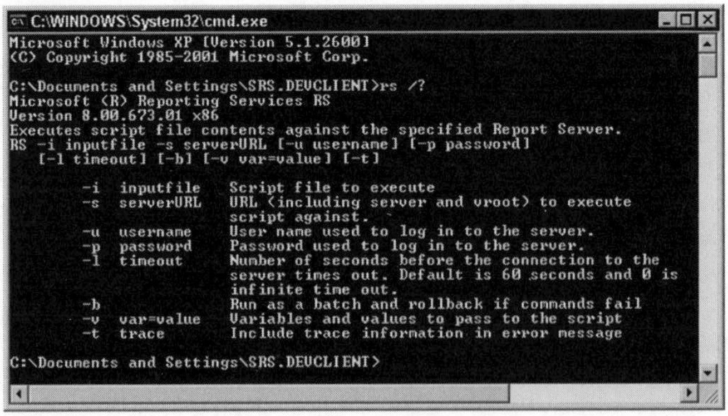

Figure 8-1

Invoking the RS utility is as simple as typing `rs` or `rs.exe` at the command prompt, and supplying the required values. The two required values are the script to run (`/i` argument), and the server to run the script against (`/s` argument).

The syntax for using the RS utility is as follows:

```
rs /i <inputFile> /s <serverURL> [/u <username>] [/p <password>] [/l <timeout>]
[/b] [/v <var=value>] [/t]
```

The arguments (parameters) can be indicated by using the `/` or `-` symbols. For example, the input file value can be provided using `-i` or `/i` and the filename. It's a matter of personal preference and in some cases company style guide. The arguments themselves are case insensitive except for the password value. You can have as many spaces as you want between the argument indicator and the value you're providing.

The script file must be a fully qualified path to the `.rss` file. For example, let's say that your scripts are located in the `C:\ReportServer\Scripts` directory. If you navigate to that location in the command window, the path value that you'll provide to the RS utility will be as simple as the filename itself.

The `serverURL` value is made up of the protocol, server, and virtual directory to execute the script. By default, the RS utility will attempt to connect to the resource using `https`. If you specify `http`, the RS utility will only use `http`. If you specify https and it's not supported on the server, the RS utility will return an error.

By default, the RS utility will authenticate against the target Report Server instance using the credentials provided by the user running the script. Both the username and password arguments are optional arguments and can be used to provide different credentials. The script itself can provide credential values through the `rs` object, but hardcoded credentials are a security threat. It's better to have the script authenticate credentials passed by the user at runtime; the username must include the domain name and user account.

The `timeout` value is an optional argument and is used to specify the number of seconds before the connection to the server times out. The default value is eight seconds. Providing a value of zero means the connection never times out.

If you want your script to run as a batch, you can indicate that by using the optional `/b` argument. Batches are particularly useful when you need to be sure that the same action is performed on multiple machines; for example, when running a script against multiple machines in a server farm. A batch runs as a type of mini transaction where failure of commands within the script causes the batch to roll back. This argument doesn't take any values. The RS utility default bahaviour is to run scripts without creating a batch.

Your VB.NET script can also contain variables with user-provided values. These variables are not declared in the script and are available globally to any member within the script. The values are supplied using `/v` arguments for each variable, which are provided as `name=value` pairs. The following code shows an example:

```
rs /i DeployReports.rss /s http://localhost/reportserver/reportservice.asmx /v
targetURL= http://localhost/reportserver/reportservice.asmx
```

Quotes around the value are optional unless the value contains spaces. The /v argument is optional unless your script uses a variable value that's not declared in the script. If the script takes an argument that the user doesn't supply, the script will not compile.

The /t argument is also optional; it turns on tracing to view request processing and capture information about returned errors.

When your script runs, the RS utility creates an instance of the scripting engine to run it. The VB.NET scripting engine uses the same code base as VB.NET, so you have access to standard VB.NET functionality from within your script. You'll take a closer look at the hosting environment capabilities and limitations throughout the rest of this chapter.

RS Utility Errors

It will be helpful to be aware of the errors that the RS utility can return. Knowing the exceptions can help you avoid raising them. Briefly, the RS utility errors include:

- ❑ CompilerFailed: If the RS utility is unable to compile your script it will return an error to indicate what the problem was.

- ❑ ConnectionFailed: The utility could not connect to the server.

- ❑ DuplicateCommandLineOption: Command line arguments provided more than once, except for the /v argument.

- ❑ DuplicateVariable: Same variable provided more than once.

- ❑ InvalidAuthorizationMethod: The server doesn't recognize your authorization method.

- ❑ InvalidCommandLineOption: Check the syntax by running /?. Usually it's the result of a typing error.

- ❑ InvalidTimeoutValue: The value for this argument must be a positive integer.

- ❑ InvalidVariableName: The variable name doesn't match what the script is expecting.

- ❑ InvalidVariableSpecification: Variables must be provided using the name=value syntax. Use quotes if the variable value contains spaces.

- ❑ MissingOptionValue: You specified the argument, but forgot the value (or it's in a form the compiler doesn't recognize).

- ❑ MissingRequiredOption: Input file and server URL are required.

- ❑ MissingSomeAuthorizationValues: Username and password are optional but paired.

- ❑ ScriptException: The script lets an unhandled exception fall off the Main method. You need to investigate the error and consider adding some additional exception handling.

If the Reporting Service returns an exception, it will be a SoapException containing the specific error message. As you'll see in the next section, there is no way to catch a SoapException in the script, so you'll need to configure a generic catch block to catch these exceptions.

Now that you have an understanding of how the RS utility works, let's take a look at configuring a development environment and building a script to deploy content.

Script Development

Before you begin creating an effective development harness, it's important to know the elements you have to work with. A Reporting Service script file is simply a Unicode or UTF-8 text file which is a 16-bit character-encoding standard supported by many languages. It simplifies the localization of text and data, providing a data exchange format by defining code values for each character. The latest Microsoft operating systems use it for character and string manipulation.

The script project that follows is done using Visual Studio .NET. Let's take a look at the requirements for the script.

Script Format Requirements

The file must contain a `Main` method .The `Main` method is used by the script host as the entry point into your code. For this environment, the `Main` method can take no parameters. When the `Main` method completes, your script is done. You can make calls to methods outside of the `Main` method. For the script to compile, it needs to contain at least this code:

```
Public Sub Main()
      'code to process server content goes here
End Sub
```

The script file can contain user-defined variables and methods. The variables can be module-level, which means they're available to all members in the file. User-defined variables (those provided by the user at runtime) are not declared in the code.

The host environment doesn't understand overloaded methods so you can't use them in your code. The script file does not contain `Imports` statements, which would otherwise indicate namespaces that are in use.

Namespaces Available

Not all namespaces in the .NET Framework base class library are available for use in your scripts. The RS hosting utility provides access to the Reporting Services Web Service interface as well as to classes contained in four namespaces described in the following sections.

System

Most of the classes in this namespace reside in the `mscorlib` assembly. This namespace is home to data types, such as integer and string, as well as to utility classes, such as the `Array`, `Console`, and `Convert` classes.

System.IO

Classes in this namespace provide access to the file system. Several encapsulate static or instance methods for performing file and directory manipulation. Streams and different types of readers and writers belong to this namespace. Although a few classes in this namespace are in the System assembly, most of them are located in mscorlib.

System.Xml

The System.Xml namespace is primarily located in the System.Xml assembly. This namespace provides access to most of the classes needed to create and read XML documents including:

- ❑ XmlDocument
- ❑ XmlElement
- ❑ XmlTextReader
- ❑ XmlTextWriter
- ❑ XmlValidatingReader

This namespace does not provide access to the following classes:

- ❑ XmlSchema
- ❑ XPathDocument
- ❑ XslTransform

System.Web.Services

This namespace contains relatively few classes, primarily the WebMethodAttribute and WebServiceAttribute. These attribute classes are applied to classes and methods, enabling them to be exposed as web services and web methods.

Reporting Services Web Service

Access to the Reporting Services Web Service interface is made through the RS utility script host. The RS utility proxy provides full access to the Web Service members.

It may be helpful to note the namespaces that are not available:

- ❑ Microsoft.VisualBasic
- ❑ System.Text
- ❑ System.Web.Services.Protocols

The Microsoft.VisualBasic namespace contains global functions that many VB users rely upon. The System.Text is home to the StringBuilder and encoding classes, and System.Web.Services.Protocols is where the SoapException class lives.

Building a Script Development Harness

The process of creating and maintaining a management script file can be cumbersome. Frequently, scripts are written using a text editor or other scripting tools. Depending on the developer, the file may then be ported to Visual Studio for testing. Once the code is stable, the extra Visual Studio bits are removed or commented out to create a proper script file once again.

Personally, I think the typical process of running a file in Visual Studio to check it and then commenting out the extra code to make it work as a dedicated script is basically a hack. There are better ways of making a script file work in both the development and production environments.

The technique outlined in this chapter uses the conditional compilation capabilities of the .NET compilers that are used when a script runs. By using conditional compilation, a script file simply toggles from one environment to the other. It's ideal for development because the developer has the support of code completion and *IntelliSense*. The development environment provides sophisticated debugging capabilities, and the file can be managed as part of a VS.NET project. The conditional compilation approach enables scripting projects to be managed like every other project in the production development environment while providing a completely suitable code file for the script host at runtime.

Although the script file contains VB.NET code, an `.rss` script file, as it is, will not compile in the Visual Studio development environment. But that's not the only confusing aspect of the script file. For example, although the file acts as a VB.NET module, it doesn't contain module statements. To help matters, the script can contain undeclared variables and runs against an unseen web service proxy class. Having a good development harness can go a long way in creating an efficient environment for script development.

Creating the Console Project

Visual Studio is a robust development tool that's familiar to most .NET developers. Its IntelliSense, code completion, and debugging capabilities help ease the development of `.rss` scripts as well. If you plan on creating multiple scripts for the RS utility, it can be helpful to group them under a single solution. For this, start with a blank solution and add script projects as needed.

In Visual Studio, select File | New | Blank Solution from the menu bar. This will open the New Project dialog box as shown in Figure 8-2:

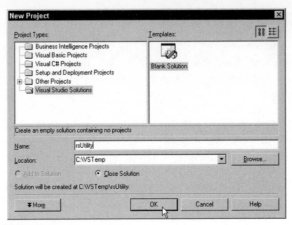

Figure 8-2

Name the blank solution rsUtility and click OK to create the solution. You now have a container for all your RS utility script projects. To add the first project, right click the solution in the Solution Explorer and select Add | New Project to open another New Project dialog box. This time select Visual Basic Projects in the Project Types pane. You'll see the various pre-built project templates in the right pane. Choose the Console Application template and give the project an appropriate name, in this case, DeployReports as shown in Figure 8-3:

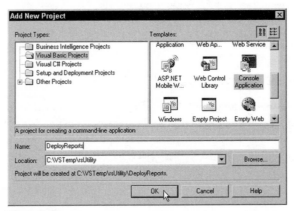

Figure 8-3

When the project is added to the solution, the `Module1.vb` file opens in the code window. Notice that the file already includes the `Main` method contained in a module called `Module1`. Rename the `Module1.vb` file to `DeployReports.vb` in the Solution Explorer.

Now that the rough framework is in place, let's further define the environment you'll be working in.

Adding Imports Statements

Remember, you only have access to certain namespaces from within the .rss script. The RS hosting utility provides the namespace access. The script file itself does not contain any Imports statements. The console application template includes several Imports statements already, and you'll need to modify those to suit the project.

To do this, right click the DeployReports project in the Solution Explorer and select Properties. That will bring up the DeployReports Property Pages box. In the Common Properties folder in the left pane, click the Imports group. Notice that in the Project imports box, five namespaces are already listed:

- ❏ Microsoft.VisualBasic
- ❏ System
- ❏ System.Collections
- ❏ System.Data
- ❏ System.Diagnostics

Select and remove all but the System and System.Diagnostics namespaces. The System.Diagnostics namespace is included for debugging purposes. Then, add System.IO, System.Web.Services, and System.Xml. Your new imports list will include:

- ❏ System
- ❏ System.Diagnostics
- ❏ System.IO
- ❏ System.Web.Services
- ❏ System.Xml

The completed property page will be similar to Figure 8-4:

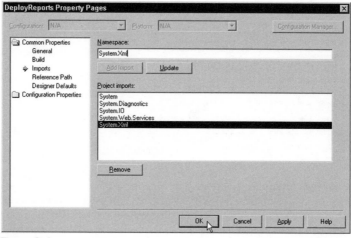

Figure 8-4

Adding References

Now you'll need to modify the assembly references for the project. First, remove the references that are not needed. In the Solution Explorer, open the References folder to view the current assembly references. Remove the System.Data reference by right clicking it and selecting Remove from the context menu. Then right click the References folder and select Add Reference.

In the Add Reference dialog box, ensure that you're viewing the .NET tab. Select the System.Web.Services assembly by clicking the component name, and then click the Select button. That will add the component to the list of Selected Components in the bottom list box. Click OK to add the reference to your project.

For development, you'll also need to reference the Reporting Services Web Service. To do that, right click the References folder in the Solution Explorer and select Add Web Reference to bring up the Add Web Reference dialog box. This form contains a browser pane, an address bar, and a couple of other items. In the address bar, type the URL of the Report Server you want to code against. The default URL is http<s>://<servername>/reportserver/reportservice.asmx.

If you've pointed at a valid web service, the Add Reference button will be enabled. Before you click it, however, give the web reference a name; in this case, the reference is called ReportServer. Figure 8-5 shows a completed web reference dialog box:

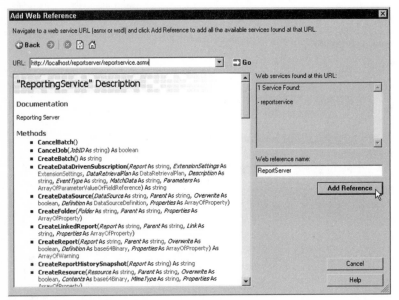

Figure 8-5

Clicking the Add Reference button invokes the wsdl.exe utility. The wsdl.exe checks the WSDL document for the web service and creates a proxy class that acts as your local interface to the remote web service. You're creating a web service proxy in the same way that the RS utility creates it for your hosted script. Now you can code against that web service as if it were a local object, because in proxy form, it is a local object.

The completed solution and project hierarchy is shown in Figure 8-6. Note that the reference to the **System.Data** assembly has been deleted. The RS utility host doesn't provide access to its content, so the reference is deleted from the development environment.

Figure 8-6

Now, let's start working with the code. In the code editor, change the name of the module to **DeployReports**. Although it isn't required, it's a good practice to add a section of commented lines containing information about the file. Make some space above the module declaration to add a file summary:

```
#Region ' File Summary'
'==================================================================
'   Development File:     DeployReports.vb
'   Production File:      DeployReports.rss
'
'   Description:
'           This module is an approach to building Reporting
'           Service scripts hosted by the RS utility.
'           The devEnvironment bool value allows toggling the
'           file between development (.vb) and production (.rss).
'
'           The DeployReports script iterates through the Report
'           Server items on a source machine, deploying the .rdl
'           report definitions and properties to a target machine.
'           Actions and results are logged to an XML file.
'
'   Required Variable:
'           This value must be provided at runtime when hosted by
'           the rs utility (using the /v parameter).
'
'           Name: targetURL
'           Value: http(s) URL of the target Reporting Service machine.
'                  Must have same folder structure as source machine.
'                  Must use same credentials as the source machine.
'
'------------------------------------------------------------------
'           SQL Reporting Services Beta 2
'           .NET Framework 1.1
'           Visual Studio .NET 2003
'           Jan 2004; James Counihan; Seattle USA
'//================================================================
#End Region
```

The commented section is wrapped by a conditional compilation directive. The `#Region` directive allows the wrapped section to be closed (collapsed) while working in other regions of the file. It's a sample use of a conditional compilation directive. The next step is to structure the code to work in both development and runtime environments, which is done by using other conditional compilation directives.

Using Conditional Compilation

The file you're creating is meant to work in both the Visual Studio development environment and the hosted RS utility production environment. To save development time, it would be nice to have a single place to toggle the file for use in each of the environments. Conditional compilation enables you to do that.

Conditional compilation involves the use of compiler directives. For the **DeployReports** project you'll use two directives: a constant definition and statements to compile different blocks of code depending on the constant value. Conditional directives are indicated using the # symbol at the start of the code statement. You may recognize the `#Region` and `#End Region` directives that wrap generated code sections in a Windows form or a web form application.

In the `DeployReports.vb` file, make some space above the module `DeployReports` statement. In that area at the top of the file, enter the following statements:

```
#Region ' Dev/Prod Toggle '

'Set value to True if hosted by Visual Studio;
'Set value to False if hosted by the rs utility.
#Const devEnvironment = True

#End Region
```

A data type declaration is not part of the statement. There's a Visual Basic .NET background compiler that will check syntax as you code, based on the value you've toggled `devEnvironment`to. As part of your imperative code statements you'll use `#If...Then...#Else` statements to block code based on the environment. Configuring the file for hosting by the RS utility then becomes a matter of setting the `devEnvironment` value to `False` and giving the file an `.rss` extension.

In fact, the `Module` statement itself needs the conditional compilation block applied to it. The `Module` statement isn't used in the hosted RS utility environment so you'll need to wrap it with the conditional check. If this is a development environment, compile the embedded statement into the assembly, if not, skip it.

```
#If devEnvironment Then
Module DeployReports
#End If
```

The RS utility compiles the script file when it's first invoked and the compiler in that hosted environment understands the conditional compilation statements.

The next section of code is an area for global variable declaration. Three string variables are declared: `m_logFile`, `m_logDir`, and `m_logPath`. They contain values for the file name, directory path, and concatenated path of where you want the log file to be saved.

```
#Region ' Global Vars '

    'Name of the log file. This code creates xml output.
    Dim m_logFile As String = 'EventLog.xml'
    'Directory to save the log to.
    Dim m_logDir As String = '/Report Deployment Log'
    'Full path
    Dim m_logPath As String = m_logDir & '/' & m_logFile

    'Not a user-defined value
    Dim m_errFlag As Boolean = False

#End Region
```

This code writes XML output to the `EventLog.xml` file in the **Report Deployment Log** directory of the current drive. If the file does not exist, it will be created. The `m_errFlag` Boolean value is used for error handling to determine whether to throw the exception or handle it internally. Now you're ready to go in and start adding code to the `Main` method.

Accessing Server Items

The `Main` method is the host entry point to your application. In the RS utility environment the `Main` method takes no arguments. Runtime variable values can be passed to your script but you use a different technique to do that. You'll read about using that technique later in this chapter. Before that, let's add some code to the file.

In the code body of the `Main` method, declare the `traceMessage` and `timeStamp` string variables and the `reportCount` integer field. These are used to display processing information in the console window and to write nodes to the XML log file.

```
#Region ' Main()'

    Sub Main()

        Dim traceMessage, timeStamp As String
        Dim reportCount As Integer
```

In the development environment, you'll need to connect to the `ReportServer` instance to begin performing actions on it but as the RS utility hosting environment provides the connection, this step isn't necessary.

Creating the Proxy Instance

Because you need to create your own web service connection in one environment and not in the other, conditional compilation is an ideal solution. Additionally, how you qualify the classes you're working with in code is different for each environment. For example, previously you added a web reference to the project. The reference was named **ReportServer**. Through the reference you have access to the types and methods it defines.

```
Dim catItems(), catItem As ReportServer.CatalogItem
```

However, the web service is available globally in the hosted RS utility environment. Qualifying classes uses a different syntax:

```
Dim catItems(), catItem As CatalogItem
```

Both of these statements do the same thing that is declaring variables representing an array of `CatalogItems` and a single `CatalogItem`. The `ReportServer.CatalogItem` statement compiles in Visual Studio, the other compiles in the RS utility environment.

Additionally, you need to create an instance of the web service proxy class that was created locally by the `wsdl.exe` utility when you added the web reference:

```
'create an instance of the Report Server
' Web service proxy
Dim rs As New ReportServer.ReportingService
```

As in the RS utiltiy environment, the reference is called `rs`. This chapter will continue to refer to the `rs` reference as the `rs` object. The `New` keyword allocates memory on the managed heap and then the `ReportingService` constructor is invoked to instantiate it. This statement is not needed in the RS utility environment. The complete conditional code block is as follows:

```
#If devEnvironment Then
        Dim catItems(), catItem As ReportServer.CatalogItem

        'create an instance of the Report Server
        ' Web service proxy
        Dim rs As New ReportServer.ReportingService

        'var value supplied by the user at runtime;
        ' set here for development to deploy the
        ' reports right back to the source machine.
        Dim targetURL As String = rs.Url 'development value
#Else
        Dim catItems(), catItem As CatalogItem
#End If
```

The (`devEnvironment = true`) embedded statements include a string variable declaration:

```
Dim targetURL As String = rs.Url 'development value
```

This statement allows you to set a `targetURL` value at design time rather than retrieving one from the user at runtime. For development, this value is set equal to the URL property value of the `rs` object web service reference. This will allow the script to run and it will overwrite the existing content on the development machine. For the production environment, it would be better to allow the user to provide the `targetURL` value.

Passing Variable Values to the Script

The `targetURL` value is used in the script regardless of which environment the code runs in. When hosted by the RS utility though, the variable is never declared in the code. The RS utility will expect the variable value to be set when the utility is invoked. The RS utility syntax provides an optional `/v` argument, which is used to set values for the undeclared variables. In this case, the user will need to provide the `targetURL` value in order for the script to compile. When the script is completed, the variable value will be passed as follows:

```
rs /i DeployReports.rss /s http://localhost/reportserver/reportservice.asmx /v
targetURL= http://localhost/reportserver/reportservice.asmx
```

To read more about running this file, see the *Running the Script* section later in this chapter.

Retrieving Items

Before you can perform any actions on the Report Server instance, your code must be authenticated. The Report Server won't allow any methods to be invoked without authenticating the user tied to the request and authorizing that the user has permission to perform the request. You could use credential values provided by the user at runtime, but for ease, the code uses the identity of the user currently logged in. The following lines show the `credentials` property of the `rs` object being assigned the value of the shared `DefaultCredentials` property of the `CredentialCache` object:

```
'set credentials, so we'll be let through
rs.Credentials = System.Net.CredentialCache.DefaultCredentials
```

The authentication mechanisms you implement should be based on your security policy. Be sure to modify this code to support your chosen security policy.

> **In the production environment, it is preferable to have the username and password values supplied by the user at runtime.**

In this script, you'll be looking at each of the items in the source server to find reports to deploy. The Reporting Service `ListChildren` web method returns an array of catalog items that can be iterated through:

```
'get array of server catalog items
catItems = rs.ListChildren("/", True)
```

The returned results are available in the `catItems` array.

Building Message Content

The next Report Server actions involve processing the returned `CatalogItems`. Before proceeding, this is a good time to start logging the initial actions and displaying feedback to the user.

There are two places to output messages, the console and XML log file. The console will display messages regarding general actions; the log file will contain those messages in addition to actions and warnings about each item deployed.

The RS utility-provided namespaces do not give us access to the `StringBuilder` class. To increase the usability in the console window, creating the message content is done in two operations. In the initial stages of the process, the current date and time are converted to a string and then formatted:

```
'write to log & console.
'For usability in the console and xml file,
'two approaches are taken.
'Note we have no access to the stringbuilder class.
timeStamp = DateTime.Now.ToString("G")
```

The display message is then built in chunks for display in the console. The message text is built using the properties of the `rs` object reference and the `catItems` array. The chunks are split in the way you want the content to be displayed in the console:

```
'build message elements
Dim temp(6) As String
temp(0) = "** DeployReports script for Reporting Services ** "
temp(1) = "Copying report definitions and properties from"
temp(2) = "(source URL) " & rs.Url & " to"
temp(3) = "(target URL) " & targetURL & ";  "
temp(4) = "Total server items to process: " & catItems.Length & ";  "
temp(5) = "Start date/time: " & timeStamp & "."
```

Once the message content is built, it writes values to the console:

```
'for readability in the console, display in chunks
Console.WriteLine()
Console.WriteLine(temp(0))
Console.WriteLine()
Console.WriteLine(temp(1))
Console.WriteLine(temp(2))
Console.WriteLine(temp(3))
Console.WriteLine()
Console.WriteLine(temp(4))
Console.WriteLine(temp(5))
Console.WriteLine("Logging to: " & m_logPath)
Console.WriteLine()
```

Then concatenate the message chunks to create the string written to the XML log. Because the chunks are array elements, a `For ... Next` loop works:

```
'concatenate the values to create the log entry
Dim i As Integer
For i = 0 To temp.Length - 1
    traceMessage &= temp(i)
Next
```

Finally, the concatenated `traceMessage` value is passed to a method for logging. The `traceMessage` variable will be used again later in the code, so once the message is logged, it's cleared to make it ready for the next use:

```
'write to the log
LogComment(traceMessage)
traceMessage = ""
```

It would be nice to have access to the `System.Text` namespace where the `StringBuilder` class is located. During informal testing, we've found that the `StringBuilder` class is about 300% faster at string concatenation than the `String` class. This is a relatively short operation though, so the performance penalty is reasonable.

With the status displayed and the first actions logged, it's time to start processing the items in the database.

Retrieving Reports

The content in a Report Server database includes folders, data sources, reports, and so on. Now that you have a listing of each item in the Report Server database, you'll need to loop through them to identify the reports to be deployed.

Retrieving Report Items

The items returned from the `ListChildren` method are available in the array of `CatalogItems`, `catItems`. The `catItems` variable is an instance of `System.Array`, which provides the ability to iterate through each of the elements contained in it. There are different ways to perform the iteration, but for this purpose using a `For ... Each` loop is clean and efficient:

```
'process catalog items
For Each catItem In catItems
```

Perform a test on each item to determine the item type. The Report Server exposes an `ItemTypeEnum` enumeration. It has six values that you can compare the current array element with:

❑ `DataSource`

❑ `Folder`

❑ `LinkedReport`

❑ `Report`

❑ `Resource`

❑ `Unknown`

This script tests each array element to see if it's a report. If the `CatalogItem` is a report, then it performs additional processing on it. How the `ItemType` enumeration is qualified will be different for each of the development and production environments. That calls for a second conditional compilation code block.

```
#If devEnvironment Then
            If catItem.Type = ReportServer.ItemTypeEnum.Report Then
                Dim warnings() As ReportServer.Warning
#Else
            If catItem.Type = ItemTypeEnum.Report Then
                Dim warnings() As Warning
#End If
```

The array of warnings holds information about the processing of the report item. You'll also need information about the location of the report item later, so a variable is declared and its value set using the `Path` property of the current report `CatalogItem`:

```
Dim itemPath As String = catItem.Path
```

Getting Report Definitions

The next section of the script file is where actions performed on the Report Server could raise exceptions. .NET introduced the use of structured exception handling using `Try … Catch` blocks. The code that may raise an exception is wrapped in a `Try` block, and then a `Catch` block is configured to catch any exceptions that are raised in the `Try` block:

```
'process report
Try
```

The `Catch` and `End Try` statements can be entered now and then space can be created between them to add more logic.

The report definition is an `.rdl` file in the Report Server database. The Reporting Service Web Service exposes a `GetReportDefinition` method, which can be used to get the definition. The method returns a `Byte` array, so a variable is created to hold the returned result:

```
'get report definition
Dim reportDefinition() As Byte = _
                        rs.GetReportDefinition(itemPath)
```

Later in the code, you'll need to pass a string value that the parent directory of the report. To get that value, the `Substring` method of the `itemPath` string variable is invoked. The parameters passed narrow down the resulting string to the parent directory name without any "/" characters:

```
Dim parentDir As String = itemPath.Substring(0,
            (itemPath.Length - catItem.Name.Length) - 1)
```

Once you've got the report definition, you can change non-protected (non read-only) report property values. You can also deploy the report to another machine.

Deploying Reports

While you've got the current report definition, you can toggle the URL property of the `rs` object Report Server reference to point to the target machine. That value will come from the user-provided `targetURL` variable:

```
'deploy to target machine
rs.Url = targetURL
```

Now that the code is pointed at the `targetURL`, you can deploy the report.

The CreateReport Method

The Reporting Service `CreateReport` method writes a report definition to a target address. This method takes parameters to indicate the name of the report to create, the directory to create it in, a Boolean value indicating whether to overwrite an existing definition, a byte array which is the report definition, and an array of property items for report properties that you might want to change.

For testing purposes, the parent directory parameter of the `CreateReport` method can be set to a value other than the current location of the source report. For example, a parent directory value of / will cause the reports to be written to the root directory of the Reporting Service. You can then open Report Manager and view the newly deployed reports in the `Home` directory:

```
warnings = rs.CreateReport(catItem.Name, parentDir, True,
                reportDefinition, Nothing)
```

If there's something to know about the report creation process, the `CreateReport` method will return an array of warning objects. Each array element contains information about a specific warning that was raised while creating the report. Warnings will not prevent the report from being created. You'll have to write warnings to the log file, along with information about the deployed report. For readability in the log file the, deployment is logged first followed by any warnings:

```
'for readability: log the deployment, then any warnings
LogEvent(catItem)
If Not (warnings Is Nothing) Then
    #If devEnvironment Then
        Dim warning As ReportServer.Warning
        #Else
        Dim warning As Warning
        #End If
        traceMessage = warnings.Length.ToString & _
        ' deployment warning(s) for the " & catItem.Name & "
            report: "
        For Each warning In warnings
        traceMessage &= warning.Message & " "
    Next warning
    LogComment(traceMessage)
    traceMessage = ""
End If

reportCount += 1
```

A conditional compilation block is used to separate how the `Warning` class is qualified as a data type for the `warning` variable. The `warning` variable is used to represent each element in the `warnings` array to build a string containing each element value, so that the completed string can be written to the log.

That completes the `Try` block and the processing of this report item. A `reportCount` variable value is incremented, which will be used in the building of a final message for display and logging. The next step in the process is configuring the `Catch` block.

Error Handling

In this script, error handling is limited to logging errors returned while retrieving or creating the report. If a script error occurs, the exception is written to the console:

```
        Catch ex As Exception
            If errFlag Then
                Console.WriteLine("Error processing: " & ex.ToString)
            Else
                LogError(ex, catItem)
            End If
            'reportCount = 0
        End Try
    End If
Next 'catalogItem
```

Exceptions caught by the RS utility host will cause execution to stop.

Logging Events

The script logs general information on the script run, actions performed on report items, and exceptions. Each log entry is an XML node, which can either be an element or a comment. Elements are used for recording report item actions and errors, while comments are used for general information and report deployment warnings.

The `#Region` ... `#End` Region directive wraps this group of utility methods, which are used for writing to the log. Each of the methods invokes a utility that checks for the existence of the log file.

Opening the File

The `GetLogFile` is invoked even before the logging methods attempt to write any content to the XML file. This function checks for the existence of the `m_logDir` and `m_logFile` values and creates them if they don't exist. The `System.Xml` namespace contains the `XmlDocument` class used here:

```
    Public Function GetLogFile() As XmlDocument
        Dim xmlDoc As XmlDocument
```

If the XML file exists, it is opened. The `Load` method of the `XmlDocument` opens the existing file so that the contents can be appended:

```
        If File.Exists(m_logPath) Then
            xmlDoc = New XmlDocument
            xmlDoc.Load(m_logPath)
```

If a new XML file is created, the XML declarations and root element are added to the document. This code block uses the shared (static in C#) CreateDirectory method of the Directory class, which is in the System.IO namespace. As the member is shared, it's invoked on the class rather than as an instance of the class. Additionally, the LoadXml method of the XmlDocument is invoked so a string can be passed defining the foundation of the XML content:

```
        Else
            If Not (Directory.Exists(m_logDir)) Then
            Directory.CreateDirectory(m_logDir)
            'create the new xml doc
            xmlDoc = New XmlDocument
            xmlDoc.LoadXml('<?xml version='1.0' encoding='utf-8' ?>
                        <events> </events>')
        End If
```

In both cases, a reference to the XmlDocument is returned for the logging methods to work with:

```
        Return xmlDoc
    End Function
```

Now that the document has been returned, the logging members can write to it.

Writing XML Nodes

There are three logging members in the script:

❑   LogEvent

❑   LogComment

❑   LogError

The methods are invoked depending on which node type is needed. The LogEvent code is walked through here; the other methods work in almost the same way but with different data types passed as parameters. This would typically be a situation for overloaded versions of the same method but that's not an option in the RS utility environment. Because the different parameter data types are qualified differently in each environment, this is also a case for using conditional compilation. In this case, the method signatures are blocked using the #If...Then...#Else directive:

```
#If devEnvironment Then
    Public Sub LogEvent(ByVal reportItem As ReportServer.CatalogItem) 'Report
    Server.
#Else
    Public Sub LogEvent(ByVal reportItem As CatalogItem)
#End If
```

The method body begins with declaring a string to hold a timestamp value for the log entry. Then the `GetLogFile` method is called to retrieve the `XmlDocument` to log to:

```
        Dim timeStamp As String
        Try
            Dim logDoc As XmlDocument = GetLogFile()
```

Each `event` is logged as separate event elements. The elements are empty and contain their data as attribute values. In this code, the `CreateElement` method of the `XmlDocument` is invoked and passed a parameter, which is the name of the element to create:

```
            Dim elem As XmlElement = logDoc.CreateElement("event")
```

The `timeStamp` variable is assigned a formatted value. Attributes are given values using the `SetAttribute` method of the `XmlElement`. Two parameters are passed to the method, the name of the attribute and its value:

```
            timeStamp = DateTime.Now.ToString("T")
            With elem
                .SetAttribute("eventType", "deployment")
                .SetAttribute("reportItem", reportItem.Path)
                .SetAttribute("sizeBytes", reportItem.Size)
                .SetAttribute("timeStamp", timeStamp)
            End With
```

The newly created element is then added as a child element to the root node and the file changes are saved. If an error occurs while processing the entry, you write the details to the log and continue:

```
            logDoc.DocumentElement.AppendChild(elem)
            logDoc.Save(m_logPath)
        Catch ex As Exception
            LogError(ex, reportItem)
        End Try
    End Sub
```

This code will output an XML element format as:

```
    <event eventType="deployment" reportItem="/RSExplorer/Company Sales"
        sizeBytes="17274" timeStamp="8:41:35 PM" />
```

The `LogError` method also logs `event` elements, but the `eventType` attribute value is `error`. The error `Message` property is written to the log. The method code is presented here for completeness:

```
#If devEnvironment Then
    Public Sub LogError(ByVal err As System.Exception, ByVal reportItem As
                        ReportServer.CatalogItem) 'ReportServer.
#Else
    Public Sub LogError(ByVal err As System.Exception, ByVal reportItem As
                        CatalogItem)
#End If
        Dim timeStamp As String
```

```
        Try
            Dim logDoc As XmlDocument = GetLogFile()
            Dim elem As XmlElement = logDoc.CreateElement("event")
            timeStamp = DateTime.Now.ToString("T")

            With elem
                .SetAttribute("eventType", "error")
                If Not (reportItem Is Nothing) Then
                .SetAttribute("itemToProcess", reportItem.Name)
                .SetAttribute("errorMessage", err.Message)
                .SetAttribute("timeStamp", timeStamp)
            End With
            logDoc.DocumentElement.AppendChild(elem)
            logDoc.Save(m_logPath)
        Catch ex As Exception
            m_errFlag = True
            Throw ex
        End Try
    End Sub
```

The `LogComment` method takes a string parameter and writes it to the file as an XML comment. Because this method takes a `String` data type parameter the method signature doesn't have to be wrapped in a conditional compilation block. Again, this method code is provided for completeness. The code bundle is also downloadable from www.wrox.com.

```
    Public Sub LogComment(ByVal comment As String)
        Try
            Dim logDoc As XmlDocument = GetLogFile()
            Dim node As XmlComment = logDoc.CreateComment(comment)
            logDoc.DocumentElement.AppendChild(node)
            logDoc.Save(m_logPath)
        Catch ex As Exception
            LogError(ex, Nothing)
        End Try

    End Sub
```

With the addition of the four logging members, the `DeployReports` script file is complete and ready to run.

Running the Script

Running the script in the development environment is simply a matter of pressing F5 on your keyboard. This will compile the assembly just before the CLR steps into the `Main` method. The script can be debugged using techniques such as setting breakpoints and stepping through code. In the production environment the script will be run at the command prompt as part of a scheduled batch file, which itself is a script file.

Once the code is clean and bug-free in the development environment, it's ready to be toggled so it can be hosted by the RS utility. Simply set the `devEnvironment` value to `False` and change the file extension to `.rss`. The script file is now ready for running in the RS utility environment.

To run the script, open the command prompt and navigate to the directory containing the script file. Navigating in the console is easily done by typing `cd` and a space at the command prompt. Then open Windows Explorer and navigate to the directory containing the script file. Enable the Show full path in address bar setting of Windows Explorer. Drag the folder icon in the Windows Explorer address bar into the console window. The console window will be activated and the directory path added; press Enter to have the console navigate to that directory.

Then invoke the RS utility by typing `rs` at the command prompt and supply values for the needed arguments. For this script, the RS utility will need to know the URL of the source Report Server instance, the name of the script file, and a value for the `targetURL` variable within the script.

A sample command would be as follows:

```
rs /i DeployReports.rss /s http://localhost/reportserver/reportservice.asmx
/v targetURL= http://localhost/reportserver/reportservice.asmx
```

This syntax invokes the RS utility to have it run the `DeployReports.rss` input file against the server URL `http://localhost/reportserver/reportservice.asmx` (the default Report Server location on the local machine). The `targetURL` variable value has been set to the same URL as the source machine. This is suitable for development and testing as this will cause the script to write the deployed report definitions back over the reports on the source machine.

In a production environment, the `targetURL` value would be different from the source. Ideally, the script would also run by itself.

Scheduling the Script

A frequently heard request is how to automate the running of a microsoft script according to a schedule. Invoking the RS utility can be done using the Task Scheduler. In Microsoft Windows XP, go to Control Panel and select Scheduled Tasks.

That will open a window listing of any tasks already scheduled along with the option to Add Scheduled Task. Double click that item to open the Schedule Task Wizard. Click Next to start the process of scheduling your script run.

The first step is to choose which program to run as shown in Figure 8-7:

Figure 8-7

Click the **Browse** button to browse to the `rs.exe` utility. It is located in `C:\Program Files\Microsoft SQL Server\80\Tools\Binn`.

Select the `rs.exe` program and click **Open**. That will bring you to the next step in the wizard where you can give the task a descriptive name and indicate how often you want the task to run. For this demonstration, the **One time only** option is selected as shown in Figure 8-8:

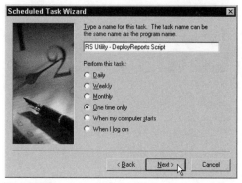

Figure 8-8

Clicking the **Next** button will bring you to a form where you can set the time for the task to run. The options for configuring the run time vary depending on the time interval you've chosen. Choose a time that's appropriate for you and click **Next**.

The next form is an opportunity to provide the credentials that you want the request to be performed under. Enter appropriate values and click **Next** as shown in Figure 8-9:

Figure 8-9

At the next form, check the box to access advanced properties, as shown in Figure 8-10:

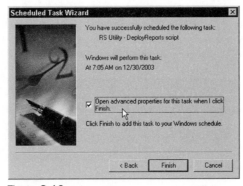

Figure 8-10

Clicking Finish will open the property pages dialog box for the task as shown in Figure 8-11:

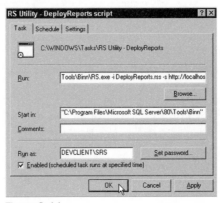

Figure 8-11

On the Task tab, the Run textbox is where you provide the command line arguments that the RS utility needs to run. For example, the input file, Report Server URL, and so on are added as arguments to the command listed in the Run textbox.

You can also access this dialog box by opening the task again after completing the Schedule Task Wizard process. Note that you can access the schedule and other settings for this task by using the tabs.

Summary

Scripting is a tool that allows you to automate the administration and management of a Report Server instance, its content, and metadata. The WMI-flavored interface exposed by Reporting Services and other Microsoft application servers is powerful and flexible.

Reporting Services provides several command line utilities including the RS utility. This utility runs scripts written in Visual Basic .NET code contained in files with a particular structure. Note that the RS utility provides access to a limited number of base class library namespaces.

In this chapter, you've read about the capabilities and limitations of scripts written for hosting by the RS utility. A structure for the script file was presented, which uses the conditional compilation capabilities of both Visual Studio .NET and the RS utility runtime environment. The script deploys report definitions from a source machine to a target machine while logging actions to an XML file. Creating scripts in Visual Studio .NET provides a rich, familiar development environment. Conditional compilation creates a file that easily toggles between development and production environments.

Scripting is but one of the features of Reporting Services. The next chapter describes how to programmatically render reports including accessing reports using HTTP requests and submitting parameters to reports using query strings.

URL Access and Programmatic Rendering

The main focus of Reporting Services is to be a flexible reporting tool that can be easily incorporated in different applications. There are a number of scenarios where the Report Viewer provided by Reporting Services will not meet report delivery needs. For example, many organizations maintain corporate reporting portals. In these situations, developers might need a way to display numerous reports in a web environment. Reporting Services can also be embedded into any line of business applications. Developers might want to use Reporting Services to create invoices or purchase orders directly from their applications. For other organizations, the default Report Viewer might not provide a broad security architecture.

All of these issues can be solved with the features available in Reporting Services. In this chapter, you will take a look at the two methods for rendering reports in Reporting Services. They are:

❑ Using URLs to access reports

❑ Using the Reporting Services Web Service to programmatically render reports

URL access allows you to quickly incorporate Reporting Services reports in applications such as web portals. Programmatic rendering allows for creating custom interfaces. Developers can do anything from implementing their own security architecture around Reporting Services to creating their own parameter interface.

By the end of this chapter, you will know about:

❑ The syntax and structure for accessing Reporting Services through the URL

❑ The reporting items that can be accessed through the URL

❑ The parameter options that can be passed to the URL to control report output

❑ Creating a Windows application that renders reports to the file system

❑ Creating a web application that returns rendered reports to the browser

URL Access

Reporting Service's main means for accessing reports is through HTTP requests. These requests can be made through URLs in a web browser or a custom application. By passing parameters in the URL, you can specify the report item, set the output format, and perform a number of other tasks. In the next few sections, you will look at the features available through URL requests, URL syntax, passing parameters, and setting the output format.

URL Syntax

The basic URL syntax is as follows:

http://server/virtualroot?[/pathinfo]&[prefix:]param=value[&[prefix:]param=value]...n]

Here is a quick look at retrieving the list of items under the Professional SQL Reporting Services folder:

The parameters in the syntax are as follows:

❑   server: Specifies the instance of Report Server you would like to access. To access your local machine, you can either type the machine name or use the localhost alias.

❑   virtualroot: Specifies the IIS virtual directory you specified during the setup. When installing Reporting Services, you must enter two virtual directories: one for the Report Manager and one for the Reporting Services Web Service. By default, the virtual directory you would access is reportserver.

❑   pathinfo: After specifying the server and virtual directory to the Reporting Services Web Service, you can pass a number of parameters to access report objects. The first parameter you pass is pathinfo, which specifies the path to the resource you want to access. To access the root of the Report Server, you can simply place a single forward slash ().

Once you have listed the path, you can pass various parameters. These parameters will depend on the type of object you are referencing. Reports will have a number of parameters to specify properties such as the rendering format. Each parameter is separated by an ampersand (&) and contains a name=value pair for the parameter.

http://localhost/reportserver?%2fProfessional+SQL+Reporting+Services&rs:Command=ListChildren

Now that you've taken a look at the basic URL syntax, let's see how it is implemented in each of the Reporting Services objects.

Accessing Reporting Services Objects

URL requests are not limited to just reports. You can access a number of Reporting Services items. These include:

❑   Folders

❑   Data Sources

❑　Resources

❑　Reports

In this section, you will look at accessing each of the items listed above. You will go through sample URLs and look at items provided in the Professional SQL Reporting Services project.

Folders

Accessing folders will be your starting point for looking at URL requests. Let's take a look at the simplest URL request you can make:

http://localhost/reportserver

With this request, you can see a listing of all reports, data sources, resources, and folders in the root directory of the Reporting Server as shown in Figure 9-1. To access another server, simply replace localhost with the name of the server.

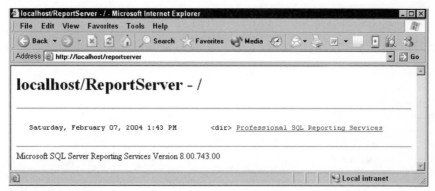

Figure 9-1

To see how other folder URL requests work, simply click on any of the <dir> links. Clicking the Professional SQL Reporting Services link will give you the following URL:

http://localhost/reportserver?%2fProfessional+SQL+Reporting+Services&rs:Command=ListChildren

This URL contains the following items:

❑　**Path to the report**: %2fProfessional+SQL+Reporting+Services

❑　**Command to list the contents of the directory**: rs:Command=ListChildren

You'll take a closer look at the URL parameters in the Reporting Services URL Parameters section later in the chapter.

Data Sources

Through URL requests, you can also view the contents of data sources. Let's again take a look at the Professional SQL Reporting Services folder. Enter the following URL to view the contents of this folder:

http://localhost/reportserver?%2fProfessional+SQL+Reporting+Services&rs:Command=ListChildren

You should see the listing of items as shown in Figure 9-2:

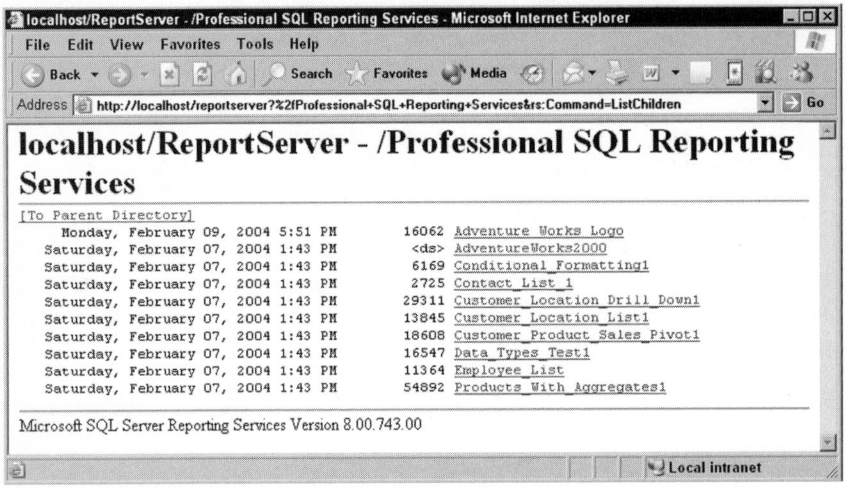

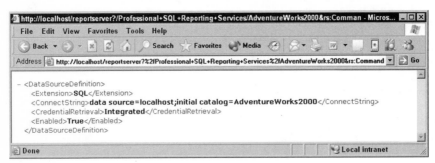

Figure 9-2

You will notice that one of the items listed is AdventureWorks2000. This item is a data source by the <ds> tag next to the item name. If you follow the AdventureWorks2000 link, you will be able to view the contents of that data source. Figure 9-3 shows the AdventureWorks2000 data source contents:

Figure 9-3

Let's take a look at the URL used to view the AdventureWorks2000 data source:

http://localhost/reportserver?%2fProfessional+SQL+Reporting+Services%2fAdventureWorks2000&rs:Command=GetDataSourceContents

This URL contains the following items:

❑ **Path to the data source**: %2fProfessional+SQL+Reporting+Services%2fAdventureWorks2000

❑ **Command to view the data source content**: rs:Command=GetDataSourceContents

Viewing the data source allows you to quickly see how your data source is configured. Notice that this information is returned in XML format. This allows you to easily work with the data source information. If you have your own reporting application that shares a single connection, you could use this URL to dynamically load this data source information. This information could then be used to make other database connections in your application.

Resources

Resources are items that you use in your reports like images or additional resources that have been added to your Report Server folder, such as Word and Excel documents. You can use URLs to access resources stored in the Report Server. Depending on the type of resources you reference, you will either be prompted to open or save a file, such as a Word or Excel document, or the resource will be rendered directly in the browser. In the Professional SQL Reporting Services folder, a resource for the Adventure Works logo is added. This image can be directly rendered in your browser. Let's take a look at the following URL:

http://localhost/reportserver?%2fProfessional+SQL+Reporting+Services%2fAdventure+Works+Logo&rs:Command=GetResourceContents

See Figure 9-4 for the output:

Figure 9-4

The URL contains the following contents:

❑ **Path to the resource**: %2fProfessional+SQL+Reporting+Services%2fAdventure+Works+Logo

❑ **Command to retrieve the resource content**: rs:Command=GetResourceContent

You can use this information in other applications. If you want to reference the Adventure Works logo from a web page, you could simply set the src attribute of an image tag (<img>) to reference the earlier URL .

Resources can also be incredibly handy for storing documents. In your reporting solution, you might want to store *readme* files to accompany your reports. You can store these documents as resources on the Report Server and then apply different properties to them, such as security. Your application could then point to the resource URL to allow downloading of the document.

Reports

The most important objects you can access through the URL are your reports. This section provides a quick look at the syntax for accessing reports. Later we'll discuss the various parameters you can pass to change things such as report parameters, output formats, and other items.

The basic syntax for accessing a report is very similar to accessing all of your other resources. You should first specify a path to the report and then provide the commands for its output. Let's look at the basic URL for accessing your Customer Product Sales Pivot report:

http://localhost/reportserver?%2fProfessional+SQL+Reporting+Services%2fCustomer_Product_Sales_Pivot1&rs:Command=Render

View the Customer Product Sales Pivot report as in Figure 9-5:

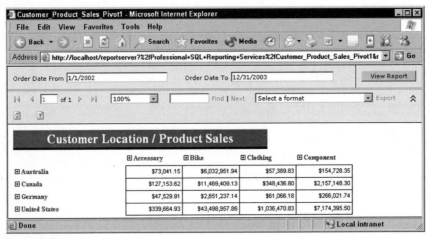

Figure 9-5

The URL contains the following contents:

❏ **Path to the resource**: %2fProfessional+SQL+Reporting+Services%2fCustomer_Product_Sales_Pivot1

❏ **Command to retrieve the resource content**: rs:Command=Render

Using URLs is the easiest and most convenient way to embed Reporting Services reports in your applications. You can simply create your own links that point to the various report URLs. You are probably asking yourself, "That's nice! I can access a report, but how do I pass parameters and change the output format?" In the next section, you'll take a look at all the possible parameters you can pass through the URL including setting report parameters and output format.

Reporting Services URL Parameters

Now that you have seen the basics of obtaining items from your Report Server using URLs, let's take a look at passing some parameters. The next few sections will move through how parameters are passed to Reporting Services and the available values for these parameters. The majority of the parameter functionality will be focused on report rendering, but some items will also apply to your data source, resources, and folder.

Parameter Prefixes

The first thing you need to take a look at is the different parameter prefixes in Reporting Services. There are four main parameter prefixes in Reporting Services: rs, rc, dsp, and dsu. The following sections will take a look at these prefixes in detail.

rs Prefix

In the earlier examples, you saw the parameter rs:Command. This parameter contains the prefix rs. The rs prefix is used to send commands to the Report Server. The following URL shows an example of the rs prefix being used to call the Command parameter and pass the ListChildren argument to it:

http://localhost/reportserver?%2fProfessional+SQL+Reporting+Services&rs:Command=ListChildren

rc Prefix

The second main parameter prefix in Reporting Services is the rc prefix. This prefix is used to interact with the given report output format. For example, if you are outputting your report as HTML, you can control the HTML viewer. You can use this prefix to pass parameters that do things such as hide toolbars or control the initial state of toggle items. The following URL calls the Product Sales Pivot report and turns off the parameter inputs:

http://localhost/reportserver?%2fProfessional+SQL+Reporting+Services%2fCustomer_Product_Sales_Pivot1&
rs:Command=Render&rc:Parameters=False

Figure 9-6 shows how rc:Parameters is used to hide parameters in the HTML viewer:

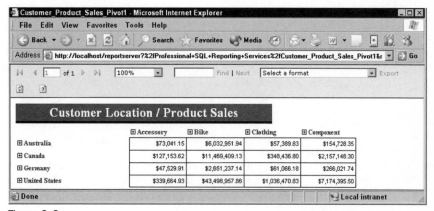

Figure 9-6

Notice that the parameter dialog is not visible in the HTML viewer.

dsu and dsp Prefixes

Parameter prefixes can also be used to send database credentials. Use the dsu prefix to pass the data source username and dsp to pass the data source password. In any Reporting Services report, you could incorporate multiple data sources. So, you need a way to specify which data source the credentials should be passed to. That's where the prefixes come in. The full syntax to use these prefixes is as follows:

    [dsu | dsp]:datasourcename=value

If you want to pass the user name guest with a password guestPass to your AdventureWorks2000 data source, you will use the following URL parameters:

&dsu:AdventureWorks2000=guest&dsp:AdventureWorks2000=guestPass

> **You should be aware that these credentials will be passed as clear text over the Internet and will be visible to the end user. You can encrypt the URL using the *Secure Sockets Layer (SSL)* on your web server. This will prevent the information from being sent as clear text over the Internet, but will not prevent the end user from viewing the credentials that you use. Make sure you consider these factors in your reporting solution architecture.**

Now that you have seen the different parameter prefixes in Reporting Services, we'll move on to the available parameters that can be used with the rs and rc prefixes.

Parameters

First, let's take a look at the parameters that can be used with the `rs` prefix. The following table lists the three available values and their uses:

Parameter	Use
Command	The Command parameter is used to send instructions to the Report Server about the item being retrieved. Available values return the report item and set session timeout information.
Format	The Format parameter is used when rendering reports. Any rendering formats available on the report server can be passed using this parameter.
Snapshot	The Snapshot parameter is used to retrieve historical report snapshots. Once a report has been stored in snapshot history, it is assigned a time/date stamp to uniquely identify that report. Passing this time/date stamp will return the appropriate report.

Now that you have seen the different rs parameters, let's take a look at some of their available values.

Command Parameter

The Command parameter is your main parameter for setting the output of a given report item. It can also be used for resetting a user's session information, which guarantees that a report is not rendered from the session cache. Here is a listing of the possible values that can be passed to the Command parameter:

Value	Use
GetDataSourceContents	The GetDataSourceContents command can be used to return data source information in an XML format. You can use this parameter on shared data source items.
GetResourceContents	The GetResourceContents command will return the binary of your Reporting Services resources. You can use this to retrieve report resources, such as images, via the URL.
ListChildren	The ListChildren command is used in combination with a Reporting Services folder. This value allows us to view a list of all items in a given folder.
Render	The Render command is probably the most commonly used command value. It allows you to render your report via the URL.
ResetSessionTimeout	The ResetSessionTimeout command can be used to refresh a user's session cache. Because Reporting Services works via HTTP, it is crucial for the server to maintain state information about the user. However, if you want to ensure that a report is executed each time the user views a report, this state information needs to be refreshed. Use this parameter to reset the user's sessions and remove any session cache information.

Format Parameter

The Format parameter is the main parameter for controlling the report output. The available values for this parameter are determined by the different rendering extensions available on your Report Server. The following table shows the output formats available with the default installation of Reporting Services:

Value	Output
Web Formats	
HTML3.2	HTML version 3.2 output. This format is used for older browser versions.
HTML4.0	HTML version 4.0 output. This format supports newer browser versions such as Internet Explorer 4.0 and above.

Table continued on following page

Value	Output
Web Formats (continued)	
MHTML	MHTML standard output. This output format is used for sending HTML documents in email. Using this format will embed all resources, such as images, into the MHTML document instead of referencing external URLs.
Print Formats	
IMAGE	The IMAGE format allows you to render your reports to a number of different Graphics Device Interfaces (GDI) such as BMP, PNG, GIF, or TIFF.
PDF	The Portable Document Format (PDF) can also be used for viewing and printing documents.
Data Formats	
EXCEL	Excel XP and Excel 2003 output. Users can use this format to further manipulate report information.
CSV	Comma Separated Value (CSV) format. CSV output is handy for consuming report data through applications that work with CSV files.
XML	Extensible Markup Language (XML) format. XML can be used by numerous applications to consume report data.
Control Format	
NULL	The NULL provider allows you to execute reports without rendering. This can be very useful when working with reports that have cached instances. You can use the NULL format to execute the report for the first time and thereby storing the cached instance.

When you set the rendering formats via the URL, the report will either be rendered directly in the browser or you will be prompted to save the output file. Let's take a look at rendering the Customer Product Sales Pivot report in PDF format. Enter the following URL using the rs:Format=PDF parameter:

http://localhost/reportserver?%2fProfessional+SQL+Reporting+Services%2fCustomer_Product_Sales_Pivot1&
rs:Command=Render&rs:Format=PDF

Figure 9-7 shows the output:

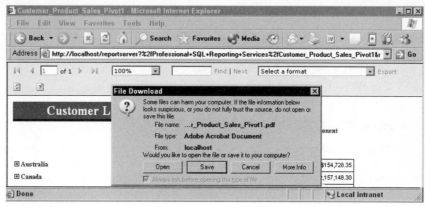

Figure 9-7

Notice that the browser will now prompt you to save the rendered report. This can be easily incorporated into your own custom applications or portals. You can simply give your users a link containing the rs:Format parameter and automatically output the correct format.

Setting Device Information

Now that you have seen the various output formats available in Reporting Services, you need to take a look at the different device information settings for the various formats. The Format parameter allows you to specify the type of format you want, but each format has specific settings that can be useful to you. For example, if you specify the IMAGE format, you get an output in TIFF. What if you wanted a Bitmap or JPEG image? Well, to output in a different image format, all you need to do is to just specify device information when passing the URL. Let's take a look at outputting your Customer Product Sales Pivot report in JPEG format using the following URL (Figure 9-8 shows the output):

http://localhost/reportserver?%2fProfessional+SQL+Reporting+Services%2fCustomer_Product_Sales_Pivot1& rs:Command=Render&rs:Format=IMAGE&rc:OutputFormat=JPEG

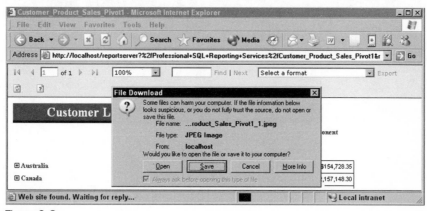

Figure 9-8

Notice that the file type sent back to you is a JPEG image. There are numerous device information settings you can use for each of the rendering extensions. Each device information setting is prefixed using the rc prefix. The following syntax can be used for passing device information:

http://server/virtualroot?/pathinfo&rs:Format=format&rc:param=value[&rc:param=value...n]

Now that you have seen the different output formats and commands you can pass to Reporting Services, let's take a look at passing information to your individual reports.

Passing Report Information through the URL

The previous sections illustrated how a URL can be used to control report rendering In the next section, you will look at how a URL can be used to control report execution. This section starts with an explanation of passing report parameters. These are the parameters that you define while authoring your report. Finally, you'll see how historical snapshots can be rendered using the URL.

Report Parameters

Many of your reports have parameters to control all kinds of behavior. You can use parameters to alter your query, filter datasets and tables, and even change the appearance of your reports. Reporting Services allows you to pass this information directly via a URL request. In the earlier section, you saw a lot about the parameter prefixes and the available values that can be sent to the Reporting Services. With report parameters, you simply need to remove the prefix and directly call the parameter name.

Your Customer Product Sales Pivot report accepts two parameters: OrderDateFrom and OrderDateTo. You might want to allow your users to update these parameters through a custom interface you define. When you call the report, you will need to provide these parameters in the URL as shown here:

http://localhost/reportserver?%2fProfessional+SQL+Reporting+Services%2fCustomer_Product_Sales_Pivot1&rs:Command=Render&OrderDateFrom=12/1/2003&OrderDateTo=12/31/2003

Let's take a look at calling the report with an OrderDateFrom value of 12/1/2003 and OrderDateTo value of 12/31/2003 (see Figure 9-9):

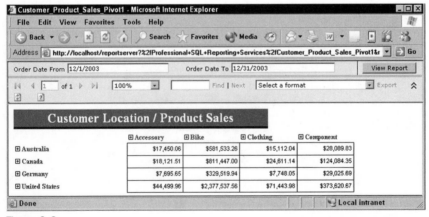

Figure 9-9

Notice that by passing the parameters in your URL, the HTML viewer updates to reflect the values. The parameter name that you use in the URL is defined in the report definition. Since your Report Parameters are called OrderDateFrom and OrderDateTo, these names are used in your URL.

Now that you have seen how to pass report parameters to the URL, let's look at passing snapshot IDs to render historical execution snapshots.

Rendering Snapshot History

One of the major features of Reporting Services is the ability to create execution snapshots of reports. Say you have a report where the data updates on a monthly basis. Once the data is updated, it does not change for another month. A perfect example of this would be monthly financial statements. If your data only changes once a month, there is no reason to query your database every time you need a report. So, you can use execution snapshots to store this information after the query has been executed. Going along the same lines as a monthly report, what should happen when your data updates from say January to February? You don't want to lose the January snapshot once the February information is available. That is where historical snapshots come into play. When you create the February snapshot, you go and add January to the snapshot history and so on for each subsequent month.

Now that you have execution snapshots stored in history you need some way to access them. Reporting Services gives you a very easy way to do this. As you have already seen, each report has a report path that can be used to render the report. To render a historical snapshot, you simply need to add a parameter for the historical snapshot ID.

The syntax to pass your snapshot ID is as follows:

http://server/virtualroot?[/pathinfo]&rs:Snapshot=snapshotid

The snapshot ID for your historical snapshot will be the time and date stamp of when the report was added to the history. The time is adjusted to GMT based on the time zone where the historical snapshot was added.

URL Rendering Summary

Through URL rendering, you have seen the various commands that can be passed to Reporting Services that can be used to control the report item display, the format to use, and snapshot information using the rs prefix. Once you have created your commands for the Report Server, you can pass parameters specific to the output format. Using the rc prefix and the device information parameters, you can specify things such as encoding and what items to display in the HTML viewer. After you have specified the report item, you need to know how to output it. You can pass parameters to your report by simply passing the parameter name and value combination.

In the next section, let's take a look at the second part of rendering Reporting Service reports. You can use URLs for simple web applications and web portals, but sometimes you need finer control over report access and rendering. To achieve this, we'll use the Reporting Service Web Service to programmatically render your reports.

Programmatic Rendering

Reporting Services gives you two main methods for rendering your reports. Rendering using a URL is very handy and easy to implement in many situations, but it does have its limitations. When rendering from the URL, you have to make sure that you use the security infrastructure provided with Reporting Services. For some applications, such as public web sites, you might want to implement your own security. In that case, rendering from the URL will not provide the functionality you need. In this section, you will take a look at rendering reports using the Reporting Services Web Service.

You'll connect to the Reporting Services Web Service, return a list of available reports, retrieve their parameters, and finally render the report. Let's take a look at two implementations of programmatic rendering. The first implementation is using a Windows form to render reports to a file. This will help you to understand the basic principles without a lot of interface work. The second implementation will take you through rendering through an ASP.NET page. You'll see some of the items that need to be considered when working through a web application.

Common Scenarios

Before you look at the actual programming code for rendering reports, it is important to understand a couple of scenarios where it is reasonable to do so. There are two scenarios that are commonly experienced while working with clients. They do not represent the *only* scenarios where you would write your own rendering code, but do illustrate how and when custom code can be used. Let's look at each of these scenarios.

Custom Security

Probably the biggest question I get when working with clients is, "How do I use Reporting Services if I don't want to implement their security infrastructure?" Reporting Services requires you to connect to reports using a Windows identity. In many organizations, this is just not possible. They have mixed environments or non-trusted domains that do not allow for identification to the Report Server. Some clients also have largescale authentication and authorization infrastructures already implemented.

You can still use Reporting Services in these situations. Using your own security infrastructure involves creating both authentication and authorization code in your environment. After you have determined that a user can access a report, a Windows identity that you define can be used to connect to reports. To hide this security implementation, the Reporting Services Web Service can be employed. You can render reports directly to a browser or file without passing the original user identity to the Report Server.

Server-Side Parameters

While URL rendering is by far the easiest way to incorporate Reporting Services in your applications, it does have some limitations. When you send information via a URL, it is very easy for a user to change that URL or see what it is that you pass.

By using the Reporting Services Web Service you can easily hide the details of how you retrieve report information. Parameters are passed through your code instead of the URL. This gives you complete control over how that information is retrieved without exposing it to the users. Let's take a look at your first rendering application.

Rendering through Windows

In this section, we'll take a look at the mechanics of rendering using the Reporting Service Web Service. We are going to build a simple Windows application that returns a list of reports from the Report Server. Once we have the list of reports, we'll use the web service to return a list of report parameters. After entering any report parameters, we'll render the report to a file. These steps will illustrate the main components of rendering through program code.

Building the Application Interface

To start, you need to build your application interface. Let's start by building a simple Windows form; Figure 9-10 shows the design view of your form:

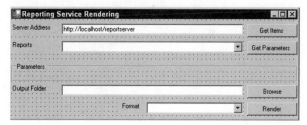

Figure 9-10

This form will allow you to query a given Report Server to return a list of reports. Once it has returned the reports, you can use it to access a list of parameters for the reports. Finally, you'll need to render the report to a given folder location.

Setting Up the Reporting Service Web Service

Before you can get into rendering reports, you need to first set up a reference to the Reporting Service Web Service. Once you have created your web reference, you can start to develop the application. The next few figures show you how to create a reference to the web service. Start by adding a web reference to your project.

Open the Solution Explorer and right click on the Reference folder. Click the Add Web Reference menu item to open the Add Web Reference dialog as in Figure 9-11:

Figure 9-11

In the Add Web Reference dialog, enter the location of web service in the URL dialog. This URL will depend on the Report Server name and the installed location of the Report Server virtual directory. By default, the Report Server virtual directory is located under the root as /reportserver. For the default virtual directory on a local machine, enter the following URL:
http://localhost/reportserver/reportservice.asmx?wsdl.

Once you have entered the URL, hit Enter to view a description of the web service. Enter a name for the new web reference and hit Add Reference. The dialog should look like Figure 9-12 when filled in:

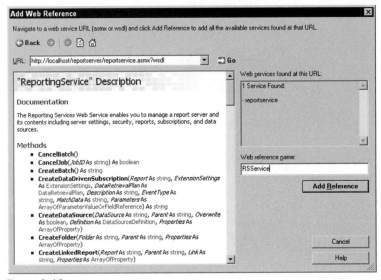

Figure 9-12

Now that you have referenced the web service, you are ready to start writing your code. The first thing you can do is add a using (C#) or Imports VB. (VB.NET) statements to your code. The first part of the using statement will be the application name followed by the web reference name. I have called my C# project Rendering and my VB.NET project RenderingVB.

C#

```
using System;
using System.Drawing;
using System.Collections;
using System.ComponentModel;
using System.Windows.Forms;
using Rendering.RSService;
```

VB.NET

```
Imports System
Imports System.Drawing
Imports System.Collections
Imports System.ComponentModel
Imports System.Windows.Forms
Imports RenderingVB.RSService
```

After you have added the `using` or `Imports` statement, you need to create an instance of the `ReportingService` object. This is the main object that will be used to retrieve a list of reports and their associated parameters, and then render the report. At the top of the Windows form class code, create the declarations shown in the following sections.

C#

```
private ReportingService _rs = new ReportingService();
```

VB.NET

```
Private _rs As New ReportingService
```

Next, you need to set the security credentials that will be used by Reporting Services. In your code, pass the credentials of the currently logged on user. If you already have your own custom authentication and authorization method in place, you could pass a system identification you define instead of the current user.

Open the Form Load event in the windows form, this is a suitable place for setting the credentials. Inside this event, set the `ReportingService` object's `Credentials` property to `System.Net.CredentialCache.DefaultCredentials`. This will give the web service the credentials of the currently logged-on user.

C#

```
_rs.Credentials = System.Net.CredentialCache.DefaultCredentials;
```

VB.NET

```
_rs.Credentials = System.Net.CredentialCache.DefaultCredentials
```

The final piece you need to add to the Form Load event is the code to populate your drop-down list. This code will add all the format names to the list along with appropriate extensions for each. Let's begin by creating a small class that helps you populate the drop-down.

C#

```
/*  Helper class for format extensions. */
private class Format
{
    private string _name;
    private string _extension;

    public Format(string name, string extension)
    {
        _name = name;
        _extension = extension;
    }

    public string Name
    {
        get{return _name;}
    }
```

```
    public string Extension
    {
        get{return _extension;}
    }
}
```

VB.NET

```
'  Helper class for format extensions.
Private Class Format
    Private _name As String
    Private _extension As String

    Public Sub New(ByVal name As String, ByVal extension As String)
        name = name
        extension = extension
    End Sub

    Public ReadOnly Property Name() As String
        Get
            Return _name
        End Get
    End Property

    Public ReadOnly Property Extension() As String
        Get
            Return _extension
        End Get
    End Property
End Class
```

With these classes you can finish off your `FormLoad` event code. Add the few last lines of code to populate your format combo box.

C#

```
private void frmMain_Load(object sender, System.EventArgs e)
{
    rs.Credentials = System.Net.CredentialCache.DefaultCredentials;
    //load the format values
    Format[] formats = new Format[7];
    formats[0] = new Format("Excel", ".xls");
    formats[1] = new Format("HTML3.2", ".html");
    formats[2] = new Format("HTML4.0", ".html");
    formats[3] = new Format("XML", ".xml");
    formats[4] = new Format("CSV", ".csv");
    formats[5] = new Format("PDF", ".pdf");
    formats[6] = new Format("IMAGE", ".tif");

    cboFormat.DataSource = formats;
    cboFormat.DisplayMember = "Name";
    cboFormat.ValueMember = "Name";
}
```

VB.NET

```vb.net
Private Sub frmMain_Load(ByVal sender As Object, _
    ByVal e As System.EventArgs) Handles MyBase.Load

    rs.Credentials = System.Net.CredentialCache.DefaultCredentials
    'load the format values
    Dim formats(6) As Format
    formats(0) = New Format("Excel", ".xls")
    formats(1) = New Format("HTML3.2", ".html")
    formats(2) = New Format("HTML4.0", ".html")
    formats(3) = New Format("XML", ".xml")
    formats(4) = New Format("CSV", ".csv")
    formats(5) = New Format("PDF", ".pdf")
    formats(6) = New Format("IMAGE", ".tif")

    cboFormat.DataSource = formats
    cboFormat.DisplayMember = "Name"
    cboFormat.ValueMember = "Name"
End Sub
```

You have now created an instance of the `ReportingService` object, passed the logged-on user's credentials to it, and populated the format drop-down list. In the next section, we'll take a look at connecting to the Report Server and retrieving a list of available reports.

Retrieving Report Information

Now that you have set up the Reporting Service Web Service, you need to retrieve your list of reports. To do this, specify the Report Server you want to query and then call the `ListChildren` method of the `ReportingService` object. `ListChildren` returns a list of all items including data sources, resources, and reports. Once you have retrieved the list, you will need to pull out only report items. Finally, you will add the report items to the drop-down.

Let's start by setting the URL to your Report Server. Open the click event of the **Get Items** button to start your code.

C#

```csharp
_rs.Url = txtServer.Text + "/ReportService.asmx";
```

VB.NET

```vb.net
_rs.Url = txtServer.Text & "/ReportService.asmx"
```

The preceding code uses the server location specified in the **Server Address** textbox concatenated with the reference to the Reporting Service Web Service.

Once the URL for the web service is set, you can get the list of reports. Create an array of `CatalogItem` objects and then call the `ListChildren` method. This method takes two parameters, the folder path on the Report Server and a Boolean value indicating whether or not to recur the directory.

C#

```
CatalogItem[] items;
items = _rs.ListChildren("/", true);
```

VB.NET

```
Dim items() As CatalogItem
items = _rs.ListChildren("/", True)
```

The last step is to loop through the returned list of items and add them to a drop-down list. Similar to how the formats were loaded, create a class to help data-bind the report items. Let's take a look at the code for this class.

C#

```
private class ReportItem
{
    private string _name;
    private string _path;

    public ReportItem(string name, string path)
    {
        name = name;
        path = path;
    }

    public string Name
    {
        get{return _name;}
    }

    public string Path
    {
        get{return _path;}
    }
}
```

VB.NET

```
Private Class ReportItem
    Private _name As String
    Private _path As String

    Public Sub New(ByVal name As String, ByVal path As String)
        _name = name
        _path = path
    End Sub

    Public ReadOnly Property Name() As String
        Get
            Return _name
        End Get
    End Property
```

```
        Public ReadOnly Property Path() As String
            Get
                Return _path
            End Get
        End Property
    End Class
```

Using the `ReportItem` class just created, you can now add the report catalog items to the combo box. The following code is for the `GetItems` button click event including populating the report drop-down.

C#

```csharp
private void btnGetItems_Click(object sender, System.EventArgs e)
{
    //set the path to the report server
    _rs.Url = txtServer.Text + "/ReportService.asmx";

    //return a list of items from the report server
    CatalogItem[] items;
    items = _rs.ListChildren("/", true);

    //populate your report combo box
    cboReports.Items.Clear();
    foreach(CatalogItem item in items)
    {
        if(item.Type == ItemTypeEnum.Report)
        {
            cboReports.Items.Add(new ReportItem(item.Name, item.Path));
        }
    }

    cboReports.DisplayMember = "Name";
    cboReports.ValueMember = "Path";
}
```

VB.NET

```vbnet
Private Sub btnGetItems_Click(ByVal sender As Object, _
    ByVal e As System.EventArgs) Handles btnGetItems.Click

    'set the path to the report server
    _rs.Url = txtServer.Text & "/ReportService.asmx"
    'return a list of items from the report server
    Dim items() As CatalogItem
    items = _rs.ListChildren("/", True)
    'populate your report combo box
    cboReports.Items.Clear()
    Dim item As CatalogItem
    For Each item In items
        If item.Type = ItemTypeEnum.Report Then
            cboReports.Items.Add(New ReportItem(item.Name, item.Path))
        End If
    Next item
```

```
        cboReports.DisplayMember = "Name"
        cboReports.ValueMember = "Path"
End Sub
```

You will now be able to open your form and return a list of report items. In the next section you will look at retrieving the parameters for a report.

Retrieving Report Parameters

The next area of programmatic rendering consists of retrieving a list of parameters for your report. This bit of code can be used in a number of scenarios. The parameter interface that is provided by Reporting Services works well for simple parameters. However, it does not handle many thing, like multi-select parameters or more advanced interfaces such as calendar controls. Being able to return a list of parameters allows you to create your own dynamic interface.

In the following example, we will create a simple list of parameters. For each parameter, we will dynamically add a label control and textbox to your form. This example will also include the GetParameters click event to run your code. First thing you need to do is identify the report that is selected in your report drop-down list.

C#

```
    ReportItem reportItem = (ReportItem)cboReports.SelectedItem;
```

VB.NET

```
    Dim reportItem As ReportItem = CType(cboReports.SelectedItem, ReportItem)
```

This creates a new ReportItem variable using the selected item of your combo box. The ReportItem class created in the previous section contains a Name and Path property. You can use this Path property to retrieve your list of parameters.

To return your list of parameters, call the GetReportParameters method or the ReportingService object. This method has two functions. It returns a list of parameters and can validate parameters against the available values defined when creating the report. Let's take a look at the arguments of the GetReportParameters method:

- ❑ Report: This is the path to the report you want to retrieve.
- ❑ HistoryID: The ID used to identify any historical snapshots of your report.
- ❑ ForRendering: This Boolean argument can be used to retrieve the parameters that were set when the report was executed. For example, you might create a snapshot of your report or receive it in an email subscription. In both cases, the report is executed before the user views it. By setting the ForRendering property to true, you can retrieve these values and use them in your own custom interface.
- ❑ ParameterValues: The ParameterValues argument can be used to validate the values assigned to a parameter. This can be useful in guaranteeing that the parameter values you pass to your report match the parameter values accepted by the report.
- ❑ Credentials: The database credentials to use when validating your query based parameters.

Since you are not working with historical reports or validating values, a number of the properties will not be set. The following code can be used for calling the `GetReportParameters` method.

C#

```
ReportParameter[] parameters;
parameters = _rs.GetReportParameters(reportItem.Path, null, false, null, null);
```

VB.NET

```
Dim parameters() As ReportParameter
            parameters = _rs.GetReportParameters(reportItem.Path, Nothing, False,
                    Nothing, Nothing)
```

The last piece of work to do is to create a user interface for your parameters. The `ReportParameter` objects returned by Reporting Services contain information useful for creating a custom interface. Some of the key properties include the parameter data type, prompt, and valid values. All of these can be used to define your own interface. Finish your code by simply adding a label and textbox to your form for each `ReportParameter`. Following is the completed `GetParameter` click event code.

C#

```
private void btnParameters_Click(object sender, System.EventArgs e)
{
    //return the list of parameters for the report item
    ReportItem reportItem = (ReportItem)cboReports.SelectedItem;
    ReportParameter[] parameters;
    parameters = _rs.GetReportParameters(reportItem.Path, null, false, null,
                                null);
    //add the parameters to the parameter list UI
    int left = 10;
    int top = 20;
    foreach(ReportParameter parameter in parameters)
    {
        Label label = new Label();
        TextBox textBox = new TextBox();

        label.Text = parameter.Prompt;
        label.Left = left;
        label.Top = top;

        textBox.Name = parameter.Name;
        textBox.Text = parameter.DefaultValues[0];
        textBox.Left = left + 150;
        textBox.Top = top;
        top +=25;

        grpParamInfo.Controls.Add(label);
        grpParamInfo.Controls.Add(textBox);
    }
}
```

VB.NET

```
Private Sub btnParameters_Click(ByVal sender As Object, ByVal e As _
    System.EventArgs) Handles btnParameters.Click

    'return the list of parameters for the report item
    Dim reportItem As ReportItem = CType(cboReports.SelectedItem, ReportItem)

    Dim parameters() As ReportParameter
                parameters = _rs.GetReportParameters(reportItem.Path, Nothing, _
                                                  False, _Nothing, Nothing)
    'add the parameters to the parameter list UI
    Dim left As Integer = 10
    Dim top As Integer = 20
    Dim parameter As ReportParameter
    For Each parameter In parameters
        Dim label As New Label
        Dim textBox As New TextBox
        label.Text = parameter.Prompt
        label.Left = left
        label.Top = top

        textBox.Name = parameter.Name
        textBox.Text = parameter.DefaultValues(0)
        textBox.Left = left + 150
        textBox.Top = top
        top += 25

        grpParamInfo.Controls.Add(label)
        grpParamInfo.Controls.Add(textBox)
    Next parameter
End Sub
```

Now that you have retrieved your list of reports and built a parameter list, let's take a look at outputting the report to a file.

Rendering a Report to a File System

In this section, you'll take a look at rendering your report to a file. Using the `ReportingService` object's `Render` method, you can retrieve a byte array that contains the final report. This byte array can be used in a number of different ways. In this example, you will write the byte array to a file using the file system object. Later you will take a look at another example that writes the byte array to the HTTP `Response` object.

Before you get into the rendering code, let's look at the different parameters of the `Render` method:

Parameter	Data Type	Description
Report	String	Path to the report in Reporting Services.
Format	String	Output format of the report: HTML3.2, HTML4.0, MHTML, IMAGE, PDF, EXCEL, CSV, XML, NULL.
HistoryID (optional)	String	History ID used to render historical snapshots.
DeviceInfo	String	Information used by a specified rendering format. For example, specifying the image type (.gif,.jpeg) with the IMAGE format.
Parameters	ParameterValue Array	Input parameter value array used to render the report.
Credentials	DataSourceCredentials Array	Array of data source credentials used to connect to the data sources for a report. These credentials contain the username, login password, and data source name.
ShowHideToggle	String	Changes initial toggle state of the report.
Encoding (out)	String	Output returned from Reporting Services containing the encoding of the report. The encoding parameter is used to correctly decode the returned byte array.
MimeType (out)	String	Output returned from Reporting Services containing the MIME type of the underlying report. Useful when rendering a report to the web. The MIME type can be passed to the Response object to ensure that the browser correctly handles the document returned.
ParametersUsed (out)	ParameterValue Array	Output of parameter values used to execute the report. Can include query parameters used for the creation of an execution snapshot. Important when developing the application user interface.
Warnings (out)	Warning Array	Output of any warnings from Reporting Services.
StreamIds (out)	String Array	Output of stream IDs that can be used with the Render Stream method.

The parameters of the `Render` method are similar to the values that can be passed using URL rendering. In your Windows application, you will be mostly interested in the `Report`, `Format`, and `Encoding` parameters. These parameters allow you to correctly return your report and stream it to the file system.

Now that you have seen the basics around the `Render` method, let's take a look at the code you need to write for your **Render** button click event. The first thing you need to do in your code is retrieve the selected report and output format. Use the `Format` and `ReportItem` classes created earlier to retrieve the selected items in your drop-downs.

C#

```
Format format = (Format)cboFormat.SelectedItem;
ReportItem reportItem = (ReportItem)cboReports.SelectedItem;
```

VB.NET

```
Dim format As Format = CType(cboFormat.SelectedItem, Format)
Dim reportItem As ReportItem = CType(cboReports.SelectedItem, ReportItem)
```

You need to retrieve the input parameters specified by the user. Then, you need to create a new function that loops through the textboxes you've created earlier to retrieve their values and return an array of `ParameterValue` objects.

C#

```
private ParameterValue[] GetParameters()
{
    ArrayList controls = new ArrayList();

    //get the values from the parameter controls
    int len = grpParamInfo.Controls.Count;
    for(int i=0;i<len;i++)
    {
        if(grpParamInfo.Controls[i] is TextBox)
        {
            controls.Add(grpParamInfo.Controls[i]);
        }
    }

    //add the control information to parameter info objects
    len = controls.Count;
    ParameterValue[] returnValues = new ParameterValue[len];
    for(int i=0;i<len;i++)
    {
        returnValues[i] = new ParameterValue();
        returnValues[i].Name = ((TextBox)controls[i]).Name;
        returnValues[i].Value = ((TextBox)controls[i]).Text;
    }

    return returnValues;
}
```

VB.NET

```vb
Private Function GetParameters() As ParameterValue()
    Dim controls As New ArrayList

    'get the values from the parameter controls
    Dim len As Integer = grpParamInfo.Controls.Count
    Dim i As Integer
    For i = 0 To len - 1
        If TypeOf grpParamInfo.Controls(i) Is TextBox Then
            controls.Add(grpParamInfo.Controls(i))
        End If
    Next i

    'add the control information to parameter info objects
    len = controls.Count - 1
    Dim returnValues(len) As ParameterValue
        For i = 0 To len
            returnValues(i) = New ParameterValue
            returnValues(i).Name = CType(controls(i), TextBox).Name
            returnValues(i).Value = CType(controls(i), TextBox).Text
        Next i

    Return returnValues
End Function
```

You can now use the `GetParameter` function to build an array of input parameters. You can add the following code to your `Render` click event to retrieve the input parameters.

C#

```csharp
ParameterValue[] parameters = GetParameters();
```

VB.NET

```vb
Dim parameters As ParameterValue() = GetParameters()
```

Now that you have your list of input parameters, you are almost ready to call the `Render` method. For this, you need to declare variables that will be used for the MIME type, encoding, output parameters, warnings, and stream IDs. These are all output parameters of the `Render` method. This step is necessary when working in C#, but can be avoided in VB.NET by passing `Nothing` into the unused parameters. The final variable you will need for the `Render` method is an array of bytes. This byte array can then be written to the file system.

C#

```csharp
string encoding;
string mimeType;
ParameterValue[] parametersUsed;
Warning[] warnings;
string[] streamIds;

//render the report
byte[] data;
```

```
data = _rs.Render(reportItem.Path, format.Name,
        null, null, parameters, null, null, out encoding, out mimeType,
        out parametersUsed, out warnings, out streamIds);
```

VB.NET

```
Dim encoding As String
Dim mimeType As String
Dim parametersUsed() As ParameterValue
Dim warnings() As Warning
Dim streamIds() As String

'render the report
Dim data() As Byte
data = _rs.Render(reportItem.Path, format.Name, Nothing, Nothing, _
        parameters, Nothing, Nothing, encoding, mimeType, _
        parametersUsed, warnings, streamIds)
```

Finally, you need to take the byte array returned from the Render method and write it to the file system. Use the output path specified in the output textbox along with the report name and format file extension to open a file stream. Following is the entire Render button click event along with the final piece of code for writing the file to the file system.

C#

```
private void btnRender_Click(object sender, System.EventArgs e)
{
    //get the format and report item from the comboboxes
    Format format = (Format)cboFormat.SelectedItem;
    ReportItem reportItem = (ReportItem)cboReports.SelectedItem;

    //set up variables needed to call render method
    ParameterValue[] parameters = GetParameters();

    string encoding;
    string mimeType;
    ParameterValue[] parametersUsed;
    Warning[] warnings;
    string[] streamIds;

    //render the report
    byte[] data;
    data = _rs.Render(reportItem.Path, format.Name,
            null, null, parameters, null, null, out encoding, out mimeType,
            out parametersUsed, out warnings, out streamIds);
    //create a file stream to write the output
    string fileName = txtOutputLocation.Text + "\\" +
    reportItem.Name + format.Extension;

    System.IO.FileStream fs = new System.IO.FileStream(fileName, System.IO.FileMode
                              .OpenOrCreate);

    System.IO.BinaryWriter writer = new System.IO.BinaryWriter(fs);
    writer.Write(data, 0, data.Length);
```

```
        writer.Close();
        fs.Close();
        MessageBox.Show("File written to: " + fileName);
    }
```

VB.NET

```
    Private Sub btnRender_Click(ByVal sender As Object, ByVal e As System.EventArgs) _
                        Handles btnRender.Click

        'get the format and report item from the comboboxes
        Dim format As Format = CType(cboFormat.SelectedItem, Format)
        Dim reportItem As ReportItem = CType(cboReports.SelectedItem, ReportItem)
        'set up variables needed to call render method
        Dim parameters As ParameterValue() = GetParameters()
        Dim encoding As String
        Dim mimeType As String
        Dim parametersUsed() As ParameterValue
        Dim warnings() As Warning
        Dim streamIds() As String

        'render the report
        Dim data() As Byte
        data = _rs.Render(reportItem.Path, format.Name, Nothing, Nothing, _
                parameters, Nothing, Nothing, encoding, mimeType, _
                parametersUsed, warnings, streamIds)
        'create a file stream to write the output
        Dim fileName As String = txtOutputLocation.Text & "\" & reportItem.Name & _
                            format.Extension

        Dim fs As New System.IO.FileStream(fileName, System.IO.FileMode.OpenOrCreate)

        Dim writer As New System.IO.BinaryWriter(fs)
        writer.Write(data, 0, data.Length)
        writer.Close()
        fs.Close()
        MessageBox.Show(("File written to: " + fileName))
    End Sub
```

Now that you have completed the code for rendering the application, let's try it out. You need to build and run the project. When the form opens, enter your server information in the **Server Address** textbox and click the **Get Items** button that you can see in Figure 9-13:

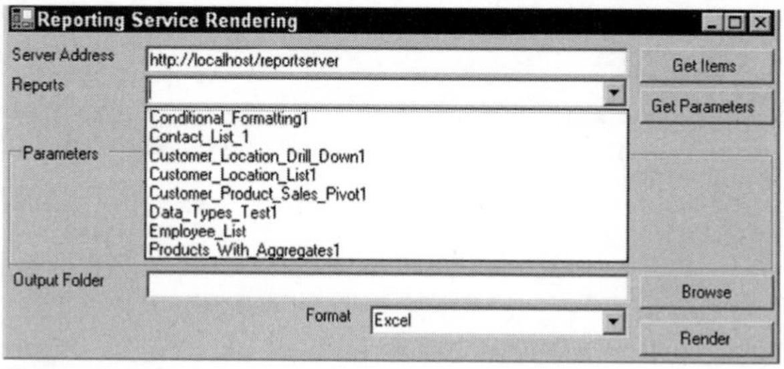

Figure 9-13

You can select the Customer_Product_Sales_Pivot1 report from the report list (Figure 9-14) and click the Get Parameters button. This will give you two parameters, Order Date To and Order Date From.

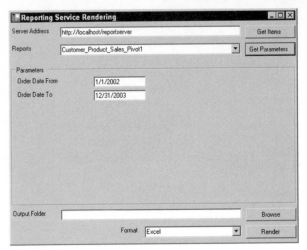

Figure 9-14

Finally, enter the Output Folder (C:) and the rendering Format as PDF. Once these items have been specified you can click the Render button to render your report. When the rendering is complete, you will receive a message box letting you know that the file has been written to the specified location as shown in Figure 9-15:

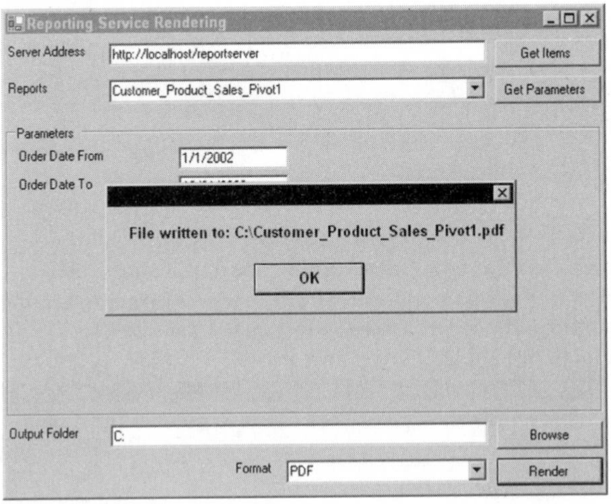

Figure 9-15

You can now search for and open the file `Customer_Product_Sales_Pivot1.pdf` in Adobe Acrobat.

Rendering a Report to the File System Summary

In this section, you learnt the basic steps of rendering a report to the file system:

❑ Using the `ReportingService` object's `ListChildren` method to return a list of reports.

❑ Using the `ReportingService` object's `GetReportParameters` method to return a list of report parameters.

❑ Using the `Render` method of the `ReportingService` object to output your report in a given format.

These basic steps can be used in numerous applications to render a report. Using these methods, users can create their own custom list of reports, customer report parameter pages, and output the report using the returned byte array. In the next section, you will use some of these same steps to render a report to the web via the `Response` object.

Rendering to the Web

In the preceding section, you saw the mechanics of rendering to a file system. However, most of today's applications are written for the web. Along with URL requests, you can also use the Reporting Services Web Service to render reports programmatically to the web.

While doing this, most of your steps will be identical to rendering to the file system; you simply change the interface. Using the `ListChildren` method, developers can easily bind reports to an ASP.NET data grid or create a tree view of available reports. Likewise, developers could also use the `GetParameters` method to create their own parameter interface.

Since you have seen both the `ListChilden` and `GetParameters` methods, in this section, you will work more with the specifics around developing ASP.NET applications. You'll look at changes that can be made to the `web.config` file to pass credential information to Reporting Services. Then you will look at the mechanics of rendering to the ASP.NET `Response` object.

Using Integrated Authentication

There are two main components to every security model, authentication and authorization. In Reporting Services, you can use Windows Integrated Security within an ASP.NET application to authenticate users.

> **Before you start your example, you need to ensure that your application is configured to use Integrated Security.**

After creating a new ASP.NET web application, you need to open IIS and change some settings of the virtual directory.

In the sample created for this chapter, the virtual directory created in IIS is called `WebRenderingCS` and `WebRenderingVB` for the C# and Visual Basic .NET projects respectively. To set the virtual directories to use integrated authentication, you need to check their settings in IIS. In Figure 9-16, the appropriate IIS settings are shown.

Make sure that the **Anonymous access** has been turned off and **Integrated Windows** authentication has been turned on.

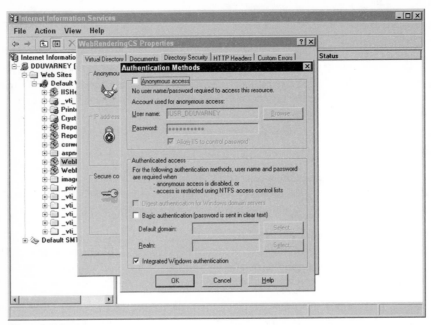

Figure 9-16

Using Integrated Authentication in an ASP.NET web application is the easiest way to take advantage of the security features in Reporting Services. Using this method allows developers to concentrate on other areas of an application without having to build their own authentication mechanism. It also allows for taking full advantage of the Reporting Services role-based security model.

After updating the IIS settings to use Integrated Authentication, you will have to make some modifications to your ASP.NET web application.

Modifying the web.config File

In the web application created for this demonstration, you want to pass the user's security credentials to the Reporting Services Web Service. To accomplish this, you have to allow your ASP.NET application to *impersonate* the currently logged on user. Setting up impersonation requires adding the following line of code to the `web.config` file; place this line after the authorization tag in the file:

```
<identity impersonate="true" />
```

Setting Up the Reporting Service Web Service

Just like in any Windows application, you need to set a reference to the Reporting Services Web Service. The details for creating the reference are identical to those found in the *Rendering Through Windows* section, so we will not go into the details here.

For this example, we have added a web reference to http://localhost/reportserver/reportservice.asmx?wsdl and named it RSService.

Rendering to the Response Object

Now that you have set up Integrated Authentication and modified the `web.config` file, you're ready to write some code. In this application, you will have one page that takes in a report path and format from the URL. You'll use this information to call the `Render` method of the Reporting Services object and write that information back to the response stream.

This sample will use one ASP.NET page called `Render.aspx`. Place your code sample in the `Page_Load` event of the page. This would be a logical approach when developing an application around Reporting Services. It allows you to have one point of entry to the Report Server. The page could then be referenced from other areas of an application.

Let's add some code to the pages `Page_Load` event to retrieve the report path and format from the HTTP Request.

C#

```csharp
string path = Request.Params["Path"];
string format = Request.Params["Format"];
```

VB.NET

```vbnet
Dim path As String = Request.Params("Path")
Dim format As String = Request.Params("Format")
```

Now that you have the report path and format, you can start setting up the `ReportingService` object. Like you did with the Windows application, you will create an instance of the `ReportingService` object and then set the credentials to the credentials of the currently logged-on user.

C#

```csharp
//create the ReportingService object
ReportingService rs = new ReportingService();

//set the credentials to be passed to Reporting Services
rs.Credentials = System.Net.CredentialCache.DefaultCredentials;
```

VB.NET

```vbnet
'create the ReportingService object
Dim rs As New ReportingService

'set the credentials to be passed to Reporting Services
rs.Credentials = System.Net.CredentialCache.DefaultCredentials
```

Once the Reporting Service object has been created and your credentials set, you can go ahead and render the report. You will create variables to pass any report parameters (none in this example) and capture the reports encoding, MIME type, parameters used, warnings, and stream IDs. The key output parameter, which you'll render your report through, is the MIME type. This parameter will tell the HTTP Response what type of document is being passed back. The following code renders your report to the web application. You should notice that it is identical to the code used in the Windows application.

C#

```csharp
ParameterValue[] parameters = new ParameterValue[0];
string encoding;
string mimeType;
ParameterValue[] parametersUsed;
Warning[] warnings;
string[] streamIds;

//render the report
byte[] data;
data = rs.Render(path, format, null, null, parameters, null, null,
        out encoding, out mimeType, out parametersUsed,
        out warnings, out streamIds);
```

VB.NET

```vbnet
Dim parameters As ParameterValue()
Dim encoding As String
Dim mimeType As String
Dim parametersUsed As ParameterValue()
Dim warnings As Warning()
Dim streamIds As String()

'render the report
Dim data As Byte()
data = rs.Render(path, format, Nothing, Nothing, parameters, _
                Nothing, Nothing, encoding, mimeType, parametersUsed, _
                warnings, streamIds)
```

The Render method of the ReportingService object passes back a byte array that can be used in a number of ways. For the web, you will write this information directly back to the HTTP Response object. Before you write back the data though, you need to set some information about the report, namely, the report MIME type and a file name. You will start by assembling a file name for the report. To do this, you use the name of the report followed by an extension that you determine using the value returned in the MIME type parameter. Following is a sample function for determining a file extension based on the MIME type. There are a number of MIME types that can be passed back from Reporting Services that are not shown here, so you might want to add more code to this function for your application needs.

C#

```csharp
string GetExtension(string mimeType)
{
    string retVal="";

    switch(mimeType)
```

```
    {
        case "text/html": //HTML3.2, HTML4.0
            retVal = "html";
            break;
        case "multipart/related": //MHTML
            retVal = "html";
            break;
        case "text/xml":  //XML
            retVal = "xml";
            break;
        case "text/plain":  //CSV
            retVal = "csv";
            break;
        case "image/tiff":  //IMAGE
            retVal = "tif";
            break;
        case "application/pdf":  //PDF
            retVal = "pdf";
            break;
        case "application/vnd.ms-excel": //EXCEL
            retVal = "xls";
            break;
    }
```

VB.NET

```
Public Function GetExtension(ByVal mimeType As String) As String
    Dim retVal As String

    Select Case mimeType
        Case "text/html"  'HTML3.2, HTML4.0
            retVal = "html"
        Case "multipart/related"  'MHTML
            retVal = "html"
        Case "text/xml"  'XML
            retVal = "xml"
        Case "text/plain"  'CSV
            retVal = "csv"
        Case "image/tiff"  'IMAGE
            retVal = "tif"
        Case "application/pdf"  'PDF
            retVal = "pdf"
        Case "application/vnd.ms-excel"  'EXCEL
            retVal = "xls"
    End Select

    Return retVal
End Function
```

Now that you have a function to return the appropriate file extension, you can construct a complete file name. Following is the code to use the report path information long with the MIME type to create the file name.

C#

```
string extension = GetExtension(mimeType);
string reportName = path.Substring(path.LastIndexOf("/") + 1);
string fileName = reportName + "." + extension;
```

VB.NET

```
Dim extension As String = GetExtension(mimeType)
Dim reportName As String = path.Substring(path.LastIndexOf("/") + 1)
Dim fileName As String = reportName & "." & extension
```

Finally, you need to put it all together by writing the data and file information back to the Response object. For this, you:

❑ Start by clearing out any information that is already in the response buffer.

❑ Set the content type of the response equal to the MIME type of your rendered report.

❑ If your report is in a format other than HTML, make sure to attach your file name information to the response.

❑ Finally, use the BinaryWrite method to write the rendered report byte array directly to the Response object.

Following is the completed code for the Page_Load event.

C#

```
private void Page_Load(object sender, System.EventArgs e)
{
    //get the path and output format from the query string
    string path = Request.Params["Path"];
    string format = Request.Params["Format"];

    //create the ReportingService object
    ReportingService rs = new ReportingService();

    //set the credentials to be passed to Reporting Services
    rs.Credentials = System.Net.CredentialCache.DefaultCredentials;

    ParameterValue[] parameters = new ParameterValue[0];
    string encoding;
    string mimeType;
    ParameterValue[] parametersUsed;
    Warning[] warnings;
    string[] streamIds;

    //render the report
    byte[] data;
    data = rs.Render(path, format, null, null, parameters, null, null,
            out encoding, out mimeType, out parametersUsed,
            out warnings, out streamIds);
    //determine if format is rendered to the web or a file.
    string extension = GetExtension(mimeType);
```

```
string reportName = path.Substring(path.LastIndexOf("/") + 1);
string fileName = reportName + "." + extension;
```

```
//write the report back to the Response object
Response.Clear();
Response.ContentType = mimeType;
//add the file name to the response if it is not a web browser format.
if(mimeType!="text/html")
    Response.AddHeader("Content-Disposition", "attachment; filename=" +
                        fileName);

Response.BinaryWrite(data);
```
```
}
```

VB.NET

```
Private Sub Page_Load(ByVal sender As System.Object, ByVal e As System.EventArgs)_
                Handles MyBase.Load

    'get the path and output format from the query string
    Dim path As String = Request.Params("Path")
    Dim format As String = Request.Params("Format")

    'create the ReportingService object
    Dim rs As New ReportingService

    'set the credentials to be passed to Reporting Services
    rs.Credentials = System.Net.CredentialCache.DefaultCredentials

    Dim parameters As ParameterValue()
    Dim encoding As String
    Dim mimeType As String
    Dim parametersUsed As ParameterValue()
    Dim warnings As Warning()
    Dim streamIds As String()

    'render the report
    Dim data As Byte()
    data = rs.Render(path, format, Nothing, Nothing, parameters, _
            Nothing, Nothing, encoding, mimeType, parametersUsed, _
            warnings, streamIds)

    'determine if format is rendered to the web or a file.
    Dim extension As String = GetExtension(mimeType)
    Dim reportName As String = path.Substring(path.LastIndexOf("/") + 1)
    Dim fileName As String = reportName & "." & extension
```

```
    'write the report back to the Response object
    Response.Clear()
    Response.ContentType = mimeType
    'add the file name to the response if it is not a web browser format.
    If mimeType <> "text/html" Then
        Response.AddHeader("Content-Disposition", "attachment; filename=" &
                            fileName)
    End If
```

```
      Response.BinaryWrite(data)
End Sub
```

This example quickly demonstrates some of the key pieces of code that can be used to to render reports to the web. You first need to set the security context for the application by configuring Windows Integrated authentication and allowing impersonation from your application. Next, you retrieve a report from Reporting Services by specifying the report path and format. Finally, you use the rendered report data along with its associated MIME type to render the report using the HTTP `Response` object.

Now that the code for your web application is complete, let's take a look at using your `Render.aspx` page. You can use a simple query string to render your report. A sample query string that renders the Employee List report from the Professional Reporting Services sample reports in HTML 4.0 format is as follows:

http://localhost/WebRenderingCS/Render.aspx?Path=%2fProfessional+SQL+Reporting+Services%2fEmployee_List&Format=HTML4.0

This URL does the following:

❑ It calls the `Render.aspx` page from your C# project.

❑ It passes in the required parameters, the path (Professional SQL Reporting Services/Employee List) and the Format (HTML 4.0).

If you place this URL in the Internet Explorer, you'll get the following HTML output as shown in Figure 9-17:

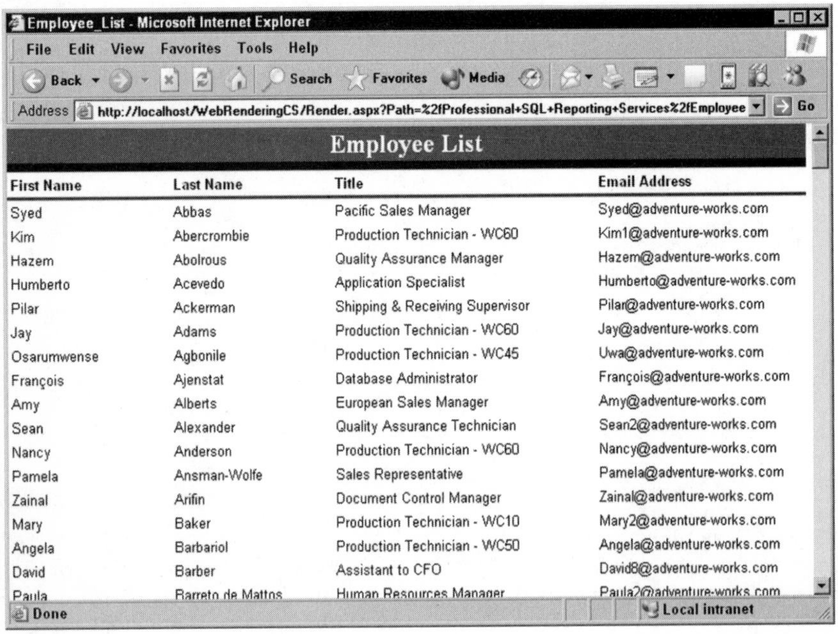

Figure 9-17

Notice that when you enter HTML 4.0 as the output format, the report data is rendered directly in the browser. In your code, set the MIME type of your HTTP Response to `text/html` in this scenario. When the browser receives the response, it recognizes the MIME type and renders it directly to the browser.

Let's take a quick look at rendering in a format that does not go directly to the browser. Use the following URL to render the same Employee List report, but in the EXCEL format:

http://localhost/WebRenderingCS/Render.aspx?Path=%2fProfessional+SQL+Reporting+Services%2fEmployee _List&Format=EXCEL

Figure 9-18 shows the result:

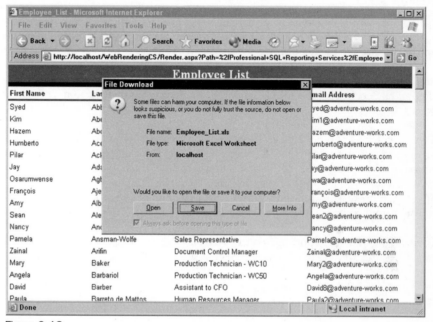

Figure 9-18

Notice this time that when you set the format to EXCEL, you are prompted to save to the file system. In this case, the MIME type needs to be set to `application/vnd.ms-excel`. You also need to add header information to the `Response` object that contains the file name `Employee_List.xls`. The MIME type notifies Internet Explorer that you are sending a file and the added header gives it the appropriate file name.

Rendering to the Web Summary

In this section, you saw some of the base mechanics around rendering a report using an ASP.NET application. To start with, you need to pass the currently logged on user's credentials. This is accomplished by setting the application virtual directory to use Integrated Windows authentication, and then modifying the `web.config` file for the application to use impersonation. In the code, you need to call the Reporting Services Web Service to retrieve the report along with content information such as

MIME type. Once you have the binary report data, you can write that information directly back to the `Response` object.

Rendering reports directly through an ASP.NET application can be very helpful. It allows developers to create their own interface for items such as parameters. A key point to remember is that Report Manager uses the same Reporting Services Web Service that we used here. So, anything that you can do from the Report Manager, can also be done through your own code. This adds an incredible amount of flexibility for developers of custom applications.

Summary

In this chapter, we saw the two main ways to render reports from Reporting Services. The first part of the chapter focused on rendering reports via URL requests. The second part looked at rendering reports programmatically through the Reporting Services Web Service.

URL rendering gives you a quick way to add Reporting Services reports to your own applications. You can add Reporting Services reports to custom portals or create your own custom report links in other applications.

Programmatic rendering of reports gives developers the greatest amount of flexibility. Since the Reporting Services API is implemented as a web service, you can call it from a number of different types of applications including .NET Windows applications, ASP.NET web applications, and .NET console applications. You can even use this web service from Visual Basic 6.0 or VBA applications using Microsoft's SOAP library. This flexibility allows for the creation of a number of applications including those that use custom security or pass parameter information stored in other application databases.

With URL rendering and the Reporting Services Web Service, developers can quickly and easily incorporate Reporting Services into their own custom-built applications.

10

Report Caching and Subscriptions

This chapter will deal with some of the most compelling and exciting capabilities of Reporting Services. If used appropriately, report caching, snapshots, and history provide an efficient, scalable solution for delivering reports to thousands of users without unnecessarily taxing server resources. Subscriptions give users reports delivered in any format when they need them. You will use the *Report Manager* interface to create and manage subscriptions and then take a look at using .NET code and script to create custom solutions for programmers and administrators.

Report Delivery

Reports may be delivered to users in different ways. Using the Report Manager interface, you've primarily seen reports delivered *on-demand*. This means that when a user requests a report, a query is executed, parameters are used to filter data, and the report is rendered in real-time. Although on-demand delivery has the advantage of presenting the most timely report data, it may not always be the most optimal method and best use of system resources if a report is to be viewed multiple times. Two other delivery methods, caching and subscriptions, give users additional options to make reports available immediately when needed.

Caching can be used to conserve system resources by rendering reports less often while serving more users. There are three different ways to cache reports that affect the ability to revisit a report snapshot stored in history or to apply client-side filtering without retrieving additional data from a data source.

Caching

It's important that you differentiate between the general concept of caching and a specific type of report caching that is referred to as the *cached instance* of a report. In general terms, report caching means that a copy of an executed report (and possibly a copy of its data) is held on the Report Server in memory and/or in the Report Server database. Before you try to differentiate between *cached instances*, *snapshots*, and *snapshot history*, we need to discuss some of the details about what goes on when reports are rendered on the server. In their infinite wisdom, our good friends at Microsoft devised an intelligent method for managing report delivery. The result is a mechanism that balances efficiency and flexibility. It is a three-phased approach that encompasses the server-side report definition, an intermediate rendering of a report independent from any specific rendering format and a cache of its data, and then the final rendering in a specified format.

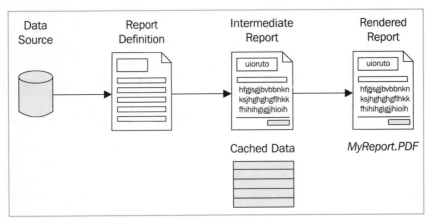

Figure 10-1

After a report is deployed to the Report Server, its definition is stored in the *Report Server Database*. Before the final rendered report is outputted, an image of the report and its data is produced on the server in an *intermediate report format*. The intermediate report format describes the placement of data, items, regions, and pages before it is rendered to a specific output format.

The intermediate rendering format is the foundation of report caching. For reports that are rendered *on demand* in real time, the intermediate format is held in memory on the Report Server. When a report is cached, the intermediate format image is written to disk in the `ReportServerTempDB` database (one of the two databases that comprise the Report Server). This enables the report data and definition to be retrieved once and outputted in different rendering formats or multiple times in the same rendering format. This way, the retrieval of report data which is typically the most time consuming process, is performed once and reused multiple times, thus dramatically improving performance. This also makes it possible for a single cached instance to produce different outputs based on report parameters that filter data on the cached data store. The final rendering is performed against the intermediate format using a designated rendering extension.

In order to set up any implementation of caching, security credentials must be provided for the data source of a report. If you are using shared data sources, this only needs to be set up once on the shared data source.

Cached Instances

If a report is configured to cache report instances when a user first requests the report with a unique combination of parameter values (assuming the report takes parameters), the intermediate form of the report and its data are stored in the Report Server database. Each unique combination of parameters may produce a separate cached instance. A significant difference between a cached instance and a snapshot is that a cached instance is rendered the first time a user requests the report with unique parameters. Cached reports are configured to expire after a specific period or on a schedule, after which the report cache is flushed and the report is cached again on the next request. The cache will also be flushed automatically when a report definition is modified and redeployed, caching options are changed, or the report is deleted.

> **Keep in mind when using cached instances that users viewing a report will have no indication that the report is rendered from a cached instance and will not see new data entered since the report was cached.**

If the report is rendered from a cached instance, this means that data presented in the report could potentially be out of date without the user's knowledge. For this reason it may be a good idea to update cached instances frequently, especially for a transactional database where data changes often. In the case of a data warehouse, it might make sense to synchronize cached report updates with batch data updates to the warehouse database.

Snapshots

A *snapshot* is a static, cached copy of a rendered report. Snapshots are created before users request reports and are usually created and refreshed on a prescribed schedule. Because snapshots are rendered beforehand, users cannot interactively supply parameter values. Reports that require parameters must be configured with these values ahead of time.

Often, a particular report needs to be generated at a predetermined interval, for example, a monthly sales report. So if the report were created at the end of January, users would want to see the January report throughout February. They do not expect the February data to be seen in the January report. These types of reports are best created upfront, without waiting for the first user to request it, because the report is expected to be available at the end of January. Therefore, you can now instruct Reporting Services to create the report pro-actively and keep it ready for users.

History

Report snapshots may be placed into history. This means that when another snapshot is created for a report, it doesn't overwrite the previous snapshot. Any of these individual snapshots for the same report may be retrieved from history until the history is cleared or reaches its maximum size. Reports may manually or automatically be placed into history based on a schedule when a snapshot is created.

The following table compares the features of various types of cached reports:

	Cached Instance	Snapshot	History
Creation	Created with the first user request using a unique combination of parameters.	Created on a schedule before the first user requests a report.	Like a standard snapshot; history entries can be created on a schedule or snapshots may be added to history manually by users.
Lifespan	Cache automatically expires after a designated time has elapsed or based on a designated schedule.	A Report snapshot is overwritten when the next scheduled snapshot is created.	History entries don't typically expire but may be overwritten when a designated number of history entries has been reached.
Typical Scenarios	To optimize performance and conserve resources when users use different parameter values.	For static reports that do not require user interaction, a snapshot can be created with pre-selected parameter values. It's not optimal if reports have several parameter options.	Preserves snapshots for archival and future reference. Appropriate for keeping a static view of data that changes.

Storing Parameters

Since report snapshots and subscriptions are executed without the user's interaction, all parameter values must be supplied in the report configuration so they may be presented to the rendering engine at the time of unattended report execution. Although defaults can be set for parameters, reports configured to execute as a cached instance can be interactive and, therefore, do not require parameter values to be stored. You can look at some examples of the configuration pages in Report Manager in the following section.

Parameterized Filters

In Chapter 3, we discussed a number of query and filter techniques. In brief, these included using parameterized queries in the database (by using either ad hoc SQL statements or stored procedures), filtering data in the report, or a combination of the two.

You will recall that report parameters that are derived from query parameters cause data to be filtered at the data source. Additional report parameters may be added to filter data on the report server using filter expressions. Unlike query parameters that will cause multiple report instances to be cached (each instance for a different combination of parameters), filter parameters in a cached instance simply filter the data stored with the cached report. Filter expressions are applied to the cached data and will not cause additional instances to be cached.

Configuring Credentials for Data Sources

If you have created reports where data sources use Windows Integrated security or don't store credentials in the connection string, you will need to make a configuration change before you can enable caching or add subscriptions for these reports. Some types of cached reports are executed before a user actually views the report. For this reason, the security credentials needed to retrieve data from the data source must be stored to execute the report ahead of time.

Storing Credentials

Data sources used by cached reports (either cached instances or report snapshots) must use stored credentials. This information is stored in encrypted form with the shared data source or the report definition in the Report Server database. If this is not set up prior to attempting to create a cached report or subscription, a warning will be displayed similar to the Figure 10-2:

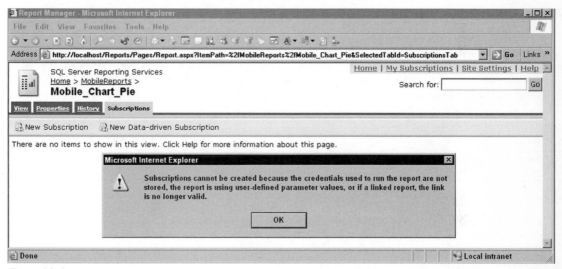

Figure 10-2

This is easily remedied. Shared data sources make it much easier to configure caching for multiple reports. In Report Manager, open the folder containing the reports and data sources. Data sources appear different from reports and are shown with a small globe icon. Click a data source link to open the Properties page. You can view properties for the AdventureWorks2000 data source as shown in Figure 10-3:

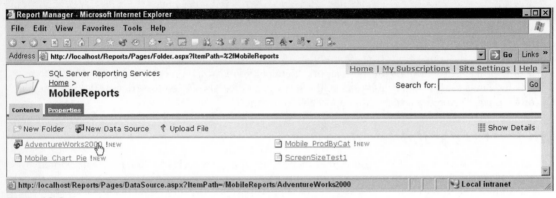

Figure 10-3

If you are not using a shared data source, you can get the same settings in the Data Sources tab on the Properties page of a specific report.

In the data source Properties page, select Connect Using: Credentials stored securely in the report server. Enter a username and password to authenticate to the data source as shown in Figure 10-4. This information is stored as an encrypted string in the Report Server database. With this setting in place, you will be able to configure caching and create subscriptions.

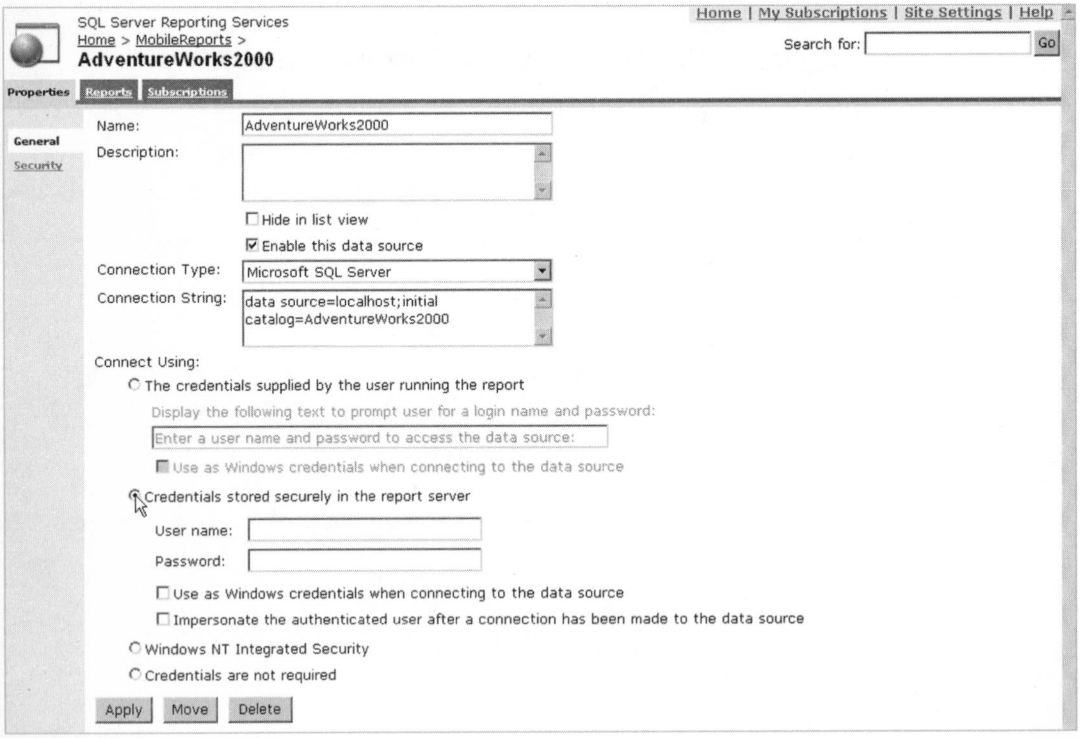

SQL Server Reporting Services
Home > MobileReports >
AdventureWorks2000
Home | My Subscriptions | Site Settings | Help
Search for: [   ] Go

Properties Reports Subscriptions

General
Security

Name: [AdventureWorks2000]

Description: [   ]

☐ Hide in list view
☑ Enable this data source

Connection Type: [Microsoft SQL Server ▾]

Connection String: [data source=localhost;initial catalog=AdventureWorks2000]

Connect Using:

○ The credentials supplied by the user running the report

  Display the following text to prompt user for a login name and password:

  [Enter a user name and password to access the data source:]

  ☐ Use as Windows credentials when connecting to the data source

◉ Credentials stored securely in the report server

  User name: [   ]

  Password: [   ]

  ☐ Use as Windows credentials when connecting to the data source

  ☐ Impersonate the authenticated user after a connection has been made to the data source

○ Windows NT Integrated Security

○ Credentials are not required

[Apply] [Move] [Delete]

Figure 10-4

352

Depending on how the database or database server is configured, different options on this page may be appropriate. If you are using SQL Server and authenticating with Windows Integrated Security, check the box labeled Use as Windows credentials when connecting to the data source. These settings should be sufficient to enable caching and subscriptions. Click Apply to save your settings.

Linked Reports

In Chapter 1, you were presented a once common scenario where slight variations in reporting requirements would lead to the creation of several different reports. Rather than creating individual reports that may be filtered on different criteria or use different security settings, you can use one report and store a different set of settings to match each requirement. A linked report is a configuration profile for a report that can store a separate set of configuration settings. Any number of linked reports can be created for a base report.

For example, let's say that you have a sales summary report that presents data filtered on a country parameter and an optional parameter to filter on more specific regions within the country. You want to cache several versions of the region-specific reports (one for each region using supplied parameter values) such that the data is current or within a range of three hours. The Sales Manager only runs the report for the entire country once a week and wants to always see the latest, up-to-the-minute sales data. In this case, you can create a linked report for each of the regions with default values provided for the country and regional parameters.

> **Default parameter values can only be specified for non-query-based parameters. In cases where you would like to have an interactive version of the report with query-based parameters and another version for caching, you should either use subscriptions or save a separate copy of the report without query-based parameters.**

In the sales summary report example, the Sales Manager's report is rendered live using interactive parameter selections. Another copy of the report is saved without query-based parameters and is configured as a cached instance. This report would serve as the base for linked reports that have the country and regional parameter values provided.

Configuring Cached Reports

Caching options are configured for each report using settings on the Execution tab on the Properties page. To begin, select the report in Report Manager. In this example, I've created a version of the Product Sales by Location report without query-based parameters so you can specify default values and name this modified report Product Sales By Location (cache). The new report has been deployed. Open it in *Report Manager* and as you can see in Figure 10-5, the Order Date parameters are requested without drop-down lists:

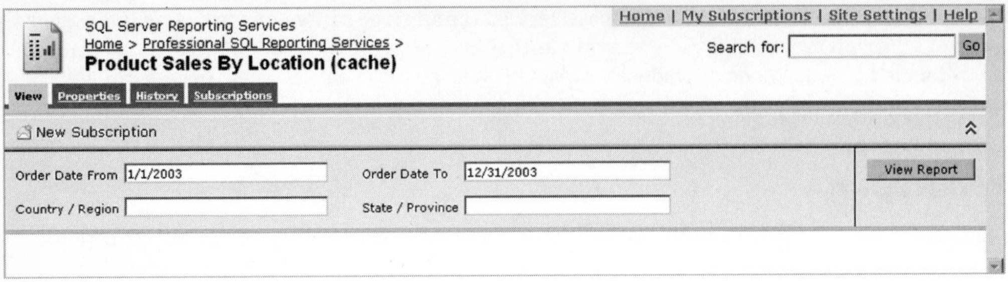

Figure 10-5

Now select the Properties tab to create a linked report. On the Properties page, click the Create Linked Report button to add the linked report as illustrated in Figure 10-6:

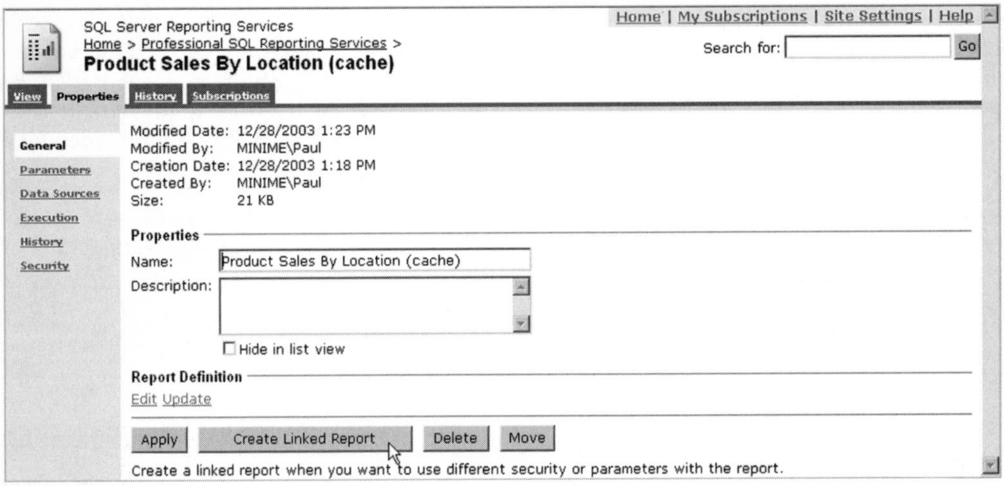

Figure 10-6

In the linked report page that you see in Figure 10-7, enter a name for the linked report and optionally, a description. In this example, we create a linked report for our general purpose Product Sales report that will be used to view sales summary data for the state of Arizona. I'm naming the linked report Product Sales-Arizona.

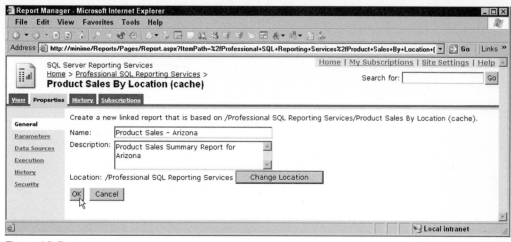

Figure 10-7

The linked report can now be treated just like any other report with its own set of configuration settings. Click the Parameters link on the left side of the Properties page.

Based on the specifications for this report, specify the default parameter values for the cached report as you can see in Figure 10-8. The order date range was already given default values in the Report Designer. Set the CountryRegionCode to US and the StateProvinceName to Arizona. It is necessary to select the Has Default checkbox to enter a default value. If you want the user to be able to change a parameter value from the default, leave the corresponding Prompt User checkbox checked. The Prompt String setting simply modifies the label text for the parameter on the Report Manager page. Apply these settings when completed.

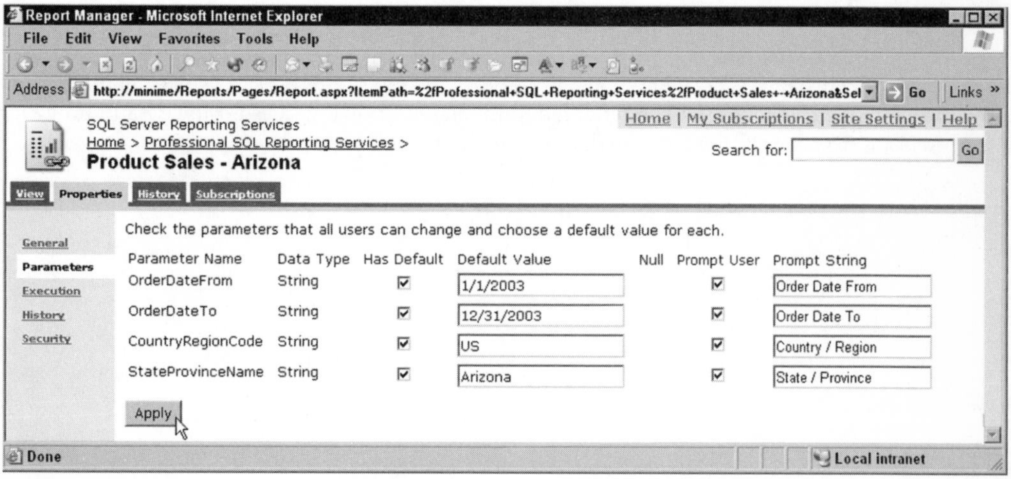

Figure 10-8

Using the Execution link, you can specify caching options. As you can see in Figure 10-9, this page may be used to create a snapshot, to enable snapshot history, or to configure a cached instance of the report.

To enable a cached instance to be generated the first time the report is rendered, select the radio button labeled Render this report with the most recent data, and the second radio button in this group labeled Cache a temporary copy of the report. Set this cached instance to expire after three hours by entering 180 minutes into the corresponding textbox in this setting as shown in Figure 10-9, and then apply these settings when completed:

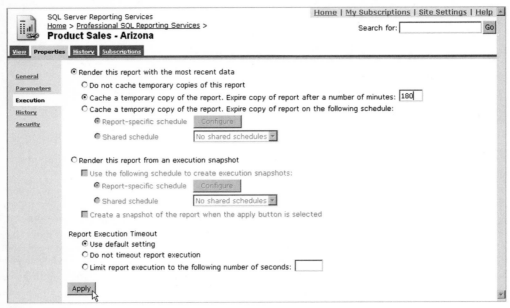

Figure 10-9

The cached report instance is created when a user views the report. In this case, since default parameter values are provided, the report will be rendered immediately showing sales for the default range for the state of Arizona. You can see the generated report in Figure 10-10:

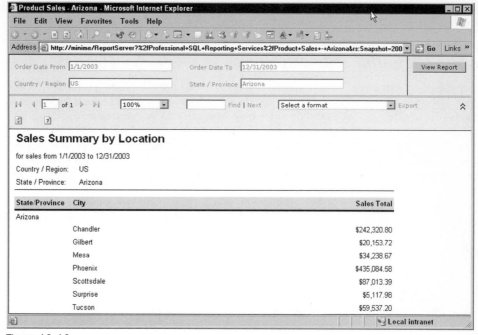

Figure 10-10

After the first request, subsequent visits to this report within three hours should show the same content very quickly as the report is rendered from the cached instance rather than the typical database query execution and report rendering process.

Creating a snapshot is very similar to creating a cached instance. On the Execution tab, select options for creating a snapshot rather than a cached instance. The snapshot is generated immediately or on a specified schedule (without user interaction) rather than on the first user's request.

Subscriptions

What a useful and convenient feature this is! As a manager, you may need to do a bi-weekly status report for your people. When you travel, you might like to have a current, up-to-date employee directory on your PDA at all times. As new products are added to your line of products and pricing information changes, you'd like the updated product catalog in front of your people so they're never working with outdated information. Using subscriptions makes all of this possible, simply and easily.

When I began to use SQL Server Reporting Services in the first beta version, I was thoroughly impressed with the many new features. The ability to output reports using different rendering formats was compelling. The simple Report Manager interface was nice and the ability to program reports to integrate them into my applications was cool. I thought the product team at Microsoft had done a terrific job. But this feature is icing on the cake! When I started playing with subscriptions, I thought, "Wow, this is just too good to be true!"

The subscription engine renders a report any time you want it. It renders it in the format you need and delivers it using the method you choose – either by email or to a file in any folder.

Snapshot-Triggered Subscriptions

Subscriptions can be triggered when a snapshot gets updated rather than being directly tied to a schedule. If the snapshot is refreshed on a schedule, this effectively will cause the subscription to deliver a report on the schedule for the snapshot. Since snapshots can also be updated manually, using this technique can guarantee that users receive updated reports regardless of the method used to refresh the snapshot. For example, at the end of each month, after you bulk-load new data into your decision-support database you update the related snapshots. Triggering subscriptions on the snapshot updates brings the process into balance without concern for the coordination of scheduled events.

The option to create a snapshot-triggered subscription is only available when the report execution is based on a subscription. After setting up a snapshot for your report, add a subscription. Figure 10-11 shows you how to set the appropriate report delivery options. Under the Subscription Processing Options, select the radio button to run the subscription when the report content is refreshed.

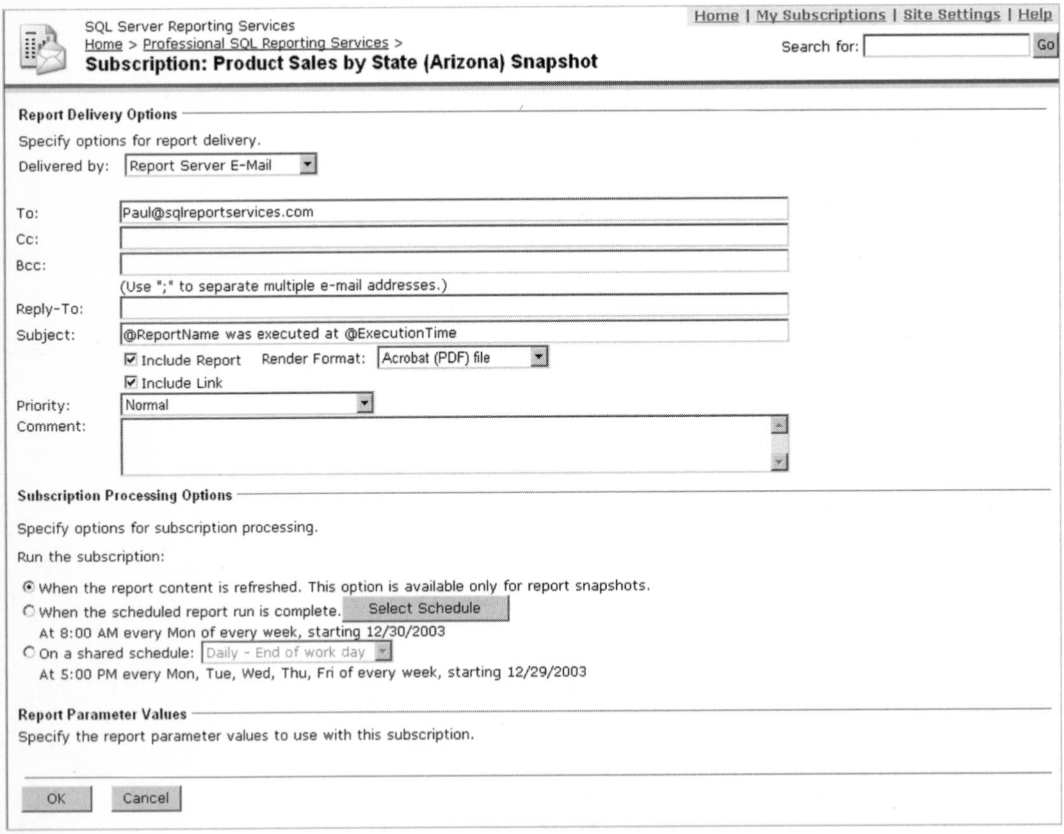

Figure 10-11

Schedule-Triggered Subscriptions

The most common type of subscriptions will likely be based on a shared or an individual schedule. The scheduling mechanism is based on the *SQL Server Agent* that fires and executes events at specific times.

Individual and Shared Schedules

There are advantages of using both the types of scheduling options. Creating a shared schedule makes it easier to schedule multiple events to run at the same time and individual schedules don't have to be set up for each event. This may be an appropriate solution when you need to run several reports during off-peak hours when the server isn't busy with live user requests. Although this may be more convenient, a significant penalty is realized when the server tries to run demanding jobs at the same time. For reports that are long, perform complex calculations, or consume a lot of data, you may want to stagger the schedules to prevent this condition.

To create a shared schedule, click the Site Settings link in the Report Manager. On the Site Settings page, click Manage Shared Schedules (see Figure 10-12):

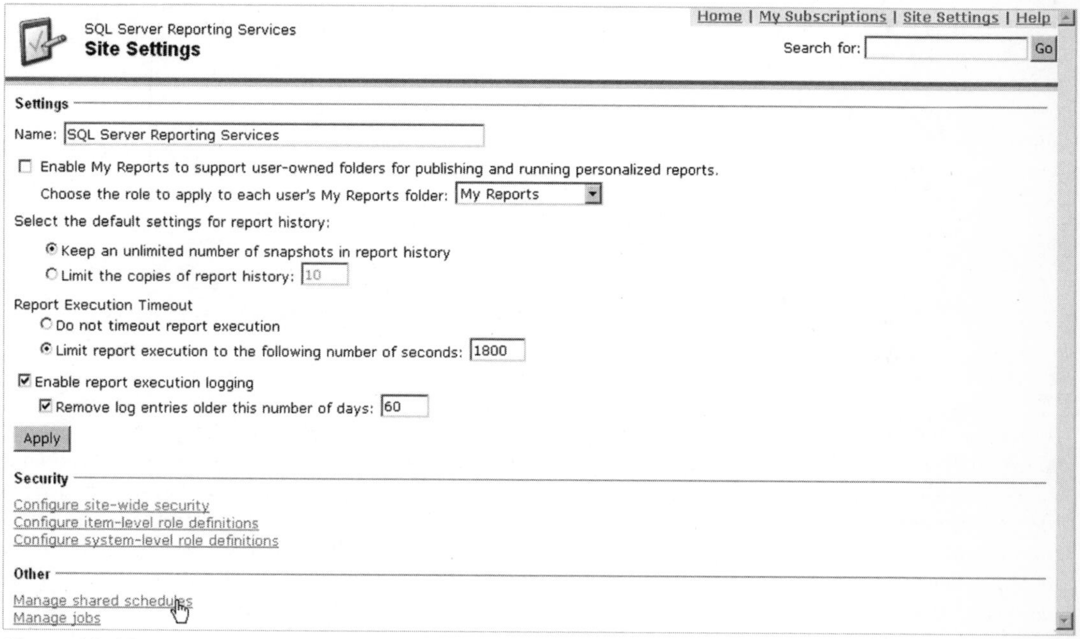

Figure 10-12

On the next page (shown in Figure 10-13), click New Schedule and fill out the details in the Scheduling page. These options are similar to setting a recurring appointment in Microsoft Outlook.

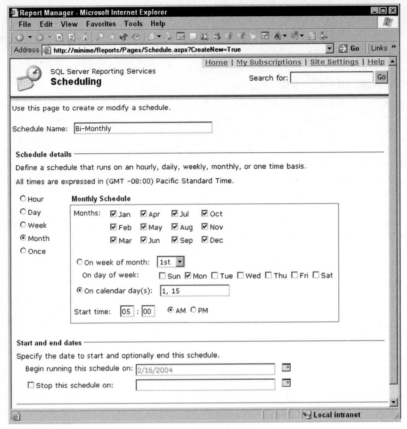

Figure 10-13

As you can see in Figure 10-13, by default, the start date is set to the current date and no end date is specified. If you would like the schedule to expire then you must set the end date. The start and end dates can only be set by using the calendar controls. Click on the corresponding calendar icon to display the calendar control (Figure 10-14) and then navigate to the date using the calendar's back (<) and forward (>) buttons and then select the dates. To enable the end date, the Stop this schedule on checkbox must be checked. Clicking the end date calendar icon will check this box for you. Click OK to accept the new schedule. The shared schedule will now be available for selection in all pages that prompt for a schedule.

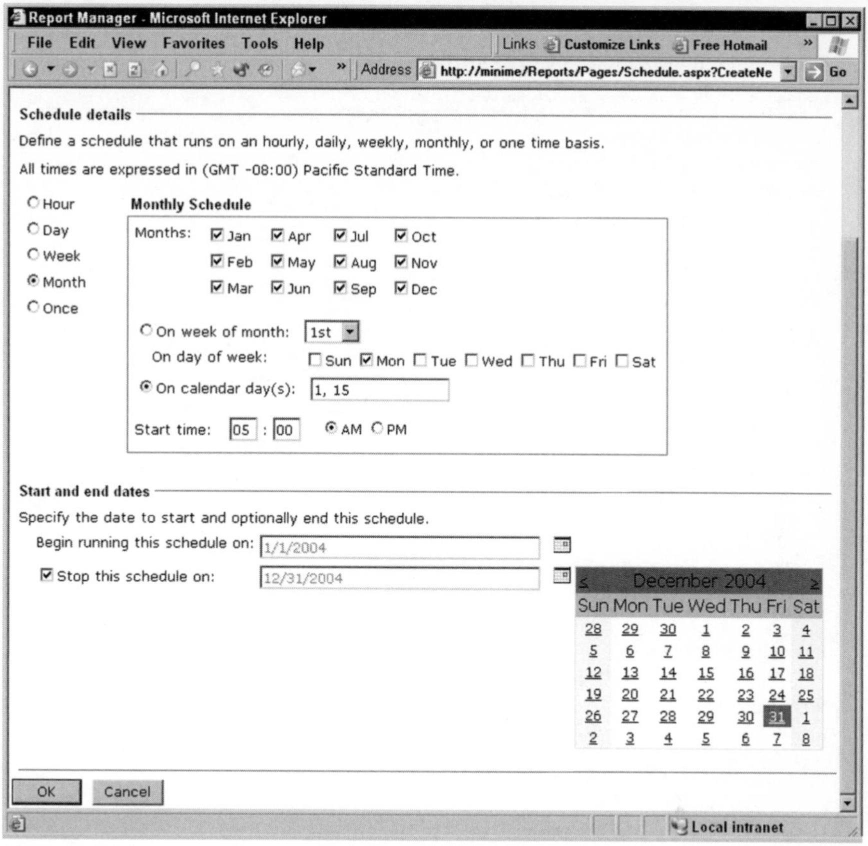

Figure 10-14

Configuring Email Delivery

When Reporting Services is first installed, the setup wizard prompts for the mail server name and address information. Launching the setup wizard again will not prompt for this information again. To modify or set the email server information, you must edit the `RSReportServer.config` file. Email options are set under the `RSEMailDPConfiguration` element in the Delivery section of this file. For more information about modifying configuration settings, please refer to Chapter 1.

File Share Subscriptions

Specifying a file share subscription is very simple. On the Subscriptions link for a report, click Add Subscription. On the Report Delivery Options page, under Delivered By, select Report Server File Share from the drop-down list. See Figure 10-15:

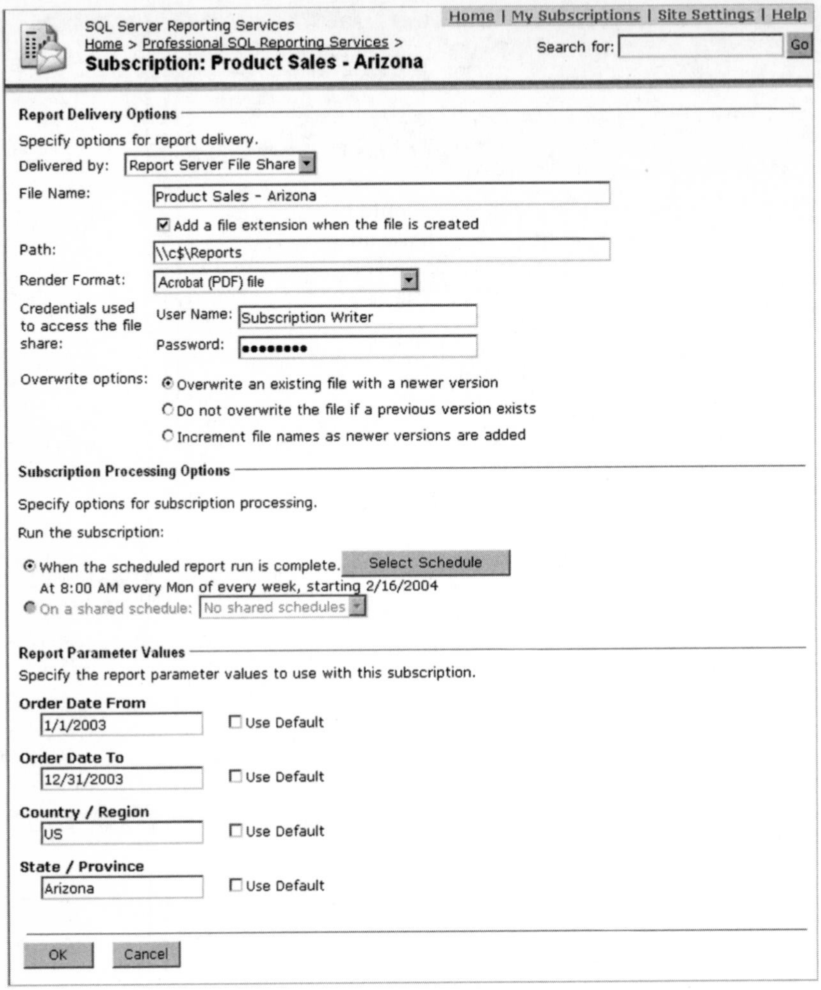

Figure 10-15

You will typically want to specify credentials for a user and then assign this user write permissions on the shared folder. The example in Figure 10-15 shows a user created specifically for our file subscriptions called Subscription Writer. This user has been granted write permissions on the folder.

Enter a valid UNC file path into the Path text box. A local file system path is not acceptable input. If you are entering a local path, follow these steps:

1. Using Windows Explorer, create a file share for the local path. This is easily done by right clicking on the folder and selecting Sharing. Create the share using the Sharing tab.

2. Using the Permissions options on the Sharing tab, grant a user read and write access to this shared folder.

3. Click OK on the Sharing Permissions dialog to accept the file share settings.

4. In Windows Explorer, navigate to My Network Places (or Network Neighborhood in Windows NT). Continue to drill-down to the network share on the server. Typically, this will be under Entire Network\ Microsoft Windows Network\ (your domain or workgroup name)\ (server name)\ (file share name).

5. Copy the path from the address box in Windows Explorer and paste it into the Path textbox.

The Universal Naming Convention (UNC) path should be in the form \\server name\share name. Although it usually is not recommended, you can use an administrative user's credentials to write the subscription output file. In this case, you could use an administrative share (such as c$) rather than create a new share. In any case, the system administrator should be involved in this decision.

Pocket PC Report File Updates

If you would like to have a subscription that updates file-based reports for a Pocket PC device, you can output report files across the network to the synchronization folder for a device. When a mobile device partnership is created using Microsoft ActiveSync on a user's personal computer, a folder is designated for automatic file synchronization. Any files that are modified or written to this folder will be automatically synchronized with the Pocket PC device. This folder is found under the user's My Documents folder and is typically named (mobile device name) My Documents. For example, if your device name were Freds Pocket PC, the synchronization folder would be named Freds Pocket PC My Documents. Any subfolders are also synchronized so you could create a subfolder called Reports and write report files to this location.

When creating file shares for machines across the network, the My Documents folder location can be remapped by the user and is profile-specific. The default location for My Documents is C:\Documents and Settings\(user profile name)\My Documents. Make sure that the user writing to the remote computer from the Report Server has been granted write access to the output folder.

Data-Driven Subscriptions

A data-driven subscription is a subscription where the report recipient information is provided by a query. In addition to the list of recipients, several subscription-specific properties can be based on values returned by a query as well. This makes some very interesting and creative solutions possible.

Reporting Services doesn't provide a database by default so you do have to do a little work to prepare a data-driven subscription, but it's actually quite simple. The data can be stored in practically any form as long as the necessary values are available in columns returned by the query. At the very least, the only requirement is a list of names or email addresses. Every property may use either a static value (assigned when the subscription is created) or values from each row in the query. The query could return information that can be used to customize a report; this implies that for every subscription recipient, a report may be rendered in a different format, sent to a different file share, or sent using a different subject line, priority flag, and so on.

Unlike the Report Designer, tools to assist with building expressions are not offered. If you are not versed in the practice of creating a connection string or Transact SQL expressions, it is recommended that you use the Report Designer to create these expressions as discussed in Chapters 2 and 3. The connection string and query expressions may be copied from the respective designer tool and pasted into these textboxes. File paths must also be typed into these pages as no browsing feature is offered.

The following properties are available for email subscriptions:

Property	Description
To (required)	Email address or alias of recipient
CC	Carbon copy email address or alias
BCC	Blind carbon copy email address or alias
Reply-To	Address or alias for recipient to reply
Include Report	True/False– Include report as embedded content (defaults to True)
Render Format (required)	Report rendering format (defaults to web archive). A single file rendering format is recommended for subscriptions, such as MHTML rather than HTML
Priority	Email message priority (defaults to Normal)
Subject	Email subject line
Comment	Text added to the message subject
Include Link	True/False – Include report as linked file (defaults to True)

The following properties are available for file-share subscriptions:

Property	Description
File name (required)	File name without the path. Omit the extension if the File Extension property is set to True.
File Extension (required)	True/False – Generate file extension based on the Render Format.
Path	UNC path not including the file name or trailing slash.
Render Format (required)	Report rendering format for output file. Single file rendering format is advised for subscriptions, such as MHTML rather than HTML.
Use Credentials (required)	True/False – Use specified credentials or system process.
User Name	Required if Use Credentials is True.
Password	Required if Use Credentials is True.
Write Mode	Auto increment to add an auto-incrementing number to file name. Overwrite to replace existing file.

Managing Subscriptions

It is likely that the most significant subscription management task will be to verify if subscriptions are running as scheduled. The outcome of subscription events is recorded in the server's Application Log and more specific details are written to individual log files with the date/timestamp in each file name. Over time, hundreds of these files may be produced and should be backed-up and/or deleted.

Events in the Application Log are recorded with the `Source` property value of Report Server and SQL Server Reporting Service. There is no method to directly read or consolidate the individual log files. However, Reporting Services ships with SQL script files, which will enable you to import this data into tables for analysis using SQL Server DTS. These files are contained on the product CD in the Extras folder.

> *For more information about importing and using log file information, search the Reporting Services Books Online for the topic Querying and Reporting on Report Execution Log Data. Like other advanced features, this can be a powerful tool for administrators but it's a little cumbersome to set up.*

Now the good news. Simplified subscription log information is easy to obtain in the Report Manager. To get information for a specific report, select the Subscription tab. The status for the last execution is displayed for each subscription and snapshot. A summary view of all reports accessible to the current user is also available on the My Subscriptions tab (see Figure 10-16). These execution summaries can be used to diagnose subscription errors including service and permission related problems.

			Report ↓	Description	Folder	Trigger	Last Run	Status
		Edit	Employee List	Save in \\MiniMe\c$\Temp\Employee List.xls as Employee_List	/Professional SQL Reporting Services	TimedSubscription	12/26/2003 6:45 PM	Failure writing file Employee_List.xls : The network location cannot be reached. For information about network troubleshooting, see Windows Help.
		Edit	Mobile Chart Pie	Send e-mail to Barney@Rubble.com	/MobileReports	TimedSubscription		New Subscription
		Edit	Mobile Chart Pie	Send e-mail to Fred@Flintstone.com	/MobileReports	TimedSubscription		New Subscription
		Edit	Mobile Chart Pie	Send e-mail to Paul@sqlreportservices.com	/MobileReports	TimedSubscription	12/27/2003 11:00 AM	Failure sending mail: The server rejected the sender address. The server response was: 501 5.5.4 Invalid Address
		Edit	Product Sales – Arizona	Send e-mail to Paul@sqlreportservices.com	/Professional SQL Reporting Services	TimedSubscription	12/29/2003 6:52 AM	Failure sending mail: The server rejected the sender address. The server response was: 501 5.5.4 Invalid Address
		Edit	Product Sales by Location – US States	Send monthly US Sales report	/Professional SQL Reporting Services	SnapshotUpdated		New Subscription
		Edit	Product Sales by State (Arizona)	Send e-mail to Paul@sqlreportservices.com	/Professional SQL Reporting Services	TimedSubscription	12/28/2003 1:00 PM	Failure sending mail: Default value or value provided for the report parameter 'StateProvinceName' is not a valid value.
		Edit	Product Sales by State (Arizona) Snapshot	Send e-mail to Paul@sqlreportservices.com	/Professional SQL Reporting Services	SnapshotUpdated	12/30/2003 7:00 PM	Failure sending mail: The server rejected the sender address. The server response was: 501 5.5.4 Invalid Address
		Edit	Stores By Territory for CategoryID 1	Save in \\c$\Temp\Sales_By_Territory (CategoryID 1).xls as Stores_By_Territory for CategoryID 1	/Professional SQL Reporting Services	TimedSubscription	12/26/2003 6:50 PM	Failure writing file Stores_By_Territory for CategoryID 1.xls : The network location cannot be reached. For information about network troubleshooting, see Windows Help.

Figure 10-16

Using the Reporting Service Web Service

The ReportingService Web Service object exposes methods for managing subscriptions. The following table lists these methods and associated arguments. Remember that *webmethods* (programmatic methods for a `webservice` class) don't support overloaded calls or optional arguments. For arguments that don't require a value, you can pass a `Null` (C#) or `Nothing` (VB).

Method	Arguments
CreateDataDrivenSubscription	Report, ExtensionSettings, DataRetrievalPlan, Description, EventType, MatchData, Parameters()
CreateSubscription	Report, ExtensionSettings, Description, EventType, MatchData, Parameters()
DeleteSubscription	SubscriptionID
GetSubscriptionProperties	SubscriptionID, ExtensionSettings, Description, Active, Status, EventType, MatchData, Parameters()
ListSchedules	-
ListSubscriptions	Report, Owner
ListSubscriptionsUsingDataSource	DataSource
SetDataDrivenSubscriptionProperties	DataDrivenSubscriptionID, ExtentionSettings, DataRetrievalPlan, Description, EventType, MatchData, Parameters()
SetSubscriptionProperties	SubscripionID, ExtensionSettings, Description, EventType, MatchData, Parameters()

Let's look at a few examples of some subscription management routines. To obtain a list of subscriptions with associated properties for a report, you can use the `ListSubscriptions` method and use it by passing in a report name. This returns a collection of `Subscription` objects.

Let's take a look at a sample application to view and create subscriptions. I'm not going to take you through this example step-by-step, but I will give you enough information to reproduce the subscription-related code. As you can see in Figure 10-17, I've added two `ComboBoxes`, two `Buttons`, and a `ListView` control to a form in a Windows application project. The `Panel` and the other controls at the bottom will be used later to create new subscriptions. The `Panel` is invisible and the **New Subscription** button is disabled. The click event of the **Get Subscription** button enables the other button because you create the `ReportService` object in this event.

The `ListSubscriptions` event takes two optional arguments. Now, if you were paying attention, you would have caught that webmethods don't support optional arguments! In this sense, arguments that don't have required values can accept the value `Nothing` (VB) or `null` (C#), making these methods somewhat polymorphic (behaving differently under different conditions); this method behaves like this. If you pass the path and report name for the `Report` argument, all subscriptions are returned. If you pass the username for the *Owner*, subscriptions owned by this user are returned, and if you pass nothing, all subscriptions on the server are returned. I've written some conditional statements that check the two combo boxes and pass the appropriate values.

Figure 10-17

In the declaration section of the form class module, you declare an object variable for the web service proxy class. The code to implement this in VB.NET is as follows:

```
Private rs As New localhost_RS.ReportingService
```

The code in C# is as follows:

```
private localhost_RS.ReportingService rs = new localhost_RS.ReportingService();
```

The **Get Subscription** button uses two object variables to hold the report pathname and/or owner name supplied by the user. You use object type variables so you can pass the value `Nothing` (VB) or `null` (C#) in case no values are provided.

After attaching the current user's security credentials to the web service proxy object, you use the `ListSubscriptions` method to iterate through each subscription object and write associated properties to list and view sub items. The `ListView` control will show each of these values in separate columns if displayed in `Detail` mode. The last step is to enable the **New Subscription** button. This button will be used in the next example. The code to implement this in VB.NET and C# follows.

VB.NET

```
Private Sub btnGetSubscriptions_Click( _
                ByVal sender As System.Object, ByVal e As System.EventArgs) _
                Handles btnGetSubscriptions.Click
    Dim subscr As localhost_RS.Subscription
    Dim strReport As String = IIf(Me.cboReport.Text <> "", Me.cboReport.Text,
                            Nothing)
    Dim strOwner As String = IIf(Me.cboOwner.Text <> "", Me.cboOwner.Text, Nothing)
```

```
      rs.Credentials = System.Net.CredentialCache.DefaultCredentials
      '-- Loop through subscriptions collection, add to listview
   For Each subscr In rs.ListSubscriptions(strReport, strOwner)
      Dim ListItem As New ListViewItem
      With ListItem
         .Text = subscr.Description
         .SubItems.Add(subscr.Owner)
         .SubItems.Add(subscr.EventType)
         .SubItems.Add(subscr.LastExecuted)
         .SubItems.Add(subscr.Status)
      End With
      Me.lstvwSubscriptions.Items.Add(ListItem)
   Next
   '-- Enable new subscription button
   Me.btnNewSubscription.Enabled = True
End Sub
```

C#

```csharp
private void btnGetSubscriptions_Click(object sender, System.EventArgs e)
{
    string strReport = null;
    string strOwner = null;
    if(this.cboReport.Text!= "")
    {
        strReport = this.cboReport.Text;
    }
    if(this.cboOwner.Text!= "")
    {
        strOwner = this.cboOwner.Text;
    }
    rs.Credentials = System.Net.CredentialCache.DefaultCredentials;

    foreach (localhost_RS.Subscription subscr in rs.ListSubscriptions(strReport,
             strOwner))
    {
        ListViewItem  ListItem = new ListViewItem();
        ListItem.Text = subscr.Description;
        ListItem.SubItems.Add(subscr.Owner.ToString());
        ListItem.SubItems.Add(subscr.EventType.ToString());
        ListItem.SubItems.Add(subscr.LastExecuted.ToShortDateString());
        ListItem.SubItems.Add(subscr.Status.ToString());
        this.lstvwSubscriptions.Items.Add(ListItem);
    }
    this.btnNewSubscription.Enabled = true;
}
```

Figure 10-18 shows what the form looks like when the application is run and `my computer\user name` is passed:

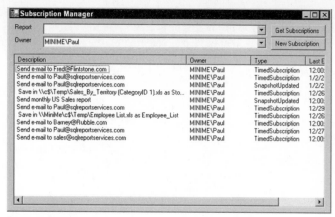

Figure 10-18

You can add a new subscription using the `CreateSubscription` method. Arguments passed to this method are as follows:

1. `ExtensionSettings`: This argument is required and can be a little tricky. The `ExtensionSettings` object contains two properties. The `Extension` property is a string indicating the type of delivery extension. The `ParameterValues` property is an object of type `ParameterValueOrFieldReference` that contains an array of `ParameterValue` objects. Each element is a name/value pair. Depending on the subscription type, a different list of parameter name/value pairs is passed using this array. These parameters correspond to the items presented on the Report Delivery Options section of the Snapshot page in Report Manager.

2. `EventType`: This argument takes a string to set either `TimedSubscription` or `SnapshotUpdate`.

3. `MatchData`: This argument accepts multiple types and values depending on the `EventType` argument; these include the `ScheduleID` for a shared schedule or a string containing the XML element content for the schedule. Shared schedule information may be obtained using the `ListSchedules` method to enumerate the server's schedules.

4. `Parameters`: This argument is an array of `ParameterValue` objects. It is used to supply report parameters as name/value pairs.

Now, let's put it all together in a sample application. Using the same form as the previous example, I've placed two textboxes, two combo boxes, and a button on the `Panel` control at the bottom of the form as seen in Figure 10-19:

Figure 10-19

At the top of this form, the New Subscription button was enabled at the end of the Get Subscriptions button click event code. In the click event of this button, you set the Visible property of the panel to True and get a list of shared subscriptions that have been created on the Report Server, adding the Description for each schedule to the Schedule combo box. For the following code, you'll look at VB.NET and C# language examples side-by-side.

VB.NET

```
Private Sub btnNewSubscription_Click( ByVal sender As System.Object, _
                                      ByVal e As System.EventArgs) _
                                      Handles btnNewSubscription.Click

    Me.Panel1.Visible = True

    Dim sched As localhost_RS.Schedule
    For Each sched In rs.ListSchedules
        Me.cboSchedules.Items.Add(sched.Description)
    Next
End Sub
```

C#

```
private void btnNewSubscription_Click(object sender, System.EventArgs e)
{
    this.Panel1.Visible = true;
    foreach (localhost_RS.Schedule sched in rs.ListSchedules())
    {
        this.cboSchedules.Items.Add(sched.Description);
    }
}
```

After a schedule is selected from the schedule combo box, the SelectedIndex value will correspond to the index of the corresponding schedule. Let's use this to obtain the ScheduleID value and pass it to the CreateSubscription method.

After entering a description, recipient email address, and selecting a rendering format, the user clicks the Add Subscription button. In this click event, you set up the values and objects passed as arguments to the CreateSubscription method. Let's see how to do this in the following sections.

The selected item in the Schedule combo box corresponds to a member of the Schedules collection returned by the ListSchedules method. There is only one method to obtain these items, so you use a loop to resolve the selection and exit when the counter variable matches the SelectedIndex property of the combo box.

VB.NET

```
'-- Get selected schedule
Dim sched As localhost_RS.Schedule
Dim iSchedCounter As Int16
For Each sched In rs.ListSchedules
    iSchedCounter += 1
    If iSchedCounter = Me.cboSchedules.SelectedIndex() Then Exit For
Next
```

C#

```csharp
//-- Get selected schedule
localhost_RS.Schedule scheduleItem = null;
Int16 iSchedCounter = 0;
foreach (localhost_RS.Schedule sched in rs.ListSchedules())
{
    iSchedCounter += 1;
    if (iSchedCounter == this.cboSchedules.SelectedIndex)
    {
        scheduleItem = sched;
        break;
    }
}
```

You can now obtain the `ScheduleID` property of the `Schedule` object using the `sched` variable.

Next, you create an `ExtensionSettings` object and set its `Extension` property to indicate that this subscription will use the email delivery extension as follows.

VB.NET

```vbnet
Dim extset As New localhost_RS.ExtensionSettings
extset.Extension = "Report Server Email"
```

C#

```csharp
localhost_RS.ExtensionSettings extset = new localhost_RS.ExtensionSettings();
extset.Extension = "Report Server Email";
```

Now for the extension-specific properties of the `ExtensionSettings` object. The `ParameterValues` property is set to an object of type `ParameterValueOrFieldReference` and is a five-element array. You also create five corresponding `ParameterValue` objects. For each of these objects, you set the `Name` and `Value` properties and then add them to the array.

VB.NET

```vbnet
'-- Create Parameter Values array
Dim ParamVals(5) As localhost_RS.ParameterValueOrFieldReference
extset.ParameterValues = ParamVals

'-- Populate the Extension Parameters
Dim pvTo As New localhost_RS.ParameterValue
pvTo.Name = "TO"
pvTo.Value = Me.txtEMailTo.Text
extset.ParameterValues(0) = pvTo
Dim pvIncludeRpt As New localhost_RS.ParameterValue
pvIncludeRpt.Name = "IncludeReport"
pvIncludeRpt.Value = "True"
extset.ParameterValues(1) = pvIncludeRpt

Dim pvRenderFormat As New localhost_RS.ParameterValue
pvRenderFormat.Name = "RenderFormat"
pvRenderFormat.Value = Me.cboRenderFormat.Text
extset.ParameterValues(2) = pvRenderFormat
```

```
        Dim pvPriority As New localhost_RS.ParameterValue
        pvPriority.Name = "Priority"
        pvPriority.Value = "NORMAL"
        extset.ParameterValues(3) = pvPriority

        Dim pvSubject As New localhost_RS.ParameterValue
        pvSubject.Name = "Subject"
        pvSubject.Value = "@ReportName was executed at @ExtensionTime"
        extset.ParameterValues(4) = pvSubject
```

C#

```
    //-- Create Parameter Values array
    localhost_RS.ParameterValueOrFieldReference[] ParamVals = new
            Subscriptions_CS.localhost_RS.ParameterValueOrFieldReference[5];
    extset.ParameterValues = ParamVals;

    //-- Populate the Extension Parameters
    localhost_RS.ParameterValue  pvTo = new localhost_RS.ParameterValue();
    pvTo.Name = "TO";
    pvTo.Value = this.txtEMailTo.Text;
    extset.ParameterValues[0] = pvTo;

    localhost_RS.ParameterValue  pvIncludeRpt = new localhost_RS.ParameterValue();
    pvIncludeRpt.Name = "IncludeReport";
    pvIncludeRpt.Value = "true";
    extset.ParameterValues[1] = pvIncludeRpt;

    localhost_RS.ParameterValue  pvRenderFormat = new
                                        localhost_RS.ParameterValue();
    pvRenderFormat.Name = "RenderFormat";
    pvRenderFormat.Value = this.cboRenderFormat.Text;
    extset.ParameterValues[2] = pvRenderFormat;

    localhost_RS.ParameterValue  pvPriority = new localhost_RS.ParameterValue();
    pvPriority.Name = "Priority";
    pvPriority.Value = "NORMAL";
    extset.ParameterValues[3] = pvPriority;

    localhost_RS.ParameterValue  pvSubject = new localhost_RS.ParameterValue();
    pvSubject.Name = "Subject";
    pvSubject.Value = "@ReportName was executed at @ExtensionTime";
    extset.ParameterValues[4] = pvSubject;
```

The report you are using doesn't require any parameters, so you have everything necessary to actually create the subscription. Call this method by passing `Nothing` in place of a `Parameters` array.

VB.NET

```
    '-- Create the Subscription (no report parameters in last arg)
    rs.CreateSubscription(Me.cboReport.Text, _
                        extset, _
                        Me.txtDescription.Text, _
                        "TimedSubscription", _
```

```
                                    sched.ScheduleID, _
                                    Nothing)
```

C#

```csharp
//-- Create the Subscription (no report parameters in last arg)
rs.CreateSubscription(this.cboReport.Text,
                      extset,
                      this.txtDescription.Text,
                      "TimedSubscription",
                      scheduleItem.ScheduleID,
                      null);
```

Now let's look at the entire routine put together. Here's all of the **Add Subscription** button click event code in both VB.NET and C#.

VB.NET

```vbnet
Private Sub btnAddSubscription_Click(ByVal sender As System.Object, _
                                     ByVal e As System.EventArgs)
                                     Handles btnAddSubscription.Click
    '-- Get selected schedule
    Dim sched As localhost_RS.Schedule
    Dim iSchedCounter As Int16
    For Each sched In rs.ListSchedules
        iSchedCounter += 1
        If iSchedCounter = Me.cboSchedules.SelectedIndex() _
                    Then Exit For
    Next

    Dim extset As New localhost_RS.ExtensionSettings
    extset.Extension = "Report Server Email"

    '-- Create Parameter Values array
    Dim ParamVals(5) As localhost_RS.ParameterValueOrFieldReference
    extset.ParameterValues = ParamVals

    '-- Populate the Extension Parameters
    Dim pvTo As New localhost_RS.ParameterValue
    pvTo.Name = "TO"
    pvTo.Value = Me.txtEMailTo.Text
    extset.ParameterValues(0) = pvTo
    Dim pvIncludeRpt As New localhost_RS.ParameterValue
    pvIncludeRpt.Name = "IncludeReport"
    pvIncludeRpt.Value = "True"
    extset.ParameterValues(1) = pvIncludeRpt

    Dim pvRenderFormat As New localhost_RS.ParameterValue
    pvRenderFormat.Name = "RenderFormat"
    pvRenderFormat.Value = Me.cboRenderFormat.Text
    extset.ParameterValues(2) = pvRenderFormat
    Dim pvPriority As New localhost_RS.ParameterValue
    pvPriority.Name = "Priority"
    pvPriority.Value = "NORMAL"
    extset.ParameterValues(3) = pvPriority
```

```vbnet
        Dim pvSubject As New localhost_RS.ParameterValue
        pvSubject.Name = "Subject"
        pvSubject.Value = "@ReportName was executed at @ExtensionTime"
        extset.ParameterValues(4) = pvSubject

        '-- Create the Subscription (no report parameters in last arg)
        rs.CreateSubscription(Me.cboReport.Text, _
                        extset, _
                        Me.txtDescription.Text, _
                        "TimedSubscription", _
                        sched.ScheduleID, _
                        Nothing)
End Sub
```

C#

```csharp
private void btnAddSubscription_Click(object sender, System.EventArgs e)
{
    //-- Get selected schedule
    localhost_RS.Schedule scheduleItem = null;
    Int16 iSchedCounter = 0;
    foreach (localhost_RS.Schedule sched in rs.ListSchedules())
    {
        iSchedCounter += 1;
        if (iSchedCounter == this.cboSchedules.SelectedIndex)
        {
        scheduleItem = sched;
        break;
          }
    }
    localhost_RS.ExtensionSettings  extset = new localhost_RS.ExtensionSettings();
    extset.Extension = "Report Server Email";

    //-- Create Parameter Values array
    localhost_RS.ParameterValueOrFieldReference[] ParamVals = new
    Subscriptions_CS.localhost_RS.ParameterValueOrFieldReference[5];
    extset.ParameterValues = ParamVals;

    //-- Populate the Extension Parameters
    localhost_RS.ParameterValue  pvTo = new localhost_RS.ParameterValue();
    pvTo.Name = "TO";
    pvTo.Value = this.txtEMailTo.Text;
    extset.ParameterValues[0] = pvTo;

    localhost_RS.ParameterValue  pvIncludeRpt = new localhost_RS.ParameterValue();
    pvIncludeRpt.Name = "IncludeReport";
    pvIncludeRpt.Value = "true";
    extset.ParameterValues[1] = pvIncludeRpt;
    localhost_RS.ParameterValue  pvRenderFormat = new
                                            localhost_RS.ParameterValue();
    pvRenderFormat.Name = "RenderFormat";
    pvRenderFormat.Value = this.cboRenderFormat.Text;
    extset.ParameterValues[2] = pvRenderFormat;

     localhost_RS.ParameterValue  pvPriority = new localhost_RS.ParameterValue();
```

```
        pvPriority.Name = "Priority";
        pvPriority.Value = "NORMAL";
        extset.ParameterValues[3] = pvPriority;

        localhost_RS.ParameterValue  pvSubject = new localhost_RS.ParameterValue();
        pvSubject.Name = "Subject";
        pvSubject.Value = "@ReportName was executed at @ExtensionTime";
        extset.ParameterValues[4] = pvSubject;

        //-- Create the Subscription (no report parameters in last arg)
        rs.CreateSubscription(this.cboReport.Text,
                extset,
                this.txtDescription.Text,
                "TimedSubscription",
                scheduleItem.ScheduleID,
                null);
    }
```

Managing Subscriptions Using Script

Using script, you can perform almost any task in a .NET application but scripts are run at the command line in text mode. As we discussed in Chapter 8, a Reporting Services script file is written using Visual Basic .NET code and has nearly all the capabilities of a console application.

We will use the GetSubscriptions button code from the Subscription Manager application above. However, there are some modifications for this to work in console mode rather than as a Windows form. The VB Script code is saved in a file called List_Subscriptions.rss.

```
Sub Main()
    Dim subscr as Subscription
    Console.WriteLine()
    Console.Write("Report: ")
    Dim strReport as String = Console.ReadLine()
    Console.Write("Owner: ")
    Dim strOwner as String = Console.ReadLine()
    rs.Credentials = System.Net.CredentialCache.DefaultCredentials
    If sReport = "" Then strReport = Nothing
    If sOwner = "" Then strOwner = Nothing

    Console.WriteLine()
    Console.WriteLine("*************************************************************")
    Console.WriteLine("Subscriptions for:")
    Console.WriteLine("Report: " & sReport)
    Console.WriteLine("Owner:  " & sOwner)
    Console.WriteLine("------------------------------------------------------------")
    For Each subscr In rs.ListSubscriptions(strReport, strOwner)
        Console.WriteLine(subscr.Description)
    Next
    Console.WriteLine("------------------------------------------------------------")
End Sub
```

Let's examine the code, grasp the logic, and then run the script.

In a Reporting Services script, the Reporting Service Web Service is invoked automatically and all related classes are accessible without additional references. As you can see in this code, you declare a `Subscription` object using the variable `subscr`.

Using the `Console` object, you use the `ReadLine` method to obtain a value from the user and the `Write` and `WriteLine` methods to send text to the console (command line).

You can use two string variables, `sReport` and `sOwner` to capture input from the user and then convert these values to object types using the variables `oReport` and `oOwner`. This is necessary so you can pass the `Nothing` value to the `ListSubscriptions` method in case the user doesn't provide a value. Next, you iterate through the `Subscriptions` collection and write out the list to the console.

Open a command window, change to the folder containing the report, and issue a command to execute the script, which looks like Figure 10-20:

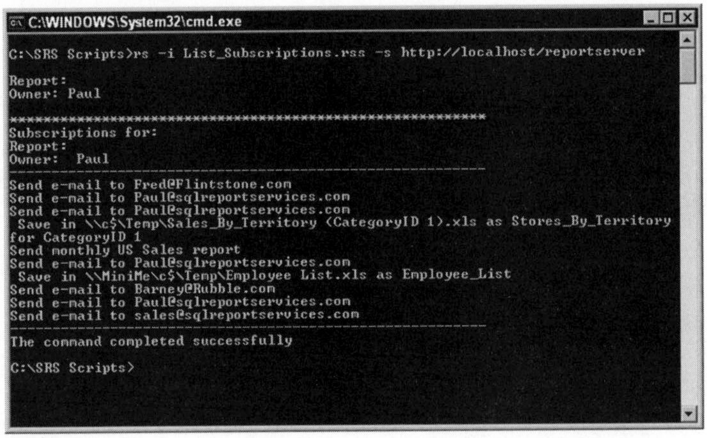

Figure 10-20

The result is a list of all subscriptions on the server for which I am the owner. By using scripts, you should be able to apply almost any VB.NET code that is simplified to work in the console environment.

Summary

Reporting Services has several options for report delivery including on-demand reporting where the data is queried and reports are generated upon request. Although this provides the most timely report data, it may not be the most practical solution.

Caching report content gives us a range of scalable and extensible options. A cached instance can hold both the report content and a portion of data in the report server database so the data can be filtered and reports can be rendered to different formats after the cached report is created without taxing the data source.

Snapshots are static, cached reports that can be generated before users need them and can be delivered in a variety of ways that may include subscriptions and history.

Subscriptions deliver reports on a shared or individual schedule and can be sent via email or a shared folder. Delivery extensions can also be written to provide additional delivery mechanisms. We've explored some custom subscription management solutions. Using the Reporting Services Web Service or scripting host provider, custom applications can be written to create and manage your own subscriptions and report delivery solutions.

Report Definition Language

In the previous chapters, we have demonstrated how reports can be created for SQL Server Reporting Services using Visual Studio and the Report Designer tool. The goal of this chapter is to give you a better understanding of how reports are built, what is happening in the background, and how your reporting requirements are communicated to SQL Server Reporting Services using *Report Definition Language (RDL)*. We will discuss the technology that makes it all possible and RDL itself. We will finish the chapter by demonstrating the creation of simple RDL tags using the .NET Framework XML classes and by creating a full blown report using a freeware tool called *CodeSmith*.

In short, this chapter covers:

❑ The underlying technology behind RDL and related definitions, such as XML naming rules, elements, attributes, documents, namespaces, and schema.

❑ What is RDL?

❑ Creating RDL

RDL – Underlying Technology

Microsoft's RDL is a XML grammar that allows us to define reports. It is based on open standards and designed to communicate your reporting needs to SQL Server Reporting Services, but can be consumed by any tool that understands its structure. The Visual Studio Report Designer provides a graphical user interface that allows you to design reports in a *What You See Is What You Get (WYSIWYG)* type of environment. Behind the scenes, the Visual Designer is actually creating a RDL document based on the following technologies that you can use to communicate your reporting requirements to Reporting Services:

❑ XML

❑ XML Schema

❑   RDL

❑   XML Web Services

What Is XML?

XML is an acronym that stands for *Extensible Markup Language*, a specification developed by the *World Wide Web Consortium* (W3C). XML is a pared-down version of *Standard Generalized MarkUp Language* (*SGML*), designed especially for web documents. It allows designers to create their own customized tags, enabling the definition, transmission, validation, and interpretation of data between applications as also between organizations.

XML has strong syntactical rules that facilitate its use in machine-to-machine as well as human communication. These rules only define what constitutes an XML document, but do not define or limit its use in any way. This means that you are in full control of the tags you use and the representation of different data in your documents. In order to further discuss RDL, the structure and makeup of XML must be more fully explored. The scenario for this discussion is an XML document that needs to be created to represent the inventory for a hypothetical car dealership called Ali's Auto.

XML Naming Rules

The rules of XML naming are common among all of the pieces used to build an XML document and should be first discussed because of this. There are no rules that govern what you name the pieces of your document, but there are rules on how you name them:

❑   Names must start with letters or an underscore.

❑   Names cannot start with numbers.

❑   Names cannot contain spaces.

❑   Items cannot begin with "xml" as it is a reserved word.

There are many schools of thought on XML naming conventions, but the XML 1.0 specification only addresses what characters may be used and where.

XML Elements

The basic building block of an XML document is the *element*. Examine the text below:

```
<Car>Pontiac Grand Prix</Car>
```

The text between the < and > characters is known as a XML tag. The <Car> tag above is known as the start tag. The </Car> tag is its duplicate with the exception of the / character, which marks it as the end tag. In XML, this matching is required. The text Pontiac Grand Prix is known as the element content. These tags and everything within them together constitute a XML element. In cases where a tag has no content, it is legal to add a / to the starting tag to indicate an empty tag:

```
<Car/>
```

When creating XML elements, there are rules that must be followed:

- ❑ Elements must follow XML naming rules
- ❑ Every start tag must have a matching end tag
- ❑ Tags cannot overlap

XML is extensible in that it allows you to fully control all the tags that you use to describe your data. The following XML fragment demonstrates changing the Car tag to provide information that is more detailed:

```
<Car>
   <Make>Pontiac</Make>
   <Model>Grand Prix</Model>
</Car>
```

The `<Make>` and `<Model>` tags have been added to give you additional granularity when accessing your Car data. Notice that they are nested within the `<Car>` tag. This indicates that they belong to or provide additional information about the `<Car>` tag. *Nesting* is normally used to indicate relationships between the data being represented in an XML Document.

XML Attributes

Another much used part of an XML document is the *attribute*. An attribute is typically used to provide detailed information about an XML element although this is not a formal requirement. Attributes are attached to the start tag of an XML element.

```
<Car Vin="BR549">
   <Make>Pontiac</Make>
   <Model>Grand Prix</Model>
</Car>
```

The above Car element has now been modified to provide more information about the car. In this instance, a vehicle identification number attribute was added to the start tag of the Car element. Because of the flexible nature of XML, a more attribute-centric version of the Car element could be created without violating any XML rules:

```
<Car Vin="BR549" Make="Pontiac" Model="Grand Prix" />
```

Although the text of the last two code blocks is very different, they are functionally equivalent. Just like elements, attributes also have rules that they must abide by:

- ❑ Attributes must be unique within their element.
- ❑ Attributes must have content.
- ❑ Attribute content must be enclosed with quotes.

The type of quotes that you use to enclose the contents of your attributes is not important, but you must be consistent in their usage.

You might have to decide between using attributes and elements in your report design. Both can serve the same purpose, but there are some tradeoffs you need to take into account. If you are in a situation where you have limited bandwidth, you could use attribute-centric XML, otherwise use element-centric XML. However, mixing the two is a bad design strategy.

XML Documents

XML documents are a mixture of elements and attributes organized to represent some data. In this section, let's discuss how to declare your documents as an XML document, and how detailed information and instructions can be sent to applications that will parse or use your XML data. The concept of a *'well-formed'* XML document will also be introduced.

An XML document is identified by the inclusion of an XML declaration similar to:

```
<?xml version="1.0" ?>
```

This XML declaration should be the first thing encountered in the document. It is used to identify the document as an XML document, as well as to provide additional version or encoding information. Currently, the version information is not really used as there is only one XML specification, but this information is in place in case additional versions of the XML specification should ever occur. It would indicate to the application that was reading or *"parsing"* the XML, which specification and rules to enforce. Let's modify the above XML fragment example to provide it with an XML declaration.

```
<?xml version="1.0" encoding="utf-8" ?>
<Car Vin="BR549">
    <Make>Pontiac</Make>
    <Model>Grand Prix</Model>
</Car>
```

While the XML above allows you to represent a car, there is still a problem. The ability to represent more than one car must be added. In order to do this, you need to create a common outer element that will be the container for all the other elements in our document. This outermost element is known as the *root* or *document* element. To prepare for the eventuality that other types of vehicles besides cars might need to be represented, the outer element could be named `Vehicles`:

```
<?xml version="1.0" encoding="utf-8" ?>
<Vehicles>
    <Car Vin="BR549">
        <Make>Pontiac</Make>
        <Model>Grand Prix</Model>
    </Car>
</Vehicles>
```

The document designed to represent vehicles for Ali's Auto is almost complete. It now complies with all the rules required for it to be considered "well formed" XML.

❑ The document has an XML declaration.

❑ It is composed of one or more elements.

- ❑ All document entities conform to the XML naming rules.

- ❑ All document entities meet rules for their type (elements, attributes, namespaces, and so on).

- ❑ The XML tags are properly nested (no overlapping tags).

A well formed XML document simply follows all the rules governing the creation of XML. These rules provide and enforce a common standard for machine and program readability, which is one of the primary purposes of XML. It is important to note that nowhere do these rules address what should be contained in a document. This issue will be addressed in the XML Schema section that follows.

XML Namespaces

When using XML, you might need to combine XML documents. It is likely that names used by you might have been used by others. This would be troublesome if not for the concept of *namespaces*. XML namespaces allow developers to uniquely identify their element names and relationships. This allows the developer to avoid name collisions with elements that have the same names but are defined in different vocabularies. Typically developers use *Uniform Resource Identifiers* (*URIs*) as namespaces and specifically *Uniform Resource Locators* (*URLs*), because the naming standards for Internet domains guarantee that each domain name is unique. See the following example:

```
<?xml version="1.0" encoding="utf-8" ?>
<Vehicles xmlns="http://sqlreportservices.com/AliAuto">
    <Car Vin="BR549">
      <Make>Pontiac</Make>
      <Model>Grand Prix</Model>
    </Car>
</Vehicles>
```

This allows the multiple tags with the same name to maintain their individuality. A combined document might look similar to the document that follows:

```
<?xml version="1.0" encoding="utf-8" ?>
<Vehicles xmlns="http://sqlreportservices.com/AliAuto"
    xmlns:JJ="http://sqlreportservices.com/JanicesJalopies"
    xmlns:LL="http://sqlreportservices.com/LeweysLemons">
    <Car Vin="BR549">
      <Make>Pontiac</Make>
      <Model>Grand Prix</Model>
    </Car>
    <JJ:Car>
      <JJ:Vin>BR549</JJ:Vin>
      <JJ:Make>Pontiac</JJ:Make>
      <JJ:Model>Grand Prix</JJ:Model>
    </JJ:Car>
    <LL:Car Vin="BR549" Make="Pontiac" Model="Grand Prix" />
</Vehicles>
```

Notice that the namespace declared for Ali's Auto has no prefix. It is the default namespace of the document, and all entities will be processed in that context unless a prefix is specified. This leads us into the next topic of discussion, XML Schema.

XML Schema

Ali's Auto has now identified the information that is important for their use, and come up with an XML structure to represent that information. Next, they need to ensure that all of their XML documents match this structure. The most recent and powerful way to perform this function is by using an *XML Schema*.

An XML Schema is a formal specification that defines how information is to be represented in an XML document. It defines the structure of the document and the elements that are allowed. It defines the relationships between elements, their order, and can also define their data types. An XML Schema document is another example of the power and flexibility of XML, which is used to create the schema itself.

Let's start out by creating our solution. The steps are as follows:

1. Create the solution by choosing File | New | Blank Solution. Change the name of the solution to `RDLSolution`.

2. Add the language-specific project by choosing File | Add Project | New Project. Use the empty project template.

3. Change the name of the project to `XMLProject`.

4. Add an XML document to the project by selecting File | Add New Item | File.

5. Select an XML file and change the name of the file to `AliAuto.xml`.

6. Edit the XML so that it matches the text in Figure 11-1:

```
Start Page  AliAuto.xml
    <?xml version="1.0" encoding="iso-8859-1"?>
    <Vehicles xmlns="http://sqlreportservices/AliAuto">
        <Car Vin="BR549">
            <Make>Pontiac</Make>
            <Model>Grand Prix</Model>
        </Car>
    </Vehicles>
 □ XML   ⊕ Data
```

Figure 11-1

Now that we have created our document using the facilities provided by Visual Studio, it is time to make use of another tool that is available. We want to make a Schema to enforce the structure of our XML document. Choose XML | Create Schema from the Visual Studio Menu as shown in Figure 11-2. Ensure that the cursor is inside the document to make this choice visible.

Figure 11-2

This can have several effects on both the document and the project. If no namespace is identified in your document, then Visual Studio creates a default namespace. Visual Studio will modify the `Vehicle` element by adding an `xmlns` attribute with a value of `http://tempuri.org/AliAuto.xsd`. The value that Visual Studio inserts into the tag is not actually unique; it is a place holder for your custom namespace. Split "tempuri" and you literally have "temp" and "uri". The idea is to create a unique namespace that identifies the elements from this particular XML document.

```
<Vehicle xmlns="http://tempuri.org/AliAuto.xsd">
```

Since we have already defined a namespace for the document, a new XML Schema document has been added to our project but no namespace was specified. XML Schema documents have an .xsd file extension; in the example described earlier, this file is called AliAuto.xsd. You can see that it has been added to the **XMLProject** project in Figure 11-3:

Figure 11-3

An XML Schema document is used to verify that a particular document meets the structure, naming, and type information required for a specific document. Open AliAuto.xsd and you should be able to see something similar to Figure 11-4:

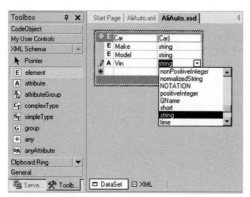

Figure 11-4

This image is the **DataSet** view provided by Visual Studio for working with Schema documents. It displays the Car element as well as the other attributes and elements that should be nested within that tag. The data types of the individual elements are also displayed and can be modified. Notice the toolbar on the left. It contains the design objects for creating and working with all types of XML Schema definitions. The **DataSet** view is a visual schema design surface that abstracts what is going on behind the scenes. To see the actual XML that gets generated is used to enforce the structure of XML documents for Ali's Auto, click on the **XML** tab at the bottom:

```
<?xml version="1.0" ?>
<xs:schema id="Vehicle" targetNamespace=":http://sqlreportservices.com/AliAuto"
 xmlns="http://sqlreportservices.com/AliAuto"
 xmlns:xs="http://www.w3.org/2001/XMLSchema"
 attributeFormDefault="qualified" elementFormDefault="qualified">
 <xs:element name="Vehicle" >
    <xs:complexType>
     <xs:choice maxOccurs="unbounded">
      <xs:element name="Car">
        <xs:complexType>
         <xs:sequence>
           <xs:element name="Make" type="xs:string" minOccurs="0" />
           <xs:element name="Model" type="xs:string" minOccurs="0"/>
         </xs:sequence>
         <xs:attribute name="Vin" form="unqualified" type="xs:string" />
        </xs:complexType>
      </xs:element>
     </xs:choice>
    </xs:complexType>
 </xs:element>
</xs:schema>
```

This XML should be similar to what is generated by Visual Studio for your XML document. This version has been edited to remove the Microsoft-specific namespaces so that it is more readable. The deletion of these unused tags has no effect on the ability of this document to enforce the XML rules defined by Ali's Auto.

After examining the document, you should notice that almost all of the tags are prefixed by xs. This indicates that these tags are defined by the XML Schema definition maintained by the W3C:

```
<xs:schema id="Vehicle" targetNamespace="http://tempuri.org/AliAuto.xsd"
 xmlns="http://sqlreportservices.com/AliAuto"
 xmlns:xs="http://www.w3.org/2001/XMLSchema"
 attributeFormDefault="qualified" elementFormDefault="qualified">
```

For the most part, Schema documents are almost self explanatory. The <Vehicle> tag is a complex tag, which means that it is composed of other tags. It is unlimited in the number of times that it can occur in a document, which is indicated by the maxOccurs="unbounded" attribute tag:

```
<xs:element name="Vehicl"
    <xs:complexType>
      <xs:choice maxOccurs="unbounded">
```

After the schema has been created for Ali's Auto, you may validate the document by selecting XML|
Validate XML Data from the Visual Studio Menu. The results of the document are displayed in the status window if there are no errors. See Figure 11-5:

Figure 11-5

To demonstrate both the effectiveness of an XML Schema and show what happens when the data is invalid, the document needs to be modified. The schema document for Ali's Auto specifies the order of the Make and Model elements. This is indicated by the elements being placed in the confines of the XML Schema sequence element:

```
<xs:sequence>
    <xs:element name="Make" type="xs:string" minOccurs="0" />
    <xs:element name="Model" type="xs:string" minOccurs="0"/>
</xs:sequence>
```

Changing the order of the elements should cause the document to fail validation. Edit the XML document to reverse the element order in the first <Car> tag as shown in Figure 11-6:

Figure 11-6

Because the schema document specifies the order that these tags should be in, the document now fails validation. When errors occur, the error message is placed in the **Task Pane** of Visual Studio. Validating with the reversed element order causes the message in Figure 11-7 to appear:

Description
Click here to add a new task
The element 'http://sqlreportservices/AliAuto:Car' has invalid child element 'http://sqlreportservices/AliAuto:Make'. An error occurred at , (5, 4).

Figure 11-7

The ability to define the elements and structural relationships that are valid in a particular context vastly increases the flexibility and functionality of XML in data processing. The combination of a standard XML document format and a schema to validate that format combine to create what is commonly known as an *XML Vocabulary*. XML Vocabularies allow you to define a standard mechanism for machine-to-machine communication using XML and to validate that communication at both ends of the transaction. There are several well known vocabularies in place today:

❑ **Channel definition format**: Used to "*push*" web pages

❑ **XHTML**: Attempt at structuring HTML

❑ **XSL**: XML stylesheets (XML transformation and formatting)

New XML vocabularies are being created at a frantic pace. They can be extremely useful for facilitating communications between businesses and software. Many vertical industry vocabularies have and are being developed.

What Is RDL?

RDL promotes interoperability of reporting tools by defining a common schema facilitating the exchange of report definitions between most reporting tools. However, you need to be clear about the fact that RDL is a schema definition and not a programming language, interface, or a protocol, nor does it specify guidelines for report processing or the passing of report definitions between applications.

As mentioned earlier, RDL is the XML vocabulary that defines the communication of reporting definitions to SQL Server Reporting Services. The purpose of the previous section on the XML technology was to provide the insight you need to closely examine RDL.

Let's start by adding a new project to the existing RDLSolution. Select File | Add Project | New Project from the Visual Studio menu. Next, select the Business Intelligence Project section and the Report Project template. Change the name of the project to Master Detail as shown in Figure 11-8:

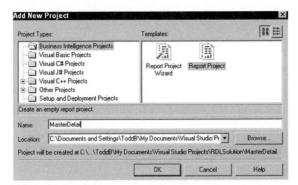

Figure 11-8

Figure 11-9 shows that a new reporting project has been added to the solution. The method used to create this project is kind of convoluted because Microsoft, in trying to be helpful, has made it almost difficult to create a blank report. The standard report creation mechanism is wizard-based, which is helpful in a production environment, but does not facilitate the examination of RDL modifications. This is needed to enable you to examine the underlying RDL as controls are added or data connection settings are changed:

Figure 11-9

The next step is to add a report to the **Master Detail** Project. Highlight the **Reports** folder and right click to bring up the context menu. Specifically avoid the **Add New Report** menu choice because it will start the report wizard. Choose **Add | Add New Item** as shown in Figure 11-10:

Figure 11-10

This will bring up the **Add New Item** dialog box, where the **Report** object should be chosen as in Figure 11-11. A blank report will then be created and added to the project:

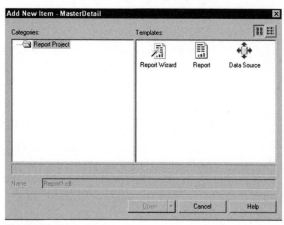

Figure 11-11

After the blank report has been added, you will see a design surface like Figure 11-12. During this walkthrough, the visual controls provided in the Report Designer toolbox will be added to the design surface and the corresponding RDL examined.

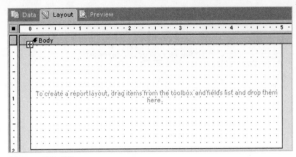

Figure 11-12

Document RDL

In order to view the RDL that gets generated during the process of dragging and dropping the visual controls, the file that contains the RDL must be selected. This is done in the Solution Explorer window. In this window, right-click on the file to invoke the context menu as you can see in Figure 11-13. Select the View Code option (this can also be done from the Visual Studio menu).

Figure 11-13

After the View Code option is chosen, there should be two views of the report open in Visual Studio. The first view is the Visual Design view into which we will place our visual controls. The second is the XML view of the report, which we will examine after placing controls on the design surface. The RDL for an empty report is as follows:

```xml
<?xml version="1.0" encoding="utf-8"?>
<Report
  xmlns="http://schemas.microsoft.com/sqlserver/reporting/2003/10/reportdefinition"
  xmlns:rd="http://schemas.microsoft.com/SQLServer/reporting/reportdesigner">
  <RightMargin>1in</RightMargin>

  <Body>
    <Style />
    <Height>2in</Height>
  </Body>

  <TopMargin>1in</TopMargin>
  <Width>5in</Width>
  <LeftMargin>1in</LeftMargin>
  <rd:SnapToGrid>true</rd:SnapToGrid>
  <rd:DrawGrid>true</rd:DrawGrid>
  <rd:ReportID>6d3a29b0-6216-4880-857f-1fd355497048</rd:ReportID>
```

```
    <BottomMargin>1in</BottomMargin>
    </Report>
```

Notice that there are two namespaces at the top of the document. The first namespace is used to define the elements that belong to the report definition. This is also the default namespace of the document, which means that any tags that do not contain a prefix are defined within the context of this namespace:

```
xmlns="http://schemas.microsoft.com/sqlserver/reporting/2003/10/reportdefinition"
```

The second namespace that you see is specific to the designer:

```
xmlns:rd="http://schemas.microsoft.com/SQLServer/reporting/reportdesigner">
```

The designer-specific tags are used to control the behavior of the Visual Studio Report Designer. All of the tags that belong to the designer namespace will be prefixed with rd to resolve any name clashes, should they occur.

```
<rd:SnapToGrid>true</rd:SnapToGrid>
<rd:DrawGrid>true</rd:DrawGrid>
<rd:ReportID>6d3a29b0-6216-4880-857f-1fd355497048</rd:ReportID>
```

These tags are represented in the Properties window for the document in the Design Section, and any changes made to these properties will be reflected in the RDL itself. Change the SnapToGrid property to False. See Figure 11-14:

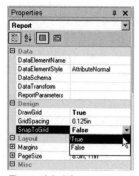

Figure 11-14

The following snippet of RDL illustrates how changing properties in the design window changes the RDL text in the document itself. It reflects the change in the value of the SnapToGrid property. This is true not only for the document properties, but also for the data that you choose to use and every visual control that you use in your report design:

```
<rd:SnapToGrid>false</rd:SnapToGrid>
    <rd:DrawGrid>true</rd:DrawGrid>
    <rd:ReportID>6d3a29b0-6216-4880-857f-1fd355497048</rd:ReportID>
```

Data RDL

In previous chapters, the AdventureWorks database has been used for all of the examples. To maintain consistency, this section will also use this database. In order to create a simple report, you first need to create the data definition that will be used to populate your report. Choose the Data tab of the report designer and select New Dataset... from the drop-down list box as seen in Figure 11-15:

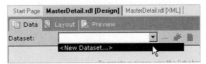

Figure 11-15

This will cause the Data Link Properties dialog to appear. Edit your connection settings to resemble those shown in Figure 11-16:

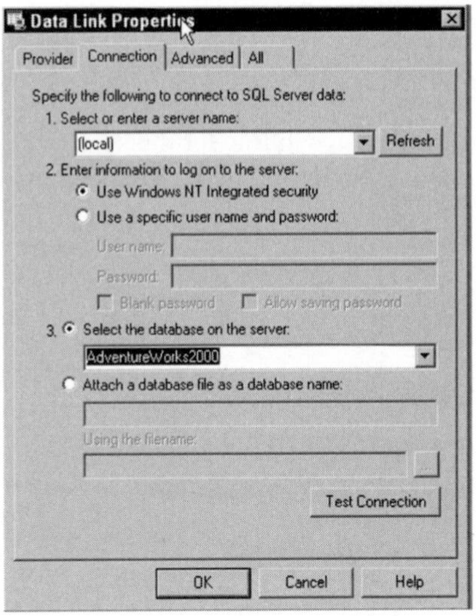

Figure 11-16

After the connection to the database has been successfully made, the Query Designer window appears. This window is very similar to that seen in Access or Visual Studio, so a detailed explanation is not included here. Before you add any actual data to the report, examine the changes made to the RDL by the addition of a valid database connection.

After examining the RDL, you will notice that two new sections have been added to the document by the designer. The following RDL section is the <DataSources> section. This tag contains nested tags that identify the data provider used as well as the connection string properties needed to connect to the data store.

The content inside the <rd:DataSourceID> is a *Globally Unique Identifier (GUID)* that enables the designer to track individual data sources. Reporting projects might contain several different data sources, and it also supports the concept of a shared data source in which many different reports use the same data connection. In fact, the data source is conceptually equivalent to the Connection object in traditional ADO. If Integrated Security is used, a tag in the RDL indicates this:

```
<DataSources>
  <DataSource Name="AdventureWorks2000">
    <rd:DataSourceID>6740a68a-aaa7-42fb-8025-57eed884a359</rd:DataSourceID>
    <ConnectionProperties>
      <DataProvider>SQL</DataProvider>
      <ConnectString>data source=(local);
                     initial catalog=AdventureWorks2000</ConnectString>
      <IntegratedSecurity>true</IntegratedSecurity>
    </ConnectionProperties>
  </DataSource>
</DataSources>
```

The second section added to the report is the `<DataSets>` section. It contains tags to name the dataset, relate the dataset to a specific query, and a `<DataSourceName>` tag that is used to link a particular dataset to a data source:

```
<DataSets>
  <DataSet Name="AdventureWorks2000">
    <Query>
      <DataSourceName>AdventureWorks2000</DataSourceName>
      <CommandText />
    </Query>
  </DataSet>
</DataSets>
```

At this point, the `<CommandText>` tag in this code is empty, but that will soon change when you add database content to your report. Click on the **Add Table** button on the **Query Designer** toolbar as shown in Figure 11-17:

Figure 11-17

This will cause a table selection dialog box to be shown. For the purpose of this example, we will keep the data access portion very simple by adding just the **Contact** table. After adding the table, check the **FirstName, MiddleName,** and **LastName** boxes. As we add or delete tables and fields using **Query Designer,** the SQL statement is created in the SQL window at the bottom. The result is shown in Figure 11-18:

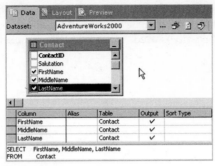

Figure 11-18

You can now examine the results of the addition of data to your report by switching over to the XML View of the report. The `<DataSources>` tag remains unmodified, but there have been significant changes to the `<DataSets>` tag:

```xml
<DataSets>
  <DataSet Name="AdventureWorks2000">
    <Fields>
      <Field Name="FirstName">
        <DataField>FirstName</DataField>
        <rd:TypeName>System.String</rd:TypeName>
      </Field>
      <Field Name="MiddleName">
        <DataField>MiddleName</DataField>
        <rd:TypeName>System.String</rd:TypeName>
      </Field>
      <Field Name="LastName">
        <DataField>LastName</DataField>
        <rd:TypeName>System.String</rd:TypeName>
      </Field>
    </Fields>
    <Query>
      <DataSourceName>AdventureWorks2000</DataSourceName>
      <CommandText>SELECT FirstName, MiddleName, LastName FROM Contact
      </CommandText>
    </Query>
  </DataSet>
</DataSets>
```

The first and most obvious change to the `<DataSets>` tag is the addition of a `<Fields>` tag with nested `<Field>` elements within. The `<Fields>` tag represents the collection that is returned by querying the data store:

```xml
<Field Name="FirstName">
  <DataField>FirstName</DataField>
  <rd:TypeName>System.String</rd:TypeName>
</Field>
```

Each <Field> tag has two additional nested elements, the <DataField> tag and the <rd:TypeName> tag. The <DataField> tag is not required to be unique, and contains the information needed to access the data or calculate its value. The <rd:TypeName> is used to provide design time support for working with and editing the value contained in a <DataField> tag.

The Name attribute of the <Field> element must be unique among the elements. It is an alias that the report uses to access the data. The SQL statement is modified to return a different field name if a name collision occurs. This is demonstrated in the following code. To illustrate name collision, the tables and selected field names have been temporarily modified to use related tables with identical field names. Notice in the following code that the ProductSubCategory.ProductCategoryID is returned as Expr1 in the SQL statement and that the <Fields> collection has been modified to reflect that change:

```
<DataSets>
  <DataSet Name="AdventureWorks2000">
    <Fields>
      <Field Name="ProductCategoryID">
      <DataField>ProductCategoryID</DataField>
      <rd:TypeName>System.Byte</rd:TypeName>
      </Field>
      <Field Name="Expr1">
        <DataField>Expr1</DataField>
        <rd:TypeName>System.Byte</rd:TypeName>
      </Field>
    </Fields>
      <Query>
        <DataSourceName>AdventureWorks2000</DataSourceName>
        <CommandText>SELECT ProductCategory.ProductCategoryID,
                  ProductSubCategory.ProductCategoryID AS Expr1
                  FROM ProductSubCategory INNER JOIN ProductCategory ON
                  ProductSubCategory.ProductCategoryID =
                  ProductCategory.ProductCategoryID</CommandText>
      </Query>
  </DataSet>
</DataSets>
```

Each <Field> tag has two additional nested elements, the <DataField> tag and the <rd:TypeName> tag. The <DataField> tag is not required to be unique and contains the information needed to access the data or calculate its value. The Visual Design Controls support the use of the <Value> element and extract the actual data values used during report processing with the following syntax:

```
<Value>=First(Fields!FullName.Value)</Value>
```

The statement is effectively requesting the first FullName field from the Fields collection for the current result set. The <rd:TypeName> is used to provide design time support for working with and editing the value contained in a data field. Now that you understand how data is modeled and extracted based on RDL, let's move on to the Visual Design Controls that generate the RDL and help present data to the user.

Control RDL

There are nine visual design controls that ship with Reporting Services. Figure 11-19 shows a `Textbox` control added to report. They each generate RDL based on their purpose. After creating an empty report, you can view the tags that each control generates by simply dragging and dropping them onto the design surface. The corresponding RDL can be viewed through the View Code option.

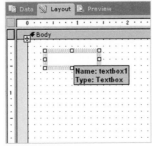

Figure 11-19

In the following sections, we will study the RDL generated by these nine controls.

> **The complex controls cause many pages of RDL to be added to the report, and in those cases, only the skeleton of the RDL has been included here instead of using actual default values.**

TextBox

The RDL generated by the `Textbox` control is displayed in the following code snippet. The `Textbox` is a simple placeholder for information that needs to be displayed. The `<Value>` tag contains the formula or expression that will be used to provide the needed data. The `Textbox` can be used as a standalone control or contained within sophisticated controls that use it to output their results.

```
<Textbox Name="textbox1">
  <Style>
    <PaddingLeft>2pt</PaddingLeft>
    <PaddingBottom>2pt</PaddingBottom>
    <PaddingTop>2pt</PaddingTop>
    <PaddingRight>2pt</PaddingRight>
  </Style>
  <Top>0.25in</Top>
  <rd:DefaultName>textbox1</rd:DefaultName>
  <Height>0.25in</Height>
  <Width>1in</Width>
  <CanGrow>true</CanGrow>
  <Value />
  <Left>0.375in</Left>
</Textbox>
```

Line

The `Line` control is used only for visual effect. The style, size, and position of the line can be modified in the Visual Designer. It is primarily used to provide context separation within reports:

```
<Line Name="line1">
  <Top>0.53125in</Top>
  <Width>1in</Width>
  <Height>1in</Height>
  <Style>
    <BorderStyle>
      <Default>Solid</Default>
    </BorderStyle>
  </Style>
  <Left>1.23958in</Left>
</Line>
```

Rectangle

A `Rectangle` is a container control. It is used to group other controls on a report so that they can be presented or moved as one unit. It is the conceptual equivalent of a panel control in Windows application development. The RDL below is generated by a `Rectangle` control that contains a `Line`:

```
<Rectangle Name="rectangle1">
  <Top>1.39583in</Top>
  <ReportItems>
    <Line Name="line2">
      <Top>0.11458in</Top>
      <Height>1in</Height>
      <Width>1in</Width>
      <Style>
        <BorderStyle>
          <Default>Solid</Default>
        </BorderStyle>
      </Style>
      <Left>0.3125in</Left>
    </Line>
  </ReportItems>
  <Height>1.47917in</Height>
  <Width>2in</Width>
  <Left>1.34375in</Left>
</Rectangle>
```

Table

The `Table` control is used to group or relate repetitive data items. Dropping a `Table` control onto a blank report causes four pages of RDL to be generated, which is too much to display here. The RDL displayed below is a skeleton based on Reporting Services Books Online. A summary of the `Table` control is that it creates a collection of rows and columns that can be sorted and grouped like the *Data Grid* control used by developers. The combination of a row and column corresponds to a cell, which uses a nested `TextBox` control to display the data.

```
<Table Name="table1">
  <Style />
```

397

```
    <Top />
    <Left />
    <ZIndex />
    <Visibility />
    <ToolTip />
    <Label />
    <Bookmark />
    <Custom />
    <KeepTogether />
    <NoRows />
    <DataSetName />
    <PageBreakAtStart />
    <PageBreakAtEnd />
    <Filters />
    <TableColumns />
    <Header />
    <TableGroups />
    <Details />
    <Footer />
</Table>
```

Matrix

The `Matrix` control is a two-axis grid with drill-down capability on both axes. It is very similar to the `Table` control except for its dual axis capabilities. It is the Reporting Services equivalent of the *Pivot Table*. The `Matrix` is composed of rows and columns that use the `Textbox` to render all of the results. The following code snippet is a skeleton of the RDL generated by the `Matrix` control:

```
<Matrix Name="matrix1">
    <Style />
    <Top />
    <Left />
    <ZIndex />
    <Visibility />
    <ToolTip />
    <Label />
    <Bookmark />
    <Custom />
    <KeepTogether />
    <NoRows />
    <DataSetName />
    <PageBreakAtStart/>
    <PageBreakAtEnd />
    <Filters />
    <Corner />
    <ColumnGroupings />
    <RowGroupings />
    <MatrixRows />
    <MatrixColumns />
    <LayoutDirection />
    <GroupsBeforeRowHeaders />
</Matrix>
```

List

A `List` is a data region that is repeated with each group or row in a result set. It is used for repeating records and allows simple grouping with nested tags being repeated for each record. The following example list will group on each repetition of `CustomerID` from the `NorthWind` database:

```
<List Name="list1">
  <Style />
  <Height>1in</Height>
  <Top>0.875in</Top>
  <ZIndex>1</ZIndex>
  <Grouping Name="CustomerGroup">
    <GroupExpressions>
      <GroupExpression>=Fields!CustomerID.Value</GroupExpression>
    </GroupExpressions>
  </Grouping>
  <DataSetName>Northwind</DataSetName>
  <Width>2in</Width>
  <Left>0.375in</Left>
</List>
```

Image

The `Image` control is used to display images on a report. The images that you add to a report have three storage options. The image may be embedded in the report, stored in the database, or added to the project. The following example is that of an embedded image. Adding the `Image` control causes two tags to be added. The first tag, `<Image>`, contains all of the display information:

```
<Image Name="ovals">
  <Top>0.94792in</Top>
  <Height>0.16667in</Height>
  <Width>0.41667in</Width>
  <Source>Embedded</Source>
  <Style />
  <Value>ovals</Value>
  <Left>0.875in</Left>
  <Sizing>AutoSize</Sizing>
</Image>
```

The second tag, `<EmbeddedImages>`, is a collection that contains the data for each image that is embedded into the report. Inside the `<EmbeddedImage>` tag is located the MIME type of the image and the encoded values that make up the image:

```
<EmbeddedImages>
<EmbeddedImage Name="ovals">
  <MIMEType>image/gif</MIMEType>
  <ImageData>R0lGODlhKAAQAOYAADMAAOe7b16p1eXw921DO72ppuvIjJHG55t+eFMhGebe3oW93r/c
7vLduYizwXlRSUAIAODX1u/Vp9LFwo5sZ8Oxrvz7+Gmv17GZlsu8uea/eWYzM920cPbnz/ju3NDm8uP
XzaJyRabQ50MNAG+03l8xJ+nEhL+dfKaMh/j29qHEz/HYrToBAE4bENbp8/Ht7NTKqs07lu3n55HE4f
jiu67T6eu+hRZI4OHhJztC6NA2MCTX7dhBahTCMoReuCIc8uVz4O9fLxeEemwoaHAEixA7FD6zEaOh
wymFJiypaJGAEo3Pqqjw2C6IKkIFKNJjUQKEFXz5bDk5wBKgFEMZINAbwoLäJhM4oQUw4YQLFQH/oAp
cdAPAKxYtEGQRFMWcVw0Sfghy0euXgAUfEsmgsKHEDSIRHzhp4WGAx4pcgz7MyJHDBxRJk1L0UMQkEu
BJiBMjDgQAOw==</ImageData>
```

```
    </EmbeddedImage>
  </EmbeddedImages>
```

MIME stands for Multipart Internet Mail Extension. MIME types were originally designed so that mail messages could contain nontext data like images and documents. They are used to identify the specific encoding mechanism used to store or serialize data. When an embedded image is used, a binary representation of the image is stored, and when rendered the appropriate MIME type is sent as part of the stream payload to indicate how the binary data should be processed.

Subreport

The `Subreport` control emits RDL text that allows a report to be embedded within the body of the main report. The `Subreport` can be parameterized and repeat with other data region controls.

```
<Subreport Name="subreport1">
  <Style />
  <Top>1.44792in</Top>
  <ReportName />
  <Width>3in</Width>
  <Left>2.29167in</Left>
</Subreport>
```

Chart

The `Chart` control emits the RDL that allows Reporting Services to create a graphical representation of data. The `Chart` control is able to represent two-dimensional data using nine chart types: Column, Bar, Line, Pie, Scatter, Bubble, Area, Doughnut, and Stock.

```
<Chart Name="chart1">
  <Style />
  <Top />
  <Left />
  <Height />
  <Width />
  <ZIndex />
  <Visibility />
  <ToolTip />
  <Label />
  <Bookmark />
  <Custom />
  <KeepTogether />
  <NoRows />
  <DataSetName />
  <PageBreakAtStart/>
  <PageBreakAtEnd />
  <Filters />
  <Grouping />
  <Sorting />
  <ReportItems />
  <Parameters />
  <DataFields />
  <ChartDefinition />
</Chart>
```

Creating RDL

Creating an RDL document is not a trivial task. It requires a detailed understanding of XML and Reporting Services processing. In addition, you should expect a plethora of third party tools to emerge that generate Reporting Services-compatible RDL. Although most developers use tools provided by Microsoft or third parties to create report definitions, it is important to understand how you could, if needed, create or modify an RDL document.

In this section, we will cover two methods to create RDL. We will use the XML classes within the .NET framework to emit a simple RDL tag followed by a more practical example, where you begin with a report template and modify the RDL based upon a different data source. The second example will use a third party tool called CodeSmith.

RDL with .NET

Because a full blown discussion of XML programming in .NET is beyond the scope of this book, this section will only demonstrate the creation of a simple RDL tag using the .NET Framework classes. The following code snippets assume that you are familiar with Visual Studio and C#.

> *For a more detailed discussion of this topic, see XML Programming Bible by Wiley Press (ISBN 0-7645-3829-2).*

The following code snippet is a simple console application. It has one static method that creates the XML for a `Textbox`:

```
static void Main(string[] args)
{
    CreateXML.GenerateRDL();
}
public static void GenerateRDL()
{
    MemoryStream stream = new MemoryStream();
    XmlTextWriter writer = new XmlTextWriter(stream,Encoding.UTF8);
    writer.Formatting = Formatting.Indented;

    writer.WriteStartElement("Textbox"); //begin textbox
    writer.WriteAttributeString("Name","textbox1");

    writer.WriteStartElement("Style"); // begin style
    writer.WriteElementString("PaddingLeft","2pt");
    writer.WriteElementString("PaddingBottom","2pt");
    writer.WriteElementString("PaddingTop","2pt");
    writer.WriteElementString("Paddingright","2pt");
    writer.WriteEndElement();// end style

    writer.WriteElementString("Top","0.25in");
    writer.WriteElementString("rd:DefaultName","textbox1");
    writer.WriteElementString("Height","0.25in");
    writer.WriteElementString("Width","1in");
    writer.WriteElementString("CanGrow","true");
    writer.WriteElementString("Value","");
```

```
    writer.WriteElementString("Left","0.375");
    writer.WriteEndElement();   // end textbox

    writer.Flush();
    stream.Position=0;

    StreamReader sr = new StreamReader(stream);

    Console.WriteLine(sr.ReadToEnd());
    sr.Close();
}
```

A more object-oriented approach could also be taken. One idea might be to create your own object model for all of the RDL objects. You could create a Textbox object with properties that map to the RDL tags and override the ToString method with code while replacing the values with those from the object. The result of running this code is shown in Figure 11-20:

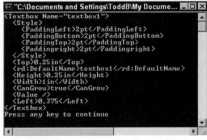

Figure 11-20

RDL with CodeSmith

Developers spend a significant amount of their time doing redundant work. The process is not only boring, but also error prone. The idea behind automating the creation of repetitive code is to decrease errors and increase maintainability. RDL is non-proprietary in nature, and hence, a third party tool can also be used to create a report. The following criteria were used when selecting a tool for this demonstration:

❏   Free

❏   Powerful

❏   Flexible

❏   Preferably created using .NET

❏   Not created specifically to illustrate this concept

CodeSmith, created by Eric J. Smith, is a free template-based code generator that meets all of these criteria. It consists of four related tools, three of which are available at no cost:

- ❑ **CodeSmith Console**: It is a command line application that can be used to batch build sophisticated projects using CodeSmith templates and XML property sets.

- ❑ **CodeSmith Explorer**: It is a graphical user interface to the generation engine. It allows developers to browse templates, add and modify template properties, and view the results.

- ❑ **CodeSmith Visual Studio Addin**: It is an add-in to Visual Studio that allows the generation of code from XML property sets from within Visual Studio. This paradigm is very similar to ASP code-behind pages.

- ❑ **CodeSmith Studio**: It is a template development environment with syntax highlighting that will soon be available for a minimal charge. CodeSmith's syntax is almost identical to ASP.NET, and anyone who is familiar with that syntax should easily be able to produce code with it. It even uses the compilers that ship with the .NET Framework to compile the template code, resulting in the ability to write templates in any of the pure .NET-compatible languages: Visual Basic .NET, C#, or J# CodeSmith enjoys strong support, both from the creator and a growing community of active developers.

The scenario for the following example is that we have created a standard report format that needs to be replicated with different data sources. The original report used for this example was created using Visual Studio and is based upon a two-table join of related database tables. Retracing the steps to create a common look and feel changing the data source and the control value tags is both time consuming and error prone. Our design goal is that we should be able to pick two related tables from any data source, choose the fields that we want displayed, and generate the appropriate report based on the new data sources. Let's start by looking at the original report design (see Figure 11-21).

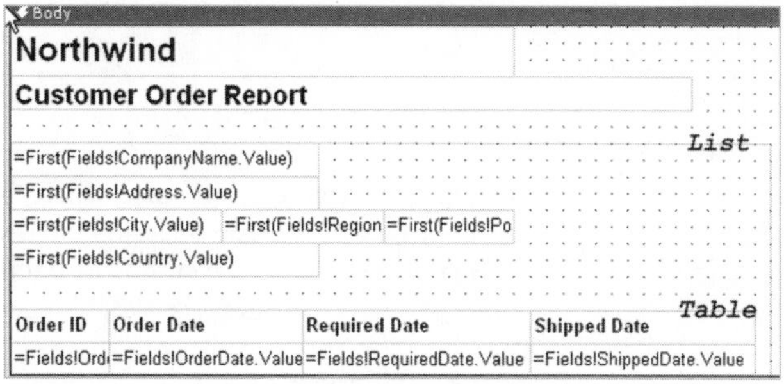

Figure 11-21

This report was designed using the NorthWind database that ships with SQL Server. It is a Master Detail relationship report based on an inner join of the `Customer` and `Order` tables. The top two boxes in the report are `Textbox` controls that contain the name of the database and the name of the report. The third box from top is a `List` control. It has been set up to group on the primary key value from the `Master` table. This will cause all controls and fields to be repeated for each row in the `Customer` table. The last box on the report is a `Table` control. The `Table` control has been set up to group on the `OrderID` Field. In the final report, a table will be output that contains the order information from that particular customer. The report resembles Figure 11-22 when processed:

Figure 11-22

Now that the design of the report is done and it renders correctly, we need to make our efforts more repeatable. A template needs to be created that will allow us to choose any Master and Detail table, specify the fields that need to be displayed, and automatically have a new report generated. For the purpose of this demonstration, we will be using the CodeSmith Explorer to set the report properties and generate reports. There are five values that vary between the reports that will be generated, and we need to create properties that will allow the user to edit and change those values. The values are:

❑ Master Table

❑ Master Table Display Columns

❑ Detail Table

❑ Detail Table Display Columns

❑ Report Name

Let's examine the key portions of the template and examine the generation of a Master Detail Report. The template that we will use is called `MasterDetail.cst`. You need to install CodeSmith and then click on the template provided with the book code samples to execute it. The following window shown in Figure 11-23 will appear:

Figure 11-23

*You can download the template used for the following example from
http://www.ericjsmith.net/codesmith/.*

Notice that the window looks exactly like the property window used to set design time values in Visual
Studio and that there are five editable properties that map to the varying report values described earlier.
These properties are defined within the template and are used to dynamically generate our reports.The
property at the bottom of the form is the **ReportName** property and is used to set the name of the report.
The report name is stored in a variable called `ReportName` of type `string`. The default value is
`Master/Detail Report` and it is created using the following code:

```
<%@ Property Name="ReportName" Type="System.String" Default="Master/Detail Report"
             Category="Summary" Description="The name of the report." %>
```

The default value inserted by this property directive for **ReportName** is acceptable, so you don't need to
modify it. Select the **MasterTable** property; this will cause the **Table Picker** window to appear
(see Figure 11-24):

Figure 11-24

CodeSmith would display any known data sources in the **Data Source** listbox above, but because this is
the first time that any data source is being accessed, a data source must be specified. This is done by
clicking on the ellipses displayed in the upper right hand corner (see Figure 11-24) which causes the **Data
Source Manager** window to appear, which you can see in Figure 11-25:

Figure 11-25

Click the **Add** button; this will cause the **Data Source** window to be displayed. Edit the **Connection**
properties for the data source connection as shown in Figure 11-26 to connect to your database:

Figure 11-26

The connection information is verified upon pressing the OK button. If your connection settings are correct, the Data Source Manager window will now have an entry (see Figure 11-27):

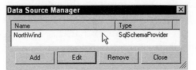

Figure 11-27

Now, if you close the Data Source Manager window, it will cause the Table Picker window to be displayed and it should be populated with the available tables as seen in Figure 11-28:

Figure 11-28

Choose the Customers table by clicking the Select button. This causes the Table Picker window to close, and the report property window to come to the forefront as shown in Figure 11-29:

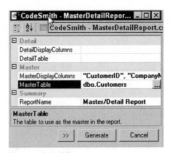

Figure 11-29

You can see from Figure 11-29 that the MasterTable property has been set to dbo.Customers and the fields from that table have been copied into the MasterDisplayColumns property field. Next, you need to set the table value for the Detail section of the report. Because you have a valid data source, the table list from Figure 11-28 is displayed. Select the Orders table and the chart properties window will be displayed with the information shown in Figure 11-30:

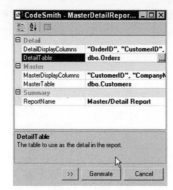

Figure 11-30

All that remains for generating a new report is to choose the fields that we want to display. These properties have already been set from the code for our Master and Detail tables, but the default behavior is all fields and we may want to change this.

Edit the Columns property for both the Master and Detail tables by clicking on those property fields. A custom type editor has been associated with each property, which will cause the String Collection Editor window to be displayed as in Figure 11-31:

Figure 11-31

Finally, you need to delete unwanted fields from the report. You can generate the report by pressing the Generate button displayed at the bottom of Figure 11-30. This causes our template to use the properties that we have set to generate the RDL, the results of which are shown in Figure 11-32:

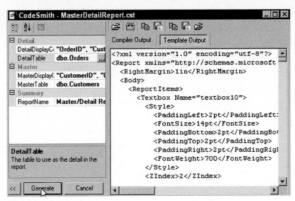

Figure 11-32

The report created by this template matches the report shown in Figure 11-25. The main benefit it provides is that the users of this template may create and use this reports with a common look and feel based on different tables and fields with no additional effort. Our efforts to create a flexible, repeatable solution have been successful.

Although a full-blown example of template creation is beyond the scope of this book, it is important to display an example of how the RDL from the original report and the templated code work together. The following code snippet illustrates the mixed ASP.NET-like code that generates the table cell headers for the Detail records. Only the template code has been highlighted here:

```
<TableCells>
    <% for (int i = 0; i < DetailDisplayColumns.Count; i++) {%>
<TableCell>
    <ReportItems>
    <Textbox Name="<%= DetailDisplayColumns[i] %> Header">
      <Style>
       <PaddingLeft>2pt</PaddingLeft>
       <TextAlign>Left</TextAlign>
       <PaddingBottom>2pt</PaddingBottom>
       <PaddingTop>2pt</PaddingTop>
       <PaddingRight>2pt</PaddingRight>
       <FontWeight>700</FontWeight>
      </Style>
      <ZIndex>7</ZIndex>
      <rd:DefaultName><%= DetailDisplayColumns[i]%> Header</rd:DefaultName>
      <CanGrow>true</CanGrow>
      <CanShrink>true</CanShrink>
      <Value><%= DetailDisplayColumns[i] %></Value>
    </Textbox>
    </ReportItems>
    </TableCell>
  <% } %>
```

Notice that the code almost resembles the use of traditional ASP. CodeSmith uses a mixed text and tag solution that generates dynamic output based on changing properties. Automatic or template-based code generation cannot eliminate all of your coding but can be intelligently applied to improve quality and reduce the effort involved in code maintenance.

There is, however, a small disadvantage associated with using a third party tool like CodeSmith. In case of errors, you might need to examine three levels of code to determine the source: Reporting Services, Visual Studio, and CodeSmith.

Summary

Microsoft's use of XML-based RDL is huge step forward toward common report definition formats. It opens up a brand new revenue stream for tool vendors, and allows existing reporting solutions to export their proprietary reports into an open extensible format for use by Reporting Services or any other future tools that are able to emit or consume RDL. Our simple examples using both the .NET Framework classes and CodeSmith illustrate this point. The ability to buy or build these tools give us that have been sorely lacking in the reporting arena for years.

12

Extending Reporting Services

Earlier chapters focused on building and managing reports and interfacing with Reporting Services through the exposed Reporting Service Web Service. All of these topics are crucial to using and understanding Report Services, but we also want to address those situations where the built-in functionality provided by Reporting Services does not fully meet your needs.

In this chapter, you will learn about the extensibility of Reporting Services and the areas that currently support customization. These include:

❑   Extensibility options

❑   Reasons for extending SQL Server Reporting Services

❑   How to create custom extensions

❑   How to install custom extensions

Overview

As you learned in Chapter 2, Reporting Services is a robust and scalable product for enterprise report processing. In addition, Microsoft has built Reporting Services using a modular extensible architecture that gives users the ability to customize, extend, and expand the product to support their enterprise Business Intelligence (BI) reporting needs. Reporting Services currently supports extending its behavior in the following areas:

❑   **Data processing extensions**: Custom data providers can allow you to access any type of data store using a consistent programming model. Currently supported providers include ODBC, OLEDB, Oracle, and SQL.

Chapter 12

❑ **Delivery extensions**: Delivery extensions allow you to deliver reports to users or groups of users according to a schedule. Email and network file shares are the delivery mechanisms currently built into the product.

❑ **Delivery management extensions**: Management extensions are user interface components that allow a user to control the delivery of reports through Report Manager.

❑ **Custom report objects**: Custom report objects are .NET assemblies that allow you to add custom functionality to report processing.

The Missing Pieces

Reporting Services supplies a good deal of extensibility out of the box. This is especially impressive when you consider its status as a first release product. There are, however, key pieces of the product that you would expect to be extensible where customization is blatantly absent.

Security Extensions

Reporting Services currently supports only Integrated Windows Security and SQL Server security. This is a glaring omission by the designers of the product. Most companies have heterogeneous networks with multiple operating systems (OS) and products. In a perfect world, all of our networks, applications, and resources would support some form of single sign-on, or at least would allow us to build this ourselves. By limiting Reporting Services to a Windows-only environment, Microsoft has severely restricted its customer base.

Postings at the beta news groups indicate that they are aware of this issue and is actively working towards resolution. There is an unimplemented placeholder interface called `IAuthorizationExtension` *in the Reporting Services Interface assembly. There are no guarantees, however, that this functionality would make it into the Release to Market 1.0 version.*

Rendering Extensions

Rendering extensions control the type of document that gets created when a report is processed. Theoretically, you could have Report Services create any type of document given the ability to extend the product in this area. Microsoft has indicated support for custom rendering in future versions but not in the 1.0 release. Currently, Microsoft provides the following rendering extensions out of the box:

❑ **HTML**: The HTML extension will generate HTML 3.2 for use with older browsers and HTML 4.0 for browsers that support the dynamic HTML standard.

❑ **MHTML**: MHTML is another HTML standard created to allow disconnected viewing of HTML documents. All the images in the page are encoded into the document, which increases its size, but allows it to be viewed both online and offline.

❑ **Excel**: The Excel extension creates Microsoft Excel-specific MHTML.

❑ **CSV**: The Comma Separated Values extension emit data fields separated by commas. The first row of the CSV result contains the field names for the data.

❑ **Image**: The image extension allows you to export reports as images in the EMF, GIF, JPEG, PNG, TIFF, and WMF formats.

❑ **PDF**: This extension allows the generation of reports in the PDF format.

Extensible Report Designer Classes

Microsoft's tool for creating Reports is the Report Designer. Report Designer is integrated into Visual Studio .NET and uses a development paradigm that is very similar to building Windows forms. You drag and drop controls onto the design template and set properties to change the behavior of the control. Unlike Windows forms, the Report Designer classes are sealed, preventing programmers from extending them and adding functionality.

Microsoft team members have indicated that decisions about the object model for Reporting Controls is still ongoing and are not commiting to either timelines or functionality. There is, however, a placeholder in the RDL object model called *CustomReportItem* that suggests that the capability to create custom Report controls at some time in the future would be available. Since the Designer ultimately creates XML, it is possible to overcome this limitation by creating your own object model to create RDL. In fact, many third parties such as *Proclarity* and *Sorfware Artisans* are already extending their tools to emit Reporting Services compatible RDL.

Business Opportunities

Microsoft has a long history of creating and fostering an ecosystem around their products. SQL Server already has many third party products that can be used to enhance its capabilities, ease development, and make managing the product easier. Searching the Internet revealed literally hundreds of products built to enhance your SQL Server experience. Reporting Services will be no exception. This chapter introduces you to most of the areas within Reporting Services that allow customization and offer opportunities to create add-on products that provide value to customers. Some areas of opportunity include creating:

❑ Delivery extensions that work with third party products like IBM MQSeries.

❑ Rendering extensions to support other presentation formats such as Macromedia Flash or Microsoft PowerPoint.

❑ Custom security extensions to allow the use of Reporting Services in heterogeneous environments.

❑ Entire Business Intelligence (BI) reporting solutions for various business products.

Common Extension Interfaces

Reporting Services uses common interfaces to allow expanding the product in a standard way. Most of these interfaces are used to allow Reporting Services to interact with a variety of different objects without any knowledge of their architecture or implementation. This is a commonly used way of allowing product extension and standardizing object creation and interaction used in *Object Oriented Programming* (*OOP*).

What Is an Interface?

Most C/C++ developers are intimately familiar with interfaces. The entire COM programming model is based upon them. Visual Basic developers have used interfaces for years, but the VB programming environment hid this from programmers. In fact, Reporting Services itself is exposed to developers through a web service interface. In order to provide complete coverage of Extending Reporting Services, a definition and explanation of interfaces is required. So what is an interface?

> **An interface is a presepecified definition that forms a contract between software components and defines how they communicate.**

This sounds great, but what does it mean? In Reporting Services, the primary class of all extension components must implement the `IExtension` interface. This is illustrated in the code snippets provided in the following section.

IExtension

All developers who want to extend Reporting Services must build a method called `SetConfiguration` into the initial class used in their components. This method matches the method signature in the following code sample. They must also create a property called `LocalizedName` that returns the name of the component based on the language being used for coding (Russian, German, Italian, and so on). Once the programmers have met these requirements, they are said to have implemented the interface.

C#

The code in C# that extends the `IExtension` interface is as follows:

```
public interface IExtension
{
        void SetConfiguration(string configuration);
        string LocalizedName{ get; }
}
```

VB.NET

A Visual Basic example that implements the `IExtension` interface is shown here:

```
Imports Microsoft.ReportingServices.Interfaces
Public Class MyExtension Implements IExtension

    Public ReadOnly Property LocalizedName() As String _
        Implements IExtension.LocalizedName
        Get
           'write code to return the localized name of the component
        End Get
    End Property
```

```
    Public Sub SetConfiguration(ByVal configuration As String) _
        Implements IExtension.SetConfiguration
        'write code to configure your component to allow configuration
    End Sub

End Class
```

IDisposable

The IDisposable interface is very common, although it is not a Reporting Services—specific interface. It is commonly used throughout the .NET Framework. The purpose of the IDisposable interface is to provide a common way of releasing references to non-memory resources such as a database connection. Let's see the definition of IDisposable.

C#

```
public interface IDisposable
{
    void Dispose();
}
```

VB.NET

```
Public Interface IDisposable
        Sub Dispose()
End Interface
```

Many of the input/output related objects in the .NET Framework implement the IDisposable interface due to their interaction with non-memory resources. The extensions we will create for Reporting Services are no exception. A full discussion of resource management, however, is beyond the scope of this book. Our code will not actually do anything in IDisposable, but will have an empty or NOOP operation to meet the interface requirements of the specific object.

Interface Language Differences

There are differences in the way that VB.NET and C# require interface methods to be declared. C# supports implicit interface definitions. If the method names and signatures match those of an interface implemented by the class, then the class methods are automatically mapped to their associated interface methods. VB.NET requires explicit interface implementation. In order to be mapped correctly, VB.NET requires that you specify that the method is implementing a certain interface. This is done with the Implements keyword as follows:

```
Public Sub Dispose() Implements IDataReader.Dispose
        'Data Providers often work with non-memory resources.  If this
        'is the case implement the IDisposable Interface.
End Sub
```

Data Processing Extensions

Reporting Services allows you to access data from traditional data sources such as relational databases using the existing .NET data providers. The following providers are supplied as part of the .NET Framework supplied by Microsoft:

❑   ODBC

❑   OLEDB

❑   Oracle

❑   SQLClient

Data processing extensions are components that allow you to access data for use within Reporting Services. If that implies a .NET data provider to you, then congratulations are in order. These two types of data access objects are very similar and are based on a common set of interface definitions. If you have already built a custom .NET data provider, you may use that provider with Reporting Services with no modification. However, you also can extend your existing provider to provide additional functionality.

In this chapter, we will discuss the similarities and differences between a standard .NET data provider and a Reporting Services Data Processing Extension. Let's start with some architectural information about data providers in general, and then dive into the details of creating a custom data processing extension. The .NET Framework has a data access object model that is very similar to that used in traditional COM-based ADO. The ADO.NET object model is shown in Figure 12-1:

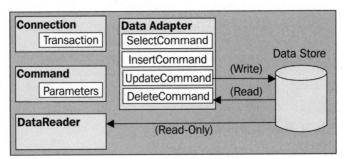

Figure 12-1

The RS data provider is essentially the same as the ADO data provider, except for the fact that it requires wrappers around .NET providers to support the RS required interfaces. The programming paradigm is very similar as well.

The basic steps for working with a data source are as follows:

❑   Make a connection to a data source.

❑   Issue a command to manipulate data.

❑   Retrieve the results of your query.

These actions map directly to the objects above, although a `DataAdapter` implementation is not needed because Reporting Services only *reads* the data.

The following table summarizes the objects that are normally created in a data processing extension, and provides a description of the object responsibilities:

Object	Description
Connection	Establishes a connection to a specific data source.
Command	Executes a command against a data source. Exposes a `Parameters` collection and can execute within the scope of a transaction.
DataReader	Provides access to data using a forward-only, read-only stream.
DataAdapter	Responsible for retrieving data and for resolving updates with the data source. This object is not required for a Reporting Services Data Processing Extension because of the read-only nature of Reporting Services.

Each of these objects contains implementation-specific code needed to create a connection, issue commands, or read and update data. Microsoft has enforced a consistent data access mechanism by basing these objects on a set of standard interfaces. Figure 12-2 shows the interfaces that may be implemented when creating a data processing extension, although not all of them are required:

Figure 12-2

The following table indicates the interfaces that must be implemented to build a custom data processing extension:

Interface	Description
IDbConnection	Unique session with a data source
IDbTransaction	Local transaction (non-distributed)
IDbCommand	Represents query command methods to be executed against a data source

Table continued on following page

Interface	Description
IDataParameter	Methods to support passing parameters to a Command object
IDataParameterCollection	Collection of parameters
IDataReader	Methods used to read a forward-only, read-only data stream
IExtension	Reporting Services-specific interface that supports localization and is implemented by all SRS extensions

Creating a Custom Data Processing Extension

Creating a full blown data provider is no trivial task. The goal of this walkthrough is familiarize you with the .NET data access mechanism, as well as help you create and install a custom Reporting Services Data Extension. Our implementation is simplified in that it does not support transactions. It should also be noted that an ODBC driver already exists that could be used for this task.

Let's look at the scenario for this walkthrough. You regularly receive student data from a third party over which you have no control. The information is sent in a CSV file with a specific layout. There is an immediate need to create a formatted hard copy of this data for use as a roster. After some research, you realize the Reporting Services will meet your needs. You decided to make your efforts reusable by creating a custom data extension.

Creating the Project

Let's start by creating our projectby choosing File | New | Project. Change the name of the Project to CSVDataExtension. Use the Class Library template. The name of the assembly needs to change to reflect our custom namespace. Choose Project | Properties and change the assembly name to Wrox.Professional.ReportingServices.CSVDataExtension.

Most of the classes created for this project have common requirements. Most of them have empty default constructors, and all of them require the use of some common namespaces. The code below is a skeleton of how each class should look after you create it. Replace the ClassName with the name of the class you are working on. This will allow you to concentrate only on the differences between the objects that will be created in your data extension project.

C#

```csharp
using System;
using Microsoft.ReportingServices.DataProcessing;

namespace Wrox.Professional.ReportingServices.CSVDataExtension
{
    public class CSVClassName
    {
    }
}
```

VB.NET

```
Imports System;
Imports Microsoft.ReportingServices.DataProcessing;

Namespace Wrox.Professional.ReportingServices.CSVDataExtension
    Public Class CSVClassName

    End Class
End Namespace
```

Creating the CSVConnection Object

The `Connection` object is responsible for connecting to the data source and providing a mechanism for accessing both the data processing extension—specific transaction and command objects. These responsibilities are enforced through the `IDbConnection` interface.

To add the `CSVConection` class to the project, choose **Project | Add Class** from the menu. Change the name of the class to **CSVConnection**. After the class definition, the `IDisposable.Dispose` method must be added to this class. This was discussed earlier in the section on interfaces.

Namespaces are used to bring assemblies that you have referenced into scope. You will be using the following namespaces in the `CSVConnection` class. Add the `Interfaces` namespace definition to the top of your file.

C#

```
using System;
using Microsoft.ReportingServices.DataProcessing;
using Microsoft.ReportingServices.Interfaces;
```

VB.NET

```
Imports System
Imports Microsoft.ReportingServices.DataProcessing
Imports Microsoft.ReportingServices.Interfaces
```

Variable Declarations

The following variables are used later in the code. The `m_connString` variable holds the connection string that will be used to connect to the data source. The `m_state` variable holds the value of the state of the current connection. The `System.Data.ConnectionState` is an enumeration that represents all the possible states of a connection.

C#

```
private string  m_connString;
private System.Data.ConnectionState  m_state = System.Data.ConnectionState.Closed;
```

VB.NET

```
Private m_connString As String
Private m_state As System.Data.ConnectionState = System.Data.ConnectionState.Closed
```

Constructors

The CSVConnection object has an empty default constructor, as well as an overloaded constructor that allows the developer to create the object and initialize the connection string in one line of code.

C#

```
public CSVConnection(string connString)
{
        //contructor with connection string
        m_connString = connString;
}
```

VB.NET

```
Public Sub New(ByVal connString As String)
        'contructor with connection string
        m_connString = connString
End Sub
```

Implementing IDbConnection

The IDbConnection interface is the standard mechanism that data providers use to control the use of the Connection object. These properties and methods help you make changes to the connection settings, open and close the connection, and associate the connection with a valid transaction. Your Connection object does not support transactions due to its read-only nature and because you are working against a file system, which is not a resource manager.

C#

```
public interface IDbConnection : IDisposable, IExtension
{
        IDbTransaction BeginTransaction();
        IDbCommand CreateCommand();
        void Open();
        void Close();
        string ConnectionString { get; set; }
        int ConnectionTimeout { get; }
}
```

VB.NET

```
Public Interface IDbConnection
    Inherits IDisposable, IExtension
        Function BeginTransaction() As IDbTransaction
        Function CreateCommand() As IDbCommand
        Sub Open()
        Sub Close()
        Property ConnectionString() As String
        Property ConnectionTimeout() As Integer
End Interface
```

Implementing IDisposable

The Connection object is also required to implement the IDisposable interface. Since it is the first object of the extension that Reporting Services will create, the CSVConnection object must also implement the IExtension interface that was discussed in the *Common Extension Interfaces* section of this chapter. Add the following language-specific statements to your code to force the CVSConnection object to implement these interfaces.

C#

```
namespace Wrox.Professional.ReportingServices.CSVDataExtension
{
    public class CSVConnection: IDbConnection, IExtension
    {
        private string   m_connString;
```

VB.NET

```
Namespace Wrox.Professional.ReportingServices.CSVDataExtension
    Public Class CSVConnection
        Implements IDbConnection
        Implements IExtension
        Private m_connString As String
```

BeginTransaction Function

The BeginTransaction function is primarily responsible for initiating a new transaction and returning a reference to a valid, implementation-specific transaction object. The file system, which is our data store, does not support transactions, but this method is required by the interface. You need to ensure that the developer who will use your object in code is aware of that fact. This is done by throwing a NotSupportedException.

C#

```
public IDbTransaction BeginTransaction()
{
    //example doesn't support transactions
    throw new NotSupportedException("Transactions not supported");
}
```

VB.NET

```
Public Function BeginTransaction() As IDbTransaction _
    Implements IDbConnection.BeginTransaction
    'example doesn't support transactions
    Throw New NotSupportedException("Transactions not supported")
End Function
```

CreateCommand Function

The Createcommand function is responsible for creating and returning a reference to a valid implementation-specific Command object. The method uses an overloaded constructor of the custom Command object in order to pass that object a reference to the current connection.

C#

```csharp
public IDbCommand CreateCommand()
{
    // Return a new instance of the implementation-specific command object
    return new CSVCommand(this);
}
```

VB.NET

```vbnet
Public Function CreateCommand() As IDbCommand _
        Implements IDbConnection.CreateCommand
        'Return a new instance of the implementation
        'specific command object
        Return New CSVCommand(Me)
End Function
```

Open Method

In a full data provider implementation, the Open method is used to make a data source—specific connection. Your implementation does not actually support connections, but you can trick Reporting Services into thinking that it does. You can do this by implementing the Open method and changing the value of the ConnectionState property to indicate that the connection is valid and open. The current value of the connection state is stored inside a private variable called m_state, which you can change to indicate an open connection.

C#

```csharp
public void Open()
{
    // set the connection state to open and return
    m_state = System.Data.ConnectionState.Open;
    return;
}
```

VB.NET

```vbnet
Public Sub Open() Implements IDbConnection.Open
    ' set the connection state to open and return
    m_state = System.Data.ConnectionState.Open
    Return
End Sub
```

Close Method

The Close method is used to close your data source—specific connection. You trick Reporting Services by creating the Close method and changing the value of the ConnectionState property to indicate that the connection is closed. Your Close method is exactly the same as your Open method with the exception that it sets the value of m_state to closed to indicate that the connection was closed correctly.

C#

```csharp
public void Close()
{
    //set the connection state to close and return
```

```
        m_state = System.Data.ConnectionState.Closed;
        return;
}
```

VB.NET

```
Public Sub Close() Implements IDbConnection.Close
        ' set the connection state to close and return
        m_state = System.Data.ConnectionState.Closed
        Return
End Sub
```

ConnectionString Property

The ConnectionString property allows you to set the connection string through code. This property uses a private variable to store the current connection string, which is used to provide the information needed to connect to the data source. Most developers are familiar with this property because of its frequent use in both traditional ADO and ADO.NET. The ConnectionString property is used to indicate the file that you are going to parse. The user of your data processing extension should input the path to the file they wish to parse into the connection string. We are storing the connection string in the m_connString private member variable .

C#

```
public string ConnectionString
{
        Get {return m_connString;}
        Set {m_connString = value;}
}
```

VB.NET

```
Public Property ConnectionString() As String _
        Implements IDbConnection.ConnectionString
        Get
                Return m_connString
        End Get
        Set(ByVal Value As String)
                m_connString = Value
        End Set
End Property
```

ConnectionTimeout Property

The ConnectionTimeout property allows you to set the timeout property of the connection. This is used to control how long the interval for connecting to the source should be before an error is thrown. Your class does not actually use this value, but it is implemented for consistency and due to interface requirements. Returning a value of 0 indicates that there is an infinite timeout period.

C#

```
public int ConnectionTimeout
{
        get
        {
                // Returns the connection time-out value.
```

```
            // Zero indicates an indefinite time-out period.
            return 0;
        }
    }
```

VB.NET

```
Public ReadOnly Property ConnectionTimeout() As Integer _
      Implements IDbConnection.ConnectionTimeout
      Get       ' Returns the connection time-out value.
                ' Zero indicates an indefinite time-out period.
                Return 0
      End Get
End Property
```

Creating the CSVParameter Class

The CSVParameter class is not needed until the Command class is created, but because of that dependency you do need to create it. The Parameter object is used to send parameters to the Command object that can be used in executing commands against the data source. Despite the fact that this class is not used to perform any work, the interface requirements of the Command class force you to create it. This class also has interface requirements; it is required to support the IDataParameter interface defined in the Reporting Services Data Processing Extension assembly.

To add the CSVParameter class to the project, choose Project | Add Class from the menu and change the name to CSVParameter.

Declarations

The following declarations are used internally to hold both the value and the name of the parameter. The name is stored in a string variable called m_paramName. Because the value variable might contain any type of value, the m_value is declared as an Object type.

C#

```
String   m_paramName;
Object   m_value;
```

VB.NET

```
Dim m_paramName As String
Dim m_value As Object
```

Implementing IDataParameter

The IDataParameter interface enforces that your custom parameter class allow a programmer to get and set the name and value of the current parameter.

C#

```
public interface IDataParameter
{
        string ParameterName { get; set; }
```

```
        object Value { get; set; }
    }
```

VB.NET

```
Public Interface IDataParameter
    Property ParameterName() As String
    Property Value() As Object
End Interface
```

Modify the class code to force the CSVParameter class to implement IDataParameter.

C#

```
namespace Wrox.Professional.ReportingServices.CSVDataExtension
{
    public class CSVDataParameter : IDataParameter
    {
        string   m_paramName;
```

VB.NET

```
Namespace Wrox.Professional.ReportingServices.CSVDataExtension
    Public Class CSVDataParameter
        Implements IDataParameter
        Dim m_paramName As String
```

ParameterName Property

The ParameterName property is used to store the name of the parameter in a string variable called m_paramName. This field is typically used to map to parameters in stored procedures but is unused in your implementation.

C#

```
public String ParameterName
{
        get { return m_paramName; }
        set { m_paramName = value; }
}
```

VB.NET

```
Public Property ParameterName() As String _
        Implements IDataParameter.ParameterName
            Get
                Return m_paramName
            End Get
            Set(ByVal Value As String)
                m_paramName = value
            End Set
End Property
```

Value Property

The `Value` property is similar to the name created earlier in that it is not actually used. The value is stored in an object variable called `m_value`.

C#

```csharp
public object Value
{
        get
        {
            return m_value;
        }
        set
        {
            m_value    = value;
        }
}
```

VB.NET

```vbnet
Public Property Value() As Object _
        Implements IDataParameter.Value
            Get
                    Return m_value
            End Get
            Set(ByVal Value As Object)
                    m_value = Value
            End Set
End Property
```

Creating the CSVParameterCollection Class

The `CSVParameterCollection` class is simply a collection of `Parameter` objects. Although you could have created a custom collection class that implements all of the required methods, an easier route exists. The `IDataParameterCollection` interface is basically a subset of the `IList` interface used to define other objects in the .NET Framework. By using an object already available, you reduce the required coding effort considerably.

To add the `CSVParameterCollection` class to the project, choose **Project | Add Class** from the menu. Change the name of the class to `CSVParameterCollection`.

There is no need to create custom constructors or member variables for use in your collection class. This is because you can use the internal variables and constructors that exist inside the `ArrayList` base class that this class inherits from. The properties that you create will be mapped directly to properties and methods that exist in the `ArrayList` class.

Namespaces

The `CSVParameterCollection` class uses the standard namespaces discussed earlier. There is an additional namespace that is needed because of the use of `ArrayList`. You must add the `System.Collections` namespace.

C#

```
using System;
using Microsoft.ReportingServices.DataProcessing;
using System.Collections;
```

VB.NET

```
Imports System
Imports Microsoft.ReportingServices.DataProcessing
Imports System.Collections
```

Implementing IDataParameterCollection

The `IDataParameterCollection` interface defines a custom `Add` method as well as provides methods to access the members of this collection through the `IEnumerable` interface. The `ArrayList` base class implements this interface. Your class will use the parent class properties and methods to service its needs.

C#

```
public interface IDataParameterCollection : IEnumerable
{
        int Add(IDataParameter parameter);
}
```

VB.NET

```
Public Interface IDataParameterCollection
    Inherits IEnumerable
    Function Add(ByVal parameter As IDataParameter) As Integer
End Interface
```

You can modify the code to enforce the implementation of `IDataParameterCollection` as well as to be able to gain the functionality inherited from the `ArrayList` class.

C#

```
namespace Wrox.Professional.ReportingServices.CSVDataExtension
{
    public class CSVDataParameterCollection : ArrayList, IDataParameterCollection
    {
```

VB.NET

```
Namespace Wrox.Professional.ReportingServices.CSVDataExtension
    Public Class CSVDataParameterCollection
        Inherits ArrayList
        Implements IDataParameterCollection
```

Since most of the functionality of the `CSVDataParameterCollection` class exists in its parent class, all that needs to be done is to create the custom `Add` method required by the `IDataParameter` interface. This method is used by the custom collection to add parameters to an instance of the `Collection` object.

C#

```
public int Add(IDataParameter value)
{
        if (((CSVDataParameter)value).ParameterName != null)
        {
            return base.Add(value);
        }
        else
            throw new ArgumentException("parameter must be named");
}
```

VB.NET

```
Public Overloads Function Add(ByVal value As IDataParameter) As Integer _
        Implements IDataParameterCollection.Add
                If Not (CType(value, CSVDataParameter)).ParameterName Is Nothing Then
                    Return MyBase.Add(value)
                Else
                    Throw New ArgumentException("parameter must be named")
                End If
End Function
```

Creating the CSVCommand Class

The Command object is responsible for sending commands to the data source. This is enforced by making the object implement the IDbCommand interface, which supplies a standard mechanism for passing in commands to be executed against the data source as well as parameters that might be needed in the process of executing these commands. It also defines a property that allows the developer to associate the command with a transaction object. Your implementation is simplified in that it does not support transactions.

To add the CSVCommand class to the project, choose Project | Add Class from the menu. Change the name of the class to CSVCommand. Then go on declaring some variables.

C#

```
CSVConnection    m_connection;
String           m_cmdText;
```

VB.NET

```
Dim m_connection As CSVConnection
Dim m_cmdText As String
```

Constructors

You would want the users of your processing extension to be forced to create the Command object either through the CreateCommand method of the IDbConnection interface or by passing in a valid CSVConnection object as a parameter. The purpose of this is to ensure that you have access to the connection string that is needed to locate the CSV file you intend to parse. This can be accomplished by declaring the default constructor of your command object to be private. This prevents the developer from creating the CSVCommand object without the correct initialization.

C#

```
private CSVCommand()
{
        //force creation of the object through the IDBCommand
        //interface or with a valid connection
}

public CSVCommand(CSVConnection connection)
{
        //overloaded constructor to accept current Connection object
        m_connection = connection;
        this.m_cmdText = this.m_connection.ConnectionString;
}
```

VB.NET

```
Private Sub New()

End Sub

Public Sub New(ByVal connection As CSVConnection)
        'overloaded constructor to accept current connection object
        m_connection = connection
        Me.CommandText = Me.m_connection.ConnectionString
End Sub
```

Implementing IDbCommand

The required interface for all `Command` objects is called `IDbCommand`. It consists of methods that allow the developer to pass commands and parameters to the `Command` object. The most interesting method of this object is the `ExecuteReader` method, which contains the object-specific code to read data from our CSV data source.

C#

```
public interface IDbCommand : IDisposable
{
        void Cancel();
        IDataReader ExecuteReader(CommandBehavior behavior);
        string CommandText { get; set; }
        int CommandTimeout { get; set; }
        CommandType CommandType { get; set; }
        IDataParameter CreateParameter();
        IDataParameterCollection Parameters { get; }
        IDbTransaction Transaction { get; set; }
}
```

VB.NET

```
Public Interface IDbCommand
    Inherits IDisposable
    Sub Cancel()
    Function ExecuteReader(ByVal behavior As CommandBehavior) As IDataReader
    Property CommandText() As String
```

```
        Property CommandTimeout() As Integer
        Property CommandType() As CommandType
        Function CreateParameter() As IDataParameter
        Property Parameters() As IDataParameterCollection
        Property Transaction() As IDbTransaction
    End Interface
```

You need to add the following `Implements` statements to your code using language-specific syntax to force the `CVSCommand` object to implement these interfaces.

C#

```
namespace Wrox.Professional.ReportingServices.CSVDataExtension
{
    public class CSVCommand: IDbCommand
    {
        CSVConnection m_connection;
```

VB.NET

```
Namespace Wrox.Professional.ReportingServices.CSVDataExtension
    Public Class CSVCommand
        Implements IDbCommand
        Dim m_connection As CSVConnection
```

Cancel Method

The `Cancel` method is typically used to cancel a method that has been *queued*. Most implementations of data providers are multi-threaded and support the issue of multiple commands against the data store. You have only created this method to support the `IDbCommand` interface requirements and should inform the developer of your lack of support by throwing a `NotSupportedException`.

C#

```
public void Cancel()
{
        // not supported
        throw new NotSupportedException();
}
```

VB.NET

```
Public Sub Cancel()_
        Implements IDbCommand.Cancel
        ' Not supported
        Throw New NotSupportedException
End Sub
```

ExecuteReader Function

The `ExecuteReader` method returns an extension-specific reader object to the caller so they may loop through and read the data. The `CSVCommand` object creates an instance of your custom reader object. An internal method is then executed passing in the `m_cmdText` variable that you filled from the `CSVConnection.ConnectionString` property. Your `CSVReader` implementation knows how to use this information to gain a reference to the supplied CSV file. A reference to your custom data reader is then returned.

C#

```csharp
public IDataReader ExecuteReader()
{
        //Verify a valid connnection
        if (m_connection == null || m_connection.State !=
                        System.Data.ConnectionState.Open)
            throw new InvalidOperationException("Connection must be valid and
                                            open.");
        // Execute the command and return a datareader
        CSVDataReader reader = new CSVDataReader();
        reader.GetFile();
        // The getfile methods opens a stream to the file
        // specified in the command text

        return reader;
}
```

VB.NET

```vbnet
Public Function ExecuteReader() As IDataReader
        'Verify a valid connnection
        If m_connection Is Nothing Or m_connection.State <>
                        System.Data.ConnectionState.Open Then
            Throw New InvalidOperationException("Connection must be valid and
                                            open.")
        End If
        'Execute the command and return a datareader
        Dim reader As CSVDataReader = New CSVDataReader()
        reader.GetFile(m_cmdText)
        'The getfile methods open a stream to the file
        'Specified in the command text
        Return reader
End Function
```

CommandText Property

Reporting Services does not manually create a separate Command object. It uses the CreateCommand method of the IDBConnection interface to return an implementation-specific command object. This object maps the ConnectionString property of the CSVConnection object to the CommandText of the command object to provide the path to the file that you are going to parse using your custom data extension. Due to this, you do need not allow the programmer to change the CommandText property from code. You need to create this property as a read-only property, but are forced to make it read/write based on interface requirements. Therefore, you need to create both the set and get methods, even though the set method is effectively empty, (it contains a NOOP operation).

C#

```csharp
public string CommandText
{
                //string used to specify the filepath
```

```
       get { return m_cmdText; }
       set {//NOOP}
}
```

VB.NET

```
Public Property CommandText() As String _
        Implements IDbCommand.CommandText
            Get
                Return m_cmdText
            End Get
            Set(ByVal Value As String)
                'NOOP
            End Set
        End Property
```

CommandTimeout Property

The `CommandTimeout` property is used to specify how long the `Command` object should wait for the results of an executed command before throwing an exception. You do not actually use this value, but it must be implemented due to interface requirements. You don't allow the developer to actually set this value through code, but return the default value of 30 seconds.

C#

```
public int CommandTimeout
{
        // Implemented the Property for consistency but it is not used.
        get {return 30;}
        set {//NOOP}
}
```

VB.NET

```
Public Property CommandTimeout() As Integer _
        Implements IDbCommand.CommandTimeout
            Get
                Return 30
            End Get
            Set(ByVal Value As Integer)
                'NOOP
            End Set
End Property
```

CommandType Property

Most data processing extensions allow the developer to pass in a command as text, or they can pass in a fully initialized `Command` object for the Execute reader method to examine and use. The `CSVCommand` class only accepts text, and any other type of will cause your component to throw a `NotSupported` Exception.

C#

```
public CommandType CommandType
{
        // supports only a text commandType
```

```
                    get {return CommandType.Text;}
                    set {if (value != CommandType.Text) throw new NotSupportedException();}
        }
```

VB.NET

```
Public Property CommandType() As CommandType _
        Implements IDbCommand.CommandType
            Get
                Return CommandType.Text
            End Get
            Set(ByVal Value As CommandType)
                If Value <> CommandType.Text Then
                    Throw New NotSupportedException
                End If
            End Set
        End Property
```

CreateParameter Function

The `CreateParameter` function returns an extension-specific parameter to the `Command` object. The method must be supported due to the interface requirements, even though it is not actually used. The `CSVParameter` object is a simple class that implements another interface called `IdataParameter`, which allows it to be returned as an object of the interface type.

C#

```
public IDataParameter CreateParameter()
{
    //return CSVDataParameter
    return new CSVDataParameter();
}
```

VB.NET

```
Public Function CreateParameter() As IDataParameter _
        Implements IDbCommand.CreateParameter
            Return New CSVDataParameter
End Function
```

Parameters Property

The `Parameters` property returns a collection that implements the `IDataParameterCollection` interface. Your custom collection class is the `CSVParameterCollection` and satisfies these requirements. The `Parameters` property allows the developer to index into the `Parameters` collection to set or get the parameter values.

C#

```
IDataParameterCollection IDbCommand.Parameters
{
    //Indicate that our provider does not support parameters
    get {throw new NotSupportedException("Parameters not supported");}
}
```

VB.NET

```
Public ReadOnly Property IDbCommandParameters() As IDataParameterCollection _
        Implements IDbCommand.Parameters
            Get 'indicate that parameters are not supported
                Throw New NotImplementedException("Parameters are not supported")
            End Get
End Property
```

Creating the DataReader Object

The data reader is the workhorse of your extension. Everything you have done to this point is to get to your custom CVSDataReader object. The behavior of the data reader is enforced by the IDbDataReader interface, which supplies methods to indicate the number, names, and types of the fields that will be read. It also allows the object to actually access the data.

To add the CSVDataReader class to the project, choose **Project | Add Class** from the menu. Change the name of the class to **CSVDataReader**. After adding the class, add the custom namespace and edit the class definition.

Declarations

The variables of the CSVDataReader hold of all the information that you will use to build the properties supported by the CSVDataReader class. The m_currentRow variable is used to store the value of the current row as the data is being read from your CSV data file. The string array m_names contains the names of the fields that will be read, while the m_types array provides access to the type of data that will be read. As the data is read, it will be loaded into an array of the object type called m_cols. Data from the file will be read by an internal StreamReader class called sr.

C#

```
internal int          m_currentRow;
internal String[]     m_names = {"Name","EmailAddress"};
internal Type[]       m_types = {typeof(String),typeof(String)};
internal bject[]      m_cols = new object[2];
internal int          m_fieldCount = 2;
private StreamReader   sr;
```

VB.NET

```
Friend    m_currentRow As Integer
Friend    m_names() As String = {"Name", "EmailAddress"}
Friend    m_types() As Type = {Type.GetType("string"),Type.GetType("string")}
Friend    m_cols() As Object = New Object(2) {}
Friend    m_fieldCount As Integer = 2
Private   sr As StreamReader
```

Implementing IDbDataReader

The IDbDataReader interface enforces consistency in working with data. It provides properties and methods that allow you to examine the data and its types as well as the Read method that will actually do the dirty work.

C#

```
public interface IDataReader : IDisposable
{
        Type GetFieldType(int fieldIndex);
        string GetName(int fieldIndex);
        int GetOrdinal(string fieldName);
        object GetValue(int fieldIndex);
        bool Read();
        int FieldCount {get;}
}
```

VB.NET

```
Public Interface IDataReader
    Inherits IDisposable
    Function GetFieldType(ByVal fieldIndex As Integer) As Type
    Function GetName(ByVal fieldIndex As Integer) As String
    Function GetOrdinal(ByVal fieldName As String) As Integer
    Function GetValue(ByVal fieldIndex As Integer) As Object
    Function Read() As Boolean
    Property FieldCount() As Integer
End Interface
```

You need to modify your class definition to force the custom `CSVDataReader` class to support the interface requirements.

C#

```
namespace Wrox.Professional.ReportingServices.CSVDataExtension
{
    public class CSVDataReader : IDataReader
    {
        internal int            m_currentRow;
```

VB.NET

```
Namespace Wrox.Professional.ReportingServices.CSVDataExtension
    Public Class CSVDataReader
        Implements IDataReader
```

GetFieldType Function

This property returns the type of data at a particular position within the stream that is being read. This data is used to allow the developer to store the data being read in the correct datatype upon retrieval from the data reader.

C#

```
public Type GetFieldType(int i)
{
        // Return the actual Type class for the data type.
        return m_types[i];
}
```

VB.NET

```
Public Function GetFieldType(ByVal i As Integer) As Type _
        Implements IDataReader.GetFieldType
            'Return the actual Type class for the data type.
            Return m_types(i)
End Function
```

GetName Function

The GetName method allows the developer to retrieve a data field from the DataReader object by passing in the name of the field to be read.

C#

```
public string GetName(int i)
{
        Return m_names[i];
}
```

VB.NET

```
Public Function GetName(ByVal i As Integer) As String _
        Implements IDataReader.GetName
            ' returns name of current column
            Return m_names(i)
End Function
```

GetOrdinal Function

The GetName method allows the developer to index data based on its position within the DataReader stream.

C#

```
public int GetOrdinal(string name)
{
        // Look for the ordinal of the column with the same name and return it.
        // Returns -1 if not found
        return Array.IndexOf(m_names, name);
}
```

VB.NET

```
Public Function GetOrdinal(ByVal name As String) As Integer _
        Implements IDataReader.GetOrdinal
            ' Look for the ordinal of the column with the same name and return it.
            ' Returns -1 if not found
            Return Array.IndexOf(m_names, name)
End Function
```

GetValue Function

The GetValue function retrieves the actual value from the data stream. All of these methods are typically used together. The developer pulls the type information from the stream, creates variables of the correct type to hold this data, and gets the values of the data using the GetValue function.

C#

```csharp
public Object GetValue(int i)
{
    //returns column value
    return m_cols[i];
}
```

VB.NET

```vbnet
Public Function GetValue(ByVal i As Integer) As Object _
        Implements IDataReader.GetValue
            'returns column value
            Return m_cols(i)
End Function
```

Read Method

The Read method is the workhorse of the CSVDataReader class. The function loops through the CSV data line by line. As each line is read, it is split into individual data fields and placed into the m_cols object collection based on the delimiter field delimStr. If a line is successfully read, this is indicated to the user of your extension by incrementing the row count variable m_currentRow and by returning a Boolean value. As long as true is returned, data is successfully read. False is returned when the internal StreamReader hits the end of the file.

C#

```csharp
public bool Read()
{
        //Implement the Methods to open the CSV File
        string line;
        string delimStr = ",";
        char [] delimiter = delimStr.ToCharArray();

        while ((line = sr.ReadLine()) != null)
        {
            m_currentRow++;
            m_cols = line.Split(delimiter);
            return true;
        }
        return false;
}
```

VB.NET

```vbnet
Public Function Read() As Boolean _
    Implements IDataReader.Read
    'Implement the Methods to open the CSV File
    Dim line As String
    Dim delimStr As String = ","
    Dim delimiter() As Char = delimStr.ToCharArray()
    Do
        line = sr.ReadLine
        If Not (line) Is Nothing Then
            m_currentRow = m_currentRow + 1
```

```
                    m_cols = line.Split(delimiter)
                    Return True
            Else
                    Return False
            End If
        Loop
    End Function
```

FieldCount Property

The `FieldCount` property returns the number of fields or columns available in each row of data that the `Read` method returns.

C#

```
public int FieldCount
{
        // Return the count of the number of columns,
        get { return m_fieldCount; }
}
```

VB.NET

```
Public ReadOnly Property FieldCount() As Integer _
        Implements IDataReader.FieldCount
            Get
                    Return m_fieldCount
            End Get
End Property
```

Installing the CSVDataProcessing Extension

After creating your custom data processing extension, you must install it to enable access to it. The installation process is actually pretty simple. Since your extension will be used by both the developer and Reporting Services, it requires installation in more than one location.

Reporting Services has a standard location where extensions should be installed. This location is a subdirectory below the installation directory of SQL Server itself. I will refer to the SQL Server installation path as `InstallPath`. On my machine, this directory is `C:\Program Files\Microsoft SQL Server\MSSQL\`.

The directory that you will install the extension into is the `bin` directory of the Report Server: `InstallPath\Reporting Services\ReportServer\bin`. Copy your custom data processing extension assembly into this directory. The extension is now in the correct location, but we need to inform Reporting Services of its presence. This is done by editing the configuration file that Reporting Services uses for its settings. This file is called `RSReportServer.config` and is located in the `InstallPath\Reporting Services\` directory. Open this file and look for the `<Data>` section. Within this section, you should see entries similar to the following:

```
<Data>
      <Permissions>
          <PermissionSet class="System.Security.NamedPermissionSet" version="1"
```

```
                        Unrestricted="true" Name="FullTrust"
                        Description="Allows full access to all resources"/>
        </Permissions>
        <Extension Name="SQL"
            Type="Microsoft.ReportingServices.DataExtensions.SqlConnectionWrapper,
                Microsoft.ReportingServices.DataExtensions"/>
        <Extension Name="OLEDB"
            Type="Microsoft.ReportingServices.DataExtensions.OleDbConnectionWrapper,
                Microsoft.ReportingServices.DataExtensions"/>
        <Extension Name="ORACLE"
            Type="Microsoft.ReportingServices.DataExtensions.OracleClient
             ConnectionWrapper, Microsoft.ReportingServices.DataExtensions"/>
        <Extension Name="ODBC"
            Type="Microsoft.ReportingServices.DataExtensions.OdbcConnection
                Wrapper,Microsoft.ReportingServices.DataExtensions"/>
        <Extension Name="CSV"
            Type="Wrox.Professional.ReportingServices.CSVDataExtension.CSVConnection,
                Wrox.Professional.ReportingServices.CSVDataExtension"/>
    </Data>
```

Add the CSV entry that you see in the highlighted code snippet. Save the file and your installation of the CSV extension for the Report Server portion is complete.

The next task is installing the extension on your development machine so that you can use it in the Report Designer. This is also done by copying the file to a specific directory of your development machine and making an entry in the configuration file so that the Designer is aware of the extension.

Copy your extension to the InstallPath\80\Tools\Report Designer directory. The configuration file of the Designer is in the same directory. It is called RSReportDesigner.config. Insert the same information that you inserted at the server-side extension at the end of the <Data> section in this file.

```
    <Data>

        <Extension Name="ODBC"
            Type="Microsoft.ReportingServices.DataExtensions.OdbcConnection
                Wrapper, Microsoft.ReportingServices.DataExtensions"/>
        <Extension Name="CSV"
            Type="Wrox.Professional.ReportingServices.CSVDataExtension.CSVConnection,
                Wrox.Professional.ReportingServices.CSVDataExtension"/>
    </Data>
```

Testing the CSVDataExtension

In order to test the extension, a report that uses the custom extension must be created. You also need to create a CSV file to contain your data or use the one provided in the sample code. The data needs to be in a two column format as shown here:

```
    Name, Email Address
```

Add a new project to your existing solution. Create the project by choosing File | Add Project | New Project. Change the name of the project to TestReport. If the development environment is set up correctly, you will see the Business Intelligence template folder. Choose the Report Library template.

After the project has been created, you need to add a report. Add the report by selecting File I Add New Item I Report. Change the name of the report to Roster. There is no dataset associated with the report. Create a new dataset by clicking on the drop-down list and select New Dataset as shown in Figure 12-3:

Figure 12-3

After the new dataset is created, the Data Source window will pop up. Edit the Name property displayed in the text box to something like CSVDataSource and select the CSV type. If the CSV type is not available, then review your installation of the extension. The result should look like the image shown in Figure 12-4:

Figure 12-4

Next, we must set up the security. Select the Credentials tab and ensure that Windows Integrated Security is selected as shown in Figure 12-5:

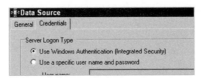

Figure 12-5

Select OK and now you can design the visual aspects of the report. Select the Toolbox tab of the tool box window. Drag and drop a List Control onto the design surface. Next, select the Fields tab of the tool box window. That should display the available field names for the report. There should be two fields: Name and Email Address. Drag and drop the field names into the list box. The layout of the report should be similar to that shown in Figure 12-6:

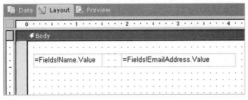

Figure 12-6

Now, select the Preview tab to view the results of your work. This should appear as shown in Figure 12-7. This view will depend on the data in the file that you use:

Figure 12-7

Summary

In this section, we have learned about the extensibility options available in SQL Reporting Services and some of the business opportunites created. Microsoft has created a flexible and powerful reporting solution that allows us to modify its behavior by implementing the interfaces required by the particular extension type. This functionality is sure to create a third party market for tools as well as allow the enterprise developer to create custom solutions for the unque needs of their business.

We also discussed the data access methods used by the .NET Framework and specifically how to create a custom data processing extension to work with non-relational data. Our example is very simple and does not stand alone as an application, although it could be easily extended to provide additional functionality, such as support for variable numbers of fields and field names. The primary purpose of the example in this chapter was to familiarize the reader with the requirements for creating and installing an extension. This type of extension was chosen because it is used on the server for report processing and on the developer machine for report creation.

Deployment Strategies

It might seem that placing all the chapters about how to use Reporting Services before information on how to design a solution and deploy it is a bit like putting the cart before the horse. We believe that this work should first provide you with details and training on what Reporting Services can do and how it can be accomplished. This should have revealed some horizons to you about what you might be able to accomplish with this tool. Now with all the knowledge and skills you have acquired, we would like to provide some direction for your solution and how to deploy it.

We will be reviewing some information that has already been presented so that we can build on that. By the time we finish you should have sufficient information to deploy a solution in a variety of scenarios.

Architecture Review

In the following section, we will review the different architectural components of Reporting Services. Understanding the different components will help you understand how those components can be deployed. Let's start by reviewing each of the major functional areas of Reporting Services: the Report Server and Report Server database. The section will finish with a look at three different deployment scenarios: small, medium/large, and enterprise. You should be able to identify the appropriate deployment scenario for your organization.

Reporting Services Components

Before we cover deployment, you need to take a look at each of the components of Reporting Services. Each component needs to be considered when deploying Reporting Services. The components to consider can be grouped into three categories:

❑   Interfaces to Reporting Services

❑   Report Server

❏   Report Server database

The interfaces you will look at include Report Manager and client applications. Both will use the Reporting Services Web Service to communicate with Reporting Services. With these items you will need to think about IIS deployment along with application authentication.

Deployment of the Report Server will affect processing of reports, scheduled execution, and connection by clients. Here you will look at the major functions of Report Server and how they can be scaled out and up to handle larger volumes of data.

Finally, you'll look at the Report Server database. All metadata for Reporting Services is stored in two SQL databases. Our major considerations here are how the Report Server connects to these two databases and how these databases can be scaled.

Report Manager

Report Manager is the primary tool for managing and configuring reports. You could break Report Manager into three main areas:

❏   Report organization

❏   Report management

❏   Site management

Report Organization

It is the ability to logically group reports into a hierarchical structure. Through the use of folders, Reporting Services users can organize reports based on their business requirements. Report folders give you the ability to set properties such as description and security. Careful consideration should be given to the logical organization of reports before starting with Reporting Services. Proper organization will ensure that users can easily navigate folders to find reports as well as assist in setting up secure access to data.

Report Management

As the name implies, report management allows you to manage individual reports. You can set descriptions of reports, manage parameter default values and prompts, manage report data sources, set executions properties, view report history, and set security on individual items. All of these areas are crucial to successfully managing Reporting Services.

Site Management

The final area of report management is site management. From Report Manager, you can set various site properties as well as define site-level and item-level security roles. Site management really has to do mainly with managing the Report Server itself. You can set information such as report execution timeouts, shared schedules, and whether or not to enable logging. Some of these items can also be set through Reporting Services configuration files that will be covered in the *Server Configuration Files* section later in this chapter.

Security is a major issue for any system. Reporting Services implements a *role-based* security model. This model can be applied to both individual items such as reports and folders as well as the Report Manager site. Through Report Manager, system administrators can define site-level and item-level roles and manage existing roles.

In order to prevent system lockouts, Reporting Services does not allow the BUILTIN\Administrator group to be removed from the system administrator role assignment. This means that any member of BUILTIN\Administrators group will have the ability to change their security settings on individual reports. This should be taken into consideration when deciding which server to deploy Reporting Services to.

> *Report Manager is an ASP.NET application built on top of the Reporting Services Web Service. Why is this important? Well, anything that Microsoft has done in the Report Manager, you can do in your own code. If you don't like the management interface or simply want to build enhancements, you can do that by calling the web service.*

Clients

The final components you'll look at in the architecture are Reporting Services clients. They are divided into two categories:

- ❑   Report Designer
- ❑   Report Consumer

Each component will need to interact with Reporting Services and be considered in your final deployment.

Report Designer

A Report Designer is any application that needs to publish report definitions to Reporting Services. You will need to use Microsoft's Designer in Visual Studio .NET for this discussion, although the same principles would apply to any third party design tool.

Through the Reporting Services Web Service, designers can publish *Report Definition Language* (RDL) files. This process reads the report definition and stores it in the Report Server database. When deploying Reporting Services, you must ensure that report design tools are able to connect to the Reporting Services Web Service.

Report Consumer

Report Consumers can come in just about any form. They could be ASP.NET web applications, Windows Forms applications, or just about anything that can consume web services. For this reason, it is much more difficult to generalize how every consumer will connect to Reporting Services.

The key point to remember is that the application must communicate with Reporting Services through the Reporting Services Web Service. For this reason, you will need a valid HTTP connection to the Report Server. You will also need to pass the user's credentials to the Report Server. Depending on your application's design, this could come in numerous forms.

Consider a Report Consumer deployed over the Internet versus an Intranet. If you deploy your consumer over the Internet, you will have to find some way to pass authentication to Reporting Services. This could come through basic authentication over SSL, ASP.NET Forms authentication, or your own custom security model. You will need to consider any consumer deployment of this type when configuring Reporting Services.

Reporting Services Web Service

The Reporting Services Web Service is the main entry point into Reporting Services. Microsoft has taken all of the API calls for Reporting Services and created a platform independent interface using web services. The Reporting Services Web Service relies on the .NET Framework and IIS for implementation. When you install Reporting Services, you will be required to have both of these components.

Because the interface to Reporting Services is hosted in IIS, you can take advantage of a number of its features. To scale applications, you have one of the two options:

- ❑   Scale up
- ❑   Scale out

Scale Up

Scaling up requires adding additional powerful hardware to an existing server to increase output. This can be very handy for small deployments and is often a less expensive approach. Purchasing hardware can be cheaper than most software licenses.

Scale Out

Scaling out, on the other hand, means adding additional servers and then allowing them to work together to increase output. This option is the most robust but often requires additional software licenses. Deployment of Reporting Services in a web farm configuration will be outlined later in the chapter.

The Reporting Services Web Service handles all communication with the Reporting Server. It allows for cross-platform independence and gives us a deployment option that both scales up and scales out.

Report Server

The Report Server is the key component of Reporting Services. The Report Server component is responsible for handling report processing, which includes data processing and rendering along with handling security authorization, scheduled report execution, and delivery.

Report Server Databases

To perform all of its operations, Reporting Services must have a store for the services metadata. This includes things such as user role assignments, report definitions and the Report Server's folder hierarchy.

Microsoft has decided to store this metadata in Microsoft SQL Server. SQL Server is a robust and well-established relational database management system (RDBMS). Storing data in SQL Server allows Reporting Services to take advantage of features such as transaction logging, data page caching, and sophisticated backup utilities.

Let's take a look at the two databases used by Reporting Services:

- ❑ `ReportServer`
- ❑ `ReportServerTempDB`

The use of these two databases is crucial to Reporting Services operation. It allows you to physically separate the Report Server and its underlying metadata store.

ReportServer

The `ReportServer` database is the main metadata store for Reporting Services. This database contains all report definitions, data source definitions, schedules, security assignments, snapshots, and snapshot history. In order for Reporting Services to function properly, it must be able to establish a connection to this database.

The `ReportServer` can reside on either the same machine or a different machine than the installation of Reporting Services. This allows administrators to scale SQL Server resources separately from Report Server resources. Later in the chapter, you will see how separating the Report Server from the underlying metadata store can be used in larger deployments.

ReportServerTempDB

The `ReportServerTempDB` database is responsible for storing short-lived metadata such as the user's session cache and cached instances. This database is also crucial to the operation of Reporting Services and is installed on the same SQL Server as the `ReportServer` database.

Because the information in this database is temporary, it is not necessary to perform regular backups. Backup strategies will be discussed later in the chapter.

Reporting Services Components Illustrated

Figure 13-1 is a diagram of the Reporting Services components. When looking at the diagram, you should be aware of the different physical components involved. The two major components include the Report Server and `ReportServer` database. Later in the chapter, you will see how these components can be separated to meet large scale reporting needs.

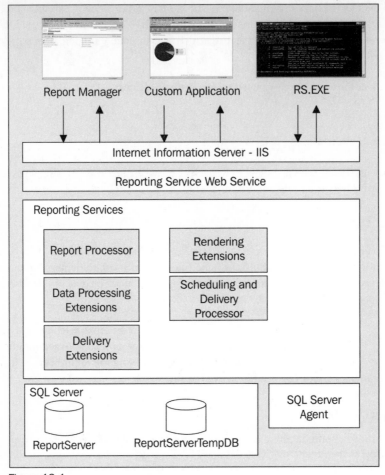

Figure 13-1

Reporting Services Deployment Scenarios

Now that you have reviewed the components of Reporting Services, let's take a look at different deployment scenarios. The deployment scenarios are broken down into different size categories. You will first look at small deployments. These deployments would consist of single-server setups for smaller user groups. Then you will look at medium to large deployments. In this scenario, you'll look at separating the report processing and Report Server *metadata*. Finally, you will go over enterprise size deployments. Here you will see how Reporting Services can be scaled out using multiple web servers to handle report processing.

In this section, we will illustrate how Reporting Services can be scaled out by adding more servers. In certain scenarios, you might want to consider scaling up Reporting Services. By scaling up you are adding additional resources to the current server instead of adding additional servers. This option does not afford as much scalability as additional machines but can save considerable amount of money on licensing and maintenance.

Small Deployment

For a small deployment of Reporting Services, it is acceptable to place both the Report Server and `ReportServer`, database on one machine. This allows you to take advantage of an existing SQL Server license. If a machine already has SQL Server 2000 installed, you can install Reporting Services on that same machine with no additional licensing costs. A single server deployment is most commonly used in departmental type reporting scenarios. This setup can easily support a user base of up to 50 users.

While installing Reporting Services, you need to specify the local SQL Server as the location for the `ReportServer` and `ReportServerTempDB`. This server must be running IIS, SQL Server 2003 (SP3a) and the .NET Framework. The installation will also install the Report Manager application along with the Reporting Services Web Service. You will also need to specify an SMTP server when sending email subscriptions.

Let's take a look at the deployment of Reporting Services on a single server. Figure 13-2 shows the various components of Reporting Services (clients, Report Manager, Reporting Service, and Reporting Service database):

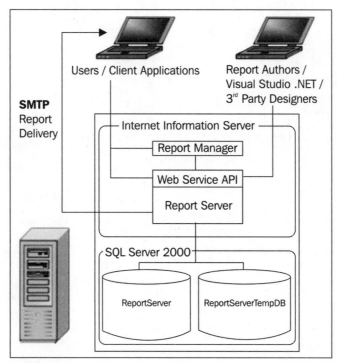

Figure 13-2

Medium/Large Deployment

The next type of deployment scenario you might consider is a medium to large-scale deployment. This deployment would be suitable for supporting the reporting needs of a small organization, or taking advantage of existing SQL Server resources.

In this scenario, Reporting Services is installed on one server containing IIS and the .NET Framework. During the installation, you can point to a remote server to house the `ReportServer` and `ReportServerTempDB` database. The installation server will contain the Report Manager, Report Services Web Service, and Report Server.

The advantage to this architecture is the separation of report processing and metadata processing. Multiple machines allows for allocating different resources for the two separate tasks. There are, however, a couple of disadvantages to this setup. First, there will be increased network traffic between the two servers. Installing additional or gigabit network adapters can overcome some of this. The second disadvantage is licensing; when you install Reporting Services on a separate machine, you will be required to have SQL licenses for both. Be sure to check the Microsoft web site for specific licensing details.

Figure 13-3 illustrates deploying Reporting Services on multiple servers:

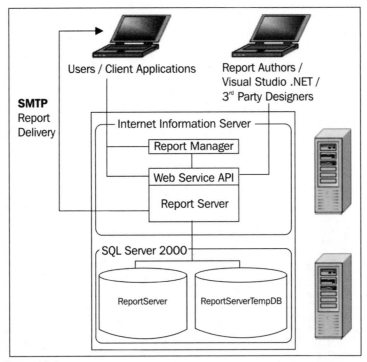

Figure 13-3

Enterprise Deployment

One key feature of Reporting Services is its ability to scale out for an enterprise environment. Its web-based interface along with its integration with SQL Server allow for large-scale deployments.

In an enterprise deployment, you will start out by installing Reporting Services on one server containing IIS and the .NET Framework. During installation, the Report Server database should be installed on a remote SQL Server. For each additional machine, you need to install Reporting Services again and point its database to the shared SQL Server. Once all of the machines have been configured, you can use production scaling and clustering tools such as Microsoft Application Center, to maintain the web farm environment. You can also take advantage of Network Load Balancing to improve the performance of SQL Server.

This scenario takes advantage of available Microsoft technologies as well as multiple machines. The upside is that processing power can now be distributed among numerous machines. However, the setup and maintenance of a web farm environment will take considerably more resources. You will also have to pay additional licensing fees for each installation of SQL Server and Reporting Services.

Figure 13-4 illustrates a web farm deployment with three web servers and two SQL Servers:

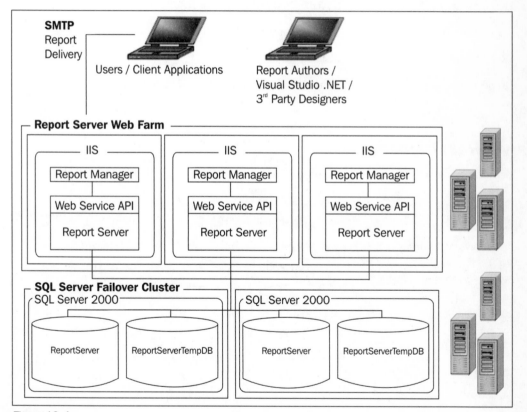

Figure 13-4

System Requirements and Prerequisites

Before deploying Reporting Services, there are some configuration aspects that need to be considered and some key decisions made.

A Report Server installation consists of the following:

❑ A web server that hosts the server-side components, usually Microsoft IIS

❑ An instance of SQL Server to host the database on which Report Services is built

❑ User accounts with the necessary security permissions to create the database on the SQL Server instance that will be hosting the Reporting Services database

❑ An SMTP server that will deliver reports via email

The prerequisites for each of these components are given in the following table. These elements are required for the setup to run successfully.

Component	System Requirements
Report Server	IIS 5.0 or higher web server; ASP.NET
Report Manager	IIS 5.0 or higher web server; ASP.NET
Report Server database	Instance SQL Server 2000 SP3
Report Designer	Workstation with any edition of Visual Studio .NET 2003

Server Requirements

Operating system requirements for the server components are shown in the following table:

Operating System	Operating System-Specific Requirements
Windows 2000 Server with Service Pack 4 (SP4) or later Windows 2000 Advanced Server with SP4 or later Windows 2000 Datacenter Server with SP4 or later	Internet Information Services 5.0 SQL Server 2000a with Service Pack 3a SQL Server Agent
Windows XP Professional with Service Pack 1 or later	Internet Information Services 5.0 SQL Server 2000a with Service Pack 3a SQL Server Agent

Operating System	Operating System-Specific Requirements
Windows Server 2003, Standard Edition Windows Server 2003, Enterprise Edition Windows Server 2003, Datacenter Edition	Computer configured as an application server ASP.NET SQL Server 2000a with Service Pack 3a SQL Server Agent

Prior to running setup, both Report Server and Report Manager require IIS to be installed and running. When running the Reporting Services installation, a number of components will need to be updated for the installation to run correctly. The following components may be updated:

❑ Windows Installer 2.0

❑ Windows .NET Framework version 1.1

❑ Microsoft SQL Server 2000 Reporting Services setup support files

> **Once installed, these components cannot be rolled back or uninstalled.**

By the yard stick of the hardware currently available in the market place today, the hardware requirements for a Report Server installation are very ordinary. Minimum hardware requirements are shown in the following table:

Component	Hardware Requirement
Processor	500 MHz Pentium II – class processor required, 600-MHz Pentium III (or higher) – class processor recommended
Memory	256 MB minimum for server components, 512 MB recommended
Hard Disk	100 MB on the installation drive

It cannot be emphasized enough that these represent minimum requirements. These requirements are adequate for a development environment or even a small installation with a limited number of users. However as the number of users of the system increases, a minimalist system can become bogged down.

In my experience, all of the Windows server operating systems outlined in the earlier table perform better with more memory. "More is always better" may indeed be true when discussing server RAM. As some vendors sell systems based on 2 GHz processors for less than $300 (without monitor), it would make sense for a production system to use a processor substantially more powerful than a 500 MHz.

Licenses

Reporting Services is licensed as a component of SQL Server 2000. A valid SQL Server license is required for each machine on which Reporting Services or any of its components are installed. If your installation uses a web farm to deliver reports, each server in the farm will need a license, even though SQL Server itself may not be installed on these machines.

Report Server Database

All folders, report definitions, data sources, subscriptions, metadata, and so on are stored in a SQL Server relational database. The setup process installs and configures the database on a machine already running an instance of SQL Server 2000. The instance of SQL Server can be on the local machine or a remote instance. Installing multiple instances of Reporting Services on a single server is not supported.

> **The Reporting Services database can only be installed on Developer, Standard, and Enterprise editions of SQL Server 2000. It cannot be installed on the Personal edition (also known as MSDE).**

.NET Framework Requirement

Both Report Server and Report Manager require Microsoft .NET Framework version 1.1. If the .NET Framework version 1.1 is not installed, the setup process for Reporting Services will install it. The setup process will also register ASP.NET in IIS if it has not already been registered.

> **To install Reporting Services on Windows Server 2003 you must manually enable ASP.NET.**

Configuring Windows Server 2003 Application Server

As a security measure, Windows Server 2003 is installed with nearly all services turned off. To configure a Windows Server 2003 machine in preparation for installing Reporting Services, the server must be configured as an IIS application server and have ASP.NET enabled. This is done using the Configure Your Server Wizard or from the Add / Remove Programs tool in the control panel as in Figure 13-5.

To configure the application server using the wizard, start the wizard. If you are shown an information screen, click Next. Select Application server as shown in Figure 13-5 and click Next:

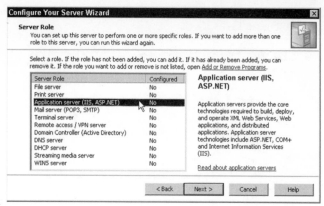

Figure 13-5

On page 2 of the wizard, be sure to check the checkbox marked Enable ASP.NET as shown in Figure 13-6:

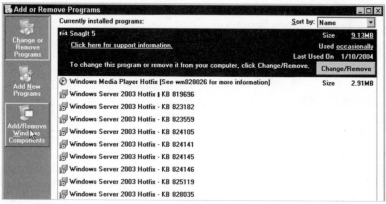

Figure 13-6

If you use the Add / Remove Programs tool in the Control Panel to configure your server, after starting the tool, click on the large button on the left labeled Add/Remove Windows Components as shown in Figure 13-7:

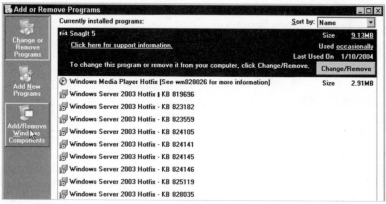

Figure 13-7

The Windows Components Wizard will then be displayed. Check the Application Server checkbox and then click the Details button as in Figure 13-8:

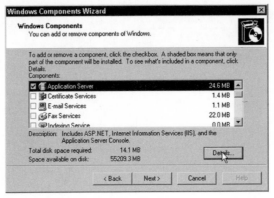

Figure 13-8

Be sure to check the ASP.NET checkbox as in Figure 13-9. Click the OK button to close the Application Server details dialog box. Finally click the Next button on the Windows Components Wizard to perform the setup.

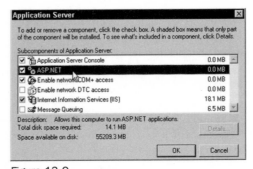

Figure 13-9

After IIS and ASP.NET have been configured, your server is ready to install Reporting Services. The server that is to host the SQL Server database must, of course, have SQL Server installed before the Reporting Services database can be installed.

Client Requirements

Consumers of Reporting Services reports generally view the output and manage the server through a web browser. There are no operating system requirements for users to view published reports. The only requirement is that the client workstation must have a browser that supports HTML 3.2.

Internet Explorer 6.0 with Service Pack 1 is required for client workstations that will access and manage a report server using Report Manager. Additionally, scripting must be enabled when using Report

Manager. To enable scripting, you need to click on Tools in the Internet Explorer window and select Internet Options. Then click on the Security tab and then on the Custom Level button. Scroll down to Scripting settings and enable the Active scripting option.

Report Designer Requirements

The Report Designer will run on any version of the following operating systems as long as all the current service packs have been applied:

- ❑ Windows 2000
- ❑ Windows XP
- ❑ Windows Server 2003

The tool requires Microsoft Visual Studio .NET 2003. Any edition of Visual Studio .NET 2003 can be used for designing reports. However, Visual Studio .NET 2002 cannot be used for designing reports. For developing applications that consume the Reporting Services Web Service, either Visual Studio .NET 2002 or Visual Studio .NET 2003 can be used.

If reports are to be rendered into formats other than HTML, such as PDF or XLS, appropriate software tools (Adobe Acrobat Reader or Excel) will be required for viewing the output.

Accounts and Credentials

While running the Reporting Services setup, a number of pages will prompt you for credentials. Before you run setup, this is a good time to understand what credentials are required and why.

Reporting Services components need credentials for:

- ❑ The `ReportServer` service needs a credential to operate as a Windows Service.
- ❑ The Report Server machine must connect to the Report Server SQL Server database at *runtime,* as this is where all information about any item is stored.
- ❑ A computer being added to a web farm must have credentials to connect to a report server that already exists in a web farm.

Installation

The user running setup on a server must be a member of the Administrators group on the target installation system. One of the first screens encountered during the install asks you to select account under which the Windows service will run.

While running setup, a credential must be provided to the SQL Server that has permissions to:

- ❑ Create the Report Server database
- ❑ Create logins
- ❑ Create roles
- ❑ Assign permissions to users

This set of installation credentials can use either SQL Server Authentication or Windows Authentication. If it is undesirable for the user running setup to use their own credentials, then the command line setup utility should be used where alternative credentials can be entered.

As all these credentials can be a bit confusing, so let's spend some time on the details of these accounts in the installation walkthrough.

Ongoing Operations

For operating Reporting Services after installation has completed successfully, the Report Server will need to be in the database owner role for the `ReportServer` database and have local system administrator privileges to start the Report Server Windows service. This account can be a local system account or a Windows domain account. While using a local account, remember that the account must be a member of the local system administrators group.

Installation and Configuration

By far the easiest method of installing Reporting Services is to use the GUI setup program. The setup program includes a wizard for specifying installation options. Setup prompts for login credentials, virtual directory names, and other information depending on the components selected for installation.

All components are installed locally with the exception of the `ReportServer` database. The database can be installed either on a local or remote SQL Server instance. The installation can install all components or specific components selected at the start of the process. By far the simplest installation is to install all the components on a single system.

It is also possible to install Reporting Services from a command prompt. For devout adherents to the command line interface, refer to the setup help file. The help file also provides a great deal of detail on using the wizard and the choices that need to be made during the installation.

Running Setup

Before running setup, an important item should be checked. The *Distributed Transaction Coordinator* (*DTC*) service is required for setup to complete successfully. Before running setup, use the Services tool in the Control Panel to make sure that the service is installed and that its Startup type is set to Automatic or Manual. Setup will fail if the DTC service is disabled.

Let's go through the setup wizard in detail. Start the installation process by double clicking on `setup.exe` or by inserting the product CD into your CD drive and selecting the option to install Reporting Services. After you agree to the license for the product some support files will be installed on your machine to allow setup to run. If you cancel or abort the setup process the support files will not be uninstalled. Once the support files have been installed successfully click the Next button.

The next step is to evaluate your system and make sure that the prerequisites are installed. These are things like .NET Framework 1.1 and ASP.NET; the process will also look for the existence of Visual Studio .NET 2003 to determine if the design tools can be installed on your machine. Once your machine has passed the prerequisites check, click the Next button.

You now finally come to the start screen for the install wizard. Click the Next button. Fill out the registration information so you can get to where you actually have to make some decisions as in Figure 13-10:

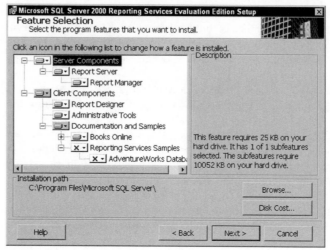

Figure 13-10

This is the screen where you indicate which parts of Reporting Services you want to have installed on the target machine. If the prerequisite check found that Visual Studio .NET 2003 is installed on your machine, then the option to install the Report Designer will be shown. Otherwise this screen will give the option to install the server components, administrative tools, and documentation. For your walkthrough, it does not matter if you choose to install the Report Designer. You will be focusing on the server component installation.

The samples and the AdventureWorks database are good tools to explore the capabilities of Reporting Services. However, some database administrators view sample or demonstration databases on a production server as a potential security problem. Installation of these samples will likely depend on your security policies and the intended use of this Reporting Services installation.

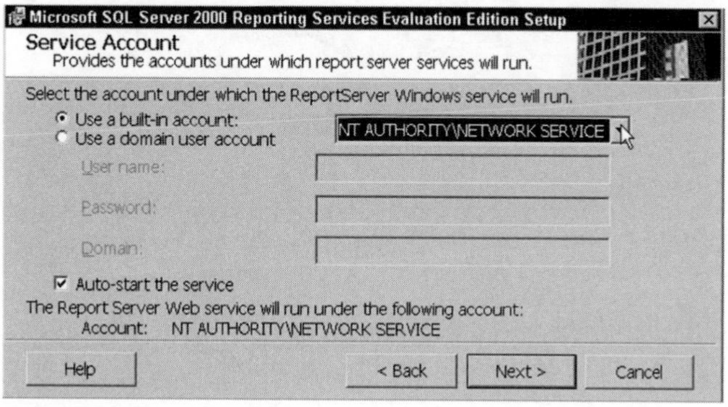

Figure 13-11

This page of the wizard, as shown in Figure 13-11, determines under which account the Windows service will run. The choices are for a built-in system account or a Windows domain account. Under most circumstances, you will want to run the service using a built-in account. For Windows 2000 and XP, this will be the local system account. For Windows Server, you have the choice of using the local system account or the NT AUTHORITY\NETWORK SERVICE account. If you choose to use a domain user account to run the service, make sure that the account has permissions to logon as a service. It is recommended that you use the local system account for Windows 2000 and XP and that the NETWORK SERVICE account be used for Windows Server 2003. The Auto-start the service check box should be checked.

The names of the virtual directories are not important, but they can be specified to be something different from the default values. The two checkboxes on the form are of some interest.

If you are setting up a server the primary function of which will be to deliver Reporting Services reports, you may want to make the default web page for the server be the local Report Manager virtual directory. To do this, check the box labeled Redirect the default Web site. This will cause the Report Manager application to come up by using only the machine name in the URL of a browser.

If you are setting up Reporting Services to be exposed to the Internet you may want to use *Secure Sockets Layer (SSL)* connections to the web service and Report Manager. This will ensure that any information sent over the Internet to the server will be encrypted for security as in Figure 13-12:

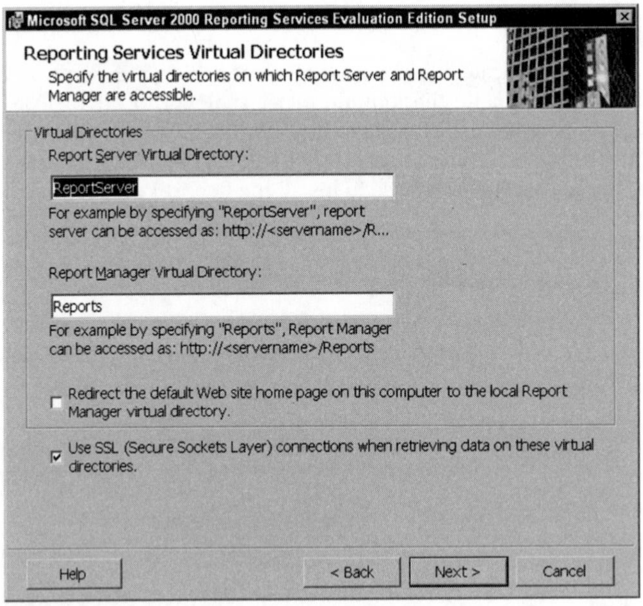

Figure 13-12

You then come to the database settings as shown in Figure 13-13. The settings on this page determine whether the configuration will be on a single server or multiple servers as part of the configuration.

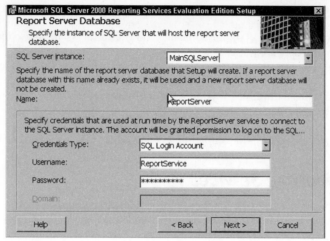

Figure 13-13

SQL Server Instance

If SQL Server has already been installed on the machine the default value here will be the name of the default SQL Server instance on your machine. If SQL Server has not been installed on the machine, you will need to give the name of a SQL Server instance on another machine. Choosing an instance on a different machine is necessary if you want keep the web service and the database separate or if you want to install the service on a web farm.

Database Name

The default name of the database is ReportServer, however, any valid SQL Server database name can be used. The name chosen for the database must be unique on the server where the database is to be installed.

Database Credential

For this credential, you can specify a Windows domain account, a SQL Server login, or a service account. Any of the three account types can be used, but some thought and care should go into the selection of the account. The credential specified must have permission to create the database if it does not exist. If you are using an existing database on a different server, this account must have database owner permission to the ReportServer and ReportServerTempDB databases. If your SQL Server 2000 database server is a Windows Server 2003 machine, Reporting Services must use SQL Server authentication to connect to the ReportServer database. If Windows authentication is used for a Windows Server 2003 database server, schedules and subscriptions will fail with an internal error (rsInternalError).

Finishing the Setup

The next step is to specify the email server name and the From address to be used for reports that are sent to users via email. These are less critical to the operation of Reporting Services except when it comes to the *push* delivery of reports. Be sure to use a valid server and address. The last step before the process actually starts is to specify the license model and number of licenses. This is identical to SQL Server licensing and in fact is just a duplicate of your SQL Server license. You should use the same license model as your database server.

With any luck, the process will run to completion and announce that it was successful.

Scaling Up Reporting Services

To configure a multi-server Reporting Services environment or an enterprise-size web farm of Report Servers, the same setup procedure is used. The only difference comes at the database configuration page. If you enter the name of a SQL Server instance that is not on the local machine, the wizard page immediately after the database setup will be shown as in Figure 13-14:

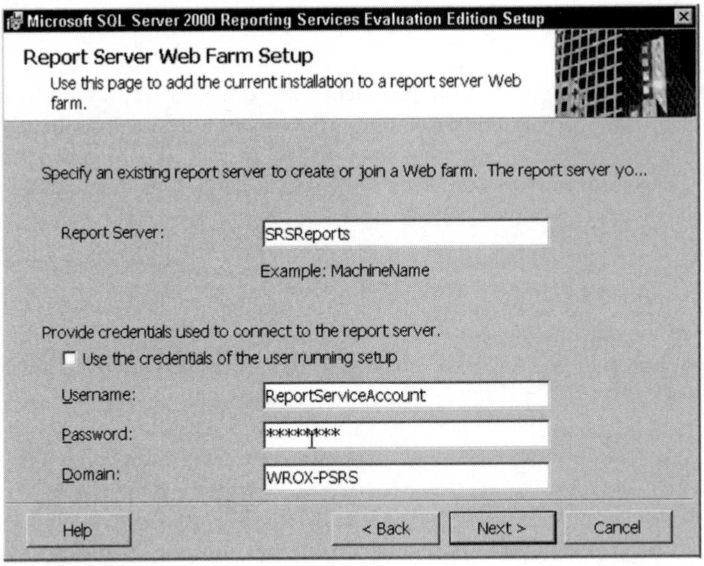

Figure 13-14

This page is used for all of the scaled up installations that separate the web server from the database server.

Report Server

The name of a computer in a Windows domain must be specified here. If this is the first server that will be running the web service only, you should enter the name of the machine on which you are running the setup program. If you have already installed a report server and want to add another server to the farm, then you should specify the name of a server that already is a member of the farm. All the computers that make up a web farm must be in the same domain or in a trusted domain.

Credentials

The credential must be a Windows domain account with permission to administer the Report Server on the web farm. This account should be a member of local administrators group on the machines in the farm. This is simplified greatly if the account is a member of the domain administrators group.

> *Carefully choose the account you want to use here. This credential is not saved; it is only used for the installation process. If you select an account with insufficient permissions, the process will fail.*

Server Configuration Files

Reporting Services installs the following files that contain configuration settings for the Report Server Web Service, Report Manager Web application, Reporting Services service, and Report Designer at the locations described in the following table:

Configuration File	Default Install Location
RSReportServer.config	Program Files\Microsoft SQL Server\MSSQL\Reporting Services\ReportServer
RSWebApplication.config	Program Files\Microsoft SQL Server\MSSQL\Reporting Services\ReportManager
ReportingServicesService.exe.config	Program Files\Microsoft SQL Server\MSSQL\Reporting Services\ReportServer\bin
RSReportDesigner.config	Program Files\Microsoft SQL Server\80\Tools\Report Designer

The .config files are XML files that can be edited with any XML editor. They are contained in the physical directories where the web application and the web service are installed. The most interesting of the files is RSReportServer.config.

RSReportServer.config contains information such as data connection strings, which are encrypted for security reasons, values for SQL Server Agent jobs, and extensions that contains properties to control the Report Server.

Extension	Properties
Data processing extension	Child elements in the `Data` element
Rendering extension	Child elements in the `Render` element
Delivery extension	Child elements in the `Delivery` element
Delivery UI extension	Child elements in the `Delivery` UI element
Event processing extension	Child elements in the `EventProcessing` element

These extensions can be modified and customized by programming the web service. The detailed format of the `RSReportServer.config` file is detailed in Books Online.

The other configuration files take care of the other areas of Reporting Services. `RSWebApplication.config` contains settings for the Report Manager interface. `ReportingServicesService.exe.config` has information pertaining to the Reporting Services Windows services. Most importantly, this file contains information for configuring the level of tracing performed by the service. The final configuration file, `RSReportDesigner.config`, contains settings that are used by Visual Studio .NET. These settings are similar to those found in `RSReportServer.config`. In the next section, you'll look at working with the `RSReportServer.config` file.

Configuring Using the Command Line Utility

Since `RSReportServer.config` is an XML file, it can be edited by any text editor. However, the data connection information is encrypted for security reasons. In order to modify encrypted information, a command line tool, rsconfig, which comes with Reporting Services must be used. If the database connection information for the web service must be modified, Reporting Services could be uninstalled and re-installed. However using `rs.config` to change the connection information is a much faster and less complicated solution.

The syntax for `rs.config` is as follows:

```
rsconfig -s YourSQLServer -m YourComputerName -d ReportServerDatabaseName -a SQL
-u YourUserName -p YourPassword
```

The parameters for `rs.config` are as follows:

❑   -m computername: The name of the computer on which the report server is installed. This is optional unless you are managing a remote computer.

❑   -s servername: The name of the SQL Server instance on which the Report Server database is installed. Optional if the instance is on a local computer. The *default* value is the default SQL Server instance installed on the computer that is specified by the computername argument.

❑   -d databasename: The name of the Report Server database.

❑ `-a authorization method`: Allowable values are `windows` or `sql`. Use `windows` to specify that the Report Server should use Windows credentials when connecting to the Report Server database. Use `sql` to specify that the report server should use SQL Server credentials when connecting to the Report Server database.

❑ `-u [domain\]username`: Specifies a user name. The value is case sensitive if you are using Windows Authentication.

❑ `-p password`: Specifies the password to use with the `username` argument. You can set this argument to a blank value if the account does not require a password.

A more detailed explanation of the parameters for `rsconfig.exe` is found in Books Online.

Administrative Issues

In this section, you will take a look at common administrative issues in Reporting Services. Let's start by identifying disk space requirements for the Report Server database. Then we can move on to backup and restore of the Report Server database along with the Report Server encryption key. You'll look at security administration and demonstrate some of the common security tasks. Finally, you'll look at performance monitoring and administration of Reporting Services log files.

Database Space Requirements

There is no set formula for calculating how much disk space Reporting Services will consume. However, you will learn those factors that will significantly increase disk space along with the database tables that should be monitored closely.

To understand how Reporting Services consumes disk space, you have to look back at some concepts demonstrated earlier in the book. The major area you need to consider is *report caching*. When Reporting Services caches reports, it caches both the report definition and data. This is why it is difficult to definitively state how much disk space Reporting Services will consume. It is partly based on the number of reports that are cached and the size of data returned in those reports. Following is a list of factors that will contribute to increased disk space:

❑ Total number of reports
❑ Total number of active sessions
❑ Number of report cached instances
❑ Length of time reports are cached
❑ Total number of report snapshots
❑ Total number of report snapshots in history
❑ Amount of report data returned in individual reports

All of these factors will have a considerable impact on the size of the Report Server database. To monitor this size, there are a couple of key tables to monitor. First, you should watch the size of the `Catalog` table in the `ReportServer` database. This table contains all report definitions. The more the report definitions, the larger the size of this table.

The second and most important table to monitor is the ChunkData table. You will find this table in both the ReportServer and ReportServerTempDB databases. In the ReportServer database, the ChunkData table contains all report snapshots. So, the number of report snapshots along with the size of data in the snapshots will affect this table. The ChunkData table in the ReportServerTempDB contains all temporary cache information. This includes individual session cache data and report cached instances. The size of this table will increase with more active connections and long expire times on cached instances. You can monitor the size of these tables through the task pad in SQL Server Enterprise Manager.

Backup and Restore

The key effectively manage to any system is to take proper backup of application data. There are two items that need to be backed up to ensure proper disaster recovery of Reporting Services. First you will look at the backup of the ReportServer database. Then we will discuss how Reporting Services uses encryption keys and why these keys need to be backed up.

Report Server Database Backup

We have discussed in this chapter that the metadata store for Reporting Services lies in Microsoft SQL Server. The backup utilities in SQL Server can be used to backup both the ReportServer and ReportServerTempDB database. However, it is not necessary to backup both databases.

Again, you need to recognize what data is stored in each of the two Report Server databases. The ReportServer database contains crucial information that must be backed up. It contains all of the report definitions, security role assignments, and report snapshots. ReportServerTempDB is less crucial to backup. It contains temporary information such as session caches and cached instances. If the database were to fail, the information in ReportServerTempDB would be restored as soon as operations began again. However, if you had set up a specific schedule that populated cached instances, such as scheduling delivery to the *null* provider, you would want to back this database up.

Encryption Key Backup

There are a number of items stored securely in each Report Server instance. This includes connection information, credentials, and server accounts. This information is encrypted using an encryption key that is created when Reporting Services is installed. There are a number of scenarios where you might need to reinstall Reporting Services. If you reinstall Reporting Services, you will need to also restore this encryption key. If it is not restored, data stored in the ReportServer database will not be property retrieved.

After Reporting Services is installed, you should backup the encryption key. Microsoft has supplied a utility called rskeymgmt that will copy the encryption key to the file system. This utility will also allow you to remove any encrypted information in case your encryption key cannot be restored.

To backup the encryption key, you will have to use the following command line switches:

- ❑ -e: Does not take a value and tells the utility to extract the encryption key
- ❑ -f: Specifies where on the file system to store the encryption key
- ❑ –p: Specifies a password to be associated with the key file

This password will be needed later when restoring the encryption key file. Let's take a quick look at backing up the Report Server key. See Figure 13-15:

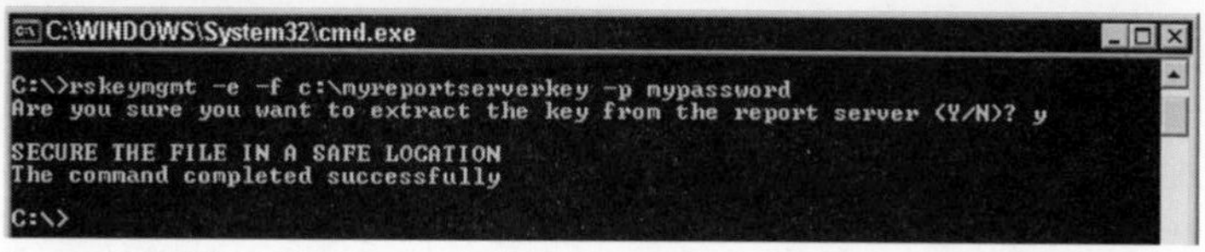

Figure 13-15

You can see that the encryption key has been backed up to the file system. This file can then be moved to another media for safe storage.

To restore the encryption key, you will use the rs.keymgmt utility. With the restore, you will use the -f and -p switch as shown earlier, but instead of specifying the extract key, here you will specify the -a (apply) key. Figure 13-16 shows a screenshot of restoring the encryption key:

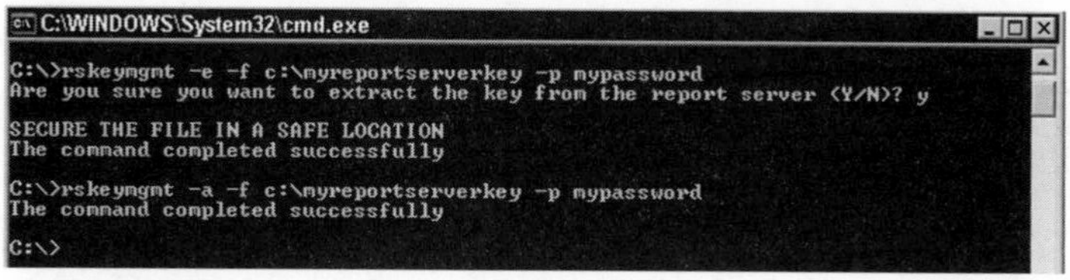

Figure 13-16

> If you use the rs.keymgmt utility to restore your encryption key, you will have to reactivate the instance of Report Server.

Use the following command line to reactivate a local copy of report server:

```
rsactivate -c "C:\Program Files\Microsoft SQL Server\MSSQL\Reporting
Services\ReportServer\RSReportServer.config" -r
```

Security Administration

Reporting Services uses a role-based security model. This model combines Windows NT users and groups and Reporting Services roles to set security on a securable object. In this section, you will look at the different types of securable objects, the predefined roles for each, and creating role assignments.

In Reporting Services, there are two different types of securable objects:

❑   Report Server site

❑   Report Server items

Report Server Site

When defining roles for the Report Server site, you are defining how users can work with and administer Reporting Services. Report Server items are the folders, data sources, connections, and reports contained within a Report Server instance. Let's take a look at the roles that can be defined for each.

For each securable object type, there is a certain set of tasks that can be defined. Role definitions are used to represent a set of tasks that can be performed. Once a role definition has been created, it is associated with a securable object and a Windows NT user or group to create a role assignment. Let's walk through creating a role assignment for the Home folder.

Report Server Items

First, navigate to the properties of your Home folder using Report Manager. Enter the following URL into your browser:

http://localhost/Reports/Pages/Folder.aspx?SelectedTabId=PropertiesTab

You can view the properties as shown in Figure 13-17:

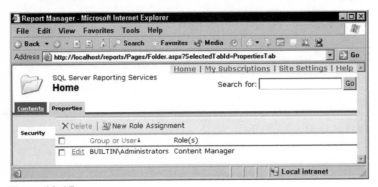

Figure 13-17

You can see on the Home folder that there is one role assignment defined for the BUILTIN\Administrators group. The role assigned is Content Manager. So, this is an associate between the Home folder (securable object), BUILTIN\Administrators group (user/group), and Content Manager (role definition). Now let's add a new role assignment for the guest account. You need the guest account to have browse permissions on the Home folder. Click the New Role Assignment button to create the association.

Here enter the group you would like to give permissions to, Guests, and the role to associate them with, Browser. Clicking OK will create the role assignment as shown in Figure 13-18:

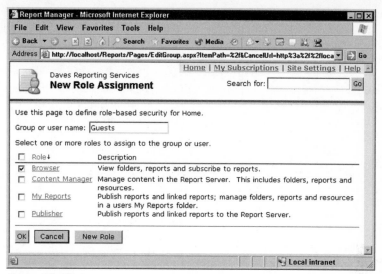

Figure 13-18

You can see that you have defined two role assignments for the Home folder as in Figure 13-19:

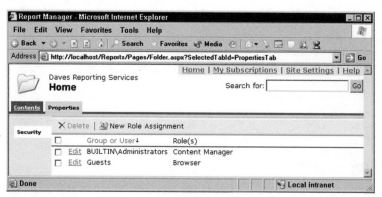

Figure 13-19

The key to remember here is the relationship between a securable object, role definition, and Windows user/group. The combination of these three items creates a role assignment and sets permissions in Reporting Services.

Server Monitoring

Microsoft Reporting Services also comes equipped with a couple of server monitoring options. The first option is log files. Log files capture information such as events sent to the application log, exceptions from Reporting Services, and SOAP messages sent to and from the server. The second server monitoring option is *Windows Performance Counters*. Reporting Services provides over 30 performance counters including the number of active sessions, number of report executions, and cache hit ratios. These options allow you to troubleshoot problems as well as monitor current resource utilization. Let's look in detail at each monitoring option.

There are three main log files used by Reporting Services. The log files can be found under the SQL Server install directory at `<Instance (Default MSSQL)>\Reporting Services\Log Files`. In this folder, you will find trace log files that are created daily. The description of each of the three log files is as follows:

Log File	Description
`ReportServerService_<timestamp>.log`	This log contains information about the Reporting Service service.
`ReportServerWebApp_<timestamp>.log`	This log contains information for the Report Manager Web application.
`ReportServer_<timestamp>.log`	This log contains information for the Report Server processing engine.

There are numerous counters that can be viewed using Windows Performance Monitor. A few of the main counters include Active Sessions, Report Requests, Total Reports Executed, and Total Requests. There are also a number of counters that can be used to monitor report cache information. Using these counters can help pinpoint bottlenecks in Reporting Services.

You can manage the amount of information that is stored in the trace logs through the `ReportingServicesService.exe.config` configuration file. However, the logs files are not deleted. You should make sure that you monitor the log files directory and remove files as appropriate.

Execution Log

You can also monitor Reporting Services through the Reporting Services Execution log. When reports are executed, log entries are stored in the `ReportServer` database's `ExecutionLog` table. This table includes information about which report is executed, the duration of execution and other metrics that can be used to monitor performance. By default, Reporting Services maintains these entries for 60 days. You can change this value through the Report Manager. To do this, go to the following link:

http://localhost/Reports/Pages/Settings.aspx

This opens Reporting Services **Site Settings** as shown in Figure 13-20:

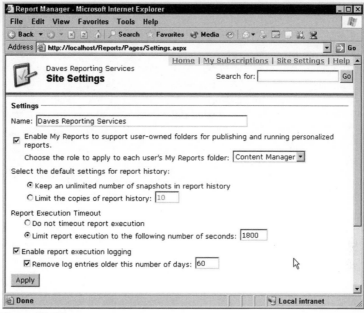

Figure 13-20

Notice that at the bottom of the screen you can specify when to remove log entries along with turning on and off execution logging.

Summary

In this chapter you have reviewed architecture, discussed installation planning, performed an installation, and discussed administering a Reporting Services solution. This chapter should serve as a foundation upon which you can build your level of skill with the product. A more detailed explanation of the features is available through BOL that is included with Reporting Services. It is a good tool for further investigation of the product.

This foundation will be sufficient to get you started in a productive installation.

14

Designing
Business Intelligence
Reporting Solutions

It's time to change our vantage point once again. Now that you understand the many capabilities of SQL Server Reporting Services, let us discuss how to apply these features to solve real problems. We will take a look at some of the high-level business drivers, challenges, and the climate of Business Intelligence (BI).

The objective of this chapter is not to give you all the details necessary to create an entire solution but to discuss the considerations and high-level objectives for a complete BI or reporting solution. We will show you some example solutions and discuss their components. It is said that you can give a man a fish and feed him for a day but you can *teach* a man to fish and feed him for a lifetime! In this chapter, we will talk about *why…* and *how* to fish.

Business decision-makers face many of the same questions now as in decades past. How to increase revenue, identify and increase the profitability of key customers, and recognize market trends are familiar questions to leaders and managers at all levels within a business organization. One of the largest differences between today's decision-makers and those of twenty years ago is that today's manager must be faster and more informed.

Even the process of identifying a company's most valuable customers can involve analyzing data from multiple data sources and customer touch-points. For example, the information of a single customer can be located in sales and marketing data stores, a web application database, and in satellite offices closer to the customer's geographical location. Capturing the data to get an aggregate view, enabling you to identify your most profitable customers is one example of how businesses can increase performance through BI. The goal is being an agile company that's able to compete more effectively in the marketplace, ultimately increasing profitability and reducing costs while responding to changing market conditions with both speed and precision.

In this chapter, you'll read about recommended approaches to BI solution design, as well as see how two companies implement Reporting Services solutions in their own environments. The chapter concludes with tips for enterprise development and an overall summary of how to approach your next Reporting Services solution.

Approaching Solution Design

Reporting solutions often exhibit the kind of behavior seen in company web applications; they tend to start small, and increase in size and complexity quickly. Allowing for this growth while maintaining usability and manageability can be a significant challenge.

Define the Business Problem

Using the term *solution* suggests that something needs to be fixed. The natural conclusion of this line of reasoning is that a problem exists! The fact is that not all business solutions are necessarily a fix for something broken, however, a solution must have a clear purpose. The *problem* might simply be that we recognize an opportunity that we would like to pursue. If our information tells us that customers will need a product or service, the problem might be that we aren't currently selling that product or the service. Whatever the case, the business need, opportunity or problem must drive the solution.

Business solutions are remedies for business problems. It's often easy to lose sight of this fundamental truth as programmers and other technical professionals immerse themselves in designing applications. Every element of the system must be designed for this purpose. From the login dialog to the browse lists and reports—every feature exists for the sole purpose of meeting a stated business need and solving a business problem. Business intelligence tools support the goal that business decision makers are informed and empowered through visibility to important information.

Performance Gaps

A performance gap is a problem that stems for the inability to perform optimally. This might be a measure of response time, profitability, quality, or the low-level of customer satisfaction. Performance gaps must be in the form of measurable and quantifiable values.

Missed Opportunity Costs

Lost or missed opportunity costs can be difficult to quantify because the desired goal has not yet been attained. It's imperative to fully understand and define the conditions and implications of seizing an opportunity. The perceived goal must be clearly defined in terms or values that are both measurable and specific enough to define. Setting goals such as *improving performance* and *increasing production* are too ambiguous to either recognize or measure an acceptable degree of success.

Consider the classic case of the small, home-based, thriving business that grows and expands to the small office. Suddenly the one-guy-company entrepreneur must contend with factors like rent, payroll and labor laws (did I mention corporate taxes?). This scenario has stifled the energy of countless small business owners. Moving from the small, one-person business to the moderate-sized office business might open doors of opportunity, but this comes at an increased cost and management overhead. Having visibility to lost opportunities, as well as our capacity to accommodate such opportunities, can help business grow at the right time and in the right way.

Another significant factor to consider in business is the cost of not seizing an opportunity. Often the current state of business simply cannot be maintained. Take, for example, the thousands of businesses over the past decade that were doing just fine selling their products exclusively through retail stores. Some competitors recognized the opportunity to go on-line and sell offer products on the World Wide Web. Since that time, markets have undergone drastic changes and latecomers have been forced to do the same out of sheer survival.

Current State/Future State

Before we can understand where we are going, we have to understand where we are. In order to accurately describe the intended state of a solution, it's important to fully understand the current conditions and environment. Many times, replacing a system or implementing a new tool can introduce new elements into an environment that can cause additional problems or affect other elements. The better we can understand the current state, the better we may be able to define the desired future state of the solution.

Business Goals and Objectives

Possibly one of the greatest challenges in developing a new solution is to fully understand its purpose. It's easy to lose sight of the bigger picture. Users, customers, IT professionals, and business executives have different goals and relatively different perspectives and requirements. No one perspective is necessarily more important than the other (unless one is paying our salary, their needs are far more important than those any others!).

What should ideally drive a business solution is, well, the business. The needs of the business keep it alive. A healthy business is founded on goals and objectives that serve its customers, employees, and shareholders. So, naturally, the ultimate purpose for a business solution is to meet the needs of the business and everyone who makes the business work. This may sound a bit idealistic but it's a fundamental principle that is all too often realized too late after expensive IT projects fail.

Direction

I just can't talk about IT project goals without telling one of my favorite stories.

Long ago, in the medieval times, a small kingdom had suffered many attacks from surrounding enemies. The king sent out his knights, charged to strengthen his armies. A certain valiant knight rode into a small, fortressed village in the kingdom. He looked up at the wooden fortress wall outside of the village and noticed dozens of arrows that had been shot into the wall from the same direction. Each arrow was shot directly into the bull's-eye of one of several different targets painted on the wall.

Figure 14-1

The knight asked a man passing by where the arrows had originated. The man told him that they were shot into the wall from the vicinity of a small cottage, on the edge of the woods, across a large field from the village wall. The knight was impressed and wanted to meet the person responsible for such an impressive feat. He rode his steed across the field to the cottage and dismounted.

The knight knocked on the cottage door. A young boy of about fourteen years old opened the front door and was startled to see, standing in his doorway, this towering knight in his armor, shield and sword. The knight sternly spoke to the boy and asked to speak with the person responsible for the arrows in the fortress wall. The boy sheepishly replied that he had done it and wanted to know if there would be a punishment. The knight chuckled and told the boy he was impressed with his skill and wanted to see a demonstration.

The boy quickly disappeared and zealously returned with his hand-carved bow and quiver full of arrows. He nervously fumbled through the arrows and pulled the straightest arrow he could find from the quiver. The boy excitedly explained that archery was his passion and that he lived for the bow. He spent long hours practicing daily. Together they stood on the front porch as the boy drew back the arrow and let it sail across the field in the direction of the fortress wall.

The knight and the boy walked together across the field to find the arrow and when they reached the wall, the knight searched through all of the arrows, looking for the one that had most recently been thrust into the wood. The knight didn't notice that the boy scrambled away and then quickly returned while he was searching for the arrow. It didn't take the knight long to find the new arrow because it was nowhere near a target. As the knight turned to the boy with a puzzled look (although the boy had run away and returned), he was standing in the same place. The young man looked at the knight with a big grin on his face—and a bucket of paint in his hands—that he used to paint a target around the arrow..

This is the standard operating procedure for many IT project teams. We reason that as long as we have a general direction it ought to be good enough. However, the larger the project and the greater the impact it will have on a business, the more important it is to define its scope and specific purpose. It is no longer feasible to sketch out a rough project plan and then fill-in the gaps and details as the project progresses—bolting on features and appendages here and there. This is what Doctor Frankenstein did with his creation, and unless we would like to have similar results, we shouldn't do that same.

Solution Design

Nearly all business systems share some common attributes. We will briefly discuss these common elements of design and then apply these principles to business intelligence and reporting solutions.

Successful solution design includes effectively addressing many areas within an organization. sales, marketing, operations, manufacturing, and accounting department personnel and applications can all provide data to and consume the data from Reporting Services. Start bringing in BizTalk Server, SharePoint Portal Server, Commerce Server and Content Management Server into the solution mix and you've got a rapidly escalating quantity of data and an equally escalating need to effectively manage it. It's important that your reporting solution help users access the reports they need, rather than making it difficult for them. Good reporting solutions address four key questions:

- ❏ Is it secure?
- ❏ Is it manageable?

❑   Is it available when needed?

❑   Is it scalable?

Reports must be available to users across an organization. Like any critical Web application, a Reporting Services solution must satisfactorily address those questions to remain a viable solution as it matures. Balance is important; an impregnable application that nobody wants to use fails to fulfill its purpose.

Security

Often addressed after the fact, security is a topic that should be addressed early—even as early as the envisioning phase of the solution development process. It's important to implement multiple barriers or layers of defense in your architecture. By having multiple layers of security in place that are configured to work together, you create a defense-in-depth strategy that doesn't rely on any single point in the infrastructure to secure it. When designing such a strategy, it's important to address three key aspects of the solution:

❑   **The network topology and host infrastructure**: This includes the use of firewalls at the perimeter and mechanisms like digital certificates to secure communication.

❑   **The reporting solution architecture and design**: This aspect of the solution includes appropriate error handling (fail securely—and test it to be sure), input validation (never trust user input), and content structure (based on permissions).

❑   **The component-level interactions that are made**: Here, interactions between the logical tiers of the application architecture are examined to ensure that functions such as data access and ASP.NET control processing are performed securely.

During the design phase, document all of the access requirements for your solution, including the Report Server content structure. Define the *Access Control Lists (ACLs)* used to support the security policy. The idea is to be explicit about who has access permission and who doesn't at each point in the system, and configure each element in the structure to support the chosen policies.

In a simple extranet scenario, Figure 14-2 shows the use of a SSL connection between the client and the ISA perimeter firewall, securing communication in transit. IIS is configured to use digital certificates, and handles the task of authenticating users. Web applications are held in a DMZ, which is further removed from the internal domain by another ISA firewall. IPSEC can be used internally, encrypting communication in transit on the network if required. This is an example of breaking the network into manageable sections, and using devices such as routers and firewalls to protect each section.

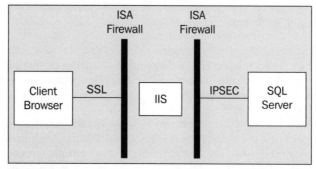

Figure 14-2

A well-known security doctrine says, "Run with just enough privileges to get the job done, and no more." Allowing users or applications more privileges than required for the task exposes unnecessary vulnerabilities and increases the security threat. Reporting Services functionality is exposed as a Web Service, which is fundamentally an ASP.NET application running on IIS. Report Manager is an ASP.NET application that provides a GUI interface to the Web service. Each application server in the overall solution architecture has its own security mechanisms that can be configured to suit requirements. For example, IIS can be configured to authenticate users, or the CLR can handle the task using its own authentication mechanism. To make the most of the capabilities of each element in the solution, you'll want to develop an overall security policy and then configure each element to support the policy. Use the security mechanisms in each application server, so they don't have to rely entirely on the network mechanisms for protection.

Manageability

Manageability refers to the ongoing operations required to keep the infrastructure, technologies, and processes of the solution healthy. Ideally, operations are performed using a pro-active approach rather than being forced to continually respond to whatever the current, urgent need is. The tasks typically associated with system management include:

❑ **Content management**: The Report Server content must grow in a controlled fashion as requirements change and the solution matures.

❑ **System monitoring**: Use performance monitors and logs to spot bottlenecks and flag elements of the system that might not be running at full health.

❑ **Remote server management**: Report Server solutions are frequently deployed to multiple servers at multiple end points. Using code to automate the deployment and management process eases the maintenance workload.

Typically, there's a close relationship between manageability and the other goals you're trying to achieve. Effective management tools and techniques are important to your ability to address the other areas of the solution. For example, regular system monitoring can have a direct impact on application availability. Frequently, decisions made in one area directly affect those made in other areas. For example, the content structure you choose can affect both security and manageability.

Availability

Availability is the ability of the application to recover from component or infrastructure failures. Typically the domain of IT operations, availability includes controlling how changes are made to the system, isolating trouble spots, and implementing fallback policies in the event of a failure. Success in this area requires planning for failure.

As with security, it's important to not rely on any one element in the system. For example, having a single IIS instance to handle incoming HTTP requests means a critical single point failure in the system. Increasing the number of servers creates redundancy in the system so that requests can be serviced even in the event of a failure.

The front end of the system can be made redundant by using cloned, load-balanced servers in a Web farm. Each server has instances of IIS, the Report Service, and Report Manager if that functionality is also required. Availability can be increased yet again by having multiple server farms at alternate end points. For example, the service can be deployed to server farms in multiple cities. Applications that consume the web service content can be written to self-heal themselves if waiting for a response from a service end point times out. Having Microsoft Windows Server 2003 available on your network provides you the ability to do that, because of the Universal Description Discovery and Integration (UDDI) service it provides.

UDDI is a standards-based store of Web service listings. The listing data is communicated to the store using XML and HTTP, using the same mechanisms as regular web services. Each listing contains information about the company exposing the service, a description of the service, and details about the server end-points and protocols. In the event of a web service end point failure, the consuming application can abort the original request and send a request to the UDDI server for a listing of available, identical services. Once the collection of listings is received, the application sends a request to a selected service and the application process continues. Figure 14-3 is a diagram of the resulting interactions:

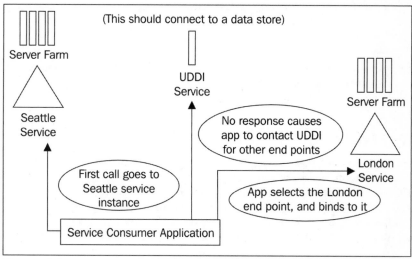

Figure 14-3

The Reporting Services application scales well to different environments. The topology you select will depend on the load you expect, or more specifically, the number of HTTP requests the server will be expected to service. Use performance counters to monitor the CPU usage and number of cache hits as requests are sent to the server. Aim for a high load of 80-85% of CPU capacity, to allow for spikes in usage.

Back-end data stores can also use clustering for fail over protection. Like the front end, back end nodes can be distributed across geographical locations to help ensure availability. In both cases, be sure you have a program in place to manage and stay up-to-date on application updates and patches.

Scalability

Scalability is the ability of the application to handle an increasing user load. Reporting Service is a web application, giving you the ability to use multiple mechanisms to support increasing user loads. Both front-end web servers and back-end application servers can scale. There are two main ways to scale: scaling up and scaling out.

Scaling up involves increasing the capacity of a component in the system. For example, you might scale up the processor in a machine or increase the RAM.

Scaling out increases the number of components so they can handle increased load together. For example, adding more machines to handle HTTP requests would result in creation of a web server farm. There are significant performance capabilities when using multiple machines to share the workload. Sharing the workload includes having separate machines for the Reporting Services application, the SQL Server data store, and other application servers used in the system.

Each component in the solution may have its own techniques and tools for scaling. For example, ASP.NET provides many scaling capabilities. Caching is an excellent way to increase the ability of your servers to handle an increasing load. For example, you can cache the output for processing an HTTP request so the next request for that resource is pulled straight from cache. The request is never processed in the traditional sense. You can set the cache expiration value so that the cache gets refreshed periodically.

Moving management applications off to separate machines, and implementing functionality like Component Services are both techniques that can enable a solution to handle increased load. Web servers benefit greatest from increases in processor power, while storage components benefit from increases in disk space and I/O speed.

Transactional and Decision-Support Data

There are generally two categories of data storage systems used to manage business information. When most people hear the term *database system*, they probably think of a Relational Database Management Systems (RDBMS). This is by far the most common and most often used type of database for collecting, managing, and providing reporting for transactional data. The other category, OLAP (On-Line Analytical Processing), is more specialized and is used only for advanced reporting and decision-support. We'll discuss some of the differences and design strategies for these two types of data storage.

On-line Transactional database systems (OLTP) are typically based on relational data stores that are queried using structured query language (SQL). OLAP systems, typically based on multidimensional, hierarchal structures, are queried using specialized languages such as multidimensional expressions (MDX).

Back in the 1960s and early 1970s, computer systems made it feasible for large businesses to track large volumes of information. They designed systems to keep track of customers, accounts, products, inventory, invoices, vendors, shipments, manufacturing processes, measurements, quality control and the like. A data revolution was underway. However, as the companies who provided these systems tried to maintain them and interoperate with others, they quickly learned that there was more to information management than just writing values out to a file.

In the 1970s, a mathematician named Edgar Codd, working for IBM, wrote a series of articles about design principles for relational data stores. The point of his work was not so much as to how to build products to manage data but how to design database systems for effective storage and retrieval— whether implemented as tables in a client-server database product or as flat or delimited text files. The eventual outcome was a generation of products designed for managing moderate to huge volumes of data and making that data accessible to hundreds or thousands of users via current computer and networking technologies. Dr. Codd's work (along with the efforts of Ray Boyce and Chris Date) has driven the capabilities and features of modern relational database products, mainly patterned after the work of Oracle and IBM. Boyce and Codd established the rules of Normal Form (BCNF), a short list of rules for designing relationships and structures within databases.

Concurrency

One of the main goals for relational systems is typically to allow multiple users the ability to enter data, make modifications, and access information all at the same time. A basic assumption in these systems is that users will need access to data immediately after it is entered into the data store. Unfortunately this ability can often expose data in a partial or inconsistent state. In some environments, it may only be appropriate to make records available for reporting after an item (such as an invoice or order) has been "closed" or completed.

For this and other reasons, decision-support systems are typically based on read-only databases. Using either relational storage or special-purpose OLAP data sources, transactional data is loaded into these data stores at regular, scheduled intervals using ETL (Extract/Transform/Load) tools.

Strategic Latency

Making this data visible for immediate reporting can adversely affect the accuracy of report data. In a system where data will only be retrieved, these capabilities don't add value and require design elements that may not support the purpose of the solution. Reporting and decision-support systems are usually not updated in real-time. Depending on how important the most recent data is in management decisions, regular load intervals may be scheduled daily, weekly, or monthly. This gives time in the process for *scrubbing* data so it is presented in a reliable state and assuring that values are consistent throughout the data store.

If users understand that weekly sales summaries are made available by Monday morning, reports can be produced at the appropriate times with no question about the accuracy of the information they contain. Using caching, snapshots and subscriptions; reports can be produced for thousands of users from a moderate server. By coordinating the scheduled weekly data load, report cache refresh and subscription delivery; everyone has accurate information in a well-coordinated fashion.

Why Be Normal?

The rules of normal form were specifically written to support concurrent, consistent, transactional data. Most large-scale, transactional databases consist of scores of tables; some have hundreds. Most tables may be used to store look-up values and to bridge multi-entity relationships so values aren't stored redundantly throughout the database. All of this data organization can have an adverse effect for data retrieval. The values describing our reporting facts are spread across many tables. This requires complex queries to traverse joins between all of the tables.

The rules that govern transactional systems are often not applied (at least not strictly) to decision support systems. For example, a product sales fact table in our decision-support database might contain the product name and category name text values repeated many times across different records to avoid joining it to a product table via a foreign key surrogate value. In a transactional system, this would be a no-no! In the data warehouse, this isn't an issue due to the fact that the data can't be changed and, therefore repeated values should be consistent.

Understanding Business Intelligence

As you have seen, we have many choices for data storage, query techniques, languages, and tools. One of the greatest challenges for any business is to select a set of tools and products and integrate them into long-term solutions. The essence of BI is to make appropriate selections to assemble an enterprise architecture to provide these capabilities. A functional BI solution empowers business leaders to make informed decisions that will carry a business to its goals. Whether this is increased sales, competitive viability, improved processes or all of these, BI is the finger on the pulse of a business.

In terms of technology, a BI solution is the total integration of information gathering and data collection, the effective storage of data, the extractions and collaboration of various business unit data silos, and finally the aggregation of all this information into a consumable form. It should be simple and uncomplicated yet encompass all important business processes and activities.

Possibly one of the greatest lessons I've learned from Microsoft's approach to building software is the concept of zero-defect. Contrary to the name, this doesn't mean that a product must be perfect or even better than anything else. The concept of zero-defect is that we define the quality of a product or service in measurable terms before we build it, and then, throughout the construction of that product, we continually monitor its quality against the specification. With rigid quality assurance practices in place, we assure that our solution is good enough to meet the standard set at the beginning of the process. Likewise, a business intelligence solution should be used to set thresholds and acceptance criteria—and then to measure business performance against predefined marks.

Reporting information must be standardized, qualified, and comparative—it has consistent interval, form, and is exposable to extractions and operations (aggregation, analysis, and data mining etc.) Creating reports to guide business decisions is the primary driver for gathering and maintaining information in our organization with the accuracy of these reports often determining the success or failure of a business process, campaign, or the business itself.

BI Process Lifecycle

With BI, we do our best to simplify processes but business is not always simple. If your business was easy, more people would be doing it. As a business consultant, I've entered many business environments charged with simplifying processes and building reporting solutions to help ease complexity. As outsiders, we tend to cut through the details and quickly define core processes. On many occasions, I remember thinking, *"what's wrong with these people. Don't they realize that their business is simple? Why don't they just go from step A to Z rather than executing all of the convoluted steps in between?"* Months later, having worked along side people and just beginning to realize the complexity of an environment, did I start to appreciate how delicate and complicated some business processes can be.

BI needs to deal with the complexities of, while providing a means to simplify the flow of critical information through a business as much as possible. Like your business, the flow of information isn't always linear. Our BI solution recognizes dependencies as well as the parallel nature of business processes. The intelligence part comes from the dynamic, iterative nature of these processes.

Each process is aware of *state* (current information particular to its position in time and relative to the whole business process.) The process is informed, dynamic, and intelligent. All processes roll up into and depend on the *business case*. The business case, in turn, qualifies state and process through quality assurance and control. State and processes have tolerance, extractions rules, storage and maintenance rules, and operational requirements. BI is an iterative process with ongoing qualifying of information through structure, context, and operations. BI's lifecycle completes as the Business Case changes, proactively and intelligently.

Information Gathering

Business related information may be gathered at many points. Collecting or *transacting* information applies to any point or process that acquires data that will reside within the BI solution. Whether it is an internal or external source, the data comes into or back into the information pool accessible to BI processes. Many companies have invested heavily in ERP (Enterprise Resource Planning) systems that gather a tremendous volume of data but without effective aggregation and analysis tools, all of this information becomes overwhelming.

Processes for gathering data fall into *interactive* or *automated* types. Data-quality is enforced by applications that host these processes. Both types can depend upon diverse storage systems as intermediate and/or final caching structures for a process. Often, it makes sense for data to exist in duplicate—at least for a time—until archived records are removed from transactional systems and summarized records are stored for reporting. Data marts and data warehouse solutions isolate reporting from transactional data management, both to preserve integrity and conserve system resources.

Data Scrubbing and Consolidation

Data is collected as records that define informational context through association with other records. Often, isolated values must be extrapolated into multiple tables with lookup keys and category codes to support the context of these values. This is often one of the most cumbersome tasks; extracting from a non-normalized, flat-structured or ad-hoc collection if informational facts, meaningful values that fit neatly into our data store.

I recall a data warehouse consulting project in the mid nineties at the same paper mill I mentioned in Chapter 1. The inventory management system was a special-purpose mainframe system that had been in operation for decades. Most of its data was stored in a just a few flat text files. Critical values had been hand-keyed into the green screen applications with no validation for product descriptions, production lines and machines, inventory locations, product categories, status codes, etc. After we built a normalized staging database, we automated the extraction and wrote scripts to scrub the data as it was loaded. When a new lookup value (such as a location or product category was encountered), we added this to our lookup tables to maintain referential integrity.

The result: hundreds of slight mis-spellings and abbreviations that represented duplicate values already present in the lookup tables. Without validating data as it was input into the inventory system, we continued to collect garbage in the data warehouse. Working with the mill workers who entered most of the data, we could manually fix over 99% of the data but a certain percentage of the records simply had to be tossed out.

Data Staging and Transformation

The process of decision-support data consolidation is often called *ETL* (*Extract*, *Transform* and *Load*). A number of tools are offered to move and manipulate data as it is staged for loading into a data warehouse. The SQL Server arsenal includes a very powerful tool for this purpose. Data Transformation Services (DTS) can be used to "pump" large quantities of data from data sources to data destinations with nearly limitless capabilities. Transformations may be performed using complex scripting and query logic. A transformation package consists of steps that can execute queries, scripts, applications, import, export, send email, and log events. Each transform moves data from one connection to another.

The selection is typically based on a SQL expression and each column may be validated, parsed, combined or otherwise manipulated with a program script (using either VBScript of Jscript.) Dependencies may be established between each step to create branching logic. Execution steps may be performed based on a previous step's successful completion or failure.

The DTS designer offers simple drag-and-drop symbols and wizard dialogs to make this complex process easy to perform. The DTS package depicted in Figure 14-4 illustrates the transformation and loading of data from four regional data marts, importing a text file from the corporate mainframe, running an external utility and three script files to scrub and validate data rows. The graphic nature of DTS makes this package relatively simple to design and easy to follow its data-flow and logic.

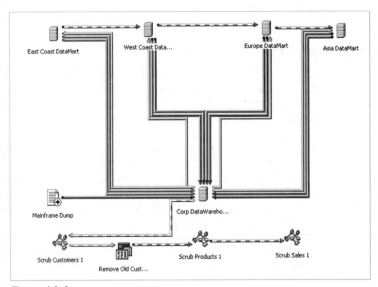

Figure 14-4

Indexing Strategies

Adding indexes to a table can accelerate data retrieval, support joins and enforce record uniqueness. In a transactional system, indexing can impede performance, as indexes must be updated as and when records are inserted, deleted or modified. This is a classic trade-off between performance and functionality. A typical OLTP database will have an index to enforce the primary key constraint on each table. Additional indexes will support foreign-key relationships and columns most often used to for sorting and selection should be indexed. Additionally, if data is most often retrieved or joined on one particular column, building the tables using a clustered index will speed data retrieval without significant impact on typical query performance. When designing the usual multi-purpose database, it is necessary to strike an appropriate balance between optimal transaction processing and query performance.

Since decision-support databases exist for the sole purpose of data retrieval, tables should typically be heavily indexed. There is much to be considered and there are a number of variables. If some tables will always have records sorted in a particular order, a clustered index will support this goal but can work against additional queries on the same table. Typically, use multiple, non-clustered indexes on tables and composite, multi-column indexes to support commonly used queries that sort by multiple columns.

Decision-Support

To remedy the issues of traditional relational database design, we simply break the rules! This is not done in the transactional database but in a separate database designed exclusively for decision-support. New data is loaded at regular intervals into the decision-support database. Often called a data warehouse, this becomes a central repository for historical and relatively current data. A data warehouse can be fed from many sources. In large organizations, data is often collected through departmental systems that store data in separate stores. These databases are often referred to as data silos. Each may be structured and designed to support its own process and user needs. Over time, data silos may exist on different platforms and locations; it'll be virtually impossible to connect and share them in real time.

In this environment, the data warehouse becomes the central point for reliable and consistent reporting information (see Figure 14-5). After data from various locations and sources has been scrubbed and transformed, the information it represents should be accurate and results should be predictable.

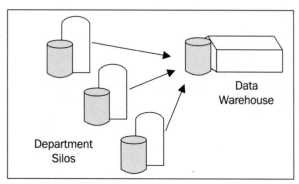

Figure 14-5

Sometimes this data consolidation must be performed in stages. Take, for example, a large business with several regional locations. Each location has several departments, each with their own disparate data collection and storage systems. In this case, we recognize individual data silos at the department level. Each night, data is collected into a site-specific data warehouse, called a *data mart*. At the end of the week, the data marts are consolidated into a central data warehouse where the data is further aggregated and made available at the corporate level.

Depending upon the disparity of these data structures, consolidation may require a staging database. This provides an intermediate platform for collecting and transforming the data structure before it loads into the data warehouse or any other final destination. In Figure 14-6, data marts feed a central data warehouse but not all data analysis may be performed in a central location. Figure 14-7 shows data marts that may also be fed from the central data warehouse as well as local silos. Reports may be generated from the data marts as well as the central data warehouse.

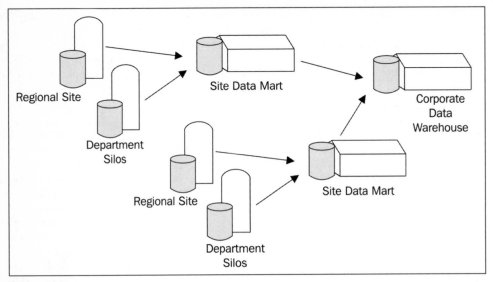

Figure 14-6

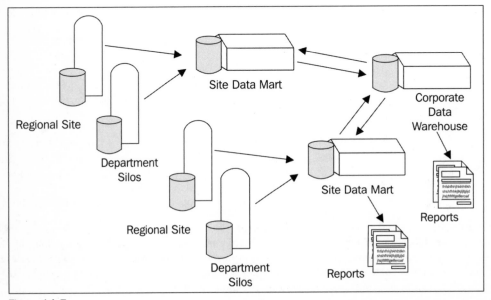

Figure 14-7

Query Languages

Reporting Services supports practically any query language as long as there is a capable driver or data provider for the product that can return a standard result set. The query language is passed directly to the data source and it's the job of the driver and data source to parse and execute the query. This means that if you are using an Oracle database, you would write your queries in PL/SQL. If you are using Informix, MySQL, Sybase, Access, or any other database product, you simply write your queries in the native dialect of SQL or any appropriate query language.

Multidimensional Expressions (MDX)

Microsoft Analysis Services and other OLAP data sources use MDX, a query expression language specifically designed to query cube structures. Rather than addressing data using rows and columns, cube structures are addressable using *tuples* and *slices*. By slicing cube data along different dimensions, we resolve dimensional intersections that represent aggregated data points. MDX expressions convert the multidimensional structure of a cube into flat row and column structures, which is why we can use these expressions in Reporting Services.

OLAP and SQL Server Analysis Services

Decision support data stores are specifically designed for reporting. At some point, relational storage and structured query language may no longer meet data warehouse requirements. When tables reach millions of rows, a traditional database may not deliver acceptable performance or function at all! In order to achieve acceptable performance, a data warehouse is typically designed with pre-aggregated values so all of the functions and calculations don't have to be applied each time a query is processed.

OLAP databases are specifically engineered to support special data structures and associated query languages for this purpose. Microsoft SQL Server Analysis Services defines cube structures as multidimensional hierarchies supporting the concepts of facts and dimensions. Data can be stored in a relational database, in a multidimensional storage structure, or parts of the data can be stored in both.

OLAP queries are designed to be interactive. This is where SQL and MDX differ significantly. In a SQL query, a single result set is returned to the client. MDX queries are tightly coupled to the OLAP database and provide continual drill-down and discovery into the cube structures using interactive tools. In SQL Server 2000, Reporting Services doesn't support this capability. It only allows MDX queries to return a flat result set—much like a SQL query. However, despite this limitation, reports using MDX expressions against OLAP sources can still be far more efficient than using SQL to query the source databases.

SQL Server's relational store can effectively store hundreds of millions of data rows but lacks the tools to deliver multidimensional cube data and drill-downs. Microsoft's data warehouse solution includes both the relational storage engine and a multidimensional engine optimized to consolidate large volumes of data and to build pre-aggregated results for multiple dimensions of values. Analysis Services simplifies the complexities of transactional systems and provides a simple interface to create intricate cubes, dimensions and calculated measures.

As the volume of data increases, different storage options may be appropriate. Cube data can be maintained in the relational store using a method called *Relational On-line Analytical Processing (ROLAP)*, in a multidimensional structure (MOLAP), or a combination of the two. Let's take a look at a simple OLAP report using MDX expressions. Figure 14-8 shows an OLAP cube in the SQL Server Analysis Services Cube Editor. This cube is based on the AdventureWorksDW sample data warehouse database.

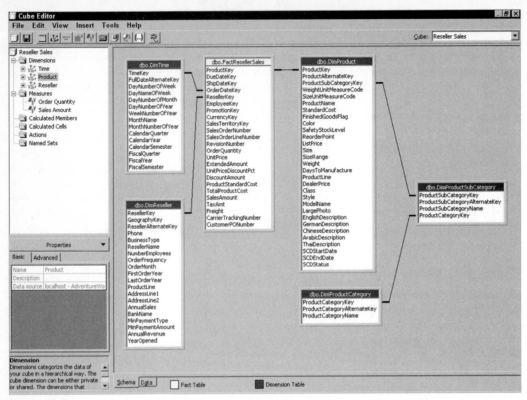

Figure 14-8

To create the report, we define two datasets using a shared data source. In Figure 14-9, the data source uses the OLE DB Provider for OLAP Services:

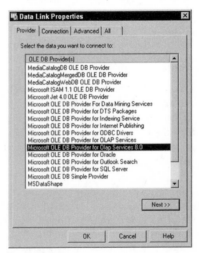

Figure 14-9

Two datasets are used to represent the cube data. The first dataset is used to populate a parameter list from our `Time` dimension. The following MDX query retrieves date values at several levels based on the dimension definition in the cube including the year, quarter and month.

```
With
     MEMBER Measures.DateKey as '[Time].CurrentMember.UniqueName'
     MEMBER Measures.DateName as 'Space([Time].CurrentMember.Level.Ordinal*2) +
[Time].CurrentMember.Name'
Select
     {Measures.DateKey, Measures.DateName} on Columns,
     [Time].Members on Rows
FROM [Reseller Sales]
```

We'll define a parameter called `TimePeriod` in the report and set the source of this parameter to this dataset in the designer. When the report is opened in Report Manager, the parameter list looks like this (see Figure 14-10):

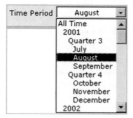

Figure 14-10

The report itself will be based on a dataset called DataDetail. This MDX expression is entered into the generic query builder as a literal string preceded by an equal sign. Note that in order to insert line breaks for improved readability, we must parse the string with double quotes and then concatenate it with ampersands. The filtering criteria of this expression refers to the `TimePeriod` parameter in the `WHERE` clause.

```
="SELECT NON EMPTY HIERARCHIZE({[Product].[Category].Members, "
& " [Product].[Sub Category].Members, "
& "[Product].[Product Name].Members}) ON ROWS, "
& "{[Sales Amount]} ON COLUMNS "
& "FROM [Reseller Sales] "
& "WHERE " & Parameters!TimePeriod.Value
```

The report uses a simple matrix data range to display values along two axes. The report will have product category, subcategory, and product name groupings on the rows. A more sophisticated report might also have column groupings and could support drill-down capabilities like the matrix report we looked at in Chapter 3.

The end result (shown in Figure 14-11) is a report displaying product sales with automatic rollup summaries on the category and subcategory rows:

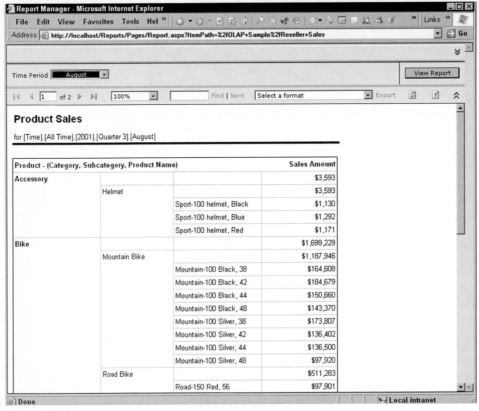

Figure 14-11

Figure 14-11 shows this report executed for the month of August selected from the `TimePeriod` parameter list. A textbox near the top of the report shows the parameter value. In this example, the parameter value is `[Time].[All Time].[2001].[Quarter 3].[August].`

Architecting BI Solutions

In order to serve a large user base and, perhaps, use in various locations; multiple database servers are often necessary. There are a number of options which we'll consider in the following sections.

Farms and Gardens

No, this is not a magazine title. Database servers, component application servers and web servers can incorporate clustering technology to form scalable hosting platforms for large enterprise solutions. Web page processing and report rendering can be very resource-intensive and a single server—regardless of its processor speed or memory—may not have the capacity to manage all requests at a given time.

A web farm is a virtual server comprised of multiple physical servers that run in tandem sharing a single IP address. As web requests are presented to the virtual server, the clustering service finds the most available server in the cluster to handle the request. This technology allows banks of relatively inexpensive PCs to provide the computing horsepower of midrange and small mainframe systems. Smaller-scale operations can start at the fraction of the cost and add hardware, scaling-out as needed. Clustering capabilities were first introduced in a stand-alone product (code-name *WolfPack* Server for Windows NT 4.0) and then incorporated into Windows 2000 Advanced Server. Clustering is now a standard feature of Windows Server 2003 Enterprise and Datacenter Editions.

A web garden is simply a web server residing on a scaled-up machine, consisting of multiple processors. Individual processors may be assigned to specific services and processes or they can collectively service processes in tandem.

Federating and Partitioning Data

Clustering and replication technology have made it possible and relatively easy to use multiple servers to host enterprise-scale databases. One advantage of the Windows distributed network platform is that we don't have to put all data on a single storage device or host it on the same server. Often times, bottlenecks can be resolved by simply spreading data access across the network, either putting data closer to users or sharing the workload. SQL Server can remotely access other database servers so that data can be made available at different locations.

Partitioning data is a matter of placing the data for a single database on different storage media. Hard drives and other storage hardware are usually the slowest part of the system. When data stored on three different hard disks is accessed, queries may be able to run three times faster (assuming there are no other bottlenecks).

The strategy of federating data is that multiple database servers will host supporting data. Through linked servers that bridge the collective data, queries on one server can access the data on other servers. This shares the resources of all servers. To support large volumes of data, very fast or dedicated network connections may be required between the database servers.

Reporting Solution Design

An effective reporting solution addresses both the external network environment and the internal structure of content in the Report Server.

System Environments

One size does not fit all—large organizations with sophisticated needs require more capable system configurations than small operations. In Chapter 13, we had discussed specifics of server deployment and configuration details. Now, we will take a brief look at some of the considerations that influence the design and planning for appropriately sized business intelligence solutions.

Small Environments

Small businesses can realize the benefits of Reporting Services with a single server. Figure 14-12 shows an example of a small-business architecture:

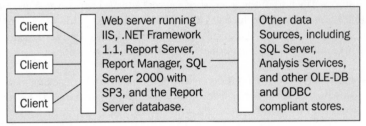

Figure 14-12

Many smaller businesses have IIS applications and SQL Server running on the same box. If the server has sufficient resources, simply adding Report Server to the installed programs will work. Additional data sources on other machines can be accessed as required.

Medium Environments

Medium-sized businesses are likely to place enough load on the reporting structure to warrant spreading that load across multiple machines, as shown in Figure 14-13:

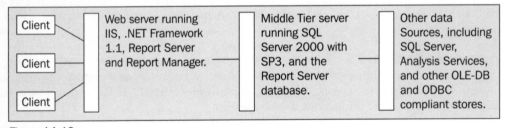

Figure 14-13

This architecture will allow the web server to handle more requests than in the smaller environment reducing the need to scale out with more machines. Note that you can also scale up at this point by increasing the capacity of the components in the server.

Large Environments

When the number of requests hitting the server becomes too many for a single machine, scaling out with more machines is an effective way to handle increased load (Figure 14-14):

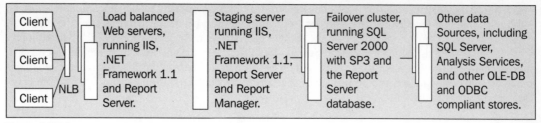

Figure 14-14

The Report Manager application isn't deployed to the front-end server farm. It's a level back on a dedicated staging server, keeping the load-balanced servers focused on handling report requests. Report Manager can run on a background machine. Updated Report Server content is then deployed to the cloned farm machines using scheduled scripts.

Content Organization

Similar to the organic nature of intranet sites, Report Server content tends to grow with little central management or control. Departments and teams create their own folders, and sometimes groups are created to restrict access to the folder contents. Frequently, the folder structure mirrors the organizational structure of the company. Although these approaches are often easier, they won't necessarily provide the anticipated return.

Unplanned growth in the content structure can often result in a difficult-to-manage combination of non-conventional folder names and mixed report content blended with checkerboard permissions. A frequent cause of ad hoc designs is a reluctance of administrators to enforce the concept of running with least privileges. Too many users with too many permissions leaves too many people deciding how best to organize and secure the content. The server content and server environment can become difficult to use and maintain. The larger your environment, the more crucial it is to use discipline. Remember how intertwined security, manageability, availability, and scalability are. Here is where the pain of poor choices can come back to haunt you.

Another more disciplined, systematic approach to develop a content structure is based on security.

Security-Based Content Structure

This is a design of solution based on how security is implemented using groups and users. This approach allows you to take full advantage of the hierarchical structure of Reporting Services content and leverage the inheritance of security policies by folder child items.

One of the most effective techniques to use when developing the Report Server content structure uses security as its foundation. This approach works with the hierarchical structure of how the Report Server organizes content. Each content folder in Report Server inherits the permissions of its parent folder, along with the other report and resource items located there. Structure your content based on how you want to control access, keeping more secure content in folders nested below a more permissive parent.

Consider, for example, a small manufacturing company with five hundred employees. The company operates in a single location and is divided into organizational departments. Each department has report needs based on work groups and users. The reports are needed primarily by department managers, although some manufacturing team leads use reports to monitor production. In this case, the content structure consisted of separate folders at the root for each department. Users within each department were added to a group which had permission to that folder. Within each department folder, access to more sensitive resources was further restricted by creating nested sub-folder. The restricted content was moved to the nested folder, and permissions set accordingly. Figure 14-15 shows you an example of how the content was structured:

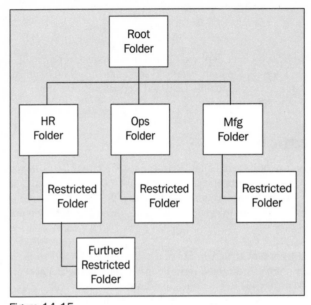

Figure 14-15

Using this structure, generally available reports are at the Root or Home level. Operations-only reports are in the Managers folder, with access permitted only to Operations department members. This is duplicated for each department, with each nested content node typically restricting access further.

Solution Profiles

The following are two solutions that demonstrate implementations of Reporting Services in a real business solution environment.

Linked Reports for Multiple Field Offices

A computer retailer based in New York has 150 outlets on the east coast of the United States. The stores are grouped into ten regions. It's a moderate operation with each retail shop doing between $1-2 million in sales per year. The parts for each computer are sourced and assembled at the home office, and delivered to each storefront by truck. Retail performance goals are set by the main office. Each retail shop has daily, weekly, and monthly sales goals for each item and system the company sells. The retail stores use a mix of static and dynamic reports to track sales data for each period. Dynamic reports are viewed via browser and secure Internet connection, while static reports are emailed to store managers each morning. The set of reports used by the retail stores is consistent among all stores.

The main office uses reports to provide aggregate and detail views of retail sales. Additionally, separate departments have their own reporting requirements. For example, the warehouse is continually monitoring inventory levels and attempting to forecast demand. There, the staff is trying to keep enough stock on hand for short-term production needs, without overbuying and ending up with an overstock of outdated components.

Because each of the retail stores uses essentially the same report set, a strategy using linked reports is employed. In the Report Server root, a folder was made for each region and the main office, along with a Retail Master folder (Figure 14-16):

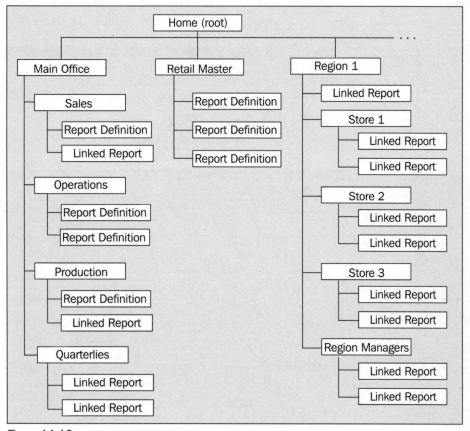

Figure 14-16

Each region folder has a child folder for every retail store in that region. The Retail Master folder contains the actual reports that the retail stores use. The Master folder is locked down, preventing access to anyone other than developers and report managers. The region-level and store-level folders have user groups configured so only the users in that region or store have permission to access it. The retail stores use linked reports to view the data, which allows additional control. For example, linked reports provide a filtering capability. Each office gets the same set of reports, but users only have access to reports that are rendered using the data for that office. Folder permissions for the main office work the same way, with permissions granted by office user group. The structure of the content and report linking was designed in the planning phase of the development process. Naming conventions were also established for folders, reports, data sources, and schedules.

For this particular solution, one of the key features of Reporting Services is the ability to connect to many different data stores. Because this company had invested in applications for different departments, data is spread among SQL Server, OLE DB, ODBC, and IBM DB2 data stores. Implementing a Reporting Services solution enables managers and key decision-makers to aggregate data from disparate stores into a single, comprehensive report.

Scout-Master.com

Scout-Master.com allows Boy Scout leaders to manage their unit records online. See Figure 14-17.

Figure 14-17

The challenge facing these organizations is that every boy, parent, and leader has to keep track of dozens of individual awards, requirements, and their goals, progress and status. Using a secure web-based database solution has made this daunting task more manageable. Over the years, desktop software has been developed for scout records management but this doesn't provide visibility to anyone but the unit leader who has the program running on their home PC. The web-based solution connects everyone and automatically sends email reminders for calendar events, goals, and award deadlines. Over the past two years, hundreds of scout troops had signed-up to use the site to keep track of their membership, contacts, calendar activities, meeting plans, and award progress.

The project started small when the Microsoft .NET Framework was in beta stage and eventually went commercial. About a year ago, the first design was unplugged and the entire site was re-architected using Visual Studio.NET. The web solution is a three-tier design built on SQL Server 2000, .NET business classes, ASP.NET Web user controls, web forms and mobile web forms. A few months ago, the site was moved from a commercial Internet service provider host to a dedicated server running Windows Server 2003 Web Server Edition.

Master.com are two-fold. Based on a user's position in the unit, they should have access to different reports. Some reports will only provide detail information for a boy and will be available to the scout, his parents, and award counselors. Other reports will be available only to certain unit members with privileges based on their leadership position. Reports can be viewed in real time or may be saved on the server for download or off-line viewing. Figure 14-18 shows a merit badge requirements report rendered to a secondary browser window from a page within the ASP.NET web forms application:

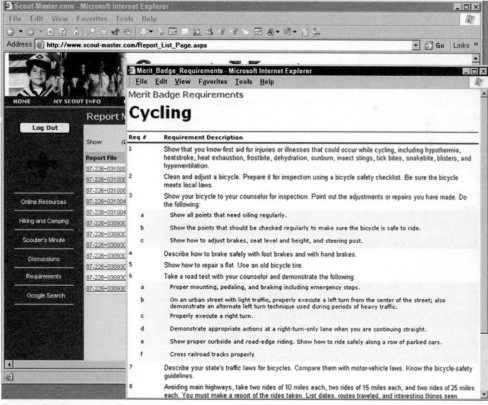

Figure 14-18

Many scout leaders have hand-held PDA devices and would like to save membership rosters and summary reports to files so they may be viewed when they aren't connected to the Internet (unfortunately most scout summer camps don't have wireless Internet access.)

SQL Reporting Services has been easy to implement within the application. All reports are rendered from code behind web user controls and the process is completely invisible from users. They simply see a list of available reports. Custom web forms prompt users for report parameters and criteria and the reports are simply delivered in the web browser as part of their application experience. Users are also given the option to download report files in a variety of formats (including PDF and Excel) in a layout suitable for their PDAs.

Some users have expressed concerns about keeping their unit records only on a commercial site rather than having the data in their possession. Reporting Services provided an easy solution and is used to let privileged users retrieve data backups. A set of reports was designed to return the bulk of unit membership data, rendering these records in XML and CSV file formats. This gives subscribers the ability to off-load their data for safe-keeping and to import records into their own spreadsheets or ad-hoc databases. If nothing else, it gives users a safety blanket, knowing that their current data is in their possession.

In all, the reporting solution has been rock solid since it was originally written using the beta 1 version of Reporting Services. It was easy to program and offers all of the features needed to meet the system requirements.

Reporting Solution Development Environment

Questions frequently come up about effective environments for team ASP.NET application development. For example, it's surprising how many developers write code logged in an account that's a member of the local Administrators group. It's also rare to see development computers configured with services running as something other than the Administrator. The idea of managing the environment so as to help users to run with least privileges applies to development as much as it does to users of the Report Server content. Creating applications that don't need elevated privileges to run help create a safer environment for everyone. There are a few more good practices that are worth mentioning, starting with the idea of isolated development.

Isolated Development

There are several approaches that you can take when working on complex web applications in a team environment. They differ mostly in *where* the code files are worked on and stored. Provisions include making code files available to each member of the development team. Generally, the different development environment models are referred to as *isolated*, *semi-isolated*, and *non-isolated*.

An isolated development environment is one where development work is done in isolation on your local machine. The master source code files can be located on a file share or managed using a tool like Visual Source Safe. In a semi-isolated environment, developers work on their files located on a common web server. Debugging also takes place on that server. When debugging a web application, IIS is blocked—which effectively prevents other developers from running their own code. A non-isolated environment takes that one step further, by having all developers working with one set of files in a single virtual folder on the server using Front Page extensions or by some technique that's similar to this. Don't do that! It's too easy to mess stuff up.

In the development of an island that is your workstation, each developer works with separate local copies of the application. Creation and debugging are done safely away from other developers and the non-dev environments. With more than three or four developers, you'll also benefit from some type of source control. Migrate your work to a server for building, testing, or staging and eventual deployment to the production boxes.

Using Source Safe

Microsoft's Visual Source Safe (VSS) is a proven and effective tool for source control. It integrates with Visual Studio .NET, enabling you to run. VSS also integrates with Visual Studio and Reporting Services solutions. For example, you can check out a report definition .rdl file for development or testing. Be sure to use the VSS hooks and menus in Visual Studio, rather than using the VSS Explorer interface. The VSS menus in VS.NET provide easy access to code check-in & out, and utilities like WinDiff for comparing two files for differences. Implementing source code control can really help make the development process more efficient and easier to manage. Adding a build process will do the same.

Staging Reports

In an enterprise environment, reports should be staged to a server. There, they can be managed using Report Manager and deployed to target machines using scripts. If the staging server is also used for testing, its hardware and software configuration should mirror the production machines as closely as possible.

One Reporting Service environment had report development work being done by individuals in different departments of the company. The reports all ran on the same Report Server instance which serviced the moderate reporting load. In that case, developers deployed their work to their My Reports folder. Administrators have access permission to each users My Reports folder. It was a simple process for the admin to move the reports from each My Reports folder to the staging machine. Once there, the process of testing and managing continues.

Summary

Business intelligence solutions, like any business solutions, must be carefully planned and scoped to avoid common pitfalls. Business solutions are created to solve business problems and to enable business leaders to take advantage of the opportunities in a timely manner. Every feature should be traceable back to a stated business requirement. Design considerations like scalability, available up-time, and performance should be clearly defined before the system is designed and constructed.

Most small to mid-scale reporting solutions will likely be based on databases designed for transactional data processing. Systems in this category often require design compromises data entry and query performance.

Data warehouses are used to collect read-only data using storage optimized for data retrieval. SQL Server Analysis Services stores data in hierarchal cube structures that are queried using Multidimensional Expressions (MDX,) a query language optimized for complex pivots and data mining. Reporting Services supports MDX queries through the OLE DB OLAP data provider.

Troubleshooting

In any development project or system implementation, even code that cannot possibly break may need to be fixed. Reporting Services is a tool written and used by people. As long as we continue to have software written and used by people, we can expect that from time to time problems will occur. Hopefully this appendix will be a useful tool in helping you navigate the bumps in the Reporting Services deployment process.

Resources

Even though this is a new product, there are a number of resources available to help you work out difficult problems with Reporting Services. Microsoft server products have generally been put into production environments before they are available for retail sale. Reporting Services is no different. A good place to start with is the Reporting Services web site:

http://www.microsoft.com/sql/reporting/default.asp

This site is a vital resource for articles, support, and downloads.

Reporting Services Books Online

All the documentation for Reporting Services is contained in the Books Online (BOL) help file. While accurate, the information in BOL is sometimes too brief to be of much help. BOL does provide authoritative information and should be one of the first resources used when in need of help.

http://msdn.microsoft.com/library/default.asp?url=/library/en-us/RSPORTAL/HTM/
rs_gts_portal_3vqd .asp

Microsoft Knowledge Base

Relevant knowledge base (KB) articles are linked to the details of error messages from BOL. The KB can also be searched from http://support.microsoft.com. The KB contains the most recent information about issues and problems associated with Microsoft products.

Microsoft Newsgroups

Microsoft provides many public newsgroups on a variety of topics for SQL Server. At the time of writing, Reporting Services was still in beta testing stage and did not have a public newsgroup. However, without the aid of the beta newsgroup for this product it would have been extremely difficult to complete this book. Using a newsgroup gives you the advantage of hundreds of heads working together on a difficult problem.

http://www.microsoft.com/sql/community/newsgroups/dgbrowser/en-us/default.mspx?dg=microsoft.public. sqlserver.reportingsvcs

MSDN

MSDN provides a duplication of the development tools documentation. You can find links on MSDN to other resources, such as articles from MSDN magazine and other publications as well at:

http://msdn.microsoft.com/

Tools

The Reporting Services Windows service and Web Service both keep log files of their processes and errors. The log files are found in:

```
C:\Program Files\Microsoft SQL Server\MSSQL\Reporting Services\LogFiles
```

The web service logs, by default, begin with `ReportServer`. The Windows service logs begin with `ReportServerService`. The log files are text files that can be viewed with Notepad or any other text editor. In the event of problems, this should be a source to see what is happening as the service runs.

The tracing level is controlled by the configuration file:

```
C:\Program Files\Microsoft SQL Server\MSSQL\Reporting Services\ReportServer\bin
\ReportingServicesService.exe.config
```

The tracing level can be adjusted by editing the value of `DefaultTraceSwitch`. Acceptable values for this switch are described in the following table:

Value	Description
0	Disables tracing
1	Exceptions and restarts
2	Exceptions, restarts, warnings
3	Exceptions, restarts, warnings, status messages (default)
4	Verbose mode

The setup process sets the logging level to 3 by default. The tracing can be made more thorough or turned off completely.

Installation Errors

For the writing of this book, particularly in trying to set up a web farm, a persistent error was the problem in getting the Reporting Services Web Service to start:

Activation error 1603
Failure activating the web service

There are several reasons why the web service might bot start:

❑ ASP.NET on Windows Server 2003 does not run as a Network Service

❑ Report Server Windows service was not running during setup

❑ ASP.NET 1.1.4322 is not registered with Internet Information Services (IIS).

❑ The default web site is mapped to an IP address instead of being mapped to 'All Unassigned'

❑ Problem with the service public key

❑ Microsoft IIS configuration for the default web site includes settings that the setup program did not expect

To resolve issues with the service failing to start, be sure to check the log files and look for specific errors regarding the starting of the service. Try running the key management utility (`rskeymgmt.exe`) and deleting any security keys, after which you will need to run `rsConfig.exe` and `rsActivate.exe`.

The last item in the list, like many Windows application errors from the past, may not be viewed as especially helpful. This is rather a catch-all reason. If you have checked each of the other items in the list, it might be time to uninstall IIS and reinstall it with the default parameters.

Credentials Errors

Credentials always represent a potential source of problems. Make sure that the Windows service runs under the proper account. For Windows Server 2003 it should run as a Network Service.

Make sure that the credential that connects to the `ReportServer` database has `dbo` permission on:

- ❏ `ReportServer`
- ❏ `ReportServerTempDB`

And public permission on:

- ❏ `master`
- ❏ `tempdb`

For reports that are to be distributed via subscription, make sure that the report uses a credential stored securely on the server.

Changing Database Connection Information

The data source for Reporting Services may have to be moved to a different server or the credentials might need to be changed. Any time the database connection information for the web service must be modified, the `rsconfig` should be used.

The syntax for `rsconfig` is as follows:

```
rsconfig -sYourSQLServer -mYourComputerName -dReportServerDatabaseName
-aSQL -uYourUserName -pYourPassword
```

The complete syntax is found in BOL.

The following is a brief summary of some of the possible errors when using Reporting Services.

Service Errors

The errors listed below have to do with the Windows service and the web service. The log files can be very helpful in figuring out the details of the problem.

Error	Reasons
`rsReportServerNotActivated`	The installation has not been activated. The rsActivate utility will need to be run to start it.
`rsReportServerDisabled`	The service is unable to encrypt or decrypt data managed by the SQL Server.
`rsReportServerDatabaseLogonFailed`	The logon used by the web service to connect to the SQL database has failed.

Error	Reasons
rsServerBusy	The server is too busy to process your request; retry later.
rsServerConfigurationError	Problems in the Report Server configuration files. Check the details in the error logs.
rsInvalidReportServerDatabase	The database used by the Report Server is either in a format that is invalid, or it is corrupt and cannot be read.
rsInternalError	An internal error has occurred. Check the error log for details and how to address it.
rsAccessDenied	The user trying to perform an operation does not have sufficient permission to perform the operation.
rsSecureConnectionRequired	https (SSL) connection is required to perform the operation you are trying to perform.

Data Access Errors

Errors in this section deal with the data used in reports and access to it.

Error	Reasons
rsDataSourceDisabled	A report cannot be processed because its data source has been disabled.
rsDataSourceNotFound	The report data source cannot be found by the service.
rsInvalidDataSourceCredentialSetting	Action cannot be completed because the needed credentials are not stored on the server.
rsInvalidDataSourceReference	Action cannot be completed because the data source connection information has been deleted.

Report Errors

The following errors deal with the rendering and delivery of reports.

Error	Reasons
rsDeliveryExtensionNotFound	The delivery extension is not registered with Report Server.
rsInvalidReportLink	The report link for a linked report is no longer valid.
rsInvalidSearchOperator	The value entered for a search operator is not valid.
rsParameterTypeMismatch	The value entered for a parameter does not match the data type expected for the parameter.
rsReadOnlyReportParameter	The parameter is read-only and may not be modified.
rsReportHistoryNotFound	Snapshots for this report have not been saved, or the snapshot being searched for was not saved.
rsReportMayNotBeScheduled	A schedule for this report is not found. If it was scheduled, check to make sure that the database credentials are saved in the database.
rsReportNotReady	The report is still being rendered and not yet ready for viewing.
rsReportParameterTypeMismatch	The value provided for a report parameter does not match the expected parameter type.
rsReportParameterValueNotSet	There is no default for the report parameter and the user has not supplied a value.
rsReportTimeoutExpired	The length of time allowed for the operation has been exceeded. The operation has been cancelled.
rsUnknownReportParameter	You have tried to set the value of an unknown report parameter.

Subscription Errors

Errors in this section deal with subscriptions.

Error	Reasons
rsCannotActivateSubscription	The subscription cannot be activated. The delivery extension no longer exists.
rsCannotSubscribeToEvent	The referenced event cannot be subscribed to.

Error	Reasons
rsDeliveryExtensionNotFound	The delivery extension, that which been attempted to be used, is not defined on this report server.
rsJobWasCanceled	The job has been cancelled by an administrator.
rsScheduleAlreadyExists	You have attempted to create or rename a schedule that already exists.
rsScheduleNotFound	The referenced schedule cannot be found in the report server database.
rsSchedulerNotResponding	The scheduling engine has hung and is not responding.
rsSubscriptionNotFound	The referenced subscription cannot be found in the report server database.
rsTaskNotFound	The references task does not exist or cannot be found.

Migrating Access Reports

The following Access report controls, property settings, and other report elements will be converted to report items in SQL Server Reporting Services if supported.

Controls

Control	Converted to Item
Label	Textbox
Textbox	Textbox
Option Group	(unsupported)
Toggle Button	(unsupported)
Option Button	(unsupported)
Check Box	(unsupported)
Combo Box	(unsupported)
List Box	(unsupported)
Command Button	(unsupported)
Image	Image
Unbound Object Frame	(unsupported)
Bound Object Frame	(unsupported)

Table continued on following page

Control	Converted to Item
Page Break	(unsupported)
Tab Control	(unsupported)
Sub form	Subreport
Sub report	Subreport
Line	Line
Rectangle	Rectangle
ActiveX Controls	(unsupported)

Property Settings

Property	Supported
BackColor	Yes
BackStyle	Yes
BorderColor	Yes
BorderStyle	Yes
BorderWidth	Yes
BottomMargin	Yes
CanGrow (section)	No
CanGrow (textbox)	Yes
CanShrink (section)	No
CanShrink (textbox)	Yes
Caption	Yes
DecimalPlaces	No
FastLaserPrinting	No
Filter	No
FilterOn	No
FontBold	Yes

Property	Supported
FontItalic	Yes
FontName	Yes
FontSize	Yes
FontUnderline	Yes
FontWeight	Yes
ForceNewPage	Yes
ForeColor	Yes
Format	No
FormatConditions	No
GrpKeepTogether	No
Height	Yes
HideDuplicates	Yes
Hyperlink	Yes
IsHyperlink	Yes
IsVisible	Yes
KeepTogether (group)	Yes
KeepTogether (section)	No
Left	Yes
LeftMargin	Yes
LineSlant	Yes
LineSpacing	Yes
LinkChildFields	Yes
LinkMasterFields	Yes
NewRowOrCol	Yes
NumeralShapes	No

Table continued on following page

Property	Supported
Orientation	No
PageFooter	Yes
PageHeader	Yes
Pages	Yes
PaintPalette	No
PaletteSource	No
Picture	Yes
PictureAlignment	No
PicturePages	No
PictureSizeMode	No
PictureTiling (image)	No
PictureTiling (report)	Yes
ReadingOrder	Yes
RepeatSection	Yes
RightMargin	Yes
RunningSum	Yes
ScrollBars	No
SizeMode	Yes
SpecialEffect	No
TextAlign	Yes
Top	Yes
TopMargin	Yes
Vertical	No
Width	Yes

Functions

Nearly all common expression functions (VBA and Access SQL) are supported by Reporting Services or have Visual Basic .NET equivalents. The following domain aggregate functions are not supported and do not have equivalent functionality. Equivalent aggregate functions exist in Transact SQL, but these need to be applied within a query rather than on item properties.

Function	Supported
DAvg	No
DCount	No
DFirst	No
DLast	No
DLookup	No
DMax	No
DMin	No
DStDev	No
DStDevP	No
DSum	No
DVar	No
DVarP	No

Report Elements

Element	Supported	Comment
VBA Code Modules	Yes	
Events	No	
Parameterized queries	Yes	
Expression functions	Yes	Reporting Services supports most VBA or Access SQL functions that are allowed in Access property expressions. All supported functions are converted to the Visual

Table continued on following page

513

Element	Supported	Comment
Expression functions (continued)		Basic .NET equivalents. The most significant functions, commonly used in Access expressions and not supported by Reporting Services are the domain aggregate functions.
Access data source – Access tables	Yes	Connection string refers to the original Access database.
Access data source – linked tables	No	Connection string refers to the original Access database not the source of the linked tables.
Remote data source in Access Data Project (ADP)	Partial	ODBC and OLEDB sources are supported but certain characters are not allowed in names (';', '<', or '>').
Group section	Yes	Appropriate sorting and grouping properties are applied to detail sections. Nested groupings are created for additional group sections.
Field names and variable	Yes	Names are converted according to Reporting Services rules. Field names that are the same as control/item names are modified and names containing spaces are modified. Any variable names that don't correspond to fields are converted to report parameters.
Image formats	Yes	All image formats are converted to BMP and stored as embedded images.

During report conversion, the Access database or project is opened during the report conversion process. Although the conversion engine handles most unsupported conversion issues gracefully, errors can cause the process to stall under some conditions. In this case, the Access database may be left with open locks on it and you won't be able to open the database. In this case, delete the corresponding ldb file after closing Visual Studio. In extreme cases, you may need to reboot the computer first.

Reporting Services Object Model

Reporting Services exposes its Application Program Interface (API) through the Reporting Services Web Service that interacts with the actual Reporting Server. This appendix is meant to be a quick reference to the programmatic functionality that Reporting Services exposes through this web service.

Relevant code for both C# and VB.NET has been provided in this chapter. Book formatting constraints may cause the code lines to wrap. However, note that the VB.NET code lines should reside on one line in the code editor, note that no underscore has been inserted in such cases.

CancelBatch

This method cancels a batch of commands that are created by using `CreateBatch` and associated with a particular `BatchID`. The `BatchID` can be changed to a value equal to the `BatchID` generated when the batch was created through the `BatchHeaderValue` property of the web service. When `CancelBatch` is called, any calls associated with that `BatchID` value cannot be executed.

C#

```
public void CancelBatch();
```

VB.NET

```
Public Sub CancelBatch()
```

CancelJob

A job is a task that a report server is actively processing. CancelJob cancels execution of a job by passing in the JobID associated with that job.

C#

```
public bool CancelJob(string JobID);
```

VB.NET

```
Public Function CancelJob(ByVal JobID As String) As Boolean
```

CreateBatch

The CreateBatch method creates a batch that allows the execution of multiple methods within the scope of a single transaction. Upon execution, this method returns a BatchID. This batch identifier is used to group commands and can be accessed through the BatchHeaderValue property of the web service.

C#

```
public string CreateBatch();
```

VB.NET

```
Public Function CreateBatch() As String
```

CreateDataDrivenSubscription

This method creates a data-driven subscription for a specified report. It requires passing in the extension settings for the preferred delivery mechanism as well as the DataRetrievalPlan and event type that will cause the report to be delivered. The return value is a unique identifier for the new subscription.

C#

```
public string CreateDataDrivenSubscription(string Report, ExtensionSettings
ExtensionSettings, DataRetrievalPlan DataRetrievalPlan, string Description,
string EventType, string MatchData, ParameterValueOrFieldReference[] Parameters);
```

VB.NET

```
Public Function CreateDataDrivenSubscription(ByVal Report As String, ByVal
ExtensionSettings As ExtensionSettings, ByVal DataRetrievalPlan As
DataRetrievalPlan, ByVal Description As String, ByVal EventType As String, ByVal
MatchData As String, ByVal Parameters As ParameterValueOrFieldReference()) As
String
```

CreateDataSource

This method creates a new data source in the Reporting Server database. It is sensitive because it contains username and password information, and depending on the settings of the server, may require that it be executed only over SSL.

C#

```
public void CreateDataSource(string DataSource, string Parent, bool Overwrite,
DataSourceDefinition Definition, Property[] Properties);
```

VB.NET

```
Public Sub CreateDataSource(ByVal DataSource As String, ByVal Parent As String,
ByVal Overwrite As Boolean, ByVal Definition As DataSourceDefinition, ByVal
Properties As Property())
```

CreateFolder

The CreateFolder method creates a logical folder on the Reporting Server in which items such as reports or data sources may be placed. If you are creating a nested folder hierarchy, then you must pass in the full path of the parent folder. In addition, you must pass a collection of custom properties for the folder. These properties can be used to search by or provide detailed information about the folder.

C#

```
public void CreateFolder(string Folder, string Parent, Property[] Properties);
```

VB.NET

```
Public Sub CreateFolder(ByVal Folder As String, ByVal Parent As String, ByVal
Properties As Property())
```

CreateLinkedReport

A linked report is defined as a report that does not contain a full report definition in the Reporting Server, and is primarily created for the purpose of being included in other reports. This method creates a report and requires that you pass in the name of the linked report, the path of the report, the path to the report definition upon which you are basing the report, and the report properties.

C#

```
public void CreateLinkedReport(string Report, string Parent, string Link,
Property[] Properties);
```

VB.NET

```
Public Sub CreateLinkedReport(ByVal Report As String, ByVal Parent As String,
ByVal Link As String, ByVal Properties As Property())
```

CreateReport

The CreateReport method adds a new report to the Reporting Server database. It requires that you pass in the path where you want the report to be created, a Boolean value indicating whether you want an existing report with the same name to be overridden, the report itself, and any custom properties that you would like applied to the report.

C#

```
public Warnings[] CreateReport(string Report, string Parent, bool Overwrite,
byte[] Definition, Property[] Properties, [out] ref Warning[] Warnings);
```

VB.NET

```
Public Function CreateReport(ByVal Report As String, ByVal Parent As String, ByVal
Overwrite As Boolean, ByVal Definition As Byte(), ByVal Properties As Property())
As Warning()
```

CreateReportHistorySnapshot

A snapshot of a report is a view of that report frozen at a certain point in time. This method generates a report history snapshot of a specified report. All the subreport items and parameters are also stored as history. A string is returned which is a unique snapshot identifier.

C#

```
public string CreateReportHistorySnapshot(string Report, [out] ref Warning[]
Warnings);
```

VB.NET

```
Public Function CreateReportHistorySnapshot(ByVal Report As String, ByRef Warnings
As Warning()) As String
```

CreateResource

This method adds a new resource to the Reporting Server database. It requires that you pass in the resource, the parent directory, a Boolean value indicating whether to overwrite an existing resource with the same name, the MIME type of the resource, and any properties that you want to specify.

C#

```
public void CreateResource(string Resource, string Parent, bool Overwrite, byte[]
Contents, string MimeType, Property[] Properties);
```

VB.NET

```
Public Sub CreateResource(ByVal Resource As String, ByVal Parent As String, ByVal
Overwrite As Boolean, ByVal Contents As Byte(), ByVal MimeType As String, ByVal
Properties As Property())
```

CreateRole

This method creates a new security role in the Reporting Server database. The required fields are a string role name, a description of the role, and a collection of tasks that you want the role to perform represented by task IDs.

C#

```csharp
public void CreateRole(string Name, string Description, Task[] Tasks);
```

VB.NET

```vbnet
Public Sub CreateRole(ByVal Name As String, ByVal Description As String, ByVal Tasks As Task())
```

CreateSchedule

The `CreateSchedule` method allows the developer to create a shared schedule that can be used by a subscription to deliver reports. The name of the schedule and a `ScheduleDefinition` object that describes the schedule are the required parameters. The return value is a unique schedule ID that identifies the newly created schedule.

C#

```csharp
public string CreateSchedule(string Name, ScheduleDefinition ScheduleDefinition);
```

VB.NET

```vbnet
Public Function CreateSchedule(ByVal Name As String, ByVal ScheduleDefinition As ScheduleDefinition) as String
```

CreateSubscription

Creates a subscription for a specified report in the Reporting Server database. The required parameters are the name of the report, the delivery extension to use, a user friendly description, the event that will cause the subscription to be run, and match data that is needed by the `EventType` object. This method returns a unique subscription ID for the newly created subscription.

C#

```csharp
public string CreateSubscription(string Report, ExtensionSettings ExtensionSettings, string Description, string EventType, string MatchData, ParameterValue[] Parameters);
```

VB.NET

```
Public Function CreateSubscription(ByVal Report As String, ByVal ExtensionSettings
As ExtensionSettings, ByVal Description As String, ByVal EventType As String,
ByVal MatchData As String, ByVal Parameters As ParameterValue()) As String
```

DeleteItem

The DeleteItem method deletes a specified item from the Reporting Server database as well as any objects that are related to that item, such as properties, subscriptions, or snapshots. It takes the full path to the item to be deleted as a string parameter.

C#

```
public void DeleteItem(string Item);
```

VB.NET

```
Public Sub DeleteItem(ByVal Item As String)
```

DeleteReportHistorySnapshot

This method deletes an individual report history snapshot for a specified report. It requires that you pass in the path to the report and an identifier for the specific history to be removed.

C#

```
public void DeleteReportHistorySnapshot(string Report, string HistoryID);
```

VB.NET

```
Public Sub DeleteReportHistorySnapshot(ByVal Report As String, ByVal HistoryID As
String)
```

DeleteRole

It deletes a specified role from the Reporting Server database. In addition, all the policies associated with this role are also deleted. It requires you to pass in the name of the role to be deleted.

C#

```
public void DeleteRole(string Name);
```

VB.NET

```
Public Sub DeleteRole(ByVal Name As String)
```

DeleteSchedule

The `DeleteSchedule` method deletes a specific schedule from the Reporting Server database. Any reports that were scheduled to run based on this schedule will no longer be processed. It requires passing in a string value representing the ID of the schedule.

C#

```
public void DeleteSchedule(string ScheduleID);
```

VB.NET

```
Public Sub DeleteSchedule(ByVal ScheduleID As String)
```

DeleteSubscription

This method allows the user to delete a subscription to a specified report. Executing the method requires the subscription ID of the subscription to be deleted.

C#

```
public void DeleteSubscription(string SubscriptionID);
```

VB.NET

```
Public Sub DeleteSubscription(ByVal SubscriptionID As String)
```

DisableDataSource

This method allows the developer to disable a specific data source. Reports and subscriptions that use the specified data source will not run. It requires passing in the name of the data source that is to be disabled.

C#

```
public void DisableDataSource(string DataSource);
```

VB.NET

```
Public Sub DisableDataSource(ByVal DataSource As String)
```

EnableDataSource

This method enables a data source that was previously disabled.

C#

```
public void EnableDataSource(string DataSource);
```

VB.NET

```
Public Sub EnableDataSource(ByVal DataSource As String)
```

ExecuteBatch

A batch identifier is returned when the `CreateBatch` Method is used. To execute a batch, the developer sets the `BatchHeaderValue` property of the web service proxy class to the appropriate batch ID. All methods that are associated with this batch ID will execute within the scope of a single database transaction.

C#

```
public void ExecuteBatch();
```

VB.NET

```
Public Sub ExecuteBatch()
```

FindItems

`FindItems` returns items that match the specified search criteria. The required parameters are the folder to search, logical operators `AND` and `OR`, and a collection of search conditions. The return value is the `CatalogItem` collection.

C#

```
public CatalogItem[] FindItems(string Folder, BooleanOperatorEnum BooleanOperator,
SearchCondition[] Conditions)
```

VB.NET

```
Public Function FindItems(ByVal Folder As String, ByVal BooleanOperator As
BooleanOperatorEnum, ByVal Conditions As SearchCondition())As CatalogItem())
```

FireEvent

`FireEvent` causes an event to be fired. Required parameters are the event to be fired and the data required by the event.

C#

```
public void FireEvent(string EventType, string EventData);
```

```
Public Sub FireEvent(ByVal EventType As String, ByVal EventData As String)
```

FlushCache

`FlushCache` invalidates the cache for an individual report. The name of the report is the only parameter passed to this method.

C#

```
public void FlushCache(string Report);
```

VB.NET

```
Public Sub FlushCache(ByVal Report As String)
```

GetCacheOptions

This method returns the cache configuration for a report and the `ExpirationDefinition` settings that describe when the cached copy of the report expires. The return value is a Boolean value indicating whether the report is in the cache or not.

C#

```
public bool GetCacheOptions(string Report, [out] ref ExpirationDefinition
                                                            Expiration );
```

VB.NET

```
Public Function GetCacheOptions(ByVal Report As String, [out] ByRef Expiration As
ExpirationDefinition) As Boolean
```

GetDataDrivenSubscriptionProperties

This method returns the properties of a data-driven subscription. The required parameter is the ID of the subscription. The other parameters are declared but not initialized. They will be returned with valid values representing the settings of the subscription. They are the extension settings, the data retrieval plan, a description of the subscription, the current status of the subscription, the type of event that causes the subscription to fire, and the match data for the event.

C#

```
public string GetDataDrivenSubscriptionProperties(string
DataDrivenSubscriptionID, [out] ref ExtensionSettings ExtensionSettings, [out]
ref DataRetrievalPlan DataRetrievalPlan, [out] ref string Description, [out] ref
ActiveState Active, [out] ref string Status, [out] ref string EventType, [out] ref
string MatchData, [out] ref ParameterValueOrFieldReference[] Parameters);
```

VB.NET

```
Public Function GetDataDrivenSubscriptionProperties(ByVal DataDrivenSubscriptionID
As String,[out] ByRef ExtensionSettings As ExtensionSettings, [out] ByRef
DataRetrievalPlan As DataRetrievalPlan, [out] ByRef Description As String, [out]
ByRef Active As ActiveState, [out] ByRef Status As String, [out] ByRef EventType
As String, [out] ByRef MatchData As String, [out] ByRef Parameters As
ParameterValueOr FieldReference())
```

GetDataSourceContents

GetDataSourceContents returns a DataSourceDefinition object representing the contents of a data source. The required parameter is the name of the data source.

C#

```
public DataSourceDefinition GetDataSourceContents(string DataSource);
```

VB.NET

```
Public Function GetDataSourceContents(ByVal DataSource As String) As DataSource
Definition
```

GetExecutionOptions

This method returns the execution options and associated settings for an individual report. The required parameters are the name of the report and an uninitialized ScheduleDefinition object. This object will be returned with its properties set to the values for the report. The return value is an enum datatype that indicates whether the report is based on live data or a snapshot.

C#

```
public ExecutionSettingEnum GetExecutionOptions(string Report, [out] ref
ExecutionSettingEnum ExecutionSetting, [out] ref ScheduleDefinitionOrReference
Schedule);
```

VB.NET

```
Public Function GetExecutionOptions(ByVal Report As String,[out] ByRef Schedule As
ScheduleDefinitionOrReference) As ExecutionSettingEnum
```

GetExtensionSettings

This method requires that you to pass in the name of an extension. The return value is an array of known parameters for the specific extension.

C#

```
public ExtensionParameter[] GetExtensionSettings(string Extension);
```

VB.NET

```
Public Function GetExtensionSettings(ByVal Extension As String)As
ExtensionParameter())
```

GetItemType

It retrieves the type of an item, if it exists in the Reporting Server database. The required parameter is the name of the object. The return value is an enumeration representing the type of object.

C#

```
public ItemTypeEnum GetItemType(string Item);
```

VB.NET

```
Public Function GetItemType(ByVal Item As String)
```

GetPermissions

GetPermissions returns a string array containing a list of user permissions that are associated with a particular item in the Reporting Server database. The required input parameter is a string representing the name of the item.

C#

```
public void GetPermissions(string Item, [out] ref string[] Permissions);
```

VB.NET

```
Public Sub GetPermissions(ByVal Item As String, [out] ByRef Permissions As _
String())
```

GetPolicies

GetPolicies returns an array of Policy objects that are associated with a particular item as well as a Boolean value indicating whether the item inherits those policies from its parent.

C#

```
public Policy[] Policies,  GetPolicies(string Item, [out] ref bool InheritParent);
```

VB.NET

```
Public Function GetPolicies(ByVal Item As String, [out] ByRef Policies As
Policy(), [out] ByRef InheritParent As Boolean)
```

GetProperties

GetProperties returns property values for a particular report object. You need to pass in an array of Property objects with names initialized and the method returns those objects with their values set.

C#

```
public Property[] GetProperties(string Item, Property[] Properties);
```

VB.NET

```
Public Function GetProperties(ByVal Item As String, ByVal Properties As
Property()) As Property()
```

GetRenderResource

GetRenderResource returns the resource for a specified rendering extension format. It requires that you pass in the format to use for processing device-specific information and the MIME type of the resource. It returns the resource as a base-64 encoded byte array.

C#

```
public void GetRenderResource(string Format, string DeviceInfo, [out] ref byte[]
Result, [out] ref string MimeType);
```

VB.NET

```
Public Sub GetRenderResource(ByVal Format As String, ByVal DeviceInfo As String,
[out] ByRef Result As Byte(), [out] ByRef MimeType As String)
```

GetReportDataSourcePrompts

This method returns an array of DataSourcePrompt objects. These are used to present prompts to the user for required connection values such as username and password. The only parameter is a string representing the full path to the data resource.

C#

```
public DataSourcePrompt[] GetReportDataSourcePrompts(string Report)
```

VB.NET

```
Public Function GetReportDataSourcePrompts(ByVal Report As String) As
DataSourcePrompt()
```

GetReportDataSources

While using this method, a developer passes in the full path to a report and this method returns an array of DataSource objects that are associated with that report.

C#

```
public DataSource[] GetReportDataSources(string Report);
```

VB.NET

```
Public Function GetReportDataSources(ByVal Report As String) As DataSource()
```

GetReportDefinition

This method retrieves the report definition for a report in base-64 encoded byte format. It can then be converted into Report Definition Language (RDL) for use in tools such as Visual Studio.

C#

```
public byte[] GetReportDefinition(string Report);
```

VB.NET

```
Public Function GetReportDefinition(ByVal Report As String)As Byte()
```

GetReportHistoryLimit

This method returns an integer that indicates the number of snapshot history reports to maintain. The required parameters are the name of the report, a Boolean value that will be altered in the method to reflect whether the report has its own limit or uses the system limit, and an integer that will be returned with the value of the current system limit.

C#

```
public int GetReportHistoryLimit(string Report, [out] ref bool IsSystem, [out] ref
int SystemLimit);
```

VB.NET

```
Public Function GetReportHistoryLimit(ByVal Report As String, , ByRef IsSystem As
Boolean, ByRef SystemLimit As Integer)
```

GetReportHistoryOptions

This method returns the report history snapshot options and properties that are generated for a report by passing in the report name. The method returns a Boolean variable that indicates whether the report allows the creation of manual snapshots. The property information is retrieved by output parameters, which indicate whether snapshots have been kept and a schedule definition is associated with the report.

C#

```
public bool GetReportHistoryOptions(string Report,[out] ref bool
KeepExecutionSnapshots, [out] ref ScheduleDefinitionOrReference Schedule);
```

VB.NET

```
Public Function GetReportHistoryOptions(ByVal Report As String,[out] ByRef
KeepExecutionSnapshots As Boolean, [out] ByRef Schedule As
ScheduleDefinitionOrReference) as Bool
```

GetReportLink

The GetReportLink method returns the full path of the report, the report definition of which is used for the specified linked report. The only parameter is the name of the report referred for the report definition.

C#

```
public string GetReportLink(string Report, [out] ref string Link);
```

VB.NET

```
Public Sub GetReportLink(ByVal Report As String) As String
```

GetReportParameters

This method returns report parameters for a specified report. The first parameter is the name of the report. The next two parameters are used together. If a HistoryId is provided and the ForRendering parameter is set to true, the returned properties belong to a snapshot of the provided report. The ParameterValues argument can be used to verify valid parameters against a report. The Credentials parameter returns the credentials to use to validate and check the parameters.

C#

```
public ReportParameter[] GetReportParameters(string Report, string HistoryID, bool
ForRendering, ParameterValue[] Values, DataSourceCredentials[] Credentials)
Parameters);
```

VB.NET

```
Public Function GetReportParameters(ByVal Report As String, ByVal HistoryID As
String, ByVal ForRendering As Boolean, ByVal Values As ParameterValue(), ByVal
Credentials As DataSourceCredentials()) As ReportParameter()
```

GetResourceContents

This method requires the developer to pass in the resource that needs retrieval. The method returns a MIME type and the value of the resource as a base-64 encoded byte array.

C#

```
Public byte[] GetResourceContents(string Resource, [out] ref string MimeType);
```

VB.NET

```
Public Function GetResourceContents(ByVal Resource As String, ByRef MimeType As String) As Byte()
```

GetRoleProperties

This method returns a collection of tasks associated with a given role. The description string argument will contain the description for the role.

C#

```
public Task[] GetRoleProperties(string Name, [out] ref string Description);
```

VB.NET

```
Public Function GetRoleProperties(ByVal Name As String, ByRef Description As String) as Task()
```

GetScheduleProperties

This method returns a Schedule object containing the schedule definition for a single shared schedule by passing in a specific schedule ID.

C#

```
public Schedule GetScheduleProperties(string ScheduleID);
```

VB.NET

```
Public Function GetScheduleProperties(ByVal ScheduleID As String) As Schedule
```

GetServerDateTime

This method is described in the documentation but does not exist in the Beta version. It supposedly returns the current date and time of the computer that is running the report server scheduler. It exists in the internal Reporting Server classes but is not exposed through the WSDL-generated proxy class.

C#

```
public DateTime GetServerDateTime();
```

VB.NET

```
Public Function GetServerDateTime()
```

GetSubscriptionProperties

The GetSubscriptionProperties method returns a subscription and the associated information for a specified report in the Reporting Server database. The required parameters are the name of the report, a delivery extension object, a string to hold a user-friendly description, an Event object, and match data that is needed by the EventType object. It also returns a string representing the owner of the subscription. All of the parameters except the subscription have no initial value, but return the settings for the subscription after the method executes.

C#

```
public string GetSubscriptionProperties(string SubscriptionID, [out] ref
ExtensionSettings ExtensionSettings, [out] ref string Description, [out] ref
ActiveState Active, [out] ref string Status, [out] ref string EventType, [out] ref
string MatchData, [out] ref ParameterValue[] Parameters);
```

VB.NET

```
Public Sub GetSubscriptionProperties(ByVal SubscriptionID As String, [out] ByRef
ExtensionSettings As ExtensionSettings, [out] ByRef Description As String, [out]
ByRef Active As ActiveState, [out] ByRef Status As String, [out] ByRef EventType
As String, [out] ByRef MatchData As String, [out] ByRef Parameters As
ParameterValue())
```

GetSystemPermissions

This retrieves a string array representing the system permissions of the current user. An example of a valid permission is the Create Roles permission.

C#

```
public string[] GetSystemPermissions();
```

VB.NET

```
Public Function GetSystemPermissions( ) as String()
```

GetSystemPolicies

This method returns an array of `Policy` objects representing groups and associated roles.

C#

```
public Policy[] GetSystemPolicies();
```

VB.NET

```
Public Function GetSystemPolicies() As Policy()
```

GetSystemProperties

This method requires passing in an array of `Property` objects with names initialized to the properties that you are interested in. The method returns this array of properties with their values from the system indicating the system status.

C#

```
public Property[] GetSystemProperties(Property[] Properties, [out] ref Property[]
Values);
```

VB.NET

```
Public Function GetSystemProperties(ByVal Properties As Property()) As Property()
```

InheritParentSecurity

This method deletes all the policies associated with an item, thereby causing it to inherit policies from its parent.

C#

```
public void InheritParentSecurity(string Item);
```

VB.NET

```
Public Sub InheritParentSecurity(ByVal Item As String)
```

ListChildren

This method returns a `CatalogItem` array when passed a string value representing a specified folder. A Boolean value that indicates whether the search should be recursive and traverse the entire directory structure of the path below the specified folder is also required.

C#

```
public CatalogItem[] ListChildren(string Item, bool Recursive);
```

VB.NET

```
Public Function ListChildren(ByVal Item As String, ByVal Recursive As Boolean) As
CatalogItem()
```

ListEvents

This method returns an array of events that are defined on the report server.

C#

```
Public Event[] ListEvents()
```

VB.NET

```
Public Function CancelBatch() As Event
```

ListExtensions

It returns a list of Extension objects that are configured for a given extension type such as delivery, rendering, or data. The parameter is an enumeration representing all of the extension types.

C#

```
public Extension[] ListExtensions(ExtensionTypeEnum ExtensionType );
```

VB.NET

```
Public Sub ListExtensions(ByVal ExtensionType As ExtensionTypeEnum) As Extension()
```

ListJobs

This method returns an array of Jobs that represent information about currently running jobs on the report server.

C#

```
public Jobs[] ListJobs();
```

VB.NET

```
Public Function ListJobs()As Job()
```

ListLinkedReports

The ListLinkedReports method returns an array of catalog items that are linked to the specified report.

C#

```
    public CatalogItem[] ListLinkedReports(string Report);
```

VB.NET

```
    Public Function ListLinkedReports(ByVal Report As String) As CatalogItem()
```

ListReportHistory

This method returns an array of report history snapshots and their properties for a specified report.

C#

```
    public ReportHistorySnapshot[] ListReportHistory(string Report)
```

VB.NET

```
    Public Function ListReportHistory(ByVal Report As String)As ReportHistorySnapshot()
```

ListReportsUsingDataSource

This method returns an array of reports that are associated with a shared data source.

C#

```
    public CatalogItem[] ListReportsUsingDataSource(string DataSource);
```

VB.NET

```
    Public Function ListReportsUsingDataSource(ByVal DataSource As String)As
    CatalogItem()
```

ListRoles

It returns an array of Roles defined on the report server from which their names and descriptions can be extracted.

C#

```
    public Roles[] ListRoles();
```

VB.NET

```
    Public Function ListRoles() As Role()
```

ListScheduledReports

This method returns an array of reports that are associated with a shared schedule.

C#

```
public CatalogItem[] ListScheduledReports(string ScheduleID);
```

VB.NET

```
Public Function ListScheduledReports(ByVal ScheduleID As String) As CatalogItem()
```

ListSchedules

This method returns an array containing all the shared schedules on the report server.

C#

```
public Schedule[] ListSchedules();
```

VB.NET

```
Public Function ListSchedules()As Schedule()
```

ListSecureMethods

It returns a string array of methods that require a secure connection when invoked.

C#

```
public string[] ListSecureMethods();
```

VB.NET

```
Public Function ListSecureMethods() As String()
```

ListSubscriptions

The ListSubscriptions method returns an array of Subscription objects that have been created for a given report for a specific user. This array includes both standard and data-driven subscriptions.

C#

```
public Subscription[] ListSubscriptions(string Report, string Owner);
```

VB.NET

```
Public Function ListSubscriptions(ByVal Report As String, ByVal Owner As String)
As Subscription()
```

ListSubscriptionsUsingDataSource

This method returns a list of subscriptions associated with a given data source.

C#

```
public Subscription[] ListSubscriptionsUsingDataSource(string DataSource);
```

VB.NET

```
Public Function ListSubscriptionsUsingDataSource(ByVal DataSource As String) As
Subscription()
```

ListSystemRoles

It returns an array of Role objects from which the names and descriptions of system roles can be extracted.

C#

```
public Role[] ListSystemRoles();
```

VB.NET

```
Public Sub ListSystemRoles() As Role()
```

ListSystemTasks

The ListSystemTasks method returns an array of Task objects from which system task information can be extracted. System level tasks are specific to the Reporting Server, such as managing shared schedules or server roles.

C#

```
public Task[] ListSystemTasks();
```

VB.NET

```
Public Function ListSystemTasks() As Task()
```

ListTasks

This method returns an array of Task objects from which item task information may be extracted. An example of an item-level task is viewing a folder or a report.

C#

```
public Task[] ListTasks();
```

VB.NET

```
Public Function ListTasks() As Task()
```

MoveItem

The MoveItem method moves or renames an item in the Reporting Server database; required parameters are the original location and the destination path.

C#

```
public void MoveItem(string Item, string Target);
```

VB.NET

```
Public Sub MoveItem(ByVal Item As String, ByVal Target As String)
```

PauseSchedule

This method pauses the execution of a given shared schedule. The required parameter is the associated schedule ID.

C#

```
public void PauseSchedule(string ScheduleID);
```

VB.NET

```
Public Sub PauseSchedule(ByVal ScheduleID As String)
```

PrepareQuery

This method returns a dataset containing the fields retrieved by the delivery query for a data-driven subscription. The parameters are the data source to be used, the data definition object, and a Boolean value to indicate whether the data definition has changed.

C#

```
public DataSetDefinition PrepareQuery(DataSource datasource, DataSetDefinition
dataset, Boolean changed);
```

VB.NET

```
Public Sub PrepareQuery(ByVal DataSource As DataSource, ByVal DataSet As
DataSetDefinition, ByRef Changed As Boolean)
```

Render

The Render method processes a specified report and renders it in a specified format. The required parameters are the report name, the report format (HTML, PDF, and so on), a history ID if a snapshot is to be used, an XML string providing device-specific information, the report parameters, the credentials used to access the data, a toggle to show or hide the ID, the encoding mechanism (UTF-8, UTF-16, and so on), an array of parameters to be filled with the used parameters if the report is a snapshot, a Warning collection to be filled with any warnings that occur, and a collection of streams representing any external resources. The return value is an array of bytes representing the rendered stream.

C#

```
public byte Render(string Report, string Format, string HistoryID, string
DeviceInfo, ParameterValue[] Parameters, DataSourceCredentials[] Credentials,
string ShowHideToggle, [out] ref string Encoding, [out] ref string MimeType, [out]
ref ParameterValue[] ParametersUsed, [out] ref Warning[] Warnings, [out] ref
string[] StreamIds);
```

VB.NET

```
Public Function Render(ByVal Report As String, ByVal Format As String, ByVal
HistoryID As String, ByVal DeviceInfo As String, ByVal Parameters As
ParameterValue(), ByVal Credentials As DataSourceCredentials(), ByVal
ShowHideToggle As String, [out] ByRef Encoding As String, [out] ByRef MimeType As
String, [out] ByRef ParametersUsed As ParameterValue(), [out] ByRef Warnings As
Warning(), [out] ByRef StreamIds As String())
```

RenderStream

The RenderStream method returns a byte array of the requested stream associated with a rendered report. This method is called to render a specific external resource, such as an image, within a report.

C#

```
public byte RenderStream(string Report, string Format, string StreamID, string
HistoryID, string DeviceInfo, ParameterValue[] Parameters, [out] ref string
Encoding, [out] ref string MimeType);
```

VB.NET

```
Public Sub RenderStream(ByVal Report As String, ByVal Format As String, ByVal
StreamID As String, ByVal HistoryID As String, ByVal DeviceInfo As String, ByVal
Parameters As ParameterValue(), ByRef Encoding As String, ByRef MimeType As
String)
```

ResumeSchedule

This method is used to resume from a shared schedule that has been paused.

C#

```
public void ResumeSchedule(string ScheduleID);
```

VB.NET

```
Public Sub ResumeSchedule(ByVal ScheduleID As String)
```

SetCacheOptions

This method configures caching options for a specified report. Parameters of the report, a Boolean value that indicates whether to create a cache of the report, and an expiration definition or date that controls how long the report is in the cache are passed to this function.

C#

```
public void SetCacheOptions(string Report, bool CacheReport, ExpirationDefinition
Expiration);
```

VB.NET

```
Public Sub SetCacheOptions(ByVal Report As String, ByVal CacheReport As Boolean,
ByVal Expiration As ExpirationDefinition)
```

SetDataDrivenSubscriptionProperties

This method sets the properties of a data-driven subscription.

C#

```
public void SetDataDrivenSubscriptionProperties(string DataDrivenSubscriptionID,
ExtensionSettings ExtensionSettings, DataRetrievalPlan DataRetrievalPlan, string
Description, string EventType, string MatchData, ParameterValueOrFieldReference[]
Parameters);
```

VB.NET

```
Public Sub SetDataDrivenSubscriptionProperties(ByVal DataDrivenSubscriptionID As
String, ByVal ExtensionSettings As ExtensionSettings, ByVal DataRetrievalPlan As
DataRetrievalPlan, ByVal Description As String, ByVal EventType As String, ByVal
MatchData As String, ByVal Parameters As ParameterValueOrFieldReference())
```

SetDataSourceContents

It replaces the contents of an existing data source. The parameters are the name of the source and a data definition object defining all the source properties.

C#

```
public void SetDataSourceContents(string DataSource, DataSourceDefinition
Definition);
```

VB.NET

```
Public Sub SetDataSourceContents(ByVal DataSource As String, ByVal Definition As
DataSourceDefinition)
```

SetExecutionOptions

This method sets the execution options and the associated execution properties for an individual report. The first parameter is the name of the report, followed by an enumeration indicating whether the report should be excuted in real-time or scheduled. The third parameter, `Schedule`, is only used if the execution is scheduled.

C#

```
public void SetExecutionOptions(string Report, ExecutionSettingEnum
ExecutionSetting, ScheduleDefinitionOrReference Schedule);
```

VB.NET

```
Public Sub SetExecutionOptions(ByVal Report As String, ByVal ExecutionSetting As
ExecutionSettingEnum, ByVal Schedule As ScheduleDefinitionOrReference)
```

SetPolicies

This method sets the policies that are associated with a specified item. The required parameters are the item and an array of `Policy` objects to place on the specified item.

C#

```
public void SetPolicies(string Item, Policy[] Policies);
```

VB.NET

```
Public Sub SetPolicies(ByVal Item As String, ByVal Policies As Policy())
```

SetProperties

It sets the properties that are associated with a specified item. The required parameters are the item for which you will set properties and an array of `Property` objects to place on the specified item.

C#

```
public void SetProperties(string Item, Property[] Properties);
```

VB.NET

```
Public Sub SetProperties(ByVal Item As String, ByVal Properties As Property())
```

SetReportDataSources

It sets the data sources that are associated with a specified item. The required parameters are the item in question and an array of data source objects to place on the specified item.

C#

```
public void SetReportDataSources(string Report, DataSource[] DataSources);
```

VB.NET

```
Public Sub SetReportDataSources(ByVal Report As String, ByVal DataSources As
DataSource())
```

SetReportDefinition

The `SetReportDefinition` method is used to change a report definition for a specified report. The required parameters are the name of the report, followed by an array of bytes that are the report definition. The return value is an array of warnings informing the developer of problems that occur.

C#

```
public Warning[] SetReportDefinition(string Report, byte[] Definition);
```

VB.NET

```
Public Function SetReportDefinition(ByVal Report As String, ByVal Definition As
Byte()) As Warning()
```

SetReportHistoryLimit

This allows the developer to specify the number of snapshots of a report that the report server retains. The required parameters are the name of the report, a Boolean value indicating whether the default system limit should be used or a specific limit.

C#

```
public void SetReportHistoryLimit(string Report, bool UseSystem, int
HistoryLimit);
```

VB.NET

```
Public Sub SetReportHistoryLimit(ByVal Report As String, ByVal UseSystem As
Boolean, ByVal HistoryLimit As Integer)
```

SetReportHistoryOptions

This method allows the developer to sets report history options that control snapshot creation and lifetime. The required parameters are the name of the report, a Boolean value that controls whether manual snapshots can be created, and a Boolean value indicating whether snapshot histories should be maintained. You also need to pass in the schedule the snapshot should be created against.

C#

```
public void SetReportHistoryOptions(string Report, bool
EnableManualSnapshotCreation, bool KeepExecutionSnapshots,
ScheduleDefinitionOrReference Schedule);
```

VB.NET

```
Public Sub SetReportHistoryOptions(ByVal Report As String, ByVal
EnableManualSnapshotCreation As Boolean, ByVal KeepExecutionSnapshots As
Boolean, ByVal Schedule As ScheduleDefinitionOrReference)
```

SetReportLink

A linked report does not contain a full report definition. This method allows you to specify the report that contains the full definition for the report. A linked report may be linked to more than one report definition.

C#

```
public void SetReportLink(string Report, string Link);
```

VB.NET

```
Public Sub SetReportLink(ByVal Report As String, ByVal Link As String)
```

SetReportParameters

This method allows the developer to specify parameters to a report that it needs in order to be processed. The parameters are the name of the report and a collection of parameters, the names of which much match those defined in the report.

C#

```
public void SetReportParameters(string Report, ReportParameter[] Parameters);
```

VB.NET

```
Public Sub SetReportParameters(ByVal Report As String, ByVal Parameters As
ReportParameter())
```

SetResourceContents

Resources such as images are stored as byte arrays. The SetResourceContents method allows the developer to replace the contents of an existing resource by passing in a byte array representing the new value. The required parameters are the resource to be accessed, the byte array that contains the value, and the MIME type of the resource.

C#

```
public void SetResourceContents(string Resource, byte[] Contents, string
MimeType);
```

VB.NET

```
Public Sub SetResourceContents(ByVal Resource As String, ByVal Contents As Byte(),
ByVal MimeType As String)
```

SetRoleProperties

This method allows the developer to associate a group of tasks with a specified role. The required parameters are the role name and the array of tasks to associate with the role.

C#

```
public void SetRoleProperties(string Name, string Description, Task[] Tasks);
```

VB.NET

```
Public Sub SetRoleProperties(ByVal Name As String, ByVal Description As String,
ByVal Tasks As Task())
```

SetScheduleProperties

This method allows the developer to sets the properties of a shared schedule. The required parameters are the name of the report, the schedule ID, and a schedule definition object that contains the schedule properties for the report.

C#

```
public void SetScheduleProperties(string Name, string ScheduleID,
ScheduleDefinition ScheduleDefinition);
```

VB.NET

```
Public Sub SetScheduleProperties(ByVal Name As String, ByVal ScheduleID As String,
ByVal ScheduleDefinition As ScheduleDefinition)
```

SetSubscriptionProperties

This method allows the developer to set the properties of a shared subscription. The required parameters are the name of the report, the subscription ID, delivery-specific setting information, a description of the subscription, the event that causes the subscription to run, match data used by the specific type of event used, and the parameters for the report.

C#

```
public void SetSubscriptionProperties(string SubscriptionID, ExtensionSettings
ExtensionSettings, string Description, string EventType, string MatchData,
ParameterValue[] Parameters);
```

VB.NET

```
Public Sub SetSubscriptionProperties(ByVal SubscriptionID As String, ByVal
ExtensionSettings As ExtensionSettings, ByVal Description As String, ByVal
EventType As String, ByVal MatchData As String, ByVal Parameters As
ParameterValue())
```

SetSystemPolicies

This allows the developer to set system policies by passing in an array of `Policy` objects.

C#

```
public void SetSystemPolicies(Policy[] Policies);
```

VB.NET

```
Public Sub SetSystemPolicies(ByVal Policies As Policy())
```

SetSystemProperties

This method allows the developer to set system properties by passing in an array of `Property` objects.

C#

```
public void SetSystemProperties(Property[] Properties);
```

VB.NET

```
Public Sub SetSystemProperties(ByVal Properties As Property())
```

UpdateReportExecutionSnapshot

This method creates a report history snapshot for a specific report.

C#

```
public void UpdateReportExecutionSnapshot(string Report);
```

VB.NET

```
Public Sub UpdateReportExecutionSnapshot(ByVal Report As String)
```

ValidateExtensionSettings

This method allows the developer to validate the Reporting Services extension settings. The required parameters are the name of the extension and an array of parameter values to verify. The method returns an array of extension parameter objects with initialized values if they are valid and error messages if they are not.

C#

```
public ExtensionParameter[] ValidateExtensionSettings(string Extension,
ParameterValueOrFieldReference[] ParameterValues);
```

VB.NET

```
Public Function ValidateExtensionSettings (ByVal Extension As String, ByVal
ParameterValues As ParameterValueOrFieldReference()) ParameterErrors As
ExtensionParameter())
```

The Reporting Services Web Service proxy class contains several properties that are used to control how Reporting Services handles various requests. These properties and a description of their impact on Reporting Services are discussed in the following sections.

BatchHeaderValue

This value is used to group multi-method operations against the Reporting Services Web Service.

C#

```
public BatchHeader BatchHeaderValue { get; set; }
```

VB.NET

```
Public Property BatchHeaderValue() As BatchHeader
```

ItemNamespaceHeaderValue

This value is used to retrieve properties for a specific item by setting either the ID or the name of the property in the ItemNamespaceHeader.

C#

```
public ItemNamespaceHeader ItenNamespaceHeaderValue { get; set; }
```

VB.NET

```
Public Property BatchHeaderValue() As BatchHeader
```

ServerInfoHeaderValue

This property contains server-related information such as the edition of Reporting Services and the version information.

C#

```
public ServerInfoHeader ServerInfoHeaderValue { get; set; }
```

VB.NET

```
Public Property ServerInfoHeaderValue() As ServerInfoHeader
```

SessionInfoHeaderValue

This property contains information about the current session such as the session ID and the session expiration time.

C#

```
public SessionInfoHeader SessionInfoHeaderValue { get; set; }
```

VB.NET

```
Public Property SessionInfoHeaderValue() As SessionInfoHeader
```

Transact SQL Query Functions and Expressions

Every organization should establish a standard for programming and database object naming conventions. This appendix includes some suggested naming standards and a simplified reference of common Transact SQL functions and statements for use in query expressions.

Naming Conventions

Although a universal, industry-wide naming convention doesn't exist, most experienced database professionals agree on some basic conventions. Agreeing on a universal standard is not nearly as important as an organization having a set of standards upon which they can agree upon, support, and maintain. The following is a list of some of the common objects with some suggested naming conventions.

Tables

Table names are not typically prefixed. Some database designers use the `tbl` prefix but this is less common in client/server databases than in desktop databases like `Access`. Table names in SQL Server can be in mixed case. Because older database systems have not had a history of supporting mixed-case names, many tenured database professionals still do not use them. A long-standing tradition has been to separate logical words in table names using underscores. You must not try to use any other punctuation character. Although SQL Server supports spaces in names, many professionals don't believe this is a good practice. If spaces are used in object names, the name must be enclosed in square brackets. For example:

```
[Customer Orders].[Customer First Name]
```

In any case, keep names simple yet descriptive.

Bear in mind that as a database grows in size and supporting tables are added, it is common for tables to be added with names that will be very similar to others. For this reason, it is recommended that you be more descriptive as you name tables. Many database professionals also have strong feelings about pluralization of table names. Some argue that a table name describes a single instance of a data entity, therefore the name should be singular. In either case just be consistent. Names may end with numbers only with a good reason but should begin with a letter. Some examples are:

```
Customer_Order
CustomerOrder
ProductSupplier
```

Columns

Column naming rules (and variations) are similar to tables. Again, it's more important to be consistent within your organization than to conform to a universal naming rule. You should be more concerned about describing the purpose of a column in its name than keeping it short. Column names shouldn't contain spaces and may contain underscores. No other punctuation should be used.

Views

Prefix views with v, vw, or vw_. Because views can represent complex queries it is important to describe its purpose in the name. You could begin the name with the main table or entity name. For example:

```
vw_CustomerOrderDetailByProductCategory
```

Stored Procedures

Do not prefix stored procedures with sp_. This is reserved for system-stored procedures. There are two schools of thought for stored procedure naming. The traditional convention is to use a prefix that describes the type of operation a procedure will perform for a table or entity. For example:

```
Get_Customer
Ins_Customer
Upd_Customer
Del_Customer
```

The other idea is that if the procedure name begins with the name of the table, all of the related stored procedures will be listed along with the table. For example:

```
Customer
Customer_Del
Customer_Get
Customer_Ins
Customer_Upd
```

User-Defined Functions

Because user-defined functions have been offered only since the release of SQL Server 2000, there has been little time for naming standards to evolve. A simple rule is to prefix all function names with `fn_`. For example:

```
fn_FirstName ( )
fn_CustomersWithOrders ( )
```

When calling a stored procedure, you must use a two-part or multi-part name that identifies the owner. For example, `DBO.fn_CustomersWithOrders ( )`.

Multi-Part Names

All database objects can be identified using up to four name elements. When programming across servers or multiple databases, it may be necessary to use more than just the object name to identify an object. The complete object name has four parts separated by periods:

```
SERVER.DATABASE.OWNER.OBJECT
```

For example:

```
Production5.CompanySalesDB.DBO.CustomerOrder
```

Depending on the scope of the reference or code, only part of the name may be necessary:

```
CompanySalesDB.DBO.CustomerOrder
DBO.CustomerOrder
CustomerOrder
```

Functions

The following Transact SQL functions are grouped by category:

Numeric Manipulation

Function Name	Description
CEILING (numeric_value)	Converts numeric expressions to actual numeric values. For example, a numeric expression with currency symbol and thousand separator. CEILING ($1,234.0) Returns 1234.
COS (numeric value)	Cosine of an angle.
COT (numeric value)	Cotangent of an angle.

Table continued on following page

549

Function Name	Description
DEGREES (numeric)	Converts radians to degrees.
EXP (float)	Returns the exponent for a float value.
FLOOR (numeric)	Used to round a numeric value to the largest integer not greater than the value.
ISNUMERIC (value)	Indicates whether a value can be converted to a number. Returns 1 or 0.
LOG (Float)	Returns the logarithm of a value.
LOG10 (Float)	Returns the 10-based logarithm of a value.
PI ()	Returns the constant value of Pi.
POWER (value, exponent value)	Calculates the exponent (value raised to the exponent_value).
TAN (numeric value)	Returns the tangent of a value.

String Manipulation

Function Name	Description
CHAR (Integer)	Returns a character from the ASCII character code CHAR (65) Returns A
CHARINDEX (target value string, whole_string string) CHARINDEX (target value string, whole_string string, start_position Integer)	Returns an integer indicating the starting position of the first occurrence of the target value that is found within the whole_string value. Often used to locate delimiting characters within a column or static value.
DATALENGTH (string value)	Returns the number of characters in a variable-length string.
LEFT (string_value, end_character_int)	Returns a string value that is the left-most characters ending with the end_character.
LEN (string value)	Returns an integer indicating the length of a string.
LOWER (string value)	Converts all characters of a string to lower case.

Function Name	Description
LTRIM (string value)	Trims spaces from the left side (leading) for a string.
NCHAR (character code)	Returns a Unicode character for an integer character code. Similar to CHAR but handles Unicode character set.
PATINDEX (pattern_string, value)	Returns the index (integer of the staring position) of a search pattern string found within another string. The pattern_string is any string with wild card characters that could be passed to the LIKE operator.
QUOTENAME (string_value) QUOTENAME (string_value, quote_string)	Accepts a string with embedded quotes (', ", [or]) and returns a string with double instances of quote characters to indicate that they are literal.
REPLACE (target_string, replace_characters, new_characters)	In the first string, replaces occurrences of the second string with the third string.
REPLICATE (string_value, repeat_int_value)	Returns a string that consists of the string_value repeated a specified number of times.
REVERSE (string_value)	Returns a string with characters of the input string in reverse order.
RIGHT (string_value, length_int)	Returns the right-most part of a string. Like the LEFT function but reads from the right-most part of the string.
RTRIM (string_value)	Removes spaces from the right of a string (trailing).
SOUNDEX (string_value)	Returns a four character string to represent a comparative phonetic equivalent. Typically used for sound-alike comparisons.
SPACE (repeat_int_value)	Returns a string of spaces (one space repeated a specified number of times).
STR (value)	Converts a value to a string.
STUFF (string_value, start_int, length_int, replace_with_string)	Replaces characters in the string_value with characters in the replace_with_string, starting at start_int for a length or length_int. STUFF ('abcdefghij', 2, 4, 'wxyz') Returns abwxyzghij

Table continued on following page

Function Name	Description
SUBSTRING (string_value, start_int, length_int)	Returns part of a string from the start_int for a length of length_int. To return all characters to the right of the starting position, use a length value that is equal to or greater than any possible value. SUBSTRING ('abcdefghi', 3, 4) Returns cdef SUBSTRING ('abcdefghi', 3, 1000) Returns cdefghi
UNICODE (single_character)	Returns the Unicode character code for a string character.
UPPER (string_value)	Converts a string to upper case characters.

Mathematical

Function Name	Description
ABS (numeric_value)	Absolute value for a number.
ACOS (numeric_value)	Angle from a cosine.
ASIN (numeric_value)	Angle from a sine.
ATAN (numeric_value)	Angle from a tangent.
ATN2 (low_range, high_range)	Angle from a range of two tangents.
RADIANS (numeric_value)	Converts degrees to radians.
RAND (numeric_seed)	Returns a fractional random number between 0 and 1
ROUND (numeric_value, length) ROUND (numeric_value, length, operation)	Rounds a number to a given length. Optionally truncates if operation argument is greater than 0.
SIGN (numeric_value)	Returns + or – for a positive or negative numeric value.
SIN (radians_numeric)	Returns the sine of an angle.
SQUARE (numeric_value)	Returns the square of a value.
SQRT (numeric_value)	Returns the square root of a value.

Dates

Function Name	Description
DATEADD (datepart, number, date_value)	Returns a datetime value after adding or subtracting a specified period to the input date_value. The datepart is a named constant (Year, Month, Day). Number is an integer (positive or negative) for the number of datepart units to add to the date_value. DATEADD (Month, 3, '12/25/2003') Returns 3/25/2004
DATEDIFF (datepart, start_date, end_date)	Returns an integer for the number of datepart units that separate the start_date from the end_date values. DATEDIFF (Day, '12/25/2003', '3/25/2004') Returns 91
DATENAME (datepart, date_value)	Returns the specified datepart value for a date as a string. DATENAME (Month, '1/7/2004') Returns January
DATEPART (datepart, date_value)	Returns the specified datepart value for a date as an integer. DATENAME (Month, '1/7/2004') Returns January
DAY (date_value)	Returns an integer for the Day datepart of the date_value.
GETDATE ()	Returns the current date and time.
GETUTCDATE ()	Returns the current date and time of Universal or Greenwich Mean Time.
ISDATE (value)	Indicates whether a value can be converted to a date. Returns 1 or 0
MONTH (date_value)	Returns the month number for a date.
YEAR (date_value)	Returns a four position–integer representing the year part for a date.

Aggregate Functions

Function	Returns
AVG (value)	Average for a group or range.
COUNT (column_name) COUNT (*)	Aggregate count of rows not including nulls. Using * counts all rows regardless of nulls.
COUNT_BIG (column_name) COUNT_BIG (*)	Aggregate count of rows not including nulls. Using * counts all rows regardless of nulls.
MAX (value)	Aggregate function returns the highest value in the group or range.
MIN (value)	Smallest value in the group or range.
STDEV (value)	Standard deviation of a group or range.
STDEVP (value)	Standard deviation for a population of a group or range.
SUM (value)	Sum of a group or range.
VAR (value)	Variance of a group or range.
VARP (value)	Variance of a population for a group or range.

Grouping Variations

Function	Returns
GROUP BY column_name GROUP BY column_name, column_name, ...	Rolls up a result set by a column value or unique combination of column values. All columns returned in the query must have aggregate functions or be in the GROUP BY list.

GROUPING (column_name)	An aggregate function that returns a bit value indicating whether the row is the result of a *ROLLUP* or *CUBE* group summary.
	
	```SELECT ProdID, OrderID, GROUPING (OrderID), SUM (Amt)```
	```FROM ProdSales```
	```GROUP BY ProdID, OrderID```

HAVING criteria	Used to qualify an expression evaluated after GROUP BY and aggregate functions have been applied to a result set.
	
	```SELECT ProdID, OrderID, SUM (Amt)```
	```FROM ProdSales```
	```GROUP BY ProdID, OrderID```
	```HAVING SUM (Amt) > 500```
	
	Note that the SUM function is not actually performed again. This is treated only as an expression to qualify rows returned.

Type Conversion and Formatting

Function	Returns
`CAST (value AS type)`	Converts a value (of any acceptable type) to an explicit data type. `CAST (1234 AS VarChar(10))` This can also be achieved using the `CONVERT` function.

`CONVERT (type, value)`
`CONVERT (type, value, style)`
	Converts a value to an explicit data type. Optionally applies a style (format) to values such as numbers and dates. Style is an integer value—(found in MSDN Library & SQL Books On Line).
	
	`CONVERT (VarChar(10), 1234)`
	
	`CONVERT (VarChar(10), @DateValue,101)`
	
	Returns 1/7/2004

Logic

Function	Returns
`COALESCE (expr, expr, expr, …)`	Returns the first non-null value from a list of any number of expressions. `COALESCE (null, 'abc', 'def')` Returns abc
`ISNULL (value)`	Indicates whether a value is null. Returns 1 or 0.
`NULLIF (value1, value2)`	Returns null if two values are equal, otherwise returns the first value.

Query Criteria

Function	Returns
`CONTAINS (column_name, 'search criteria')` `CONTAINS (*, 'search criteria')`	Valid only with full-text indexing enabled. Provides more extensive search and criteria–matching capabilities than the standard `WHERE` and `LIKE` operators. Using * applies criteria to all full text– indexed columns in the table. Several optional rules and conditions can be applied to use complex matching expressions. For example `WHERE CONTAINS (*,'apples')`

Function	Returns

`FREETEXT (column_name, 'search criteria')`
 	
`FREETEXT (*, 'search criteria')`
	Valid only with full-text indexing enabled. Provides more extensive search and criteria matching capabilities than the standard `WHERE` and `LIKE` operators. Performs approximate text matching and can return a comparative rating for the match.
	
	Expressions may contain operators such as `AND`, `OR` and `NEAR`.
	
	Using `*` applies criteria to all full-text indexed columns in the table.

`IN (value, value, value, …)`	Used to match one set of criteria against a list of values. Effectively replaces multiple `OR` statements. `SELECT * FROM Customers WHERE State IN ('WA', 'OR', 'CA')`

Configuration Files

Following the pattern set in .NET, configuration information is stored in XML files in SQL Server Reporting Services. Configuration information is easy to modify and the file structures are easily readable.

XML Basics

If you need to modify any settings in these files, it's important to understand the essentials of XML document structure and form. XML data is organized into elements and attributes. Like in HTML, an element is called a tag. Tags consist of opening tags and closing tags and can also contain nested element tags. The following code snippet is a simplified example of an XML element structure:

```
<FirstElement>First Element Value
   <SecondElement>Second Element Value
   </SecondElement>
</FirstElement>
```

Note that in XML, carriage returns, spaces, and tabs are ignored. These are added only to increase human readability other than in element names and values.

In the first example, element values are sandwiched between opening and closing element tags. Values can also be defined using attributes contained in the opening element tag. The following is an example of values stored in an element's attributes:

```
<FirstElement Attribute1="Attribute 1 Value" Attrubute2="Attribute 2 Value">
   <SecondElement Attribute1="Attribute 1 Value"></SecondElement>
</FirstElement>
```

Attribute values are enclosed in double-quotes and element values are not. Element values can still be used in combination with attributes. They are removed from the example for simplicity. Since the second element is opened and closed with no element value or nested elements, an optional convention may be used to open and close the element in a single tag using the format used for the <SecondElement> element:

```
<FirstElement Attribute1="Attribute 1 Value" Attribute="Attribute 2 Value">
  <SecondElement Attribute1="Attribute 1 Value" />
</FirstElement>
```

Configuration Files

Four files are used to manage various configuration settings for the server and design environment. We've simplified the XML file layout for each of these configuration files below:

The RSReportServer.config File

All settings that apply to the report server, including connections, security, caching, and subscription delivery options.

Default install path:
C:\Program Files\Microsoft SQL Server\MSSQL\Reporting Services\ReportServer

Settings:
Configuration
  Dsn
    ConnectionType
    LogonUser
    LogonDomain
    LogonCred
    InstanceId
    InstallationID
    SecureConnectionLevel
    InstanceName
    ProcessRecycleOptions
    CleanupCycleMinutes
    SqlCommandTimeoutSeconds
    MaxActiveReqForOneUser
    DatabaseQueryTimeout
    RunningRequestsScavengerCycle
    RunningRequestsDbCycle
    RunningRequestsAge
    MaxScheduleWait
    DisplayErrorLink
    ReportCodePermissions/Permissions
    ReportExpressions/Permissions
    CustomAssemblies/Permissions
  Service
    IsSchedulingService
    IsNotificationService

```
      IsEventService
      PollingInterval
      MemoryLimit
      RecycleTime
      MaxAppDomainUnloadTime
      MaxQueueThreads
      UrlRoot
      UnattendedExecutionAccount/UserName/Password/Domain
  Extensions
    Delivery/Configuration
      RSEmailDPConfiguration
        SMTPServer
        SMTPServerPort
        SMTPAccountName
        SMTPConnectionTimeout
        SMTPServerPickupDirectory
        SMTPUseSSL
        SendUsing
        SMTPAuthenticate/From
        EmbeddedRenderFormats/RenderingExtension
        PrivilegedUserRenderFormats
        ExcludedRenderFormats/RenderingExtension
        SendEmailToUserAlias
        DefaultHostName
        PermittedHosts
    Render
      Permissions
        Extension(s)  (XML,NULL,CSV,IMAGE,PDF,HTML4.0,HTML3.2,MHTML,EXCEL,HTMLOWC)
        Configuration
          OWCConfiguration
          OWCDownloadLocation  (Languages)
    Data
      Permission
      Extension(s)  (SQL,OLEDB,ORACLE,ODBC)
    Security
      EventProcessing
        Extension(s)/Type(s) (ReportHistorySnapshotCreated,
                              TimedSubscription,SnapshotUpdated)
```

The RSWebApplication.config File

Settings that apply the Report Manager web application. Most settings correspond to options in the Report Manager application configuration pages.

Default install path:
C:\Program Files\Microsoft SQL Server\MSSQL\Reporting Services\ReportManager

Settings:
Configuration
```
  UI
    ReportServerUrl
  Extensions
    DeliveryUI
```

```
     Extension
        DefaultDeliveryExtension
        Configuration
           RSEmailDPConfiguration
     DefaultRenderingExtension
        Extension
           Configuration
              FileShare
   DefaultRenderingExtension
   MaxActiveReqForOneUser
   DisplayErrorLink
```

The ReportingServicesService.exex.config File

Enables tracing and logging of certain server events that include restarts, exceptions, warnings and status messages. Some settings are used to manage the trace and log files and tracing output options.

Default install path:
C:\Program Files\Microsoft SQL Server\MSSQL\Reporting Services\ReportServer\bin

Settings:
Configuration
```
  configSections
     name
  system.diagnostics
     switches
        DefaultTraceSwitch
  RStrace
```
FileName
```
  Prefix
  TraceListeners
  TraceFileMode
  Components
```

The RSReportDesigner.config File

Used to manage and configure custom data processing and rendering extensions. Also sets designer preview and rendering options.

Default install path:
C:\Program Files\Microsoft SQL Server\80\Tools\Report Designer

Settings:
Configuration
```
  SecureConnectionLevel
  InstanceName
  KeepSnapshotsInMemory
  SessionCookies
  SessionTimeoutMinutes
  ReportCodePermissions
     ReportExpressions
        CustomAssemblies
        Default
```

```
    PermissionSet
      IPermission/class
Extensions
Render
       Permissions
PermissionSet/class/version/Unrestricted/Name/Description
   Extension(s)  (XML,CSV,IMAGE,PDF,HTML4.0,HTML3.2,MHTML,EXCEL,HTMLOWC)
Data
   Permissions
PermissionSet/class/version/Unrestricted/Name/Description
   Extension(s)  (SQL,OLEDB,ORACLE,ODBC)
Designer
   Extension(s)  (SQL,OLEDB,ORACLE,ODBC)
```

Index

Index

A Guide to the Index

The index is arranged hierarchically, in alphabetical order, with symbols preceding the letter A. Most second-level entries and many third-level entries also occur as first-level entries. This is to ensure that users find the information they require however they choose to search for it.

Q

X